To Kay from Olla ...IL1...
Christmas 19

D1587425

MacDIARMID

C. M. Grieve
Di...Pepi del 1923

MacDIARMID

Christopher Murray Grieve

A Critical Biography

Alan Bold

JOHN MURRAY

For Valda

The publisher acknowledges subsidy
from the Scottish Arts Council
towards the publication of this volume

Text © Alan Bold 1988
MacDiarmid quotations © Valda Grieve 1988

First published 1988
by John Murray (Publishers) Ltd
50 Albemarle Street, London w1x 4BD

Typeset, printed and bound in Great Britain
by Butler & Tanner Ltd
Frome and London

British Library Cataloguing in Publication Data

Bold, Alan, *1943–*
MacDiarmid: a critical biography.
1. Poetry in English: Poetry in Scottish dialects.
MacDiarmid, Hugh, 1892–1978—Biographies
I. Title
821'.912

ISBN 0–7195–4585–4

FRONTISPIECE: MacDiarmid, as seen by David Foggie in 1933, the year he settled in the Shetland island of Whalsay; islanders remember him as an intense man who 'disliked all authority'.

Contents

Contents

Illustrations

Sources of Illustrations

Frontispiece: The Scotsman Publications Ltd; 2, 6, 7, 8, 9, 12, 13: Edinburgh University Library; 3, 5, 11, 14, 15, 18, 19, 21, 32, 34, 35: Mrs Valda Grieve; 4: Rev. A. J. MacKichan; 10: Morag Enticknap; 16: Sorley MacLean; 17, 23: W. R. Aitken; 20: Dairmid & Alasdair Gunn; 22: Aberdeen *Press & Journal*; 24: Charles Nicoll; 25: *Scottish Sunday Express*; 26: Mrs Mary Johnstone; 27: Mrs Hazel Goodsir Smith; 28: Emilio Coia & The Scotsman Publications Ltd; 29: George Outram & Co Ltd; 30, 31: Michael Peto/*Observer*; 33: Claddagh Records; 36: *Irish Times*; 37: Duncan Glen. The handwritten extract on p. 220 is reproduced by courtesy of the Trustees of the National Library of Scotland.

Prologue

I first became conscious of the name Hugh MacDiarmid when I was a pupil at Broughton Secondary School in the 1950s. I had left the school in 1958, aged fifteen, worked as an apprentice baker then impulsively decided to return to Broughton in the vague hope of doing something more demanding than putting the lids on pies. Teaching music at Broughton, at that time, was the composer Ronald Stevenson who told me, first, that Scotland had a great living poet called MacDiarmid and that, when the poet was still known as Christopher Murray Grieve, he himself had attended Broughton when it was a Junior Student Centre about half a century before. 'Chris Grieve is a great man,' Ronald assured me.

Not only did Ronald revere MacDiarmid, he knew Chris Grieve. Ronald stayed at Townfoot House, West Linton, some ten miles from Brownsbank Cottage, near Biggar, where the poet lived with his wife Valda. I became a regular visitor to Townfoot House and Ronald lent me books by MacDiarmid: as a great admirer of Ezra Pound I was first given *In Memoriam James Joyce* to read and, on completing it, wrote to the author in effusive terms. He replied with his characteristic courtesy and invited me out to Brownsbank Cottage. I was, however, hesitant about dropping in on such a formidable figure. I was a student at Edinburgh University when I first met MacDiarmid in 1962. He had come to speak to students and read a few of his early lyrics: 'The Watergaw', 'Crowdieknowe', 'The Eemis Stane' and others. He had an accent that veered between Border Scots and cultivated English and several eccentricities of pronunciation. When he talked about the dangers of nuclear war, the epithet was delivered as 'knuck-leer'.

In his books, MacDiarmid seemed an impossibly erudite and argumentative man. In private, however, he was unfailingly friendly. He wrote a long introduction to my first volume of verse, welcomed me to his home, came to our house on 29 June 1963 to celebrate our wedding. When I moved to Balbirnie, in Fife, in 1975 I asked him and his friend Norman MacCaig to read at an exhibition of my Illuminated Poems at Kirkcaldy Art Gallery. The occasion provided an example of his personal determination and courage. He accepted my invitation with a quali-

9

fication, in a letter of 2 October 1975, about an accident sustained in Glasgow at the home of his son Michael:

> I'd have had no hesitation in replying to your letter that of course I'd be very pleased to take part with Norman MacCaig and you on Friday Dec. 5 in Kirkcaldy Art Gallery – if I could. ... Valda was away in Spain, I was moving about in Edinburgh, Glasgow, Dumbarton, Perthshire and Fifeshire, and got your letter at Michael's house in Glasgow. The following day, however, I fell down an awkward stair with a bend in it. I had a sore toe and think I must have inadvertently put pressure on it, causing me to miss a step. Anyhow I swivelled round and severely cut my back. I am still only able to shuffle about, and suffering from all manner of aches and pains.
>
> However 5th Dec. is a good while ahead and I've no reason to doubt but that I'll be OK again and able to keep that date with you.

He did indeed keep the date. He was eighty-three at the time and a minor matter like a fall down a stair was not enough to put MacDiarmid out of commission.

After the reading there was a fascinating glimpse of an essential part of MacDiarmid's personality. With a few friends we retired for a private party at the Station Hotel. Much drink was taken, the mood was relaxed, the conversation was inconsequential. Suddenly MacDiarmid said he wanted to say something. He stood up and launched into an eloquent speech about the cultural claims of the Gaelic language. Had he been given the opportunity, he said, he would have written his poetry in Gaelic. The convivial Chris Grieve had become the forceful MacDiarmid, self-conscious of his destiny as the poetic voice of a nation. He was never complacent, he always felt there were urgent challenges. Although he had revitalised the Scots language through his lyrics and achieved artistic immortality with *A Drunk Man Looks at the Thistle*, he was not about to rest on his laurels. He was a restless man, always capable of intellectual provocation.

The last time I saw MacDiarmid was in the early autumn of 1978, the year he died. I had not been out to his house for some time and knew he was ill. Henry Stamper, the actor who portrayed the poet in a memorable one-man stage production, was living in a cottage near to my own. He suggested we should 'go out and see Chris'. We took the train to Edinburgh, then the bus to Biggar, carrying with us an afternoon's supply of whisky. Blended whisky. We should have known better. MacDiarmid looked with disdain at the bottle and pointed to an unopened bottle of Glenmorangie, his favourite malt. 'We'll have some of that lemonade,' he chuckled. Henry did the honours then retired to another room with Valda, leaving me alone with MacDiarmid. I had no sensation of looking into the face of a dying man, though the poet had only weeks to live. I felt instead that I was in the presence of an unquencheable vitality. His mind was sharp, his comments perceptive, his jokes (and he loved puns and bawdy jokes) excellent. 'Your shadow's not getting any smaller, Alan,' he said with a reference to my increasing bulk. 'Of course, I've always said that Scotland needs substance.' Such chatter was punctuated with pointed remarks about the lack of intellectual integrity in Scotland. 'Too many lowbrows,' said MacDiarmid. He laughed a lot. Even while he suffered agonies from the cancer that was consuming him, he exuded optimism.

For MacDiarmid, that day and always, everyday life was something to be approached with flexibility. Art was another matter: the essence of life and not be to trifled with. 'Poetry', he said in *In Memoriam James Joyce*, 'is human existence come to life' (757).*

Taking his cue from Shestov and other irrationalists, MacDiarmid put no intrinsic value on consistency. Indeed, in his work, he often appeared to put forth a mass of contradictions. Though he admitted to being tone deaf he expatiated on music, numbering Schoenberg and the esoteric Sorabji among his favourite composers. In his autobiography, *Lucky Poet*, he described himself as a mystic and a Marxist, an atheist and an Advaitin. Introducing *In Memoriam James Joyce* he declared he had no supernatural faith yet stated, in the poem itself, (paraphrasing a sentence from the *Autobiography* of John Cowper Powys), 'The astronomical universe is *not* all there is' (822). At various times he named David Hume, C. H. Douglas and John Maclean as the greatest Scot of all, though few had a greater claim to that title than himself.

Politically, MacDiarmid was a Nationalist with a poor opinion of the nation he lived in; a Communist who scorned the low intellectual level of the proletariat; an advocate of Social Credit who had little interest in economics. Philosophically he could accept the mysticism of Plotinus and the scepticism of Hume, the determinism of Marx and the existentialism of Kierkegaard, the quietism of Shankara and the supermania of Nietzsche. He was both positivist and irrationalist, realist and romantic, isolationist and internationalist. Brought up in the Christian church, he denounced institutional religion yet affirmed 'I believe in ... the ineluctable certainty of the resurrection' (480).

Still, MacDiarmid felt justified in drawing attention to the unity of

* See footnote on p. 15 for an explanation of the parentheses.

his artistic achievement, citing 'the complex vision of everything in one' (823). All his work, he realised, emanated from 'a single creative ray' (823). He believed that 'The universal *is* the particular' (845) and knew that the source of his art was himself, hence his fascination with his own personality, his belief in a creative evolution of the individual upwards into 'self-universal' (877), his dislike of mob-morality. Pluralistic by nature, he held that his spiritual self was indivisible.

MacDiarmid the visionary poet of the spirit does not immediately seem to square with MacDiarmid the controversial public figure, forever immersing himself in argument, forever fighting literary and political battles. He wanted it that way and took great delight in confusing his admirers. Those who anticipated a fierce revolutionary were confronted with a philosophical romantic and vice versa. MacDiarmid resisted classification and rejected labels. He was the nationalist, the Marxist, the agnostic, the mystic, the political poet, the contemplative poet, the linguistic champion of Synthetic Scots, the upholder of Synthetic English, the traditionalist, the modernist: all of these things. Above all, though, he was an individual with an imperishable spirit. Such, certainly, is the theme of his masterpiece, *A Drunk Man Looks at the Thistle*; a poem that contains the complexity of the man.

While MacDiarmid was no confessional poet, in the critical sense of that term, he was an intensely subjective writer. His work is illuminated by his life and the more one knows about the man the more one is able to appreciate his art as the outcome of a constant battle, an internal struggle that reached a triumphant artistic conclusion. This book is an attempt to come to terms with the man who created some of the greatest poetry of the twentieth, or any other, century. It does not regard Grieve the man as beyond criticism and does not approach MacDiarmid the thinker as infallible. It does, however, respect MacDiarmid as a unique individual and a major poet.

Acknowledgements

My first vote of thanks goes to Valda Grieve who discussed various aspects of her late husband's life in detail with me at her home at Brownsbank, Biggar, and who read the text of this book in typescript. I am also greatly indebted to Michael Grieve, the poet's son, who proved – as ever – a most helpful and supportive friend; and to Michael's wife Deirdre for information and encouragement. As executors of the Estate of Hugh MacDiarmid, Valda and Michael have graciously allowed me to quote copyright work by MacDiarmid. Without them I could not have produced this book. Though it is a critical biography, not a hagiography, Valda and Michael made no conditions, allowing me free range to interpret MacDiarmid as I saw fit.

I would like to acknowledge the generosity of the Scottish Arts Council in giving me a research grant, and the interest that Walter Cairns, Literature Director of the Scottish Arts Council, has taken in the project. I also thank the Phoenix Trust for an additional grant.

Much of the research for this book has been done at the National Library of Scotland and Edinburgh University Library. I wish to thank E. F. D. Roberts, Librarian of the National Library of Scotland, and his helpful staff; and Brenda Moon, Librarian of Edinburgh University, and the equally helpful staff of the Special Collection.

For permission to use their texts of previously unpublished poems by MacDiarmid, as identified in the Notes, I am grateful to Edinburgh University Library and to the University of Delaware Library. For permission to quote seven lines from *The Collected Poems of W. B. Yeats* I thank Michael B. Yeats and Macmillan London Ltd. My discussion of MacDiarmid's 'Lament for the Great Music' adapts a passage from my critical study *MacDiarmid: The Terrible Crystal*, published by Routledge & Kegan Paul in 1983.

My friend W. R. Aitken – the leading bibliographical authority on MacDiarmid and co-editor, with Michael Grieve, of *The Complete Poems of Hugh MacDiarmid* (the Penguin edition of which I have used as my standard poetic text throughout) – kindly supplied the Selected Bibliography for this book, and for this, and other kindnesses, I am greatly obliged.

13

My skilful and attentive editor, Duncan McAra, commissioned the book and patiently saw it through its various stages. His efforts have been much appreciated.

While writing this book I have been sustained, as always, by my wife Alice. I have also discussed ideas with, and extracted information from, friends and colleagues. The following list identifies only names but those cited all helped in important ways: Isabella Andrews; John Bett; Valentina Bold; Ern Brooks; George Bruce; Duncan Cameron; Linda Christie; Alex Clark; Hugh M. Douglas-Hamilton; Lord James Douglas-Hamilton; Sheila Duffy; Kulgin Duval; Morag Enticknap; Revd Inglis Finnie; Lilias Scott Forbes; Hywel Francis; Graham Greene; Colin Hamilton; Bernard Landis; Maurice Lindsay; John Linklater; Frank McAdams; Mary MacDonald; Revd A. J. MacKichan; Sorley MacLean; George Matthews; Ian Milner; John Montague; Hugo Moore; Timothy D. Murray; the late Norman Nicholson; Eileen O'Casey; Eleanor Pearson; Sadie Pritchard; John Roberts; Douglas Rome; Trevor & Hannah Royle; George Scott; J. C. Scott; Earl of Selkirk; Judith Sutherland; David C. Sutton; Henry Grant Taylor; J. W. W. Thomson; Fred Urquhart; Jack Webster; Arnold Wesker; Jean White; Robert Blair Wilkie; Colin Wilson.

A. B.

1

The Muckle Toon

> Gin scenic beauty had been a' I sook
> I never need ha' left the Muckle Toon.
> I saw it there as weel as ony man
> (As I'll sune prove); and sin syne I've gane roon'
> Hauf o' the warld wi' faculties undulled
> And no' seen't equalled.
>
> 'Kinsfolk' (1147)*

THE little Border mill town of Langholm, in Dumfriesshire, rarely occupies a central position in affairs of international importance. Its rugby football team is occasionally cited in the sports pages of Scottish newspapers; its annual Common Riding festival is a popular event in the Borders; its facilities for trout and salmon fishing are appreciated by anglers; its tweeds and woollens are known for their quality. Only occasionally does Langholm – twenty miles north of Carlisle, and seventy miles south of Edinburgh – attract wider attention. One such occasion occurred on 10 March 1972, when Neil Armstrong, the first man on the moon, became the first freeman of Langholm. The astronaut who had uttered the famous words 'That's one small step for man, one giant

---

*Parentheses with verse quotations refer to page numbers in Michael Grieve and W. R. Aitken (eds.), *The Complete Poems of Hugh MacDiarmid* (Harmondsworth: Penguin Books, 1985, 2 vols.).

leap for mankind' (on 20 July 1969) was welcomed enthusiastically in Langholm as a nominal descendant of the Armstrong clan who had caused havoc in the Borders in the sixteenth century.

As hundreds of local people crowded into the town square. Armstrong was received by the Provost, James Grieve, and the Town Clerk, Edward Armstrong, and presented with various gifts: a travelling rug of the Lunar tartan, made specially for the occasion by the Esk Valley Textile Company of Langholm, which hoped to market the design 'throughout the world'[1]; three suit-lengths from the local tweed mills, a present from the townspeople; and (to contain his burgess ticket of finest calf vellum) a wooden casket, fashioned in the form of Hollows Tower, once the stronghold of the notorious freebooter Johnnie Armstrong of Gilnockie, four miles south of Langholm. Neil Armstrong said that he now considered Langholm as his home town, then spent the night as guest of the Duke and Duchess of Buccleuch at Drumlanrig Castle. Langholm, it was felt, had risen to the occasion.

By contrast, when Hugh MacDiarmid was buried in Langholm Cemetery on Wednesday, 13 September 1978, the occasion was observed mainly by outsiders. Hundreds of them descended on Langholm to stand by the graveside in the drizzle, to honour MacDiarmid as one of the most gifted poets of the twentieth century and as one of the most individual Scots of his generation. The former town clerk, Mr Armstrong, did not attend the funeral; and the former Provost, Mr Grieve, likewise stayed away, feeling that his presence would amount to an insult since he had long opposed the idea of giving MacDiarmid an official honour equal to that bestowed on Neil Armstrong. More than forty years before the astronaut's historic landing on the moon MacDiarmid had been there imaginatively. He was moonstruck, looking at the reflected light and thinking of eternity:

> An' the roarin' o' oceans noo'
> Is peerieweerie to me:
> Thunner's a tinklin bell: an' Time
> Whuds like a flee.   (24)

That is the unmistakable voice of Hugh MacDiarmid, the visionary who sought universal insights and who devoted his life to a series of artistic, intellectual and social ideals. Behind the creation of the visionary there is the making of a man. Hugh MacDiarmid was a pseudonym adopted in 1922, the *annus mirabilis* of modernism, the year of James Joyce's

Ulysses and T.S. Eliot's *The Waste Land*. The poet was buried in the textile town where the man had been born in 1892 with the name Christopher Murray Grieve.

When Hugh MacDiarmid said he had 'no use for anything between genius and the working man'[2] he was, with characteristic immodesty, defining himself as well as declaring his faith in a socialist future. It is entirely appropriate that the birthplace of Scotland's most pugnacious poet should have a grand conceit of itself. At the time of Grieve's birth, Langholm was a small town with a population of less than four thousand yet gloried in the title of the Muckle Toon – the big town. Surrounded by hills that dominate the district of Eskdale, Langholm (meaning long holm) is built, as the name suggests, on flat land. It stretches along the banks of the river Esk which is joined, at the centre of Langholm, by the rivers Wauchope and Ewes; 'A perfect maze/O' waters is aboot the Muckle Toon' (314), according to MacDiarmid, who also claimed to have 'spent most of my early boyhood in the river, actually, physically, building islands in the river and cooking eels that we speared'.[3]

There is, as MacDiarmid was fond of pointing out, a saying 'Out of the world and into Langholm' (the poem 'The Dog Pool' begins by alluding to the phrase). Lying in a hollow among hills Langholm gives the impression of being a world on its own. For MacDiarmid it was a superior world, a personal Eden:

> After journeying over most of Scotland, England and central, southern and eastern Europe, as well as America, Siberia and China, I am of the opinion that 'my native place' – the Muckle Toon of Langholm, in Dumfriesshire – is the bonniest place I know: by virtue not of the little burgh in itself (though that has its treasurable aspects, and on nights when, as boys, we used to thread its dim streets playing 'Jock, Shine the Light', and race over the one bridge, past the factory, and over the other, with the lamp reflections wriggling like eels at intervals in the racing water, had an indubitable magic of its own), but by virtue of the wonderful variety and quality of the scenery in which it is set.[4]

As a boy, Christopher Grieve took full advantage of the landscape around Langholm. He sledged on the Lamb Hill, gathered wild raspberries ('hines') in the Langfall, collected nuts and crab-apples in the Scrog Nut Wood, walked past the Kernigal Wood to reach the top of Warbla, climbed to the shoulder of Whita Hill (where the Hound Trail starts at 5 a.m. for the Common Riding). By getting out and about Grieve could penetrate the five glens that encircle the town: Eskdale, Wauchopedale, Tarrasdale, Ewesdale and the Dean Banks. He felt that Langholm offered 'the manifold and multiform grandeur and delight of Scotland in minia-ture – as if quickened and thrown into high relief by the proximity of England'.[5] Langholm, as local inhabitants are quick to confirm, is a mere eight miles from England.

It is not surprising, therefore, that the prose and poetry of Hugh MacDiarmid are rich in topographical references to Langholm. His short stories describe, for example, 'The Common Riding', the traditional pivot of Langholm life; 'Murtholm Hill', where Grieve sledged as a boy; 'The Waterside', about the area, near the Suspension Bridge (or Swing Brig), inhabited by millworkers. His poems mention such sights as the Fairy Loup waterfall, the Factory Gullets and the Skipper's Pool ('Water of Life'); Tarras Water, which rises in a boggy wasteland ('Tarras'); and the 100-foot-high white sandstone obelisk erected on Whita Hill in 1835 to honour Sir John Malcolm, one of the Four Knights of Eskdale ('The Monument'). Several images arise from memories of adventures in the Langfall, the big wood that stands on lands owned by the Duke of Buccleuch. Past the ruins of Langholm Castle there is a sawmill and nearby a winding path, known as the Curly Snake, coils up through a copse till it eventually runs into the Langfall. The Curly Snake haunted the poet's imagination and probably constituted itself as the ground-plan of his mind. MacDiarmid's long poem *To Circumjack Cencrastus* is subtitled the Curly Snake and in it he asks lovingly:

> And hoo should I forget the Langfall
> On mornings when the hines were ripe but een
> Ahint the glintin' leafs were brichter still
> Than sunned dew on them, lips reider than the fruit,
> And I filled baith my basket and my hert
> > Mony and mony a time? (271)

Significantly, since MacDiarmid mentions 'a second and far more drastic and irrevocable expulsion from the Garden of Eden'[6] when contemplating the distance between him and Langholm in the 1930s, there is, near the Langfall, a parting of the hills known locally as the Gates of Eden.

A Langholm Eden had its limitations. Inside the town economic and architectural divisions partly determined each individual's perception of place. The land was owned by the aristocracy, the imposing homes were possessed by the millowners, the more humble houses were rented by those who worked in the mills or served the community. In Langholm, Grieve was part of a social structure based on class and wealth. Among the many complexities of his personality there was, as a result of his upbringing in Langholm, a complicated attitude to social strata. Though he relished the 'tremendous proletarian virtue'[7] of Langholm and 'hated the gentry ... loathed the gentry'[8] he learned to like the ring of aristocratic titles and would, as an adult, draw attention to the fact that his admirers included 'men like the Duke of Hamilton, his brother the Earl of Selkirk and others'.[9] Similarly, he would identify the man who introduced his first book of Scots lyrics as Lord Tweedsmuir rather than John Buchan.[10] This fascination with titles is built into the romance of the Borders. We have it on J. G. Lockhart's authority that his father-in law Sir Walter Scott would have 'at the highest elevation of his literary renown ... considered losing all that at a change of the wind, as nothing, compared to parting with his place as the Cadet of Harden and Clansman of Buccleuch'.[11] It was because Grieve the Borderer understood this attitude that he publicly deplored it, condemning both Sir Walter Scott and Lord Tweedsmuir as reactionary representatives of 'the pro-English type of Scottish literature'.[12]

Grieve could not escape the haunting presence of Border history. The house in which he was born was in Arkinholm Terrace, a row of houses named after a historic battle fought at Langholm. On 1 May 1455 the Black Douglas brothers, who then controlled the district, were defeated by a combined army of prominent Border families at the battle of Arkinholm. Having broken the power of the Black Douglases the other aristocratic families were free to dispute their rights to Langholm which lay within the Debateable Land, so called because the Border line between Scotland and England was so often contested. A charter of 1621, granting the lands of Langholm to the Earl of Nithsdale, conferred on the town the status of a free burgh of barony. The barony passed into the possession of the Buccleuch family – still big landowners around Langholm – and in 1687 Langholm was erected into a burgh of regality for the Duchess of Buccleuch.

During the eighteenth century Langholm laid the foundations for its commercial future. It was well placed to establish trade with the north of England as well as the south of Scotland and when it founded a cotton factory in 1788 it had a commodity, cotton yarn, to market in Carlisle and Glasgow. Working men and women were attracted to Langholm by the prospect of employment; by 1791 its population of less than two thousand was larger than that of Hawick and Galashiels combined. When Dorothy Wordsworth visited Langholm on 23 September 1803 she was impressed by its air of prosperity:

> The town, as we approached, from a hill, looked very pretty, the houses being roofed with blue slates, and standing close to the river Esk, here a large river, that scattered its waters wide over a stony channel. The inn neat and comfortable – exceedingly clean: I could hardly believe we were still in Scotland.[13]

Having built a new part of the town – Meikleholm – at the end of the eighteenth century, Langholm continued to prosper and provide employment. In 1832 it began to make plaids and check trouserings for shepherds and rapidly established itself as a substantial tweed town. By 1881 it had a population of 4612, the highest ever recorded for the burgh.

Langholm expanded by combining ambition with native ingenuity. For example the problem of mobility was solved by constructing the series of four bridges that spanned the Esk. Inevitably, local men of talent began to assert themselves. William Julius Mickle, author of 'Cumnor Hall' (which suggested the subject of *Kenilworth* to Scott) and the song 'The Mariner's Wife' (with the refrain 'For there's nae luck about the house'), was born in 1735 in a parish manse on the ruins of Wauchope Castle and subsequently translated Camoens's *Lusiad* (published 1771-5 by subscription). Thomas Telford, the great civil engineer, was the son of a Westerkirk shepherd. Apprenticed to a mason in Langholm, he worked on Langholm Bridge in 1775. Nicknamed the 'Colossus of Roads' by his friend, the Poet Laureate Robert Southey, Telford was responsible for the creation of Langholm Library, a gesture that would reverberate through Grieve's life.

The first penny newspaper in Scotland, the *Eskdale and Liddesdale Advertiser*, was founded in Langholm in 1848. As an adolescent Grieve supported, in its pages, the attribution to William Julius Mickle of 'The Mariner's Wife':

> For there's nae luck about the house,
>   There's nae luck at a',
> There's nae luck about the house,
>   When our gudeman's awa.

He also published the result of his genealogical researches in the *Eskdale and Liddesdale Advertiser*.[14] Grieve found an aristocratic connection for his mother:

> Her great-great-grandfather had been the Laird of Castlemilk, but had been a typical reckless, hard-drinking, heavy-gambling laird of his time, and had gambled away his estates on the turn of the card to, I think, one of the well-known Border family of Bell-Irving, or to one of the Buchanan-Jardines, who now own the property in question.[15]

But then Grieve was fond of making family connections, including links with John Grieve (1781-1836), a poet friend of James Hogg, the Ettrick Shepherd; and William Laidlaw (1780-1845), Sir Walter Scott's amanuensis and steward at Abbotsford.[16] The first section of *In Memoriam James Joyce* makes exalted intellectual connections:

> And my own kinsmen, Lindley Murray, the father of English
>   Grammar,
> And Alexander Murray, who studied the languages
> Of Western Asia and North-East Africa and Lappish
> And wrote the 'History of European Languages'   (745)

The poet's autobiography *Lucky Poet* likewise names Alexander Murray (1775-1813) and Lindley Murray (1745-1826) as kinsmen, praising the former as a shepherd lad who became one of the greatest linguists of his time. 'This', the poet declares, 'is the blood that is in my veins.'[17]

Grieve's immediate ancestors were not, however, lairds or linguistic scholars but hard-working Borderers devoted to the Bible. His paternal grandfather John was a woollen weaver, his maternal grandfather Andrew Graham was a mole-catcher and farm labourer. John Grieve was a short, lively, jocular man who wore, the one time his grandson Christopher saw him, a transparent, butter-coloured waistcoat. He made a vivid impression on Christopher:

> I caught him in the act of taking some medicine of a vivid red colour, and somehow or other got it into my childish head that he was drinking blood, and thought of him with horror – not unmixed with envy – for years afterwards. I resemble him physically (in point of leanness and agility, though I am considerably taller) and facially (a big brow and all the features squeezed into the lower half of my face); but when I was a lad the older folk used to tell me I took after him in another respect – 'juist like your grandfaither,' they used to say, 'aye amang the lassies'.[18]

Despite this piece of local lore, John Grieve settled for one wife. He married Christina Murray on 14 February 1857 at Gretna and their son James was born, on 20 May 1863, in a rented house in Henry Street, Langholm. John Grieve supported his family with the money he earned as a power-loom tuner in a tweed mill. He died, a widower, in 1898.

Andrew Graham, the mole-catcher, lived at Kirtleton Lodge, on Kirtleton Farm, near Waterbeck, a village on the Beck Water, some ten miles south-west of Langholm. He married Isabella Carruthers and their daughter Elizabeth Graham was born on 25 October 1856 in Kirktonhill at Westerkirk, almost five miles north-west of Langholm. Andrew Graham died in his ninety-sixth year after slipping and falling down the stone steps of his cottage. 'He was the first man I saw die,' Grieve noted, 'and I remember to this day the ragged wounds on his forehead where he had hit the ground.'[19] Andrew Graham was buried, beside his wife, in Crowdieknowe churchyard in Middlebie parish. His white-bearded figure is resurrected in the apocalyptic vision Hugh MacDiarmid created in a lyric about Crowdieknowe churchyard:

> Oh to be at Crowdieknowe
> When the last trumpet blaws,
> An' see the deid come loupin' owre
> The auld grey wa's.
>
> Muckle men wi' tousled beards,
> I grat at as a bairn
> 'll scramble fare the croodit clay
> Wi' feck o' swearin'.   (26)

As a boy Grieve often visited his mother's relatives and friends in Wauchope, Eskdalemuir, Middlebie, Dalbeattie and Tundergarth and hoped his familiarity with the Scottish agricultural folk 'made it at any rate possible that I would in due course become a great national poet of Scotland'.[20]

James Grieve, the poet's father, became a postman in Langholm and courted Elizabeth Graham at Kirtleton Lodge where she worked as a domestic servant. She was more than six years his senior: when they married, on 15 October 1891, James was twenty-eight, Elizabeth was going on thirty-five. Conducted at Kirtleton Lodge by James Monilaws, minister of the Church of Scotland in Middlebie, the ceremony was witnessed by John Laidlaw and Annie Hetherington. James and Elizabeth Grieve rented a house in Arkinholm Terrace and there, at 9.30 a.m. on

11 August 1892, Dr John Gill delivered their first son. They gave him two Christian names, Christopher Murray, after his paternal grandmother Christina Murray, and his first name was regularly abbreviated to Christie or Kirsty. Elizabeth Grieve described her first-born as 'an eaten an' spewed lookin' wee thing wi' een like twa burned holes in a blanket'.[21] The comment is incorporated into *A Drunk Man Looks at the Thistle* when, describing a forsaken child, the narrator declares:

> Dod! It's an eaten and a spewed-like thing,
> Fell like a little-bodies' changeling,
> And it's nae credit t'ye that you s'ud bring
> The like to life – yet, gi'en a mither's love,
> – Hee, hee! – wha kens hoo't micht improve?   (104)

The notion of surpassing the circumstances of birth is a crucial issue in the work and life of Hugh MacDiarmid.

The infant Christopher's introduction to his native land was unfortunate, his 'first bit of bad luck'.[22] During the winter that followed his birth the Esk froze so solidly that carts and horses could go on it for as far as twenty miles. Elizabeth Grieve wrapped Christopher in a Shetland shawl and took him to the door of her hillside house in Arkinholm Terrace so he could savour the sight of the townspeople, skating on the river. 'Alas,' Grieve lamented, 'my infant eyesight could not carry so far ... and there was I, poor little mite, so unfortunate as to be unable to see it, though I was held outside for the purpose.'[23] Fourteen months after that memorable winter Elizabeth gave birth, on 7 April 1894, to a second son in Arkinholm Terrace. Andrew Graham Grieve was named after Elizabeth's father and his arrival was greatly resented by Kirsty who attempted to get rid of this rival:

> I was caught in the act of trying to commit my first murder – attempting, in short, to smash in the head of my newly-born brother with a poker, and, when I was disarmed, continuing to insist that, despite that horrible red-faced object, I 'was still Mummy's boy, too'.[24]

Even allowing for Grieve's habit of hyperbole the anecdote is instructive; the brothers were never close and later in life were not even on speaking terms.

When Christopher was four and Andrew two, the Grieves moved to a house in Henry Street, where their grandfather John Grieve had lived. A year after that Christopher enrolled at Langholm infant school then, when he was seven, entered the primary department of Langholm Academy. The year he started at the Academy, 1899, his father obtained accommodation in Library Buildings, Parliament Square. On street level, the new Grieve home was situated behind the post office where James Grieve worked. Elizabeth Grieve was employed as caretaker to the Langholm Library, in the same building and above the post office. Christopher was now in one of the busiest parts of Langholm, his home adjacent to the Town Hall where, as part of the Common Riding ceremony, the Cornet and his horsemen received the town's standard from the Provost. His 'incredibly happy'[25] boyhood developed in Library Buildings for he was not too far from a rich landscape like that at the Langfall; he was given annual evidence of a rural tradition in the Common Riding; he had constant and easy access to the resources of the town library; and – though he could be critical of them – he appreciated the concern his parents had for him. Though James Grieve never earned more than thirty-seven shillings a week he provided the members of his family with a strong sense of their own worth.

James Grieve was a slim, raven-haired, clear-eyed, ruddy-complexioned townsman of Langholm. As a rural postman his route ran up the Ewes Road to Fiddleton Toll – 'They ken a' that opens and steeks,/Frae Fiddleton Bar to Callister Ha'' (334) – and he travelled it by bike. He was devoutly religious, holding such pronounced presbyterian views that he would not have the poems of Robert Burns in the house presumably so he could not be contaminated by the satirical thrust of such works as 'Holy Willie's Prayer' and 'Address to the Unco Guid'. Up the hill from his post office house Langholm South United Free Church had been built in Drove Road, in 1883, to serve the needs of the Townfoot congregation. James Grieve attended religiously as a worshipper, as a church elder and as superintendent of the Sunday School to which both his sons were sent. His friends, drawn from those townsfolk of Langholm who shared his principles, included Adam Ferguson, who became a minister in Dundee; and James Leishman, who 'rose from rural postman to a high position in the Civil Service in Scotland'.[26] James Grieve's involvement in church work meant that ministers and church officers often visited him and young Kirsty was fascinated by the contrast between their Christian calling and their love of malicious gossip.

At the time of the Boer War, James Grieve stood out against local patriotic opinion by declaring pro-Boer sympathies. Stubborn by nature he supported the Liberal Party but became increasingly interested in the aims of the Labour Party (founded in 1900 as the Labour Representation

Committee). As a member of the Postmen's Federation he attended Co-operative and Trade Union meetings; in his son's opinion he was moving 'steadily towards the Socialist position'.[27] Four MacDiarmid poems feature James Grieve – 'The Watergaw', 'At My Father's Grave', 'Kinsfolk' and 'Fatherless in Boyhood' – and indicate a quietly resolute, kindly man. In one of them, 'Kinsfolk', the man to whom Burns was 'taboo'[28] is portrayed as a serious, sober figure similar to the father in Burns's 'The Cotter's Saturday Night':

> He had his differences but a host o' freen's
> At ane wi' him on maist things and at serious odds
> In nane, a kindly, gin conscientious man,
> Fearless but peacefu', and to man's and God's
> Service gi'en owre according to his lichts
>   But fondest o' his ain fireside o' nichts.   (1148)

A more vivid verbal portait is created in 'Fatherless in Boyhood':

> Your bike-wheels ga'en like bees-wings doon the road,
> Or, your face scarlet frae the icy wind,
> Openin' your big broon bag and showin' in'd
> Cakes, apples, oranges, a wondrous load,
> Frae hogmanayin' a' the way up Ewes,
> Or 'mang your books, as queer a lot to me
> As ony library frae Mars might be,
> Or voicin' Trade Union and Co-operative views
> Or some religious line   (1250)

James Grieve's interests did not include writing though he did compose some sermons.

James Grieve's wife Elizabeth did, on the other hand, write verse as her son remembered: 'I once saw poems (very bad!) my mother had written before she was married'.[29] If anything she was more of a biblical fundamentalist than the poet's father, irritating Christopher with phrases like 'Ah! wait till you see the light', 'You see, you haven't been washed in the blood of the Lamb yet', 'Every prospect pleases, and only Man is vile'.[30] The poet sensed that both his parents, by earnestly holding to religious ideals, made the Grieve family conspicuous in Langholm so that the earthier locals 'were apt to jeer at them a little'.[31] This sensation of being cut off from the community is a recurrent theme for MacDiarmid, who regarded himself as 'a sort of Ishmael'.[32] It clearly goes back to his

25

childhood. Christopher and Andrew were kept tidier and better dressed than other boys in Langholm, even attired in Highland dress of the green Graham tartan for special occasions. Consequently the two boys were 'jeered at as "Mother's angels" '.[33] Even as a boy Christopher preferred to keep his own company. On holidays he chose his companions carefully.

One of Elizabeth Grieve's brothers was a gamekeeper on an estate near Dingwall, the market-town of Ross and Cromarty, eighteen miles north of Inverness. Some of Christopher's earliest holidays were spent with his uncle. He was delighted to hear Gaelic spoken by the Ross-shire woman who was his uncle's second wife. He even attempted 'to learn a little Gaelic'.[34] This experience was crucial in the light of later years for, as Hugh MacDiarmid, the poet argued the case for restoring Gaelic as Scotland's most glorious language. Grieve was sensitive to linguistic subtleties, noting that Langholm Scots differed from Hawick Scots and Canonbie Scots, so the sound of Gaelic must have been a revelation to him.

Another holiday introduced him to the Cumbrian dialect (as an adult he admired Susanna Blamire who wrote in both Cumbrian and Scots).[35] Two boyhood holidays took him to Millom, in Cumberland, where he stayed with the Littles, relatives of his mother. He got on well with the girls – Annie, Eleanor and Janet – who showed him the countryside around Millom. On one trip they took him to Furness Abbey, near Barrow-in-Furness. Christopher buried a penny under a tree in Furness Abbey, marked the tree, and told the girls that one day he would come back to find it. On these Millom holidays he made friends with a Captain Fairclough, captain in this context being a term used in the iron-ore mines. Fairclough, the harbour master, lived with his three daughters in an isolated stone house. As often as he could, Grieve visited Harbour House (now ruined) which stood on a lonely part of the shore where the estuarine mudflats gave way to the dunes of the true coast.

Back in Langholm, Christopher indulged in various outdoor pleasures. Perhaps impressed by his father's prowess as a postman on a bike he 'early won the reputation of being a dare-devil cyclist'.[36] He went on long walks, covering (by his own estimation) as many as thirty-two miles on a good day. He clambered over the hills or immersed himself in the woods, the Langfall or Whitshiels (pronounced 'Whuchulls' in Langholm):

Here I dung doon the squirrels wi' my sling
And made the lassies brooches o' their paws,
Set girns for rabbits and for arnuts socht,
Herried my nests and blew the eggs, and lit
Fires o' fir-burrs and hag in tinker style.   (1092)

Cycling and walking offered an opportunity for solitude and he 'preferred bein' alane – wi his ain thochts'.[37] Nevertheless he was thrilled each year at the sight of the whole population of Langholm turning out to celebrate the Common Riding, a pageant deriving from the old custom of riding round the boundaries of a burgh. Now held every last Friday in July, this spectacular communal ceremony dates from a court decision of 1759 which recognised that the burgesses of Langholm had legal rights in the common lands, principally the Common Moss and the Kilngreen. Around 1765 Bauldy Beattie, the town-drummer, or crier, was employed to maintain the boundary marches. For more than fifty years Bauldy Beattie walked the marches and also proclaimed the Langholm Fair at the Market Place. Langholm Fair (no longer held) was once one of the most important lamb sales in Scotland; the Langholm coat of arms depicts a lamb as well as the spade, thistle and salt-herring-and-barley-bannock emblems of the Common Riding. Every year, from the time he could stand until he left Langholm at the age of sixteen, Christopher Grieve would have heard the Crying of the Fair in words that were mainly traditional, though the mention of the Town Council (established in 1893, a year after the poet's birth) is a Victorian addition:

This is to gie notice, that there is a muckle Fair to be hadden i' the muckle Toun o' the Langholm on the 15th day o' July, auld style, upon His Grace the Duke of Buccleuch's Merk-land for the space o' aucht days and upwards, and ony hustrin, custrin, land-louper or dub-scouper or gae-by-the-gate swinger, wha come here to breed ony hurdrum or durdrum, huliments or bruliments, hagglements or bragglements or squabblements, or to molest this public Fair shall be ta'en be order o' the Baillie and the Toun Council and his lugs be nailed to the Tron wi' a twalpenny nail, until he sit doon on his hob-shanks and pray nine times for the King and thrice for the muckle Laird o' Ralton ... and A'll awa' hame and hae a barley bannock and a saut herring tae ma denner be way o' auld style.[38]

Thus was Scots publicly preserved in Langholm. All his life Grieve acknowledged that the Scots he used had its linguistic roots in Langholm, insisting that he spoke 'a racy Scots',[39] that 'English ... is not my native language',[40] and that 'I was born into a Scots-speaking community and my own parents and all those round about spoke Scots'.[41]

If Bauldy Beattie's precedent of Crying the Fair in Scots was followed closely, the Common Riding evolved by departing from his pedestrian inspection of the marches. From 1816 the boundaries were examined by men on horseback and this Riding developed as a race. A Cornet, or leader, was chosen and in the games organised for the annual festival he acted as Master of Ceremonies. The pattern of the Common Riding was well established in Grieve's boyhood. It begins with a 5 a.m. call to the Hound Trail on the shoulder of Whita Hill. Each Common Riding morning the Provost formally hands the town flag over to the Cornet. After the Presentation of the Standard and the Crying of the Fair the Cornet leads scores of horsemen up the Kirk Wynd towards Whita Hill. The ceremony ends when the Provost receives the standard at the close of day. In the procession led by the Cornet, various emblems are carried in addition to the flag: a barley-bannock and salted herring fastened to a wooden dish by a large nail; a spade, used for cutting the sod at different points of the Common; an eight-foot thistle grown in the garden at the Townfoot; and the floral crown. The Scottish symbolism of the thistle is obvious, Langholm demanding a gigantic specimen:

> The biggest and shapeliest was chosen, but it was an unwritten law – and a point o' honour wi' the gairdener – that it had to be at least aucht fit high wi' the tap aboot as muckle in diameter. Tied to the tap o' a flag pole it made a bonny sicht, wallopin' a' owre the lift, an' a hunner roses dancin' in't, a ferlie o' purple and green.[42]

Other emblems have a local symbolism (the bannock and herring signifying the Duke of Buccleuch's rights in the mills and fisheries) but it was the combination of image and archetype (thistle and crown) that had such a lasting impression on Christopher Grieve. As Hugh MacDiarmid he saluted the Common Riding ceremony in *A Drunk Man Looks at the Thistle*:

> Drums in the Walligate,[43] pipes in the air,
> Come and hear the cryin' o' the Fair.
>
> A' as it used to be, when I was a loon
> On Common-Ridin' Day in the Muckle Toon.
>
> The bearer twirls the Bannock-and-Saut-Herrin',
> The Croon o' Roses through the lift is farin',

The aucht-fit thistle wallops on hie;
In heather besoms a' the hills gang by.   (97)

Apart from the Common Riding, Christopher Grieve avoided group activities with the exceptions of church and Sunday School. 'I was always a loner,'[44] he admitted. Even as a boy he had 'no use for going about with any gang or group'.[45] He was happiest going up the stairs from his father's post office house to Langholm Library to which his mother had the keys. Langholm Library had been established in 1800. Under the will of Thomas Telford the sum of £1000 was left to the parish minister of Langholm on the understanding that the interest would be used for the purchase of books. As suitable accommodation was needed to house the books adequately the Duke of Buccleuch was approached; he provided a free site, charging only a nominal feu-duty of five shillings. Alexander Reid, the millowner, gave £1000 towards the erection of a building on condition that the same sum was raised by the members. Eventually, in 1878, the Library Buildings were erected and Robert Scott was appointed Librarian, a position he held for more than forty years.

To Christopher Grieve the library was the most exciting place in Langholm. There he was transported into a wider world, reversing the proverbial wisdom of his birthplace by going, vicariously at least, out of Langholm and into the world. He read avidly about the bitter winter Washington's men spent at Valley Forge, thrilled to the tale of the great march of the Mormons, delighted in the Wild Western panache of Joaquin Miller (the Poet of the Sierras), immersed himself in other American writers such as Mark Twain and Francis Bret Harte. Christopher Grieve looked on the library as a treasure house, as he explained in one of the most enthusiastic passages of his autobiography *Lucky Poet*:

I had constant access to it [from the age of seven], and used to fill a big washing-basket with books and bring it downstairs as often as I wanted to. My parents never interfered with or supervised my reading in any way, nor were they ever in the least inclined to deprecate my 'wasting my time reading'. There were upwards of twelve thousand books in the library (though it was strangely deficient in Scottish books), and a fair number of new books, chiefly novels, was constantly bought. Before I left home (when I was fourteen [actually sixteen]) I could go up into that library in the dark and find any book I wanted. ... I can still remember not only where about on the shelves all sorts of books were, but whereabouts in the books themselves were favourite passages or portions that interested me specially for one reason or another...[46]

Christopher was (and remained all his life) a bookworm, burrowing into the pages of the books that filled his basket. This early obsession with reading cut him off from his contemporaries who were inclined to look on him as distinctly odd. Apparently he was called 'Lassie-boy',[47] an insult that still irked him in the 1920s when he wrote Scots short stories about his Langholm boyhood: he resented being treated as if he was 'a kind o' lassie-boy'[48] or 'Jessie-like'[49] because he stayed in with his books. His mother criticised him for being indoors so often, unlike his robust brother Andrew who was forever out on the golf-course, caddying for several shillings a week. The first paragraph of the story 'Andy' (clearly Christopher's brother is the eponymous Andy) suggests how his parents reacted to the apprentice intellectual in the house:

> She'd nae patience wi' him – 'aye sittin' in a corner mumpin' owre a book!' If it had been his schulebooks it wadna hae been sae bad – but poetry and novels and guid kens what! Stuffin' his heid wi' a lot o' useless nonsense. His faither was faur owre saft wi' him. 'Let the laddie abee,' he aye said; 'there's waur things than readin'!' ... What he couldna stand was Andy aye yabble-yabbling aboot things he felt sma' and silly in comparison wi' nature or books.[50]

Andrew's behaviour was in complete contrast to Christopher's; Andrew was an open-air boy who had little use for books except as a means to passing his exams, which he did more successfully than his brother.[51] Christopher resented Andrew, had no wish to compete with him as an angler or a caddy on the golf-course. Christopher felt more at home with more mature minds.

Arguably the greatest influence on Christopher Grieve's boyhood was not his father or his mother but the minister of the church he attended. This man, T. S. Cairncross, was not only a Christian by profession but a poet by aspiration. He had a wide range of interests, wrote book reviews for the *Irish Times* and liked to visit literary landmarks. Though his correspondence with Christopher Grieve has not survived[52] there is a postcard, showing Wordsworth's grave in Grasmere churchyard, addressed to Master Christie Grieve: 'Thought you might be interested in having in your collection a view of the tombstone of the man who wrote the Ode to Immortality'.[53]

Thomas Scott Cairncross (1872-1961) was born in Lesmahagow, a town and parish in Lanarkshire, five miles south-west of Lanark on the river Nethan.[54] He was educated locally, took his Bachelor of Divinity degree at Glasgow University, then completed his theological training by spending a year at the United Presbyterian Hall in Edinburgh. In 1900, the year Cairncross qualified as a minister, the thousand parishes of the Free Church of Scotland joined the six hundred congregations of the United Presbyterian Church to form the United Free Church of Scotland.[55] Cairncross's first charge was as minister of Langholm South United Free Church from 1901 to 1907. These six years cover a formative part of Grieve's life who was nine when Cairncross arrived in Langholm and fifteen when the minister left the Muckle Toon to become minister at Old Kilpatrick Church, Bowling, Dunbartonshire.

What most impressed Christopher was that the minister was also a poet. In 1905, when Grieve was a thirteen-year-old Sunday School teacher in Langholm South United Free Church, Cairncross published – under the imprint Robert Scott of Langholm – his first collection, *The Return of the Master*. The book pays tribute to such favourite writers as W. E. Henley and Bliss Carman and makes imaginative use of imagery associated with Langholm. 'Saint Thorwald and Whita Well' is a poem in dialect Scots beginning:

> There's a well in the Border Country,
> And for miles and miles, roun' and roun',
> There's nane in the Border Country
> Like Whita by Langholm toun.

'Crying the Fair', invoking the custom that is a central part of the Common Riding Ceremony, separates the speaker from the townspeople:

> For where they dance upon the Castleholm
>   Or throng the Green,
> Or ride the Common, or 'The Langholm' roam,
>   One grief I ween,
>
> Stays as the Thistle and the Bannock proudly pass
>   And dims the eye,
> That of the hearth where gay go lad and lass,
>   No child am I.

The showpiece of the collection is a poem called, simply, 'Langholm':

> It lies by the heather slopes,
> Where God spilt the wine of the moorland
> Brimming the beaker of hills. Lone it lies
> A rude outpost: challenging stars and dawn,
> And down from remoteness
> And the Balladland of the Forest
> The Pictish Esk trails glory,
> Rippling the quiet eaves
> With the gold of the sun.
>
> Here casts the angler,
> Half-hid in shadow; his eyes
> Veiled with rapt contemplation,
> Where raider and reiver darted and harried.
> Those mild terrible eyes
> Came down from Flodden.
>
> He hints and bends over the crystal waters
> In large content,
> The Roman Road all empty
> By death's stern, sure outlawing,
> With here in great spaces of the wind and sunshine
> Life at the full!
>
> O Border shadow!
> A silhouette of silence and old years
> Ever abide: now the clang of the long day over,
> The little town shall fold itself to rest
> With through its dreams the chequered river gleaming
> In luminous peace!

It is an impressive, elegantly expressed, descriptive poem. The notion that the local minister could compose such verse astounded Christopher. 'I thought that was great stuff when I was a boy,'[56] he admitted. Grieve included the poem in the first book he produced, the anthology *Northern Numbers*; and he quoted it in its entirety in *Lucky Poet*, published when he was a man of fifty-one. He claimed 'Basically, I don't think I've been influenced by anybody at all'[57] but, as will be seen, there are echoes of Cairncross's 'Langholm' in the early poems of Christopher Grieve.

Evidently Cairncross was not a quietly conventional minister. When he first encountered Christopher Grieve, Cairncross was attracted by the earnest intelligence of the boy though he found him, at times, an unsettling influence in Sunday School and at the Bible class the minister held in his home one evening each week. It is likely that Christopher had his first serious discussions on socialism with Cairncross who was intensely interested in the subject. While in Langholm, Cairncross worked on the essays assembled as *The Steps of the Pulpit* (1910), his second book. This discursive work considers the relative merits of socialism and Christianity. Sceptical of socialism as a surrogate religion, Cairncross argues that spiritual strength is superior to economic planning:

> The feeling I have is that Britain today is not needing socialism so much as the Spirit of Christ. ... Of course, if the Socialist has a better rule than that one of Christ given in the Sermon on the Mount, 'Therefore all things whatsoever ye would that men should do to you, do ye even so to them', if he has a better rule than that, I have an open mind. It was Christ who said that. I go by Him. ... Even if Socialism comes it is not likely to supersede the need of the gospel of Christ. ... The defect of much Socialistic pleading today is that it has no Christ.[58]

Long after he had renounced institutional Christianity, Christopher Grieve referred to 'the tremendous sayings of the Sermon on the Mount'.[59]

As Hugh MacDiarmid, the poet never eliminated the figure of Christ from his work, nor did he abandon the spiritual insights he absorbed as a youngster in Langholm. During his evolution as an artist he ingeniously adapted some of his early beliefs rather than completely rejecting them. For example, the intellectual elitism of MacDiarmid is an extension of the doctrine of the elect so crucial to the Calvinistic tradition of the Scottish kirk. It seems certain that MacDiarmid derived from the New Testament his own gospel of salvation through self-sacrifice: it is one of the major themes of *A Drunk Man Looks at the Thistle*, one of the main contentions of the unfinished epic *Cornish Heroic Song for Valda Trevlyn*. A poem collected in 1934, the year he joined the Communist Party of Great Britain, unambiguously declares a faith in 'the ineluctable certainty of the resurrection' (480). Such a statement does not mean that Mac-Diarmid, the self-styled Communist, was a closet Christian or that he was insincere in his many assertions of atheism.[60] He was, to cite his favourite Whitman quotation, a man who contained multitudes. Cairncross's beloved Wordsworth offered the paradox that the child is father of the man; behind the adult MacDiarmid was the youth who

spent six years of his life learning literary and theological lessons from
T. S. Cairncross.

With his accomplishment as the author of *The Return of the Master*
and his intellectual sophistication, Cairncross must have seemed an
idiosyncratic incomer to the natives of Langholm. *Lucky Poet* refers to a
minister

> who married a local mill-girl, sent her to Atholl Crescent in Edinburgh to
> learn domestic economy, to the vast amusement of the Langholm folk, and
> who took a church in another part of Scotland, after such a time of salty
> gossip and 'personalities' of all kinds in Langholm that he retaliated by
> writing a book about it and giving the townsfolk a terrible showing-up.[61]

Cairncross wrote such a book. His novel *Blawearie* was suppressed until
1911 precisely because of its unflattering comments on easily identifiable
Langholm characters. It describes Christopher Grieve's birthplace as a
tightly closed community:

> It has always been a mystery to me that Blawearie [i.e. Langholm] has never
> loved the stranger, for it is the stranger who keeps it alive. He keeps shop
> for it, finances its mills, heals its sick, preaches its gospel, makes its will, and
> tells of its beauty in story and song.[62]

Langholm, Cairncross lamented elsewhere, 'does not love the incomer'.[63]

Christopher Grieve, who was awarded several certificates for Bible
knowledge, looked on Cairncross as more than a minister: because he
could share his love of literature with the man he saw him as an
inspirational figure and a friend. Such like-minded friends were difficult
to find in Langholm. Christopher was encouraged in his 'omnivorous
reading'[64] by two of his cousins as well as by Cairncross. Some of
Christopher's cousins were millworkers, earning around fifteen shillings
a week, but the Laidlaw brothers had other ambitions. John Laidlaw
worked as a printer in Langholm; he also contributed topical poems to
local newspapers. Christopher greatly admired John's 'sardonic turn of
expression and ... faculty of biting invective'.[65] By a fortunate coincidence John's wife, Maggie Cairns, was on the staff of Langholm Library
and hoped for 'great things'[66] from Christopher.

Bob Laidlaw, ten years older than Christopher, also submitted verse
and prose to local papers. He worked in an office as a young man (later
setting up as a shoe repairer and retailer). When his young cousin was
twelve, Bob taught Christopher shorthand. A great admirer of the

sentimental style of J. M. Barrie (*Margaret Ogilvy* and *Sentimental Tommy* appeared when Christopher was four, *Peter Pan* when he was twelve), Bob also kept up to date with literary periodicals. The poet said that Bob 'gave a definite Scottish twist to my already well-developed tastes as a reader, and a modern twist as well'.[67] When Bob died, Grieve wrote to John Laidlaw:

> he and I had been so friendly in my early teens and I owed so much to him then − teaching me shorthand and lending me literary papers and books and talking with me on all sorts of subjects I was interested in.[68]

From such tributes it seems likely that Bob Laidlaw is the friend referred to in an autobiographical poem:

> I can't remember anything before I was six.[69]
> Aren't I backward? − But, later, in my early teens
> I had a friend who taught me to remember everything.
> (I mean everything about Scotland, of course.
> Thanks largely to him I have lived my life
> Fully and happily − finding fact
> Not only delightful but sufficient
> And needing no escapes into fantasy.)   (654)

Bob Laidlaw married T. S. Cairncross's sister-in-law Alice and refused to have anything to do with his cousin Christopher following the appearance of an attack on the minister in *Lucky Poet*.[70]

As he approached his adolescence, Christopher's interests were not exclusively confined to books. Outside the house, moreover, he was not always following the Curly Snake to the Langfall, or fishing (somewhat reluctantly) with his father and brother, or cycling 'fifty to a hundred miles in a day'.[71] He had a natural curiosity about sex:

> I remember how even as a boy I watched
> The courting couples go out the Ewes road − the girls
> Walking along so neat and ladylike
> While coming down the street but as soon as they got in the dark
> Siding up like heifers, or coming back
> Stop (where I stood hidden) to fix up.   (1032)

Probably Christopher's experience, at the time, was limited to such voyeurism. There is a story, 'Murtholm Hill', in which twelve-year-old Christopher's daring on a sledge impresses a girl of his own age though he is alarmingly unsure of himself with girls since 'in dealin' wi' lassies there was a haill complicated way o' gan' on he didna ken the first letter o' '.[72] One of his favourite anecdotes concerned a Border farmer who, on finding his son coupled with a servant girl, muttered 'Yech, Jock, you're an awful lad. You'll be smokin' next.'[73] Possibly Christopher associated smoking with maturity, both social and sexual, for he was smoking cigarettes before he was thirteen (later preferring a pipe, though he continued to smoke cigarettes).

In school he continued his voyeuristic study of sex. When he was twelve he transferred from the primary to the secondary department of Langholm Academy

> And I remember – when the teacher was temporarily out of the room – one of the country lads ... giving a very able object-lesson in sexual intercourse on the top of one of the desks with one of our class-mates, a sonsy wench.[74]

Notwithstanding such eagerly observed incidents, Grieve's feeling of isolation from his contemporaries was confirmed at school. He felt that the women teachers were hostile to him on account of his working-class background and that one in particular hated him 'venomously'.[75] Still, Grieve pronounced Langholm Academy a 'great school',[76] but more for its spirit of abandon than its scholastic standards. Corporal punishment – striking the palms of pupils with a leather strap known as the tawse – was practised in the school. Grieve relished the sight of a teacher going to a table drawer for his tawse only to find that it had been sliced into little pieces. On another occasion a friend of Grieve's threw a frameless slate at one of the teachers; it split a door panel as 'Black Jock' Howie, the headmaster, entered the room. 'If', Grieve observed, 'he'd been a fraction of a second earlier (as we wished he had) he'd have been sliced in two.'[77] Grieve had no athletic aspirations though rugby (which he enjoyed in his Army days) was a secular religion in Langholm. He had only one fist fight at school and that against an expert boxer. Grieve won by accident when his first tentative punch blooded the nose of his more muscular opponent.

Throughout his life Christopher Grieve railed against the anglicisation of Scottish education; as he put it, in *Lucky Poet*, Scotland's traditionally autonomous educational system was 'utterly de-Scoticized and adapted in the most shocking fashion to suit the exigencies of English Imperialism and the Capitalist system'.[78] Though Langholm boys and girls spoke Scots in the streets of the town they were conditioned to associate English with intelligence and were physically punished if they lapsed into the vernacular. Apart from some Burns lovesongs – 'one or two of the more hackneyed'[79] – pupils were not made aware of the glories of Scottish literature and knew nothing of writers of the stature of Dunbar, Henryson and Gavin Douglas. Again, though Langholm was in the heart of the balladland (see Cairncross's poem 'Langholm' on p. 32) the Border ballads were not part of the curriculum. Grieve got to know 'perhaps one of the ballads'[80] at school.

No doubt the ballad Grieve learned at Langholm Academy was 'Johnnie Armstrong' (numbered 169 in Francis James Child's classic collection of popular ballads) because of its local connotations. Langholm Castle (now in ruins) was built in the sixteenth century by the Armstrongs, whose kinsman Johnnie was the ill-fated reiver of the ballad. Around 1528 Johnnie Armstrong built his stronghold, Hollows Tower, at Gilnockie, a brisk ride from Langholm. His Border raids against the English infuriated James V who had to put up with English protests about a man acting as if he was a law unto himself. In 1530 the Scottish king levied an army to pacify the Debateable Land, trapping Johnnie Armstrong into a meeting with a false promise of safe conduct. The ballad emphasises the independence of Johnnie who bargains for his life with his great possessions (including 'gude Inglish gilt' and 'four and twenty ganging mills') before he is hanged at Carlenrig chapel. The variant printed in Allan Ramsay's two-volume anthology, *The Ever Green* (1724), closes with a characteristically anti-English flourish:

> John murdred was at Carlinrigg,
>> And all his galant companie:
> But Scotland's heart was never sae wae,
>> To see sae mony brave men die.

> Because they savd their country deir
>> Frae Englishmen; nane were sae bauld,
> Whyle Johnie livd on the border-syde,
>> Nane of them durst cum neir his hald.

The impact of such patriotic sentiments on Grieve can readily be imagined. He claimed to come 'Frae battles, mair than ballads' (1150) yet, in the Border ballads, battles are a way of life. Something of the feuding spirit of Johnnie Armstrong motivated Grieve.

One of Grieve's teachers at Langholm Academy knew 'Johnnie Armstrong' (and other ballads) 'almost by heart'.[81] Francis George Scott was born in Hawick on 25 January 1880. Educated at Hawick Academy and Brand's Teviot Grove Academy, Scott displayed an early aptitude for music and developed a talent for versifying in his teens. He studied English, under George Saintsbury, at Edinburgh University but abandoned the course without taking a degree. Instead he qualified as a teacher at Moray House College of Education, Edinburgh. In November 1903 he became a teacher of English at Langholm Academy. Thus this fiercely argumentative, emphatically Scottish personality came into the youthful world of Christopher Grieve. Years after, F. G. Scott would emerge as the most melodically gifted Scottish composer of his time, the man who set MacDiarmid lyrics to music, the mentor to whom *A Drunk Man Looks at the Thistle* is dedicated. In 1905, when Grieve was thirteen and Scott twenty-five, the two careers collided – 'and collided is the correct word'.[82] Grieve was then a lonely schoolboy and Scott a frustrated composer.

As told by Grieve, the first encounter between the two was routine:

> I was a boy of about thirteen in the sixth standard. I am afraid most of we boys had a cynical attitude towards our teachers ... We were all juvenile delinquents, and consequently up to pranks which today would condemn us to a remand home or Borstal. Our delinquencies were practised inside as well as outside school, and woe betide the teacher who was not an effective disciplinarian. Mr Scott was. As far as I recall, he thrashed me only once. I have no doubt I well deserved it. If I thought F. G. a brute, I recognise that he was a just brute. As a matter of fact I was his blue-eyed boy, the star pupil ... I think that the basis that was laid then for our later friendship and collaboration was the fact that we were both imbued with the frontier spirit.[83]

Scott's approach to education was flexible. When he set his class the annual essay on 'How I spent my holidays' he noticed that Grieve alone was unable to begin writing. 'Don't worry, Christopher,' Scott said as his pupil puzzled over his task, 'there's something in that big head of yours that will come out some day.'[84]

It was through Scott that Grieve was given a special interest in science and botany. 'He was', Grieve explained to Scott's nephew (by marriage) George Bruce, 'very keen on botany, and he used to send me out to the moors to find things and come back and show them.'[85] Scott's fellow English teacher William Burt also felt that Grieve had artistic potential. Without mentioning them by name, Grieve grouped Scott and Burt together in a compliment: 'Two of the men who were teachers at Langholm Academy when I was a boy [are] among the strictly limited number of the best brains in Scotland'.[86] Scott and Burt lost contact with Grieve when their pupil left school; the three were reunited in 1923 after Burt drew Scott's attention to poems by Hugh MacDiarmid appearing in the *Scottish Chapbook*. Until the grand reunion neither Scott nor Burt realised that MacDiarmid was none other than the Christopher Grieve they had taught.

John Howie, the headmaster, agreed with Scott and Burt that Grieve had an artistic temperament that might prove decisive; as the pupil once scored only two per cent in mathematics[87] and showed no inclination to compete with others in school examinations, however, it was felt that Christopher's future was unpredictable. Howie told James Grieve that his son would succeed if he did not ruin his life through recklessness or 'sheer carelessness'.[88] James Grieve told Christopher that he should seek security in the teaching profession. Already Christopher was contemplating a life that would leave him free to do creative work. He thought he might become a gamekeeper or a farm labourer (like his grandfather Andrew Graham) or a gardener. Asked by his parents to outline his intentions, he appalled them by telling them he intended to take to the roads as a tramp. Worse was to follow. 'Pressed,' Grieve recalled, 'I admitted that what I really was going to be was a poet; and that, I think, horrified them even more.'[89] An exhausting argument ensued, settled only when Christopher promised his parents that he would, indeed, seek a career in schoolteaching.

Despite this assurance to James and Elizabeth Grieve, Christopher was not happy with his decision. Looking back on it he indulged in a typical polemic against teachers in general, lambasting the majority of them as

hopeless Safety-Firsters, continually bending the knee to Baal in this connexion or that, or grovelling altogether, obliged, in order to secure their jobs, to tout and belly-crawl, and pull all manner of dirty little strings in the most ignominious fashion, the conscienceless agents of the Powers-that-be, destitute of any vocation for teaching, and themselves indifferently educated and utterly destitute of culture...[90]

In Langholm he was anxious to avoid any betrayal of his working-class origins. Though they had little sympathy with him, he cared passionately about the predicament of the working men and women of Langholm. His cousins who worked in the mills clattered in their clogs through the streets in the early morning and came back in the night when the mills were closed and all for fifteen shillings a week. Grieve, conscious of the 'beat of the wooden clogs upon the pavement',[91] concluded that the solution to the problems of the workers lay in socialism. At the age of sixteen (in 1908, the year he left school) he became a member of the Independent Labour Party — founded in 1893, the year after Grieve's birth, under the influence of the Lanarkshire miner Keir Hardie. Around the same time Grieve also joined the Territorial Army (or Territorial Force as it was originally called when established in 1908).

On 1 July 1908 the local paper, the *Eskdale and Liddesdale Advertiser*, reported that Christopher Grieve had gained an Intermediate Certificate, qualifying him as a Junior Student which meant that he would leave Langholm for Edinburgh. Just over four months later the same paper published a three-stanza poem called 'Memories of Langholm'.[92] It was attributed to Alister K. Laidlaw. Few readers would have guessed that the name concealed the identity of the recently departed Kirsty Grieve:

> Here is no gorgeous rioting of gold
>   Blue, or gleaming red,
> In skies, unutterably cold,
>   Hopeless and dead.
> The vision which no more delights these eyes,
>   In bright remembrance glows,
> There is a glory in the western skies;
>   Esk ripples rose.
>
> How horrible the clatter and the noise
>   That jars eternally!
> There is no music in the voice
>   Of the city.
> But, Oh! the sweet sad song Ewes used to sing
>   Is ringing in my ears.
> Its magic tinkling still will ring
>   Throughout the years.

God! Here is gloom and stricken loneliness,
    And barren, withered boles,
Gaunt, stark, loom through the mistiness,
    And men, like moles,
Potter in the darkness. Great God! Does gorse
    Still glow on Whita's slope?
Does Esk ream with its old wild force?
    Sea-winds blow hope?

2

A Man Sae
Shunned

What speculations maun a man sae shunned
No' ha'e until at last the reason's brocht
To view acceptable, as the fact may be
 On different grun's to them and me.
 'Charisma and My Relatives'   (302)

THAT embattled Borderer Thomas Carlyle set out, on the eve of his
fourteenth birthday in November 1809, to walk the hundred miles
from his native Ecclefechan to Edinburgh so that he could attend the
university in the capital of Scotland. Christopher Grieve – who 'kent
that Ecclefechan stood/As pairt o' an eternal mood' (144) – by contrast,
had an easier passage to Edinburgh than Carlyle. In 1908 he took the
branch line from Langholm to Riddings – an eight-mile journey lasting
almost an hour[1] – then caught the Carlisle-Edinburgh train.

When he arrived in Edinburgh to attend Broughton Junior Student
Centre Grieve's immediate problem was how to adapt to the change he
experienced between the small, familiar rural community in which he
had spent his boyhood and the rather daunting capital city in which he
now found himself. For all its cultural credentials, Edinburgh did not
instantly appeal to Grieve who did not like 'Edinburgh (or any city very
much), for I have never been able to find one that was not full of

reminders of the fact that Cain, the murderer, was also the first city-builder'.[2] Out of Langholm and into another world, Grieve was homesick as the poem 'Memories of Langholm' discloses. He complains of cold skies and endless noise, of gloom and loneliness, men who 'like moles,/Potter in the darkness'. Impressively, he had rapidly written a poem expressing the emotions of homesickness; significantly, he had submitted to a Langholm paper under a pseudonym linking him with his Langholm cousins. Grieve was not yet sure of his own identity.

If he felt insecure in Edinburgh then there were interesting compensations. Grieve took the opportunity, in his first year in Edinburgh, to join the Edinburgh University branch of the Fabian Society.[3] This made him a member of three organisations, the others being the ILP and the Territorial Army. He was, at least in his own opinion, a reluctant and somewhat subversive temporary citizen of a big city. Aware of both the architectural elegance and the 'loathsome'[4] slums of Edinburgh, Grieve turned to the chore of training as a teacher. At sixteen he was a small,[5] wiry youth with fair hair – 'towsy hair of the colour of teased rope'[6] – and, even at this early age, dark lines under his eyes, the result of his constant reading. His only physical peculiarities, too small to be noticed, were 'two holes, like piercings for earrings, at the upper ends of the joinings of my ears to my head'.[7] He arrived at Broughton Junior Student Centre wearing a Norfolk jacket and knickerbockers. His appearance in 1908 has been preserved in a sympathetic verbal portrait by his English teacher, George Ogilvie:

> I remember vividly Grieve's arrival among us. I see the little, slimly built figure in hodden grey, the small, sharp-featured face with its piercing eyes, the striking head with its broad brow and great mass of flaxen curly hair. He hailed from Langholm, and had a Border accent you could have cut with a knife. I am afraid some of the city students smiled at first at the newcomer, but he very speedily won their respect. He certainly very quickly established himself in mine. ... He was not, it must be admitted, a model student; in some subjects, frankly, he had no interest. As a matter of fact he became the despair of most of his teachers. Yet none of them could help liking him. He had a most engaging ingenuousness, and I have yet to meet the infant who could look as innocent as Grieve.[8]

Ogilvie was the Principal Teacher of English at Broughton from 1904 to 1928, and remained one of the most influential men in Grieve's life. An engineer's son, Ogilvie was born in Glasgow in 1871; when his mother died the family moved to Kilmarnock and George left Kilmarnock

Academy at the age of fifteen to serve his time as a draughtsman at Barclay's Engineering Works. During his seven years' engineering apprenticeship Ogilvie joined the Kilmarnock Christian Union, one of the evangelical organisations formed in the wake of the wave of revivalism that swept Britain in the 1870s after the meetings held by the Americans Dwight Lyman Moody and Ira David Sankey. Ogilvie was appointed President of the Young Men's Fellowship, a branch of the Christian Union, and preached eloquently in the streets of Kilmarnock.

Ogilvie was always an inquisitive Christian, interested in biblical debate. Scotland, in the 1880s, was theologically disturbed by the case of William Robertson Smith who, for expressing advanced views of the historicity of the earlier books of the Bible, had been deposed as Professor of Old Testament at the Free Church College in Aberdeen in 1881. After Smith's dismissal the so-called Higher Criticism was widely discussed in Scotland by Christians interested in coming to terms with, for example, the theory of evolution. Eagerly involved in contemporary analyses of theological issues, Ogilvie decided to go to university to prepare for the ministry.

He won a bursary examination to Glasgow University in 1894 and the following year moved into the Students' Settlement, established by Professor Henry Drummond and others in Possil Road in the city's Garscube district. George and his brother Archibald shared a double bedroom for which the joint rent (board and lodging) was twenty-five shillings a week. Along with the thirteen other settlers (as those in residence were called) George and Archibald tested their religious principles in practical circumstances. George preached against the social evils of drink at temperance meetings while Archibald visited the poor people of Garscube. In 1897 George and Archibald became Joint Wardens of the Settlement. For George, his work for the Settlement was a moving and instructive experience, giving him glimpses of the deprivation that prevailed in areas such as Garscube. 'It was little', he admitted 'we could do for those poor devils. The area was poverty-stricken, and they were filthy, bug-infested and drink-sodden.'[9] A successor of his at Broughton suggested that he 'began to find his Christian faith broadening out inconveniently widely, till the idea of preaching on orthodox lines became increasingly difficult for him'.[10] As a result he switched from divinity to literature and graduated in 1899 with a First Class Honours degree in English. He had already trained as a teacher at the Episcopal Church Normal College (during his university course, from September to February 1897-8).

After teaching in Glasgow and Fife Ogilvie was, in 1904, appointed Principal Teacher of English at the new Pupil Teacher Centre at Broughton (subsequently Broughton Higher Grade School and Junior Student Centre and, eventually, Broughton Secondary School). A mature man of thirty-three when he took the job at Broughton, Ogilvie was still a committed Christian; he became an elder of Lothian Road Church and a close friend of the minister, the Revd Robert Drummond. He was also a convinced socialist, as Grieve was pleased to discover:

> He had ... a revolutionary note. It may seem absurd to call Ogilvie a revolutionary. He was far too gentle, too humble, too self-effacing to fill the stereotype of that role – yet perhaps it is the quiet revolutionaries who are the most revolutionary. Ordinary working men and women with whom he came in contact instinctively felt that he was their friend. This was not to be wondered at, because his Socialism sprang from his heart; his faith in Socialism was founded on something more durable than Socialist polemics or mental gymnastics. He believed that we were all made of the same common clay, and that good men may become evil in certain circumstances, and that evil men may be uplifted. He treated all men as equal, irrespective of their rank or social position, and his contempt was reserved for the snob alone.[11]

Grieve's admiration was reciprocated. His first essay, an unseen done in class, seemed to Ogilvie the 'finest bit of work'[12] he ever received at Broughton. From that day onwards Ogilvie decided 'to keep my eye on Grieve'.[13] He was certainly not disappointed by his pupil's creative progress.

Like Christopher Grieve, George Ogilvie was small and wiry. Outside the classroom he wore a bowler hat at a dandy's tilt, inside the school he had few personal affectations. He spoke in a soft voice, the highlight of his lessons being his readings from the works of his favourite poets from Palgrave's *Golden Treasury:* Shakespeare, Milton, Burns (on whom he compiled a school textbook), Shelley, Tennyson. While Grieve delighted in these classroom performances, Ogilvie never let him forget that he was in Edinburgh for a purpose. Grieve attended Broughton as a junior student, a pupil-teacher; that is he was required to continue his education while completing his three-year course of teacher training. He was, initially at least, a dutiful pupil. The *Eskdale & Liddesdale Advertiser* (30 Dec. 1908) reported that Grieve had passed in Higher Grade English and the Broughton School Register recorded that he had scored 83 in Lower English, 87 in Higher English, 68 in Honours English. His parents were pleased with this evidence of scholastic progress.

James Grieve would not have approved of the iconoclastic direction his son's thoughts were taking. After school hours Grieve was drawn into discussion by Ogilvie who introduced his pupil to the *New Age*, the radical weekly edited from 1907 to 1922 by A. R. Orage (who was to be a friend to MacDiarmid in the years to come). As a member of the ILP and Edinburgh University Fabian Society, Grieve was taken by the paper's progressive tone and he found Orage's editorial line stimulating for its insistence that the ordinary man could, with a supreme effort of will, surpass himself and become almost superhuman. Thanks to the efforts of Herbert Spencer, Social Darwinism – advancing evolution as the ultimate universal principle – was a commonplace with English intellectuals of the Edwardian age. Orage applied a European interpret- ation to the evolutionary idea, exalting the individual above the broad Spencerian drift of humanity.

Orage trained as a teacher and in 1893 took a teaching job in Leeds where he joined the ILP, immersed himself in theosophy and formed a close friendship with the literary journalist Holbrook Jackson. In 1905 Orage abandoned his career as a teacher and moved to London in an attempt to make a reputation as a writer. A year later he brought out a book that was to have a considerable impact on Grieve. *Friedrich Nietzsche: The Dionysian Spirit of the Age* was published by T. N. Foulis, the Edinburgh firm who would later (in 1923) publish the first number of Grieve's anthology *Northern Numbers*. Orage apotheosised Nietzsche as the 'greatest immoralist the modern world has seen',[14] punctuating his exposition with pages of aphorisms selected from Nietzsche's works. 'Become what thou art'[15] was one of those aphorisms. It was treated with the grandeur of a gospel by the *Scottish Chapbook* of 1923 which proclaimed 'the slogan of a Scottish literary revival must be the Nietz- schean "Become what you are" '.[16] Thus spake MacDiarmid.

Friedrich Nietzsche elucidated the concept of the dynamic Dionysian movement, stressed the German's moral relativism, promoted the will to power. Orage cautioned that man would not inevitably evolve into Superman but pointed out that this would require immense determination on the part of the individual:

> Remembering that Nietzsche denied any purpose in nature other than man's will, the creation of the Superman may not be left to chance. ... Thus the Superman, if he is to appear at all, must be willed – in plain words, be bred.[17]

46

The Nietzschean doctrine was expanded in *Nietzsche in Outline and Aphorism* (1907) and linked to theosophical thought in *Consciousness: Animal, Human, and Superman* (1907). Animal consciousness, Orage argued, possessed a unity compared to the duality of human consciousness. The way forward was to make possible the extension of consciousness through the creation of the Superman:

> Perhaps the sure way [towards the extension of consciousness] is to raise, to deepen, and to extend our human faculties; for as man is only an intensified animal, an ecstatic animal, if you will, superman is no more than an intensified man, man made ecstatic. Therefore it is that superman is not the contradiction but the fulfilment of man...[18]

Edinburgh was the appropriate place for Grieve to respond to these ideas for the authorised translation of Nietzsche's work was published in the capital; Helen Zimmern's translation of *Beyond Good and Evil* appeared in 1907 over the imprint of the Good European Society, the Darien Press.

In 1907 Orage and Holbrook Jackson made a successful bid, with the backing of George Bernard Shaw who put up half the capital, for the *New Age*. When it was founded, in 1894, the *New Age* served the interests of the Liberal party but Orage was adamant that the weekly would operate as an intellectual organ of socialism, particularly the theory of Guild Socialism which urged the trade unions to evolve – or will themselves – into national guilds conscious of craftsmanship. Orage preached the Nietzschean gospel in the pages of the *New Age* of which, by 1908, he was sole editor. In his first six months as editor Orage obtained contributions by Shaw, Belloc, Havelock Ellis, John Galsworthy and H. G. Wells who wrote, in June 1907 in the *New Age*, that the essence of socialism was to give birth to the 'complex systematic idea' of a higher civilisation. The *New Age* was a minority paper (22,000 was the highest circulation it ever achieved). Its readers thought of themselves as an élite. George Ogilvie and Christopher Grieve, teacher and pupil, considered they were among those participating in the evolutionary movement upwards to a higher civilisation.

Both were the sons of working men, both had a Presbyterian upbringing, both believed they could surpass themselves through intellectual effort. Whereas Ogilvie saw no conflict between his socialism, his *New*

Age Nietzscheanism and his position as a kirk elder, Grieve was convinced that the church was an institution contaminated by what Nietzsche condemned as the slave-morality of an irrelevant ethic. An antinomian before he was fourteen, Grieve at sixteen was a socialist and something of a Nietzschean. What Grieve valued in Nietzsche was

> the value to European thought of his logical exposure of undogmatic Christianity ... his antithesis of Dionysian and Apollonian, his conception of the Eternal Recurrence, his challenge to objective science divorced from society, his exaltation of the individual, his searching analysis of the values of democracy and nationalism ... his devastating attack on the social philosophers who thought that you could destroy the whole basis of the Christian religion and yet retain a few of its ethical principles.[19]

Coincidentally, another Scottish (or, more exactly, Orcadian) poet also felt, as a young man, he could surpass himself by attending to Nietzschean injunctions. As an impoverished clerk, in Glasgow, Edwin Muir wrote to Orage and was advised to concentrate on one writer. Muir chose Nietzsche. Nietzsche saw man as 'a rope connecting animal and Superman — a rope across a precipice'.[20] Like Edwin Muir, Christopher Grieve wanted to make his way across that precipice.

Arnold Bennett (under the pseudonym 'Jacob Tonson') and F. S. Flint (a champion of French poetry) had started columns in the *New Age* in 1908; in 1909 T. S. Hulme introduced *New Age* readers to the philosophy of Henri Bergson who claimed — *L'Évolution créatrice* (1907) — that the creative urge and not natural selection animated evolution. Reinforced by his reading, Grieve was sure that the artist, the poet, had a unique role to play in the evolutionary drama but also realised that the tightrope walk across the precipice was fraught with danger. One of his favourite poets, John Davidson, committed suicide at the age of fifty-one on 23 March 1909. Davidson had been brought up in Greenock where his father was an Evangelical Union minister; when he went to London he published poems, rich in scientific imagery, exploring the Nietzschean notion of the artist as superman. As a result of economic and emotional difficulties, Davidson was subject to fits of depression and eventually drowned himself in the English Channel, recalling the fate of 'A Runnable Stag':

> The stag, the buoyant stag, the stag
> That slept at last in a jewelled bed
> Under the sheltering ocean spread,
> The stag, the runnable stag.

Grieve took Davidson's death as a personal blow, feeling as if 'the bottom had fallen out of my world'.[21] The moment endured, for Hugh MacDiarmid composed a poignant address to the dead Davidson:

> I remember one death in my boyhood
> That next to my father's, and darker, endures;
> Not Queen Victoria's, but Davidson, yours,
> And something in me has always stood
> Since then looking down the sandslope
> On your small black shape by the edge of the sea,
> – A bullet-hole through a great scene's beauty,
> God through the wrong end of a telescope.   (362)

(It is worth noting that several MacDiarmid poems later address dead writers: Dostoevsky in *A Drunk Man Looks at the Thistle*, Rilke in 'Vestigia Nulla Retrorsum', Doughty in 'Stony Limits', Joyce in *In Memoriam James Joyce*.)

Grieve saw Davidson as a pioneer of scientifically orientated verse and described him as 'the only Scottish poet to whom I owe anything at all',[22] a characteristic exaggeration. Approaching the age of seventeen when Davidson died, Grieve identified with a writer who had also been a pupil-teacher (at the Highlanders' Academy in Greenock). With his perception of himself as a modern Ishmael, Grieve could take his stand with Davidson's 'The Testament of a Man Forbid' (1901):

> Mankind has cast me out. When I became
> So close a comrade of the day and night,
> Of earth and of the seasons of the year,
> And so submissive in my love of life
> And study of the world that I unknew
> The past and names renowned, religion, art,
> Inventions, thoughts, and deeds, as men unknow
> What good and evil fate befell their souls
> Before their bodies gave them residence,
> (How the old letter haunts the spirit still!
> As if the soul were other than the sum
> The body's powers make up – a golden coin,
> Amount of so much silver, so much bronze!)
> I said, rejoicing, 'Now I stand erect,
> And am that which I am.'

The Nietzschean thrust of the last two lines quoted and the parenthetical aside were not lost on Grieve. He knew that the traditional iambic rhythm hardly contained the intellectual indignation of the speaker who is compelled to keep his own company. Davidson's Man Forbid is not only isolated by society but conscious of his place in a vast cosmos, a universe empty of the God whom Nietzsche pronounced dead:

> So I went forth for evermore forbid
> The company of men. The Universe,
> Systems and suns and all that breathes and is,
> Appeared at first in that dread solitude
> Only the momentary, insolent
> Irruption of a glittering fantasy
> Into the silent, empty Infinite.
> But eyes and ears were given to me again:
> With these a man may do; with these, endure.

Davidson's vision of the individual as a creative component of the universe was absorbed by Grieve. The immortal Drunk Man of Mac-Diarmid was anxious to 'unite/Man and the Infinite' (98).

In Edinburgh Grieve was not entirely 'forbid/The company of men'. He had adopted Ogilvie as his mentor (as he had adopted Cairncross in Langholm) and his contemporaries included some who shared his passion for literature. Grieve was numbered Entry 342 in the Broughton Register. Entry 349 was Mary Baird Aitken. She returned to Broughton as a teacher and, in 1944, published the novel *Soon Bright Day* about the great Scottish radical Thomas Muir of Huntershill. Her description of Ogilvie as 'the man with the opal mind'[23] pleased Grieve. Inspired by Ogilvie, other Broughton students of Grieve's generation went on to write books. Edward Albert collaborated with Ogilvie on *A Practical Course in Secondary English* (1913) before achieving some success as a minor novelist. Roderick Watson Kerr (1893-1960), a year younger than Grieve, published a volume of war poems under the title *War Daubs* (1919). In 1922 Kerr founded with his fellow student John Gould (and George Malcolm Thomson) the Porpoise Press which published Scottish poets and novelists before becoming a subsidiary of Faber & Faber.

Grieve's closest friend at Broughton was another youth Ogilvie thought had literary promise. John Bogue Nisbet (Entry 277 in the Broughton Register) was a year older than Grieve: he was born in Reston, Berwickshire, in June 1891. In 1907 Ogilvie had founded a School

Literary and Debating Society, also the *Broughton Magazine*. The Summer 1909 issue of the magazine contained a chilling tale about death and disaster in a fishing village. Calling his story 'Sea Weed and Sand' Nisbet signed it with his initials J. N. His description of the reaction of the village women to the loss of the fishing fleet has a Gothic intensity:

> They howl and shriek, but their shrieking is not heard. They can hear nothing but the furies around them – see nothing but the glimmer of the foam. Now and then a black form approaches the rocks, through the phosphorescent gleam, a chilling shriek pierces the elements, and the waves dash and grind and churn as before. In this crowd of maniacs, on the rocks at the harbour-head, there are a few men, peasants and old fishermen, striving their utmost to hold these women, raving to tear the sea to pieces.[24]

Doubtless attracted by Nisbet's inventive intelligence, Grieve befriended the older youth. The pair spent the summer holidays of 1909 cycling and camping in Berwickshire. To Grieve, Nisbet was 'infinitely more than a brother, a very spiritual familiar'.[25] They had similar interests. Nisbet, like Grieve, was a socialist and an ardent reader of poetry. Both bought (or borrowed) copies of a book published in 1909, Jethro Bithell's anthology of *Contemporary German Poetry*. Bithell's little book was a revelation, introducing Grieve and Nisbet to translated versions of the verse of Rilke, Frank Wedekind, Carl Spitteler, Else Lasker-Schüller and others. Even the introduction excited Grieve. Bithell's praise of Else Lasker-Schüller as 'one flame of passion, consuming and consumed'[26] is echoed in Grieve's sonnet 'Consummation', beginning 'Ablaze yet unconsumed I lay in thee' (14). Gratifyingly for Grieve, Bithell's introduction ended on a note of Nietzschean affirmation:

> Darwin, Walt Whitman, Baudelaire, Verlaine, Nietzsche: these are the poets who have most influenced the poetry of the last decades in Germany. Has all this influence been for the good of literature? That is too early to decide. But one thing is certain: the lyric poets march with Ibsen towards an ideal which can only be approached by subverting all that is false and insincere.[27]

That had an optimistic ring. Grieve and Nisbet believed that they, too, were the enemies of the false and insincere.

In his second year as a junior student, Grieve was appointed editor of the school magazine by Ogilvie, its founder. The third editor of the *Broughton Magazine*, he was responsible for the first three numbers of the third volume. His first issue contained a fair amount of the editor's own work: a facetious preface, a story 'The Black Monkey', the 'Centre Notes', a poem 'The Land Beyond Quadratics', contributions to the humour column. The poem 'The Land Beyond Quadratics' is unexceptional, nowhere near the level of 'Memories of Langholm'. It is clearly written by a clever youth who has read the light verse of Belloc as well as the children's verse of Stevenson. It invokes a land devoted to endless self-indulgence as two quatrains show:

> Everlasting cigars to infinity sprout
>   In that many-coloured land,
> And pulverised surds go up the spout,
>   To the rant of a German band.

> Pumps at corners yield strawberry jam;
>   Automatic machines, ginger beer.
> The streets are paved with rashers of ham –
>   'My eye,' to quote Keats, 'if it don't look queer.'[28]

More substantial is 'The Black Monkey', an absorbing tale taking its cue from H. G. Wells's scientific romances. A brilliant science student – from Langholm – inherits a fortune and leaves college to get married. Beside himself with grief, on the death of his beloved in a car crash, he vows to find the secret of eternal life. An experiment to prolong his life transforms him into a black monkey before the ageing process is abruptly accelerated. It is the most accomplished piece of writing in the magazine. On other pages Grieve's friend Nisbet wrote up the affairs of the Literary Society. He noted that in a school debate on 19 October 1909 Grieve made an eloquent appeal on behalf of Blood and Thunder Literature. He lost the motion. Still, Grieve was one of the most colourful members of the Literary Society. Giving a stump speech on 'Vegetation in Morocco' he managed to achieve maximum effect by wrapping himself in a large table-cloth.

Manifestly, Grieve was enjoying himself at Broughton. Sensitive and introspective as he could be, there was a side of him that loved the limelight. The poetic soul had a histrionic spirit. On 9 and 10 December 1909 both Grieve and Nisbet acted – as Jarvis and Leontine respectively – in the school production of Goldsmith's boisterous comedy *The Good-Natured Man*. Six hundred saw the two performances which brought the school a profit of two shillings. On 23 January Broughton staged a mock-election. Grieve, standing as an Independent Women's Suffrage candidate, came bottom of the poll with eight votes (compared to sixty-one for the successful Liberal candidate).

Editor of the school magazine and Ogilvie's protégé, Grieve was treated by his fellow students as the literary star of the Junior Student Centre in 1910. However, his interests went further than the conventional subject-matter of poetry. From the precedent of John Davidson he was persuaded that the serious poet should be familiar with scientific developments. Accordingly he and Nisbet turned up at school, on the evening of 18 February 1910, to listen to a talk by Peter Ross, Principal Teacher of Mathematics at Broughton. Author of a textbook on algebra, Ross was a vivacious character who had become engrossed in astronomy, then a rapidly expanding science; for example, Einstein's Special Theory of Relativity had, in 1905, made startling assumptions about the speed of light. Ross's lecture dealt mainly with the solar system. According to Nisbet, Ross had a faculty for making astronomy intelligible to the lay members of his audience:

> Mr Ross gave a Lecture which was interesting from first to last, and without so much as a single sentence that was dull or uninteresting ... He took us to each planet and star in turn, and allowed us to make our bow and to add each to our list of acquaintances. Indeed, sometimes we got so vivid a picture that we imagined we heard these great bodies dancing in the upper airs.[29]

Grieve must have been enraptured by the lecture. He began to see the space between the stars as profound with meaning. It is, indeed, tempting to speculate that Ross's talk (and others like it) led indirectly to the astronomical conceits of the early MacDiarmid:

> Mars is braw in crammasy,
> Venus in a green silk goun,
> The auld mune shak's her gowden feathers,
> Their starry talk's a wheen o' blethers   (17)

For a spectacular reason, the year 1910 caused many thousands to think about the depths of space. Astronomically the year marked the return of Halley's Comet, which came closest to the Earth in May. The event caused considerable panic, not only in the popular press. Camille Flammarion – founder of Juvisy Observatory, author of such works as *Catalogue of Movement in Double and Multiple Stars* (1878) and a man to whom Grieve wrote in 1911 – concluded that the poison gas in the comet's tail could be catastrophic and predicted, wrongly, that 'the cyanogen gas would impregnate the atmosphere and possibly snuff out all life on the planet'.[30] Seeking copy for his third and last issue of the *Broughton Magazine*, Grieve asked Ogilvie for a contribution. Ogilvie wrote 'Two Valedictory Poems from any Teacher to any Pupil Leaving School'. In less than twenty minutes Grieve completed a reply along the same stylistic lines, juxtaposing a sonnet with three quatrains of light verse. The comet made its appearance in the second of Grieve's 'Two Valedictory Poems to any Teacher from any Pupil Leaving School':

> Sir, you're very like a comet
>   Whose orbit is a closed ellipse.
> The phlegm with which you roam it
>   Gives me pips.[31]

Ogilvie had no hesitation in saying that 'Grieve carried off the honours in the exchange of compliments'.[32]

By now Grieve was a regular guest at Ogilvie's home in Cluny Gardens. He accompanied Ogilvie to the Lothian Road Church Literary and Debating Society, becoming friendly with the minister, the Revd Dr Robert Drummond. One of Grieve's earliest stories, 'A Limelight from a Solitary Wing' (collected in *Annals of the Five Senses*) focuses on his state of mind in the spring of 1910 in the light of his involvement with the Literary Society in Lothian Road. Grieve depicts himself as – simultaneously – a lonely seeker after spiritual truth, a lost soul in search of likeminded companions, an intellectual elitist, a socialist exulting in the common cause of humankind. Psychologically taut with tension, he takes comfort from the thought that he is a part, however small, of a majestically mysterious universe:

> Thus would he stand with his eyes widened at the mysteries around him, remembering that, in spite of all his book-lore, what he knew was but a trifle and that the smallest detail of the world was infinitely greater than his own immortal mind, and recognising, too, in that prodigiousness of the universe a safeguarding excellence, since it must hold infinite resources and he might allow it some credit without accusing himself of improvidence. Since the fish were still spawning in the waters and a million mothers were smiling at their babies and the publishers' catalogues were increasing in number and growing in size and interest, he found fresh courage to be a mere man and to commit the rest to the numberer of the stars.[33]

The complexity of the world creates contradictions, Grieve implies; the attempt to cope imaginatively with the universe is an end in itself. Therefore he feels that the 'redeeming inconsistency'[34] of his character is a notable virtue.

On 6 May 1910, the month that Halley's Comet passed closest to the Earth, George V succeeded to the throne on the death of his father. A. R. Orage announced, in the *New Age* of 12 May 1910, that the 'last genuine link with the Victorian age has been broken with the death of King Edward VII'.[35] Devouring the *New Age* with the hunger of the neophyte, Grieve welcomed what, indeed, seemed to be the dawn of a new age. He had various views on the future. If he was occasionally overwhelmed by the apparent inconsistency of his opinions – the conflict, for example, between his socialism and his supermania – he was certain he had in him the power to become a genuine poet. The Dionysian man, he was inclined to believe, had no need to cultivate consistency. He had Nietzsche's assurance on that. The title alone, *Beyond Good and Evil*, agitated him – 'Guid and Ill' (91) are counterpointed in *A Drunk Man Looks at the Thistle* – but the refutation of rationalism was an inspiration. In his first chapter, 'Prejudices of Philosophers', Nietzsche wrote:

> The problem of the value of truth presented itself before us ... The falseness of an opinion is not for us any objection to it ... The question is, how far an opinion is life-furthering, life-preserving, species-preserving, perhaps species-rearing ... *To recognise untruth as a condition of life:* that is certainly to impugn the traditional ideas of value in a dangerous manner, and a philosophy which ventures to do so, has thereby alone placed itself beyond good and evil ... It is certainly not the least charm of a theory that it is refutable; it is precisely thereby that it attracts the more subtle minds ... All psychology hitherto has run aground on moral prejudices and timidities, it has not dared to launch out into the depths ... The power of moral prejudices has penetrated deeply into the most intellectual world, the world apparently most indifferent and unprejudiced, and has obviously operated in an injurious, obstructive, blinding, and distorting manner ... We sail away right *over* morality, we crush out, we destroy perhaps the remains of our own morality by daring to make our voyage thither ... Never yet did a *profounder* world of insight reveal itself to daring travellers and adventurers ...[36]

Like many young men of his generation, Grieve was seduced by the audacity of Nietzsche's approach.

Nietzsche's invitation to set forth on an amoral voyage was one thing; committing an irresponsible act was another. Grieve's adventure beyond good and evil amounted to little more than a schoolboy prank that seriously backfired. On 17 January 1911 it was discovered that Broughton had been entered overnight and that books and postage stamps, to the value of three shillings, had been stolen. Four of the stolen books were science reference works belonging to the School Board; the other four volumes belonged to Ogilvie. The headmaster, John Watson, must have adhered to Victorian standards of morality for he was not amused. He reported the theft to the police. Detectives investigated the burglary on 19 January and, as a result of their inquiries, two third-year junior students – Andrew Sutherland and William Blackhall – were placed under arrest. On admitting he had taken and stolen the science reference books, Sutherland was put under probation. Blackhall maintained his innocence with regard to Ogilvie's books. Predictably, Ogilvie did not want to pursue the matter so the case against Blackhall was dropped.

Grieve was involved in the theft of Ogilvie's books but his fellow students were unwilling to give evidence against him and Blackhall (for this act of solidarity six students were formally reprimanded by the School Board on 1 February). Ogilvie was anxious to avoid a scandal and, thanks to his intervention, Christopher Grieve was allowed to resign from the school on 27 January 1911. The Broughton school log puts it diplomatically: 'Christopher Grieve, Junior Student, resigned on grounds of health and mistaking his vocation.'[37] His friends were not so fortunate. Sutherland was expelled from Broughton on 1 February; Blackhall, after being reinstated with a punitive £5 cut in his allowance, left the school on 17 February and emigrated to Canada.

In effect, Grieve had been rejected by Broughton but not by Ogilvie. Albert Mackie, who attended Broughton some time after Grieve and edited the *Broughton Magazine* in 1922-3, put it at its simplest when he said 'Christopher was put out for pinching books'.[38] Grieve's version of his departure from Broughton was at variance with the somewhat ignominious truth. He wrote defiantly:

My father died suddenly before I was finished at the Junior Student Centre. I took immediate advantage of the fact to abandon my plans for becoming a teacher. That is one thing which I have never, for one moment, regretted. ... If I had gone on and qualified and become a teacher, my sojourn in the profession would have been of short duration in any event, and I would have been dismissed as Thomas Davidson and John Maclean and my friend, A. S. Neill, were dismissed.[39]

In fact, Grieve 'left Broughton under a cloud'[40] eight days before the death of his father.

James Grieve was proud of his record of unbroken service as a rural postman. He had never been ill in his life until, in the winter of 1910, he caught a chill after attending a funeral. Christopher Grieve was adamant on the subject of his father's fitness; 'He'd never had an illness in his life,'[41] he said; he'd 'never ailed' (1251). Tragically, James Grieve's chill developed into pneumonia. Christopher bitterly resented the treatment of this condition:

> Now at that time, he belonged to the trade union – the Postmen's Federation as it was called then – and they paid one shilling a week for medical attendence, and the local doctor was an old Tory who had no use for shilling-a-week patients. So, when he was called to my father, he simply stuffed him with a dose of – injected a dose of morphia, said to my mother, 'He'll be all right when he comes out of that'. Of course, he didn't come out of it. His heart gave way and he died at forty-seven.[42]

There is perhaps a dark element of wishful thinking in that account, as if Grieve wanted to blame someone, rather than something, for the death of his father. James Grieve's death certificate records that he died at Library Buildings, Langholm, at 5.15 a.m. on 3 February 1911. Doctor Robert Watt confirmed that the cause of death was acute lobar pneumonia sustained over six days. The certificate was signed by James Grieve's brother, Thomas, of 25 Eskdale Place, Langholm.

Before he died, so Christopher was told by his mother, his father 'turned and gied a lang/Last look at pictures o' my brither and me/Hung on the wa' aside the bed' (1148). James Grieve may well have felt a sense of wonder as he thought of the contrasting personalities of his two sons. Christopher had left Langholm for Edinburgh to train as a teacher, a conventionally respectable career that was now closed to him. Andrew had, in 1909 at the age of fifteen, gone to Burton-on-Trent to work as a boy clerk in the Inland Revenue and was conscientiously applying himself to a steady job. Grieve dwelt on the meaning of his father's final look for years. It became the basis for 'The Watergaw', the first Scots poem attributed to Hugh MacDiarmid:

Ae weet forenicht i' the yow-trummle
I saw yon antrin thing,
A watergaw wi' its chitterin' licht
Ayont the on-ding;
An' I thocht o' the last wild look ye gied
Afore ye deed!

There was nae reek i' the laverock's hoose
That nicht – an' nane i' mine;
But I hae thocht o' that foolish licht
Ever sin' syne;
An' I think that mebbe at last I ken
What your look meant then.   (17)

No longer a junior student on a bursary, Christopher Grieve had to look for a job – in Edinburgh, for he was not willing to return to Langholm discredited. For all his authentic 'indifference to money-making and material comfort'[43] he needed to support himself somehow. Saddened by the fuss that had been made over a minor misdemeanour at Broughton, George Ogilvie was instrumental in getting Grieve a job as a journalist with the *Edinburgh Evening Dispatch*. Grieve found this a grimmer situation than the one he had enjoyed (with reservations) at Broughton Junior Student Centre. His immediate boss was Isaac Donald, chief reporter of the *Dispatch*. An irascible man, Donald irritated Grieve. Donald treated his office juniors as inferiors and satisfied his cruel sense of humour by sending young reporters on impossible errands. It amused him greatly to embarrass his reporters by disparaging them in front of others. He must have been irked by the rebellious spirit of Christopher Grieve, never a man to turn the other cheek. Even at eighteen, Grieve found it difficult to suffer fools gladly. And he felt that Donald was 'a very obnoxious kind of fool'.[44] From the start of their relationship Donald disliked Grieve and the feeling was returned.

House policy on the *Dispatch* was to retain all books sent to the paper for review. The most literate reporters, such as Grieve, were asked to write a brief account of a book then return it to the office shelves. Grieve had a better idea, as he explained to Ogilvie:

I did some book reviewing on the *Dispatch*. My wage left practically nothing over after paying my 'digs'. I was anxious to get on. I was trying to do free-lance articles in my spare time. I found it very difficult indeed to buy the necessary paper, envelopes and stamps to send them on their rounds. I got practically no return except in rejection slips. It was borne in upon me that the cause of this was that my articles were not typed. The cost of having them typed was a problem. I thought however that if I could surmount this difficulty it was only a question of time before I would 'arrive'. As books for review were handed to me I reviewed them – then sold them to second-hand shops – getting a few shillings for each which I used to get my stuff typed and sent out. I ordered the same books at a bookseller's and when they came gave them to the *Dispatch*. ... Selling the review copies gave me working capital: getting the others on account gave me the necessary time.[45]

It all sounds ingenuous enough. Grieve never learned to type, always turning out copy (as well as presenting his poems) in manuscript. Undoubtedly he had to pay for typing as well as paper and postage when he submitted his work to periodicals in 1911. He may have been acting amorally (Nietzsche again) but did not feel he was perpetrating a serious fraud or committing an outrageous crime. Isaac Donald thought differently.

Grieve suffered an attack of jaundice, while employed by the *Dispatch*, and was unable to turn up for work. He had run up an account with a bookseller who, in his absence from the *Dispatch*, brought the matter to the attention of his employers. Donald pounced on the opportunity to incriminate Grieve. An experienced reporter, he put the unkindest possible interpretation on the story. Donald believed that Grieve had unlawfully removed review books from the *Dispatch* office and that he had obtained new books from the bookseller on false pretences by claiming he was ordering them on behalf of the *Dispatch*. He was not interested in Grieve's side of the story. The day Grieve returned to the *Dispatch* to resume his journalistic duties he was dismissed.

For the second time in the space of a year Grieve had been rejected by those he saw as representatives of the bourgeois world. The headmaster of Broughton had suspected him of stealing books, now the chief reporter of an established Edinburgh newspaper had accused him of the same. It is ironic, considering these two charges, that when Grieve later was under attack for plagiarism in 1965 he replied by confidently quoting T. S. Eliot's dictum 'Minor poets borrow, major poets steal'.[46]

Though Grieve had lost his job as a result of his idiosyncratic strategy there was a major compensation: he had placed an article in his favourite journal, the *New Age*. Orage's weekly was as magisterial as ever. It did not so much inform its public as assault it with ideas. On 9 February 1911, for example, Arnold Bennett wrote that the 'crying need of the day' required a complete and faithful translation of the works of

Dostoevsky. 'It is', Bennett commanded, 'the duty of one or other of our publishers to commission Mrs Constance Garnett to do it.'[47] Six weeks later the publisher Heinemann dutifully announced the principal novels of Dostoevsky would be issued in translations by Constance Garnett. The literary powers of the land evidently attended to the *New Age*. On 23 February Bennett asked rhetorically 'Who among you has ever heard of Paul Valéry?'[48] Grieve was certainly among those rushing to find out more about this apparently neglected Frenchman.

Orage paid nothing to most of his contributors, hence the weekly's nickname the 'No Wage'. No matter. Grieve desperately wanted to appear in the pages of a publication he once praised extravagantly as 'the most brilliant journal that has ever been written in English'.[49] 'The Young Astrology', by C. M. Grieve, was printed in the *New Age* of 20 July 1911.

Grieve's little essay is an oddity, revealing his desire to escape from the everyday world into the sphere of speculation. It also shows an obsession with great men and their mental attributes. After spending three paragraphs seeking to demonstrate the 'strictly empirical character' of astrology (then, as now, dismissed by scientists as a spurious exercise in self-indulgence) Grieve comes to his central thesis:

> We hold that the theory of traducianism is perfectly correct, so far as merely terrestrial factors are concerned; but that man being a product not only of the earth but of the universe there are cosmic factors to be taken into account which are usually ignored. We further affirm that the two theories, taken together, are found to confirm and complete each other in the exactest fashion, parental generation supplying the needful element of constancy, sidereal influence the no less needful element of variability. The physical conditions of conception are substantially the same, but the face of the heavens alters from hour to hour. We add as a corollary from these views that a stupendous reincarnation is actually in progress on a much grander scale than, and in a very different manner from, metempsychosis.[50]

Grieve's sources, in the above quotation, are not difficult to discover. From *New Age* exchanges on eugenics he had some insight into current biological theories. His use of astronomical terms like 'sidereal' was prompted by Peter Ross's outline of the solar system. The image of man as a 'product ... of the universe' was derived from John Davidson's notion of the individual as the embodiment of the universe. The irrationalism – the emphasis on variability – came, of course, from Nietzsche.

Having stated his terms, Grieve launched into astrological assumptions. He suggests that insanity is associated with individuals whose birthdays coincide with the influence of Saturn, Mars or Uranus on Mercury and the moon. By contrast cases of the highest poetic genius – he cites Shakespeare, Wordsworth, Byron, Shelley and Keats – occur at the opposition of Mercury and the moon. 'The Young Astrology' is a curious blend of journalistic fact and far-fetched speculation. As such it was not out of place in the *New Age*. Always a student of theosophy, Orage welcomed esoteric articles and eventually (in 1922) abandoned the editorship of the weekly to enter the Gurdjieff Institute near Fontainebleau. The important thing to Grieve was that Orage had accepted his article. Its merit was beside the point.

To ensure that George Ogilvie, a regular reader of the *New Age*, scrutinised the article Grieve sent him a cutting of 'The Young Astrology'. He was still interested enough in Broughton to nudge Ogilvie into showing the piece to Peter Ross. However, Ross was nonplussed by Grieve's argument. Ogilvie told Grieve so – not in person but by letter for Grieve was already elsewhere. By October 1911 Christopher Grieve was in Wales. He wrote to tell Ogilvie he would never again live in Edinburgh and that it was unlikely he would ever see his old teacher again. He got one of these predictions right.

Christopher Grieve had matured in Edinburgh but was still tormented by the contradictions in his character. Because he read everything he could lay his hands on he could be confused by his desire to see subjects and objects from several angles simultaneously. He was always eager 'to plunge into the full current of the most inconsistent movements, seeking ... to find ground upon which he might stand foursquare'.[51] Occasionally he was bewildered by the breadth of his reading and his response to it. His problem was not duality but plurality. When his intellectual élitism clashed with his socialism he felt that the only sure synthesis was his own personality. At times he suspected himself of solipsism, of treating his self-existence as the only certainty. At other times he was intimidated by the achievements of the great men he read so that he suffered from a 'sense of personal insignificance, of physical inadequacy – of having paralysed his creative faculties by over-reading'.[52]

The main collision of interests was the contest between his upbringing and his aspirations. His sensibility was saturated in Christian imagery, he remembered the faith of his father and T. S. Cairncross whose *Blawearie* was published in 1911. Moreover, the older men who sympathised with him in Edinburgh were practising Christians – Ogilvie and the Revd

Robert Drummond. Yet he endorsed Nietzsche's – and John Davidson's – vision of a Godless universe, kept up-to-date with the scientific exploration of the cosmos, believed the 'brotherhood of man ... fundamentally essential to the real and endless advance of humanity'.[53] For all his cultivation of energetic independence the approval of others mattered deeply to him.

Edinburgh brought Grieve close to individuals he valued greatly. He had found in George Ogilvie a similar spirit and in John Bogue Nisbet a firm friend. Now, physically at any rate, he was drifting away from them. They had their own lives to consider. Ogilvie, in Broughton, was working on his book, *A Practical Course in Secondary English*. Nisbet was about to embark on an Honours English course at Edinburgh University where he became Secretary, then President, of the Fabian Society. Grieve's father was dead, his brother Andrew (admittedly never a close companion) was working in Burton-on-Trent. Grieve decided that his future was emphatically what he himself made of it through sheer determination. He would 'plough a lonely furrow and concentrate upon matters in which there is no competition and in which to achieve effects which are *sui generis* is the very essence of the task'.[54] Wales was welcome in that it took him away from Edinburgh and the twin loss of a career and his first job. He must have reflected on Davidson's phrase 'Mankind has cast me out'. As he saw it, a section of mankind had cast him out of the capital of Scotland.

3

An Ardent Spirit

Sae an ardent spirit
Should submerge a' it's learned
And enjoy to the full
Whatna leisure it's earned.
'De Profundis'   (441)

H AVING been rejected by the small world of local journalism in
Edinburgh, Grieve decided to enter what he felt would be the larger
world of radical political journalism. The only outlet for him, however,
was outside Scotland and so he moved to South Wales, celebrating his
nineteenth birthday in Ebbw Vale, Monmouthshire, on 11 August 1911.
He was a long way from home, living in a narrow valley twenty miles
north of Cardiff and the coast. Sixteen years of his life had passed in a
small Scottish Border burgh, three years in a capital city. Now he was
confronted with the impact of industrialism.

In 1801 the population of Wales was 587,000 and evenly distributed
throughout the country; by 1911 the population had expanded to
2,421,000 and five-eighths of the Welsh people lived in the southern
industrial counties of Glamorgan and Monmouthshire. Under Liberal
patronage, nationalism had flourished in Wales from 1886 to 1895 in
Cymru Fydd (Future Wales) but the movement disintegrated as a result

of internal squabbles and the hostility of South Wales industrialists. (*Plaid Cymru*, the Welsh Nationalist Party, was formed in 1925.) When Grieve came to the country the majority of Welsh people spoke English: in 1911 there were 947,366 Welsh speakers which was almost twice the population of Wales a century earlier but less than half the total population.

As a result of industrialisation Wales was no longer synonymous, in the popular mind, with Methodism. A stronghold of the Liberal party, it was moving steadily towards a more radical outlook in response to the demands of working men and women. In the General Election of January 1906, which resulted in a Liberal landslide at Westminster, not one Conservative was returned from the thirty-four Welsh constituencies. With the exception of the second seat in Merthyr Tydfil, won by Keir Hardie for the Labour Representation Committee, all the seats went to the Liberals. Four of those returned as Liberals were miners – Liberal-Labour members, 'Lib-Labs'. In 1908 the Miners' Federation of Great Britain voted in favour of affiliation to the Labour Party (as the Labour Representation Committee called itself after the 1906 election) and the four Welsh Lib-Labs were moved from the Liberal to the Labour benches.

One of the Welsh mining MPs, Tom Richards (1859-1931), represented West Monmouthshire and resented the exclusively Labour label. Secretary of the South Wales Miners' Federation when he first stood for Parliament, Richards was a moderate with 'unimpeachable Liberal credentials'.[1] He was also on the editorial committee of the *Monmouthshire Labour News*, a paper published by the South Wales Miners' Federation, and it was this paper that employed Grieve as a reporter. In Ebbw Vale, Grieve felt he was 'in a good position, earning good money, working fifteen or sixteen hours a day'.[2] Almost immediately he arrived in Wales he had his 'first taste of war corresponding'.[3] South Wales was tense and turbulent. Ebbw Vale, where Grieve lived at 55 Harcourt Street, had just witnessed the closure of its old steel-making blast furnace. It was made more economically reliant on coal, like the adjacent towns; in Tredegar (where Aneurin Bevan had been born in 1897), a couple of miles to the west, ninety per cent of the population earned their living from the pits.

Working-class anger had intensified in the South Wales coalfield as a result of the Cambrian Combine strike in the Rhondda which lasted ten months until 15 August 1911. There had been battles between miners and police, the cavalry had been sent in by the Home Secretary, Winston Churchill, and fixed bayonets were used by the infantry. The strike was concluded said Michael Foot, the Labour MP who succeeded Aneurin Bevan in Ebbw Vale, 'in pitiful defeat and bitter reproaches that the men had been betrayed by their leaders'.[4] One day after the miners' strike ended so disastrously, British railwaymen went on strike, an action that inevitably caused further hardship in Wales.

As resentment built up in South Wales the anger of working men was directed towards an easier target than the police or the government. Some Jewish landlords had bought slum property and raised rents to a level that was unacceptable to people already impoverished by low wages and infuriated at the collapse of the Cambrian Combine strike. Grieve was indignant to learn of 'the almost incredibly inhuman system of rack-renting and blood-sucking on the part of the Jews in the district'.[5] In his capacity as reporter for the *Monmouthshire Labour News* he witnessed the anti-Jewish riots that broke out in South Wales.

On 19 August 1911 some two hundred men, some of them singing favourite Welsh hymns, began to attack and loot Jewish shops in Tredegar; reinforcements from Ebbw Vale left the police outnumbered and men of the Worcester Regiment from Cardiff were called in. On Monday, 21 August, Jewish shops at Ebbw Vale and Rhymney were pillaged. On Tuesday the riots spread to Victoria, Cwm, Waunllwyd, Abertysswg and Brynmawr. On Wednesday, Jewish premises were attacked at Bargoed in Glamorgan. Abruptly the violence stopped, as a historian of the period explained:

> That weekend, quite suddenly, the disturbances ended. However, the events left behind an unsettling trail of destruction and some commentators were prompted to draw an analogy between the riots and the blood-stained pogroms which were taking place in Tsarist Russia.[6]

Grieve told Ogilvie, in a letter, that he had not slept for four consecutive nights during the riots and was the only reporter present at a strategic meeting of the rioters. 'The riots', he added, 'were almost as admirably directed as the present Chinese revolution.'[7]

A compulsive communicator, Grieve needed an audience for his activities and was willing to settle for an audience of one if he could convey his most intimate thoughts. Occupied most of the time by his job as a reporter in Wales, he craved contact with a sympathetic soul and it was in Ebbw Vale that he started a correspondence with his old teacher. 'Please let us keep up a correspondence,'[8] he implored George Ogilvie in the postscript to a letter of October 1911. The two kept up the correspondence for almost twenty years, during which time Grieve became MacDiarmid, shook Scottish poetry to its linguistic roots and gravitated to more and more extreme political positions. Grieve found the proletarian socialism of Ebbw Vale intoxicating; 'It's like living on the top of a volcano down here,'[9] he enthused to Ogilvie.

Ebbw Vale had grown up round the iron-works established at the end of the eighteenth century. At the beginning of the twentieth century the huge Ebbw Vale Steel, Iron and Coal company made its own steel and manufactured its own plant, supplying its own limestone and making coke from its own coal. However, as local ore contained too much phosphorus, iron ore was imported from Spain and Norway. This contributed to the decline of Ebbw Vale. The workers were desperate men, not detached intellectual readers of the *New Age*. In such an ambience, emphasising the class divisions between employees and employers, the élitism of Grieve's Edinburgh days was inadequate. An earthier outlook was needed if he was to relate to the Welsh workers. Grieve was fortunate in finding, in the area, a fellow Scot who not only preached a simple socialist gospel but expressed his faith in the human qualities of the Celtic peoples.

Founder Chairman of the Independent Labour Party in 1893, Keir Hardie was elected to Parliament (as a Labour Representation Committee candidate) by the mining constituency of Merthyr Tydfil in 1900. His socialism was based on Burns and the Bible rather than on the dialectical materialism of Marx. Hardie, who learned lessons in public speaking from Nonconformist chapel ministers, felt at home in Wales: he spoke in favour of disestablishment, temperance and land reform. He was in accord with the idea of Home Rule in Wales, he praised the Welsh language and he learned the Welsh national anthem. The *Merthyr Pioneer*, the newspaper he founded in 1911, displayed a strong Welsh-language bias and was edited by the socialist bard and Independent minister, the Revd Thomas Nicholas of Glais (near Swansea). After winning Merthyr Tydfil for the LRC in 1906 Hardie was elected the first Chairman of the Parliamentary Labour Party.

For Keir Hardie there was a political welcome in Wales where his socialism was seen as not entirely antipathetic to the progressive tendencies of Welsh Liberalism. By 1910 the ILP had ninety-five branches in South Wales, compared to nine in North Wales. Grieve wanted to extend the ILP presence in Wales. He made a point of seeking out Keir Hardie: 'I walked over to Merthyr Tydfil from Ebbw Vale to meet Keir Hardie and used to write for his paper, the *Merthyr Pioneer*.'[10] In a letter of 24 October 1911 to George Ogilvie, Grieve proudly disclosed that he was responsible for the further spread of the ILP:

> I have already been instrumental in forming four new branches of the ILP down here. In Tredegar a policeman took my name and address on the grounds that it was illegal to speak off the top of a soap-box.
>
> I asked him if a match box was within the meaning of the act and he put something else down in his note-book: what I do not know.
>
> However, as a branch of 25 members was the outcome, I can afford to be generous.[11]

Grieve's ILP activism, his 'youth and natural tactlessness'[12] and his general attitude of belligerence displeased Tom Richards, MP, a man Grieve disliked as a cautious careerist. Once more Grieve was up against authority, feeling himself 'shipwrecked on hidden rocks of implacable liberalism and non-conformity suddenly in bright seas of labourist activity'.[13] He accused Richards and his colleagues on the editorial committee of the *Monmouthshire Labour News* of hypocrisy. It was decided to discontinue the paper and thus dispense with Grieve's services.

George Bernard Shaw – patron of Orage's *New Age*, creative evolutionist, self-styled intellectual superman – had Jack Tanner, the hero of *Man and Superman* (1903), boast that the 'true artist will let ... his mother drudge for his living at seventy, sooner than work at anything but his art'.[14] Having lost his second job as a reporter in succession, Grieve attempted to adopt this Shavian tactic. Elizabeth Grieve was, in 1912, fifty-five not seventy but Grieve admitted to living 'practically, as Bernard Shaw did, off my widowed mother'.[15] He spent much of his time in Langholm reading in the library. Otherwise he tried to earn enough from freelance writing to pay for his cigarettes, pipe tobacco and newspapers.

During the year 1912 Grieve submitted verse and prose to Scottish journals. Some of his work was accepted. 'The Cabbage', a poem published anonymously in the *Glasgow Herald* of 21 February 1912, shows the influence of John Davidson. The third section of Davidson's 'Snow' – from *Fleet Street and Other Poems* (1909) – gives poetic and scientific substance to an object usually taken for granted by poets:

> Once I saw upon an object-glass,
>   Martyred underneath a microscope,
> One elaborate snow-flake slowly pass,
>   Dying hard, beyond the reach of hope.

> Still from shape to shape the crystal changed,
>   Writhing in its agony; and still,
> Less and less elaborate, arranged
>   Potently the angle of its will.

Similarly, Grieve invoked the metamorphic magic he associated with the common cabbage:

> Once upon your blades, laid row on row,
>   I saw the eggs of butterflies
> And other wingèd things that go
>   Like rainbow flakes through summer skies.
>
> To me, bemused, it seemed as though
>   These eggs grew vital in their cup;
> And suddenly – like clouds of snow –
>   Your countless butterflies went up.[16]

The simile 'like clouds of snow' harks back to Grieve's stylistic source, Davidson's 'Snow'.

On 15 March 1912 the *People's Journal,* a popular Scottish periodical, featured an anonymous parody of Thomas De Quincey's classic *Confessions of an English Opium Eater* by 'Our Special Commissioner'. Under the lurid headline 'All Night in a British Opium "Joint"' and above a photograph of an unidentified Grieve lying on a couch with a long pipe in his mouth, the article purported to be 'The Confessions of a Scotch opium smoker'. It established that Grieve had been in Liverpool, on his way to and from South Wales. From that fact the article took off into fantasy. Guided by his friend Corp, a habitual and indiscriminate user of drugs ('All the curious drugs and illicit decoctions of heathendom have at some time or other in his career titillated that imperturbable palate') the narrator goes by tram to Liverpool's Chinatown. The pair are admitted to the opium den by 'an aged Chinaman' and provided with the drug:

> Corp and I pulled off our boots, arranged our cushions and mats, and fell to the task of inducing the heavenly hallucinations which are said to be the result of opium smoked in the right way. Corp was an expert at the business, and could conjure the semi-fluid drug into a neat little pellet five times while I was doing it once. He fell asleep in the space of half an hour.
>   The only effect which the infernal stuff had on me was to wish I was dead. I don't believe all the poppy juice extracted east or west of Suez could

do more than violently upset a good Scotch stomach. At any rate, I got less spiritual exaltation than a smile from a *People's Journal* prize beauty would have produced any day of the week.[17]

It is an entertaining piece of fun, an example of the Scottish vein of reductive humour, bringing all the paraphernalia of opium smoking down to earth with a reference to the pictorial merits of the *People's Journal*.

More serious work was undertaken by Grieve early in the autumn of 1912. The Fabian Society formed a committee to examine the issues of land reform and rural development. It required researchers with specialist knowledge of the different parts of Britain and Grieve – a close friend of John Bogue Nisbet, Secretary of Edinburgh University Fabian Society – was made 'responsible for all the Scottish information'.[18] A draft report appeared in the *New Statesman* before the book *The Rural Problem* was published (with an acknowledgement to C. M. Grieve) in 1913 under the editorship of Henry D. Harben. Grieve's contribution to the book was a source of great satisfaction to him. During the 1930s, when he advertised the Hugh MacDiarmid Book Club, he listed (complete with mistaken title) as one of his works '*Rural Reform* (with Lord Passfield and others)'.[19] Lord Passfield is better known as Sidney Webb, founding father of the Fabian Society in 1884. Grieve, as has already been noted, liked to invoke aristocratic titles.

As the poem 'The Cabbage' and the parody 'All Night in a British Opium "Joint"' demonstrate Grieve, in 1912, was struggling to find his feet as a writer. While he felt that his omnivorous reading was, to some extent, 'a fault ... responsible for my present predicament'[20] he persisted, reading whatever came his way. From 30 November 1911 to 22 February 1912 the *New Age* published twelve articles by Ezra Pound under the title 'I Gather the Limbs of Osiris'. Already Pound was advocating poetic innovation, criticising a routine reliance on iambic rhythm and simple rhyme, urging the serious artist to avoid a derivative rhetoric:

Let the poet who has been not too long ago born make very sure of this, that no one cares to hear, in strained iambics, that he feels sprightly in spring, is uncomfortable when his sexual desires are ungratified, and that he has read about human brotherhood in last year's magazines.[21]

Grieve was attentive to Pound's creative credo of inventive individuality but unaware, as yet, of the formal distance between Poundian and Georgian verse; it was not until October 1912 that Pound coined the phrase Imagism (to describe a poem of Hilda Doolittle's he read in the

British Museum tearoom). Despite Orage's disapproval of Georgian verse, Grieve enjoyed the poems of Rupert Brooke, W. H. Davies, Walter de la Mare and D. H. Lawrence included in the first volume of *Georgian Poetry* (1912). Thanks to the *New Age* he learned of the work (or, at least, of the name) of Freud, first mentioned in Orage's weekly in 1912; and, in common with many of his *New Age* contemporaries, was staggered by the emotional sweep of Dostoevsky's *The Brothers Karamazov*, published in Constance Garnett's English translation in 1912.

Seldom in his published work did Grieve elucidate the details of his private life. His physical relationships with women were treated with discretion in his prose; in his poems he tended to idealise individuals. Nevertheless, reading and writing did not monopolise Grieve's time in Langholm. Summing up his return to his native place, in a letter to George Ogilvie, he itemised some amorous exploits:

> Philandered extensively during this period. Intimate passages with three young ladies, all English, revived in me our racial antipathy to the English ... Later fell seriously in love with a Scotch girl, a school teacher.[22]

This is the first time that Grieve has sounded the anglophobic note he gradually orchestrated into a major theme of his work. That it was provoked, in Langholm, by a triple disappointment of a sexual nature, implies a need to rationalise a series of rejections. Grieve was twenty in 1912, past the age of accepting rejection meekly.

The schoolteacher with whom he fell in love was Minnie Punton, a diminutive young woman with definite ideas of domesticity. Bonny rather than beautiful, Minnie had hopes of a secure future with Grieve, an ambition that could be fulfilled only by his finding another job. Grieve's feelings for Minnie are expressed in an early love poem that equates Eden with the Langfall, the wood approached by the path known locally in Langholm as the Curly Snake. Dedicated to 'M.P.', the poem is called 'The Curly Snake':

> Sweetheart of mine, I hope that there will be
> A Curly Snake for us in Paradise
> (Oh! All true lovers go to Paradise)
> That goes up darkly unexpected-wise,
> Behind the gardens of felicity,
> – A Curly Snake that takes its curious way
> Through heavy woods where night still lingers
> On to dark hills (unknowledged of the singers,

Who prophesy an endless-shining day)
– Dark hills and broken stars and ravelled skies
Else Paradise will not be Paradise.

If it be roses, roses everywhere
And stirless waters and a constant sun
(Dearer the moon to lovers than the sun;
Better than moon a night when there is none).
Sweetheart, we will not be all-happy there
For you and I must have a crooked way
And wild things crying strangely in the night
And cold winds on the hillside, and the play
– The unintelligible daring! – of stars' eyes
That shine out suddenly still-bright
Through loaded branches – just as here!
But ah Beloved, there can be I fear
No Curly Snake for us in Paradise.[23]

As a poetic performance by a man of twenty, 'The Curly Snake' is informative. The basic image (the serpentine road to an erotic Eden) combines a biblical allusion with a topographical landmark and is sustained intelligently. However, 'The Curly Snake' shows that Grieve could be curiously conservative in his approach to love poetry. 'The Curly Snake' pays little heed to either the aesthetic propaganda of Pound's *New Age* articles or the structural solidity of the poems anthologised in Edward Marsh's *Georgian Poetry*. Indeed, the poem is pre-Georgian in sentiment, redolent of the languid tone of some late Victorian verse. Grieve was interested in the poets associated with the Rhymers' Club of the 1890s: men such as Davidson, Ernest Dowson, Lionel Johnson, Yeats. Grieve's poem 'The Cabbage' had a sharpness derived from Davidson; 'The Curly Snake' had a Dowsonesque dying fall. Still, it shows some fundamental features of Grieve's art: the desire for difficulty ('a crooked way'), the fondness for the dark ('Better than moon a night when there is none'), the excitement of the unknown ('wild things crying strangely in the night'). What Minnie Punton thought of this tribute to her is not known. In practical terms she was adamant that her suitor should secure remunerative work.

Early in 1913 Grieve, 'buoyed up with new dreams of honour, visions of a "home of my own", etc',[24] was working for the *Clydebank and Renfrew Press*, a weekly newspaper owned by the firm of Cossar. He lived, in a house owned by a Mr Gibson, at 8 Bon-Accord Street in

Clydebank. On the north side of the river Clyde, below and adjoining Glasgow, Clydebank was a thriving industrial burgh when Grieve worked there. In 1871 the brothers James and George Thomson moved from Govan and chose the site of Clydebank (which they named after their foundry in Finnieston) for a shipyard opposite the mouth of the river Cart; the first ship was launched in 1872. Thomson's was bought by John Brown & Company (from Sheffield) in 1899 and the name of the new Clydebank company became a guarantee of quality shipbuilding: the Cunard liner *Lusitania* was built in 1906 at Clydebank. In 1882 the American firm of Singer had established a sewing machine factory at Kilbowie, thus adding to the prosperity of Clydebank. Neil Munro, the author of *Doom Castle* (1901) and *The Vital Spark* (1906, humorous tales about the adventures of a Clyde puffer), typified the attitude of Scotland's artistic establishment to the industrial towns of the Clyde:

> Whiteinch, Yoker, Clydebank, Kilbowie and Dalmuir, all on the north side of the Clyde between the Kelvin and the Kilpatrick hills, are towns whose origin is of yesterday; they are the homes of men who work in the shipyards or in the huge factory of the Singer Sewing Machine Company whose clock tower dominates the smoky valley ... With the towns named we have no pastoral associations now; their mention brings to the mind but thoughts of shrieking and insistent sirens heralding wet winter morns, the clatter of toilward feet on muddy pavements, a manner of life strenuous and unlovely.[25]

(Grieve's attitude to Munro was ambivalent since he disliked his work but dedicated his anthology *Northern Numbers* to him in 1920.)

It was at Clydebank that Grieve first heard about the political work of John Maclean, a man he considered 'the greatest leader the working class of Scotland have yet had'.[26] Surrounded by industrialism at Clydebank, the life of which hovered round the shipyard and the sewing machine factory, Grieve renewed his ILP activities in association with two men, Neil Malcolm Maclean and James Maxton, who had links with John Maclean. Neil Maclean completed his apprenticeship as a mechanic in the Singer Sewing Machine Company and remained with the firm until he was, in 1912, appointed a full-time organiser and propagandist with the Scottish Co-operative Wholesale Society. A year later he was elected to a seat on the Central Board of the Co-operative Union. Neil Maclean was a member of the ILP; whereas many in the ILP had a religious notion of socialism, Maclean, a student of Marxism, accepted the labour theory of value and understood the revolutionary implications of the class struggle. Neil Maclean had assisted John Maclean in Marxist education classes; he had noted John Maclean's support of the strike at the Singer Sewing Machine Company in April 1911.

Like John Maclean, James Maxton was a native of Pollokshaws; it was seeing John Maclean in oratorical action that converted Maxton to socialism. Son of a headmaster and graduate of Glasgow University (where he was athletically accomplished as well as academically bright) Maxton was convinced by Marx's economic analysis of the structure of capitalism though he rejected his historicism. In 1912 Maxton was elected Scottish representative on the National Administrative Council of the ILP and from 1913 to 1919 he was Chairman of the Scottish ILP.

Reporting on his progress to George Ogilvie, Grieve said that 'poor Maxton and Maclean and I were great friends and co-propagandists'.[27] He was greatly taken by Maxton's personal combination of Scottish nationalism and socialism. Maxton, a Home Ruler, as well as a member of the ILP, once declared he could 'ask for no greater job in life [than to transform] the English-ridden, capitalist-ridden, landlord-ridden Scotland, into a Scottish Socialist Commonwealth'.[28] Over the years, though, Neil Maclean and Jimmie Maxton softened their Red Clydeside sentiments as a result of their careers as Labour MPs. Grieve went further and further to the left. (In 1936 he worked on a biography of John Maclean, a task he took over from Maxton who handed over the results of his own research.)

Grieve found time, while at Clydebank, to enjoy himself. There was (so he confided to Ogilvie) 'a little interlude with a Dunoon girl, which clashed nastily with the other affaire [with Minnie Punton] owing to a rank inadvertence'.[29] There was also his enjoyment of drinking. On this issue Grieve was conspicuously at variance with ILP thinking. Keir Hardie and Jimmie Maxton both eschewed alcohol. Specifically, Hardie believed that intemperance was a major cause of working-class poverty and his views were widespread in the Labour movement; the Scottish socialist journal *Forward* (founded in 1906) refused to accept advertisements from the drinks trade and was in favour of prohibition. Grieve could happily discuss politics with the likes of Maxton, read *Forward*, then retire to a public house to drink whisky – which he thought of as 'the safest drink in the world'.[30] After spending some five months in Clydebank he left to take up a more lucrative position as a journalist in Cupar. He found, to his delight, that the Fife town was 'a boozy little hole'.[31]

Ten miles south-south-west of Dundee and with a population about twice as large as that of Langholm, Cupar was a busy little market town.

In 1913 Andrew Graham Grieve, the poet's brother, was working in Cupar for the Inland Revenue. From his lodgings at 75 Bonnygate he wrote to Christopher about a vacancy with the Innes group of newspapers. Grieve got the job and wrote for the *Fife Herald* (published every Wednesday), the *Fife Coast Chronicle* (also every Wednesday) and the *St Andrews Citizen* (every Saturday). The three newspapers, selling for one penny per copy, reported local news, school and church events, and gave considerable coverage to sport – especially golf tournaments at St Andrews. Occasionally political issues impinged on the papers: a headline of 6 August 1913 in the *Fife Herald* stated 'Scottish Home Rule Advocate Heckled at Upper Largo'.

By his own admission Grieve worked hard and drank even harder while in Cupar. Writing to the abstemious George Ogilvie, Grieve boasted of his alcoholic prowess:

> I enjoyed Cupar immensely – worked harder than I should have believed it possible for me to do and simultaneously drank like a fish, acquiring in time the art ... of accurately transcribing and telephonically transmitting while wildly intoxicated reports from the shorthand of brother-journalists, who, collapsing under the strain of work and wine, had passed into hopeless conditions which left it up to the unbowled-over one of the party to see that their papers were not 'let down'.[32]

Not surprisingly Grieve fell foul of his employers, a practice he had by now perfected. He had to move on but, before he did so, he formed a friendship with an attractive young girl of sixteen who worked as a copyholder for the Innes papers. He was eventually to marry her.

Margaret Cunningham Thomson Skinner was born on 6 February 1897 at Westfield Park, Cupar. Her father, David Thomson Skinner, was, at the time of his daughter's birth, employed as a vanman. After a couple of years in Cupar, David Skinner left to work in Methil, Fife, where he became a colliery surface foreman. Grieve, though engaged to Minnie Punton, made sure he kept in touch with Margaret – Peggy, as she liked to be called.

Ever resourceful, Grieve soon found a job in Forfar, Angus, as a journalist with the weekly *Forfar Review*. Thirteen miles north-north-east of Dundee, Forfar must have seemed, to Grieve, like a combination of Cupar and Langholm. Like Cupar, Forfar was a thriving market town. Like Langholm, it owed its prosperity to the textile trade; it contained several jute and linen mills. Standing in the middle of flat fertile country at the north-east end of the Vale of Strathmore, Forfar had been a royal burgh since the reign of David I.

Having experienced Cupar as 'a boozy little hole', Grieve discovered that Forfar was 'the booziest place in Earth'.[33] At first he drank regularly with other young men then decided that his literary dreams could only approach reality by serious application to his art. He invited his mother to join him, so he explained in a letter to Ogilvie:

> [Once] again the men with whom I was associated were jolly good fellows. Our libations were limitless. So far did this go, in fact (although my work never suffered – that is to say my work in the limited sense excluding what I am pleased to consider my life-work) that a sudden access of unaccountable good sense made me take a house, four miles in the country by Glamis Castle way, and invite my mother to keep house for me. The result was eminently satisfactory. I had an easy and well-paid-job: my mother had claims upon my time which kept me out of 'company' in my spare time, and I had peace to write.[34]

Grieve may have enjoyed the role of the writer creating in the peace and quiet of the country. However, European events made his an impossible position.

At 11 p.m. on 4 August 1914, the day after the German invasion of Belgium, Britain declared war on Germany. The orthodox view of the government's action was given in *The Times* of 5 August. Warming to the notion of a national crusade, *The Times* editorialised 'We go into the fray without hatred, without passion, without selfish ambition, or selfish ends.'[35] An entirely different attitude motivated some ardent socialists.

For the pacifist members of the ILP the war was an unmitigated disaster; on 6 August, Keir Hardie was shouted down in Aberdare and a mob, incensed by his anti-war eloquence, broke up his meeting. Over in the West of Scotland, both Jimmie Maxton and Neil Maclean opposed the war as irrelevant to the aspirations of working men and women. The position of the extreme left was succinctly stated by John Maclean. His letter of 17 September 1914 to the British Socialist Party newspaper *Justice* – which was directed by H. M. Hyndman to support the war – maintained that the working class had nothing to gain from the conflict of another class. Maclean argued:

> Capitalism has neither conscience nor morality when it is brought to bay [so] it is our business as socialists to develop 'class patriotism', refusing to murder one another for a sordid world capitalism. The absurdity of the

present situation is surely apparent when we see British socialists going out to murder German socialists with the object of crushing Kaiserism and Prussian militarism ... Let the propertied class, old and young alike, go out and defend their blessed property. When they have been disposed of, we of the working class will have something to defend, and we shall do it.[36]

This was very much a minority opinion in Scotland where workers and members of the Labour movement were swept along on a wave of anti-German feeling.

In the early stages of the war Grieve was more inclined to agree with Maclean than to join in the jingoistic fervour. This isolated him from many of his own generation. On 5 August 1914 Lord Kitchener, the newly appointed Secretary of State for War, had asked for a million men – within eight weeks he had them. He then asked for half a million more, and filled that quota by Christmas. For intellectuals, accustomed to armchair battles, the war had definite attractions. Poets well past the age for active service – including Thomas Hardy (seventy-four), Robert Bridges (seventy), Sir Henry Newbolt (fifty-two) and Rudyard Kipling (forty-nine) – signed a collective letter in *The Times* of 18 September 1914 claiming that 'Britain could not without dishonour have refused to take part in the present war'.[37] Rupert Brooke, a past President of Cambridge University Fabian Society, was initially hesitant about enlisting but soon changed his mind, eventually accepting a commission in the Royal Naval Division from the First Lord of the Admiralty, Winston Churchill. Suddenly Brooke felt his mission in life was 'to get good at beating Germans'.[38] He was twenty-seven.

Similarly, John Bogue Nisbet, a past President of Edinburgh University Fabian Society, made the war his priority. Nisbet graduated in 1914 and was appointed to a teaching position at George Watson's College, Edinburgh. During his university course he had served in the 9th Battalion Royal Scots; on the outbreak of war he heeded Kitchener's call and rejoined his regiment rather than taking up his post at George Watson's. Gazetted to the 14th Battalion Royal Scots then transferred to the 3rd Battalion, he was sent, on 17 February 1915, to France where he was attached to the 2nd Battalion. In the month that Nisbet went to the Western Front it was estimated that one in five Scottish miners had enlisted. War fever was affecting all classes of society.

The nightmarish horror of the Western Front – with soldiers dying in their millions in a landscape disfigured by barbed wire, shell-holes and rat-infested trenches – has entered the cultural consciousness of the literary world through the poems of Siegfried Sassoon, Ivor Gurney, Isaac Rosenberg, Wilfred Owen and Charles Sorley. John Bogue Nisbet died in such a landscape. The second time he was in the trenches he was shot while trying to locate German snipers. The *Edinburgh Evening News* of 22 April 1915 reported that Second Lieutenant John Nisbet, of the Royal Scots, had been killed on 13 April. A year younger than Grieve, Nisbet was not yet twenty-four.

Ten days after Nisbet's death Rupert Brooke died, on 23 April, in a French military hospital at Skyros after contracting blood poisoning on his way to Gallipoli. Before he had prepared to go with his Division to Gallipoli as part of Churchill's ill-conceived Dardanelles operation, Brooke had laid the foundations of his fame. During the last months of 1914, when Brooke was home on leave from the Navy after taking part in the defence of Antwerp, he wrote five sonnets at Rugby School (where his father was a housemaster). They first appeared in the fourth and final issue of *New Numbers* in December 1914. On Easter Sunday, 4 April 1915, Dean Inge of St Paul's preached a sermon and quoted Brooke's sonnet 'The Soldier'. As the news of Brooke's death reached England, he was cast in the role of martyred crusader by Churchill whose obituary contribution in *The Times* was as purple as Brooke's own poetry:

> He expected to die; he was willing to die for the dear England whose beauty and majesty he knew; and he advanced towards the brink in perfect serenity, with absolute conviction of the rightness of his country's cause and a heart devoid of hate for fellow-men.... Joyous, fearless, versatile, deeply instructed, with classic symmetry of mind and body, ruled by high undoubting purpose, he was all that one would wish England's noblest sons to be in days when no sacrifice but the most precious is acceptable, and the most precious is that which is most freely proferred.[39]

Not a word about Brooke's socialist past and agnostic attitude. Not a word in Churchill's sermon about the nation being other than English ('dear England ... England's noblest sons'). Still, England had an official martyr, blessed by the Dean of St Paul's and consecrated by the First Lord of the Admiralty. Ironically, Churchill's Dardanelles operation had cost the poet his life; it cost Churchill only a cabinet post in the coalition government of 1915.

Though sceptical of the emphatically English rhetoric of Churchill, Grieve was impressed by Brooke's poetry. He certainly read the five sonnets, either in *New Numbers*; or in *1914 and Other Poems* (16 June 1915), edited by Edward Marsh; or in the pamphlet *1914: Five Sonnets*, published a few months later. Their sacrificial tone, stanzaic precision and romantic passion heavily influenced Grieve's own sonnets in English. Reading 'The Soldier' he may have subconsciously substituted Scotland for England in the opening sentence: 'If I should die, think only this of me:/That there's some corner of a foreign field/That is for ever England.' If Grieve was going to fight then it would not be for 'dear England' or 'gallant little Belgium'[40] but for Scotland though in a sense that was not yet entirely clear to him.

His attitude to the war had changed and he told Ogilvie 'Nisbet's death finally settled matters'.[41] When, some time after Nisbet's death, he composed a tribute to his friend, it was a sonnet, 'In Memoriam J.B.N.' And it had stylistic features in common with Brooke's 'The Soldier'. Brooke's sestet begins 'And think', Grieve's sestet begins 'And know'; Brooke rhymes 'no less' with 'gentleness', Grieve rhymes 'may press' with 'emptiness'. Grieve alludes to the 'richer dust' of Brooke's fourth line when he speaks of 'No little dust'. The main difference between Brooke's 'The Soldier' and Grieve's 'In Memoriam J.B.N.' (apart from slight variations in the rhyme scheme) is one of mental approach for the former is forgiving ('all evil shed away') while the latter is defiantly desolate:

> And know how pitifully at the last
> My eyes shall gaze upon your emptiness,
> No little dust of any rose thou hast!
> No withered wisp of all the green and gold
> Your starveling fingers in the Night may press!
> And Life's a wind that 'twixt your bones blows cold.   (1231)

It took a World War and a personal rediscovery of Scotland to liberate Grieve from the admittedly exiguous demands of Georgian verse.[42]

Technically, since he had joined the Territorial section of the Royal Army Medical Corps in 1908, Grieve was on reserve. Accordingly he left Forfar and, in July 1915, reported to Hillsborough barracks in Sheffield. Within six months, he proudly informed George Ogilvie, he had risen from a RAMC recruit to acting Quarter-Master-Sergeant of a company one thousand strong. He had, in his own estimation, acquired both a sense of responsibility and a reputation for reliability. If he had altered his appearance externally by donning a uniform and putting on a determinedly respectable front for official purposes, then his appetites were unchanged:

Needless to say in a Sergeants' Mess sobriety is not strictly insisted upon. I drank as heavily as I possibly could without bad effect to my work and position – and it is wonderful how very heavily that is. In full rig-out with sling-sword belt, and polished crowns, and knee-breeches and tan boots, I was 'some nut' too, and English girls are notoriously 'free', especially since the war began – and I prosecuted feminist studies [of an erotic nature] to a great extent. But I got no black mark on my papers, and I never failed my C.O. or Sergeant-Major in the slightest respect.[43]

On the first day of 1916 he was at liberty to continue these 'feminist studies' without any pangs of conscience. Minnie Punton decided she could not accommodate a permanent partnership with Grieve. She celebrated the New Year of 1916 by breaking off her engagement.

While Grieve was at Hillsborough barracks, he was overwhelmed by the news of the Easter Rising in Ireland: on 24 April 1916, the day after Easter Sunday, an Irish Republic was declared and 1500 members of the Dublin Volunteer Brigade and Irish Citizen Army occupied parts of Dublin. When the Republic was proclaimed from the steps of Dublin's General Post Office, Padraic Pearse was named president of the provisional government; James Connolly as vice-president, Commandant-General, and commander of all rebel forces in Dublin. In the ferocious fighting that followed the proclamation Connolly was wounded twice, in the arm and ankle; altogether some 1351 people were killed or seriously wounded in the running battles between the Irish forces and British government troops. Pearse and Connolly agreed to an unconditional surrender, on 30 April, only to avoid further bloodshed. 'I cannot bear to see all these brave boys burn to death,'[44] Connolly told a colleague.

The leaders of the Easter Rising were arrested and sentenced to death by secret court-martial. Padraic Pearse and Thomas MacDonagh were shot on 4 May; John MacBride was shot on 5 May; Connolly, so crippled by gangrene that he had to be carried on a stretcher to the yard of Kilmainham Jail and strapped on a chair, was shot on 12 May. W. B. Yeats immortalised the names of these men in his poem 'Easter, 1916':

> I write it out in a verse –
> MacDonagh and MacBride
> And Connolly and Pearse
> Now and in time to be,
> Wherever green is worn,
> Are changed, changed utterly:
> A terrible beauty is born.[45]

Grieve was deeply moved by the Easter Rising. 'If it had been possible at all,' he revealed in an interview, 'I would have deserted at that time from the British Army and joined the Irish.'[46] Henceforth he closely connected the Scottish and Irish struggles for autonomy. Connolly, after all, had been born in Edinburgh – on 5 June 1868 at 107 Cowgate, son of an Irish immigrant who worked as a manure carter for Edinburgh Corporation – and had contributed to the Scottish socialist journals *Justice* and *Forward*. Moreover, Connolly's career inspired John Maclean, one of the major figures in Grieve's political pantheon. Grieve's postwar appraisal of his armoury credits MacDiarmid with the best Celtic qualities of the Scots and Irish:

> Scots steel tempered wi' Irish fire
> Is the weapon that I desire.   (263)

Sent to Aldershot in July 1916, for posting overseas, Grieve 'lost (by the curious custom) my acting rank of QMS; in a week or two came through in orders with the substantive (permanent) rank of Sergeant'.[47] He did not greatly care for the camaraderie of the barracks, despairing of the philistinism of his fellow soldiers: 'They certainly had no intellectual interests of any kind and except on the merest trivia it was impossible to have any sort of conversation with them.'[48] The Army had not weakened Grieve's resolve to surpass himself by the most arduous intellectual efforts. In the meantime he had to survive with other soldiers. Grieve, Sergeant 64020 of the RAMC, was detailed to go to Salonika with a complete General Hospital, the 42nd General Hospital. Almost the entire staff – 'all the doctors, nurses, and most of the rank-and-file'[49] – were Scots.

For a young man of twenty-four, as he was in the month of his departure for Greece, Christopher Grieve had little vested interest in remaining in Britain while other young men were facing a challenge abroad. He had not so far been able adequately to translate his literary dreams into the reality of print. In 1912 a couple of poems[50] had been published in the *Glasgow Herald* and a prose fantasy in the *People's Journal*, nothing really to compete with the kudos he enjoyed through his appearance in the *New Age* the previous year. His work as a reporter in Ebbw Vale, Clydebank, Cupar and Forfar left him little time for creative writing. Even when he took a house outside Forfar he had to put in the hours 'Chroniclin' the toon's sma' beer' (234) with the result that he failed to bring serious literary projects to fruition.

Although he was an astonishingly resilient character, he had added egregiously to his catalogue of rejections before leaving Britain for the first time. He had lost jobs in Ebbw Vale and Cupar (just as he had done already in Edinburgh) and Minnie Punton had renounced him. Politically he had matured through his association with stalwarts of the ILP such as Keir Hardie, Neil Maclean and Jimmie Maxton; and he had reason to be satisfied with the research he had done for the Fabian Society. Yet he was no more than a bit-player on the socialist stage, one of the many who served the leading men. The intellectual superman was not recognised as such.

In common with countless literary aspirants of his age and inclinations, Grieve had found in drink an outlet that momentarily eased his artistic frustration. He had been boozy instead of busy, in a creative sense, for sustained periods. Adding to his irritations was the stylistic uncertainty of his approach to his chosen art. John Davidson was revered as a poetic hero but his philosophical power was currently beyond Grieve's range. His most successful poem to date, 'Memories of Langholm', had drawn on the melancholy mood of T. S. Cairncross but he was metrically more cautious than the minister he had known in Langholm.

Poetically, then, Grieve was confused in 1916. He knew, through the *New Age*, about Pound and the Imagists yet was restricted by the stylistic straitjacket of Georgian writing. Artistically he could not reconcile what he experienced as an occasionally enervating duality. He could salute the Imagism of Pound whose *Ripostes* (1912) undermined the iambic authority of English verse; and he could seek security in the stanzaic safety of Brooke and the Georgians. Thus divided he was not sure of himself though he had learned from Nietzsche that self-fulfilment was essential for the creative individual. Grieve, in 1916, lacked three artistic elements crucial to the composition of authentic poetry: an inspirational theme, a flexible control of form, a language he could call his own. Raised in a Scots-speaking community he still spoke (despite the English orientation of his education) in a broad Border accent. The internal evidence of his literary productions to date suggested, through a polysyllabic pedantry, an impatience with English. For the time being his artistic impulse was not able to express something his political faith affirmed; that English was not only the idiom of past masters of poetry but also (as the Easter Rising reminded Grieve) the accent of British imperialism.

To date he had been out of Langholm and into the world only in a limited sense, exploring selected corners of Scotland, England and Wales. Intellectually this would not have mattered overmuch for his reading enabled him to cross frontiers. What he wanted to escape from was English insularity, the physical sensation of being confined to an island controlled by London. A period of exile from the island would give him the opportunity to put the matter of England in an international perspective from which to consider carefully the relative cultural merits of Scotland. It took him some time to absorb the artistic implications of this exile.

4

Thistleonica

It is a wonderful place this ancient city with its huge new population of soldiers. So many Scotsmen are here that it has been suggested that it should be called, not Thessalonica, but Thistleonica.'

C. M. Grieve, letter to George Ogilvie, 2 Sept. 1916

FOUNDED in 315 BC by King Cassandros (who named it after his queen, Thessaloniki, sister of Alexander the Great) the Greek Macedonian port of Salonika stands on the site of the Roman city of Thessalonica to whose inhabitants St Paul addressed two epistles, saying 'ye were ensamples to all that believe in Macedonia' (1:7). Built on a slope, Salonika lies in the Thermaic Gulf at the foot of the mountain of Hortiatus: for the Scottish Sergeant C. M. Grieve there were 'the wonderful associations of Salonika, with the "high Olympus" across the blue and silver waters of the gulf'.[1] Roman ruins and Byzantine ramparts remain in Salonika as monuments to a history that has included the ordeal of Roman occupation and the grandeur given to the second city of the Byzantine Empire.

From the White Tower, built in the fifteenth century, the city can be explored as an architectural odyssey, passing through time and temperament: the arch and palace of the fourth-century Emperor Galerius, the Church of St Demetrius (twice burned and re-erected, complete with some saved mosaics, after the fire of August 1917), the docks. Pictorial as well as architectural art flourished in Salonika. Its Rotunda was converted to Christian use as the Cathedral Church of St George and visually revitalised, in the late fourth century, with magnificent mosaics. In the ninth century, the cupola of Hagia Sophia was decorated with a superlative mosaic of the Ascension. During the medieval period Salonika contained more than three hundred churches and thirty monasteries though only a fraction of these remain (the Mone Latomou and, above it, the Mone Vlatadon, for example).

King George I of Greece was assassinated in Salonika, on 18 March 1913, and succeeded by King Constantine I, a brother-in-law of Kaiser William II. On 30 June the Second Balkan War opened with an attack by Bulgaria on Serbian and Greek positions; the Balkan states signed an armistice in Bucharest on 31 July, dividing up Macedonia between Greece, Serbia and Bulgaria. Territorially the Greek Prime Minister Eleutherios Venizelos was not satisfied by the extent of the acquisition and argued for a Hellenic State that would appropriate the Greek settlements in Turkey. With this aim uppermost, Venizelos sought entry into the First World War on the side of the Allies and against Turkey and Germany. As his policy was opposed by the pro-German Constantine, Venizelos set up a pro-Allied government first in Crete, then Salonika.

Having claimed Salonika as a refuelling base on the outbreak of the First World War, the Allies developed the city as a military base of the eastern Mediterranean. Predictably this policy infuriated King Constantine but encouraged Venizelos. General Maurice Sarrail, Commander-in-Chief of the Allied Armies in Macedonia, settled the issue by occupying the city and establishing a military government. Until his recall, at the end of 1917, it was Sarrail's obdurate arrogance that defined the nature of the Allied presence in Salonika. Even when the British General Staff recommended the evacuation of Salonika, on the grounds that it trapped too many troops in a location of limited strategic significance, it was decided to remain there partly as a diplomatic gesture to Sarrail's vanity. Around half a million Allied troops were based in Salonika, provoking the German joke that the city was their greatest internment camp. Grieve referred to this when debating whether the Allied forces in Salonika were 'a superfluous side-show or, as the boche boasted, "the cheapest internment camp they had"'.[2]

Historians of the First World War have tended to treat the subject of Salonika with the same lack of seriousness as the Germans. Dismissing the Allied effort in Salonika as a colossal waste of military manpower, one historian estimated that the Salonikan front consumed 'the energies of over 400,000 British troops alone, of whom 481,000 fell sick at one time or another – a ratio of 1103 hospital admissions per 1000 strength'.[3] Grieve was more responsive to Salonika and sickness:

> I didn't personally come into contact with the more horrific side of [the war]. In Salonika there was very little actual fighting. The Bulgars used to come over and pepper us at breakfast time and that sort of thing, and upset our breakfast, but the trouble there was the rampant nature of disease – malaria, blackwater fever, dysentery and so on, and the death rate was very very high for that reason ... I knew quite a lot of [the soldiers stationed at Salonika] and I saw quite a lot of them die. The death rate was very heavy.[4]

The thousands of crosses in the war cemeteries on the outskirts of the city mark the damage caused mainly by disease, not enemy action.

Sir Ronald Ross – who contributed verse to Grieve's anthology *Northern Numbers* (Second Series, 1921) and to whom Grieve's poem 'Science and Poetry' (first published in 1921) is dedicated – had experimentally verified the mosquito-theory of malaria in 1895 and had (in 1897-8) discovered the life-history of malarial parasites in mosquitoes. (He was awarded the Nobel prize for Medicine in 1902.) Prior to the First World War, Salonika had been free of malaria though not of the *Anopheles* mosquito. When troops returned from the malaria-infested marshes of the Struma Front they infected the *Anopheles* which spread the fever. 'The victims', one authority explained, 'suffered agonies of thirst and it was not unknown for a patient in his delirium to dash out into the nearby sea.'[5] Grieve was first infected by malaria in September 1916, shortly after arriving in Salonika.

Leaving Aldershot for overseas service, Sergeant Grieve was in Salonika before the end of August 1916. At the age of twenty-four, he was exhilarated by the excitement of arriving in a foreign country, seeing a historic city that let him look on Mount Olympus. Rudyard Kipling has a post-war poem, 'Salonikan Grave', ending 'It is fever, and not the fight – Time, not battle, – that slays.'[6] Soaking up his first impressions of Salonika, Grieve could not anticipate the ferocity of the fever. His feelings were expressed in a poem that recalls the colloquial vitality of Kipling's most popular verse. 'A Salonikan Storm Song' is dated 1 September 1916:

Sing ho! for life in the tented field
On a night of wind and rain
When the sun-baked ground goes suddenly soft
And the guy ropes tug and strain
And the pegs come up
And the tents go down
Sing ho, for the winds that beat and blow
Sing hey, for the showers that drown!

Sing ho, for life in the tented field
When the lively lightning plays
Blinding and brief over old Salonique
And the crowded waterways
And each bright flash leaves
The night still more black
Sing ho, for the wild fire over the hills,
Sing hey, for the thunders that crack!

Sing ho, for life in a tented field
On a night of storm and stress
Where chaos prevails and everything is
In the very deuce of a mess
And soaked and muddy and blown about
We still can laugh and sing
While the rain comes down in bucketfuls
And the wild fire has its fling![7]

It is a fairly typical piece of soldierly bravura. For the moment, anyway, both Poundian prosody and Georgian restraint seemed irrelevant.

Appointed Sergeant-Caterer of the Officers' Mess, Grieve found himself in his gastronomic element. Supervising five-course meals in his 'boots and buttons mirror-bright'[8] he warmed to his work. Arguably the best prose Grieve wrote during the war is contained in the letters he sent to Ogilvie. One of the earliest epistles from Salonika shows that love of cataloguing that was to inform his mature verse. On 20 August 1916 Grieve wrote to Ogilvie:

Brightly the beams fall on platefuls of white vegetable soup, patum peperium entrees, portions of cottage pie enlivened with rice-stuffed peppers, liberal helpings of rice and raisons, coffee pots and later when the Mess has come to the walnuts and almonds and the wine-steward is busy supplying Vin Blanc, Vin Russe, or Van Muscat de Samos (my favourite wine, recalling with every sip the wonderful tribute of a poem of Mr Sturge Moore's and

unreservedly endorsing every adjective therein), the Sergeant-Caterer and
his staff dine too. (What an awful war, to be sure!)[9]

His leisure time, he added, was given over to reading and 'a little
scribbling'.[10] In fact he had planned a whole programme of writing – on
the calibre of Scottish priests, on the impact of Sir Walter Scott on neo-
Catholicism, on Scottish Catholicism. Ogilvie would not have missed
the tendentious drift of Grieve's thought.

Over a bottle of beer Grieve reacted to a letter from Ogilvie,
reflecting how he had so far failed to realise the potential he had shown
at Broughton. This stream of consciousness brought back thoughts of
John Bogue Nisbet, 'with his splendid sensuous vitality'.[11] If he had
problems, then Grieve had also worked out a solution that must have
startled Ogilvie. He confessed to Ogilvie that he had come 'through the
pit of atheism to Roman Catholicism (adherent not member of the Church
of Rome ...)' and promised 'I shall come back and start a new Neo-
Catholic movement. I shall enter heart and body and soul into a new
Scots Nationalist propaganda.'[12] The Presbyterianism that motivated his
father and Ogilvie, his surrogate father, was thus consigned to the past.
The future was to be dedicated to the cause of neo-Catholic nationalism.

Established in the marble-floored premises of L'Orphenilat Grec, the
42nd General Hospital – to which Grieve was attached – was located
on the outskirts of Salonika towards Kalamaria. Grieve positioned himself
'in the mouth of a tent on a Balkan hillside, looking out over the ancient
city of Salonika and its crowded waterways, across the sun smitten gulf
to high Olympus'.[13] Grieve pronounced himself, in a letter of 2 September
1916 to Ogilvie, healthy and happy with his lot. Nevertheless his need
to keep in touch with Ogilvie was profound. His ambitions as a writer
were determined, to a considerable degree, by Ogilvie's approbation.
He assured Ogilvie of the extent of his dependence, telling his old
teacher that not one day passed without thoughts of him and how
necessary it was to write something fine enough to merit Ogilvie's
respect. Only by having Ogilvie as his lifeline to the literary world could
Grieve tolerate the philistinism of his everyday companions. One feature
of Salonikan life, though, particularly interested him. With six armies in
Salonika – the French, the Venizelos Greek, the Russians, the Anzacs,
the Serbs, the British – Grieve was aware of 'an incredible polyglottery'[14]
when he fraternised with other soldiers. That multilingual atmosphere
surfaced in the 1930s to pervade the poetic epic he attempted in Shetland.

Grieve's most immediate literary outlets as a soldier were the *Balkan*

News (to which he contributed some descriptive pieces) and the RAMC magazine. Ogilvie, active as ever at Grieve's old school, was keen to enhance the *Broughton Magazine* with work by his former pupil. In the issue for Christmas 1917 he printed one of Grieve's lucid letters. It opens with Sergeant Grieve camped 'on a high and airy promontory jutting out into the blue Aegean'[15] a day's sail away from the 42nd General Hospital. Suffering from a recurrence of the malaria that had infected him in September 1916 Grieve had been sent for a ten-day stint in a rest camp. He recuperated by bathing on a long stretch of beach and lying on a cliff-top watching the ships and boats on the water. Having read *Gallipoli* (1916) by John Masefield (who served with the Red Cross in the First World War) Grieve felt that the propaganda of the English poet did not do justice to the dazzling complexity of colour on view.

Just as he had been affected by the Easter Rising in Ireland, so Grieve was inspired by the Bolshevik Revolution in Russia. On 7 November (26 October, old style) 1917, Lenin led the Bolsheviks against Kerensky and (on 8 November) became chairman of the council of people's commissions (Trotsky becoming commissar for foreign affairs). Grieve was sympathetic to the Bolsheviks, admiring the élitism Lenin expounded in *What Is To be Done?* (1902). He insisted 'I'd fain have joined the Russians if that'd been possible.'[16] One of the books he planned before his demobilisation was a 20,000-word study of the Soviet state complete with a 'detailed description of the actual machinery of Bolshevik Government'.[17] The neo-Catholic nationalist was also a Communist sympathiser. 'I'll ha'e nae hauf-way hoose, but aye be whaur/Extremes meet' (87) is one of MacDiarmid's most memorable statements about himself. Extremes were beginning to meet and mingle compellingly in his mind during the First World War. Lenin, whom Grieve saw as a political superman, was one more figure to be included in the pantheon.

Grieve's reading during his Salonikan period was extremely varied. Beside his bed he had Robert Louis Stevenson's *Familiar Studies of Men and Books* (1882), Alfred George Gardiner's *Prophets, Priests and Kings* (1908), Augustine Birrell's *Selected Essays* (1909) plus copies of the *Nation*, the *Spectator*, the *Month*, the Dublin *Leader* (the Sinn Fein paper) and *New Witness* (which G. K. Chesterton edited from 1916 when his brother Cecil enlisted in the Army). In the *Little Review* of October 1917 he read Wyndham Lewis's story of the sexual seduction of 'Cantleman's Spring-Mate' and while he was enthusiastic about the aggressive ideas aired in Lewis's polemical Vorticist journal *Blast* (published from 1912 to 1915 with Pound as a regular contributor) he still enjoyed the relatively diffident work in Edward Marsh's anthologies of *Georgian Poetry*. He read Turgenev, Henry James, J. M. Synge, Galsworthy's *Fraternity* (1909, an exploration of the artificiality of urban life) and J. A. Ferguson's one-act play *Campbell of Kilmohr* (1915).

Under his pillow, he told Ogilvie, he had 'Chesterton's *Club of Queer Trades*, Alpha of the Plough's *Pebbles on the Shore*, E. V. Lucas's *A Little of Everything*'[18] while in his little Nestlé's Milk Box library he kept 'Viola Meynell's *Lot Barrow*, Stella Callaghan's *Vision*, Turgenev's *Rudin* in Constance Garnett's translation, Austin Dobson's *Fielding*, a monograph on Landseer, Archibald Marshall's *Richard Baldock*'.[19] He dropped the poetic names of Heine, Emily Dickinson – and T. S. Cairncross, just back from chaplaining in France and 'likely to contribute something good to the literature of the War'.[20] One of his favourite volumes of verse was Maurice Hewlett's *The Song of the Plow* (1916), a celebration of the indigenous English peasantry as personified by the hero Hodge who champions the cause of the Angles. As it was one of Grieve's favourite texts while he was in Salonika it is instructive to quote some lines from Hewlett's patriotic dedication to England:

> So, England, when the trumpets rang
> And young men stream'd to face the dread
> Of rocking battle, anguish wove
> A mist of glory for my head,
> Seeing you transfigured, and our love
> A living spirit, and our men
> One kindred![21]

As with Brooke's 'The Soldier', Grieve doubtless substituted Scotland for England when reading that passage.

Writing to Ogilvie, from Salonika, at the end of 1917 Grieve said he had 'actually committed to paper in rough draft ... two one-act plays, some seventy poems, and the first volume of a trilogy of autobiographic novels somewhat of a cross in nature between Gorki's *Childhood* and Wells' *Tono-Bungay*'.[22] Even making allowances for exaggeration it is likely that Grieve was working on a first novel in Salonika for what look like chapters from it make up the bulk of his first book, *Annals of the Five Senses*, as independent stories. His stated choice of models is indicative of his aim. Gorky's *Childhood* (*Detstvo*, 1913), the first part of an auto-biographic trilogy, describes the author's life up to the age of eleven when his grandfather sends him out into the world to fend for himself. Wells's *Tono-Bungay* (1909) charts the rise of a humbly-born hero, George

Ponderevo, who wins a science scholarship, stays with his uncle (whose patent medicine gives the novel its title) and finally achieves success as a builder of destroyers. What the two books have in common is the determination of an individual to surpass the poor expectations of his upbringing.

If, as seems likely, the story 'Cerebral' (which opens *Annals of the Five Senses*) was first written in Salonika as a section of an autobiographical novel, there is a more obvious model than either Gorky or Wells. Grieve had read Turgenev's *Rudin* (1856), in Constance Garnett's translation, by the beginning of 1918. When indecisive he said he was 'in a "Rudin" mood'.[23] Turgenev's hesitant hero (based on the Russian anarchist Mikhail Bakunin) is an idealistic intellectual whose obsessive egoism puts him at odds with social conventions. Eventually shot on the barricades during the 1848 Revolution in Paris, Rudin can hardly contain the complications of his cerebration:

> A profusion of ideas prevented Rudin from expressing himself cogently and precisely. Image after image poured out; analogies, now unexpectedly bold, now devastatingly apt, rose one after another ... All Rudin's thoughts seemed to be directed towards the future; [when] carried away in the flow of his own feelings, he reached heights of eloquence and poetry.[24]

By a curious coincidence, since Turgenev's first novel inspired Grieve, one of the main sources of *Rudin* is the work of a Scottish Borderer. Turgenev read *On Heroes, Hero-Worship, and the Heroic in History* (1841) in 1855 and was stirred by Thomas Carlyle's concept of the heroically imaginative man as 'he who lives in the inward sphere of things, in the True, Divine and Eternal, which exists always, unseen to most'.[25]

'Cerebral' has for its hero a Scottish freelance journalist of twenty-two, the age Grieve was when he worked for the *Forfar Review*. Rudin-like in his incessant cerebration, the protagonist is no local hack reporter but an intellectual in the process of completing (which he does in the course of the story) an article on 'The Scottish Element in Ibsen'. His mind is invaded by a 'thousand and one'[26] ideas, he is overwhelmed by impressions, 'athrill with the miracle of sentience, quivering in every filament of his perceptions with an amazing aliveness'.[27] He is solipsistically at the centre of his world, aware of others only in so far as they are necessary to his existence: he thinks of his old English master (Ogilvie) and resolves to reply to a letter from Peggy (Margaret Skinner, the girl Grieve met in Cupar).

The simultaneity of his perceptions gives the journalist a Rudin-like (or Hamlet-like) feeling that he is subjective to the point of superfluity: he is afflicted with 'a minute sense of unreality',[28] accumulates 'vague distrusts of certitude'.[29] His problem is coping with plurality:

> Every one of his separate egos became violently anarchical, creating an unthinkable Babel. Disunity and internecine hostility tore him into shreds. This passing, he would darken into lethargy, thus eventually recovering his poise in sleep, and the memories of such crises were almost indistinguishable from nightmares.[30]

Paradoxically, one of the consistent aspects of Grieve's art is his insight into the multitudinous possibilities of the human personality.

'Cerebral' is a remarkably vivid transcription of a mind almost stunned by its sensitivity to competing sensations. It is written in an English heightened to a fever pitch and punctuated with parentheses. An impressive achievement on its own, 'Cerebral' also anticipates ideas expressed in MacDiarmid's masterpiece *A Drunk Man Looks at the Thistle*. 'Cerebral' informs the reader that 'the Greeks built their altar to the Unknown God',[31] the Drunk Man burns 'endless candles to an Unkent God' (148); 'Cerebral' has a hero 'fearful of that "cursed conceit of being right which kills all noble feeling"', whether in himself or others',[32] the Drunk Man desires 'To dodge the curst conceit o' bein' richt/That damns the vast majority o' men' (87); the journalist of 'Cerebral' can 'suddenly see his brain as a writhing mass of worms',[33] the Drunk Man (identifying with the Thistle) thinks of 'The roots that wi' the worms compete' (104). There is justification for Grieve's insistence that 'under the apparent inconsistencies and contradictions [of my work] there is a basic unity [evident in] my first book, *Annals of the Five Senses* (1930 [actually 1923]), in which I express the main ideas of all my subsequent work'.[34]

As well as working on a first novel in Salonika, Grieve planned a first volume of verse. It was to be called *A Voice from Macedonia* and was to fill a gap in the Soldier Poets series published by Erskine Macdonald. Grieve was irritated by the assumption that the only soldier-poets were those serving on the Western Front. He wondered if the paucity of poetry from Salonika was due to the monotonously grim routine of death by disease – as opposed to the horrific drama of death in the trenches – but rejected this explanation. He contended that the 'same great elemental factors'[35] obtained in the Western Front and the Salonikan Front: the sacrifice of youth, the separations of lovers, the rush of death, 'the deep thoughts in the sentinel night, the sharpened memories of home constantly coming with an unspeakable newness'.[36] 'Beyond Exile', a poem first published in the *Broughton Magazine* (Summer 1919) – then anthologised in *Northern Numbers* (1920), then incongruously included in *First Hymn to Lenin and Other Poems* (1931) – is dated Salonika, 1916. Like 'Memories of Langholm', written in Edinburgh after leaving his birthplace, 'Beyond Exile' is a nostalgic exercise in the Georgian manner. Grieve equates homesickness with the separation from his sweetheart. Thinking of her (he has Margaret Skinner in mind) he prophesies that, if death comes to him, he will transcend it through a spiritual return to Scotland:

> And if I pass the utmost bourne
> > Why, then, I shall be home again –
> The quick step at the quiet door,
> > The gay eyes at the pane!   (306)

The stanzaic safety of the quatrain (rhyming *abcb*), the rhythmic monotony of the iambic tetrameters and concluding trimeter, the monosyllabic rhymes; these are all characteristic of the Georgian verse that Sergeant Grieve habitually enjoyed.

However, Grieve was also experimenting with a more fluent style, retaining rhymes but not absolutely relying on them, alternating the rhythmic length of his lines. The more inventive side of him appreciated the flexible prosody of Pound, the sensuousness of D. H. Lawrence. As a reader of the *English Review* and the *Georgian Poetry* anthologies, Grieve was familiar with Lawrence's work; for example Lawrence's 'Snap Dragon' – 'her bosom couched in the confines of her gown ... her dark deeps shook with convulsive thrills'[37] – was first published in the *English Review* in June 1912 and reprinted in *Georgian Poetry, 1911–1912*; 'Meeting Among the Mountains' appeared in the *English Review* of February 1914 and again in *Georgian Poetry, 1913–1915*.

Two frankly sexual poems – one of disgust, the other of delight – are set in Salonika. 'La Belle Terre Sans Merci' is an address to Salonika as a seductive city whose beauty invitingly tempts the beholder to an ecstasy dangerous with disease. The city is personified as a prostitute, with 'luring hills' as breasts:

> Syphilis in silver hides
> Her running wounds and rotting bones.
> Fever is clothed in gold,

Gaily-caparisoned War rides
And on the pointed stones
The dervish Dysentery whirls
Attenuate   (1199)

A companion poem, 'Spanish Girl' (collected in *Annals of the Five Senses*) pays tribute to the erotic appeal of the subject. Grieve was seeing a Spanish girl, Maregena, in February 1918. The poem conveys the sexual rapture he shared with her:

It is good to lie here
In endless mornings pale and clear
And see the roses trembling on the sill
And your breasts quivering still!
O thou whose unremitting lust
Constrains my dust!   (13)

Thoughout 'Spanish Girl' Grieve explores the many connotations of the rose which is first (as in Blake) an image of female fragility then, disturbingly, a 'scarlet light of lust / Frenzying the disjunct dust'. Alert to the sexual symbolism of the rose, Grieve sustains his passion with reference to the 'rose of light ... rose that will not let me rest'. He simulates the orgasmic moment through fervour ('Burn more intense. / Clasp me as in a vice') and the increasingly fragmentary form of the poem.

During his Salonikan period – from August 1916 to May 1918 – Grieve probably drafted the studies in early self-portraiture collected in *Annals of the Five Senses* ('Café Scene' and 'A Limelight from a Solitary Wing' which could be parts of the fictional scheme 'Cerebral' originally fitted) and such poems as the Nietzschean 'The Fool' (a variation on the death-of-God theme) and the explicitly sexual sonnet 'Consummation' (both included in *Annals of the Five Senses*). While he seldom altered the texts of his fair copies of poems he was adamant that while in Salonika his drafts would not be 'put into more final shape as long as I am in khaki'.[38] The poems he sent to his brother for safekeeping (obviously after the First World War as Andrew enlisted in 1917 and saw service in France before he was demobilised in 1919) offer a few clues to the chronology of composition. 'A Salonikan Storm Song' (see p. 86) was dated; other poems came complete with instructions, hinting that Grieve was not being entirely flippant when he told Ogilvie that, as Andrew had a job as 1st Clerk in the 4th Inland Revenue Division in Edinburgh, he intended to 'live on him'[39] immediately after the war. Two manuscript poems – the first beginning 'O singing heart, for in my blood the music is', the second beginning 'The ancient chorus of the rich blue flood' – conclude with a fraternal command to 'Call the latter "A Scots Heart Going East" and the former, "Race Memory" and send them to the *G[lasgow] Herald*'.[40] The poem beginning 'The ancient chorus of the rich blue flood' was published in 1920, in Grieve's anthology *Northern Numbers*, with the title 'Allegiance' subscribed 'Written on the Mediterranean'. The original title, 'A Scots Heart Going East', implies that it was composed on the way to Salonika (or on arrival in the city) rather than in Marseilles in 1918-19.

'Allegiance', which imposes a Georgian restraint on the dialogue-form of the popular ballads, allows a Scots Borderman to compare the felicities of his homeland with the fame of the 'rich blue flood' of classical verse. Naturally, the Scots Borderman itemises his memories of Langholm with its 'red bell-heather, green fir-fans, / And moorland mysteries and mountain hopes' (the hills around Langholm having grown mountainous in his imagination). The ending uses a typical Grievian contrast, juxtaposing royalty and romance:

> 'Praise give I freely to the mighty Queen
> Who passes now in splendour and in state,
> But ah! – my heart is hers whose shy, light eyes
> And small, swift smile elate

> 'Sealed me the servant of a cause forlorn,
> Whose dream and whose desire I cannot tell,
> Where timeless silence in the far blue hills
> Hangs like a ready bell!'   (1200)

(Those 'far blue hills' would have offended Ezra Pound who warned poets against superfluous epithets and cited a Turkish war correspondent who was caught 'red-handed babbling in his despatches of "dove-grey" hills, or else it was "pearl-pale".[41]) The 'shy, light eyes' are those of Margaret Skinner. Several of Grieve's poems to her mention the beauty of her eyes: 'Beyond Exile' speaks of 'The gay eyes at the pane' (306), 'Tryst in the Forest' begins 'With starry eyes she comes to me' (1114), 'She Whom I Love' ends with a look from 'a clear eye / That shineth by' (1114). Physically cut off from Scotland, Sergeant Grieve saw Peggy as the embodiment of the brilliantly lit land he had left behind.

Grieve had been infected by malaria in September 1916 and again in the summer of 1917. In April 1918 he had his third attack of malaria: if he looked on it philosophically he could take comfort from Nietzche's notion of eternal recurrence. That month he informed Ogilvie he had never felt better since 'the malaria microbe invaded my veins way back in September 1916'.[42] He had been involved in the establishment of a new camp, basking in the hot sun and drinking brown ale. Exposure to the fresh air had, temporarily, removed the dark rings beneath his eyes and the physical work had made him feel so fit he regretted that he had not followed his inclinations and become a gardener. Nevertheless, he had been 'definitely passed for invaliding home as a chronic malaria subject'.[43] He looked forward to seeing Ogilvie sometime during the summer, for he was determined to conclude some important business in Scotland.

By the time he left Salonika early in May 1918 Grieve's nationalist views were pronounced. He was hostile to English people as representatives of imperialism. He had already told Ogilvie that, when home in Langholm in 1912, 'Intimate passages with three young ladies, all English, revived in me our racial antipathy to the English'[44] and he added, in April 1918, that though loyal 'to certain ideals bound up in the Allied Cause I was never to say the least of it an Anglophile'.[45] An interview recorded one year before his death clarified the nationalist issue as one largely settled in the First World War:

> My recollection of the wartime and the hundreds of men that I soldiered with was that when they were Scots, or Irish, or Welsh we got on all right, but we always had a difference from the English, we didn't get on with the English at all and I became more and more anti-English as the time went on.[46]

Grieve was weary of the assumption that the British troops were fighting exclusively for the honour of England. Scotland, he was sure, had a future too.

Leaving Greece he sailed to the Gulf of Taranto, in southern Italy (figuratively in the instep of Italy) and boarded the invalid train. This train took thirteen days to move the troops from Taranto to Le Havre. On one of the many stops on this journey Grieve 'completely lost my heart to Faenza, where I stayed for some time'.[47] Eventually he arrived in England then travelled to North Wales to be treated in the malaria concentration centre near the coastal town of Rhyl. Within a month he was pronounced fit and sent to barracks in Blackpool for posting overseas. Before his departure, however, he was given a period of convalescent leave in Scotland, and in Edinburgh he had asked Peggy Skinner to marry him.

So far Grieve's love life had been fairly inconclusive. While at Broughton he had gone out with his fellow pupil Helen Christine Murray, who was three months younger than him. Since leaving Broughton he had seen Helen on a few occasions – in Edinburgh and London – and corresponded with her when she became a teacher in Essex. Apparently she had a nervous disposition, susceptible to breakdowns. Grieve believed that the story of his relationship with Helen 'would be voted quite impossible, but it is nevertheless although so sketchy and haphazard vital in different ways to both of us'.[48] Later, there was Grieve's engagement to Minnie Punton, broken off at the beginning of 1916, followed by his friendship with Maregena in Salonika. Then there was his meeting with the sixteen-year-old Peggy Skinner in Cupar. Grieve had written to her regularly from Salonika. She was serving in the Women's Auxiliary Army Corps as secretary to the Colonel of The Black Watch at Queen's Barracks, Perth.

Returning to Edinburgh at the end of May 1918, Grieve was involved in two marriage ceremonies. His mother Elizabeth was living with James Dawson, a forester, at Lammermuir Lodge, Whittingehame, in East Lothian. For the second time she was about to marry a man younger than herself: Dawson, a widower, was fifty-five whereas she was sixty-one. On 1 June 1918 James Dawson and Elizabeth Grieve were married at 8 Bank Street, Edinburgh, by declaration in the presence of Sergeant Christoper Grieve and Margaret Ann Dawson, James's sister. On 13 June Christopher Murray Grieve (described as a journalist and Sergeant in the RAMC) and Margaret Cunningham Thomson Skinner (described as a typist in the WAAC at Perth, with a civilian address at 31 Durie Street, Methil) were married at 3 East Castle Road, Edinburgh. The ceremony was conducted, according to the forms of the United Free Church of Scotland, by the Revd Robert Drummond – minister of Lothian Road Church and an old friend of Grieve's and George Ogilvie's (Grieve called in at Broughton to see Ogilvie but his old teacher was absent ill so there was little opportunity to call at his house in Cluny Gardens.) After the marriage Christopher and Peggy Grieve went to stay with the newly-married Dawsons at Lammermuir Lodge. Their short honeymoon over, Grieve reported to his Blackpool barracks while Peggy returned to Perth.

As Sergeant-Caterer for the RAMC Depot Sergeants' Mess, Grieve spent the month of August in Blackpool, where, despite his declaration, to Ogilvie, of his antipathy to the English he had a riotous time. He had good reason for his high spirits on this occasion:

> with over 300 warrant officers and senior NCOs in average daily messing strength and a great influx of visiting sergeants belonging to other units, I sold forty-five cases of whisky and ninety barrels of beer in the month – and that at a time of strict rationing, when Blackpool licence-holders had great difficulty in getting hold of the stuff – particularly the 'hard stuff' – at all, and would have given me two to three pounds a bottle if I would have diverted it to them: a feat which brought me to loggerheads with the Army authorities and led to an investigation from which I emerged with flying colours.[49]

With his Army record intact, Grieve was sent to a reception camp in Upper Normandy, near Dieppe – 'the wet muddy cold neighbourhood of Dieppe'.[50] Under the Army Education Scheme he was detailed to give lectures, three nights a week, on 'Political and Commercial Geography' and 'Civic and Town Planning'.

It was at Dieppe, on 11 November 1918, that Sergeant Grieve heard that the armistice had been signed by the Allies and Germany. The news, he informed Ogilvie, 'was taken very quietly – incalculable relief, but no mafficking'.[51] On the following day he had some further reflections on the war and his own future in peacetime:

> I myself believe that we have lost this war – in everything but actuality! When I see scores of sheep go to a slaughter-house I do not feel constrained to admire their resignation. Nor do I believe that the majority of soldiers killed were sufficiently actuated by ideals or capable of entertaining ideas to justify such terms as 'supreme self-sacrifice, etc.' . . . [Personally] my plans for the future are cut and dry . . my life-work is really done [for] various books exist complete and unchangeable in my mind [so] what remains is only to do the actual writing.[52]

One bright spark lit up the gloomy fatalism. The popular author John Buchan – then a Lt-Colonel as well as the Director of Intelligence in Beaverbrook's Ministry of Information – had expressed approval of Grieve's manuscript collection *A Voice from Macedonia*. The firm of Erskine Macdonald, to whom Grieve had first sent the manuscript (including, presumably, the poems 'A Salonikan Storm Song', 'Beyond Exile', 'La Belle Terre Sans Merci','Spanish Girl', 'Allegiance'), had not been enthusiastic enough to promise publication so Grieve had sent the poems to Buchan in his capacity as a director of Nelson's (during the war Buchan compiled Nelson's *History of the War*). Though Buchan finally decided against publishing *A Voice from Macedonia* he remained an admirer of Grieve and wrote a perceptive preface to *Sangschaw*, the first book published under the name of Hugh MacDiarmid. (*A Voice from Macedonia* was never published, the poems in it being either discarded or incorporated into other collections.)

There was to be no rapid return to civilian life for Sergeant Grieve. He was detached from the RAMC, attached to the Indian Medical Service and posted to the Sections Lahore Indian General Hospital stationed at the Château Mirabeau at Estaque, near Marseilles. He took the Boulogne-Paris express, spent a day seeing the sights of Paris, and was in Marseilles by October 1918. Almost immediately he met a French girl, who was working at the Norwegian Consulate there. Apparently he shared Christmas with her in erotic abandon, for he boasted to Ogilvie that 'in penetrating the warm secrets of Southern life my volatile temperament is running with the swift delightful smoothness of a high-grade electrical contrivance'.[53]

Early in the New Year of 1919 Grieve was back in the arms of his wife. With a period of leave in Scotland he stayed with Peggy at 35 South Street, St Andrews, and brought her to Edinburgh to meet Ogilvie. Returning to Marseilles in February he kept Ogilvie up to date with his literary progress on 23 March 1919. He had completed 'Triangular', a Vorticist study after the manner of 'Cerebral': possibly this was later reduced to the impressionistic prose piece entitled 'A Four Years' Harvest' in *Annals of the Five Senses* for this flashes back from 1919 and contains a quotation from a letter Ogilvie had sent commenting on his Salonikan manuscripts.[54] In addition Grieve had outlined a critical study of Conrad, had essayed some sketches on Marseilles and had researched his projected book on the Soviet state. Meanwhile, Peggy had been appointed his agent and was instructed to send *A Voice from Macedonia* to John Lane (The Bodley Head).

In the Château Mirabeau – set on a cliff on the periphery of Marseilles, and surrounded by woodlands, orchards and gardens – Grieve was grateful for comforts that had been denied to him for the duration of the war. One of four senior NCOs, he had his own bedroom in a little flat in the château: 'One could not be more cushily circumstanced on service.'[55] As a Sergeant, so he explained to Ogilvie, he had the status of Sub-Assistant Surgeon though his duties were routine. Sections Lahore

General Hospital was staffed by Indian doctors – 'mostly Edinburgh-trained'[56] – assisted by a personnel of Gurkhas. Its function, as a native labour hospital, was to deal with Asiatic soldiers who had broken down psychologically on the Western Front. Grieve found the work engrossing but frequently gruesome. He arrived in the aftermath of the influenza epidemic of 1918 and saw his patients, with little power of resistance, die in great numbers. Moreover, the staff 'never had fewer than three to four hundred insane to deal with'.[57] The experience informs 'A Four Years' Harvest' in which the autobiographical protagonist contemplates the suffering he has seen in Macedonia, Italy and France:

> A sensitive man who had suffered was a man, whether he had endured the monotonous epic suffering of an infantry private or the continual spectacle of pain in a Casualty Clearing Station, who returned not altogether sane. He had endured so much either in his own or the rent flesh of others that he brought back to civilisation an ardour of revolt, a sharp bitterness, made up partly of hatred and partly of pity ... He came back with an *idée fixe* – never again must men be made to suffer as in these years of war.[58]

Though he was never directly involved in fighting, during the war, he was certainly conscious of the wreckage of human lives.

While he was waiting for his demobilisation – 'I know now that I shall not get out of the Army for nearly a year yet'[59] he lamented on 23 March 1919 – Grieve took full advantage of his French situation. As a wing three-quarter he played rugby for the Marseilles Base Team: one weekend in the middle of March his team, playing at St Raphael, lost by eight points to nil 'against a crack team of French aviators ... after a swift, bitterly contested game'.[60] Defeat left Grieve with a split lip, gravelled knees and a raging thirst – soon satisfied. On the Monday after the match he went, with another player, to see Cannes before taking the night express back to Marseilles.

At the end of May he embarked on what was fondly remembered as perhaps 'the happiest of all my European experiences ... my walking tour in 1919 along the Franco-Spanish frontier and in the Pays Basque'.[61] By 4 June he was staying at the Villa de l'Annonciation in Lourdes, the town on the fringes of the Pyrénées where Bernadette Soubiros had her visions of the Virgin Mary in 1858. Though he had once claimed neo-Catholicism as his creed there was no mention of the miraculous legend of Lourdes. Grieve was more immediately interested in physical than spiritual heights. A postcard to Ogilvie from Lourdes tells of his prowess:

> I have just returned from the Franco-Spanish frontier ... Yesterday over
> fields of eternal snow I climbed right up the Brèche de Roland into Spain –
> about 3000 metres high – a wonderful experience. Tomorrow I am going
> on to Bayonne and Biarritz and thence into the Pays Basque and along the
> Silver Coast.[62]

He did not do this on his own; his walking (and climbing) tour was no
solitary exercise.

Grieve was accompanied by the young woman he had met in
Marseilles. She spoke four languages and, in the poet's opinion, was
'capable of brains and beauty in each of them'.[63] He wrote two poems
during his journey, 'Mountain Measure' (located Les Hautes-Pyrénées,
June 1919) and 'To a French Girl Friend' (located Cirque de Gavarnie,
Les Hautes-Pyrénées, June 1919). The second poem comprised two six-
line stanzas, the first of which commends human company in a manner
that is rare in Grieve's usually self-centred verse:

> You named the mountains in your eager way,
> Singling each cloud-bound peak along the chain,
> As you called them and they came to you
> And knew your hand upon their heads again,
> And I, the stranger, who had been afraid,
> Was taken into friendship too.   (1202)[64]

The mature poetry of MacDiarmid dismisses friendship as an unnecessary
distraction from the task of confronting the vastness of the universe as
an inviolable individual.

Ogilvie was pressing Grieve for verse and prose for the *Broughton
Magazine*. On 12 June Grieve sent him 'To a French Girl Friend', duly
published in the Summer of 1919. A prose contribution was a more
difficult problem. What was subsequently condensed into 'A Four Years'
Harvest' then ran to some 200,000 words so was therefore unsuitable
for the slim school magazine. Grieve decided to submit 'Casualties', a
story Ogilvie printed alongside the poem. 'Casualties' was probably
prompted by thoughts of Nisbet's death in the trenches of the Western
Front. It is an account of 'the unspeakable harvest on the Somme', a
description of the death of many men as a collective Fall of Man:

> On this dreary tract nothing remained of the gifts once showered by nature.
> But the grim legacies of man at war were countless – chaotic and half-
> buried heaps of his machinery, munitions and equipment, and the remains
> of his hasty meals. And he himself lay there, shattered in thousands, to give

a lurking horror to a treacherous and violent surface of mud and slime and unlovely litter. The very weeds which might have graced the desolation refused such holding-ground.[65]

Leaving aside the intimate letters he sent to Ogilvie, 'Casualties' contains the most uncomplicated prose Grieve wrote as a soldier. It was not, however, included in *Annals of the Five Senses* as it did not conform to the highly subjective pattern of that book.

Grieve was demobilised at the beginning of July 1919 – or, rather, he demobilised himself. He clarified his action in 1970:

> I ought to have gone to Ripon [in the West Riding of Yorkshire] for demob. but at that time there were proposals that married soldiers who had had malaria should not be demobbed for a year or so, and some of us were determined to get out of it by hook or crook.[66]

He had hoped to meet Ogilvie at a concert in Edinburgh but went straight to St Andrews on hearing that his wife had been taken ill, possibly at the news of the imminent return of the soldier. On 23 July Grieve said that Peggy's problem was a chill 'and a sort of nervous breakdown'[67] but that she was recovering. He stayed with Peggy in a 'wee house'[68] at 65 Market Street, St Andrews, and settled down to serious literary work. At Ogilvie's bidding he had successfully persuaded the Edinburgh firm of T. N. Foulis to publish a Scottish equivalent of *Georgian Poetry*; he intended to call the series *Northern Numbers* after the journal *New Numbers* that first published (in December 1914) Rupert Brooke's five famous sonnets. He was also working on a novel, fragments from which appeared as sections of *Annals of the Five Senses*.

Grieve's four years as a soldier had not changed him utterly but drastically sharpened his outlook. He no longer saw inconsistency as a vice but as an artistic virtue; he was no longer alarmed by his impetuosity. Politically he had become more extreme. Dissatisfied with the parliamentary social-ism of the ILP and the Fabian Society he was moving towards a revolutionary faith, one that took account of the failure of the Easter Rising in Ireland and the success of the Bolshevik Revolution in Russia. Having seen men die for 'gallant little Belgium' and the 'honour of England', he now held firmly nationalistic opinions about the economic state and inferior political status of Scotland. His neo-Catholicism of 1916 had been abandoned in favour of a belief in himself as a spiritual being: though far from being a believer in art for art's sake he had the aesthete's reverence for art as the purest of human activities. Poetically he was still open to both Poundian and Georgian influences but admitted a new ecstatic influence when he sampled the sprung rhythm of Gerard Manley Hopkins in *Poems*, edited by Robert Bridges, the Poet Laureate, in 1918. (Grieve quoted from Hopkins's 'God's Grandeur' and 'The Wreck of the *Deutschland*' in 'A Four Years' Harvest'.) As he sat in his room in St Andrews, the little house noisy with the chatter of three female friends of Peggy, he had the glimmerings of his 'shining vision of Alba'.[69] He had not done any physical fighting in the British Army; in peacetime he intended to be constantly on the offensive as he fought on home ground for the future of his own country.

5

Oddman Out

I would willingly share with you the fun connected with my appointment
here. It is the most incredible mixture of phantasy and reality ... I have
drafted a book entitled *Oddman Out: Notes from a Highland Pantry.*

C. M. Grieve, letter to George Ogilvie, 13 Nov. 1920

L IKE many of his follow servicemen, Christopher Grieve was not
convinced by Lloyd George's prediction, in a speech delivered thirteen days after the Armistice, that the task was now 'to make a fit
country for heroes to live in'. He had no job waiting for him in Scotland
and, while in St Andrews in the summer and autumn of 1919, depended
on the income his wife earned as secretary to a firm of solicitors. There
was little chance of his finding work as a journalist in St Andrews. He
had already worked for the Innes group, on the *St Andrews Citizen*, in
1913 and had left after a row. Grudges were not easily forgotten in the
restricted world of Scottish provincial journalism.

Andrew Lang, who studied at its ancient university (the oldest in
Scotland, founded in 1412 by Bishop Henry Wardlaw), produced the most
frequently quoted lines about St Andrews in his poem 'Almae Matres':

> *St Andrews by the Northern Sea,*
> *A haunted town it is to me!*

A little city, worn and grey,
   The grey North Ocean girds it round;
And o'er the rocks, and up the bay,
   The long sea-rollers surge and sound[1]

Grieve was not similarly inspired by St Andrews. The predominantly English ambience of Lang's alma mater may, however, have provoked the criticism of Scottish academic institutions in MacDiarmid's *To Circumjack Cencrastus*: 'Oor four Universities / Are Scots but in name' (203).

St Andrews in 1919 was not the base Grieve was looking for. Once the seat of the ecclesiastical primate of Scotland, St Andrews had been historically and theologically central to the national story. St Andrews Castle (now a ruin), for example, had figured prominently in the Reformation for there Cardinal Beaton was murdered in 1546 and John Knox became chaplain to the Protestants who occupied the Castle. By 1919 St Andrews was almost an outpost of England with many of the local population at the service of relatively affluent academics and students from England. The greatest glory of St Andrews, then as now, was the Royal and Ancient Golf Club (founded 1754), the ruling authority on the game. Grieve was to take up golf in Montrose in 1923 but had no time for it in St Andrews. In common with Edwin Muir, who lived in St Andrews in 1935, Grieve was conscious of the divisions of St Andrews: between Scots and English, between poor and rich.

Grieve obtained a job with the *Montrose Review* in 1920 but left after a few months. He felt that his employer – James Foreman, who had just assumed responsibility for the paper from his father Joseph – demanded so much of his time that he could do little creative work and was 'consequently verging upon a breakdown'.[2] He was to return to Montrose with a vengeance, poetically and literally for he produced his masterly work in Scots there, despite a bewildering variety of activities, and later portrayed Foreman as the epitome of the spiteful businessman in *To Circumjack Cencrastus*.

The next move was northwards, to a remote shooting lodge in a deer forest ten miles north-west of Alness in Ross and Cromarty. Kildermorie Lodge stands at the head of Loch Morie, the source of the river Alness, and is surrounded by mountains: Carn Chuinneag (the highest, at 2749 ft), Meall Mór (2419 ft), Carn Cas nan Gabhar (1976 ft). It was one of the Scottish properties owned by Charles William Dyson Perrins, the Worcester Sauce millionaire. Aged fifty-six in 1920, Perrins had been Mayor of Worcester (in 1897) and High Sheriff of Worcester-shire (1899). At his home in Ardross Castle, a mansion house six miles south-east of Kildermorie Lodge, he kept a collection of illuminated manuscripts and early woodcut books. Grieve may have been shown Perrins's collection but it is unlikely that he catalogued them as he claimed. In Grieve's opinion, Perrins was 'one of the most delightful and original little good-hearted freaks in Christendom'.[3]

Perrins had sufficient land around Ardross Castle to satisfy his own appetite for field-sports so rented out Kildermorie Lodge during the grouse-shooting season (which begins on the 'Glorious' Twelfth of August). Each year paying guests took over twelve of the sixteen bedrooms in the lodge, leaving the others free for staff. In residence all year was the caretaker and it was this post Grieve applied for, citing George Ogilvie as an authority on his respectability. Perrins's factor, Lt-Colonel Thomas Williamson Cuthbert, contacted Ogilvie; Grieve was appointed caretaker. Peggy was also taken on as an under-housemaid and given the task of keeping the lodge clean. During the shooting season – when butlers, footmen, personal maids and cooks crammed into the lodge – Grieve was odd-man, generally helping out. One of the books he planned at Kildermorie was to be titled *Oddman Out: Notes from a Highland Pantry*. (It was never completed.)

Despite the fact that he and his wife were employed as servants of the rich ruling class, Grieve was glad to get away from Montrose and into the Scottish Highlands. His move to Kildermorie he considered 'the most unqualifiedly successful experience I have yet made in a life of ups and downs'.[4] In October 1920 he was on his own as Peggy had left for five weeks' holiday. He took the opportunity to press on with his own poetry, congratulating himself (in a letter to Ogilvie) on completing twenty-nine sonnets in one week. Without first asking Ogilvie, he sent him the sonnets and was hurt when his mentor expressed annoyance at what he took to be presumption. 'It's a pity for your own sake', Ogilvie scolded his former pupil, 'that you don't keep a firmer hold on yourself – I don't know what your peculiar temptation is but it has had a good innings.'[5] Grieve's candid response of 2 November confessed to the sin of solipsism and then made an eloquent plea for Ogilvie's continued co-operation:

> My 'temptation' lies simply in the fact that when I recurrently reach a certain pitch everything outside me ceases to exist ... I have loved you above all men and women. You have been constantly in my thoughts ...

Do you think I want money or position or reputation? No. Do you think that [my literary work] matters to my wife, for instance? I may dedicate my poems to her but do you think she reads them? And if she did do you think she would understand them, or me? No! I need not write. I can dream my books and enjoy them in my head. But I try to write incessantly and cannot help doing so because your commendation of my work is my only desire. If my work gives you no pleasure – if my work does not satisfy you that you saw true away back in these Broughton days – it is wasted, irrespective of anything else.[6]

Grieve could not make his position any clearer – Ogilvie was his ideal audience of one, Peggy was one of the many incapable of understanding the unrecognised poet.

As well as discharging his duties as caretaker, Grieve sought out another job at Kildermorie. Some four hundred yards from Kildermorie Lodge, in a room of the head stalker's house, was a Side School where the young children of Perrins's employees were grounded in general knowledge by a single teacher. In November 1920 this teacher left to get married so Grieve took over. Officially employed by the Ross and Cromarty Education Authority as a Side School teacher, Grieve grandly described himself to Ogilvie as 'headmaster'.[7] He had a total of three pupils, all aged eleven: Betty Mackintosh, Lydia Monroe and Duncan Cameron, son of one of the stalkers. Cameron remembered Grieve teaching English and arithmetic and thought him 'a clever man, brilliant, a bit beyond us'.[8]

The major event for Grieve at Kildermorie was his first appearance in a volume of verse, albeit one edited by himself. Though his name does not figure on the title page of *Northern Numbers*, the anthology was Grieve's first book; he chose the contents and initialled the contentious foreword. Published by T. N. Foulis of 15 Frederick Street, Edinburgh, *Northern Numbers* came out in November 1920 with an acknowledgement to the precedent of Edward Marsh's *Georgian Poetry* series. Marsh had made *Georgian Poetry* a platform for his friends – principally Rupert Brooke – and Grieve followed this example by describing most of the contributors as 'close personal friends'.[9] Indeed the book contains poems by his former minister, T. S. Cairncross; his old school friend, Roderick Watson Kerr; and his brother, Andrew Graham Grieve. The other poets had reputations ranging from the secure to the established. Joseph Lee had published several collections, including *Ballads of Battle* (1916); Will H. Ogilvie's most recent volume was *The Australian and Other Verses*

(1916); John Ferguson's sonnet sequence *Thyrea* (1918) had gone through six reprints in less than three years; Donald A. Mackenzie was the author of two volumes of verse (*The Riddle of Life* and *Elves and Heroes*) as well as a number of prose works on myth and folklore. The first three names in the list of contents were very well known. Violet Jacob had produced historical novels (*The Interloper* and *Flemington* are both set in Angus) in addition to *Songs of Angus* (1915) and *More Songs of Angus* (1918). John Buchan and Neil Munro were two of the most popular writers in Britain. As Cairncross (*The Return of the Master*, 1905) and Kerr (*War Daubs*, 1919) had both brought out books, the only unknown poets in *Northern Numbers* were Christopher Grieve and his brother Andrew.

Grieve dedicated the anthology 'with affection and pride' to Neil Munro and had his reasons for doing so. It was his intention to use the big names as stepping stones to his own Scottish celebrity. He admitted as much in *Lucky Poet*:

> The well-known poets represented alongside *les jeunes* [in *Northern Numbers*] were speedily, and no doubt a trifle unceremoniously, 'dropped', and the field was left to the rising school. I have been accused of ill-faith in securing the association in this way of men who were relatively distinguished – and then dropping them. I cannot see that any ill-faith was involved at all.... Whatever use I had for the work of Neil Munro and others at the beginning, I speedily lost as I got 'further ben' in my chosen task. [Nevertheless] I was not on that account to be deemed an ingrate who had bit the hands that fed me and kicked away abruptly the ladder by which I had risen.[10]

The important point is that *Northern Numbers* was the first step in a campaign strategically masterminded by Grieve.

A few of the poems in *Northern Numbers* were in Scots (Buchan's 'Fisher Jamie', Violet Jacobs's 'The Whustlin' Lad') but English verse predominated. The most adventurous contributions were those of Cairncross and Kerr. Cairncross had derived his irregular idiom from the rhymeless poems in W. E. Henley's *In Hospital* (1898), written when Henley was in Edinburgh's Royal Infirmary receiving treatment from Joseph Lister.[11] Kerr had been a tank commander in the war and expressed his feelings with soldierly realism, as in 'From the Line' (reprinted from *War Daubs*): 'Have you seen men when they come / From shell-holes filled with scum / Of mud and blood and flesh ...?'[12] Compared to that the poem, 'June Memory', by Christopher's brother Andrew was soporific: 'And the shadows skip and chase / Elfin-wise across the sward, / Oh, in bright-eyed harmony / Sings a little bird / Privately to me.'[13]

Christopher Grieve included six of his own poems – 'La Belle Terre Sans Merci', 'Allegiance', Mountain Measure', 'To a French Girl Friend', 'Beyond Exile', 'To M[argaret] G[rieve]'. With the exception of the sexually direct 'La Belle Terre Sans Merci' they were technically timid. What the reviewers focused on was Grieve's editorial assertion that the anthology was the work of a Group, a new school of Scottish poets. His foreword drew attention to the anthology as the 'work of certain Scottish poets of today – and tomorrow!', described the venture as 'an experiment in group-publication', and bracketed the contributors as 'the present group'.[14] The *Scotsman* (20 Dec. 1920) took exception to Grieve's phrase 'close personal friends'; the *Glasgow Evening News* (23 Dec.) said it was 'difficult to believe that there is any such Group at all'.[15] Grieve replied to both comments, thus beginning his lifelong habit of using the correspondence columns of Scottish papers as a forum for his many activities and as a medium for self-publicity.

Still, Grieve was gratified by the interest shown in his anthology; delighted, for example, that his old paper, the *Edinburgh Evening Dispatch*, devoted a column of praise to *Northern Numbers* on 15 December 1920. He was already considering the contents of the second number of the anthology and glad, given his fixation with titles, to be in touch with 'Lady Glenconner, General Sir Ian Hamilton, and Sir Ronald Ross'.[16] Having included two poems by his brother Andrew in the first number, Grieve was not willing to repeat what could be construed as a policy of nepotism. An undated letter from Kildermorie to Andrew brutally undercut the artistic hopes of his brother and, incidentally, proclaimed Grieve's own poetic credo of the period:

> None of [your poems] will do – none of them come within miles and miles of doing ... If I printed one of them even as it stands I should become not a target for criticism – which wouldn't matter – but a laughing-stock ... Your 'three main ways' of writing poetry will never produce a poem or anything else in the form of art. Leaving out the difficult matters of inspiration, freedom or limitation in the choice of metrical vehicles, the qualities of diction in so far as they inhere with predilections and antipathies which suit or unsuit them for various forms and various subjects, poetry consists of 1/ Having something to say, 2/ Saying it poetically – that is to say with the maximum beauty, clarity and appropriateness. Poetry is the literature of power and the most concise medium man has devised for the expression of emotion. Any figure of speech that is not absolutely relevant,

any word which either in its sound, shape, or suggestions is not strictly congruous to the business of creating a given impression is out of place and utterly impermissible. Every word, every figure of speech, every associated idea should, as it were, emit convex rays which go to build a dome of thought or feeling. The adjectives must 'shade' together – the whole must be a harmony – with 'grace-notes' if you like; but without interruptions, digressions, irrelevancies.[17]

Grieve's assault on Andrew amounts almost to epistolary fratricide. However, the Poundian notion of poetry as a consummately crafted art of emotional precision was being tested by Grieve in the poems he composed at Kildermorie.

Settling into winter in his lodge in the wilderness, Grieve noted the 'soul-freezing frost'[18] and took the precaution of buying in provisions from the nearest village – Boath, five miles south-east of Kildermorie Lodge. He mulled over the tribute to himself in the Christmas 1920 issue of the *Broughton Magazine*. Ogilvie testified that his former pupil 'wrote poetry and prose with equal facility ... and the amazing thing was that everything he did was superlatively good'.[19] Writing to Ogilvie from Kildermorie, Grieve hoped to demonstrate that his *Sonnets of the Highland Hills* surpassed anything he had done before in terms of sustained creative effort. While he felt the sonnet form was 'not one in which I shall ever feel at home'[20] he thought there was a market for his sequence. Generally, there had been an enormous increase of interest in the Highland peaks. The Scottish Mountaineering Club was founded in 1889; Sir Hector Munro brought out his *Tables of Heights over 3000 Feet* in 1891, thus giving the term 'Munro' to Scotland's highest mountains. Though he was uplifted by the theme of ascent, Grieve was an armchair mountaineer, preferring to confront the mountains with a poetic perspective, not a physical assault. Duncan Cameron, the child he taught in the Side School at Kildermorie, remembered Grieve as a man who spent much of his time indoors.

Sometime during his stay at Kildermorie, Grieve sent *Sonnets of the Highland Hills* to Blackwell's of Oxford. They rejected the collection and no other publisher accepted the book; the sonnets survive from the pages of publications edited by Grieve himself (five of them were included in the second *Northern Numbers*). As a sequence, the sonnets allowed Grieve to indulge his love of contrast and his passion for the poetic catalogue. 'Courage', the first, names three of the mountains of Ross and Cromarty in a single line: 'With Slioch, and Ben Airidh a Char, and Ben Lair' (1205).

The effect of that is bilingual, an adumbration of the *Dìreadh* sequence of later years. If Brooke is, inevitably, a strong stylistic influence on the sonnets there is evidence that Grieve was breaking away from Georgian formality through exposure to the energetic sonnets of Gerard Manley Hopkins. Grieve's sonnets are full of exclamations, especially in the terminal lines – 'Oblivion and Eternity together!' (1207), 'Silence encompasses the patient place!' (1209), 'And keep His triumph trembling in my rhyme!' (1210), 'Eternity, my fawn among the trees!' (1210), 'A dream He lost and must forever seek!' (1211), 'My memory that is the Outer Night!' (1211), 'While through the endless void descends the Dead!' (1212). This recalls Hopkins's approach, as in 'The Starlight Night':

> Look at the stars! Look, look up at the skies!
>   O look at all the fire-folk sitting in the air!
>   The bright boroughs, the circle-citadels there!
> Down in dim woods the diamond delves! the elves'-eyes![21]

Grieve had not quite the confidence to emulate Hopkins's habit of taking metrical liberties with the fixed forms, though occasionally he elongates lines to vary the pattern of iambic pentameters – 'The urgent centuries and the waters take' (1209) is a deliberate mannerism as it would have been easy to delete the second definite article.

Apart from a few Keatsian phrases – 'He set you rapturous upon a peak' (1211), reminiscent of that peak in Darien Keats invoked 'On First looking into Chapman's Homer' – it is the Christian passion of Hopkins that touches the texture of Grieve's sonnets. Hopkins has said (in the sestet of a sonnet of 1885) 'O the mind, mind has mountains; cliffs of fall'[22] and Grieve follows Hopkins in connecting physical with spiritual ascent, though he is philosophically pessimistic where Hopkins is fundamentally optimistic. Like Hopkins, Grieve saturates his sonnets in biblical symbolism. Climbing a mountain is akin to repossessing Paradise – 'we briefly glimpse the dazzling world' (1206). A summit is analagous to the pinnacle of Pisgah from which Moses saw the Promised Land – 'Pisgah from whose summit lies sublime / The land of Promise'(1207). Thinking of Schiehallion (named, according to W. J. Watson, after the Gaelic for 'the fairy hill of the Caledonians')[23] Grieve writes

> Schiehallion and Calvary are one.
> All men at last hang broken on the Cross,
> Calling to One who gives a blackening sun.
> There is one hill up which each soul is thrust

> Ere all is levelled in eternal loss,
> The peaks and plains are one. The end is dust.   (1208)

Whereas God is dead in Nietzsche's *Thus Spake Zarathustra*, he is indifferent in Grieve's sonnets. Indeed God is, like the poet, exhausted by creation and solitary on pinnacle or plain. This particular poet broods on Oblivion and Eternity at Kildermorie, among 'Rain-beaten stones: great tussocks of dead grass' (1207).

One of the sonnets, 'Rivals', is addressed to Peggy. It contrasts the appeal of the poet with the greater appeal of the 'multitudinous and various hills' (1206) that compete for his wife's attention. Grieve loses the contest, as Peggy's passionate eyes look up to the hills. Compared to their monumental presence, he is Godforsaken:

> I know too well with what bright mysteries
> Your eyes on Braeriach turn: and how you run
> To where Schiehallion standing like a god
> Turns me to dust and ashes in the sun!   (1207)

Few, Grieve implies, go beyond the physical to the spiritual so the poet is unique in facing up to God and assuming the role of the crucified saviour. In the seventh sonnet, Grieve addresses Christ then speaks on his behalf. The sestet begins with a reference to the eyes of God:

> But how they lightened when He dreamt His dream
> And on the hill-line 'gainst the dawn foresaw
> Your slim white form exult, your white arms gleam
> Cast passionately round the neck of Time!
> Ah! still I feel God's lonely heart updraw
> And keep His triumph trembling in my rhyme!   (1210)

A letter to Ogilvie discussed the notion of 'the Lonely God – still continuing to discover Himself'.[24] Just as the poet desires to be divine, God has to create to overcome loneliness. Originally the fourth line of the sonnet 'Acme' read 'O wind of love, blow cold upon him then!'[25] but Grieve altered it to 'O Force Creative, fail within Him then!' (1210) as if he wished to usurp the biblical role of the creator. He accuses God of complacency, allowing his dream of divinity to become a nightmare for those who actually inherit the earth:

> And God himself is standing at the head
> And silently the stars are gathered round
> While through the endless void descends the Dead!   (1212)

Grieve uses the sonnets to survey the planet from a God's-eye elevation and finds the world wanting a faith, a Force Creative. The function of the poet is apparently to create the Christ in himself and to do so by creative force. If the thematic thrust of the sequence blends Nietzschean and Christian concepts, then Grieve meant it to be so. 'No!' he thundered to Ogilvie, 'I do not believe in consistency.'[26]

Having imposed on his muse the disciplined constraint of the sonnet form, Grieve surprised himself by producing other less inhibited compositions. Drying dishes one day he suddenly stopped and wrote down a poem he called 'The Following Day'. It is set in 'A remote Shooting Lodge beset with antlers of the wild red deer': stags were shot for sport at Kildermorie during the season; the stag, in Christian symbolism, stands for Christ fighting against evil. Grieve's poem inserts a cynical soldier's song into a dramatic monologue delivered by a man who identifies with Christ. The soldier's song conveys the mindlessness of the man of war:

> 'I nailed Him high
> 'Twixt earth and sky
> And Heaven shut
> Its flaming eye
> But
> Be nights as Hell
> I know full well
> My way to you, oblivous slut,
> Who all my roaring blood shall glut,
> Shall glut,
> Who all my roaring blood shall glut!'   (9)

Surprisingly, since it had been founded in 1919 as an organ opposed to experimental obfuscation in the arts, Grieve submitted 'The Following Day' to the *London Mercury*. J. C. Squire, the editor, rejected it as it contained 'things forced or not easy to understand'.[27]

Attempting to defend the poem against Ogilvie's charge of mystification, Grieve said it 'came into my head just as it stands on paper'[28] which shows that the twenty-eight-year-old instinctively cast his thoughts in a Christian context. Similarly, when he wrote a series of four articles on modern poets for the *National Outlook* he began with a decidedly Christian poet, none other than his Langholm minister T. S. Cairncross. In December 1920, when the article appeared, Cairncross was minister of Bowling Church, Old Kilpatrick, Dumbarton. (The name of his church was amusingly appropriate, for Cairncross played bowls for Scotland.) Grieve praised Cairncross as 'a scrupulous technician, a cunning innovator, a cerebral craftsman [and a] scholar rather than a folk-singer'.[29] That Cairncross embodied an artistic ideal for Grieve is obvious throughout the article. Grieve's verbal portrait of Cairncross bears an uncanny resemblance to the figure he was to cut as Hugh MacDiarmid:

> Business-like he is – making, for example, a perfect point of replying to every letter he receives by return of post. But there is no commercial side to his art. Lost in tobacco-smoke and the depths of his armchair, covering the single sheets of note-paper he fastidiously prefers with his extra-ordinarily minute calligraphy, he is lost, too, for all practical purposes, and his pen runs where his spirit listeth: and no man in Scotland escapes more cleanly from the chaos of modern civilisation than this lithe soft-eyed poet . . .[30]

Inordinately proud of this article, Grieve wrote to Ogilvie: 'The thing astounds me. Did you see it?'[31]

Ogilvie was certainly astounded by the poem his pupil dedicated to him. On 8 March 1921 Grieve enclosed the manuscript of 'A Moment in Eternity', explaining it was his only copy as he had been too ill to make another; he had, alarmingly, taken to bed fearing (correctly, as it transpired) a recrudescence of malaria. Ogilvie returned the manuscript with some pencilled comments which the poet took seriously; on Ogilvie's advice, for example, he changed the line 'Flame of creative criticism' to 'Flame of creative judgement' (7), accepting that 'Judgement is *the* word.'[32] As published (in the first issue of *Scottish Chapbook* and in *Annals of the Five Senses*) it is undoubtedly the finest poem Grieve created at Kildermorie; more than that, it ranks as one of his most accomplished poems in English. For the first time he successfully escaped from the restrictions of a regular stanza, for the first time he wrote fluently in free verse. Stylistically, the poem owes some touches to Cairncross's 'Langholm' (see p. 32): compare Cairncross's 'Brimming the beaker of hills' with Grieve's similarly alliterative 'Burgeoning in buds of brightness' (3), Cairncross's reference to 'crystal waters' with Grieve's 'crystal sources in dim hills' (5), Cairncross's 'luminous peace' with Grieve's 'luminous boughs', Cairncross's 'great spaces of the wind and sunshine' with

Grieve's 'wind ... Multitudinous and light' (5). The stately movement of Cairncross's poem, the contemplative presentation of the theme, the euphony: these are features Grieve refashioned in his own poem. However, whereas Cairncross was at the mercy of his liquid vowels, Grieve was at last the master of his medium. 'A Moment in Eternity' was more than a synthesis of his reading: it was an authentically creative achievement.

'A Moment in Eternity' is a mystical poem which imparts a heroic triumph to the struggles of the poet. Fond of the Romantics, Grieve drew deeply on his study of Wordsworth, Keats and the post-Romantic Arnold. Grieve's sensation of the 'quick sap / Of Immortality' (3) connects his poem to Wordsworth's ode 'Intimations of Immortality' (which he had discussed with Cairncross). Grieve has 'Heavenly light' (3), Wordsworth has 'celestial light'; Grieve has 'revels of radiance' (5), Wordsworth 'the radiance which was once so bright'; Grieve has 'a new light ... in God's heart' (6), Wordsworth 'a master-light of all our seeing'; Grieve has 'A shining silence' (7), Wordsworth 'the eternal Silence'.[33] The starting point of Grieve's intimation of immortality is Keats's remark (in a letter of 27 February 1818 to John Taylor) that if poetry comes not as naturally as the leaves to a tree it had better not come at all. In exploring this simile Grieve recalled Arnold's 'The Youth of Man' with its plea to the healing powers of nature; Arnold's 'Airs from the Eden of youth' drift through Grieve's poem and he shares Arnold's interest in the 'Stir of existence, / Soul of the world!'[34]

The reason that 'A Moment in Eternity' is so exceptional is that theme and subject are convincingly united. Grieve himself is the hero of the poem, the creator who rises to the challenge of poetic inspiration (again, a Romantic sentiment). Metaphorically he is a tree disturbed by the wind of God that blows through his branches. Rooted in Scotland, specifically in Kildermorie, hence the sight of the 'crystal sources in dim hills' (5), Grieve longs to exchange a lifetime on earth for a moment in eternity as he feels the creative force of a great song shaking his entire being:

> My shining passions stilled
> Shone in the sudden peace
> Like countless leaves
> Tingling with the quick sap
> Of Immortality.

> I was a multitude of leaves
> Receiving and reflecting light,
> A burning bush
> Blazing for ever unconsumed,
> Nay, ceaselessly,
> Multiplying in leaves and light
> And instantly
> Burgeoning in buds of brightness   (3)

Manifestly, this is a religious experience. The tree has become the burning bush – 'and the bush *was* not consumed' (Exodus 3:2) – from which God spoke to Moses. The poet has not only been transformed but transfigured; he is immortal, he bears 'The everlasting foliage of my soul' (4). He is a divine creation, thus his own creations are divinely inspired. If Scotland is his Promised Land, Eternity is his Eden.

Metamorphoses take the poet nearer and nearer to the source of his inspiration. The tree become a burning bush changes into 'a crystal trunk' (5), a shining column of light that moves through space – 'Meteors for roots' (5), 'A cosmos turning like a song of spheres' (6) – until it finds its place in eternity. The tree is not merely one tree among many but a new Tree of Life, 'Growing ineffably, / Central in Paradise' (7). This tree is unshakeable. In Genesis there were many trees in Eden, but principally 'the tree of life ... and the tree of knowledge of good and evil' (Genesis 2:9). A new Tree of Life goes beyond good and evil:

> I knew then that a new tree,
> A new tree and a strange,
> Stood beautifully in Heaven.
> I knew that a new light
> Stood in God's heart
> And a light unlike
> The Twice Ten Thousand lights
> That stood there,
> Shining equally with me,
> And giving and receiving increase of light
> Like the flame that I was
> Perpetually.   (6)

Grieve considers that the new tree will endure eternally. Created from a dream of God it is invested with that divine wisdom personified in Proverbs as an eternally feminine presence: 'I was set up from everlasting, from the beginning, or ever the earth was' (Proverbs 8:23). Grieve ends his poem with a prayer to the mysterious woman who is the wisdom of God:

> *O Thou,*
> *Who art the widsom of the God*
> *Whose ecstasies we are!*   (8)

He would later elaborate this idea by interpreting it through Solovyov's vision of Sophia – the Wisdom of God, the Eternal Feminine, the Principle of Creation – and Blok's use of Solovyov's work. In 'A Moment in Eternity' the concluding invocation of the wisdom of God allows the poet to assert his access to the divine source. Ultimately the source is silence (Wordsworth's 'eternal Silence'), what Grieve called 'the great reservoir out of which articulation and expression come'.[35] The tree is nourished by that silent source of wisdom:

> – Silent and steadfast tree
> Housing no birds of song,
> Void to the wind,
> But rooted in God's very self,
> Growing ineffably,
> Central in Paradise!   (7)

Grieve never abandoned his belief that the aim of poetry is to articulate the ineffable and so approach a vast spiritual silence. Poetically this ideal depends on the kind of paradox Grieve enjoyed; he saw nothing incongruous in the spectacle of a garrulous man and prolific poet urging his readers onwards to silence.

To some extent 'A Moment in Eternity' is a worthy prelude to Grieve's greatest work, that attributed to Hugh MacDiarmid. It uses the cosmic imagery that distinguishes the lyrics of *Sangschaw*, cites the silence that is the end of *A Drunk Man Looks at the Thistle*, defines the spiritual role the poet performs in his extended works in English. At the period of its composition, however, Grieve could see no future in vernacular verse; he was adamant that the serious Scottish poet should write in English. When, in 1921, the Vernacular Circle of the London Burns Club issued a manifesto designed to promote the revival of the Scots language, Grieve was vehemently opposed to the notion as a piece of reactionary impertinence. He declared that he could not 'ostrich-like cling to the formula that that is only Scottish which is in "Braid Scots"' and ridiculed 'the pedantic patriots of London, who would seemingly surrender their birthright for a mess of uncouth and obsolete synonyms'.[36] The man who disdained consistency would dramatically change his mind on the issue when he went to Montrose.

Grieve's last letter to Ogilvie from Kildermorie encloses nine poems, all in English: on 25 March 1921 he sent 'Ennui', 'A Fool' (which became 'The Fool' in *Annals of the Five Senses*), 'She Whom I Love', 'Withered Wreaths' (retitled 'A Last Song' in the second *Northern Numbers* and again in *Annals*), 'Tryst in the Forest', 'Truth', 'Two Gods', 'In Memory', 'To Margaret'. All the work he completed at Kildermorie shows how highly he regarded English, 'which is no monopoly of the Sassenach'.[37] He had high hopes of placing several works with Foulis including a volume of short stories, *Cerebral and Other Studies*; an anthology of postwar essays, *In the Tents of Time*; a monthly magazine, the *Scottish Chapbook*; and, of course, further volumes of *Northern Numbers*. Other books planned were *Oddman Out: Notes from a Highland Pantry*, *The Road to Spain* (about his Pyrenean holiday in 1919), and 'a volume of vers libre – all on Scottish subjects'.[38] As well as trying to launch the *Scottish Chapbook* as a monthly he contemplated a Scottish equivalent of the *New Statesman* but the *New Scotsman* (such was the title) was abandoned when Grieve calculated it would cost £20,000 a year to float the new weekly. Most of the Kildermorie projects were dropped though *Cerebral and Other Studies* became *Annals of the Five Senses* and the *Scottish Chapbook* duly appeared in August 1922. Both the book and the magazine were published by Grieve himself, from his address in Montrose.

Grieve left Kildermorie in 1921 because the *Montrose Review* wanted him back and were prepared to increase his salary in order to entice him away from his lodge in the wilderness. It turned out to be an astonishingly creative move but Kildermorie had assisted in the evolution of the artist. It was at Kildermorie that Grieve first exercised his imagination in a truly singular poetic manner and imposed his own personality on the material in his mind.

6

Montrose or Nazareth

And in the toon that I belang tae
– What tho'ts Montrose or Nazareth? –
Helplessly the folk continue
To lead their livin' death!

A Drunk Man Looks at the Thistle   (88)

MONTROSE was, literally, the making of Hugh MacDiarmid for it was there that Christopher Grieve created his alter ego, there he traced the visionary voyage of his immortal Drunk Man. The energy he expended during eight consecutive years at Montrose was phenomenal. As well as concentrating on his own creative work he turned out journalism for the *Montrose Review*, contributed columns to the *New Age* and *Scottish Educational Journal*, wrote syndicated articles on nationalist topics under the pseudonym 'Mountboy' and published the third *Northern Numbers* and *Annals of the Five Senses*. He founded the Scottish Centre of PEN (Poets, Playwrights, Editors, Essayists and Novelists) and founded and edited the *Scottish Chapbook*, the *Scottish Nation* and the *Northern Review*. Though there were pressures on him as a Town Councillor, Parish Councillor and Justice of the Peace he still managed to be active in the ILP, the Unemployed Union, the No-More-War Movement, the Scottish Home Rule Association and to help the National Party of

118

Scotland. In addition to all this there were domestic demands for he supported Peggy in Montrose and fathered two children, Christine and Walter, during his stay in the town.

Grieve returned to Montrose (where he had worked briefly in 1920) because James Foreman, proprietor of the *Montrose Review*, offered him a wage of £3 per week which Grieve thought handsome; it compared well with the three shillings and sixpence a week paid to an apprentice printer on the same weekly paper.[1] He had enjoyed the natural environment at Kildermorie, feeling as William Cowper did in *The Task*:

> Oh for a lodge in some vast wilderness,
> Some boundless contiguity of shade,
> Where rumour of oppression and deceit,
> Of unsuccessful or successful war,
> Might never reach me more![2]

Financially, however, he could not resist the temptation to return to rumours of oppression and deceit. Although Grieve looked on Montrose as 'a very attractive small burgh [with] a wide agricultural hinterland'[3] it was an unlikely setting for the birthplace of the self-appointed saviour of Scottish culture in the twentieth century.

With a population of less than fourteen thousand in 1921 and only the slender resources of a small Scottish coastal town, Montrose was known mainly to outsiders as the birthplace (in 1612, at the inner end of Montrose Basin) of James Graham, Marquis of Montrose, who fought first for the Covenanters then for Charles I. After attempting to raise a royalist rebellion in 1650 he was hanged in Edinburgh, a prospect that spurred him to write 'His Metrical Prayer (On the Eve of his own Execution)'. Grieve admired any man who was both rebel and poet and once compared his own difficult journey through life to going 'under Montrose's banner of white damask, the device, a lion about to leap across a rocky chasm and the motto *Nil Medium*'.[4] The motto of Montrose, the royal burgh, is less demanding than that of Montrose, the royalist rebel. It states that the sea enriches, the rose adorns (*Mare ditat, Rosa decorat*).

Half-way between Dundee and Aberdeen, Montrose (in the county of Angus) is located on a tongue of land surrounded by water on three sides: the North Sea on the east, the mouth of the river South Esk on the south, the landlocked bay of Montrose Basin (a tidal lagoon two miles square) on the west. Montrose takes its name from the Gaelic

monadh (moor) *ros* (peninsula) and its nature from the life attracted to a
harbour strategically sealed by Montrose Basin. Architecturally it is built
around the improbably wide High Street which has, near its head, the
Old Parish Church with its 220-ft-high clock-tower and spire designed
by Gillespie Graham in 1832. At 87 High Street, down a close known
as Review Close, was the office of the *Montrose Review*, one of the town's
two weekly newspapers. Whereas the *Montrose Review* was broadly
Liberal, the *Montrose Standard* (now defunct) was Conservative. The
owners of the two rival newspapers were cousins and Grieve found he
had the journalistic knack of accommodating the conflicting views of
these kinsmen: officially employed by the *Montrose Review* he 'had to
work for both [weeklies] and I wrote the leaders on both of them without
any difficulty at all'.[5]

Born in 1886 and educated at Montrose Academy, Grieve's employer
James Foreman was a man who enjoyed gardening and angling and
making money – though not spending it for, according to one of his
employees, he was 'a bit of a Scrooge'.[6] He had inherited the paper from
his father, Joseph Foreman, a Provost of Montrose and still alive when
Grieve worked for the *Montrose Review*; occasionally old Joseph came
into the office and had to be pushed up the stairs to the editorial office.
James Foreman did very little writing but produced the paper, operating
a Linotype machine, making up the pages and attending to financial
affairs. As editor-reporter of the *Montrose Review*, Grieve wrote most of
the contents, 'Pars aboot meetins, weddins, sermons, a'/The crude events
o' life-in-the raw' (234). He saw his employer in the editorial office but
often escaped to the cutting room 'to get away from Foreman'.[7] Grieve's
dislike of James Foreman is vividly communicated through MacDiarmid's
curses in *To Circumjack Cencrastus*:

> Curse on the system that can gie
> A coof like this control o' me
> – No' that he's in the least bit waur,
> Or better, than ither bosses are –
> And on the fate that gars a poet
> Toady to find a way to show it!
>
> Curse his new hoose, his business, his cigar,
> His wireless set, and motor car
> Alsatian, gauntlet gloves, plus fours and wife,
> – A'thing included in his life;

And, abune a', his herty laughter,
And – if he has yin – his hereafter. (235)

It was in Montrose that Grieve learned to write like that, in a thoroughly contemporary Scots. The transition from English to Scots involved a profound personal change.

Arriving in Montrose in April 1921, Grieve rented furnished rooms at 19 Kincardine Street and bought a new bicycle to help him get around the town. By 8 September he and Peggy had moved to rooms at 12 White's Place and there he corrected proofs of the second *Northern Numbers* and *Annals of the Five Senses* (previously entitled *Cerebral and Other Studies*) which he hoped T. N. Foulis would publish soon. Grieve submitted, to the publisher Andrew Melrose, a collection of seventy lyrics entitled *Shapes and Shadows*. Though this miscellany of 'songs and little lyrics'[8] never appeared its tone can be judged from poems that survive the period. 'The Yellow Bride', for example, consists of six lines:

Her sheaf of yellow irises,
    Those flames of love, were vain,
And vain the hue's devices
    In flowing veil and train;
The colour made too much ado –
    Her face was yellow, too![9]

It is a metrical jest after the manner of Shelley's poem 'On a Painted Woman', ending 'Though Iris has put on her clothes,/She has not put her face on.'[10]

More seriously, 'Cattle Show' (completed by September 1921) was probably also intended for *Shapes and Shadows* (before it was included in the third *Northern Numbers* and in *Stony Limits*). 'Cattle Show' displays Grieve at ease with the Imagist idiom. From a reading of T. E. Hulme's poems (printed as an addendum to Pound's *Ripostes* in 1912) he had seen how effective images were when left to speak for themselves, as in 'Autumn':

A touch of cold in the Autumn night –
I walked abroad,
And saw the ruddy moon lean over a hedge
Like a red-faced farmer.[11]

Grieve begins his poem by going 'among red faces and virile voices'. Pound had, in 1913, defined an image as 'that which presents an intellectual and emotional complex in an instant of time'[12] and Grieve cleverly contrasts two such images in order to juxtapose animal vitality with sartorial allure:

> I shall go among red faces and virile voices,
> See stylish sheep, with fine heads and well-wooled,
> And great bulls mellow to the touch,
> Brood mares of marvellous approach, and geldings
> With sharp and flinty bones and silken hair.
>
> And through th'enclosure draped in red and gold
> I shall pass on to spheres more vivid yet
> Where countesses' coque feathers gleam and glow
> And, swathed in silks, the painted ladies are
> Whose laughter plays like summer lightning there.   (462)

It is less stridently Nietzschean than Pound's 'The Garden', from *Lustra* (1916), which juxtaposes the figure of a lady ('Like a skein of loose silk blown against a wall') with the sight of 'a rabble/Of the filthy, sturdy, unkillable infants of the very poor'.[13] Grieve was finding himself as a poet in English, absorbing his influences and establishing a distinctive mood.

Even though J. C. Squire rejected 'Cattle Show' from the *London Mercury* Grieve was confident of his command of the English language. He was firmly of the opinion that the progressive Scottish poet must write in English and resist the maudlin mannerisms of contemporary dialect verse. Reinforcing his thoughts on this matter was a book he had recently read, G. Gregory Smith's *Scottish Literature* (1919). Smith argued that the so-called Revival of the eighteenth century – when Ramsay, Ferguson and Burns produced their best work in Scots – was, in the context of creative literature, the last gasp of the Scottish tongue. These poets used the vernacular to give sensuous sounds to earthy sentiments and the prose writers, conditioned since 1707 to accept English as the official language of North Britain (to which level Scotland had been reduced) disdained it as a handicap to civilised discourse. David Hume, whom Grieve hailed as 'Scotland's greatest son',[14] used Scottish words in convivial conversation but scrupulously avoided them in his philosophical writing. Scotticisms became, for the intellectuals, synonymous with vulgarisms. In 1761 Edinburgh's Select Society, of which Hume was a founder-member, employed an actor to coach its members in the southern pronunciation of English[15]; in 1779 James Beattie published his *Scoticisms, Arranged in Alphabetical Order, Designed to Correct Improprieties of Speech and Writing.*

Left to the limited devices of hordes of minor poets, post-Burnsian Scots degenerated (so Smith contended) into a medium for the humorous and the burlesque. Scots was no longer a national language but a dialect; or, rather, a mixture of dialects. Just as the Scottish novel had been restricted to the confines of the Kailyard ('cabbage-patch') by the cloying sentimentality of Barrie, Crockett and Maclaren, so vernacular verse had been bound in by the banality of the Whistle-Binkie school of versifying. The Whistlebinkies took their name[16] and their vocabulary from John Jamieson's two-volume *Etymological Dictionary of the Scottish Language* (1808-9) and produced such lines as William Carnie's 'Yet hairstin' – when the crap is gweed – wirk ye wi' scythes or heuks,/Has mony joys, and nane mair dear, than courtin' 'mang the stooks.'[17] Smith ridiculed the spectacle of poets dredging the dictionary for terms to embellish compositions in Braid (broad) Scots:

> The [problem of dialect] forces itself upon us at once when we encounter the surprising travesty called 'Braid Scots' ... It may be taken as seriously by us as most of the Latin prose of our classrooms must be by the shade of the long-suffering Cicero. We know how it was made, how our poeticule waddles in good duck fashion through his Jamieson, snapping up fat expressive words with nice little bits of green idiom for flavouring. It is never literature, and it is certainly not Scots ... It is the wastrels of dialect and her own bad housewifery, which threaten to destroy [Scotland's] vernacular credit.[18]

The author of 'Cattle Show' – the Grieve of 1921 – accepted every word of that dismissal of dialect verse. As for the Scots poems of Buchan and others he printed in his *Northern Numbers* annuals – 'I purposely included sentimental items [to give *Northern Numbers*] a quasi-popular appeal'.[19]

While Grieve was waiting for advance copies of the new *Northern Numbers* in October 1920 he made an unfortunate attempt to extricate himself from Montrose. Already weary with the excessive demands of a job that left him little leisure, he endured an additional irritant since Peggy was anxious to leave Montrose and live in Edinburgh. Grieve, as usual, turned to Ogilvie, asking him to put in a good word with George Waters, then Chief Assistant Editor of the *Scotsman* (he became Editor in 1924). Alas, when Ogilvie approached Waters he found that the story of Grieve's dismisal from the *Edinburgh Evening Dispatch* in 1911 was still talked about as a local journalistic scandal. In the circumstances, Waters was not willing to consider any application from Grieve: Ogilvie was mortified on hearing the details for the first time; Grieve apologised for the inconvenience he had caused and promised not to embarrass his loyal friend in future.

The second *Northern Numbers* annual, advertised for publication in October, continued Grieve's policy of rubbing shoulders with the rich and famous. Grieve included nine of his own poems − 'Edinburgh', 'Playmates', 'The Fool', 'The Last Song' and five of his *Sonnets of the Highland Hills* ('Courage', 'Heaven', 'Rivals', 'The Wind-Bags', 'Vale-dictory') − and retained John Buchan and John Ferguson as members of the Group he claimed to represent. New contributors included General Sir Ian Hamilton, Sir Ronald Ross, Charles Murray (author of *Hamewith*, 1900, a minor classic of Aberdeenshire dialect Scots), Alexander Gray (author of *Songs and Ballads chiefly from Heine*, 1920), the Revd Lauchlan Maclean Watt and Lewis Spence (an authority on world mythology and folklore).

Spence was a contact Grieve especially valued. Born in Broughty Ferry in 1874 and educated at Edinburgh University (where he studied dentistry) he had worked as a sub-editor with the *Scotsman*, as editor of the *Edinburgh Magazine* (1904-5), and as a sub-editor in London, with the *British Weekly* (1906-9). In 1910, the year he returned to Edinburgh, he published *Le Roi d'Ys*, a collection of elegant poems in English. A year later he formed an amateur drama group devoted to the promotion of Scottish drama. Fascinated by the occult and the legend of Atlantis, Spence hid his romantic ideals behind a respectable exterior, usually wearing bowler hat and spats. Grieve knew him as an English-language poet and an ardent Scottish nationalist. Spence was President of the Edinburgh Branch of the Scots National League, described by Grieve as 'the most promising nationalist organisation that has been formed in Scotland since the Union'.[20] Unlike the Scottish Home Rule Association, the SNL stood for separation rather than devolution. It was founded in 1921 by the London-based Highlanders William Gillies and Angus Clark in conjunction with the Hon. Ruaraidh Erskine of Mar. Spence, as poet and nationalist, was to play a part in the transformation of Grieve into MacDiarmid.

Well pleased with the reception given to his *Northern Numbers* in December 1921 − the *Edinburgh Evening News* of 13 December declared that the *Sonnets of the Highland Hills* breathed 'the real tang of the heather'[21] – Grieve chose that month to conduct 'a further stage of my guerilla warfare with the Vernacular Circle of the London Burns Club'.[22] Alarmed by the possibility of a revival of the dialect Scots mocked by Gregory Smith, Grieve put all his weight against 'the pedantic patriots of London'.[23] In 1920 the London Burns Club had established its Vernacular Circle to devise, in the words of its Honorary President William Will, 'a method for preserving from entire destruction the language in which the mentality of the Lowland Scot can best be expressed'.[24] It was the collective opinion of this Vernacular Circle that Lowland Scots – what Burns called 'plain, braid Lallans' and Stevenson singularised as 'Lallan'[25] – was being eroded by a process of anglicisation.

William Will was worried about the social stigma attached to vernacular Scots, appalled at the 'altogether erroneous but understandable idea that Scots boys are hampered in their lives out of Scotland by their native speech, and that therefore Lowland Scots must be banned'.[26] To reverse the destructive trend of this supposition, the Vernacular Circle issued a revivalist manifesto and initiated a lecture scheme to establish the high social standing of those who valued Lowland Scots. The first lecture was delivered in London on 10 January 1921 by W. A. Craigie, Professor of Anglo-Saxon at Oxford University, who advised sceptics to study 'what has been written in the new Norwegian tongue within the past twenty years'.[27] The Norwegian *Landsmaal* (literally 'land-speech') movement had enjoyed notable success. Ivar Aasen (1813-96), the philogist and poet, had formulated *Landsmaal* from the rural dialects of Norway and had published the collection *Symra* (1863) to demonstrate the poetic potential of the new language (which developed as *Nynorsk*, the second official language form of Norway). What Norwegians could do, Craigie implied, Scots could emulate. John Buchan (on 7 February) gave the second lecture and pressed for the preservation of 'those qualities which have made our race what it is'.[28] The third lecturer – Peter Giles, Master of Emmanuel College, Cambridge – spoke in favour of 'local peculiarities'[29] of language. It was the final lecture, 'The Delight of the Doric in the Diminutive' (delivered at the Scots Corporation Hall, Crane Court, Fleet Street, London, on 12 December 1921) that finally roused Grieve to epistolary action.

The *Aberdeen Free Press* of 18 December featured, on the front page, a report, headlined 'Diminutives in the Doric', on Dr J. M. Bulloch's lecture to the Vernacular Circle of the London Burns Club. The Editor of the London *Graphic* and Chairman of the Vernacular Circle, Bulloch said that the persistence of Doric diminutives ('wifie', 'laddie', etc) was

125

evidence of a quintessentially Scottish quality of mind, one at odds with 'the mind of the pukka English, who use hardly any genuine diminutives of their own'.[30] Grieve's letter, in the *Aberdeen Free Press* of 15 December, stated scornfully that 'Dr Bulloch's plea for Doric infantilism is only worthy of the critical consideration of nursery-governesses'.[31] What destroyed the Doric as a creative medium, according to Grieve, was its 'insuperable spiritual limitations'.[32] Grieve ended his letter by allying himself with the views of Gregory Smith's *Scottish Literature*.

On 21 December, Grieve was again on the offensive, replying to a letter from Bulloch. Grieve connected 'Doric infantilism' with Scotland's inhibited attitude to sex and called for a revival of interest in 'spiritual values'[33] instead of a debate on the Doric. Grieve was no passive observer of Doric revivalism but a creative artist intent on making a name for himself as a poet *au fait* with current modernistic tendencies in English verse. Apart from participating in the Doric debate, that December, he was working on a long poem, 'Water of Life', and a sequence of poems on Edinburgh to be entitled *Sic Itur ad Astra*. 'Water of Life' (of which only two sections survive, from the third *Northern Numbers*: the English fragment of that name should not be confused with two Scots poems called 'Water of Life') was a linguistically adventurous attempt to blend sexual and spiritual themes. Grieve celebrated the impregnation of the earth by the Soul and equated the daily experience of Everyman with the eternal recurrence of Christ:

> Thy name is Legion, Son of Man,
> And every day is Christmas Day
> And every morn is Easter Morn.
> Where'er the Tides of Life are borne
> You tread upon the waters still.
> You speak to them and they are wine.
> You crave them in Your agony
> And shameful vinegar is Thine.   (1214)

Grieve felt that such verse, with its abstractions and correspondences, was beyond the reach of Braid Scots. That Christmas and New Year in Montrose he was sure of the linguistic ground he occupied.

Early in the New Year of 1922 Lewis Spence created a stir with his stand on Scottish nationalism. As a former full-time journalist in Edinburgh, Spence was friendly with the editorial staff of the *Edinburgh Evening News* who regularly provided him with space to expound his views. On 2 January 1922 he contributed a poem and an article to the paper. The poem, in English, was called 'The Fiery Cross' and began 'My heart shall never sleep,/Nor shall my soul be free/Of shadow till our Scotland keep/Her tryst with liberty.'[34] (The debt to Blake's Preface to *Milton* is obvious.) The article was even more contentious. Spence despaired of the futile efforts of the SHRA and others to obtain justice for Scotland through an English Parliament and ended his plea for Scottish autonomy in a blaze of rhetoric inspired by the Declaration of Arbroath:

> Let all true Scotsmen with but one spark of the tried and ancient courage of their nation stand now in her defence – or submit to absorption, to race failure, and be included by posterity among those who were 'too proud to fight'. But that is unthinkable. Scotland shall live! Where are those who dared her conquest in the past? And where shall they be who now essay to achieve by guile what they have not the courage to attempt by force![35]

Not surprisingly, Spence's outburst provoked an angry correspondence in the *Edinburgh Evening News*.

Spence defended himself in a pugnacious letter of 9 January ('Be with us then, O Sons and daughters of the iron race of the North')[36] and was supported, on 13 January, by 'A.K.L.' who praised 'my friend Mr Spence' and declared 'no matter what the consequences Mr Spence can count upon me to assist him in taking whatever steps may be necessary to enforce the demand for a Scottish Free State'.[37] 'A.K.L.' was Grieve, using the initials of the pseudonym he attached to his poem 'Memories of Langholm' in 1908. On 16 January A.K.L. broke into verse to honour Spence as a saviour of Scotland in 'A Sonnet (to Lewis Spence in his Summons to Scotland)':

> Inspire me with an urgency of praise,
> O Scottish Muse, that I may honour him
> Whose writings most courageously outlimn
> The hopes of Scotland in these supine days.
> His is the ecstasy of love which sways
> His fellows' loins to gird and lamps to trim,
> The breath that fans the flame that has gone dim,
> The passionate hand dead dreams to raise.
>
> Thine be the cry whereto the gates must lift
> Their heads again: thine the prevailing power
> To call again the fluid mobs who drift
> To channels that a Land of Pride endower,

> – Yea, let all Scotland answer thee as do
> Our Great Dead who yet live to Scotland true.[38]

Reverting to his best Georgian manner Grieve (as A.K.L) evidently looked to Spence as an inspirational figure whose example he followed by expressing his love of Scotland in formal English verse.

On 27 January Grieve had a long letter in the *Aberdeen Free Press* summing up his views on the Doric controversy. While he had some sympathy with the view that the very best of vernacular literature should be expected and was even contemplating circulating among his friends some original examples of Doric prose, he remained an enemy of Doric revivalism:

> For the most part the Doric tradition serves to condone mental inertia – cloaking mental paucity with a trivial and ridiculously over-valued pawkiness! – and bolster up that instinctive suspicion of cleverness and culture – so strong in all peasants – which keeps the majority of the Scottish public wallowing in obsolete and really anti-national tastes – anti-national, for the latent spirit of Scotland showed its potential stature when a determined effort was made (in the last half of the 18th century) to cast off the swaddling clothes of the Doric.... Scotland stagnates in an apparently permanent literary infancy owing to the operation of certain forces of which the Doric sentiment is the principal.[39]

However, just as Grieve was fulminating against 'Doric infantilism', Lewis Spence decided publicly to combine his political nationalism with a gesture of support for the linguistic heritage of Lowland Scotland. Beginning, as he put it, to make 'tentative experiments in the application of older Scots phrases and syntax to the modern tongue'[40] Spence conducted some experiments in poetic conservation. It occurred to him that the most rational way of rehabilitating Scots was to base a modern idiom on the Middle Scots of the great Scots makars of the fifteenth and sixteenth centuries – Robert Henryson (*c.* 1420-*c.* 1490), William Dunbar (*c.* 1460-*c.* 1513), Gavin Douglas (*c.* 1475-1522). Their use of Scots as a national language resulted in a Scottish Renaissance that was undermined in 1560, when the Scottish Reformers adopted an English Bible (translated that year by English refugees in Geneva); and again in 1603, when James VI of Scotland became James I of a united kingdom and took his court to London. Spence believed that as Chaucerian English had evolved into modern English so Middle Scots could provide a model for modern Scots.

On 22 February Spence contributed two items to the *Edinburgh Evening News*: an article appealing for public support for a Scottish Free State and a poem in Scots, 'Spring in Lothian'. The first of the two stanzas in Scots reads:

> The win' gangs wailin' ower the firs,
>   The bent is smoor'd in Februar' snaws,
> The lang lee o' the lochan stirs,
>   And Spring has whispered in the thaws.
> I see the borders o' her braws
>   In gerss that gleams amang the frost;
> I ken her note within the shaws.
>   Love has returned and winter's lost.[41]

Two days later the same paper published 'An Auld Scots Sonnet' by Spence, beginning with the question 'O hert that is a garth of roses deid/How shall thy courage greet anither spring?'[42]

It was not so much the quality of Spence's Scots poems (though their stately serious tone was a marked improvement on most current vernacular verse) that gave Grieve pause for thought; it was the fact that a man Grieve admired as an intellectual had applied himself to Scots in a methodical manner. Grieve credited Spence with an 'exquisite sensory and intellectual equipment (an equipment not shared by another poet writing in Scots for five hundred years)'[43] and so had to reconsider his attitude to 'Doric infantilism' in the light of Spence's mature efforts. By the time Spence collected his Middle Scots imitations — four appeared in *The Phoenix and Other Poems* (1923), published by the Porpoise Press, co-founded by Grieve's fellow Broughtonians Roderick Watson Kerr and John Gould; thirteen in *Plumes of Time* (1926) — Spence's experiments were overshadowed by the poems of Hugh MacDiarmid. With the advancing years Spence bitterly resented the attention accorded to Grieve at his expense and was at pains to point out 'Mr MacDiarmid ... had applauded my endeavours and was fully knowledgeable concerning them'.[44] Chronologically, Spence may have been first in the field with his experimental Scots but his approach was essentially reactionary; in the Scots race towards a truly modern medium he was quickly left behind by MacDiarmid who often commented on the great gap between talent and genius.

In any context, but especially with reference to the transformation of Grieve into MacDiarmid, February 1922 witnessed a more momentous event than the inclusion of Spence's Scots poems in an Edinburgh newspaper. February 1922 was the month James Joyce's *Ulysses* was published in circumstances that stimulated Grieve, a lover of literary scandal. Parts of *Ulysses* had been appearing since March 1918 in Margaret Anderson's *Little Review*, an American journal Grieve read regularly from the time Pound was appointed its foreign editor in 1917. Promoted by Pound, the champion of all Joyce's work up to *Finnegans Wake*, *Ulysses* was received by avant garde intellectuals as an undeniably classic work of modern prose; when Margaret Anderson read the Proteus episode she realised Joyce's masterpiece was 'the most beautiful thing we'll ever have'.[45] In February 1921 Margaret Anderson and Jane Heap, her co-editor, were charged with obscenity, in New York's Court of Special Sessions, for publishing part of the masturbatory Nausicaa episode (a potent influence on MacDiarmid's poem 'Harry Semen') in the July-August 1920 issue of the *Little Review*. The outcome was a fine of fifty dollars each for the two women and an agreement to discontinue the serialisation of *Ulysses*. Sylvia Beach, who gladly made her bookshop Shakespeare & Company a shrine to Joyce in Paris (he referred to the shop as Stratford-on-Odéon), asked the author for the honour of publishing *Ulysses*. On Joyce's fortieth birthday, 2 February 1922, Miss Beach presented him with the first copy of *Ulysses*. Somehow Grieve obtained (or borrowed) a copy of Miss Beach's edition of 1000 rather than Harriet Weaver's Egoist Press edition of 2000 (subscribed in four days).[46] *Ulysses*, with its combination of cultural erudition and earthy realism, altered Grieve's outlook on literature and life. Regarding Joyce as a Celt like himself, Grieve responded readily to the Irishman's verbal virtuosity, his art of extremes, his ability to invest everyday incidents with a spiritual glow. If, somehow, Grieve could give the Scots language a Joycean modernity he would have solved his artistic problems. Slowly that thought crystallised in his mind.

As ever Grieve was pursuing his artistic interests in tandem with his political activities. On 13 March he was co-opted as an interim member of Montrose Town Council to fill a vacancy caused by resignation; on 17 March he and Peggy moved into a new council house – 'allocated to us months ago'[47] – at 16 Links Avenue, their home for the remainder of their stay in Montrose. Grieve now considered himself to be a political figure of some standing: 'I have ... blossomed out as one of the leaders of the Scottish Free State Movement and have addressed a public meeting in Dundee, issued a public challenge to an Arbroath opponent'. [48] His current literary projects included a sequence of one hundred sonnets, expressing 'the essence of the paradoxical philosophies of Blake, Nietz-sche, etc'[49] and endorsing the aesthetic of Benedetto Croce who urged modern thinkers to deal systematically with the psychological dilemmas of the nineteenth century instead of merely writing them off as irrelevant to a new age.

Several of these sonnets survive from periodicals: 'Spring, a Violin in the Void', 'The Last Chord', 'The Litany of the Blessed Virgin', 'The Rhythm of Silence', 'J. K. Huysmans', 'Amiel', 'Introduzione alla Vita Mediocre', 'Der Wunderrabinner von Barcelona', 'Miguel de Unamuno'. All are in English and most indicate Grieve's absorbing interest in European thought. The sonnet on the centenary of Henri-Frédéric Amiel, whose *Journal* (in the 1885 translation by Mrs Humphrey Ward) Grieve had long admired, looks up above the level of the Swiss writer to a 'horizon whence uprear/The forms of Nietzsche and his Russian peer/ Whom scaling not none may the future view' (1219). Nietzsche's Russian peer is Dostoevsky and the two writers would be similarly linked by MacDiarmid's Drunk Man who urges Scots to 'learn frae Dostoevski and frae Nietzsche' (106).

Enduring the 'terrible wait'[50] for Foulis to publish *Annals of the Five Senses*, Grieve learned that the firm was in financial straits and so not certain to publish the third *Northern Numbers*. Two years earlier, in 1920, Foulis had been interested in launching a monthly *Scottish Chapbook* under Grieve's editorship but now this was out of the question. None-theless, Grieve went ahead with plans for the new magazine, announcing his intentions in a letter in the *Glasgow Herald* of 15 May 1922. The *Scottish Chapbook* was to be devoted to critical essays and 'experimental poetics'[51]; it was to be a highbrow journal aimed at an educated minority. The day after printing Grieve's letter the *Glasgow Herald* published a leader (written probably by William Power, who, until he left the paper in 1926, actively opposed sentimentalism in Scottish literature). Commending the plan for the *Scottish Chapbook* the leader-writer was encouraged by Grieve's 'assurance that Scottish poets are not lagging behind their English brethren in experimental vigour and in the devising of new forms of utterance'.[52] As a result of his letter and the appreciative leader, Grieve was approached by several Scottish writers, three of whom became close personal friends and steady supporters – Helen Cruickshank, Neil Gunn and William Soutar.

The first of these, Helen Cruickshank, was amazed to discover that what was being publicised as a new movement in Scottish poetry emanated from an address in Montrose 'because I couldn't conceive of this small provincial east-coast town taking any vital interest in the future of Scots poetry'.[53] Born at Hillside, two miles from Montrose, in 1886 Helen Cruickshank had gone through Montrose Academy with James Foreman, Grieve's irksome employer, as a classmate. After a decade as a civil servant in London she returned to Scotland in 1912 to work for the National Health Insurance scheme in Edinburgh. Grieve accepted three of her poems for the third *Northern Numbers* thus initiating a friendship that was to last for the rest of his life.

Another civil servant who had worked in London was Neil Gunn. When he read Grieve's *Scottish Chapbook* announcement he was living with his wife Daisy in Lybster, a fishing village in Caithness. Gunn was born in Dunbeath, on the Caithness coast, in 1891 (he was a mere nine months older than Grieve); in 1922 he was keen to place his poems and stories so turned naturally to the energetic man in Montrose. Soon mutual admiration crept into their correspondence. Grieve published Gunn's poem 'Oh, Sun' in the twelfth issue of the *Scottish Chapbook*; four of his stories in the *Scottish Nation*; and a further three stories in the *Northern Review*. Grieve championed Gunn's early fiction – acclaiming him 'the only young Scottish prose-writer of promise'[54] on the strength of his first novel *The Grey Coast* (1926) – and even suggested to Gunn that they should collaborate on a novel. Yet Grieve was increasingly critical of what he saw as Gunn's Celtic romanticism and regarded his friend as something of a lost cause after the commercial success of *Highland River* in 1937. In the opinion of Gunn's biographers, the 'story of their later alienation is one of the saddest chapters in modern Scottish biography'.[55]

The third important Scottish writer drawn to Grieve by the *Scottish Chapbook* project was William Soutar, born in Perth in 1898. When he came across Grieve's announcement he was a student reading English (as well as Scots poems by Henryson and Dunbar in his spare time) at Edinburgh University. The day after seeing Grieve's letter he reported to his parents that 'the man who is responsible for *Northern Numbers* ... lives at Montrose' and hoped it might be possible to 'see his "highness" this summer'.[56] Responding to three poems Soutar sent him, Grieve magnanimously observed 'it is something, is it not, almost at first shot to come into the first half-hundred of contemporaries in your country'.[57] Grieve took Soutar's poem 'The Quest' – 'I like it immensely'[58] – for the first issue of the *Scottish Chapbook* and accepted three poems for the third *Northern Numbers*. Soutar's subsequent career exemplifies the truth of determination over adversity for he spent the busy last thirteen years of his literary life as a bedfast invalid after an unsuccessful operation in 1930. Even in 1922 Soutar's health troubled him. While serving in the Royal Navy during the First World War he had contracted what was later diagnosed as spondylitis (ossification of the spine). Like Helen Cruickshank, Soutar became one of Grieve's most loyal supporters; on 18 and 27 July Soutar made a pilgrimage to Montrose to see Grieve.

August 1922 was an eventful month for Grieve. As Secretary and Treasurer of the recently formed Montrose branch of the League of Nations Union, he went to Ferryden (a fishing village just south of Montrose, at the mouth of the river South Esk) to address a meeting of the No-More-War Movement. 'Mere detestation of war', Grieve reminded his audience, 'is ineffective.'[59] Peace, Grieve continued, could be ensured only through organisation – a frustrating thought as Montrose had only thirty members of the League of Nations Union, compared to sixty in Ferryden. Still, on the principle that a small group could swell to influential proportions, Grieve was hopeful of making headway; the same optimism activated his literary plans.

The first issue of the *Scottish Chapbook* – printed by James Foreman at the Review Press and published by C. M. Grieve from 16 Links Avenue – came out on 26 August 1922. On the front cover, beside a line-drawing of a lion rampant, was the motto 'Not Traditions – Precedents'. Ironically, in view of Grieve's obsessive hatred of Sir Harry Lauder, the back cover carried a full-page advertisement for Waterman's Ideal Fountain Pen as used by the 'inimitable Sir Harry Lauder'; another advertisement indicated that, as a result of the financial problems of T. N. Foulis, Grieve himself would publish the third *Northern Numbers.* Prominently placed at the beginning of the magazine was a statement of the *Chapbook* programme, which sums up Grieve's objectives at the time. He itemised his aims as follows: to support the campaign of the Vernacular Circle of the London Burns Club for the revival of the Doric; to help create a Scots National Theatre; to follow the *Northern Numbers* movement in contemporary Scottish poetry; to encourage the work of contemporary Scottish writers in English, Gaelic and Braid Scots; to develop a distinctively Scottish school of criticism; to relate Scottish literature to European developments; to 'cultivate "the lovely virtue" [and], generally, to "meddle wi' the thistle" and pick the figs'.[60] An editorial quoted from *All Things Are Possible* by the Russian irrationalist Leo Shestov. Henceforth regularly named as Grieve's favourite philosopher, Shestov refuted the notion that it is 'a vice to be unstable in one's opinion' and mocked those 'terrified even to appear inconstant in their own eyes'.[61] The *Scottish Chapbook* had no intention of cultivating consistency.

Notable poets represented in the first issue were Grieve ('A Moment in Eternity') and Soutar (who thus went into print for the first time under his own name). The first instalment of a conversation piece in English, entitled 'Nisbet: An Interlude in Post-War Glasgow', was attributed to Hugh M'Diarmid. In Salonika Grieve had thought of the dead Nisbet as a 'spiritual familiar'.[62] In 'Nisbet' his dead schoolfriend speaks as a soldier who has been gassed in France and is now in Glasgow as a poet who 'complains [of] modern Scottish acoustics [and is] trying to invent a new insubmersible sort of song'.[63] Only George Ogilvie could have guessed, from the use of Nisbet's name in the title of the contribution, that Hugh M'Diarmid and C. M. Grieve were one and the same.

For Grieve to adopt a pseudonym was nothing new: since 1911 he had attached the name Alister K. Laidlaw or the initials A.K.L. to some of his productions. Moreover there were plenty of precedents for the use of pseudonyms in Scotland where even Walter Scott had been reluctant to acknowledge his authorship of the Waverley novels. Henrietta Keddie published her *Logie Town* as Sarah Tytler; John Watson wrote his Kailyard sketches as Ian Maclaren; William Sharp became Fiona Macleod when composing his tales of the Celtic Twilight; George Douglas Brown wrote an adventure novel as Kennedy King and abbreviated his name to George Douglas for his anti-Kailyard classic *The House with the Green Shutters* (1901). Yet Grieve's choice of pseudonym is interesting as it gradually replaced his own name which was well known in literary circles in 1922. The surname Grieve is generally derived from the office of 'grieve' (farm overseer) though there was a place called the Grieve, at the confluence of Esk and Ewes at Langholm, where witches were drowned in the seventeenth century.[64] Grieve was the surname of the early nineteenth-century Border poet John Grieve and was firmly associated with Lowland Scotland so perhaps sounded too flat to a poet constantly looking up to Highland hills and mountains of the mind.

According to Grieve, he was drawn to the pseudonym Hugh MacDiarmid because of its Celtic connections:

> It was an immediate realization of this ultimate [Celtic] reach of the implications of my experiment which made me adopt, when I began writing Scots poetry, the Gaelic pseudonym of Hugh MacDiarmid (Hugh has a

traditional association and essential rightness in conjection with Mac-Diarmid) ... MacDiarmid is, of course, the Campbell clan name ...'[65]

On the subject of his given and borrowed Christian names he was typically positive in an interview in 1968:

> Various writers recently have proclaimed that despite my own refusal of the term I am a Christian, that I was properly named by my parents Christopher, and my reply to that is that I got rid of that name, of course, when I began writing. I used Hugh instead. Hugh is a very different thing – it is not a Christ-bearer. Hugh in the old Gothic is 'divine wisdom'. This is a very different thing.[66]

There was a previous literary Hugh MacDiarmid in Scotland, before Grieve appropriated the name: Hugh (Eóghan) MacDiarmid, who died in 1801, was the minister of the Gaelic Chapel of Ease, Glasgow, and at Arrochar and Comrie. In 1770 he assembled a manuscript anthology of Gaelic verse; his sermons (*Searmona*) were posthumously published in 1804.

Despite his fond recollections of the genesis of MacDiarmid, Grieve's alter ego made his début as a writer of English dialogue, not Scots verse. He was probably initially created to swell the chorus of contributors to the *Scottish Chapbook*, to add one more modernistic voice to the journal's progressive theme. If Grieve simply filled his magazine with items in his own name he could be accused of conducting a one-man band rather than an orchestrated movement. Assisted, however, by 'A. K. Laidlaw' (named as Advertisement Manager of the *Scottish Chapbook* as well as the author of 'Your Immortal Memory, Burns!' in the January 1923 issue), 'Martin Gillespie' (who reviewed Rebecca West's *The Judge* in the September 1922 issue) and 'Hugh M'Diarmid' — as well as genuinely individual authors — Grieve could occupy his editorial chair as first among equals. Having created MacDiarmid, however, he saw a new way to surpass himself. With Leo Shestov he could seek to project his alter ego on to 'the shoreless sea of imagination, the fantastic tides where everything is equally possible and impossible'.[67] With Walt Whitman he could say 'I am large, I contain multitudes'.[68] With Hugh MacDiarmid he could eschew conventions and entirely realise his potential. Gradually it dawned on the poet, as he searched for the spiritual essence of his art, that in the plurality of his being Grieve stood for the body, MacDiarmid for the soul. This metaphysical metamorphosis is the ultimate aim of the Drunk Man:

But let my soul increase in me,
God dwarfed to enter my puir thocht
Expand to his true size again,
And protoplasm's look befit
The nature o' its destiny   (125)

Grieve was not yet Hugh MacDiarmid, Scots poet, when he went to Birmingham as a representaive of Montrose Burns Club. In addition to his work as a journalist for the *Montrose Review* and his editorial efforts with the *Scottish Chapbook* he was trying to complete a novel in English, 'somewhat Henry Jamesy perhaps',[69] and still waiting for Foulis to bring out *Annals of the Five Senses* though the firm was on the brink of bankruptcy. In Birmingham Grieve was one of some 250 delegates attending the annual conference of the Burns Federation (an international body with more than three hundred affiliated clubs). The conference was held on Friday and Saturday, 1 and 2 September, and went through the routine business of re-electing, as President of the Burns Federation, Dr Duncan McNaught who had held this position for the previous thirty years and was shortly to be honoured in a sonnet by Grieve: 'Honour to him who hath established/A means to realise Burns' noblest dream' (1224). Replying to the toast to Scottish Literature, Grieve – who saw himself as the 'stormy petrel'[70] of the conference – began by quoting the opening of Rupert Brooke's 'glorious'[71] sonnet 'The Soldier'. He then made a forceful plea for defossilising Burns and giving contemporary poets credit for being as ambitious as the bard:

> Unifying love for the genius of Burns has brought us here but the great national and international dreams which inspired his muse have not yet been realised ... [Idolaters] who regard Burns as the unsurpassable genius of our race implicitly accuse Scotland of national decline. I for my part, while conscious of the immeasureable debt we owe to the past, look to the present and the future.... I believe in the future of Scottish literature just as I believe in the continuance of Scottish nationality which our presence here on this occasion exemplifies; and of which such an accent as mine is surely an incorruptible witness.[72]

The day after delivering his speech, Grieve stood beside his more conservative colleagues when he took part in the ceremony of laying a wreath on Shakespeare's grave at Stratford-on-Avon.

Considering he had spent 'a glorious and most useful time' at the Birmingham conference, Grieve returned to Montrose determined 'to transform the Burns movement at home and abroad'.[73] With thoughts of Lewis Spence's Middle Scots imitations and the linguistic magic of *Ulysses* still fresh in his mind he wondered if it would be possible to renew the spirit of Burns and not just restore the letter of his language; he contemplated how the vernacular could be approached from a new angle. On 30 September 1922 the *Dunfermline Press* printed the latest column in the 'Scottish Books and Bookmen' series Grieve was contributing to the paper. Grieve explained that a 'friend', staying with him in Montrose, had been delving into Sir James Wilson's *Lowland Scotch as Spoken in the Lower Strathearn District of Perthshire* (1915), a book that had supposedly lain unread on the shelves at 16 Links Avenue. Reminding his readers that he was identified as an enemy of Doric revivalism, Grieve admitted to possessing 'a great delight in words; and the obsolete; the distinctively local, the idiomatic, the unused attract me strongly'.[74] His 'friend' had actually constructed two poems from words and phrases preserved by Wilson so Grieve, believing that 'a Scotsman may waste his time in many a worse way than in giving a new lease of life to ancient words by means of verses such as these',[75] presented the poems to the reader. They were 'The Water Gaw' and 'The Blaward and the Skelly'; Grieve granted that in writing them his 'friend' had displayed 'some genuine poetic merit'.[76]

Most of the words for 'The Watergaw' (see p. 58) – to use the orthography authorised by MacDiarmid – came from two pages of Wilson's work. Yow-trummle ('cold weather in July after shearing'), watergaw ('indistinct rainbow') and on-ding ('beating rain or snow') are all on one page[77]; the first phrase of the second stanza 'There was nae reek i' the laverock's hoose/That nicht' (17) appears in Wilson's list of Proverbs and Sayings as 'Dhur'z nay reek ee laivruk's hoos dhe-nikht' where it is glossed as 'There's no smoke in the lark's house to-night (said when the night is cold and stormy).'[78] 'The Blaward and the Skelly' (the blue cornflower and the field mustard) was clearly conceived as part of Grieve's plans to renew the Burnsian manner for it is virtually a redaction of the first song Burns ever wrote, 'My Handsome Nell'. Here is Burns in 1773:

> O, once I lov'd a bonny lass,
>   Aye, and I love her still,
> And whilst that virtue warms my breast
>   I love my handsome Nell.[79]

Here is Grieve's 'friend' in 1922:

> The blaward and the skelly
> Are bonny as of yore
> But bonnier far was Nelly
> Whom I shall see no more.   (1212)

As experiments 'The Blaward and the Skelly' and 'The Watergaw' amount to one relative failure (for the former does not lift the two titular words into a life beyond the page) and one resounding triumph; it is almost as if Grieve was deliberately exhibiting alternatives. One of the reasons for the reverberations of 'The Watergaw' is the certainty that the poem is rooted in a deep emotional memory, the death of the poet's father. A polemicist by temperament, MacDiarmid did not like to be easily explained so resisted attempts to pin his lyric down:

> Take 'The Watergaw'. That was supposed by one writer [Burns Singer] to be a poem for my first wife – her death. She didn't die for thirty years after that, and it was also supposed to be my father's death. These sort of speculations have got to be wede awa.[80]

As can be seen, however, the textual evidence of the poem 'Kinsfolk' (also referring to James Grieve's last look) confirms the autobiographical origin of the poem.

What makes 'The Watergaw' so original a lyric is the linguistic synthesis of form, theme and emotion. Before MacDiarmid it was almost *de rigueur* for the Scots poet to write in the conversationally candid Burns stanza (originally called the Standard Habbie it should be renamed the Standard Rabbie) or in compact quatrains. 'The Watergaw' uses a rhyme-scheme *abcbdd*, linking the stanzas by placing the key word 'licht' at the end of the third line of each. The penultimate line of both stanzas is an iambic pentameter but the other lines are stressed, not counted, so the rhythm varies from line to line – four stresses, three, four, two, five, two – emphasising the weight of the Scots words. Instead of beginning the poem tentatively on an iambic foot, he opens assertively with two trochaic feet – 'Ae weet forenicht' (17) – so the poem rings out like a declaration. The trochaic start was a device MacDiarmid used in many of his Scots lyrics: 'Mars is braw in crammasy' (17), 'Thraw oot your shaddaws' (21), 'It was a wild black nicht' (25), 'Ilka hert an' hind are met' (26), 'Oh to be at Crowdieknowe' (26), 'Seil o' yer face! the send has come' (28), 'Wha kens on whatna Bethlehems' (32).

Thematically 'The Watergaw' proceeds by juxtaposition. The poet sees the rainbow through the downpour and thinks of his father's final look; the two images merge as the dying man closes his eyes on a world full of a natural beauty that may foreshadow an afterlife (a poignant sentiment, given James Grieve's religious convictions). Emotionally the strongly suggestive Scots words allow the poet to move swiftly from an actual situation to an abstract speculation as he concedes the possibility of a world beyond the watergaw: 'I think that mebbe at last I ken/What your look meant then' (17). As a Scots lyricist MacDiarmid constantly brings thoughts of eternity down to earth and gives earthly appetites a spiritual scope. 'The Watergaw' has an intellectual intricacy frequently found in MacDiarmid's greatest poems.

It was not until the third issue of the *Scottish Chapbook*, in October 1922, that 'The Watergaw' was attributed pseudonymously to 'Hugh M'Diarmid' instead of anonymously to Grieve's 'friend'. MacDiarmid's achievement did not pass without favourable editorial comment from Grieve who rejoiced in 'The Watergaw' and MacDiarmid's second contribution, 'Following Rebecca West in Edinburgh', a Scots monologue with English asides. Grieve's causerie acclaimed nothing less than a new experimental force in Scottish literature:

The work of Mr Hugh M'Diarmid, who contributes a poem and a semi-dramatic study to this issue, is peculiarly interesting because he is, I think, the first Scottish writer who has addressed himself to the question of the extendability (without psychological violence) of the Vernacular to embrace the whole range of modern culture – or, in other words, tried to make up the leeway of the language. What he has to do is to adapt an essentially rustic tongue to the very much more complex requirements of our urban civilisation – to give it all the almost illimitable suggestionability it lacks (compared, say, with contemporary English or French), but *would have had if it had continued in general use in highly cultured circles to the present day*. A modern consciousness cannot fully express in the Doric as it exists. . . . [The contemporary writer] must think himself back into the spirit of the Doric [then] carry it forward with him, accumulating all the wealth of association and idiom which progressive desuetude has withheld from it until it is adequate to his present needs [as] a twentieth-century artist who is at once a Scotsman [as well as] a 'good European' or 'Western World-Man'. . . . Stripping the unconscious form of the Vernacular of the grotesque clothes of the Canny-Sandy cum Kirriemuir elder cum Harry Lauder cult, [Mr M'Diarmid] has shown a well-knit muscular figure that has not been seen in Scottish Literature for many a long day.[81]

There MacDiarmid was projected as the saviour of the Scottish language.

'Following Rebecca West in Edinburgh' discusses Rebecca West's novel *The Judge* (1922); while appreciative of West's descriptive gifts, the monologue alternates between Scots and English to come to the conclusion that Edinburgh needs the genius of Joyce, not the talent of West, to do it justice:

> 'It tak's an almark like Joyce tae write aboot Edinburgh.... Edinburgh'll tak an almark like Joyce – a scaffie like Joyce.... It needs a Joyce tae prick ilka pluke, tae miss nowt'....
>
> I nodded to show that I understood. *Ulysses* is not staple fare – but it has made cleanliness and beauty more precious to us hasn't it? The dismally dirty and giggling sexual novels will continue to roll out under a thin pretence of psychological treatment. But Joyce! ... Somehow that stupendous uprising of the *vis comica* in his work seemed to be reflected, as I looked in the 'breengin'' masonry of the grey Metropolis.
>
> 'The verra last thing Scottish literature needs is *lady-frying*. [Martin] Gillespie's an idiot! It needs an almark like Joyce.... I'd glammoch her [Rebecca West] if I'd Joyce's virr.... Novels are juist bletherin' bagrels. Joyce has chammered them a' for the likes o' us.... it needs an almark like him tae claut a city like this.'[82]

Grieve was careful to connect MacDiarmid with Joycean experimentation so his readers might understand that this new application of the vernacular was selfconsciously modernist in intention. In October 1922 the *Scottish Chapbook* was concerned to promote MacDiarmid as a man with ambitions to be a Scottish Joyce, a committed modernist. Coincidentally that same month T. S. Eliot launched the *Criterion* and included *The Waste Land* (without notes) in his first issue. Thus Hugh MacDiarmid was born in the *annus mirabilis* of modernism, the year of *Ulysses* and *The Waste Land*.

Apart from Ogilvie, who knew that MacDiarmid's 'Nisbet' was by Grieve, the new name in Scottish literature was widely accepted as a personality distinct from the editor of the *Scottish Chapbook*. In June 1923 Grieve confided to his brother Andrew that he was MacDiarmid and a few months later told Neil Gunn 'I've a confession to make. I'm Hugh M'Diarmid. Tell it not in Gath.'[83] Although John Buchan anthologised the MacDiarmid poem 'The Bonnie Broukit Bairn' (*Scottish Chapbook*, Dec. 1922) as being by C. M. Grieve in *The Northern Muse* (Oct. 1924) Grieve still kept up his double act in public. In November 1924, Grieve would admit only that he had 'access to all that M'Diarmid has written'[84] while as late as 15 September 1925 (after the publication of *Sangschaw*) MacDiarmid, giving his address as the London office of the *New Age*, hinted that he might take legal action against anyone jumping too readily to conclusions 'as to the relations between Mr Grieve and myself'.[85] With his mischievous sense of humour, Grieve must have enjoyed the guessing game.

By being both Grieve and MacDiarmid there was a bonus that the poet appreciated: he could generate a movement from the friction of one mind on the other. A devotee of the dialectical method, Grieve could productively argue with himself. Having eulogised MacDiarmid as an important experimentalist in the *Scottish Chapbook* of October 1922 he could write one month later, in the *Dunfermline Press*, that Braid Scots would remain 'the special preserve of the *tour de force* and the *jeu d'esprit* – a backwater of the true river of Scottish national expression'; and attack 'the Chauvinistic insistence upon the Doric as a *sine qua non* of Scottish nationalism, and more particularly as the line along which the impulse of Scottish literary genius can most profitably be directed'.[86]

If he was keeping his options open in public, privately he was aware of the audacity of his experiment. Scots came to him as 'an illumination, a sudden awakening'[87] and he studied the language as he would 'a foreign language and a foreign literature [though the] language wasn't foreign to me'.[88] His vocabulary was based on Jamieson's *Dictionary*: 'I wrote my early Scots lyrics straight out of the dictionary,'[89] he acknowledged; and, again, 'I went to where the words were – to Jamieson's *Dictionary*. My early poems were written straight from that source.'[90] He read the great makars such as Gavin Douglas in whose work he found 'a synthesis of languages that was almost Joycean in its range [for Douglas] used half the languages of Europe [assimilating them], quite effectively, to the Scots basis in which he wrote'.[91] Aware that Scots had, since the Renaissance of the makars, disintegrated into regional dialects he aimed at a Synthetic Scots (as he came to call it) combining the various dialects with the richness of literary Scots. There was, literally, nothing pedestrian about his method:

I wrote a lot of Scots lyrics [while] I was going about my daily work. I had to do a lot of cycling – push-bicycle you know – all over the [Montrose] area and an idea of a poem would come into my head. I would push along and I didn't write down anything until I got home and then I wrote it down and, perhaps, improved it a little. But that was the way it was done, and I gradually accumulated a sufficient body of that sort of thing to publish books.[92]

The picture of Grieve cycling about Montrose and returning to 16 Links Avenue to write, in his book-lined garden shed, is not a complete one. The poet was, as ever, active in national and local politics. He had become local secretary of the Scottish Home Rule Association in Montrose and was in touch with a man often regarded as the 'father' of Scottish nationalism. Roland Eugene Muirhead (1868-1964) was a rich business-man, fervent nationalist and convinced socialist; when he took over his father's tannery business at Bridge-of-Weir he reorganised it on co-operative lines giving his workers a share in the firm. In 1906 he co-founded (with Tom Johnston) the Scottish socialist weekly *Forward* and in 1918, the year he joined the ILP, re-founded the old (predominantly Liberal) SHRA as a non-party organisation sympathetic to socialism. Secretary and Treasurer of the SHRA, Muirhead largely financed the movement and paid for the publication of the monthly news-sheet *Scottish Home Rule* – which, in October 1922, extended a cordial welcome to the *Scottish Chapbook* and, in November, featured Grieve's article 'Scottish Literature and Home Rule' on the front page. Inevitably Grieve saw Muirhead as a potential backer for the Scottish weekly he wanted to launch.

So far only a co-opted member of Montrose Town Council, Grieve presented himself as an Independent Socialist candidate at the local election of November 1922. He declared that he would not seek the temperance vote and asked for 'the suffrages of those who do not consider that age necessarily connotes wisdom, or youth, inability'.[93] Grieve polled 1279 votes and was duly returned as a Town Councillor and Parish Councillor. Appointed to the Water Committee, the School Management Committee and the Library Committee he took these chores seriously enough to attend almost all the Council meetings. Still, Council work had its humorous side. When George Ogilvie asked if the new weekly, assuming it materialised, would consume all his energies, Grieve replied:

> No! I shall retain my present work *plus* the weekly. No reward that letters has to bestow would tempt me to sever my connection with the Town & Parish Council, and other Boards of which I am duly elected representative here. It's too funny for words – and my sense of humour must be provided for in the first place. Other things come after that.[94]

142

Nevertheless, the demands on Grieve's time were growing as a brief look at two typical months shows.

In January 1923 Grieve brought out at his own expense (since Foulis had finally collapsed) the third *Northern Numbers* (printed by James Foreman and containing five poems by Grieve as well as work by others including Helen Cruickshank, William Soutar, the Glasgow journalist William Jeffrey, George Reston Malloch of the *New Age*). On top of that he had to bring out the sixth issue of the *Scottish Chapbook* and plan the seventh; press on with his novel (then being typed, though it never appeared); write local journalism for the *Montrose Review*, features for the *Dunfermline Press* and poems (by Grieve and MacDiarmid) for himself. He went to Dundee to speak, with Lewis Spence, about a Scottish Free State; he visited his mother in East Lothian; and he met Soutar at Mackie's tea-room in Edinburgh.

February was just as hectic. That month Grieve went to London where, on 13 February, he addressed the auld enemy, lecturing the Vernacular Circle of the London Burns Club on the subject of Scots. While in London he attempted to drum up financial support for his projected weekly. On his return to Montrose he attacked the Town Council's proposal to reduce the wages of its officials and workmen (a fight he eventually lost). The *Scottish Chapbook* of February contained the first of three instalments of 'A Theory of Scots Letters' in which Grieve made his most considered appraisal so far of the cultural character of Scotland. He quoted Orage on the artistic value of 'disinterestedness' – MacDiarmid's 'Second Hymn to Lenin' would insist on 'Disinterestedness,/Oor profoundest word yet' (327) – and Gregory Smith on the antithetical tensions of Scottish literature. He then revealed his credo:

> We base our belief in the possibility of a great Scottish Literary Renaissance, deriving its strength from the resources that lie latent and almost unsuspected in the Vernacular, upon the fact that the genius of our Vernacular enables us to secure with comparative ease the very effects and swift transitions which other literatures are for the most part unsuccessfully endeavouring to cultivate in languages that have a very different and inferior bias.... We have been enormously struck by the resemblance – the moral resemblance – between Jamieson's Etymological Dictionary of the Scottish language and James Joyce's *Ulysses*. A *vis comica* that has not yet been liberated lies bound by desuetude and misappreciation in the recesses of the Doric: and its potential uprising would be no less prodigious, uncontrollable, and utterly at variance with conventional morality than was Joyce's tremendous outpouring.[95]

143

A great Scottish Literary Renaissance: some readers must have thought that an impossibly audacious ambition for Grieve who had yet to publish a book of his own work, who made his living as a local journalist, and whose most arresting achievement to date as a Town Councillor was to persuade the School Management Committee, on 27 February, to refuse to allocate capital expenditure for the building of a new primary school in Montrose. Such people reckoned without the determination of Hugh MacDiarmid.

Looking for money to sustain his new weekly, Grieve turned to R. E. Muirhead with whose support (more moral than financial as it transpired) he launched the *Scottish Nation* on 8 May 1923 with a cover calling for the emancipation of Scotland from English influence. Grieve contributed to the *Scottish Nation* in his own name – calling, for instance, on 22 May for the recognition of Byron as a Scottish, not English, poet – and those of Hugh M'Diarmid (poems and prose) and Isobel Guthrie (on contemporary Scottish composers). He published a French translation of 'The Watergaw' by Denis Saurat and work by Soutar, Gunn, Spence, Erskine of Mar, George Reston Malloch, William Jeffrey and Pittendrigh Macgillivray. The most provocative articles by the editor were a 'Plea for a Scottish Fascism' and 'Programme for a Scottish Fascism' which ran over two issues, 5 and 19 June.

Like Pound (who, later, was almost executed for his actions in the Second World War) Grieve was subject to a Great Man syndrome, the result of his infatuation with Nietzschean supermania. Mussolini's march on Rome and formation of a Fascist government in October 1922 seemed to intellectuals such as Pound and Grieve an example of the superman in action. Though Mussolini had been installed as Prime Minister of Italy by reactionary forces (the Army and the King) Grieve declared that Mussolini's ideology was 'an experiment in patriotic Socialism ... a war of the idealist against the materialist, and the most dangerous forces of materialism are not on the Left'.[96]

An ex-serviceman himself, Grieve considered Fascism to be 'an ex-combatants' movement, composed of men who found the ideal of Italy worth dying for, and who were determined that below that ideal she should not fall'.[97] Granting differences between the national characters of Italy and Scotland, he felt that a Scottish Fascism – firmly aligned to the Left – could also spring from the frustrations of Scottish soldiers. As one who regularly chaired meetings of the Unemployed Union, Grieve further believed that the discontent of the out-of-work could be used to forge a militant movement:

> Every unemployed young Scotsman today should get out of the cities and get to the Highlands – to the vast spaces which they are forbidden to enter on pain of interdict – and *squat* there; and the Scottish Labour Party would acquire the farseeingness and dynamic force it still lacks – the unity and irresistibleness – if it kept them provisioned while they did so. Infinitely better than the dispatch of contingents of hunger-marchers to London would be the trek of great bands of unemployed ex-Service men to the Highlands and Islands to insist upon the immediate redemption of the Land Settlement promise – and it would be a sight for the gods to see the British Navy massed outside Stornoway, blockading the island, while thousands of squatters simply sat tight. If that happened – and it could, and can happen – the ex-Service men would win and Scottish history would enter on a less humiliating phase. We want a Scottish Fascism which shall be, where such laws are concerned, a lawless believer in law – a rebel believer in authority.[98]

An occupation of Stornoway was a long way, politically and geo-graphically, from a Fascist march on Rome. For all his involvement in the practical business of politics, the poet was in a world of his own, a world where Left and Right could be synthesised in a vision of Scottish land reclamation and where Fascism and Socialism were interchangeable terms for 'Just as Fascism in Italy must incline to the Left ... so already in Scottish literature and religion tendencies are manifesting themselves to meet Labour half-way and make common cause in the interest of "Scotland First"'.[99]

Grieve's appeal for a Scottish Fascism was another gesture of con-tempt for English parliamentary democracy; devolution, he thought, was useless whereas a strong Scottish nationalist government could impose its ideals on those with vested interests in the status quo by initiating, for example, an agrarian policy on the Mussolini model. Grieve diplo-matically dropped Fascism from his programme as Mussolini moved further and further to the Right; he said, in *Lucky Poet*, he had 'never once betrayed the glorious traditions of the Scottish people by preaching any submission in the face of Fascism'.[100] Looking back on his life from the vantage point of 1968 he exonerated Pound, and by implication himself, from anything but a naïve fascination with Fascism:

> [Pound] wasn't a Fascist at all. Most of my friends were Fascists in that sense. They were impressed in the early days by the actual practical achievements of Mussolini in draining the Po marshes and so on, and in partially at any rate solving the unemployment problem in Italy. Now that was a temporary thing. Mussolini's real objectives became clearer later on with the invasion of Abyssinia and so on. Well, none of us would have supported Mussolini in that, Sorabji, or Pound.[101]

The statement is not entirely true so far as Pound was concerned: he published *Jefferson and/or Mussolini* in 1935, the year Mussolini invaded Abyssinia, and resumed his broadcasts for Rome Radio eight weeks after the USA declared war on Germany and Italy, thus technically giving aid and comfort to the enemy. True, when he was taken to Washington on an indictment for treason, Pound denied any affiliation to Fascism (he was declared insane and mentally unfit for trial) but his *Pisan Cantos* (1945) portray Mussolini as a martyr: 'Thus Ben and la Clara *a Milano*/by the heels at Milano ... the twice crucified/where in history will you find it?'[102]

As George Orwell observed, there are two distinct aspects of nationalism: a patriotic devotion to a particular place; and 'the habit of identifying oneself with a single nation or other unit, placing it beyond good and evil and recognizing no other duty than that of advancing its interests'.[103] Grieve embraced both aspects, often being ferociously critical of the complacency of Scotland and at other times defending his country as an extension of himself: 'I am Scotland itself today ... Scotland will shine like the sun in my song' (1277). At its most irrational, as in his articles on Scottish Fascism, Grieve's nationalism is negative, clamouring for an unquestioning reverence for 'anything Scottish'.[104] Orwell puts such emotionalism in the context of Celtic nationalism:

> The Celt is supposed to be spiritually superior to the Saxon – simpler, more creative, less vulgar, less snobbish, etc – but the usual power-hunger is there under the surface.... Among writers, good examples of this school of thought are Hugh McDiarmid and Sean O'Casey. No modern writer, even of the stature of Yeats or Joyce, is completely free from traces of nationalism.[105]

The kindest thing that can be said about Grieve's plea for a Scottish Fascism is that it displayed an interest he had in common with some of the writers he respected most: Pound, Eliot, Yeats, Wyndham Lewis; all egoists with an élitist outlook. Moreover, he dissociated himself from reactionary romanticism, saying (in 1968) 'I was friendly with both [Eliot and Yeats] but not with many of their ideas which were of a pro-Fascist character'.[106] Consistency, after all, was the least of Grieve's concerns.

At long last *Annals of the Five Senses* was published, in May 1923, the month Grieve launched the *Scottish Nation*. He not only published it himself but sold it: the garden shed at 16 Links Avenue was designated the Scottish Poetry Book Shop and offered Grieve's first book as well as *Northern Numbers* (a reduced price for buying all three at once), the *Scottish Chapbook* and the *Scottish Nation*. *Annals* was well received: the *Scotsman* judged it 'readable and interesting ... Gracefully written and suggestive'; the *Glasgow Herald* bracketed the author with those 'modern Scottish writers who are feeling their way to a permanent place in literature'; the *Times Literary Supplement* praised Grieve's 'novel and complicated harmonies'.[107] Most satisfying to Grieve was Edwin Muir's comment, in the *New Age*, that 'except Mr Joyce nobody at present is writing more resourceful English prose'.[108] *Annals* comprised six poems ('A Moment in Eternity', 'The Fool', 'The Following Day', 'Spanish Girl', 'Consummation', 'A Last Song') and six stories (or psychological sketches as he called them): 'Cerebral', 'Café Scene', 'A Four Years' Harvest', 'Sartoria', 'The Never-Yet-Explored', 'A Limelight from a Solitary Wing'. For 'the encouragement and help he has given to a young and unknown writer'[109] the book was dedicated to John Buchan.

The title of the book borrowed a phrase from Gregory Smith's *Scottish Literature*: 'Certain conditions, or accidents, in the later national development ... leave the Muse the narrower reputation of being painfully concerned with the Annals of the Five Senses'.[110] Grieve had added this title as an afterthought, a farewell to all that he associated with his years as a soldier. As *Cerebral and Other Studies* the book (at least the prose part) had been waiting publication by Foulis since 1920. As we have seen, much of *Annals* was written before Grieve settled in Montrose – 'Cerebral' in Salonika, 'A Moment in Eternity' at Kildermorie.

Most of the psychological sketches have a fragmentary form, as if they were originally intended for larger works. The first three read like extracts from the projected fictional autobiography Grieve had mentioned to Ogilvie in his army days. Told in a third-personal narrative they explore the intellectual life of an unnamed hero who is obviously Grieve: in 'Cerebral' he is a literary journalist with a girl called Peggy; in 'Café Scene' he is cogitating furiously while taking tea; in 'A Four Years' Harvest' he is in the Sergeants' Mess at Marseilles, has a friend called Malloch (George Reston Malloch) and a wife called Peggy. The three remaining sketches show different aspects of Grieve's prose style. 'Sartoria' is an amusing portrayal of an eccentric aesthete obsessed with female attire; 'The Never-Yet-Explored' (perhaps the most polished piece of imaginative prose in the book since it combines intellectual energy with the demands of a plot and the evocation of a well-defined heroine) has affinities with the stream-of-consciousness narrative of Virginia Woolf (whose *The Voyage Out* appeared in 1915); 'A Limelight from a Solitary Wing' is a 'spiritual snapshot'[111] of Grieve as seen from a distance.

Grieve spattered his prose (as he was later to spatter his verse) with quotations, mentioning (in an acknowledgement) such fictional favourites as Conrad and Galsworthy. But the most obvious influence is that of Dostoevsky. The concentration on the problem-laden inner life of the hero, the tormented ontological anguish, the fevered imagination running riot: these are all mannerisms Grieve adopted from Dostoevsky since they were so appropriate to his own outlook and experience of malaria during the war. He could easily identify with the Dostoevskean hero, a solipsist who perceives the world in his own anxious image and anticipates an extraordinary response to his every action. Like Dostoevsky, Grieve derived mock-heroic comedy from his technique. In *Letters from the Underworld* (translated by C. J. Hogarth in 1913) Dostoevsky's clerk longs to make a tremendous impact on those who antagonise him: ' "Now is the time for me to throw bottles at them," thought I to myself. I seized up one, and – calmly poured myself out another glassful.'[112] Similarly, Grieve's hero produces a beautifully bathetic moment in 'Café Scene':

> He seized the cup again – a thin cynical light was playing round its fluted body – raised it high above his head, then brought it down with full force – and there it was nesting peacefully in its saucer, intact![113]

Dostoevsky's presence was precious to Grieve – and to MacDiarmid who, in *A Drunk Man Looks at the Thistle*, acclaimed the Russian as 'This Christ o' the neist thoosand years' (139). In *Annals* Grieve himself is compared to Christ (again, a notion built blasphemously into *A Drunk Man Looks at the Thistle*): in 'A Four Years' Harvest' he 'saw in the dark lineaments of the man he was to become ... a Christ, albeit a little cynical and with a cigarette in his mouth'.[114]

With its obsessively subjective concerns, its long catalogues, its

allusive technique, the prose in Grieve's *Annals* anticipates the ostentatiously intellectual verse MacDiarmid wrote in the 1930s, in the idiom
he called Synthetic English (drawing its diction from specialist texts as
well as from oral and literary sources). It charts his responses to his
reading and is often anthological in form, creating links between
quotations. But the showpiece of *Annals* was not the prose of 'Cerebral'
or 'Sartoria'; it was the verse of 'A Moment in Eternity'. The *Scottish
Nation* of 3 July 1923 included an essay by Denis Saurat, author of *La
Pensée de Milton* (1921), on 'A Moment in Eternity'. Saurat related
the poem to his own writing, admiring its metaphysical approach, its
'transformation of Man into ideas', its participation in 'the eternal search
for the ecstasy of joy, which is consciousness of self ever and ever more
intensified'.[115]

The interest shown by a European intellectual of Saurat's stature in
a Scottish poet was what Grieve had been hoping for, as he indicated in
a letter of June to his brother Andrew:

> I mean a Scottish Renaissance *is* coming, the pioneer stage is almost over;
> the solid creative stage is beginning. The foundations appear to have been
> well laid: we've builded better than we knew. Vide Saurat's interpretation
> of one of my poems in next week's (3rd July) S.N.
>
> Also, as Hugh M'Diarmid, I am making a name for myself – being set
> to music – translated & appearing in all sorts of Continental papers etc.[116]

French translations by Saurat (of the MacDiarmid lyrics 'The Eemis
Stane', 'The Bonnie Lowe', 'Feery-o'-the-feet', 'Cophetua') did appear in
the *Scottish Chapbook* in August 1923; Saurat also discussed MacDiarmid
in his article 'Le groupe de "la Renaissance Écossaise"' in the *Revue Anglo-
Américaine*, April 1924 (subsequently abridged in Saurat's own periodical
Marsyas). If the reference to 'all sorts of Continental papers' was an
exaggeration then the musical fanfare was prophetic, if premature. By
June 1923 only one MacDiarmid lyric had been set to music: 'Country
Life', from the November 1922 issue of the *Scottish Chapbook*. The
composer was Francis George Scott, Grieve's former teacher from Lang-
holm academy.

Saurat's interest in Grieve/MacDiarmid was stimulated by his respect
for Scott. From 1918 to 1921 Saurat had been Lecturer in French at
Glasgow University; Scott had attended one of his evening lectures and
formed a friendship based on a general love of French culture and a
particular interest in the poetry of Paul Valéry. When Saurat went to

Bordeaux University as Professor of English, Scott visited him, in 1921, and was introduced to the French composer Jean Jules Amable Roger-Ducasse (born in Bordeaux in 1873 and a student of Fauré at the Paris Conservatoire). After hearing Scott's setting of Burns's 'Ay Waukin, O', Roger-Ducasse told Saurat they had 'found the Scottish Mussorgsky'.[117]

Since leaving Langholm in 1912, Scott had worked as a teacher in Dunoon (where he met Burges Gray, the woman he married, and got to know Sir Harry Lauder, MacDiarmid's *bête noire*), then Glasgow. He was teaching at Townhead School, Glasgow, when he brought out, in 1922, two volumes of *Scottish Lyrics*, mainly settings of Burns. As a composer, Scott had pronounced views on the state of Scottish culture. He wanted a Scottish musical nationalism to evolve by taking account of the new language of European music. He admired the use Bartok had made of Hungarian folk music; he read Schoenberg's *Harmonielehere* (1911) and studied his experiments in atonalily. What Scott needed was a determinedly modernistic Scottish poet to set to music and he found his man when William Burt — formerly a fellow teacher at Langholm Academy, then teaching at Linlithgow Academy — drew his attention to the MacDiarmid poems appearing in the *Scottish Chapbook*.

'Country Life', in which MacDiarmid counterpoints the external and internal aspects of a rural scene, appealed to Scott's sense of structural concision and verbal economy (he was essentially a musical miniaturist able to imply an expansive mood in a few spare phrases) and his setting captures the eerie Gothic quality of the lyric:

> Ootside! ... Ootside!
> There's dooks that try tae fly
> An' bum-clocks bizzin' by,
> A corn-skriech an' a cay
> An' guissay i' the cray.
>
> Inside! ... Inside!
> There's golochs on the wa',
> A craidle on the ca',
> A muckle bleeze o' cones
> An' mither fochin' scones.   (31)

After reading the poem in the *Scottish Chapbook*, Scott and Burt contacted the editor and discovered him to be 'the young hopeful we both had taught'.[118] A reunion was arranged at Burt's home in Linlithgow. Burt's three-year-old son Billy recited a MacDiarmid poem, a performance greatly appreciated by the author who dedicated 'Hungry Waters' to this 'little boy at Linlithgow' (52).

The renewal of his relations with Scott was to have major reper-cussions for the poet. From 1923 to 1933 Scott set many MacDiarmid lyrics, advised his former pupil to value musicality in verse, and supplied him with the framework of *A Drunk Man Looks at the Thistle* (dedicated to Scott). He also paid hospital bills when the poet had a breakdown in 1935 and tried his best to dissuade him from packing his poems with political theory and scientific fact. For his part, Grieve paid tribute to Scott as creative artist and collaborator:

> After [Scott and I were reunited in 1923] we became the closest of friends and there can be few cases of closer collaboration between a poet and a composer. Scott is one of the few men, perhaps the only man, I have known for whom I had an unqualified respect. Simply because he so clearly and completely understood that ability of any kind depends upon self-respect and was incapable of losing his on any account. I think the world of him and his work seems to me of superlative importance to Scotland.[119]

Eventually poet and composer fell out: according to Grieve he objected to Scott's 'violent anti-semitic opinions'[120]; his attack on his great friend and warm-hearted collaborator was, understandably, resented by Scott's family.[121]

With Scott at his side in the 1920s – the poet began to spend weekends in Glasgow while the composer took regular holidays in Montrose (as well as spending summers in Salzburg for the International Festival of Contemporary Music) – Grieve could continue his Mac-Diarmid experiments in complete confidence, certain of a positive response from Scott. Scott certainly reinforced his faith in the expressive powers of Synthetic Scots. Grieve's great fear as a creative artist was 'of having paralysed his creative faculties by over-reading',[122] a problem that similarly haunted Flaubert who wrote, to Louise Colet in 1846, about 'excessive reading killing the imagination, the individual element, the one thing, after all, that has some value'.[123] His cultural nationalism (which Scott endorsed) confirmed what he had instinctively felt for some time, that in writing in English and thus reacting to the literature of a country he resented, he was submitting to an alien language – he repeatedly said, 'English ... is not my native language'.[124] Theoretically the notion of English as a foreign language may have been spurious since it was what Grieve spoke and wrote fluently. However, in practice the concept motivated MacDiarmid.

151

The poet believed, with St John (1:1), that 'In the beginning was the Word', at least so far as the genesis of poetry was concerned. By using Scots words he was not only satisfying a great emotional urge but doing so in a way that had the approval of a gifted composer, a man knowledgeable about European literature and the latest European music – the poetry of MacDiarmid is full of references to music though the poet admitted he was 'tone-deaf'.[125] When he described his poetic method he did so with reference to Scott's understanding of his approach:

> Because of a profound interest in the actual structure of language, like Mallarmé's, like Mallarmé I have always believed in the possibility of 'une poésie qui fut comme deduite de l'ensemble des propriétiés et des caractères du langage' – the act of poetry being the reverse of what it is usually thought to be; not an idea gradually shaping itself in words, but deriving entirely from words – and it was in fact (as only my friend F. G. Scott divined) in this way that I wrote all the best of my Scots poems ...[126]

With Scott clamouring for new lyrics to set, Grieve increased his output of MacDiarmid poems and was hopeful of persuading John Buchan to publish a volume of this Scots verse.

Exhilarated as he was by his new intellectual intimacy with Scott – and, through Scott, with Saurat – Grieve was nonetheless feeling the strain of his multifarious activities. In June 1923 he took up golf, realising that without exercise he could not cope with his professional, creative and political commitments. He tried to fit in eighteen holes of golf every evening apart from Sundays and found himself refreshed by the effort. He needed to be alert to keep on top of his public work. In May he had attempted, unsuccessfully, to persuade the Council to increase the wage of thirty-five shillings a week offered to a worker taken on to tend the town's golf courses during the summer; on 15 June he presided at the first public wireless concert in Montrose, at the King's Playhouse, to raise money for the unemployed. In August he presided at a concert to obtain funds to pay for a summer outing for the children of the unemployed; and also went to Ferryden to campaign for the No-More-War Movement. On 8 October he narrowly failed to convince the Town Council to affiliate with the SHRA, losing only because Provost Foreman, his employer's father, refused to give the casting vote. Councillor Grieve stood for re-election in November as an Independent Socialist on a programme including a reduction in the police force and the establishment of a municipal bank in Montrose. Returned as a Councillor, Grieve was appointed Hospitalmaster on 16 November. (Subsequently he became Convener of Parks and Gardens and a member of the Water Board.)

December saw the disappearance of two of Grieve's periodicals: the *Scottish Chapbook* closed after thirty-four weeks, on the issue of November-December and the last number of the *Scottish Nation* came out on 25 December. A week later, however, Grieve's editorial and literary labours were recognised in the *Glasgow Herald*. On the basis of his article on 'Le groupe de "la Renaissance Écossaisse"', in the April 1924 issue of the *Revue Anglo-Américaine*, the myth has grown that Denis Saurat was responsible for the critical concept of a modern Scottish Renaissance. However, Grieve himself had proclaimed a Scottish Literary Renaissance in the *Scottish Chapbook* of February 1923 and on 31 December 1923 the *Glasgow Herald* printed a first leader headed 'A Scottish Literary Renaissance'. Both Grieve and MacDiarmid were listed as leaders of the new movement:

> Discontent with London standards and with the submersion of Scottish literature has expressed itself in the publication of a Scottish literary weekly [the *Scottish Nation*] and of such collections of Scottish verse and prose as the *Scottish Chapbook* and *Northern Numbers*.... [Evidently] something infinitely ahead of the 'Whistle Binkie' order of things is represented by the very large group of contemporary Scottish writers headed by Neil Munro, John Buchan, Alexander Gray, Violet Jacob, C. M. Grieve, Edwin Muir, Hugh M'Diarmid, and John Ferguson – to mention only a few of the more prominent names.... That a genuine Scottish literary renaissance is in progress is to be deduced, not so much from the fine work achieved by the leaders of the movement as from the quality and inspiration of the work of the various rank and file.[127]

Predictably the leader put new heart into Grieve; he set about raising money to revive the weekly *Scottish Nation* as a monthly *Northern Review*.

The first issue of the *Northern Review* was published in May 1924; the fourth and final issue in September. Subtitled 'a progressive monthly of life and letters' and featuring on the front cover a map of Scotland stretching south to the Tyne (Grieve's notion of Scotia Irredenta) it was bigger than the *Scottish Chapbook*, had two assistant editors (G. P. Insh and Alexander McGill) and a London agent. It did not, though, command Grieve's undivided attention for he was, simultaneously, writing regularly for the *New Age*, the journal that had consistently edified him since he was introduced to it as a pupil at Broughton in 1908. 'Chris is to be a regular contributor to the *New Age*,' Peggy (now pregnant) told her brother-in-law Andrew on 23 March, 'so you'll probably be enlivened by his views on things and on books and their makers in particular.'[128]

The *New Age* in 1924 was no longer a cultural weekly edited by Orage; it was a sectarian organ of Social Credit dedicated to the economic theories of Major C. H. Douglas (1879-1952), the Scottish engineer. Orage met Douglas, in the *New Age* office, in 1918 and was almost immediately converted to Douglas's doctrine. Orage described Douglas as 'the Einstein of economics'[129] while Ezra Pound was sure that Douglas was 'a genius'.[130] Douglas's book *Economic Democracy* (1920) first appeared in instalments in the *New Age*, beginning in June 1919, and henceforth the weekly was given over to Social Credit. Briefly, Douglas held that the control of money by the banks led to a shortage of purchasing power. To remedy this, he advocated the payment of a national dividend to each citizen and suggested that retailers should sell commodities below cost, losses being covered by the banks. As the public would thus be enabled to purchase goods and circulate money, economic crises would be avoided. Douglas insisted that the state should lend, not borrow; he also considered that value was not synonymous with price. The dogmatic nature of Douglas's views had a great appeal for poets. Edwin Muir became a Douglasite and wrote a pamphlet, *Social Credit and the Labour Party* (1935). Pound declared that 'Major Douglas must command the unqualified respect of all save those few cliques of the irresponsible and the economically guilty'.[131]

Like Pound, Grieve acclaimed Douglas as a genius; after his death, and despite Adam Smith's eminence as an economist, Grieve called Douglas 'one of the greatest Scotsmen of the past hundred years, and, in relation to his own subject, the greatest of all time'.[132] Another *New Age* contributor was not so sure:

> [Douglas] was squat and bald, with a foghorn voice, and somewhat Jewish in appearance. This detail imparted a touch of burlesque irony to his brainless anti-Semitism. And apart from that, when he was present there was little chance for anyone else to get a word in. Nor was there the remotest likelihood that anything else but Social Credit would be discussed, or rather expounded.[133]

With the *New Age* dedicated to Social Credit, Orage felt he could leave the paper to its own devices. He turned increasingly inwards, entering Gurdjieff's Institute for the Harmonious Development of Man, at Fontainebleau, in 1922 then going to New York to publicise the meditative methods of Gurdjieff and his disciple Ouspensky. According to Grieve:

> When Orage gave up the *New Age* and went to America to promulgate the doctrines of Ouspensky and Gurdjieff I took over the literary editorship of the *New Age* and was a prolific contributor to it over my own name and various pseudonyms for several years – until, in fact, Orage returned to England [in 1931].[134]

He was certainly a prolific contributor.

Grieve's 'Mannigfaltig' column was a wide-ranging causerie, mainly reacting to books and cultural issues. On 24 April he reflected on psychoanalysis and praised Blok; on 8 May he claimed that Mikhail Saltykov, the satirist of Tsarist Russia, was a greater figure than Swift; on 3 July he discussed experimental verse and literary expressionism; on 17 July he mentioned Bergson and quoted from C. E. M. Joad's *Intro-duction to Modern Philosophy;* on 14 August he mourned the death of the Norwegian writer Arne Gaborg; on 25 September he discoursed on Strindberg and on 2 October he expatiated on Croce. The most relevant piece, considering that it was printed prior to the publication of *Sangschaw,* was a review of John Buchan's anthology *The Northern Muse.* Buchan had represented only eight living poets – including Grieve ('The Bonnie Broukit Bairn') and Violet Jacob, whom Grieve described as 'the finest poetess (writing in the Vernacular) Scotland has yet produced'[135] – and Grieve felt the book could have been much better. After comparing the verse of Burns to 'the lamentable efforts of a hen at soaring'[136] Grieve made a plea for a reappraisal of Scots as a poetic language:

> Anyone who knows anything about the Scottish vernacular knows that it is one of the subtlest, most searching, and most fully expressive of all languages. I personally think that there are reasons for regretting that Middle-English (of which Braid Scots is a variant) did not survive instead of modern English. . . . Nevertheless, there is a movement for the revival of the Scottish vernacular; a realistic Scots nationalism with a pronounced Sinn Fein element has recently asserted itself; subversive tendencies are at work which may undermine the odious morality and the false senses of humour and pathos which have hag-ridden Scottish letters; and, given a little group of determined, ruthless and competent artists, the latent potentialities of the Scottish vernacular may be realised in ways of consequence to European literature however abhorrent and unnatural to contemporary Scottish con-ventionalists. Stranger things have happened in literary history.[137]

Confining the 'little group' to Grieve and his alter ego MacDiarmid, the passage is truly prophetic.

Intent on a breakthrough in Scottish letters, Grieve needed friends he could confide in; he had yet to reach the stage where he could proclaim his indifference to the opinions of others. In the early summer of 1924 he met Helen Cruickshank for the first time, going through to Edinburgh to take tea with her in the Ravelston Elms studio of Pittendrigh Mac-gillivray, King's Sculptor in Ordinary for Scotland since 1921. Mac-gillivray was well known for such works as the colossal Burns statue in Irvine and the Byron statue in Aberdeen. He was also a poet, writing in English and in a regional Scots (using the north and south dialects of the vernacular); Grieve, who considered Macgillivray one of the few serious vernacular poets since Burns, had written about him in the *Scottish Nation* (as a sculptor on 9 October 1923, as a poet on 16 October). To Grieve, Macgillivray was an expansively romantic figure, a patriotic Scot of integrity. In the company of a Grand Old Sculptor (Macgillivray was sixty-eight in 1924) and a Grave Young Poet, Helen Cruickshank felt overawed:

> One end of the studio was dominated by a massive statue of the Marquis of Bute, commissioned for erection in Cardiff. From behind this statue emerged the slight figure of the poet. He was then about 33, his most noticeable feature being a bush of silky hair above a high forehead and two deep-set eyes. His manner was shy and modest. Macgillivray had a magnificent leonine head with white hair *en brosse* and was rather an intimidating character. I felt an insignificant humdrum Civil Servant between them.[138]

Macgillivray was one of the few men Grieve respected enough to entrust with the real identity of Hugh MacDiarmid.

Another artist Grieve came close to in 1924 was Edwin Muir. Born in Orkney in 1887, Muir did not think of himself as Scottish so much as insular and Orcadian – 'I've often told Grieve [that] I'm not Scotch, I'm an Orkneyman'.[139] Leaving Orkney at the age of fourteen, Muir went with his family to Glasgow, a move his work portrays as a descent from Eden into a nightmarish labyrinth. Muir worked in a beer-bottling factory in Glasgow, a bone-factory in Greenock, then returned to Glasgow for wartime work in a shipbuilding office. During this period his father died of a heart-attack, his brother Willie of consumption, his brother Johnnie from a brain tumour and his mother from an internal disease. He survived through his contact with Orage (under whose influence he became a Nietzschean) and through the friendships he made in Glasgow with F. G. Scott (the two met at a Guild Socialist evening) and Denis Saurat. Above all he was sustained by the woman he met in 1918; marriage to Willa Anderson, the following year, was, for Muir, 'the most important event in my life'.[140]

A comparatively late developer as a poet Muir had yet, in 1924, to publish a volume of verse – *First Poems* came out in 1925 – but he was well known as a critic with the *New Age* and the *Freeman* (an American periodical which ceased publication in 1924). His books *We Moderns* (1919) and *Latitudes* (1924) showed a familiarity with European writers revered by Grieve, such as Dostoevsky, Nietzsche and Ibsen. He had compared Grieve to Joyce in the *New Age* of 15 November 1923, contributed to the *Scottish Nation* and suggested to Grieve that 'a long poem in the language you are evolving would go tremendously'.[141] On receipt of Muir's letter Grieve began work on a poem that can be seen retrospectively as a rough preliminary sketch for *A Drunk Man Looks at the Thistle.* As published in the final issue of the *Scottish Chapbook* (Nov.-Dec. 1923) 'Braid Scots', dedicated to Muir, ends optimistically:

> Strang an' deep-suckin' are the roots I rin
> Into my race; an' a' its misery
> I'll raise into mysel' – an' towards the sun!
> Let whasae may lament the poverty
> O' mind an' saul they say aboonds to-day,
> An', coorin' frae reality, fin' bield
> For craven wits whaur cynicism hauds sway.
> – *Oor tree's nae daised wud yet but's routh o' fruit to yield.*   (1235)

Grieve later deleted the third section of 'Braid Scots' when he revised the poem as 'Gairmscoile' in *Penny Wheep.*

Towards the end of July 1924, after a four-year period abroad in Prague, Dresden, Hellerau and Sonntagberg, Edwin and Willa Muir came to Montrose to stay with Willa's mother who had a shop in the High Street. Settled in Mrs Anderson's house at 81 High Street, Muir was melancholy and anxious to leave as soon as possible. (He moved to Buckinghamshire early in 1925, returning to Montrose where Willa had a miscarriage in December; the couple then took to their travels again.) Willa, however, was glad to be back in Montrose. For her it was a satisfying homecoming. Edwin worked on *Transition* (1926), a series of essays on Joyce, Lawrence, Virginia Woolf, Eliot and others. He also let

Willa teach him golf. Naturally, Edwin and Willa Muir visited Christopher and Peggy Grieve. Willa described the Grieves 'living in a council house on the fringe of the town, where Peggy cooked the meals and washed and ironed Christopher's shirts'.[142] Willa was envious of Peggy's domestic efficiency and saw her, then pregnant with her first child, as an attractive woman who stood clinging to her husband's arm, 'looking up shyly through dark eyelashes, with a daisy-like white collarette round her neck, apparently an embodiment of the "wee wifie" loved by Scotsmen'.[143] Peggy told Willa she did not greatly care for life in 16 Links Avenue. Resenting the curiosity of her neighbours on the council estate she had put up extra net curtains as a precaution against the prying eyes of passers-by.

According to Willa, Peggy did not take kindly to Christopher's partiality for whisky. Willa noticed that Christopher got drunk easily, on a small amount of whisky, and was rarely able to resist temptation as a journalist required to attend farmers' dinners where whisky was the only drink offered. Willa witnessed a little domestic crisis caused by just such circumstances when she and Edwin arrived, unannounced, at 16 Links Avenue one evening:

> [Edwin and I] found Peggy at her wits' end, Christopher having come home from some farmers' junketing and locked himself into the bathroom, since when there had been neither sound nor movement from him. Peggy was sure he had passed out. Edwin managed to scramble from outside through the high, narrow bathroom window, found Christopher lying mother-naked, cold, insensible but alive in a completely dry bath, and unlocked the door at once. We lugged the poet into the living-room where we laid him on the hearthrug by the fire, covered him with blankets and left him to Peggy's ministrations in that respectable council house.[144]

Although they were to fall out famously twelve years later, over the publication of Muir's *Scott and Scotland*, Grieve and Muir got on well in 1924. F. G. Scott, a friend of both poets, came over from Glasgow to encourage the others. Willa was aware that Edwin seemed quiet in comparison to the two Scottish Borderers: diffident when they were defiant; modest when they were megalomaniac. Scott and Grieve were fervent about the future of the Scottish Renaissance but, said Willa, 'Edwin's interest in it was tepid, except that he was fond of F. G. Scott'.[145] Still the notion, encouraged by Willa, that Muir was something of a saint and Grieve something of a sinner was not substantiated by subsequent events. Muir and Grieve had more in common than is usually conceded:

both embraced socialism, Nietzschean supermania and Social Credit at various times; both were inspired by Orage and the *New Age*; both benefited from the friendship of F. G. Scott; both wrote Edenic poems about their native places. Ironically, as they both laid claim to the intellectual heritage of Europe, it was a Scottish issue that eventually drove a great divide between them: they differed over the status of the Scottish language.

In 1924 Grieve began his arrangement, continued for several years, of renting a holiday house for August and September in the Kincardineshire village of St Cyrus. For the pregnant Peggy the break from Montrose was welcome; for Christopher it meant he could write and relax beside a spectacular coastline and still continue with his work as he was within a cycling distance of five miles from Montrose. Writing to his mother from St Cyrus, Grieve joked 'I'm getting old, and it's time I was getting a regular move on at last.'[146] Pushed on by F. G. Scott he had completed enough MacDiarmid lyrics to make a volume of verse. His priorities were to place the book with a publisher and continue with his serious cultural criticism.

Grieve was involved on too many levels to keep up his Council work. There was not only his writing to consider: on 4 September 1924 Peggy gave birth to a daughter, Christine Elizabeth Margaret Grieve. Eight days later Grieve resigned from the Town Council, regretfully so 'as my heart has been in this work'.[147] With a child as well as a wife to support he was anxious to get away from local journalism, and Montrose, into a position that provided a better salary and more spare time to devote to the matter of Hugh MacDiarmid. Grieve was glad that he had generated such interest in this still mysterious figure. The *Scotsman* of 8 November 1924 carried an article by George Kitchin on the Scottish Renaissance group; though critical of the claims made (by Grieve and Saurat) for MacDiarmid as a new Burns, Kitchin conceded that 'there are certain pieces of his which raise him above the common level of writers in dialect [for he has] a certain high seriousness'.[148] Grieve replied angrily to Kitchin in a letter to the *Scotsman* (13 Nov.) and an article in *Forward* (22 Nov.) but privately told Ogilvie 'I welcome any sort of publicity rather than a conspiracy of silence'.[149] He was pleased to note that David Cleghorn Thomson, in the *London Mercury* of November, had congratulated Grieve on promoting the Scots verse of Hugh Mac-Diarmid.

Seeing an advertisement in the *Glasgow Herald* for the vacancy of

Keeper of the National Galleries of Scotland, Grieve applied for the job. On 10 February 1925 he wrote to Pittendrigh Macgillivray asking him to support his application; he also approached Ogilvie, R. J. Drummond, John Buchan and Herbert Grierson, Professor of Rhetoric and English Literature at Edinburgh University. Grieve did not get the job but MacDiarmid had another favour to ask of Grierson. Blackwood's – the prestigious Edinburgh firm who had recently scored commercial success with the thrillers of John Buchan (*The Thirty-Nine Steps* and *The Power-House*) – had, on 28 April 1925, accepted MacDiarmid's *Sangschaw* for publication. Two days later Grieve wrote to Grierson asking him to write an introduction to the book and offering to dedicate the poem 'I Heard Christ Sing' to him.

Grieve had met Grierson on 17 October 1924 when delivering the inaugural lecture to the Edinburgh University History Association and was encouraged then by Grierson's remarks on the revival of the Scots vernacular. Now he wanted Grierson to expand on these remarks without mentioning the connection between Grieve and MacDiarmid – 'I wish no hint given that McD is a pseudonym'[150] – but taking into account an article, 'Reviving the Scots Vernacular', Grieve had contributed to the *Scottish Educational Journal* on 6 February 1925. He also advised Grierson to read Saurat's comments on MacDiarmid and an article in the *Glasgow Herald* of 4 April 1925 in which Alexander McGill hailed MacDiarmid as an experimental poet worthy of European attention. McGill's assessment of MacDiarmid as a significant new voice in Scotland did much to promote the early reputation of the poet; it was commissioned by William Power who, as literary editor of the *Glasgow Herald*, actively encouraged MacDiarmid.

Grierson, though a figure of some eminence and repute, was flattered by the approach and eventually accepted the dedication of 'I Heard Christ Sing', though he asked Grieve to delete the fourth quatrain of the original text. The poet wrote to Grierson again, on 12 May 1925, apologising for intruding on his time but making a clear distinction between the critical prose of Grieve and the creative verse of MacDiarmid:

> McDiarmid's poems only partially illustrate Grieve's esoteric propaganda with regard to the Vernacular – for some of them are in particular dialects – not standardised Scots – and others are so little in Scots as to be quite intelligible to any intelligent Sassenach. McDiarmid is by no means committed to Grieve's position.[151]

This reveals not so much a psychological duality as an internal dialectic, a productive argument between two tendencies.

After some hesitation, Grierson decided against doing the introduction on the grounds that he was not sufficiently interested in the issues involved in contemporary vernacular verse. So Grieve turned to John Buchan who readily agreed to write a preface. On 1 June 1925 Grieve sent Blackwood's the text of Buchan's introduction; less than three weeks later his long series of 'Contemporary Scottish Studies' began in the *Scottish Educational Journal* with an article (19 June) on Buchan who was hailed as 'Dean of the Faculty of Contemporary Scottish Letters' and a man possessed of 'undoubted genius'.[152] Grieve was getting the Scottish stage ready for MacDiarmid to assume the leading role in a great national literary drama. The *Scottish Educational Journal*, the weekly paper of the Educational Institute of Scotland, was the staple diet of teachers until Grieve's fiercely polemical series brought it to the attention of the Scottish literary public at large, many of whom were infuriated by Grieve's air of omniscience. This series helped to create the kind of intellectual climate in which MacDiarmid could flourish. After all, the public was shortly to be assured by no less an authority than John Buchan that Hugh MacDiarmid was a man to be reckoned with:

> My friend [MacDiarmid] has set himself a task which is at once reactionary and revolutionary.... He would treat Scots as a living language and apply it to matters which have been foreign to it since the sixteenth century. Since there is no canon of the vernacular, he makes his own, as Burns did, and borrows words and idioms from the old masters.... It is a proof that a new spirit is to-day abroad in the North, which, as I have said, is both conservative and radical – a determination to keep Scotland in the main march of the world's interests, and at the same time to forgo no part of her ancient heritage.[153]

The wee bit sangs in *Sangschaw*, and *Penny Wheep*, would give lyrical substance to the new spirit seen by Buchan.

7

Wee Bit Sangs

Wee bit sangs are a' I need,
Wee bit sangs for auld times' sake!
Here are ferlies nae yin sees
In a bensil o' a bleeze.
                    'To One Who Urges More Ambitious Flights'   (57)

SANGSCHAW ('song-festival'), the first book by Hugh MacDiarmid (the surname was still given as M'Diarmid, with a turned comma), was published by Blackwood's on 9 September 1925 at five shillings per copy. Prominently printed on the front of the dustjacket was a publisher's note stating that some of the poems had been translated into French (by Denis Saurat) and Danish (by Carl Kjersmeier for his anthology *Liv Og Legende*); that one ('The Bonnie Broukit Bairn') had been anthologised in John Buchan's *The Northern Muse*; and that most of the lyrics had been set to music by F. G. Scott whose choral version of 'O Jesu Parvule' had won first prize in the Glasgow Orpheus Choir's competition for original compositions in 1924.[1] It was Scott who remarked that 'no one was more surprised than Chris when *Sangschaw* was so well received'.[2]

In Scotland the praise was by no means unanimous. The Aberdeen *Press and Journal* acknowledged the power of 'The Watergaw' but accused MacDiarmid (identified as C. M. Grieve) of elsewhere lapsing into 'the weirdest and most appalling cacophonies'.³ In the *Glasgow Evening Times* William Jeffrey, a friend of the poet, had no doubt that MacDiarmid had 'revivified the body of Scots poetry, and put the spark of hope into its almost moribund heart'.⁴ The *Scotsman*, while noting the strange blend of mysticism and realism in the lyrics, reserved judgement by saying 'Mr M'Diarmid does not always succeed, but in many poems he does succeed'.⁵ The *Scottish Educational Journal*, also identifying MacDiarmid as the Grieve then writing the 'Contemporary Scottish Studies' series in the same weekly, speculated whether the author's 'remarkable endowment of terse, pointed phrase can be applied on a more heroic scale'.⁶ It was the *Glasgow Herald*, with a review by Robert Bain, that gave MacDiarmid the Scottish boost he needed:

> The accomplishment of Hugh M'Diarmid is … quite unheralded. The matter is, of course, still Scottish, but it is stripped of all the trite sentimentalities and sanctimoniousness that hung over Northern verse like a drizzling mist. It is Scotland still, but revealed in sudden glimpses as by lightning or moon-break, sometimes starkly, sometimes with wonderful tenderness, but never other than vividly and imaginatively. The effect is won by a daring use of words practically obsolete … The secret of the whole thing is that Mr M'Diarmid has conceived each of his poems intensely – and could do so – and then searched out the vital word for the thing in his thought.⁷

Lewis Spence, in the *Nineteenth Century and After*, was likewise sure that 'no poetry for a century and a half has reflected so much of the authentic Scotland as the poems in Mr M'Diarmid's recent book *Sangschaw*'.⁸

Outside Scotland the reviewers were also divided. 'AE' (George William Russell, the friend of Yeats) praised the book on 3 October 1925 in the *Irish Statesman* (which he edited) then wrote to MacDiarmid asking him to contribute an article on the Scottish Renaissance to his journal.⁹ The anonymous reviewer in the *Times Literary Supplement* spent much time querying MacDiarmid's understanding of Scots words and concluded:

> Still, there is a true vein of poetry in Mr M'Diarmid – how rich, or how thin, his future work will show. And he has entered upon a fascinating if doubtful enterprise. Its success will depend above all on the early emergence of a poet of commanding genius; for the way to show that high poetry can be written in Scots is to write it. Mr M'Diarmid may not be the destined conqueror; neither his substance nor his form gives much promise of that; but he merits the praise of the pioneer. He writes in the faith without which there can be no conquest: the belief that Scotland still has something to say

to the imagination of mankind, something that she alone among the nations can say, and can say only in her native tongue.[10]

MacDiarmid replied to this review in a letter (14 Jan. 1926), convincingly defending his eclectic use of Scots.

The most intelligent review of *Sangschaw* was by Edwin Muir in an American journal, the *Saturday Review of Literature*. Acclaiming Mac-Diarmid as a 'perfectly original' poet, Muir noted his 'intellectual competence [and] modernity'. Introducing his American readers to the concept of the Scottish Renaissance, Muir pointed out that MacDiarmid had created a new literary language by synthesising the riches of all the Scottish dialects. If, Muir argued, a Scottish literary language was possible then an indigenous modern Scottish literature was possible too. Muir saluted 'Mr M'Diarmid's friend and colleague, Mr C. M. Grieve' for publicising the Scottish Renaissance Movement. However, Muir insisted, only two really significant figures had emerged from this movement: MacDiarmid and 'Mr F. G. Scott, who is attempting to do [for music] what Mr M'Diarmid is trying to do for poetry'. Muir singled out the lyric 'Country Life' because it had, he said, 'an almost fantastic economy, a crazy economy which has the effect of humour and yet conveys a kind of horror'. He ended his two-column-long review by comparing MacDiarmid to his English contemporaries:

> In curious speculation and half-fantastic thought he is certainly as original as Mr Graves; his descriptions are more economical and, I think, more vivid than Mr Blunden's, and his mysticism more organic than Mr de la Mare's. In the *quality* of his work he is not unworthy to be compared with these poets; but the question is whether he has a power, like theirs, of sustained imagination. This has still to be seen. Each of these poems is a single flash, vivid but brief. We wait for the further volume which will establish Mr M'Diarmid's title to our most serious attention.[11]

Considering that MacDiarmid was criticised, in later years, for writing excessively long poems it is interesting to see reviewers advising him to go beyond the abbreviated form of the lyric (which he did in two of the poems in *Sangschaw*). MacDiarmid, with foresight, put on the title-page of *Sangschaw* a quotation from the *Carmen Heroicum* of Terentianus Maurus: *habent sua fata libelli* ('books have their own destiny'). The destiny of *Sangschaw* was to be at once an end and a beginning: it ended the stranglehold the sentimentalists had on Scots verse and it was the first of many books by Hugh MacDiarmid. After seeing it in print the poet thought it 'like the curate's egg ... about a third of it below par, which I'm sorry I included'.[12] Unusually, he was being too modest. The only egregiously bad part of the book is the French poem, 'La Fourmilière', for Denis Saurat, and that because MacDiarmid had little feeling for the rhythm of the language.[13] The other non-Scots poem – 'In Glasgow', dedicated to F. G. Scott – abuses the ugliness of Glasgow in English. *Sangschaw* would have been stronger without these items, as an exclusively Scots collection.

Two of the poems are translations but not from the original languages as MacDiarmid suggests. Rather they transmute into Scots extant English translations from anthologies jointly edited by Babette Deutsch and Avrahm Yarmolinsky: ' "You Know Not Who I Am" ', supposedly after the German of Stefan George, reworks the translation of that title from *Contemporary German Poetry* (1923); 'The Last Trump', supposedly suggested by the Russian of Dmitry Merezhkovsky, is based on 'The Trumpet Call' from *Modern Russian Poetry* (1923). The slightest poems in the collection are the whimsical ones: 'Overinzievar' (about farm animals), 'Ex Vermibus' (about bird and worm), 'Whip-the-World' (about a bird). The finest Scots lyrics, though, are touched by genius.

MacDiarmid seems to have produced his lyrics through a poetic form of spontaneous combustion – he was illuminated by inspiration, sensible of 'a phenomenon akin to religious conversion'.[14] Decades after the publication of *Sangschaw* he suggested that the formal concision of the poems owed much to the compositional requirements of F. G. Scott, declaring 'It's the association of music and poetry that I was concerned with ... in these early lyrics, and after all I was writing them for a composer'.[15] As we know, MacDiarmid made his first poetic appearance in the *Scottish Chapbook* in October 1922 and soon afterwards F. G. Scott was on the trail that led, surprisingly, to his former pupil from Langholm. From the twenty-seven Scots poems in *Sangschaw* Scott made ten published songs: 'The Watergaw', 'The Sauchs in the Reuch Heuch Hauch', 'Moonstruck', 'The Man in the Moon', 'Reid E'en', 'Crowdieknowe', 'The Eemis Stane', 'Country Life', 'O Jesu Parvule', 'The Innumerable Christ'. It was, however, misleading of MacDiarmid to imply he wrote the poems simply as words for music. They each have a sturdy independence.

The most original poems are those that put the poet's vast store of biblical images in a context that is simultaneously cosmic and subjective. MacDiarmid, the product of a renaissance and self-appointed saviour of Scotland, identified with the biblical Christ. As a creator he also felt he had an insight into the mind of the biblical God. Yet there is nothing awkward in the poet's familiarity with God and Christ: the language he uses encourages intimacy, the Scots words have a gritty grandeur. On to his evocative vocabulary he superimposed the results of his reading, investing theological details with intellectual debate. Even when the sources are evident, MacDiarmid's imagination transcends them; as indeed his handling of Scots transcends the catalogue of words in a dictionary.

MacDiarmid's perception of Christ as a universal figure derives from J. Y. Simpson's *Man and the Attainment of Immortality* (1922). Professor of Natural Science at New College, Edinburgh, Simpson was concerned to give Christianity the benefit of modern scientific research and portray Christ as the supreme example of the evolutionary ideal:

> In relation to man, the appearance of Jesus Christ is, then, an integral part of the evolutionary process in the purpose of the unmasking Environment which in its ultimate spiritual aspect is God. ... [Moreover] it is not impossible that other worlds may know their Bethlehem, and their Calvary too. In a very real sense, the historic Jesus is for us the cosmic Christ.[16]

MacDiarmid slightly altered Simpson's phrasing in the quotation he placed at the head of 'The Innumerable Christ' – 'Other stars may have their Bethlehem, and their Calvary too' – though he knew that life can evolve only on planets, not stars.

'The Innumerable Christ' is a perfect example of MacDiarmid's ability to collapse an expansive concept into a notably dense structure: the poem contains only sixteen lines one of which ('I' mony an unco warl' the nicht') is subject to incremental repetition (the method of the traditional ballads). In the first stanza MacDiarmid transports the reader into space to view the earth as one planet among many; from the vantage point of another world the universe is no longer geocentric as 'Earth twinkles like a star' (32). The second stanza goes beyond the solar system into deep space, beyond the visible universe seen by human eyes, 'farther than their lichts can fly' (32) to listen to children crying on unknown worlds circling remote stars. The last two stanzas give the Nietzschean notion of eternal recurrence a Christian and cosmic dimension by counterpointing a remarkably pictorial quatrain with a speculative vision of a lifeless Earth:

I' mony an unco warl' the nicht
The lift gaes black as pitch at noon,
An' sideways on their chests the heids
    O' endless Christs roll doon.

An' when the earth's as cauld's the mune
An' a' its folk are lang syne deid,
On coontless stars the Babe maun cry
    An' the Crucified maun bleed.   (32)

'O Jesu Parvule' is also vividly pictorial. Mary sings a lullaby to Christ and draws him to her breast. The precocious infant draws no comfort from the contact but instead anticipates the *pietà* in which his dead body sprawls across his mother's lap: 'the byspale's nae thocht o' sleep i' the least' (31).

Two longer poems, 'Ballad of the Five Senses' and 'I Heard Christ Sing', lack the concentration of the compact lyrics but continue the task of confronting God and Christ as an equal intent on similar aims. 'Ballad of the Five Senses', a Scots restatement of the theme of 'A Moment in Eternity', rejects the limitations of the physical world then reassesses them. The poet sees the world as a shining spectacle as if newly created for his vision but realises (having studied Plato and Plotinus) that the earthly is only a shadow of the eternal. In the spiritual sphere, inhabited by a lonely God, the poet sees a tree – the same tree studied in 'A Moment in Eternity' – so that 'Wi' body and saul I socht to staun'/As in Eternity' (38). He spirits away his physical senses so he can face God:

Oot o' the way, my senses five,
I ken a' you can tell,
Oot o' the way, my thochts, for noo'
I maun face God mysel'.   (38)

The unadorned simplicity of that statement, the colloquial dismissal of earthly appetites and thoughts, the mainly monosyllabic rhythm: these all give the impression of certainty in a wildly speculative scenario.

As the poem progresses it becomes clear that a confrontation with God involves some sort of death, at the very least a renunciation of material desires; 'daith may only be/A change o' senses so's a man/Anither warl' can see' (40). MacDiarmid enriches the texture of the poem by pursuing this thought with a paradox, for the earthly world may equate to the eternal if understood in a visionary manner:

And God Himsel' sall only be
As far's a man can tell,
In this or ony ither life
A way o' lookin' at himsel'.   (40)

Just as Blake, always a major influence on the poet, could bring eternity to earth

To see a World in a Grain of Sand
And a Heaven in a Wild Flower,
Hold Infinity in the palm of your hand
And Eternity in an hour[17]

so MacDiarmid sees the sensual world as a spiritual sphere, and vice versa. He is, though, more subjective than Blake, more inclined to empathise with the creator and his human creation.

'I Heard Christ Sing' is, MacDiarmid explained, 'founded on an incident narrated in a recently discovered portion of Syriac Apocrypha'.[18] Christ stands in the centre of a ring formed by the twelve dancing disciples and sings of his destiny. MacDiarmid puts into Christ's song a plea for a second coming compatible with the earthly aspirations of humankind, for Christ hopes his rebirth will 'Be accompanied/By the spirit of man' (20). The empathy with Christ is evident in the first-personal song which is the centrepiece of a poetic triptych: its stanzas are structured in pairs linked by terminal lines and it is framed by descriptive quatrains.

From these poems MacDiarmid can be appreciated as a poet primarily seeking a spiritual exploration of outer and inner space: he is (to borrow the title of a work by Jung, with whose ideas the poet was familiar from summaries in the *New Age*) a modern man in search of his soul. Feeling the force of Nietzsche's declaration of the death of God, MacDiarmid either stands face to face with creation or portrays the bleak chaos of a Godless world. 'The Bonnie Broukit Bairn' compares the earth to a forsaken child on the point of weeping. 'Au Claire de la Lune' shows the earth as lifeless, 'littered wi' larochs o' Empires' (23) – a hint, there, of Shelley's 'Ozymandias' – or as a 'bare auld stane ... beneath the seas o' Space' (24).

'The Eemis Stane', perhaps the most haunting lyric in *Sangschaw*, lets the earth move through space like an insecure stone that, on closer inspection, becomes a tombstone with its inscription obliterated by time:

I' the how-dumb-deid o' the cauld hairst nicht
The warl' like an eemis stane
Wags i' the lift;
An' my eerie memories fa'
Like a yowdendrift.

Like a yowdendrift so's I couldna read
The words cut oot i' the stane
Had the fug o' fame
An' history's hazelraw
No' yirdit thaim.   (27)

MacDiarmid's metamorphic use of similes is designed to shock the reader into a realisation that nothing is what it seems at first sight. Appearance is illusory.

Several of the lyrics have a sexual theme, offering an erotic answer to the apparently indifferent world. 'Moonlight Among the Pines' substitutes for the moonlit hills the 'white breist' (21) of the poet's sweetheart. Similarly, 'In the Hedge-Back' creates a spark of warmth in the cold black night from 'the heat/Meltin' us utterly' (25). 'The Scarlet Woman' is a psalm – 'I ... fear nae ill' (28) clearly echoes the 23rd Psalm – for a prostitute. 'Reid E'en' makes a Scots pun on 'hert' as both hart and heart. The remaining lyrics range over topographical, comical, domestic and agricultural subjects so that the collection as a whole has great variety and vitality.

A month after the publication of *Sangschaw*, Grieve was in Edinburgh at a meeting chaired by Patrick Geddes, the sociologist who had, in 1892, established the Outlook Tower, on Castlehill, as an international centre of research into town planning and other of his many interests. As Grieve read MacDiarmid poems and F. G. Scott played MacDiarmid settings the appearance further undermined the plausibility of his pseudonym. Writing to Ogilvie about the irritations of life in Montrose – 'I loathe my work here'[19] – he agreed that the MacDiarmid pseudonym had its problems:

I agree as to the difficulties a pseudonym involves one in: but I am much more inclined to give every facility for the sort of malevolence I am encountering than otherwise. I think I'll get my own back with interest in the long run. At the same time – if only to please you – I'd shed the pseudonym now, if I could – but I can't for various reasons. There are the publishers of Scott's music, etc. to consider.[20]

The malevolence was the result of Grieve's journalism, not MacDiarmid's verse.

During the period the first three MacDiarmid books were published, Grieve's 'Contemporary Scottish Studies' series ran in the *Scottish Educational Journal* – from 19 June 1926 to 4 February 1927 (some of the articles were collected in the book *Contemporary Scottish Studies* in 1926). Grieve's highly controversial column amused and informed his admirers but enraged his enemies, several of whom (like Donald Mackenzie, a contributor to *Northern Numbers*) sent furious letters to the journal. Helen Cruickshank, buying her weekly copy from a station bookstall, was asked by the manager if she could account for the sudden interest in the paper. 'People buy it', she replied, 'to see who is being castigated by C.M. Grieve this week.'[21] (Coincidentally, Cruickshank's next-door-neighbour was Thomas Henderson, editor of the *Scottish Educational Journal*.)

Grieve savaged Scottish writers he had previously anthologised. Lauchlan Maclean Watt (four poems in the second *Northern Numbers*) was now condemned as the perpetrator of poetic 'atrocities'.[22] Charles Murray (also in the second *Northern Numbers*) had become a man who 'has not only never written a line of poetry in his life, but ... is constitutionally incapable of doing so'.[23] Neil Munro (to whom the first *Northern Numbers* was respectfully dedicated) got off comparatively lightly by being classed as 'a minor artist [lacking] the personality to make the most of the limited, yet indubitable gifts, he possesses'.[24] Everything contaminated by the Kailyard or the Celtic Twilight was dismissed: J.M. Barrie was an unscrupulously commercial dramatist not worthy of consideration in a Scottish context; Mrs Kennedy-Fraser, the folksong collector, was 'a Rip Van Winkle of Scottish musical development'.[25]

Intent on disposing of spurious notions of Scottish culture and basing his idea of an antithetical and irrationalist Scottish literature on G. Gregory Smith's book – '*Scottish Literature* is ... the first text-book I would like to place in the hands of any young Scot likely to play a part in bringing about a National Renaissance'[26] – Grieve promoted the Scottish Renaissance Movement as an antidote to the poison that had weakened the Scottish nation. He conducted his campaign of re-education by urging the Scottish public to study the fiction of Norman Douglas and Neil Gunn; the music of Francis George Scott; the painting of William McCance (art critic of the *Spectator*); the criticism of Edwin Muir; the educational theories of A.S. Neill; the plays of George Reston Malloch; the verse of nationalist poets such as Lewis Spence and Hugh Mac-

Diarmid. Older Scots were judged by the quality of their nationalism – R. B. Cunninghame Graham was projected as a heroic figure, Pittendrigh Macgillivray as a stalwart, R. E. Muirhead as a dedicated, if cautious, patriot.

Linguistically, Grieve expounded the theory of Synthetic Scots, applauded the success of the Norwegian *Landsmaal* movement, recommended the Scottish Gaelic propaganda of Erskine of Mar and the Irish Gaelic verse of Aodhagán Ó Rathaille. He favoured foreign writers, commending (in a letter replying to one of his critics) Blok, Spitteler and Valéry. He was ever anxious to give his readers the benefit of his reading. Ex-Prince D. S. Mirsky's *Contemporary Russian Literature, 1881-1925* (1926) provided fresh information on such names as Vasily Rozanov (authority on Dostoevsky whose mistress, Polina Suslova, he married) and Mayakovsky, whose iconoclastic achievements prompted Grieve to say 'A Scottish Mayakovsky at this juncture would be a Godsend'.[27] Through such tactics as the demolition by polemic of Scottish cultural institutions (the uncritical cult of Burns, for example) and the flourishing of foreign names (Bjørnson, Croce, Nietzsche, Spengler, Tristan Tzara, Miguel de Unamuno) Grieve sought to restore Scotland on the cultural map of Europe. That he did so with a total disregard for diplomacy made him new enemies whose hostility increased his sense of persecution.

In February 1926, the month he was appointed a Justice of the Peace in Montrose, Grieve was ready to take up with Blackwood's the option they had on two more MacDiarmid volumes. He had failed to persuade the firm to finance a new magazine, *Scots Art*, but Blackwood's were committed to MacDiarmid's poetry despite the small sale of *Sangschaw* (in the whole of 1926 it sold 106 copies). On 12 February 1926 the poet wrote to say he had two further collections. The first, to be called *Penny Wheep* (the title, meaning 'small ale', he had originally given to *Sangschaw*), was to comprise forty-four Scots poems and three English poems. The other book was a long poem of more than 600 lines and the poet was keen to keep it by him for a while so he could revise the text; he had already decided on *A Drunk Man Looks at the Thistle* as a title. On 3 March 1926 the manuscript of *Penny Wheep* was sent to Blackwood's; the book was published on 16 June.

The title-page of *Penny Wheep* quotes the last line of the poem 'Braid Scots' from the *Scottish Chapbook* of November-December 1923: 'Oor tree's no' daised wud yet/But routh o' fruit to yield'. Omitting the dedication to Muir, a concluding stanza from the second section and the whole of the third section, 'Braid Scots' had become 'Gairmscoile' (Gaelic for 'school-call'). A dazzling application of Scots, 'Gairmscoile' was designed to illuminate MacDiarmid's conviction that the vernacular might be used as a medium uniquely able to convey emotions by aural means. In the *Scottish Chapbook* of March 1923, Grieve had continued his exposition of 'A Theory of Scots Letters':

> The Scottish Vernacular is the only language in Western Europe instinct with those uncanny spiritual and pathological perceptions alike which constitute the uniqueness of Dostoevski's work, and word after word of Doric establishes a blood-bond in a fashion at once infinitely more thrilling and vital and less explicable than those deliberately sought after by writers such as D. H. Lawrence in the medium of English which is inferior for such purposes because it has [an] entirely different natural bias which has been so confirmed down the centuries as to be insusceptible of correction. The Scots Vernacular is a vast storehouse of just the very peculiar and subtle effects which modern European literature in general is assiduously seeking … It is an inchoate Marcel Proust – a Dostoevskian debris of ideas – an inexhaustible quarry of subtle and significant sound.[28]

What the subtle and significant sound meant for MacDiarmid and, by extension, Scotland is the theme of 'Gairmscoile'.

The prologue pushes the theory of evolution back to its animal origins. MacDiarmid implies that just as man contains the seeds of his own evolutionary future so does he also display, when stripped of the trappings of civilisation, the signs of his evolutionary past. Inside every man, so the prologue explains, is the monstrous origin of the human species; sexually this being stands inside every woman with whom he makes love:

> Aulder than mammoth or than mastodon
> Deep i' the herts o' a' men lurk scaut-heid
> Skrymmorie monsters few daur look upon.
> Brides sometimes catch their wild een, scansin' red,
> Beekin' abune the herts they thocht to lo'e
> And horror-stricken ken that i' themselves
> A like beast stan's, and lookin' love thro' and thro'
> Meets the reid een wi' een like seevun hells.
> … Nearer the twa beasts draw, and, couplin', brak
> The bubbles o' twa sauls and the haill warld gangs black. (72)

The use of the pun in the startling first stanza is inspired. In 'Reid E'en', from *Sangschaw*, MacDiarmid had punned on hearts and harts and the correspondence is pursued in the remaining two stanzas of the prologue of 'Gairmscoile'. More inventively, though, the phrase 'i' themselves/A like beast stan's' is a pun on sexual penetration. Given that clue it is evident that the coupling of the last two lines of the stanza does not refer to the penetration of bride by bridegroom – since that has already happened – but to the merging of man and the animal inside him. 'Nearer the twa beasts draw' signifies the disturbing duality of the lover who is both beast and bridegroom: at the moment of orgasm human nature is not divided. It is unified by the primitive grunts of ecstasy, what the poet calls 'nameless lo'enotes'. These lovenotes, moreover, are the ultimate cry of human creation.

Like the bride of the first stanza, the poet is seduced by the lovenotes. They go beyond good and evil: 'Forgot are guid and ill, and joy and fear' (72). Almost devastated by the dark passion of sexuality, the poet ventures into the hills to watch the horns of harts intertwine, like a crown of thorns, as he hears 'The beasts in wha's wild cries a' Scotland's destiny thrills' (72). The image speaks for itself; the poet wants a sound that is deeper, more sensual, than the acceptable speech of civilisation.

After the prologue, the poem becomes an address, in two sections, to Henrik Wergeland (1808-45), the national poet of Norway. MacDiarmid – who saw a parallel between Scottish and Norwegian literature, between his Synthetic Scots and the Norwegian *Landsmaal* – had, in a footnote to 'Braid Scots', saluted Wergeland as 'the first poet to give adequate expression to the aspirations of the new Norway'.[29] Wergeland is approached not only as a fellow poet but as a kinsman – 'thy bluid tae/Kent the rouch dirl o' an auld Scots strain' (73). In evolutionary doctrine, MacDiarmid recalls, 'The best survive' (73). For the poet – for a MacDiarmid or a Wergeland – language does not die an evolutionary death to be replaced by a higher form (Scots, in other words, is not inferior to English) for words are capable of resurrection. The primitive sounds of sexual passion are echoed in the guttural sounds of a language being reborn.

MacDiarmid dwells on the possibility of a linguistic renaissance by considering how the 'auld hauf-human cry' (73) heard in the prologue to the poem acts as a link between the past and the future as it

> Fa's like a revelation on the herts o' men
> As tho' the graves were split and the first man
> Grippit the latest wi' a freendly han'   (73)

Rebirth – renaissance – brings to mind thoughts of the Christian nativity and the poet recalls how 'the saft een o' the kine/Lichted Christ's craidle wi' their canny shine' (74). A Scottish Renaissance will be a rebirth of a forgotten language, one with a sound so fundamental it will astonish men, specifically 'the herts o' men' (which harks back to the heart/hart pun of the prologue). The resurrected language will have an emotional truth that transcends philology and etymology:

> It's soon', no sense, that faddoms the herts o' men,
> And by my sangs the rouch auld Scots I ken
> E'en herts that ha'e nae Scots'll dirl richt thro'
> As nocht else could – for here's a language rings
> Wi' datchie sesames, and names for nameless things.   (74)

Appropriately, since MacDiarmid's Scottish Renaissance looks back to the Scottish Renaissance of Dunbar and other great makars, 'Gairmscoile' is the poem in which MacDiarmid goes back to Dunbar. In 1922 MacDiarmid told Herbert Grierson 'Dunbar is my favourite poet',[30] in his 'Contemporary Scottish Studies' column he declared that the Scots of Dunbar was 'the living speech of his countrymen',[31] and in the 1920s he used the slogan 'Dunbar – Not Burns!' F. G. Scott, who had set Dunbar's 'Rorate coeli desuper' in 1922, encouraged this interest in a Scottish poet who could write majestically of love and religion but who was also capable of poems of sexual abandon ('Tretis of the Tua Mariit Wemen and the Wedo'), of searing satire and of combative flyting (scolding). Dunbar trades insults with a fellow poet in 'The Flyting of Dunbar and Kennedie' using the binding devices of alliteration and rhyme to outwit his opponent, Walter Kennedy:

> Thow crop and rute of tratouris tressonable,
>   The fathir and moder of morthour and mischeif,
> Dissaitful tyrand with serpentis tung unstable,
>   Cukcald cradoun, cowart, and commoun theif[32]

Following the example of Dunbar, MacDiarmid pours scorn on his enemies, bringing his great vituperative gifts to bear down on minor dialect poets. He names Gilbert Rae, John Smellie Martin and John J. Sutherland as abusers of Scots and therefore betrayers of Scotland:

Lan' ha'e they posed as men o' letters here,
Dounhaddin' the Doric and keepin't i' the draiks,
Drivellin' and druntin', wi' mony a datchie sneer
... But soon we'll end the hail eggtaggle, fegs!
... The auld volcanoes rummle 'neath their feet,
And a' their shoddy lives 'll soon be drush,
Danders o' Hell! They feel th'unwelcome heat,
The deltit craturs, and their sauls are slush.
For we ha'e faith in Scotland's hidden poo'ers,
The present's theirs, but a' the past and future's oors.   (75)

That last line looks back to the Nietzsche quotation the poet had
encountered in Orage's monograph of 1906: 'Man is a rope connecting
animal and Superman – a rope across a precipice.'[33] MacDiarmid had no
time for the procrastination of the present: he wanted, as 'Gairmscoile'
made clear, a leap from animal to superman.

Technically, 'Gairmscoile' shows MacDiarmid in splendidly flexible
form, able to sustain his thought over stanzas of eight and ten lines,
varying the rhyme-scheme to suit the subject so that some stanzas
conclude with a rhyming couplet, others with a quatrain. 'Sea-Serpent'
also varies the pace by refusing to accept a settled pattern: four of
the stanzas comprise seven lines, the other six comprise eight lines.
MacDiarmid's serpent is an elusive creature having some of the charac-
teristics of the subtle serpent of Genesis and the fearsome leviathan of
Job but not confined to the Garden of Eden or the sea: 'Round the cantles
o' space Leviathan flickered/Like Borealis in flicht' (49). In Scandinavian
mythology the serpent of Midgard (middle-earth) encircles the world
with the endless coils of the abyss of the ocean. MacDiarmid has given
a deep spatial dimension to this serpentine symbolism in his search for
an image large enough to contain his view of a Godforsaken universe:

Whiles a blindin' movement tak's in my life
As a quick tide swallows a sea.
I feel like a star on a starry nicht,
A'e note in a symphony,
And ken that the serpent is movin' still,
A movement that a' thing shares,
Yet it seems as tho' it twines in a nicht
When God neither kens nor cares.   (50)

Subtitled 'From "A Sea Suite"' (as is 'God Takes a Rest' from *Sangschaw*) 'Sea-Serpent' sounds a theme extensively explored in *To Circumjack Cencrastus*.

The third longish poem in *Penny Wheep*, 'Bombinations of a Chimaera', has none of the linguistic density of 'Gairmscoile' but reads like a poem composed in English then recast in Scots. It uses insistently obvious rhymes – some of the quatrains of the first section have a single rhyme (as in ill/kill/still/will) – and Blakean paradox to continue the familiar MacDiarmidian topic of taking issue with God and Christ for the sorry state of the world. Christ is congratulated for going through Hell, then criticised because he left lesser beings behind; forcing the colloquial connotations of the notion the poet adds 'God Himsel'/May gang to Hell' (62). The poem has a shrill, almost hysterical, tone as the speaker seeks around for salvation, eventually settling for a Christ-like resurrection:

> The wecht o' my body,
> The wecht o' my soul,
> Like the stane frae the mooth
> O' the sepulchre roll.   (64)

'Bombinations of a Chimaera' is a metrical exercise rather than a poem, and its inclusion in the book may have been in the mind of the reviewer who wrote, in the *Times Literary Supplement*, that MacDiarmid was occasionally guilty of 'that over-emphasis which has been the bane of Scottish literature from the first'.[34]

The same reviewer suggested that 'the new volume contains nothing quite so good as the best things in *Sangschaw*'.[35] Excepting 'Gairmscoile' and 'Empty Vessel' from the observation, that is fair comment. 'Empty Vessel' is one of MacDiarmid's most intricate lyrics, a poem that spans the centuries by interpreting a Scottish folk-song in the light of modern scientific supposition. As George Bruce discovered, 'Empty Vessel' derives from a song in David Herd's *Ancient and Modern Scottish Songs* (1776). The second stanza of 'Jenny Nettles' reads;

> I met ayont the cairnie
> Jenny Nettles. Jenny Nettles
> Singing til her bairnie
> Robin Rattles bastard
> To flee the dool upon the stool
> And ilka ane that mocks her

> She round about seeks Robin out
> To stap it in his oxter.[36]

Following the precedent of Burns, who fashioned some of his finest songs from extant folk materials, MacDiarmid creates his lyric from lines in 'Jenny Nettles':

> I met ayont the cairney
> A lass wi' tousie hair
> Singin' till a bairnie
> That was nae langer there.
>
> Wunds wi' warlds to swing
> Dinna sing sae sweet,
> The licht that bends owre a' thing
> Is less ta'en up wi't.   (66)

This folk-song is an anecdote founded on fact; to avoid the ignominy of sitting on the stool of repentance in kirk, Jenny finds the child's father. (In the folk-tale that inspired the song Jenny kills herself and is buried beneath a cairn of stones.) MacDiarmid's lyric offers no comfort but invites a conclusion through counterpoint: by implication the dead child has more meaning than a Godforsaken planet. The woman sings to her creation whereas the earth is bathed in a divine light that is indifferent to the objects it illuminates. Moreover, as George Bruce convincingly argues, MacDiarmid alludes to the theory of relativity in the line 'The licht that bends owre a' thing'.

MacDiarmid was certainly familiar with Einstein's Special and General theories of relativity (published in 1905 and 1916 respectively). The *New Age* had featured, in 1919-20, a series of articles on relativity by R. H. Western. In the Special Theory of Relativity Einstein insisted that nothing travels faster than light; reviewing Edwin Muir's *Latitudes*, in the *New Age*, MacDiarmid suggested that literary criticism would always try 'to reach a velocity just beyond that of light'.[37] In the General Theory of Relativity, Einstein established that space-time is curved and that its curvature increases wherever an object having mass is present. 'The licht that bends owre a' thing' is thus a pun that links the biblical myth of creation — 'lights in the firmament of the heaven to give light upon the earth' (Genesis 1:15) — with Einsteinian astrophysics. To accommodate Einstein (who is mentioned by name in *A Drunk Man*

Looks at the Thistle) in Scots shows how inventively MacDiarmid had revitalised the language.

An integral part of 'Empty Vessel', the scientific allusion is cunningly concealed in the folksy texture of the lyric which thus operates on two levels. Inevitably, MacDiarmid was not always so triumphant; in 'Servant Girl's Bed' the extravagant shaping idea is absent and the poet simply states the presence of 'the bonny lowe/O' Eternity' (65). That flame is less intense than the licht in 'Empty Vessel'. With his literary facility MacDiarmid could now turn out Scots lyrics with speed and confidence and some of the examples in *Penny Wheep* have the polish of a well-practised performance without the intellectual agitation that informs the poet's most distinctive work.

MacDiarmid had evolved his own formula for the lyric, moving abruptly from a concrete situation to a philosophical or theological conjecture. There were times when he felt the lyrics were 'a trick'[38] he had perfected. By the time *Penny Wheep* was published he was becoming weary of the trick. Though he said in 'To One Who Urges More Ambitious Flights': 'Wee bit sangs are a' I need' (57), that poem was written more than three years before the publication of *Penny Wheep* as it was printed in the *Scottish Chapbook* of December 1922. To a poet who loved to rise to a challenge the wee bit sang had lost some of its charm for him. Moreover, the one who urged more ambitious flights was himself: or the enlarged self that would speak in *A Drunk Man Looks at the Thistle.*

Some of the wee bit sangs were produced for light relief. 'Hungry Waters', written for William Burt's son Billy, has a child-like innocence as it pictures the old men of the sea, with seaweed for hair, devouring the Scottish coastline. 'The Bubblyjock', the second of two songs for the poet's daughter Christine, shows MacDiarmid's fondness for fantastic similes: the turkey of the title is 'hauf like a bird and hauf like a bogle', it 'twists its neck like a serpent' (71). Its final metamorphosis is attributed to its appetite

> For the bubblyjock swallowed the bagpipes
> And the blether stuck in its throat.　　(71)

Several of the poems display a sense of humour that alternates between the sexual and the morbid. 'Wheesht, Wheesht' warns against post-coital conversation; 'Feery-o'-the-Feet' tells of the danger resurrection has for the man who sleeps with a lusty widow; 'Focherty' is the song of a cuckold who hopes to get revenge in heaven when his rival is called to account by God; 'In Mysie's Bed' makes a black ram the sexual standard for Mysie's husband. In these poems MacDiarmid's tone is not erotic but earthy; the sex he celebrates is in the body, not in the mind (as with D. H. Lawrence).

Three of the poems ('Under the Greenwood Tree', 'The Three Fishes', 'The Robber') purport to be translations from the Cretan; one ('On the Threshold') from the French of Gustave Kahn. 'The Dead Liebknecht' transmutes into Scots an English translation (from Deutsch and Yarmolinsky's *Contemporary German Poetry*) of Rudolf Leonhardt's poem about the Marxist martyr, killed with Rosa Luxemburg in 1919. A closing couplet is both menacing and macabre, using the Gothic shock-tactic MacDiarmid (like Gregory Smith) prized in Scots literature:

> And wi' his white teeth shinin' yet
> The corpse lies smilin' underfit.   (57)

Other Scots poems express familiarity with God ('Supper to God'), offer idiosyncratic aperçus ('Parley of Beasts' shifts from the paired animals of Noah's Ark to the duality of modern man), amount to verbal snapshots of rural characters ('Jimsy: an Idiot', 'The Fairmer's Lass').

Penny Wheep closes with three poems in English. 'Your Immortal Memory, Burns!', the final poem, was originally attributed to A. K. Laidlaw when it appeared in the *Scottish Chapbook* of January 1923. As Laidlaw, Grieve and MacDiarmid the poet had been moved to indignation over the annual antics of boozy Burnsians, feeling that such lip- and belly-service made a mockery of Burns's genuine achievements. Debunking the Burns Cultists became a pastime of his. In 'Your Immortal Memory, Burns!' he tells his predecessor:

> Other cults die:
> But who'll deny
> That you your mob in thrall
> Will keep, O Poet Intestinal?   (77)

The satire is mild in comparison to the bitter words on the same subject in *A Drunk Man Looks at the Thistle*. But then the Drunk Man is meant to be greater than Burns – 'A greater Christ, a greater Burns' (86) – as well as larger than life as understood in Scotland.

8

Sic a Nicht

O I ha'e Silence left,

           – 'And weel ye micht,'
Sae Jean'll say, 'efter sic a nicht!'
A Drunk Man Looks at the Thistle   (167)

SINCE a great deal of confusion has arisen as to the genesis and
growth of MacDiarmid's masterpiece, *A Drunk Man Looks at the
Thistle*, it is essential to establish the facts at the outset. A year in the
making, the poem comprises 2685 lines and represents the poet's most
sustained creative endeavour. Without any doubt F.G. Scott provided
MacDiarmid with the seed he so assiduously cultivated then helped him
to cut back the growth when that seemed to threaten the main structure
for the poet 'got to the point when I ... ceased to be able to see the
forest for the trees'.[1]

MacDiarmid never had any hesitation about acknowledging Scott's
contribution to the poem. In his Author's Note to the first edition,
published on 22 November 1926, he wrote:

> This gallimaufry is dedicated to my friend, Francis George Scott, the
> composer, who suggested it and to whom, during the course of writing it,
> I have been further greatly indebted for co-operative suggestions and for

some of the most penetrating and comprehensive of modern European criticism.[2]

Interviewed some three years before his death, MacDiarmid clarified Scott's role:

> My friend the Scottish composer Francis George Scott said to me casually one day, when we were talking about poetry, 'write a poem about a drunk man looking at the thistle,' and the idea stuck in my head. And I realised that he'd presented me with a viable idea. The thistle wasn't only the symbol of Scottish nationality, but it was also a symbol of the miseries and grandeurs of the human fate in general. And I realised very quickly that it was capable of all sorts of applications and extensions so I was presented with the theme for a very long poem and a complicated poem which suited me perfectly. If somebody like F.G. Scott would suddenly say to me again something similar that gave me another objective symbol that I could use in the same way then I would write another long poem in Scots, but I've been unable personally to think of a suitable theme of that kind.[3]

Having supplied the idea of the poem Scott did for *A Drunk Man Looks at the Thistle*, according to MacDiarmid, what Pound did for Eliot's *The Waste Land* – he jettisoned the inessentials.

Scott's account, in his Autobiographical Letter of 20 May 1945 to Maurice Lindsay, gives a location for the origin of the poem. Scott recalled he 'outlined the plan and supplied the title of the poem during a rainy hike and a night in Glen Clovis [*sic*] Hotel.'[4] The hotel, in Glen Clova, was the Ogilvie Arms which had been residential since 1908. To distinguish it from another Ogilvie Arms, in Kirriemuir, it was regularly referred to as the Clova Hotel (the title it officially adopted in the 1980s). As the crow flies, Clova, on the river South Esk, is almost thirty miles inland from Montrose but the average walker would take two days to cover that distance through the undulating Angus glens. Scott was very fit, used to walking long distances. MacDiarmid, used to cycling daily around Montrose, considered himself a 'great walker' to whom thirty miles over hilly terrain was all in a day's walk; in one list of his hobbies, indeed, he included long-distance running.[5] If Scott and MacDiarmid had reached Clova after one 'rainy hike' from Montrose it would have been an epic performance, a fine physical prelude to the poem that came out of the journey.

More realistically, the two friends must have gone by branch railway lines from Montrose to Brechin, then Forfar, then Kirriemuir (J.M. Barrie's

Thrums) before hiking thirteen miles north to Clova. Both men were in optimistic mood. In 1925 Scott, after years of schoolteaching, had been appointed Lecturer in Music at Glasgow's Jordanhill Training College for Teachers. During his summer holiday, in July (the Grieves stayed at Gibson Place, Roadside, St Cyrus that August), Scott came to see MacDiarmid who had, by then, returned the proofs of *Sangschaw* to Blackwood's. Scott and MacDiarmid were buoyant: the composer because, at last, 'he was now earning his living out of music, even if not by composing'[6]; the poet because he was assured of shortly seeing a volume of his Scots verse in print. Scott and MacDiarmid wanted to consolidate the achievements of the Scottish Renaissance so Scott's suggestion for a major poem came at exactly the right time for MacDiarmid who needed a big theme to consume all his poetic energy.

On 12 February 1926 MacDiarmid told Blackwood's that his long poem, *A Drunk Man Looks at the Thistle*, stood at more than six hundred lines. The following day, a Saturday, the *Glasgow Herald* (where William Power, the paper's literary editor, pursued a pro-MacDiarmid policy) carried a column, headed 'Braid Scots in Verse', introducing six poems from 'a gallimaufry in Braid Scots, entitled *A Drunk Man Looks at the Thistle*'.[7] An introductory paragraph, undoubtedly written by Mac-Diarmid, emphasised the thematic unity of the work:

> It is a complete poem, in over 600 lines, deriving its unity from its pre-occupation with the distinctive elements in Scottish psychology which depend for their effective expression upon the hitherto unrealised pot-entialities of Braid Scots; but it is divided into various sections, affording scope for a great variety of forms, including lyrics, nonsense verse, verse libre, and translations from modern Russian, German, and French poems. The intention here has been to show that Braid Scots is adaptable to all kinds of poetry, and to a much greater variety of measures than might be supposed from the restricted practice of the last hundred years.[8]

The six poems were titled 'Hurricane', four quatrains beginning 'The wan leafs shak' atour us like the snaw' (151) in the printed text; 'Dénouement', two quatrains beginning 'Is it the munelicht or a leprosy' (94); 'Beyond Life and Death', two quatrains beginning 'My harns are seaweed – when the tide is in' (95); 'The Better Part', four quatrains beginning 'And O! to think there are members o'' (95); 'The Thistle', eight lines beginning 'Rootit on gressless peaks, whaur its erect' (92); and 'The Skeleton in the Cupboard', two quatrains beginning 'Time like a bien wife' (155).

In these poems MacDiarmid addressed Dostoevsky, catalogued hallucinations, compared his thought to the movement of moonlight, contrasted the wanderings of the Drunk Man with the odyssey of Ulysses, translated Ramaekers, and picked the skeletal bones of Truth. The fundamental plan of the poem was fixed in his imagination though his method of working gave the impression of chaos. MacDiarmid wrote on whatever bit of paper came to hand: Albert Mackie saw a poem 'scribbled on pieces of cardboard from cigarette packets'[9]; on another occasion he wrote a lyric on toilet paper.[10] Describing the text of *A Drunk Man* to Pittendrigh Macgillivray, the poet said 'until the very last moment it was a hopeless jumble of scraps of scribbled and cross-scribbled MSS'.[11]

Working in this way, MacDiarmid was possessed by the spirit of the poem, uplifted by a theme he defined as 'a beautiful soul in the making'.[12] On 22 March he told Neil Gunn that his Drunk Man was expanding – 'I fixed him up with the publishers at 600 lines but now he's over 800.'[13] Less than a month after, on 13 April, he informed J.K. Annand, editor of the *Broughton Magazine*, that the poem 'now stands upwards of 1200 lines'.[14] It was apparent to the poet that the theme was wonderfully flexible and that the Drunk Man could contain multitudes. What had started as a stream of poems now swelled into an ocean and MacDiarmid realised his poem had to be big enough to contain that ocean: 'I was never ane that thocht to pit/An ocean in a mutchkin' (87). The subject of the poem, at its simplest, was self-expansion so the form had to be large enough to deal with that assumption.

As the Drunk Man is an imaginative projection of the poet, MacDiarmid felt that everything that occurred to him had a claim on his creative attention. For nine days in May, Britain was politically shaken by the General Strike. On 4 May, responding to the call of the General Council of the Trades Union Congress, around a million and a half workers (including transport workers and printers of books and newspapers) joined the million miners already on strike. Soon there were signs that some members of the General Council – particularly J.H. Thomas, MP, a member of Ramsay Macdonald's Labour Government of 1924 – were as alarmed as the Prime Minister, Stanley Baldwin, at the prospect of revolutionary action. A deputation, including Thomas, went to see Baldwin at 10 Downing Street on 12 May and agreed to end the strike on terms humiliating to the workers.

MacDiarmid was shattered by the outcome of the nine-day strike. He explained in an interview of 1977:

I was a magistrate [Justice of the Peace] then, and I took an active part in the General Strike. We had the whole area, Angus, Forfarshire, we had it sewn up. I was speaking when the news came through of J. H. Thomas's betrayal of the strike. I was speaking to an audience mainly of railwaymen [Thomas had been a leader of the railwaymen], and they all broke down weeping. It was one of the most moving experiences I ever had – middle-aged men, most of them, weeping like children, you know. It was such a disappointment, because we knew, we knew we had it.[15]

In another recollection of that meeting, the poet told how his audience 'burst into tears – and I am not ashamed to say I did too'.[16] On 25 May he wrote to Annand, explaining that he had incorporated into *A Drunk Man* his long Ballad of the General Strike 'which I think will rank as one of the most passionate cris-de-coeur in contemporary literature'.[17]

The ballad comprises twenty-five quatrains beginning 'I saw a rose come loupin' oot/Frae a camsteerie plant' (119). In the printed text it comes just before the central section of the poem. MacDiarmid was now pressing on to a resolution of his enormous project. On 19 May the *Glasgow Herald* had published 'The Hanging Judge', four six-line stanzas beginning 'Grugous thistle, to my een' (156); on 2 June he sent 'a poem just written'[18] to Annand for the *Broughton Magazine* (it arrived too late for inclusion in the magazine). It was 'Yet Ha'e I silence Left' and is, minus the closing couplet – 'And weel ye micht,'/Sae Jean'll say, 'efter sic a nicht!' (167) – the conclusion of the published book.

Sometime in July, that is a year to the month after Scott had proposed the project, MacDiarmid wrote to the composer asking him to come to Montrose to help shape the parts of the poem into a whole. Not surprisingly, MacDiarmid was exhausted by his efforts, needful of the advice of a man he trusted. Scott responded to the call and his version of what followed is best described as melodramatic:

Christopher usually wrote his poetry in snatches: he never had any sense of form and after some months of scribbling on the back of envelopes and odd bits of paper, he sent to Glasgow an urgent call for me to come for a weekend and see the litter (and mess!) he'd been making of my bright idea, as Blackwood's were asking for the MS and there *was* no MS. It was late at night when I reached Montrose and after his wife and youngsters went off to bed, we sat down to a table, a great heap of scribbled bits of paper and a bottle of whisky. I can still see Christopher's face when I was indicating the shape the poem, or for that matter a musical composition, ought to take – he was literally flabbergasted either by the extent of my knowledge or by the whisky — it's anybody's guess! We spent until day-break sorting out the items worth keeping, Christopher arranging them on the table like a pack of cards in the order that I indicated as likely to give the best sequences, climaxes, etc. My plans necessitated a pianissimo close, after so much bustle ('the Stars like thistle's Roses flower') to be followed by ('Yet ha'e I silence left, the croon o' a') and I'm pretty certain I supplied the last two lines to bring the thing to some kind of conclusion.[19]

It is an excellent anecdote, but misleading as a result of obvious errors. First, there certainly was a manuscript of *A Drunk Man* but not a fair copy of the complete text. Second, the poet had only one youngster in 1926 so Scott's plural 'youngsters' shows his memory could, almost twenty years after the event, fail him. The most bizarre consequence of the story is the impression given that the poetic structure, like the protagonist, came under the influence of alcohol: Scott suggests that the poem was arranged by two Drunk Men shuffling bits and pieces 'like a pack of cards'.

The more Scott told the story the more pronounced was the emphasis on his intervention. William Johnstone, the Scottish painter, was a cousin of Scott who supplied him with a geographical variation on the basic theme:

Francis told me that Christopher arrived one evening at Jordanhill with a collection of poems written on the backs of envelopes, odd scraps of paper and reporter's notebooks. Francis placed a bottle of whisky on the table between them and they spread out *Drunk Man*. Taking drams from the bottle, Christopher soon fell asleep on the sofa, not stirring until the morning when Mrs Scott brought in tea, but Francis worked all night, and was still hard at work in the morning. The bottle was empty but Christopher's fragments had been edited and placed in order. The poem needed a conclusion, but they were stuck and Francis in the end wrote the final lines.[20]

Yet another version of the tale is told by a man who met Scott in Glasgow in the 1950s:

Francis George Scott ... described how he and Chris assembled the sequence of *Drunk Man*, arranging the organization of poems while both were merrily drinking, working throughout the night, so as to meet a deadline. Scott felt he was largely responsible for the organization but said both were just about drunk, so much was left to chance or happy inspiration.[21]

185

The anecdotal evidence does less than justice to a poem widely accepted as one of the greatest achievements of Scottish literature; indeed, the internal textual evidence tells a different story for *A Drunk Man* is not an arbitrary assemblage but a work with a definite shape and structure.

Scott's visit was not the end of the matter for after that exploratory night MacDiarmid worked on the poem for another month. Writing to Ogilvie, on 6 August, MacDiarmid explained what had happened when Scott came to Montrose. He also expressed his faith in the poem:

> I've let myself go in it for all I'm worth. My friend Scott (the composer) and I afterwards went over the whole thing with a small toothcomb. But we both felt that the section I've been rewriting – which comes about midway in the book and should represent the high-water mark, the peaks of highest intensity, could be improved by being recast and projected on to a different altitude of poetry altogether – made, instead of a succession of merely verbal and pictorial verses, into a series of metaphysical pictures with a definite progression, a cumulative effect – and that is what I've been so busy with. It's infernally intractable material: but I've spared no pains and put my uttermost ounce into the business. I'm out to make or break in this matter ... It's the thing as a whole I'm mainly concerned with, and if, as such, it does not take its place as a masterpiece – sui generis – one of the biggest things in the range of Scottish Literature, I shall have failed. Whole sections of it do go with a tremendous gusto and with a sweep over a tremendous range: but there are still a few movements that want suppleing and accelerating and bringing into harmony with the others in this way or that.[22]

That letter was written from Avondale, St Cyrus, where MacDiarmid was ensconced for most of August, putting finishing touches to *A Drunk Man*. By 13 August he was still not satisfied with the manuscript and planned to spend 'an intensive fortnight on it'[23] while his wife and daughter, accompanied by Peggy's sister Ina, took two weeks' holiday in Selkirk and East Lothian. On 28 August MacDiarmid sent Blackwood's the finished manuscript of *A Drunk Man Looks at the Thistle*.

Pittendrigh Macgillivray had offered to read the poem in proof, a gesture MacDiarmid warmly appreciated. To expedite publication of the poem, Blackwood's sent the poet proofs in instalments, as soon as the printer had set long sections. MacDiarmid sent Macgillivray a first batch of proofs on 23 September and soon realised that the sculptor intended to do more than merely scan the text for literals. Macgillivray tried to persuade MacDiarmid to change the title of the poem to *In Vino Veritas* and suggested that several passages should be deleted. He took exception to the racist tone of the reference to 'some wizened scrunt o' a knock-knee/Chinee' (84) and convinced MacDiarmid that at least two words should be changed. On Macgillivray's advice, MacDiarmid substituted 'bauld' for 'blate' in the line 'And I'm no juist as bauld as aince I wes' (83); and 'thingum' for 'mummy' in 'Am I a thingum mebbe that is kept/Preserved in spirits in a muckle bottle' (92).

On edge after all his efforts, MacDiarmid could react sharply to Macgillivray's critical tone. Defending his poem, in a letter of 6 October, he quoted the judgement of a friend on the complete poem:

> You have completed in my opinion the greatest poem ever produced by a Scotsman. I am not excepting Burns whose work in comparison with yours gives one a sense of restriction (and consequently power) that is bound eventually to become less and less congenial as man develops consciousness and intelligence. I'm perfectly satisfied with the architecture of the boat. I've had doubts at times about certain passages, but I can't now find a word to say against them. *I* mightn't have included them but then I'm not *you* and it's exactly for this reason, that the whole thing bodies forth the living image of C.M.G., that I have come to see it as the masterpiece it is, for what man in ten generations succeeds in getting outside his own skin. Now I feel that you have in this poem. You have limned yourself – the Scottish terrier in excelsis! The features will become more and more clear to the generations yet to come.[24]

The friend can only be F. G. Scott who was kept informed as to the progress of the poem; in his acknowledgements MacDiarmid cites Macgillivray and his wife Peggy as the only others fully familiar with the poem prior to publication.

MacDiarmid sent the corrected proofs of *A Drunk Man* to Blackwood's on 1 October. He explained to his publisher that his address, from Friday, 8 October, to the following Monday would be c/o Scott, 103 Woodville Gardens, Langside, Glasgow. Blackwood's sent the poet two sets of revise proofs on 19 October and one of these went to Macgillivray. By 1 November, MacDiarmid admitted to Macgillivray he was nervous about the fate of the poem but sure that its form was justified as it allowed him to 'experiment with the artistic expression of every different attitude ... I can conceive'.[25] MacDiarmid knew that though the Drunk Man was (initially, at least) intoxicated, the *Drunk Man* was a series of sober reflections. He used drunkenness – complete with touches of delirium tremens in lines such as 'My face has flown open like a lid' (95) or 'the worms'll breed in my corpse until/It's like a rice-puddin'' (111) — as a method encouraging contradictions since insobriety is popularly associated with inconsistency. (In practice, Mac-Diarmid's contradictions are capable of resolution.) The care he took over the composition of the poem deserves a reassessment that rejects any preconception that it was hastily flung together in one drunken night. The night that matters is the creative night of the Drunk Man, not the anecdotal night of two drunk friends.

The intellectual intricacy of *A Drunk Man Looks at the Thistle* is supported by a plausible scenario. A 'village drunk' (97) — obviously auto-biographical since he is a native of Langholm, has 'Sodgered 'neth the Grecian sky/And in Italy and Marseilles' (159), is resident in Montrose — discovers the depths of his soul when, transported by alcohol, he faces up to his personal nightmares and considers the dreams that have haunted his country. After drinking in a bar with two uncultured cronies he staggers homewards and collapses on a hillside; by the light of the full moon he sees a thistle which startles him by its symbolism. Erect, it is a reminder of his sexual self; indistinct, it is 'A symbol o' the puzzle o' man's soul' (147); immense, it is Ygdrasil, 'The tree that fills the universe' (126). As the alcoholic spirit passes out of his system, the Drunk Man is uplifted by a genuine spirituality and ends his immense monologue with an invocation to Silence.

Traditionally, the thistle is a Scottish emblem of inviolability associated with the motto *Nemo me impune lacessit* (No one provokes me with impunity, or Wha daur meddle wi' me). The Drunk Man, made reckless with the Scotch courage of whisky, is determined to grasp the thistle and risk the consequences. His intense examination of Scotland is a personal trial that leads to a transformation. As others see him, the Drunk Man is no more than 'a figure in a scene/O' Scottish life A.D. one-nine-two-five' (92). He begins, indeed, like a stereotypical Scot with a catalogue of complaints: he is getting too old for epic drinking sessions 'And I'm no' juist as bauld as aince I wes' (83); he is shaken by the deterioration of Scotch whisky 'And as the worth's gane doun the cost has risen' (83).

On one level the Drunk Man is presented as a real character, the sum of various prejudices. He uses the conversational shorthand of the garrulous bar regular, 'And ten to wan the piper is a Cockney' (84); he makes caustic comments about foreigners, for example 'some wizened scrunt o' a knock-knee/Chinee' (84); he disparages himself in such phrases as 'thieveless cronies sic as me' (85). That such a character can overcome his physical, psychological and geographical handicaps is the argument of the poem. Like his creator, the Drunk Man is steeped in a 'strong solution of books'[26] as well as a strong solution of whisky. He borrows a phrase – 'shook foil' (123) – from Hopkins, quotes Melville and parodies T. S. Eliot; he mentions Schoenberg as well as F.G. Scott; he makes a comical rhyme from Spengler's name, pairing him with the circus-owner Hengler; he drops the names of Freud and Einstein. Despite his irreverent attitude to everyday life, he reveres the Word. His cross is the burden of a defeatist Scotland but his salvation comes through culture.

At the outset of the poem, then, it is apparent that the Drunk Man has a purpose. The amoralist is intent on the moral that no individual need be limited by his birth. A child born humbly in Nazareth can become a saviour; therefore, by implication, a Scot born in a Border town can attempt the miracle of becoming 'A greater Christ, a greater Burns' (86). The Drunk Man is a Scot with a soul – a spirit greater than alcoholic spirit – and the recognition of this distances him from his fellow Scots who are dismissed as 'the feck' (85), 'the lave' (87), 'maist folk' (87), 'the vast majority o' men' (87), those Nietzsche despised as the rabble. To further differentiate between himself and the feck, the Drunk Man knocks down the Burnsian icon worshipped mindlessly by drunken Scots. He appreciates Burns, recognises him as a soulmate, and directs his attack against sentimental Scots who, lacking a real interest in poetry, turn up at Burns Suppers to take the poet's name in vain. These disciples of Burns are 'nocht but zoologically men' (85), incapable of attempting to rise to the stature of Burns. They resemble those who religiously attend churches without considering the meaning of Christ's self-sacrifice:

> As Kirks wi' Christianity ha'e dune,
> Burns Clubs wi' Burns – wi' a'thing it's the same,
> The core o' ocht is only for the few,
> Scorned by the mony, thrang wi'ts empty name.
>
> And a' the names in History mean nocht
> To maist folk but 'ideas o' their ain',
> The vera opposite o' onything
> The Deid 'ud awn gin they cam' back again.
>
> A greater Christ, a greater Burns, may come,
> The maist they'll dae is to gi'e bigger pegs
> To folly and conceit to hank their rubbish on.
> They'll cheenge folks' talk but no' their natures, fegs!   (86)

The Drunk Man is serious in his statement about the coming of 'A greater Christ, a greater Burns'; he is, however, ironic in suggesting that human nature cannot be changed since this possibility is demonstrated by the poem.

By collapsing in his cups, the Drunk Man is under the influence of alcohol. By rising 'To heichts whereo' the fules ha'e never recked' (83) he is under the influence of great cultural figures. His evolutionary ideal of self-improvement acknowledges the achievements of his predecessors. The Drunk Man's monologue synthesises the ideas he has encountered in books; his contradictions accumulate creatively as he applies the dialectic to dialect. Ostentatiously allusive, the poem draws attention to its artistic precedents.

Though the Burns Cult is scathingly satirised in *A Drunk Man*, one of the strongest influences on it is Burns's 'Tam o' Shanter'. In Burns's poem, the hero gets drunk with his crony Souter Johnie and the landlady; the Drunk Man gets similarly inebriated with his friends Cruivie and Gilsanquhar. Tam has to win home to his wife Kate, the Drunk Man has to win home to his wife Jean (the Christian name of the woman Burns married in 1788). Kate is a 'sulky sullen dame',[27] Jean 'maun natter, natter, natter' (88). On his way home, Tam has a hallucinatory encounter with the witch he calls Cutty-sark; the Drunk Man encounters woman in a bewitchingly visionary form. The poetic parallels are forced so that the reader will compare the voyage of the Drunk Man to the drunken ride of Tam o' Shanter:

> 'Noo Cutty Sark's tint that ana',
> And dances in her skin – Ha! Ha!
>
> I canna ride awa' like Tam,
> But e'en maun bide juist whaur I am.'   (109)

Other major indigenous influences come from Dunbar and the traditional ballads. MacDiarmid specifically says 'I widna gi'e five meenits wi' Dunbar/For a' the millions o' ye as ye are' (107) and works in ballad references to 'the horns o' Elfland' (89) and 'the unkent grave' (115). In Dunbar's 'Dance of the Sevin Deidly Synnis' there is a formidable catalogue of complaint and in another dream-allegory, 'The Goldyn Targe', the catalogue gives way to a vision of Beauty. MacDiarmid uses the dream device as well as alcoholic nightmare; he too has a catalogue of complaints before a vision of beauty. Stylistically, MacDiarmid eschews the aureate diction of Dunbar, preferring the earthy rhythms of the ballad. Most of *A Drunk Man* is cast in the ballad stanza, rhyming *abcb*, the form of 'Johnnie Armstrong' and other ballads of the Scottish Borders. MacDiarmid readily accepted that the poem was primarily composed as a gigantic ballad:

> Largely, the engine that motivates the whole poem and keeps it going is the ballad measure, of course. It varies — there's a lot of variation of metre and so on in the *Drunk Man* but underlying all the variations there's that continuing ballad metre. It comes back to the ballad all the time.[28]

In common with other writers of long poems, MacDiarmid owes a debt to Dante. As MacDiarmid knew, to his delight, Dante had chosen to write his masterpiece in the vernacular rather than in Latin and so exalted the language of the Italian people. Discussing Dante's poetry and the theories he expressed in *De Vulgari Eloquentia*, MacDiarmid observed:

> Dante's conclusion was that the corruption common to all the dialects made it impossible to select one rather than another as an adequate literary form, and that he who would write in the vulgar must assemble the purest elements from each dialect and construct a synthetic language that would at least possess more than a circumscribed local interest; which is precisely what he did.[29]

This was precisely what MacDiarmid attempted in his Synthetic Scots. The Drunk Man quotes from Dante's *Paradiso* and has similarities to the protagonist in the *Commedia*. Dante is thirty-five as his poem opens; MacDiarmid was thirty-four when *A Drunk Man* was published, so almost midway through his biblical journey of seventy years. Dante finds himself in a dark wood, confused as to how he came there, the Drunk Man has similarly strayed though in his case the confusion is confounded by alcohol:

> But that's aside the point! I've got fair waun'ert.
> It's no that I'm sae fou' as just deid dune,
> And dinna ken as muckle's whaur I am
> Or hoo I've come to sprawl here 'neth the mune.   (86)

Though the moon is full he is intensely aware of the darkness — a key concept in the poem — as he sprawls on his Scottish hillside in a dense growth of thistles and bracken. Dante sees a beautiful Lady (Beatrice), the Drunk Man sees Jean transfigured into a divine lady. Though it has been pointed out that MacDiarmid's opening quatrain contains an allusion to Burns's song 'Willie Brewed', which contains the line 'We are na fou', we're no that fou',[30] its sheer weight of utterance has a Dantean gravity. Compare the syllabic movement of the celebrated first line of the *Commedia* ('Nel mezzo del cammin di nostra vita') with 'I amna fou' sae muckle as tired – deid dune' (83).

Not all the influences are as obvious as those of Burns, Dunbar and Dante. When he was composing his poem, MacDiarmid was in close contact with F. G. Scott who, like his friend Saurat, greatly admired the poetry of Valéry. MacDiarmid would certainly have discussed the poetic masterpiece of a poet he described as 'the greatest influence on my ideas about poetry'.[31] Valéry's *La Jeune Parque* appeared in 1917 and was internationally acclaimed as a masterpiece (by, for example, John Middleton Murry in the *Times Literary Supplement*, 23 Aug. 1917). Four years in the writing, *La Jeune Parque* (The Young Fate) is a 512-line poem of self-discovery: the Young Fate emerges from sleep and becomes increasingly aware of her sensual and spiritual self. Valéry described the theme of the poem as 'the *transformation of a consciousness* in the course of one night'.[32] While staying at Marseilles in 1919, MacDiarmid had become aware of Valéry's reputation so he was well placed to study the poem.

Valéry's poem is occasionally echoed in *A Drunk Man*: the Young Fate broods on the spiritual depths of darkness, notes the serpentine coils of desire, offers a dialect of duality, visualises a tree in space. Valéry's Young Fate observes the tree as a source of spiritual light and life:

> Même, je m'apparus cet arbre vaporeux,
> De qui la majesté légèrement perdue
> S'abandonne à l'amour de toute l'étendue.
> L'etre immense me gagne, et de mon coeur divin
> L'encens qui brûle expire une forme sans fin...
> Tous les corps radieux tremblent dans mon essence! ...[33]

MacDiarmid describes his tree as a source of eternal light:

> The michty trunk o' Space that spreids
> Ramel o' licht that ha'e nae end,
> – The trunk wi' centuries for rings,
> Comets for fruit, November shoo'ers
> For leafs that in its Autumns fa'   (130)

Valéry is not mentioned by name in *A Drunk Man* but MacDiarmid quotes Valéry's hero Mallarmé.

Six poems by European authors are incorporated into *A Drunk Man*. From Deutsch and Yarmolinsky's *Modern Russian Poetry* MacDiarmid adapted two poems by Alexander Blok: 'The Lady Unknown' becomes the section beginning *'At darknin' hings abune the howff'* (88-9), 'The Unknown Woman' the section beginning *'I ha'e forekent ye! O I ha'e forekent'* (90). These adaptations are cleverly integrated into the plan of the poem. Blok's 'The Lady Unknown', more frequently translated into English as 'The Stranger', allows the Drunk Man to introduce the figure of a mysterious lady who is an idealised form of his wife. Written in the spring of 1906, Blok's poem describes a visit to a dive where the narrator drinks wine and seems to see in his beaker the reflection of a friend. Each evening he waits for the mysterious stranger to appear, weave her way among the drunkards, and sit alone by the window. Blok's vision blends the mystical figure of Soloviev's Sophia with the form of Lyuba, the woman he married in 1903. MacDiarmid's ability to apply, to his poem, this fusion of the fanciful and the familiar shows an intuitive understanding of a major Russian writer.

An authority on Blok has written that though the fascination of 'The Stranger' is impossible to convey in translation, the 'best approximation ... is Hugh MacDiarmid's adaptation in *A Drunk Man Looks at the Thistle* [though] this has more to do with MacDiarmid than with Alexander Blok'.[34] As reworked in Scots by MacDiarmid, the poem is an example of how a drunk man can see through the surface of reality. Whether or not the mysterious lady exists for others, she is central to his situation. As translated by Deutsch and Yarmolinsky, the second and third quatrains of Blok's poem present an almost elegant decadence:

Far off, above the alley's mustiness,
Where bored gray summerhouses lie,
The baker's sign swings gold through dustiness,
And loud and shrill the children cry.

Beyond the city stroll the exquisites,
At every dusk and all the same:
Their derbies tilted back, the pretty wits
Are playing at the ancient game.[35]

MacDiarmid alters the social emphasis, stressing the ethos of urban low-life. His Scots overlays an extant translation of Blok with the gritty quality of Robert Fergusson's descriptions of eighteenth-century Edinburgh:

> And heich abune the vennel's pokiness,
> Whaur a' the white-weshed cottons lie,
> The Inn's sign blinters in the mochiness,
> And lood and shrill the bairnies cry.

> The hauflins 'yont the burgh boonds
> Gang ilka nicht, and a' the same,
> Their bonnets cocked; their bluid that stounds
> Is playin' at a fine auld game.   (88)

The most memorable phrases ('blinters in the mochiness', 'bluid that stounds') depart so strikingly from Deutsch and Yarmolinsky that what is erroneously offered as a translation is best regarded as an inventive recreation.

MacDiarmid made two other adaptations from Deutsch and Yarmolinsky: Zinaida Hippius's 'Psyche', from *Modern Russian Poetry*, becomes the section beginning 'A shameless thing, for ilka vileness able' (94); Else Lasker-Schüler's 'Sphynx', from *Contemporary German Poetry*, becomes 'The Mune sits on my bed the nicht unsocht' (95). Two Jethro Bithell anthologies provided further material: George Ramaekers's 'The Thistle', from *Contemporary Belgian Poetry*, is retextured with Scots orthography as '*Rootit on gressless peaks, whaur its erect*' (92); Edmond Rocher's 'Love Them All', cited in the introduction to *Contemporary French Poetry*, emerges as 'A luvin' wumman is a licht' (102). The inclusion of these adaptations enriches the poem, contributes to the allusive mood MacDiarmid needed in order to give his Synthetic Scots a European application. He had told J.K. Annand, while he was working on *A Drunk Man*, that it was a formidable challenge to render European verse in Scots:

> To achieve poetry in any degree at all in Scots is extraordinarily difficult — to translate (i.e. reproduce) foreign poetry in Scots almost impossible. But I hope that to you & others as to me that very difficulty will prove a tyrannical incentive.[36]

Thematically, MacDiarmid's decision to draw, albeit vicariously, on poets foreign to Scots readers is vindicated. The Drunk Man is intended as an international figure.

Not directly used in the book, but contributing to its conclusion, is Fyodor Tyutchev's "Silentium". Twice in his prose MacDiarmid refers to 'Tyutchev's famous masterpiece Silentium' and Tyutchev is cited in *To Circumjack Cencrastus* and *In Memoriam James Joyce*.[37] MacDiarmid's invocation to Silence at the end of *A Drunk Man* was partly suggested by Avrahm Yarmolinsky's translation of 'Silentium' in *Modern Russian Poetry*. The second of three stanzas reads:

> The heart was born dumb; who can sense
> Its tremors, recondite and tense?
> And who can hear its silent cry?
> A thought when spoken is a lie.
> Uncovered springs men will pollute, –
> Drunk hidden waters, and be mute.[38]

MacDiarmid felt a strong affinity with Tyutchev whose verse divides the world between nocturnal chaos and diurnal harmony. Human nature, Tyutchev felt, repeated this division, being torn between dark passion and spiritual light. Searching for a synthesis – a higher unity – requires the individual to explore the dark and aspire to the light. MacDiarmid, who projected himself as 'Preferring darkness rather than light',[39] declares in *A Drunk Man* that 'Darkness comes closer to us than the licht' (148), a line that endorses Tyutchev's advice, in the first stanza of 'Silentium', to accept visions

> Like stars that take night's darkened route.
> Admire and scan them and be mute.[40]

Tyutchev felt regretfully that earthly desires brought darkness and chaos to human nature; MacDiarmid rejoiced that it was so.

The 'translations' of Blok, Ramaekers, Hippius, Lasker-Schüler and Rocher (as well as the use of Tyutchev) establish the Drunk Man's awareness of European poetry. When MacDiarmid admits English-language influences he clarifies his modernist credentials. Admiring the way Joyce structured *Ulysses* on Homeric lines, MacDiarmid draws on Joyce's novel for details of the odyssey of the Drunk Man. The journey of Leopold Bloom unfolds in a single day, the journey of the Drunk Man in a single night (appropriately so since the poet prefers darkness to light). Bloom's wife is the sexually alluring Molly Bloom who affirmatively utters the last words of Joyce's novel. The Drunk Man's Penelope, Jean, is also portrayed as a sexually exciting woman – an earthly embodiment of the eternal feminine – and, like Molly, Jean has the last word.

Eliot's *The Waste Land*, a poetic work comparable as well as contemporaneous with *Ulysses*, is accepted as a study of cultural atrophy and alienation. Pugnaciously, the Drunk Man offers Scotland as the ultimate example of such atrophy and alienation:

> T. S. Eliot – it's a Scottish name –
> Afore he wrote 'The Waste Land' s'ud ha'e come
> To Scotland here. He wad ha'e written
> A better poem syne – like this, by gum!   (94)

Towards the end of *A Drunk Man*, MacDiarmid pays Eliot the compliment of caricature, parodying his 'Sweeney Among the Nightingales': 'Death and the Raven drift above/The graves of Sweeney's body and soul' (150).

Philosophically, MacDiarmid conflates contradictory ideas in *A Drunk Man* as he searches for a creative synthesis. If dialect supplies the tonal texture of the poem, the dialectic justifies its wayward structure, its volatile to-ing and fro-ing. For MacDiarmid, as we have seen, the ability to suggest two, or more, concepts simultaneously was the signature of genius and he admired thinkers who endorsed this ideal of plurality. The act of perception, for practical purposes, enables the individual to escape from the chaos of infinite regression caused by a plethora of possibilities. By isolating one schematic solution – an explanation that excludes alternatives – the individual, in everyday life, clings on to the concept that most satisfyingly interprets the phenomenal world: one is, generally, either a nominalist or a realist; either a believer or an agnostic; either an idealist or a materialist; either a sensualist or an ascetic. The Drunk Man, however, is a universal figure animated by the clash of opposites. In this he follows a familiar path for Plato utilised the Socratic method, Hegel expounded the dialectic, and Oscar Wilde put the matter in an aesthetic context when he insisted that 'A Truth in art is that whose contradictory is also true.'[41]

The Drunk Man's dialectic has a physiological as well as a philosophical basis. 'Drunkenness', MacDiarmid wrote in his Author's Note to the poem, 'has a logic of its own'.[42] The Drunk Man is 'geylies mixed, like Life itsel'' (87). He explains 'I'll ha'e nae hauf-way hoose, but aye be whaur/Extremes meet' (87) then concedes that 'nae doot some foreign philosopher/Has wrocht a system oot to justify/A' this' (87). Hegel is just such a 'foreign philosopher' and the avoidance of a sequential consistency owes much to the Hegelian dialectic, a system with a ready appeal for the poet. According to Hegel the historical consciousness alone appreciates the true nature of reality by understanding it as a process of becoming. Essentially a spiritual phenomenon, reality involves a triadic movement from thesis to antithesis then to a higher synthesis, the whole movement ascending upwards to the Absolute. In terms of the Hegelian dialectic, contradiction is not evidence of incoherence but an example of creative insight. The Drunk Man is able to move towards an encounter with his absolute by accepting the contradictions in himself and his country (the two are interchangeable) as 'the routh/O' contrairies' (119), 'coonter forces' (137), 'My country's contrair qualities' (145).

In Gregory Smith's *Scottish Literature* MacDiarmid had found what he regarded as a quintessentially Scottish application of the dialectic. Smith contended that Scottish culture was distinguished by an antithetical energy, a 'zigzag of contradictions',[43] by what he categorised as the Caledonian Antisyzygy. Smith wrote:

> This mixing of contraries – 'intermingledons', to recall Burns's word – helps to explain the presence of certain qualities which have come to be considered as characteristic of Scottish literature [with its] strange combination of things unlike, of things seen in an everyday world and things which, like the elf-queen herself, neither earth nor heaven will claim ... It takes some people more time than they can spare to see the absolute propriety of a gargoyle's grinning at the elbow of a kneeling saint.[44]

Enthusiastically adopting this view of Scottish literature, MacDiarmid wanted to renew the indigenous tradition by adding to it a long poem exhibiting these very qualities. Hence the creative vigour in MacDiarmid's borrowings from Smith: the stress on Scotland's con-trariness, the ballad-magic of elfland, the direct reference in the phrase 'Grinnin' gargoyle by a saint' (96). In Smith's book MacDiarmid found academic authority for his own zigzag of contradictions; a sound professorial reason for his irrationalism.

Although MacDiarmid's philosopher-friend George Davie has con-tended that 'the "thocht" of the *Drunk Man* is not irrationalist in the technical sense – that is to say, it is not influenced by Shestov'[45] the internal evidence of the poem is against this supposition. MacDiarmid was familiar with Shestov's *All Things Are Possible* as early as 1922, four years before the completion of *A Drunk Man*, and in D. S. Mirsky's *Modern Russian Literature* (1925) found Shestov exalted as 'the greatest of modern Dostoevskeans'[46] – an important classification considering Dostoevsky's role in the poem. Shestov revered Dostoevsky and Nietzsche, two intellectual heroes of the Drunk Man. Shestov expressed a faith in a hypothetical Christian philosophy based on the Bible rather than on the commentaries of theologians; the Drunk Man separates the biblical Christ from the Church. Shestov delighted in the clash of contradictions, as does the Drunk Man. Shestov denied that philosophy should comfort, arguing instead that 'The business of philosophy is to teach man to live in uncertainty ... More briefly, the business of philosophy is not to reassure people, but to upset them.'[47] The Drunk Man says unsettlingly 'Let us enjoy deceit, this instinct in us' (149).

Shestov, who made a cult of chaos and the abyss, argued that 'genius ... is a condition of chaos and unutterable restlessness'.[48] The Drunk Man, anxious to uncover the genius in himself, says 'Genius in mankind like an antrin rose/Abune a jungly waste o' effort grows' (116) and welcomes the need for a man to 'plunge aboot in Chaos ere/He finds his needfu' fittin' there' (145). Shestov praised darkness and suggested 'perhaps the time is near when the impassioned poet, casting a last look to his past, will boldly and gladly cry: *Hide thyself, sun! O darkness, be welcome!*'[49] MacDiarmid responds in *A Drunk Man*:

> 'Let there be Licht,' said God, and there was
> A little: but He lacked the poo'er
> To licht up mair than pairt o' space at aince,
> And there is lots o' darkness that's the same
> As gin He'd never spoken
>   – Mair darkness than there's licht ...
> Darkness comes closer to us than the licht,
> And is oor natural element.   (148)

In a poem that advances by antitheses darkness is naturally contrasted to light but the declared preference for darkness indicates that MacDiarmid's use of chiaroscuro is Shestovian.

Predictably, given MacDiarmid's association with the *New Age*, Nietzschean assumptions permeate the poem. The Drunk Man's contempt for the feck is analogous to Nietzsche's hatred of the rabble, the subject of a forceful section of *Thus Spake Zarathustra*. Nietzsche's theory of eternal recurrence, the notion that every deed enacted by an individual will be endlessly repeated, is a possibility that occasionally alarms the Drunk Man who questions the quality of such deeds: 'Owre and owre, the same auld trick,/Cratur withoot climacteric' (109) he says of the biological ritual of birth. Nietzsche's irrationalism is realised in the Drunk Man's 'divine inebriety' (145) and Nietzsche's ambition to go beyond good and evil into a self-centred morality has a powerful appeal for the Drunk Man: 'It is morality, the knowledge o' Guid and Ill ... That kills a' else wi'in its reach' (91) he affirms, subsequently dismissing 'Guid and Ill that are the same,/Save as the chance licht fa's' (149).

Implicit throughout the poem is a faith in the will to power, interpreted subjectively and patriotically. The poet offers political and personal self-determination as an answer to the enervation caused by 'the Scots aboulia' (93). Of the nation he believes can rise again to greatness, the Drunk Man says 'The thistle rises and forever will' (152); as for himself, 'I in turn 'ud be an action/To pit in a concrete abstraction/My country's contrair qualities,/And mak' a unity o' these' (145). Passivity, in this poem, is held to be synonymous with defeatism.

One of the most explicit points of the poem is the ideal of spiritual enlargement, the transformation of the self into the superman. MacDiarmid had said, in 1923, that the slogan of the Scottish Renaissance 'must be the Nietzschean "become what you are" '.[50] Inside every individual, *A Drunk Man* contends, is a perpetual struggle between the ordinary everyman and the extraordinary superman. It is the responsibility of the creative individual to release the superman in himself. That thought is basic to the poem:

> And let the lesson be – to be yersel's,
> Ye needna fash gin it's to be ocht else.
> To be yersel's – and to mak' that worth bein'.
> Nae harder job to mortals has been gi'en.   (107)

Having thus stated the pursuit of self-improvement (in a Nietzschean, not Smilesean, manner) MacDiarmid repeatedly comes back to it so it will impinge on the reader's consciousness. He encourages all 'to create oorsels/As we can be' (113), regrets that 'ilka man alive is like/A quart that's squeezed into a pint' (122), despairs of limitations that 'winna let me be mysel' ' (126), speaks of 'bein' mysel', whate'er I am' (128), urges the reader 'To be yoursel', whatever that may be' (137). With Nietzsche the Drunk Man believes that the individual is capable of exalting his state of being on to a divine status. If the traditional God is dead, man must surpass himself and become God-like.

The aphorism, quoted in Orage's monograph on Nietzsche, that 'Man is a rope connecting animal and Superman',[51] is endorsed by MacDiarmid. In order to overcome his animal origins, the individual must recognise them as restrictions. The Drunk Man frequently separates the creative impulse from the animal appetite. He observes that 'man's skeleton has left/Its ancient ape-like shape ahint' (131), longs for 'heicher forms' (136), self-consciously looks for evidence of evolutionary improvement:

> And organs may develop syne
> Responsive to the need divine
> O' single-minded humankin'.
>
> The function, as it seems to me,
> O' Poetry is to bring to be
> At lang, lang last that unity. (163)

Poetry, then, offers the creative energy that allows man to overcome himself and attain his divine potential. Much of the tension of *A Drunk Man* derives from the conflict between the physical and the metaphysical aspects of humankind. Thus there are elements of self-hatred, moments of disgust at the animal nature of the sexual act. MacDiarmid's approach to evolution is not Darwinian, not a matter of biological determinism; it is adamantly Nietzschean, a matter of self-determination. One of Orage's perceptive comments on Nietzsche prompted the most frequently quoted quatrain in the poem. Orage wrote: 'In all great natures extremes meet; and readers of Nietzsche must beware of taking his materialism grossly or his metaphysics abstractly.'[52] MacDiarmid, whose poem describes the making of a great nature, writes:

> I'll ha'e nae hauf-way hoose, but aye be whaur
> Extremes meet – it's the only way I ken
> To dodge the curst conceit o' being richt
> That damns the vast majority o' men. (87)

If Nietzsche provides much of the philosophical fuel of *A Drunk Man*, then Dostoevsky functions as a specific artistic saviour, a creative man who has surpassed himself by becoming a cultural superman. Thanks to Constance Garnett's twelve volumes of translations, published from

1912 to 1920, Dostoevsky's work was widely available in Britain. By the time MacDiarmid's poem appeared readers were familiar with Dostoevsky's curious career. Linking 'Omsk and the Calton' (150) the Drunk Man makes a connection between centres of suffering in Russia and Scotland: Omsk is the Siberian penal settlement where Dostoevsky served a four-year sentence of hard labour from 1850 to 1854; Calton Gaol was once (after the old Tolbooth was demolished in 1817) Edinburgh's principal prison. The Drunk Man, conscious of the potential coming of 'A greater Christ, a greater Burns' (86), aspires to the level of Dostoevsky though the sheer scale of the effort occasionally intimidates him. Addressing Dostoevsky, in one of the most persuasive sections of the poem, the Drunk Man asks for 'a share o' your/Appallin' genius' (138) though he measures his own stature to Dostoevsky 'As ant-heap unto mountain' (138).

In 1923 MacDiarmid had claimed that Scots was 'the only language in Western Europe instinct with those uncanny spiritual and pathological perceptions alike which constitute the uniqueness of Dostoevski's work'.[53] Having read Spengler's *The Decline of the West* (*Der Untergang des Abendlandes*) he seized excitedly on the announced emergence of a new order, admiringly summarising Spengler's view of human history as a series of self-contained cultures. Spengler, MacDiarmid noted, asserted that the cultural exhaustion of the Western World pointed to a new beginning initiated by Dostoevsky. MacDiarmid quoted a passage in which Spengler canonised Dostoevsky: 'Dostoevsky is a saint ... The next thousand years belong to the Christianity of Dostoevsky.'[54] The second of Spengler's sentences is duly incorporated into *A Drunk Man* when the protagonist salutes Dostoevsky as a saviour:

> Closer than ony ither Scot,
> Closer to me than my ain thocht,
> Closer than my ain braith to me,
> As close as to the Deity
> Approachable in whom appears
> This Christ o' the neist thoosand years.   (139)

Since, MacDiarmid supposes, English society has exhausted its cultural resources an indigenous Scottish culture can rise to rebirth only by eschewing English and making its renaissance as dynamic as Dostoevsky's art. In Janko Lavrin's *Dostoevsky and His Creation* (1920), originally published in the *New Age*, MacDiarmid found a chapter he could turn to his own ends. Lavrin discusses Dostoevsky's 'Russian Idea' as 'a literary, or rather a religious-philosophical movement, based partly on Hegel, and aiming, above all, at an amalgamation of all creative philosophic, scientific, and social values with a pure Christianity'.[55] Lavrin quotes a passage from Dostoevsky's celebrated speech of 1880 at the unveiling of the Pushkin memorial in Moscow:

> I believe that we shall, without exception, understand that to be a true Russian does indeed mean to aspire finally to reconcile the contradictions of Europe, to show the end of European yearning in our Russian soul, omnihuman and all-uniting, to include within our soul by brotherly love all our brethren, and at last, it may be, to pronounce the final word of the great general harmony, of the final brotherly communion of all nations in accordance with the law of the gospel of Christ![56]

MacDiarmid responds, in *A Drunk Man*, by reciprocating this gesture of international friendship on behalf of the Scots: 'To seek the haund o' Russia as a freen'/In workin' oot mankind's great synthesis' (135). The implication is obvious as the poet has already rejected the English, calling love between Scotland and England 'a criminal emotion' (107). In what he called the 'Russo-Scottish parallelism'[57] MacDiarmid saw a salvation that eliminated the English. Dostoevsky's role in the poem is to provide an astonishing alternative to English gentility.

Yet another secondary source gave MacDiarmid material pertaining to Dostoevsky. D. S. Mirsky's *Modern Russian Literature* (1925) discussed Dostoevsky's *Diary of a Writer* (published weekly in the *Citizen*, a conservative paper edited by Dostoevsky in 1873) and the Pushkin speech as two variations on the same theme. Mirsky explained:

> In this *Diary* [Dostoevsky's] doctrine was, as before, a democratic Slavophilism, a profound belief that the Russian People (with a big P, and mainly meaning the peasants) was a *narodbogonosets* − 'a God-bearing people' ... Pushkin, said Dostoevsky, was Russia's all-in-all (*nashe vse*), for the very reason that he was a cosmopolitan, or, as Dostoevsky put it, an All-man (*vse-chelovek*). This Pan-Humanity is the national characteristic of Russia, and Russia's mission is to effect the final synthesis of all mankind.[58]

Mirsky's information was integrated into MacDiarmid's verse: '*Narodbogonosets* are my folk tae' (134), 'Scotland sall find oot its destiny,/And yield the *vse-chelovek*' (134), 'mankind's great synthesis' (135).

As well as including poems by Russian poets Blok and Hippius, and addressing Dostoevsky in his poem, MacDiarmid makes use of the mystical philosophy of another Russian: Vladimir Solovyov whose work has connections with both Dostoevsky and Blok. While teaching at Moscow University (1874-7) Solovyov met Dostoevsky and prompted the character of Alyosha in *The Brothers Karamazov*; as previously noted, Blok's mysterious lady derives from Solovyov's vision of Sophia. During the First World War, Solovyov's work was made available in the West: A. Bashky's translation of *Three Conversations Concerning War, Progress, and the End of History* appeared in 1915, Natalie Duddington's translation of *The Justification of the Good* in 1918. MacDiarmid expressed his admiration for Solovyov in a *Glasgow Herald* review of J. Y. Simpson's *Man and the Attainment of Immortality* in 1923:

> According to Solovyov there is no opposition between the universal and the individual ... [Solovyov's] Sophia is not only the perfect unity of all that is *sub specie aeternitatis*, but also the unifying power in the divided and chaotic world, the living bond between the Creator and the creature. Sophia is for ever seeking to bring back to herself the existence that has split off from the original whole, and by becoming incarnate in the lower world, to attain complete and perfect realization of the ideal union between God and the universe.[59]

Sophia, the feminine personification of Wisdom, features in the Bible as God's constant companion and partner in creation:

> The Lord possessed me in the beginning of his way, before his works of old. I was set up from everlasting, from the beginning, or ever the earth was ... When he prepared the heavens, I *was* there ... Then I was by him, *as* one brought up *with him*: and I was daily *his* delight, rejoicing always before him ... (Proverbs 8: 22, 23, 27, 30)

Solovyov restored this figure to her biblical glory.

Solovyov had three encounters with Sophia. At the age of nine, during a service in the chapel of Moscow University, he had a vision of a beautiful woman he identified subsequently as Sophia. During a leave of absence from Moscow University in 1875 he had his second vision of Sophia at the British Museum in London. She spoke to him, telling him to go to Egypt where, as light dawned on the desert, he had his final vision of Sophia. Solovyov felt he could give a rational explanation of religion though his approach is mystical to the point of vagueness; in Sophia he found a suggestive symbol which could be interpreted as the eternal body of God, the eternal soul of the world, the Wisdom of

God, the principle of creation, the Eternal Feminine, Christ's body, the Universal Church, the Kingdom of God, the Bride of Christ. Sophia, he argued, is ideal humanity eternally contained in the divine being of Christ. As the Bride of Christ, Sophia embraced both the natural and divine worlds. Seeking a unity of matter and spirit, Solovyov founded his faith on the Incarnation and perceived in the sacrifice of Christ the salvation of humankind. United by the Christian sacrifice the human species asserts its divinity.

MacDiarmid believed, with Solovyov, that the poetic act of creation allowed the individual to penetrate the actuality of the divine world. He therefore found the image of Sophia as a bride an alluring one. When he printed his poem 'Braid Scots' in the last issue of the *Scottish Chapbook* he appended a plan for the continuation of the sequence, using the title 'Scotland as Mystical Bride' for a projected section.[60] *A Drunk Man* includes such a section. The argumentative thrust of the poem enables the Drunk Man to transcend his earthly appetites and aspire to Christological heights. His companion in this process is also capable of transformation from the earthly to the eternal. As Jean, the Drunk Man's wife, she is a domestic creature enlarged by her sexuality. In the adaptation of Blok's 'The Stranger' she is the mysterious lady who tantalises the drinker. In a more exalted role she is Sophia, the mystical bride who retains her virginal purity though she has been penetrated by mankind. MacDiarmid conveys this paradox as a hauntingly beautiful ballad:

> O wha's the bride that cairries the bunch
> O' thistles blinterin' white?
> Her cuckold bridegroom little dreids
> What he sall ken this nicht.
>
> For closer than gudeman can come
> And closer to'r than hersel',
> Wha didna need her maidenheid
> Has wrocht his purpose fell.
>
> O wha's been here afore me, lass,
> And hoo did he get in?
>   *– A man that deed or I was born*
>   *This evil thing has din.*   (102-3)

Read only in a ballad context the passage suggests betrayal but in the metaphysical context of the entire poem there is an additional stress. The two questions posed in the quotation are answered by the Drunk

Man's vision of immortality. The bride is Sophia. The man that died before the bride was born is Christ whose death is only illusory since he carries the seeds of his own resurrection. As Sophia is everlasting she lives eternally through all women, including Jean; similarly, Christ is all men, including the Drunk Man.

What the Drunk Man has in common with Christ is an immortal soul. This is the final synthesis of the dialectical theses and antitheses. MacDiarmid saw in the soul a notion uniting his early Christian education with his reading of philosophers such as Plato, who emphasised the immortality of the soul; and Plotinus, who regarded the soul as a reality offering access, via the intelligence, to the ineffable first principle he called the One. For Plotinus, the mystical path towards the Absolute depended on the ability of the soul to transcend thought and unite with the One in a vision of eternity. MacDiarmid's understanding of this mystical process informs not only *A Drunk Man* but subsequent poems in which he emulates Plotinus's flight of the alone to the Alone. In 'Depth and the Chthonian Image' he speaks of 'the road a' croods ha' gane/And alane wi' the alane' (349); in *In Memoriam James Joyce* he similarly speaks of 'The Mature Art – alone with the Alone' (786). *A Drunk Man* is not only MacDiarmid's greatest poem but the repository of the poetic insights he later explored at greater length if not greater depth.

It is MacDiarmid's determination to reveal the soul of the Drunk Man – to equate him with Christ (and more, for the protagonist is potentially a greater Christ) – that gives the poem its structural strength. It has an argumentative design because the poet has a case to prove. At the outset of the Drunk Man's odyssey a strategy is announced:

> To prove my saul is Scots I maun begin
> Wi' what's still deemed Scots and the folk expect,
> And spire up syne by visible degrees
> To heichts whereo' the fules ha'e never recked.   (83)

His own imagination saturated in Christian symbolism, MacDiarmid takes the existence of the soul for granted in that quatrain. It is an assumption that is constantly made throughout *A Drunk Man* as the following phrases show: 'my saul/Blinks dozent as the owl I ken't to be' (87), 'My jaded soul' (92), 'mair than my ain soul – my nation's soul' (93), 'This horror ... is my soul' (94), 'To save your souls fu' mony o' ye are fain' (107), 'let my soul increase in me' (125), 'souls set free/Frae mortal coils' (127), 'A'thing that ony man can be's/A mockery o' his soul' (128), 'I canna thole/Aye yabblin' o' my soul' (142), 'A monstrous thistle ... A symbol o' the puzzle o' man's soul' (147), 'It hauds nae pew in ony kirk,/The soul Christ cam' to save' (152), 'Hauf his soul a Scot maun use/Indulgin' in illusions' (157), 'The nature o' man's soul is such/That it can ne'er wi' life tine touch' (158), 'the million days/Through which the soul o' man can gaze' (162). Ironically, the poem suggests that for the Drunk Man to prove his soul is Scots he must acknowledge the horror as well as the hope.

Since it is crucial to the Drunk Man's case that Scotland recognise its wretchedness in order to overcome it, MacDiarmid makes Scotland, the thistle and the Drunk Man interchangeable parts of the same problem. Fashioned in the form of the thistle, Scotland is 'a wretched weed' (125). Personified as the Drunk Man – who has a 'thistle-shape' (146) – Scotland takes a 'grisly form' (146). Yet if the thistle has been a cross on which the Scot has been crucified, if Scotland has been a 'hole' (166) in which the Scot has been entombed, if the Drunk Man has collapsed – still there is a hope of Christ-like resurrection. The thistle has its own passion, the Scot can arise from the tomb, the Drunk Man can stand up for himself (and therefore his whole country). The poet approaches this issue by posing a rhetorical question:

> The thocht o' Christ and Calvary
> Aye liddenin' in my heid;
> And a' the dour provincial thocht
> That merks the Scottish breed
> – These are the thistle's characters,
> To argie there's ane need.
> Hoo weel my verse embodies
> The thistle you can read!
> – But will a Scotsman never
> Frae this vile growth be freed?   (122)

The answer will be affirmative if the Drunk Man himself can rise above his unpromising origins, as Christ did.

Two of the most incisive couplets in the poem approach the Drunk Man's predicament in genetic terms. The first couplet expresses despair at the prospect of a world dominated by the feck, by the Nietzschean rabble, while the succeeding couplet contains a possible solution:

> Millions o' wimmen bring forth in pain
> Millions o' bairns that are no' worth ha'en'.
>
> Wull ever a wumman be big again
> Wi's muckle's a Christ? Yech, there's nae sayin'.   (103)

In other words, can a village drunk, who consorts with the likes of Cruivie and Gilsanquhar, win free of the feck and confound the circumstances of his birth? In a notable passage of self-hatred the Drunk Man laments over his attachment to the umbilical cord. Though he wants to 'be mysel'' (126) he is, biologically, a character created in his mother's womb, 'My mither's womb that reins me still' (126). Turning from his earthly mother to his spiritual father, the Drunk Man cries in the Scottish wilderness to God:

> Faither in Heaven, what gar'd ye tak'
> A village slut to mither me,
> Your mongrel o' the fire and clay?
> The trollop and the Deity share
> My writhen form as tho' I were
> A picture o' the time they had
> When Licht rejoiced to file itsel'
> And Earth upshuddered like a star.   (126)

Because the Drunk Man sees the thistle as his double he alternates between disgust and the desire for self-improvement. Still, the positive poetic thrust allows the Drunk Man and the thistle to undergo metamorphoses and the thistle has, in the setting of the poem, a beauty as well as a brutality:

> My nobler instincts sall nae mair
> This contrair shape be gi'en.
> I sall nae mair consent to live
> A life no' fit to be seen.   (120)

The poet specifically attributes that thought to the thistle, calling attention to its repulsive appearance:

> Sae ran the thocht that hid ahint
> The thistle's ugsome guise,
> Till a' at aince a rose loupt oot
> — I watched it wi' surprise.   (120)

These lines occur in MacDiarmid's ballad of the General Strike. The betrayal of proletarian aspirations is treated as another of Scotland's botched births.

Taking the biblical career of Christ as a viable precedent for his own position, the Drunk Man makes comparisons. Christ, cited in the poem as a being alive with the idea of his own divinity, has obvious advantages over the Drunk Man. Christ, complains the Drunk Man, 'had never toothick ... was never seeck' (104). Whereas the biblical child is blessed, the Drunk Man is aware of his lack of physical beauty: 'My self-tormented spirit took/The shape repeated in the thistle'. (105). MacDiarmid considers an extreme example of deprivation, a Scottish child – 'A bastard wean' (104) – born in a snowstorm. He observes 'It's an eaten and a spewed-like thing' (104), a description applied to the poet himself as a child.[61] This child is not born under a star but under the moon, a barren world that nevertheless gives birth to great poetic conceits. In a series of couplets the moon becomes Luna, a barmaid at the Craidle-and-Coffin, and the Drunk Man refuses to be one of her forsaken children:

> You needna fash to rax and strain.
> Carline, I'll *no'* be born again
>
> In ony brat you can produce.
> Carline, gi'e owre – O what's the use?   (109)

The use of enjambement separates the Drunk Man from the feck. The Drunk Man rejects the maternal moon just as he rejects his earthly mother. He is ultimately the child of himself for he delivers his own destiny, he creates the conditions in which his soul can soar.

The Drunk Man, indeed, repeatedly rejects some options in order to embrace more imaginative alternatives. At the beginning of the poem he literally and metaphorically leaves Cruivie and Gilsanquhar behind him as he staggers from the bar to find his own way home. Cruivie and Gilsanquhar are present in the poem as stereotypical Scots to be avoided by a man searching for a spiritual path. It is only when the Drunk Man is depressed by the immensity of his ambition that he identifies with his cronies, for occasionally he wishes he had 'nae mair sense/Than Cruivie and Gilsanquhar' (108). He tires of 'Cruivie's "latest" story or/Gilsanquhar's vows to sign the pledge' (124). Yet even these Scots contain a spark that could be ignited by a new Scotland, a possibility that gives the Drunk Man pause for thought:

> And faith! yestreen in Cruivie's een
> Life rocked at midnicht in a tree,
> And in Gilsanquhar's glower I saw
> The taps o' waves 'neth which the warld
> Ga'ed rowin' like a jeelyfish   (132)

The thought passes, leaving the Drunk Man with his customary conviction that the creation of the self is a solitary spiritual affair so he must
'leave the lave to dree/Their weirdless destiny' (141).

The Drunk Man's chosen companions are his ideals and soaring
spirits like himself. Instead of 'Cruivie and Gilsanquhar and the like' (83)
he allies himself with exceptional individuals, usually paired as with
Dostoevsky and Nietzsche, Christ and Burns (each separated from his
cult), Euclid and Einstein, Melville and Hawthorne. Melville is included
in the pantheon as a Scot who knew 'hoo Christ's/Corrupted into creeds
malign' (135), a reference to Melville's narrative poem *Clarel* (1876). The
Drunk Man sees the full moon as his 'muckle white whale' (108) and
hopes his monologue will enable a Scot to find 'in this form forlorn/What
Melville socht in vain frae Hawthorne' (135), namely an understanding
of darkness – for Melville saw in Hawthorne a 'mystical blackness ... [a]
great power of blackness'.[62]

If the Drunk Man can reject his cronies in favour of more heroic
figures, he cannot dismiss Jean; in the metaphysical role she fulfils she is
indispensable to his transformation. The Drunk Man may approach
Dostoevsky but recognises him as a separate being whereas Jean is part
of him, his familiar on many levels. As a sensual woman she is his wife,
a female made in the form of Peggy Grieve. Yet she is also an archetype,
an embodiment of the eternal feminine principle that urges the man
upwards. She is initially cited casually as 'The wife' (83) and the Drunk
Man calls on her for comfort when he appreciates the consequences of
his physical collapse. He might not be alone on a hillside, but in his own
bed dreaming beside Jean: *'Jean! Jean!* Gin *she*'s no here it's no' *oor* bed,/Or
else I'm dreamin' deep and canna wauken' (86). As the synthesis he is
searching for depends on the fusion of opposites, including male and
female, the Drunk Man realises that Jean, as the mysterious lady in Blok's
'The Stranger', might be his better half in more than a conversational
sense. She might be his self in its feminine aspect:

> Were you a vision o' mysel',
> Transmuted by the mellow liquor?
> Neist time I glisk you in a glass,
> I'se warrant I'll mak' siccar.   (90)

The second Blok adaptation names Jean as the 'strange Goddess' (91) and, as the phallic symbolism of the thistle swells in the Drunk Man, he suspects that the spirit of Scotland must penetrate the feminine principle. He expresses this as a phallic pun – 'And yet I feel this muckle thistle's staun'in'/Atween me and the mune as pairt o' a Plan' (92). After thoughts of his native Langholm, centred on 'Common-ridin' Day in the Muckle Toon' (97), he thinks of his wife as she was on 'her weddin' day' (98). The associations assemble. Jean is a goddess he has known as a virgin. She is an image of eternity: a moon goddess, Sophia, Penelope, Molly Bloom, the Virgin Mary, Eve. As his sexual partner she offers access to a divine dualism:

> Said my body to my mind,
> 'I've been startled whiles to find,
> When Jean has been in bed wi' me,
> A kind o' Christianity!'   (101)

Characteristically, the Drunk Man connects the physical and the metaphysical, the sexual and the spiritual. The phallic thistle is an object Jean can easily absorb but also a symbol she can understand: 'I'se warran Jean 'ud no' be lang/In findin' whence this thistle sprang' (102). It is at this point that Jean becomes a Scottish Sophia, a virginal bride 'that cairries the bunch/O' thistles blinterin' white' (102). Haunted by hallucination, the Drunk Man thinks with horror of sleeping with a skeleton, then with a whole host of women – 'ony wench/Can ser' me for a time' (113) – before coming to a paradoxical conclusion. Jean's uniqueness resides in her universality, her sexuality is symbolic:

> And Jean's nae mair my wife
> Than whisky is at times,
> Or munelicht or a thistle
> Or kittle thochts or rhymes.

> He's no a man ava',
> And lacks a proper pride,
> Gin less than a' the warld
> Can ser' him for a bride!   (114)

Just as a woman can be a world as well as a wife, the thistle can be the tree of life as well as 'a wretched weed' (125) – everything is capable of imaginative expansion for the Drunk Man. Thoughts of Jean dissolve into the botched birth of the General Strike then to thoughts 'O' chaos fenced frae Eden yet' (124). In an Edenic context Jean is Eve, the Drunk Man is Adam, the thistle is the tree of life. The Drunk Man must reconcile extremes in order to escape from his fallen state, his alcoholic collapse which is also the fall of man. All his reading of symbols and philosophies bring him back to the same basic problem of how to assert himself spiritually:

> And still the puzzle stands unsolved.
> Beauty and ugliness alike,
> And life and daith and God and man,
> Are aspects o't but nane can tell
> The secret that I'd fain find oot
> O' this bricht hive, this sorry weed,
> The tree that fills the universe,
> Or like a reistit herrin' crines.   (126)

Deliberately mixing his symbols (as earlier he might have mixed his drinks) the Drunk Man sees the central structure from several angles: as the biblical tree of life, as the Scandinavian cosmic tree Ygradsil, as a 'giant thistle' (131), as a Freudian symbol, as a Christian cross. The iconographic possibilities are endless for an intellectual but the issue is essential. The tree, with its restless roots and glorious ramifications, represents creativity:

> thistle or no', whate'er its end,
> Aiblins the force that mak's it grow
> And lets him see a kennin' mair
> Than ither folk and fend his sicht
> Agen their jealous plots awhile,
> 'll use the poo'ers it seems to waste,
> This purpose ser'd, in ither ways,
> That may be better worth the bein'   (133)

It is the creative force that enables the Drunk Man to surpass himself. Exhibited as a poem it allows the Drunk Man to transcend dogma, to throw off Presbyterian preconceptions learned in youth, to overcome domestic problems:

211

> *I'm fu' o' a stickit God.*
> *THAT's what's the maitter wi' me,*
> *Jean has stuck sic a fork in the wa'*
> *That I row in agonie.* (134)

The soul of the Drunk Man is larger than any philosophical system, hence it is ultimately beyond words − a belief the Drunk Man returns to at the end of his monologue so that a poem celebrating the creative power of poetry ends in silence.

The Drunk Man develops his insight into the creative principle by addressing Dostoevsky, the 'Christ o' the neist thoosand years' (139). With his 'baggit wife' (139), his obsession with gambling, his epilepsy Dostoevsky had more physical distractions than the Drunk Man yet surpassed them. Inspired by this example, the Drunk Man can soar above his everyday existence

> Till I can see richt through
> Ilk weakness o' my frame
> And ilka dernin' shame,
> And can employ the same
> To jouk the curse o' fame,
> Lowsed frae the dominion
> O' popular opinion,
> And risen at last abune
> This thistle like a mune
> That looks serenely doon
> On what queer things there are
> In an inferior star
> That couldna be, or see,
> Themsel's, except in me. (140-1)

This ambition involves a liberation of the spirit though the Drunk Man − forever conducting his argument with himself − sometimes despairs of the demands of his soul and would 'be free/O' my eternal me' (142). It is with Jean that he can begin to resolve the contradictions in himself, with her that he can attempt to combine the physical and the metaphysical, the body and the soul. Jean, the Eve to his Adam, can let him be entirely himself:

> *Clear my lourd flesh, and let me move*
> *In the peculiar licht o' love,*
> *As aiblins in Eternity men may*
> *When their swack souls nae mair are clogged wi' clay.*

> *Be thou the licht in which I stand*
> *Entire, in thistle-shape, as planned,*
> *And no' hauf-hidden and hauf-seen as here*
> *In munelicht, whisky, and in fleshly fear,*
>
> *In fear to look owre closely at*
> *The grisly form in which I'm caught,*
> *In sic a reelin' and imperfect licht*
> *Sprung frae incongruous elements the nicht!* (146)

Through Jean he can be more than one branch on the tree of life. He can shine through his own structure, be his own creation:

> *Syne liberate me frae this tree,*
> *As wha had there imprisoned me,*
> *The end achieved – or show me at the least*
> *Mair meanin' in't, and hope o' bein' released.* (146)

Before the Drunk Man can be liberated he must transcend the 'livin' death' (88) that is defined as the condition of a soporific humankind. Just as Dostoevsky, in his story 'The Dream of a Ridiculous Man', depicts water dripping from a coffin lid on to the eye of a man buried alive, so the Drunk Man has experienced entombment:

> I tae ha'e heard Eternity drip water
> (Aye water, water!), drap by drap
> On the a'e nerve, like lichtnin', I've become,
> And heard God passin' wi' a bobby's feet
> Ootby in the lang coffin o' the street (147)

The last couplet in the quotation perfectly illustrates MacDiarmid's ability to discern the universal in the particular; the likening of the Old Testament God to a local figure of authority indicates his critical attitude to an institutional deity. The Drunk Man, anxious to avoid religious dogma – one of the ruinations of Scotland in his opinion since he says 'The Presbyterian thistle flourishes,/And its ain roses crucifies' (152) – reaches out for a God larger than any orthodox God. He recognises the Unknown God, a mysterious and elusive divinity. In *Acts* (17:23) Paul observed in Athens an inscription to the Unknown God. In *Annals of the Five Senses* MacDiarmid (as Grieve) contemplated his unrealised potentialities 'even as the Greeks built their altar to the Unknown God'.[63] The Drunk Man aspires to the ineffable so the tree of life, the form he has assumed, is metamorphosed into a new shape, 'A mony-brainchin' candelabra' (147) that shines with the spirit of the Unknown God:

> I am the candelabra, and burn
> My endless candles to an Unkent God.
> I am the mind and meanin' o' the octopus
> That thraws its empty airms through a' th'Inane.   (148)

He is projecting his immortal soul into eternity with abandon.

Throughout the poem, the Drunk Man has identified himself with various forms — with the thistle, with the tree of life, with the many-branched candelabra. He is an individual who encompasses, through creativity, all the shapes the universe can offer. Thus every form the Drunk Man takes functions on literal, metaphoric and symbolic levels and every statement he makes has a universal application. His rise from a fallen state to resurrection is a general rebirth with particular meaning for Scotland for his soul is demonstrably Scots. Addressing Dostoevsky he connects the rebirth of Scotland with the ability of the thistle to withstand winter, for the snow

> *gethers there in drift on endless drift,*
> *Oor broken herts that it can never fill;*
> *And still — its leafs like snaw, its growth like wund —*
> *The thistle rises and forever will!* ...

> The thistle rises and forever will,
> Getherin' the generations under't.
> This is the monument o' a' they were,
> And a' they hoped and wondered.   (152)

This is a defiant declaration of faith in the political and spiritual future of Scotland.

The political rebirth necessarily involves emancipation from the imperial power of the English: 'I stand still for forces which/Were subjugated to mak' way/For England's poo'er' (157). Yet the Drunk Man who carefully separates Scotland from England — who chooses the thistle rather than the rose — is no narrow nationalist. He is a Scot with a universal outlook. The poem moves towards its finale through a sustained series of eighty-four triplets showing the cosmological vastness of the

Drunk Man's Scotocentric universe. Scotland, the Drunk Man accepts, is a speck in space, a part of an eternal great wheel. The origin of the great wheel has puzzled commentators[64] though MacDiarmid had at least two specific sources for it. Yeats's *A Vision*, the outcome of his wife's automatic writing, was privately printed and circulated in a signed and numbered edition of 600 copies at the end of 1925. Prominent in the book is the symbolism of the Great Wheel, which shows the lunar phases as completed movements of thought or life. Discussing the Great Year, the zodiacal motion, Yeats considers its length, as estimated by Macrobius and Plato, then states: 'Twelve thousand, nine hundred and fifty-four, however, is the number Tacitus gives, quoting from a lost work of Cicero's, but today we know that the true number is some twenty-six thousand years.'[65] MacDiarmid appropriates the Great Year and Great Wheel of Yeats:

> But wa'es me on the weary wheel!
> Higgledy-piggledy in't we reel,
> And little it cares hoo we may feel.

> Twenty-six thoosand years 't'll tak'
> For it to threid the Zodiac
> – A single roon o' the wheel to mak'!   (164)

Yeats also insisted that 'every Divine Birth occurs at a symbolic new Moon'.[66] The divine rebirth of the Drunk Man, a contrary creature, occurs at a full moon, partly because MacDiarmid wants to pun on the Scots 'fu' ', meaning both full and drunk: 'It isna me that's fou' at a',/But the fu' mune' (86).

MacDiarmid's vision of the great wheel had a more scientific source than Yeats's fancy. In the eighteenth century William Herschel conjectured that beyond the boundaries of the Milky Way lay island-universes, independent clusters of stars, and this was confirmed in 1923 when Edwin Hubble, using the telescope at Mount Wilson in California, proved that the so-called spiral nebulae are independent galaxies. With Hubble's proof the model of the universe changed to accommodate the image of the Milky Way galaxy rotating like a great wheel. MacDiarmid, always abreast of scientific developments, incorporated this viewpoint into his vision:

> And as I see the the great wheel spin
> There flees a licht frae't lang and thin
> That Earth is like a snaw-ba' in.   (158)

From the information he had about the great galactic wheel, MacDiarmid understood that even the sun, the nearest star to the earth, was simply a pinpoint of light in the immensity of space:

> E'en stars are seen thegither in
> A'e skime o' licht as grey as tin
> Flyin' on the wheel as 'twere a pin.
>
> Syne ither systems ray on ray
> Skinkle past in quick array
> While it is still the self-same day,
>
> A'e day o' a' the million days
> Through which the soul o' man can gaze
> Upon the wheel's incessant blaze,
>
> Upon the wheel's incessant blaze
> As it were on a single place
> The twinklin' filled the howe o' space.   (162)

The consequences of this astronomical information have a poetic justice; ideas of small and large are only relative (Einstein's name is shrewdly dropped into the argument of the great wheel section). Scotland may be small yet significant just as the sun is cosmically minute but crucial to humankind. What matters to MacDiarmid, the visionary, is understanding the impulse that moves the entire universe of which Scotland is a part: as the great wheel moves the poet sees, on an edge, 'Wee Scotland squattin' like a flea' (159). Measured on a universal scale Bannockburn and Flodden – a famous Scottish victory and a disastrous Scottish defeat – are little skirmishes in 'Little wars' (160). They are tiny aspects of a larger issue, properly seen in the spectacle of 'The wheel in silence whirlin' by' (160). The Drunk Man, with the arrogance of the artist, seeks union with 'the Will/That raised the Wheel and spins it still' (160). This force is ultimately accessible to the imagination, for the wheel will 'birl in time inside oor heids' (161).

MacDiarmid accepts the majestic sweep of the universe but rejects the determinism of man-made theology, especially Calvinist pre-destination for he refers to 'The horror o' the endless Fate/A'thing 's whirled in predestinate' (161). If all things, in a Shestovian sense, are possible Scotland can be seen as more than the sum of its internal squabbles. It can enlarge itself, be part of a union more lasting than the political union with England:

> He canna Scotland see wha yet
> Canna see the Infinite,
> And Scotland in true scale to it.   (162)

This grand vision is available to those who are 'disinterested' (163), who confront the universe with an intensity as if given 'The stars themsels instead o' een' (163).

It is the poet, the embodiment of the universal creative force, who sees both the particular and the universal, who synthesises opposites, who is most fulfilled where extremes meet. It is the poet who can unite man and the infinite. Poetry is the language that makes the human destiny divine:

> The function, as it seems to me
> O' Poetry is to bring to be
> At lang, lang last that unity   (163)

Looking at his country's history through its heroes and heroines (Knox, Claverhouse, Mary Queen of Scots, Burns, Wallace, Carlyle, Harry Lauder) the Drunk Man wonders why he should keep such company, why he should continue in such a country. The triplets become a dialogue between his sceptical self and his soul. His soul provides the answer in italics:

> 'Mercy o' Gode, I canna thole
> Wi' sic an orra mob to roll.'
> − *'Wheesht! It's for the guid o' your soul.'*   (164)

The Drunk Man persists by asking why he should be condemned forever with the Scottish 'rabble' (165). His soul then defines his destiny, reminding his self that resurrection requires a Christ-like sacrifice:

> *'A Scottish poet maun assume*
> *The burden o' his people's doom,*
> *And dee to brak' their livin' tomb.*

217

Mony ha'e tried, but a' ha'e failed.
Their sacrifice has nocht availed.
Upon the thistle they're impaled.

You maun choose but gin ye'd see
Anither category ye
Maun tine your nationality.'   (165)

So the great wheel section ends with the Drunk Man, having proved his soul is Scots, acknowledging that Scottishness is inescapable however irksome it can be. To save himself he must rescue Scotland from its past. To become 'A greater Christ, a greater Burns' (86) he must give the rabble a voice – the voice of the poet, a Drunk Man who has moved from bottled spirit to expansive spirituality. The contradictions cohere: the despised rabble, after all, comprise individuals potentially as immortal as the Drunk Man.

Physically and emotionally exhausted by his odyssey, by his nocturnal monologue, the Drunk Man turns again to Jean, the eternal feminine. His efforts to articulate the ineffable have left him almost speechless. His silence, though, has a mute meaning of its own. As has been seen, MacDiarmid was impressed by Tyutchev's poetic interpretation of silence. He must also have been fascinated to read about Ludwig Wittgenstein's *Tractatus Logico-Philosophicus* which was first published in 1921 and translated into English in 1922, the year of *The Waste Land* and *Ulysses* and 'The Watergaw'. Bertrand Russell, introducing the English translation, called the *Tractatus* 'a work of extraordinary difficulty and importance'[67] and the mystical passages at the end of the work caused a considerable stir. Establishing the demarcation between meaningful statements and metaphysical longings, Wittgenstein produced a haunting contemplation of the mystical as an ineffable phenomenon. 'There are, indeed,' he says, 'things that cannot be put into words. They *make themselves manifest*. They are what is mystical ... What we cannot speak about we must pass over in silence.'[68] MacDiarmid would certainly have delighted in Wittgenstein's final proposition.

The poet's own salute to a personified Silence is the end of *A Drunk Man* and remains one of the most mysterious parts of the poem though it is possible to read it in the light of what has gone before. It has a stately progression:

Yet ha'e I Silence left, the croon o' a'.

No' her, wha on the hills langsyne I saw
Liftin' a foreheid o' perpetual snaw.

No' her, wha in the how-dumb-deid o' nicht
Kyths, like Eternity in Time's despite.

No' her, withooten shape, wha's name is Daith,
No' Him, unkennable abies to faith

— God whom, gin e'er He saw a man, 'ud be
E'en mair dumfooner'd at the sicht than he

— But Him, whom nocht in man or Deity
Or Daith or Dreid or Laneliness can touch,
Wha's deed owre often and has seen owre much.

O I ha'e Silence left,

          — 'And weel ye micht,'
Sae Jean'll say, 'efter sic a nicht!'   (166-7)

Silence is the essence of the soul that MacDiarmid has spent the entire poem celebrating. Ultimately the salvation of his self depends of what he makes of his soul, not on other forces he has encountered. Silence is not Scotia, the physical beauty of Scotland with her 'foreheid o' perpetual snaw'. It is not Sophia, who 'Kyths, like Eternity in Time's despite'. It is not Death. It is not the Unknown God, 'Him, unkennable abies to faith'. Silence is the soul of the individual, the imperishable part of the individual.

The end of this paradoxical poem represents the greatest paradox in it: the poet, liberated by his resurrection of the Scots language, affirms the ineffable as the silence of the soul. The garrulous monologist becomes mute by accepting a wordless eloquence. All the selfconscious contradictions — between élitism and populism, between materialism and mysticism, between the body and the spirit, between the thistle and the rose, between sexuality and asceticism — are finally synthesised, fused in a vision of transcendental unity. The Scots language allowed MacDiarmid to realise his poetic potential. In *Annals of the Five Senses*, Grieve had noted that 'On all sides the mind was baffled by paradox'.[69] Grieve, however, had been reborn as MacDiarmid who was not baffled by paradox; the all-embracing sweep of his Scots enabled him to accept

Yet Ha'e I Silence Left.

Yet ha'e I Silence left, the croon o' a'.

Tho' her, wha on the hills langsyne I saw
liftin' a forehead o' perpetual snaw.

Tho' her, wha in the how-dumb-deid o' nicht
Kythes, like Eternity in Time's despite.

Tho' her, withooten shape, wha's name is Daith.

Tho' Him, unkennable abies by faith.

—God whom, gin e'er He saw a man 'ud be
E'en mair dumfoonert at the sicht than he!

But Him, whom nocht in Man or Deity,
Or Daith or Dreid or loneliness can touch,
Wha's deed owre often and has seen owre much.

O I ha'e Silence left, the croon o' a'.

Hugh M'Diarmid.

(italic)

'Yet Ha'e I Silence Left': this draft of the close of *A Drunk Man Looks at the Thistle*, from a letter of J. K. Annand (2 June 1926), lacks the concluding couplet of the published text:

> —'And weel ye micht,'
> Sae Jean'll say, 'efter sic a nicht!'

F. G. Scott said (in a letter to Maurice Lindsay, 20 May 1945), 'I'm pretty certain I supplied the last two lines to bring the thing to some kind of conclusion.' MacDiarmid, however, said (in a letter in *Lines Review*, Summer 1968), 'Scott had nothing to do with the actual writing.'

paradox as a principle of complexity. *A Drunk Man* is a poem made in the image of MacDiarmid; its structure is as unshakeable as the language he uses.

Formally, MacDiarmid avoids a linear progression in shaping this structure, for adjacent lines frequently contain contradictions. His structure now emulates a jagged thistle, now a profoundly rooted tree, now a many-branched candelabra. *A Drunk Man* is a dynamic poem, its dialectic movement of thesis and antithesis triumphantly expressed through a dialect that moves from the conspiratorial tone of drunken conversation to the elevated diction of philosophical discourse. Still, the poem has a definite narrative development in following the spiritual rise of a fallen man. If represented as a graph it would have dramatic ups and downs, peaks and troughs, but it would be seen as rising from a base beginning (alcoholic collapse) to a pinnacle (silence of the soul). MacDiarmid is determined, after all, to lift other Scots 'To heichts whereo' the fules ha'e never recked' (83) though he eschews a 'steady progress' (116). The Drunk Man's rise from his fallen state to his spiritual rebirth is charted by linguistic leaps and bounds. The end of *A Drunk Man* justifies the contrapuntal means; the eccentric form of the poem is its ethos.

Poetically, the transformation of the Grieve of *Annals* to the Mac-Diarmid of *A Drunk Man* is one of the most exhilarating spectacles of modern poetry. The difference between the writer of English and the master of Scots is startling. Grieve was not only baffled by paradox, he was inhibited by what he intuitively apprehended as the alien psychology that resided in the English language. MacDiarmid could prove his soul was Scots only by abandoning his inhibitions and allowing himself to be possessed by the Scots language. Theoretically he had proposed Synthetic Scots as a fusion of all Scotland's linguistic resources – the oral rhythms of the various dialects, the lexical density of dictionary Scots, the lyrical qualities of literary Scots – and felt that a Synthetic Scots was apposite to a poem intent on synthesis. Yet *A Drunk Man* is not dependent on theory. It is an inspirational work allowing MacDiarmid to translate the facts of his life into a linguistic fabric rich in detail and design.

The autobiographical elements of the poem are lifted into a universal dimension. Montrose becomes Nazareth, the intoxicated poet becomes the Scottish saviour, Peggy Grieve becomes Jean and her several meta-morphoses. Incidents MacDiarmid had observed are transmuted into great poetic events. For example, in the satirical attacks on the Burns

Cult at the beginning of the poem MacDiarmid draws on his memories of a London Burns Club dinner 'As G. K. Chesterton heaves up to gi'e/"The Immortal Memory" in a huge eclipse' (85). The picture fits the pattern of the poem which constantly refers to the rise of man. Chesterton's unsightly rise from his seat is thus counterpointed against the Drunk Man's spiritual struggle to rise from his recumbent position on a Scottish hillside. This gift of relating all obsessions to a central theme is masterful. From whatever angle it is approached – be it biographical, philosophical, structural, thematic – *A Drunk Man Looks at the Thistle* is a work of genius. Indeed, the theme of transforming a village drunk into 'A greater Christ, a greater Burns' (86) demanded nothing less.

Having completed the poem to his satisfaction, MacDiarmid waited anxiously for its reception. Before *A Drunk Man* was published Pittendrigh Macgillivray suggested that the poet should add an epilogue showing the Drunk Man waking up in morning sunshine. MacDiarmid went as far as composing a four-quatrain epilogue, which began:

> And yet gin I could fa' asleep
> To wauken here at fresh o' morn
> Hoo bonnie micht this thistle seem
> Wi' jinglin' dew on ilka thorn![70]

Finally, however, he decided against tampering with the text, explaining to Macgillivray that ambiguity was essential to the poem:

> In other words I do not agree with you that the true view of the thistle after all is that seen in the sunny morning or that the love of woman or child has compensations outwith a very limited sphere. Nor am I yet committed to the contrary position. But you will see that I am in no case yet to accord intimacy-candour on such intimate matters as my view of my relationship to my wife or child ... And yet I suspect that I really have made up my mind – that under an appearance of play I have all along been in deadly earnest – and that all that remains is to discover the conclusions I have long ago come to and acted upon.[71]

MacDiarmid added that he had no great hopes of critical or commercial success for the poem, admitting 'I expect little kudos, and less cash, from it.'[72] He was correct about the financial issue. Published on 22 November 1926 in an edition of five hundred copies, selling at seven shillings sixpence per copy, *A Drunk Man* had attracted only ninety-nine buyers by the end of the year.

The earliest reviews of MacDiarmid's masterpiece were, on the whole, unsympathetic. The *Glasgow Evening News*, commenting on both *Contemporary Scottish Studies* and *A Drunk Man*, suggested that 'All the worst faults of Mr Grieve's literary ideals will be found fully exemplified in the long poem which he has just published under his mysterious pseudonym of Hugh M'Diarmid.'[72] The Aberdeen *Press and Journal*, discussing *A Drunk Man* alongside Lewis Spence's *Plumes of Time*, admired MacDiarmid's intellectual energy but lamented 'He seems constitutionally debarred from selecting and cultivating the best of [his] aspirations, debarred, in fact, from anything but constant plangent grieving over his inhibitions.'[74] Writing to Ogilvie on 9 December 1926 MacDiarmid said he was 'ridiculously sensitive to what reviewers say', especially as the notices made 'sair reading'.[75]

Early in 1927, however, MacDiarmid was heartened by two reviews from men whom he respected. Oliver St John Gogarty, the friend of Joyce and the original of Buck Mulligan in *Ulysses*, enthused over *A Drunk Man* in the *Irish Statesman*:

> because in the wonderfully flexible and containing form he has chosen [MacDiarmid] has managed to become, as it were, a frenzied mouth letting the present-day soul of Scotland speak out with its metaphysic, its politic and its poetry.[76]

Without that tribute, MacDiarmid later told Gogarty, 'I don't know that I would have "continued poet" at all'.[77] MacDiarmid was also pleased with Edwin Muir's review of *A Drunk Man* even if Muir criticised him for carelessness. Muir declared that MacDiarmid was a master of the Synthetic Scots he had created for himself, then turned to the poetic outcome of the language:

> The flow, vigour, variety, wit, and originality of [*A Drunk Man*] are its greatest virtues; it is never dull, and there are very few poems of over four thousand lines which are never dull. Its main fault ... is a frequent carelessness of style; the rhymes are sometimes scrambled into their places in a hasty, slipshod manner. In spite of that, however, this is probably the only poem of importance which has appeared in Scots since the death of Burns.[78]

By the time he read these encouraging words MacDiarmid was already immersed in his next big poetic project, *To Circumjack Cencrastus*, and desperately looking around for opportunities that would remove him from Montrose.

MacDiarmid knew he had matured, miraculously, as a poet in Montrose and so the connection between the Scottish town and Nazareth, where Christ had grown up, had a special poetic justice. Yet, while the Drunk Man was willing to accept a poetic martyrdom in the cause of Scotland (which, however wretched, could rise to rebirth) MacDiarmid was not, as a man, anxious to entomb himself in Montrose. With 'The thocht o' Christ and Calvary/Aye liddenin' in my heid' (122) MacDiarmid had thoughts of escaping before Montrose became, physically as well as metaphorically, his Calvary.

1 The first photograph of Christopher Murray Grieve (born at the family home in Langholm) was taken in Carlisle, autumn 1892, with his parents Elizabeth and James Grieve. The poet later described his parents as 'very devout believers and very Churchy people'

2 Christopher Grieve (*l*) with his brother Andrew. This double portrait is discussed in *Lucky Poet*: 'There is an early photograph of my brother and myself – how slight and shy I look; how burly and self-assertive my brother looks in comparison!'

3 James Grieve was a rural postman in Langholm, where he died, of pneumonia, in 1911 aged 47. 'A laddie when he dee'd,' wrote MacDiarmid in 'Kinsfolk', 'I kent little o'm and he/Kent less o' me.'

4 Thomas Scott Cairncross, minister of Langholm South United Free Church which Grieve attended in his youth. Grieve was greatly impressed by the minister's book *The Return of the Master* (1905)

5 George Ogilvie, Grieve's English teacher at Broughton Junior Student Centre, Edinburgh, 1908-21; he was a decisive intellectual influence on Grieve who dedicated to him the poem 'A Moment in Eternity'

6 Grieve (*l*) with his cousin Bob Laidlaw; Laidlaw is praised in *Lucky Poet* and in a letter of 11 June 1949 from Grieve to Bob's brother John: 'He and I had been so friendly in my early teens and I owed so much to him then'

7 The Common Riding, Langholm, July 1912. Grieve, then 19, can be seen in the procession, his head framed between the poles supporting the Crown of Roses and the Barley Bannock (with a salt herring nailed to it)

8 Grieve with Minnie Punton, his girlfriend prior to the First World War. Writing to George Ogilvie in August 1916 Grieve explained how he 'fell seriously in love with a Scotch girl, a school teacher'

9 In 1914 Grieve was working as a journalist in Cupar, Fife. The postcard of Empire Day at Ladybank (near Cupar) shows Grieve and Minnie Punton in foreground. Written on the back is a note from Andrew Grieve to his mother, 'I have no doubt you will recognise Chris & Minnie'

10 After his close friend John Bogue Nisbet, 2nd Lt with 2nd Bn Royal Scots, was killed on 13 April 1915 Grieve decided to enlist

11 Sgt Grieve with his mother in Forfar, 1916, prior to his departure to Salonika where he served with 42nd General Hospital, RAMC, and termed the Greek city 'not Thessalonica, but Thistleonica'

12 Portrait of Grieve's first wife, Peggy, signed and dated 6 Dec. 1920. At that time the Grieves lived in Kildermorie Lodge, Alness, Ross-shire; he taught three children in a side school, she was employed as a housemaid

13 Peggy with Christine at 16 Links Avenue, Montrose. The Grieves settled there from 1922 until 1929; Christine, their first child, was born on 6 Sept. 1924

14 Edwin Muir, Francis George Scott (with his eldest son George) and MacDiarmid in Montrose, Aug. 1928. Friends at the time, MacDiarmid and Muir fell out after Muir's *Scott and Scotland* (1936)

15 Following Cunninghame Graham's near victory in the Glasgow University Rectorial Election in Oct. 1928 the National Party of Scotland celebrated in St Andrew's Hall, Glasgow: (*l–r*) the Duke of Montrose, Compton Mackenzie, Cunninghame Graham, MacDiarmid, James Valentine, John MacCormick

16 The Gaelic poet Sorley MacLean (r) spent the first week of Aug. 1935 with MacDiarmid in Whalsay, Shetland; the two poets are seen here on West Linga with MacDiarmid's son, Michael, then three, in the background. A week later MacDiarmid suffered his serious breakdown

17 Valda and Michael Grieve in Whalsay, summer 1937. MacDiarmid's major project, while living in Shetland from 1933 to 1942, was the epic *Cornish Heroic Song for Valda Trevlyn*

18 The poet with his friend Helen Cruickshank in Princes Street Gardens, Edinburgh, May 1936. One of MacDiarmid's most loyal admirers, Helen Cruickshank provided moral and financial support during his most difficult periods, such as that following his breakdown in 1935

19 MacDiarmid with Mary and Tom MacDonald on the same occasion. MacDiarmid had known MacDonald in Montrose and championed *The Albannach* (1932), the novel MacDonald wrote under the pseudonym Fionn Mac Colla

20 Neil Gunn in the 1930s. On the publication of Gunn's first novel, *The Grey Coast* (1926), MacDiarmid, in *Contemporary Scottish Studies*, described Gunn as a 'young Scottish prose-writer of promise'. After the publication of *Butcher's Broom* (1934) MacDiarmid said 'Gunn has gone completely off the rails'

21 Lewis Grassic Gibbon, who collaborated with MacDiarmid on *Scottish Scene* (1934). MacDiarmid greatly admired Gibbon's trilogy *A Scots Quair* (1932-4) and observed approvingly, in *The Company I've Kept*, that Gibbon 'gravitated to Communism and became an out-and-out Republican'

22 A caricature of the Muirs by Barbara Niven in MacDiarmid's magazine, the *Voice of Scotland* (Sept.-Nov. 1938). The caricature was Valda's idea: 'I got Barbara to do it for me – telling her exactly what I wanted.' When MacDiarmid was ill, in St Andrews in 1935, Valda had watched Willa 'sprawling on the beach in one of those modern bathing costumes … holding forth unnecessarily on her favourite topic – phallic symbolism'

WILLA AND EDWIN.

23 Writing to his brother Andrew in Oct. 1938 MacDiarmid said, 'I'm about twice as heavy (i.e. fat) now as I've ever been before, and have a full, curly but rather greyish beard to boot! (not to my boots)'

24 Under the wartime industrial conscription scheme MacDiarmid trained as a fitter in 1942 and worked in the copper shell-band section of Mechan's, Glasgow, where an industrial accident injured his legs

25 At the invitation of the Duke of Hamilton, MacDiarmid and Valda moved into the laundry cottage of Dungavel House, Strathaven, Lanarkshire, in 1949 and stayed there until the end of 1950. The poet was visited there by Arnold Wesker, then an aspiring writer of seventeen. 'It was', said Wesker, 'a memorable event for me, a boy from a council flat in Hackney, being welcomed into the home of a real writer'

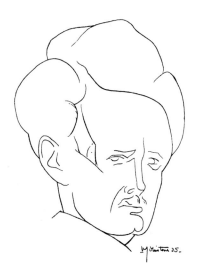

26 Line drawing by William Johnstone, reproduced on the jacket of *Second Hymn to Lenin and Other Poems* (1935). A cousin of F. G. Scott and, like MacDiarmid, a Borderer, Johnstone was an enthusiastic advocate of the Scottish Renaissance Movement. 'Water Music' is dedicated to Johnstone and the painter's first wife Flora

27 Caricature of MacDiarmid by Sydney Goodsir Smith, drawn in Sorley MacLean's flat in Queen Street, Edinburgh, 1948. Referring to Smith's ornithological nickname of Auk, in a speech of 1962, MacDiarmid said, 'the name is probably derived from the Icelandic Alka, which happily is near enough to be taken for an abbreviation of alcohol'

28 As Emilio Coia caricatured MacDiarmid in the *Scotsman* (4 Sept. 1976) shortly before the poet took part in a recital at the Netherbow Arts Centre, High Street, Edinburgh

29 Sydney Goodsir Smith, MacDiarmid and Norman MacCaig in the Peacock Hotel, Newhaven, near Leith, for the inaugural 200 Burns Club supper on 20 January 1959. 'Norman, Sydney and I may not resemble the Three Musketeers in the least,' MacDiarmid observed, 'but we make an excellent trio'

30 At Glasgow Sheriff Court in June 1952 Michael Grieve was sentenced to six months' imprisonment after being found guilty of failing to submit himself for a National Service medical examination. On his release from Saughton Prison, Edinburgh, Michael was met by his father and R. E. Muirhead

31 On 18 Feb. 1961 MacDiarmid was one of several speakers who addressed a crowd of some 20,000 in Trafalgar Square, London, at a rally dedicated to civil disobedience in the cause of nuclear disarmament. MacDiarmid is seen here with Sir Herbert Read to whom, in 1933, he had dedicated the poem 'Riding in a Fog'

32 On 14 Nov. 1970 MacDiarmid and Pound met for the first time. The two poets walked together in St Mark's Square, Venice, and had coffee in Florian's Café. MacDiarmid described Pound as 'the most lovable man I met'

33 In June 1971 Claddagh Records of Dublin released a double LP of MacDiarmid's reading of *A Drunk Man Looks at the Thistle*, and Robert Lowell attended the Scottish Arts Council's reception for the record in Edinburgh

34 After his divorce from Peggy in 1932 MacDiarmid was denied access to his children Christine and Walter. In 1953 the poet re-established relations with Christine, then living in Dundee with her doctor-husband, and he subsequently visited her in Canada, where she still lives, in Georgetown, Ontario

35 MacDiarmid did not see his son Walter again until 1963, a year after Peggy's death. Peggy had asked her children not to see their father during her lifetime and Walter honoured this request. This photo, like Pl. 34, was taken in 1975 at Brownsbank during one of Walter's visits to his father

36 On 6 July 1978, shortly before he died (on 9 Sept. in Edinburgh), MacDiarmid was awarded the honorary degree of Litt. D. at Trinity College, Dublin: (l–r) Mabel Olive Smith, Winifred Muriel Graham, Cathal William Gannon, Sir Frederick Charles Frank, MacDiarmid, Michael J. Dargan, Seán MacBride

37 The mature MacDiarmid, in mellow mood, with Valda at Brownsbank. In 'On a Raised Beach' he had written, 'let us not be afraid to die ... in death – unlike life – we lose nothing that is truly ours'

9

The 'Review'
Reporter Still

Thrang o' ideas that like fairy gowd
'll leave me the 'Review' reporter still
Waukenin' to my clung-kite faimly on a hill
O' useless croftin' whaur naething's growed
But Daith, sin Christ for an idea died
On a gey similar but less heich hillside.
Ech, weel for Christ: for he was never wed
And had nae weans clamourin' to be fed!
                    To Circumjack Cencrastus   (237)

FOR MacDiarmid 1926 had been an extraordinary year. He had
published *Penny Wheep* and *A Drunk Man Looks at the Thistle*, had
edited a selection *Robert Burns, 1759-1796* and had seen his *Contemporary
Scottish Studies* collected as a book. As a poet and polemicist he was a
force to be reckoned with in Scotland even if this fact brought little
comfort to many of his fellow Scots and little change to his professional
prospects as a journalist working on a local paper in a small Scottish
town: he was still on duty from nine to five, Monday to Friday; and
from nine to twelve, Saturday. The credo of endless creativity he had
announced in *A Drunk Man Looks at the Thistle* was difficult to sustain
in such circumstances.

In the month following the publication of *A Drunk Man* MacDiarmid was in a reflective mood. He looked gaunt but explained, in a letter of 9 December 1926 to George Ogilvie, that his lean and hungry look was entirely the result of his lack of teeth. Apparently MacDiarmid had had his teeth extracted in Salonika 'with half-a-bottle of whisky as anaesthetic'.[1] He felt that a new set of teeth would set his friends at ease. If he was temporarily toothless the Scottish terrier (as F. G. Scott described him) had lost neither his bark nor his bite. He was working on a big new poem, *To Circumjack Cencrastus*, and assured Ogilvie that *A Drunk Man* was by no means the culmination of his poetic career. He wanted to be equal, mentally and physically, to the challenge of *Cencrastus*:

> It will be an attempt to move really mighty numbers. In the nature of things such an ambition cannot be hastily consummated. It will take infinite pains – but along these lines I am satisfied that, if I cannot altogether realise my dream, I can at least achieve something well worth while ... I am frankly anxious not to die young. In many ways I am a late ripener. All my best work is still to come. I am only beginning to find myself.[2]

It would be almost four years before he completed *Cencrastus*. His promise to Neil Gunn that he meant to do *Cencrastus* 'in style though it costs my life'[3] has an ironic ring in retrospect.

MacDiarmid was keen to develop a close friendship with Gunn, a man whom he felt he could talk to as an intellectual equal. Gunn had been a valued contributor to the *Scottish Chapbook*, the *Scottish Nation* and the *Northern Review*; MacDiarmid had acclaimed Gunn's first novel, *The Grey Coast* (1926), which quoted a MacDiarmid poem, 'The Glog-Hole', on the title page. ('The Glog-Hole' was collected in *The Lucky Bag*, the only collection of verse MacDiarmid published in 1927.) The two men had in common a passionate interest in Scottish nationalism (Gunn joined the National Party of Scotland in 1929, a year after its formation), a love of literary conversation and a taste for malt whisky. Since 1923 Gunn had been an excise officer attached to Glen Mhor Distillery in Inverness where he had set up home, with his wife Daisy, in their bungalow Larachan at the north end of Dochfour Drive.

Invited to Inverness, MacDiarmid greeted the New Year of 1927 at Larachan, drinking and talking late into the night. The conversation continued over several days as the novelist and poet considered Mac-Diarmid's proposal for a collaborative novel, an experimental work using

English and Scots to isolate disparate aspects of the Scottish psychology. Though the novel did not materialise, MacDiarmid was encouraged to persevere with his Scots prose and published several autobiographical stories in Scots during 1927.[4] He told his friend that if he published a collection of these Scots stories, the book would be dedicated to Neil and Daisy Gunn.

On 25 January, the anniversary of the birth of Burns, MacDiarmid proposed the Immortal Memory at Cupar then returned to Montrose to renew his political activities. At a May Day demonstration, in the Montrose Burgh Hall, he spoke against the Trade Disputes and Trade Union Bill which intended to outlaw sympathetic strike action and introduce a contracting-in method for the payment of the political levy to the Labour Party. MacDiarmid described the Bill (eventually passed through Parliament on 27 July) as 'an odious piece of class legislation' designed 'to coerce the British working class into industrial serfdom'.[5] Memories of the failure of the General Strike were vivid and MacDiarmid was alarmed at the intention of Baldwin's government to further weaken the industrial power of working men and women.

The most promising political development, as MacDiarmid saw it, was the increasing interest in Scottish Nationalism. To encourage this he added to his burden as a journalist by beginning, in May, his weekly series of articles for the Scottish Secretariat. Roland E. Muirhead had founded the Scottish Secretariat in 1924 as a publishing concern for the distribution of Scottish material: for example it issued the *Scots Independent* (founded 1926) as a monthly journal devoted to the nationalistic debate. Through the Scottish Secretariat, MacDiarmid – using the pseudonym 'Mountboy' (after a hamlet near Montrose) – provided a weekly causerie which was syndicated to local newspapers throughout Scotland, from the *Orkney Herald* and the *Shetland News* to the *Kirkcaldy Times* and the *Kelso Chronicle*. Subjects ranged from Douglasite analyses of Scottish banking through appreciations of Scottish poets such as the Gaelic bard Alexander MacDonald to statements of the case for Scottish Nationalism. MacDiarmid received no payment for these articles, regarding his labours as necessary contributions to the Scottish cause. Several of the articles written for the Scottish Secretariat were assembled into the book *Albyn* (1927) in which the poet dismissed the Burns Cult, proposed the slogan 'Not Burns – Dunbar!', advocated the revival of Gaelic and hoped for a fusion of Social Credit, Socialism and Scottish nationalism.

That same May, MacDiarmid made another altruistic gesture by beginning his campaign to establish a Scottish Centre of PEN (Poets,

Playwrights, Editors, Essayists and Novelists). It was a subject he had discussed with Professor Herbert Grierson in 1925 and subsequently with John Galsworthy, first President of the London Centre of PEN. Now, on 16 May, MacDiarmid sent out some thirty letters to Scottish writers he considered significant including R. B. Cunninghame Graham, Neil Gunn, William Soutar, Helen Cruickshank, Lewis Spence and Compton Mackenzie, the last of whom agreed to transfer from the London to the Scottish branch. When the Scottish Centre of PEN was inaugurated in Glasgow, that summer, MacDiarmid was elected Secretary thus complicating an already busy life. Every month he attended PEN meetings, usually in Edinburgh where he stayed at Dinnieduff, the Corstorphine home of Helen Cruickshank and her mother. The poet slept over the front lobby, in a tiny guest-room with a sloping roof. Cruickshank's mother christened the room the 'Prophet's Chamber' after the story of Elijah and the pious widow who placed her small chamber at the prophet's disposal.

While the political and cultural consciousness of the Scots could be raised through the Scottish Secretariat articles and the activities of the Scottish Centre of PEN, MacDiarmid was determined to make practical progress towards his ideal of complete independence for Scotland. On 13 May the House of Commons had rejected the Government of Scotland Bill, the result of two meetings of the Scottish National Convention organised by the Scottish Home Rule Association. Prepared as a demand for Dominion status for Scotland, the Bill had been proposed by the Revd James Barr, Labour MP for Motherwell, President of the SHRA and, incidentally, Home Mission Secretary of the United Free Church of Scotland and a strong advocate of temperance.

After the defeat of Barr's Bill the SHRA called a third meeting of the Scottish National Convention at the Highlanders Institute in Glasgow on 19 November. MacDiarmid attended this as a member of the SHRA. Other organisations represented were the Scottish National Movement, founded in 1926 by Lewis Spence; and the Glasgow University Scottish Nationalist Association, founded by John MacCormick and James Valentine in 1927. The Scots National League – whose President, the Hon. Erskine of Mar, advocated sovereign independence – was not officially represented but its members made loud comments from the public gallery. The meeting was inconclusive. Lewis Spence suggested that the various nationalist groups should sink their differences and come together in a National Party of Scotland. James Barr declared that no member of the Labour Party could support such an organisation. The problem for

Scotland, MacDiarmid realised, was getting Scots to agree about political priorities. Personally he was willing to associate with any group that advanced the issue of independence. He was a member of the ILP and the SHRA; when the Hon. Erskine of Mar launched a new monthly periodical, the *Pictish Review*, in November, MacDiarmid (or Gillechriosd Mac a'Ghreidhir as he occasionally called himself in deference to Mar's Gaelic revivalism) was a prominent part of it.

At the beginning of 1928 MacDiarmid had put *Cencrastus* aside to complete a commission. He had been offered £50 by the publisher Martin Secker to translate into English a Spanish novel, *La Esclava del Señor* by Ramon Maria de Tenreiro.[6] The prospect of more money was especially welcome as Peggy was pregnant again and increasingly unhappy with her domestic lot in Montrose. As usual her husband was planning to rush about the country giving speeches at the drop of an invitation through the front door. His plans included a lecture-recital with F. G. Scott in Edinburgh, an address to the Theosophical Society of Dundee, and an attempt to 'put Burns in his place'.[7]

On 21 January, MacDiarmid made his provocative attack on Burns in time for digestion at the many anniversary dinners. Speaking in Glasgow, under the auspices of the Glasgow branch of the Scottish National Movement, he dismissed Burns as a voice from the past whose reputation counted for nothing in modern European letters. According to MacDiarmid, Burns's standing in comparison to poets such as Victor Hugo or Heine was similar to the standing of Sir Harry Lauder as a vocalist in comparison to Chaliapin. Scotland should decide, MacDiarmid argued, to forget, for the next quarter of a century at least, that Burns had ever existed. MacDiarmid criticised the Burns Federation for its indifference to contemporary Scots verse, noted that the Federation sponsored no annual prize for new work in Scots, and complained that those responsible for the Scottish Literary Revival had had no support from the Federation.

Predictably, MacDiarmid's speech was bitterly resented by dedicated Burnsians. Two Labour MPs, James Brown (South Ayrshire) and Rosslyn Mitchell (Paisley), both ardent champions of temperance and not therefore boozy Burnsians, defended Burns as a Scottish genius. Two other pillars of the Scottish Community similarly declared their allegiance to Burns: Lord Sands, speaking at the anniversary dinner in Stirling, said that Burns was the poet of Scotland as David was the Psalmist of

Israel; the Revd J. A. C. MacKellar, addressing the Albany Burns Club in Glasgow, said that MacDiarmid's attack was 'grievously foolish'.[8]

MacDiarmid returned to the attack in an article in the *Glasgow Evening Times*. He dismissed as preposterous the annual spectacle of abasement before the name of Burns and suggested that Burns was as outdated as democracy:

> My point was that if, at long last, Europe is beginning to repudiate democracy, romantic love, and other basic elements in Burns' creed, that suggests that Burns' work will speedily become more and more old-fashioned and intolerable to modern consciousness. That is at it should be. ... In conclusion, let me say that I do not object to Burns dinners on temperance grounds. ... The drinking at Burns suppers is one of the few elements in the programme which have my invariable and hearty approval. I prefer Burnsians 'speechless'.[9]

The insults were calculated to provoke and they did. MacDiarmid was succeeding in his desire to be 'Scotland's Public Enemy No 1'.[10]

With the row about Burns still resounding in Scotland, MacDiarmid was philosophical about his unpopularity in many parts of the country. His élitist outlook convinced him that the great things would be done by an avant garde and he was content to have the support of his peers, friends such as Neil Gunn. In February 1928 he was eulogised by another novelist, one much more renowned than Gunn. Writing in the *Pictish Review*, Compton Mackenzie cast MacDiarmid as a romantic hero in the great Scottish tradition:

> [Christopher Grieve] will, I hope, forgive me for insisting that his Scottish idea is precisely that for which Culloden was fought. ... All the dreams that haunt us – the salvation of Gaelic, the revival of Braid Scots, a Gaelic University in Inverness, the repopulation of the glens, a Celtic federation of independent but interdependent states, and a hundred things will only embody themselves when we have a Scottish Free State under the Crown. ... Fuse thought with action and recreate a nation. I have enough faith in Mr Grieve's poetic genius to believe that it might effect even as much as this.[11]

Mackenzie thus put his considerable authority behind the notion of MacDiarmid as the saviour of Scotland.

Only nine years older than MacDiarmid, Compton Mackenzie was a literary celebrity in 1928. The son of parents with a theatrical background, he was born in West Hartlepool because his father's touring company, the Compton Comedy Company, happened to be playing there in 1882. Mackenzie's grandfather, Charles Mackenzie, had changed his name to Henry Compton on assuming a career as an actor; Edward Montague Compton Mackenzie reverted to the family's Scottish surname as an undergraduate at Oxford. He achieved success as early as 1912 with *Carnival* and the following year *Sinister Street* made such an impact that Henry James wrote to tell the young author he had emancipated the English novel.

Mackenzie converted to Roman Catholicism in 1914, served in the Dardanelles in the First World War, and founded a successful magazine, the *Gramophone*, in 1923. Temperamentally he was an anachronism, a Jacobite at large in modern Scotland. F. G. Scott, suspicious of his motives, observed that Mackenzie saw himself as 'the Prince Charlie of a neo-Catholic Alba'.[12] MacDiarmid, however, was impressed by Mackenzie's panache and welcomed his public espousal of Scottish Nationalism. Though the two writers approached the issue of independence from different angles — MacDiarmid was republican and socialist whereas Mackenzie was romantic and committed to the union of the crowns — they were united by a vision of the spiritual rebirth of Scotland.

On 5 April Peggy gave birth to a son, Walter Ross Grieve, and MacDiarmid asked Mackenzie and Gunn to act as godfathers. Both novelists accepted the invitation and agreed to come to Montrose in mid May. Before his son's baptism took place, MacDiarmid met Mackenzie, for the first time, in Glasgow on 10 May at a conference organised by John MacCormick. The purpose of the conference was to discuss the amalgamation of the various nationalist groups — SHRA, Scots National League, Scottish National Movement, Glasgow University Scottish Nationalist Association — as a National Party of Scotland. After agreement to form such a party had been reached, Mackenzie wrote to his wife Faith about his first impressions of MacDiarmid:

> I found Grieve the poet very remarkable — a little like D. H. Lawrence, but with a harder intellect and, I think, a richer genius. I hope that between us we shall be able to steer the movement out of any kind of parochialism.[13]

The day after the conference Mackenzie addressed the Glasgow University Union, at MacCormick's request, to announce that R. B. Cunninghame Graham would stand as the Scottish Nationalist candidate at the university's forthcoming Rectorial election. As his main opponent

231

would be the Prime Minister, Stanley Baldwin, few gave Cunninghame Graham much hope of attracting more than a handful of votes.

MacDiarmid was delighted at Cunninghame Graham's return to the Scottish scene. In 1925 he had lamented Cunninghame Graham's prolonged absences from Scotland, saying that

> for those of us who are connected with either the Scottish Nationalists or the Socialist movements he has become like a curious and unseizable dream by which we are tantalisingly haunted but which we can by no means effectively recall.[14]

Born in London in 1852, the son of a Scottish laird married to the daughter of a Spanish aristocrat, Cunninghame Graham had been an outspoken Liberal MP, a prisoner after his participation in the 'Bloody Sunday' riot at Trafalgar Square in 1887, and first President of the Scottish Labour Party. A skilled writer who set some splendid short stories in Scotland (and South America), Cunninghame Graham was a flamboyant and unforgettable figure to all who met him, including Keir Hardie and Bernard Shaw. Known as 'Don Roberto', he claimed direct descent from Robert II and was usually described as a regal presence. 'He was a king among men,' said John MacCormick.[15] MacDiarmid, for his part, 'valued Cunninghame Graham beyond rubies. We will never see his like again.'[16]

After announcing Cunninghame Grahame's candidature Mackenzie travelled to Montrose to spend the weekend at 16 Links Avenue with MacDiarmid and Gunn. On Sunday, 13 May, the three writers went with Peggy and her baby to the baptism in the Scottish Episcopal Church. One incident from that weekend remained with Mackenzie. As he was in some pain from a sciatica attack, he needed an injection which MacDiarmid, drawing on his medical experience in the First World War, volunteered to give. As the needle went in, Mackenzie noted, 'the tall and distinguished figure of Neil Gunn went down on the floor in a dead faint caused by the sight of a minute drop of blood'.[17] When Gunn recovered MacDiarmid covered his embarrassment by assuring him that a dread of injections was commonplace.

On a more serious level MacDiarmid and Mackenzie discussed a strategy for the National Party of Scotland. They felt it was naïve to insist on fighting a General Election with exclusively nationalist candidates since, in the interests of practical politics and economic expediency, nationalists could contest seats as Labour candidates stressing

Home Rule as a priority. However, the NPS was constitutionally committed to exclusivity as members were debarred from standing under any other auspices. Similarly, the Labour Party was suspicious of attempts to fight NPS battles under a Labour banner. Mackenzie went from Montrose to Iona to decline the offer of standing as a Labour candidate for the Western Isles precisely because 'Home Rule was obviously not going to be a main plank on their platform at the next General Election'.[18] MacDiarmid turned down the opportunity of standing as ILP candidate for Banffshire.

MacDiarmid and Mackenzie were together again in Glasgow on 2 June for a PEN dinner at the St Enoch's Hotel in honour of the writer Gordon Bottomley. On 23 June Mackenzie was advertised as one of the speakers at the inaugural demonstration of the NPS at the King's Park, Stirling. Because Mackenzie was unable to attend Lewis Spence moved the resolution approving the formation of the NPS. Seconding the resolution, MacDiarmid made grandiose claims for the NPS's readiness to contest the next General Election:

> Funds are coming in, and men are coming in ... It is our intention to contest every Scottish constituency at the next General Election. Steps are now being taken to appoint the necessary candidates. For those of us forming the National Party who have hitherto been Conservatives, Liberals, or Socialists, these English party political divisions have lost all significance.[19]

In fact, MacDiarmid was being impossibly optimistic about NPS popular support and financial strength – and he knew it.

For the whole of July MacDiarmid took a country cottage in Brechin, seven miles west of Montrose. He felt fit and ready to respond to an invitation to attend the Tailtean Games in Dublin as the guest of the Irish Free State. Senator Oliver St John Gogarty, one of the organisers of the Tailtean Games, invited Mackenzie and the Hon. Erskine of Mar as well as MacDiarmid but Mackenzie could not go. So MacDiarmid and Erskine of Mar spent the last fortnight of August in Ireland as representatives of Scotland. For the poet it was an unforgettable experience which he talked about for the rest of his life. He had an interview with Éamon de Valera, leader of *Fianna Fáil*, and had tea with the Minister of Defence in the Cosgrave government. He flew in an Avro-Anson five-cylinder plane. He stayed in Ely Place with Gogarty who entertained him with tales of his drinking days with Joyce and took him to Joyce's favourite bars. Gogarty also drove MacDiarmid around Ireland, covering about one thousand miles in the process.

Many prominent Irish writers were introduced to MacDiarmid: F. R. Higgins, Walter Starkie, Eoin MacNeill, Seamas O'Sullivan (founder of the *Dublin Magazine*) and AE (George William Russell), editor of the *Irish Statesman*. MacDiarmid's most treasured encounter was with W. B. Yeats, a poet he had admired for years. Each Friday night Yeats went to AE's house and when MacDiarmid was in Dublin he was invited along. He noted that both AE and Yeats were highly opinionated men who delivered monologues rather than exchanging pleasantries and he regretted that nothing stronger than lemonade was served. Yeats asked Mac-Diarmid to explain Social Credit theory to him but the Scottish poet found this an impossible task given the Irish poet's indifference to the details of banking. When Yeats was ready to leave it was one o'clock in the Saturday morning. Yeats and MacDiarmid left together and walked the streets of Dublin for more than an hour. Before they parted Yeats asked MacDiarmid to excuse him; 'I must urinate,' he said, then did so in the middle of the road. MacDiarmid joined him – 'I crossed swords with him and we became very friendly after that'.[20]

Back in Montrose, in September, MacDiarmid resumed work on *Cencrastus* but found it difficult to concentrate on a poem that was shaping as a catalogue of frustrations rather than a thematically controlled composition. He was unsettled in Montrose and anxious to see more positive political developments in Scotland. R. E. Muirhead, standing as an Independent Scottish Nationalist in the May by-election in West Renfrewshire, had secured only 1667 votes. Despite this disappointing result MacDiarmid accepted an invitation from the Dundee branch of the NPS to contest the next General Election. It was a reluctant decision as he had no great faith in parliamentary progress. Meanwhile he looked for a job that would remove him from Montrose. He applied for a post as a reporter with the *Scottish Co-operator* in Glasgow and asked Muirhead to put in a good word for him. He did not get the job.

Encouraging news about another matter came from Glasgow on 27 October. The result of the Glasgow University Rectorial election showed that Baldwin, with 1014 votes, had polled only thirty-six votes more than Cunninghame Graham who was well ahead of Rosslyn Mitchell, the Labour candidate, and Lord Samuel, the Liberal.[21] For the Scottish Nationalists this was an astonishing triumph and they lost no time in parading their near-victory before the Scottish public. A few days after the announcement a public meeting was held in St Andrew's Hall in Glasgow with Cunninghame Graham as the main speaker supported by Compton Mackenzie and the Duke of Montrose (who wanted a measure of Home Rule but no separation from England so declined to join the NPS). More than three thousand people attended the celebration at which MacDiarmid and John MacCormick also spoke. MacCormick's subsequent account of MacDiarmid's contribution is acerbic:

> Grieve had joined our platform and in characteristic manner had hurled contempt at everything English. Although I have no doubt that he has done invaluable work in the whole field of Scottish literature I am certain that C. M. Grieve has been politically one of the greatest handicaps with which any national movement could have been burdened. His love of bitter controversy, his extravagant and self-assertive criticism of the English, and his woolly thinking, which could encompass within one mind the doctrines both of Major Douglas and Karl Marx, were taken by many of the more sober-minded of the Scots as sufficient excuse to condemn the whole case for Home Rule out of hand.[22]

MacDiarmid had little respect for MacCormick's qualities and subsequently wrote a poem comparing himself to MacCormick and his NPS colleagues: 'Scotland will shine like the sun in my song/While they vanish, like mists, whence they came' (1277).

Unfortunately for the NPS the euphoria associated with Cunninghame Graham's achievement seemed to evaporate rapidly. On 1 November Mackenzie and MacDiarmid were speaking in Perth. Sitting beside his friend, Mackenzie became depressed by the attitude of the audience:

> As I watched a thinnish audience listen apathetically to one of the most eloquent speeches I ever heard Grieve make I began to wonder if the country had really been shaken. For the first time I began to wonder if the policy adopted at the last [NPS] Council meeting of contesting parliamentary seats was a wise one yet awhile.[23]

Mackenzie must have recalled his conversations with MacDiarmid in Montrose. There was not sufficient money to fund a big parliamentary campaign by the NPS and both Mackenzie and MacDiarmid believed that the political consciousness of the Scots could be raised by propaganda and non-parliamentary means. The enemy was apathy.

On a personal level MacDiarmid's life was far from satisfactory. Earning around £3 for a five-and-a-half-day week MacDiarmid was finding it difficult to make ends meet now that he had two children and a wife to support and was being pressed for debts incurred in connection with the magazines he had launched in Montrose. Having written many unpaid articles for the Scottish Secretariat he turned to R. E. Muirhead for assistance. He had not yet received payment for his Spanish translation so asked Muirhead to lend him £50 which he promised to pay back at the rate of £1 per week until a fee came through from Secker. On receipt of MacDiarmid's request, Muirhead sent the money. MacDiarmid expressed his gratitude in an eloquent letter of 5 November 1928, confiding that he might have gone bankrupt but for this loan. Obviously embarrassed about being in debt to Muirhead, MacDiarmid assured his friend he would increase his efforts on behalf of Scottish Nationalism though he felt his main contribution should be poetic rather than party-political. His explanation had the force of a deeply held personal philosophy:

> I am unquestionably doing far more for Scotland when my activity issues in poetry rather than in any other form. Only that cannot be controlled; the spirit blows where it listeth. I have no silly personal pride; I do not write poetry – I am merely the vehicle for something far greater than myself. Without egoism, therefore, I know that Yeats, Mackenzie and others are right when they tell me that I am by far the greatest Scottish poet since Burns. After all what does that amount to: I may be that and still relatively negligible to Burns. In any case I know that all the best poetry I have in me is still to write. ... I stand at the very opposite pole of Scottish poetical genius from Burns: he was a great popular poet – I am essentially, and must be, an unpopular one; a poet's poet. ... My task is to be unpopular – a fighter – an enemy of accepted things; not in any captious fashion but out of profound conviction, and while I may often mistake the promptings of my heart and be merely factitious, I have reason to know that the best of my work at all events is proving a powerful influence because it springs from the deeps of the destined.[24]

Clearly MacDiarmid was in no mood to go through the routine of a parliamentary contest and was anxious to finish *Cencrastus*. All the evidence suggested that the NPS was mistaken in its decision to contest seats on an exclusively nationalist programme. Muirhead's disappointing showing in the West Renfrewshire by-election of May 1928 was matched by Lewis Spence's poor result in the North Midlothian by-election early in 1929; standing as the NPS candidate Spence received just over eight hundred votes from a poll of around 40,000. MacDiarmid decided against standing as a NPS candidate in Dundee and was justified when the results of the General Election of May 1929 were declared. Muirhead again lost his deposit in West Renfrewshire as did MacCormick, NPS candidate for the Camlachie division of Glasgow.

The General Election exposed the electoral weakness of the NPS and established a minority Labour government indifferent to Home Rule. MacDiarmid told Compton Mackenzie how downhearted he was: 'A horrible botch has been made of the first real chance we've had of creating a big National Movement and we have now a perfect mess of stupidity to clear away again.'[25] The poet was glad of an opportunity to take a break from Ramsay MacDonald's Britain. As honorary Secretary of the Scottish branch of PEN, he attended the International PEN Congress in Vienna from 24 to 29 June. He left Montrose and arrived in London early on Friday morning, 21 June, then stayed overnight at The Nook, Crowborough, with Edwin Muir who had dedicated his fiercely critical study, *John Knox* (1929), to MacDiarmid. Vienna was a revelation and MacDiarmid thought it a 'most beautiful and theatrical city'.[26] Staying in the Hotel Bristol in the Opernring he enjoyed his talks with the Socialist Mayor of Vienna, his visits to blocks of workers' flats, his trip to the wine festival at Semmering, and his epic beer-drinking sessions with Theodor Daubler, author of the epic poem *Das Nordlicht* (1910).

Edified by his visit to Vienna, MacDiarmid returned to Montrose via Jethou, the Channel Island that Compton Mackenzie leased, for £100 per year, from 1923 to 1930. The two men had two important matters to discuss. Thanks to the success of the *Gramophone*, Mackenzie now wanted to launch a companion magazine, a critical weekly devoted to the radio. It would be called *Vox*, would cost sixpence a copy, would be edited by Mackenzie and would be launched in London in November. Impressed by MacDiarmid's eagerness to escape from Montrose, Mackenzie offered him a job as the London Editor of *Vox*, a post involving the routine running of the weekly and the writing of copy on a variety of topics. MacDiarmid accepted the offer with alacrity, convinced it was the answer to his many problems. He felt that working in London for Mackenzie would be rewarding both financially and intellectually and that *Vox* had a great future in front of it. The journal, he told Mackenzie, would be 'the biggest thing since the New Journalism – and bigger; an inspiring cause to work for under an ideal leader'.[27] As far as the poet was concerned the sooner he got out of Montrose the better.

The other matter about which MacDiarmid and Mackenzie agreed was political. Having seen the NPS do so badly at the General Election, they discussed the formation of a secret society to be known as Clann Albain (the children of Scotland). Members, Mackenzie decided, should be pledged 'to foster the Celtic idea with a vision, on a far distant horizon at present, of rescuing the British Isles from being dominated by London'.[28] For MacDiarmid, still sympathetic to 'a species of Scottish Fascism',[29] it would provide opportunities to pursue illegal activities such as the occupation of Edinburgh Castle or the recovery of the Stone of Destiny from Westminster Abbey. That, at any rate, was the theory.

When MacDiarmid returned to Montrose he and Peggy made their arrangements to move to London. It was agreed that Peggy's sister Ina would accompany the family to London – to help with the housework and to do some typing in the *Vox* office. MacDiarmid took another guest with him: Tom MacDonald who, using the pseudonym Fionn Mac Colla, was to become one of the most pugnacious of modern Scottish novelists. MacDonald was born in Montrose in 1906 and brought up as a Plymouth Brother. He had an early revulsion with the Protestant faith (he was to convert to Catholicism in 1935) and a firm conviction that Scotland had been ruined by the Knoxian Reformation. He trained as a teacher in Aberdeen and, after working in Wester Ross, taught in the Scots College in Safed, Palestine. When the NPS was formed, he joined; when he returned to Scotland in 1929 he hoped he need never again leave his native land. MacDonald headed for Montrose where his family now lived at 12 Links Avenue, two doors from MacDiarmid's council house. MacDonald's family deplored the influence of MacDiarmid on the young man but that merely encouraged him in his resolve to associate himself with the poet. If that meant moving from Montrose to London, so be it. MacDonald had a first novel to write and felt he could complete this in the company of MacDiarmid.

On 16 August, MacDiarmid submitted a new collection of poems, *Fier comme un Ecossais*, to Blackwood's. That, he hoped, would compensate for his failure so far to deliver *Cencrastus*, a project he now intended to conclude in London. Before he left Montrose, MacDiarmid decided to burn the papers he could not transport to London. He had an 'almighty big bonfire'[30] in the garden of 16 Links Avenue and consigned to it all his spare copies of the *Scottish Chapbook* and the *Scottish Nation* as well as a big pile of letters from such writers as Neil Munro and John Buchan. On 9 September 1929, he took the overnight train to London, leaving behind some unpaid debts and a Scotland jolted by his activities.

10

Grief in His
Private Life

My story, on the contrary, is the story of an absolutist whose absolutes
came to grief in his private life ... But despite that tragedy (or, perhaps,
because of it) I have pulled my world together again in such wise that,
asserted more strongly than ever now, I am very unlikely to come to grief
in it a second time.

Lucky Poet, p. 44

MACDIARMID arrived in London on 10 September 1929 in high
spirits and with great expectations. For the first time in his life he
had a chance to achieve financial security and he was confident of his
creative plans. Compared to the £3 per week he earned on the *Montrose
Review*, his job on *Vox* paid a salary of £52 per month. Compton
Mackenzie had arranged for an advance of £48 which enabled Mac-
Diarmid to settle into his new house, an ex-Wesleyan manse at 18
Pyrland Road in Highbury. The new household was a busy one. As well
as Peggy, Christine (enrolled at a convent school) and the baby Walter,
the former manse accommodated Tom MacDonald, hard at work on *The
Albannach*; and Peggy's sister Ina who, it was arranged, would be
MacDiarmid's secretary at *Vox*.

The magazine itself was established in an office at 10A Soho Square,
off Oxford Street. Mackenzie, whose contribution to *Vox* was to amount

to little more than a weekly editorial (for which he was to be paid an annual salary of £2000), was convinced that radio would 'revolutionise human thought and human action as completely as did the invention of printing'.[1] In January 1927 the British Broadcasting Corporation, with John Reith as the first Director-General, had taken over from the British Broadcasting Company; Mackenzie was certain that the time was propitious for a serious critical journal devoted to broadcasting. Mackenzie's brother-in-law, Christopher Stone, London Editor of the *Gramophone*, was opposed to the launching of *Vox* but was persuaded to move from Frith Street to Soho Square to share office space with *Vox*, and to let the *Gramophone* invest £1000 in the new venture. Stone, who had published a volume of verse while a schoolboy at Eton, was not well disposed to MacDiarmid.

London's sprawling diversity offered fascinating distractions for MacDiarmid. When not absorbed in his editorial duties, planning the first issue of *Vox*, he enjoyed the social life of the capital, becoming a regular visitor to the many pubs within walking − or staggering − distance from Soho Square. North of Oxford Street there was a maze of pubs including three particularly favoured by the poet and similar spirits: the Wheatsheaf in Rathbone Place; the Marquis of Granby, a few yards north of the Wheatsheaf, on the corner of Rathbone Street and Percy Street; the Fitzroy Tavern on the corner of Charlotte Street and Windmill Street. For dedicated drinkers there were clubs that stayed open in the afternoons when the pubs closed and MacDiarmid liked David Tennant's Gargoyle Club, round the corner from Soho Square in Meard Street. In these haunts he met expatriate Scots such as the poet W. S. Graham and the painters Robert Colquhoun and Robert MacBryde. His favourite London pub was the Plough, in Museum Street, and there he drank with Tom Driberg of the *Daily Express*, the composer 'Peter Warlock' (Philip Heseltine, who died in 1930) and the Scottish writer Catherine Carswell. In the Plough he encountered the Irish writer Liam O'Flaherty 'with whom ... I straightaway had a battle-royal on the floor of the pub'.[2]

The first issue of *Vox* appeared on 9 November 1929 with a cover proudly proclaiming, under the title, that Mackenzie was editor (his first editorial discussed the Children's Hour). Using the initials A. K. L., MacDiarmid contributed 'The Cutting of an Agate' in which he defended James Agate's hostile broadcast criticism of a play and suggested that the BBC should encourage incisive comments on theatrical productions. A. K. L. was himself a hard-hitting commentator as well as an appreciative critic. In the issue of 7 December he responded to the publication of *The*

Testament of Beauty by Robert Bridges, the Poet Laureate, calling it 'a wonderful achievement, a philosophical poem, over 4000 lines long, communicating a timely and triumphant faith'.[3] By the time these words were printed in *Vox*, MacDiarmid was recuperating from a serious accident.

On Wednesday, 4 December, MacDiarmid was out late and, no doubt the worse for wear, travelled home on an open-top double-decker bus which stopped at the end of Pyrland Road. Just after midnight the bus shuddered to a halt at the poet's stop; he got up and toppled from the upper-deck, landing on the pavement on his head – or, rather, his thick head of hair. He was picked up unconscious and taken by the police first to the Metropolitan Infirmary then to Highgate Workhouse Infirmary. At 1.30 on the Thursday morning, a policeman brought Peggy news of the accident. An hour later another policeman called to confirm that MacDiarmid had severe concussion. Peggy went to her husband at 7 a.m. and was shocked by the shabbiness of the Infirmary: only the ward Sister, insisting that the patient needed rest, stopped her from taking him home immediately. Next day Peggy returned, determined to extricate MacDiarmid, and waited until he was discharged.

Restless by nature, MacDiarmid was reluctant to accept a prolonged period of absence from his work. He wrote, cheerfully enough, to tell his friends the consequences of the accident. To Gogarty, a medical man as well as a writer and regarded as Dublin's finest ear-and-throat surgeon, MacDiarmid explained on 30 December:

> I have made a wonderful recovery. Happily my skull was not fractured, largely owing to my great cushion of hair, I fancy, and to the fact that
>> it takes a lot
>> to rattle a Scot.
> But it was a narrow squeak and I am told that I must avoid mental stress and excitement, alcoholic stimulants, spiced foods, and even tobacco (but the latter I disregard as a mere General Practitioner's convention) under penalty of risking brain fever or a cerebral haemorrhage, for some considerable time to come.[4]

MacDiarmid also discussed the accident with John Buchan who, as MP for the Scottish Universities, invited him to take tea at the House of Commons. Buchan, who had twice fractured his skull, was astonished that MacDiarmid had not suffered a similar fate. Buchan must have confused the details of the discussion because when a mutual friend of both men mentioned the poet to the novelist, Buchan said 'Ah, yes! poor Grieve. Most unfortunate fellow. Always fracturing his skull!'[5]

Despite the severity of the fall, MacDiarmid resumed work with *Vox* before the end of the month: on 28 December he took issue with Buchan who suggested, in a speech, that a disembodied voice on radio was incompatible with the art of oratory. A. K. L. disagreed, contending that it was a virtue of radio to inhibit emotionalism and clarify intellectual content. His old friend Buchan, he noted, had 'no pretensions to be regarded as an orator'.[6] The year 1929 moved towards a close with MacDiarmid contentedly ensconced at *Vox* and, since he was denied drink and other distractions, determined to complete *Cencrastus* and assemble a new volume of his shorter poems. He would greet the New Year of 1930 with nothing stronger than a cup of tea.

It was during this festive season that Peggy became friendly with William McElroy, a man old enough to be her father: at the end of 1929 Peggy was thirty-two, McElroy was fifty-six. Friendly with several writers and painters, McElroy was a Scotsman with a large appetite for artistic and sexual pleasures: his wife Kate, whom he married in 1895, bore him nine children (five survived into the 1930s). As a coal-merchant he had made a fortune from the sale of slag which lay in heaps around the mines closed by the General Strike of 1926. He lived ostentatiously, renting flats, complete with servants, in Chelsea and Brighton, drawing an annual income of around £10,000 from his business. He had a Rolls-Royce car, racing stables in Rottingdean, and used some of his money to promote his cultural interests. He had, for example, financed the transfer of two plays by Sean O'Casey – *Juno and the Paycock* and *The Plough and the Stars* – to London. When O'Casey married Eileen Carey in London in 1927 McElroy was best man.

Some notion of McElroy's demanding nature can be gathered from O'Casey's play *Purple Dust* (written in 1940 and first performed in Liverpool five years later) as one of the principal characters, Cyril Poges, was modelled on the coal-merchant. As observed satirically by O'Casey, Stoke and Poges are two English businessmen who acquire an old Tudor mansion in the west of Ireland. Converts to the countryside they attempt to absorb the rural romance of Ireland and, in the process, make egregious fools of themselves. The limitations of Poges are listed in O'Casey's stage directions:

He has a fussy manner, all business over little things; wants his own way at all times; and persuades himself that whatever he thinks of doing must be for the best. He is apt to lose his temper easily, and to shout in the belief that that is the only way to make other people fall in with his opinions.[7]

Poges has a mistress, Souhaun, half his age. Again, O'Casey's directions are precise and it is reasonable to assume that Souhaun is a dramatic portrait of Peggy:

> Souhaun is a woman of thirty-three years of age. She must have been a very handsome girl and she is still very good-looking, in a more matronly way. She has [a] fine figure [and] is still attractive enough to find attention from a good many men ...[8]

In fact, as well as in O'Casey's fiction, McElroy was besotted by Peggy. Eileen O'Casey has described how McElroy would ask Peggy to parade in front of people as if she were a model then tell her 'We want to admire your legs'.[9]

Peggy must have contrasted the riches of her admirer with the struggles of her husband. On 2 January 1930, on Gogarty's advice, MacDiarmid sent some autographed copies of his books to Lord Beaverbrook at the *Daily Express* in the hope that this might lead to a column on the Scottish edition of the paper; Beaverbrook was not interested. The next day, as Blackwood's had rejected *Fier comme un Ecossais*, he sent this collection to the Porpoise Press which likewise turned it down. Meanwhile the problems of *Vox* were multiplying with every week that passed. Circulation was poor so advertisers took their custom elsewhere. On 18 January *Vox* reduced its price by fifty per cent, selling at threepence a copy. Christopher Stone then decided to dispense with the services of MacDiarmid, and his secretary Ina Skinner, in an attempt to run the magazine as a monthly prepared by the staff of the *Gramophone*. This plan came to nothing, however, and *Vox* folded with its final issue of 8 February. MacDiarmid did not even get a full month's pay as he still owed £20 of the original advance arranged by Mackenzie. Having come to London and experienced a physical fall from a bus, he now had to cope with a catastrophic financial fall.

With MacDiarmid out of a job, Peggy decided to raise money through her own talents. She agreed to type Edwin Muir's second novel, *The Three Brothers*, and she prevailed on the generosity of McElroy. Unknown to his wife Kate, who shared his Chelsea flat in Church Street when she came to London, McElroy had another address in Chelsea, in Jubilee Place. Peggy became a frequent visitor to Jubilee Place and in February was introduced to Mrs McElroy at the Grand Hotel, Brighton.

Kate McElroy said of this meeting with Peggy, 'She made it very obvious that she wanted my husband to help her in the Communist movement, and also with a book she was writing. She said they wanted men like him.'[10] Peggy, a quiet domestic creature in Montrose, was blossoming into an emancipated woman. Writing to Helen Cruickshank she mentioned that Neil and Daisy Gunn were visiting 18 Pyrland Road then said that 'Mrs G[unn] thinks I'm not nearly so nice as I was in Montrose – I'm fast now. . . . I've been having a hilarious time of late and don't feel in the least like working, I assure you.'[11]

On Easter Monday she again wrote to Cruickshank, reporting on MacDiarmid's problems with *Cencrastus*:

> He's scarcely visible these days under an accumulation of books & papers & he is certainly not in too amiable a frame of mind, but he's hatching out 'Cencrastus' & it seems a worse process than producing babies! . . . I'm accustomed [to] having my nose nipped off. I sometimes threaten to shut him in a padded room & then to stand screaming outside. Living with, or being a friend of, a poet is no joke.[12]

On a more serene level she told, in the same letter, of rambles with her husband and, incidentally, showed the sensitive side of her personality:

> We've been rambling a few times – a fortnight ago we were at Westerham & Limpsfield. I was very happy. The trouble is my pace is too fast for the other members & I've to sit on gates and dykes waiting for them every now & again. The countryside was very lovely – there were lots of catkins & wood anemones in the woods & fields of primroses & wild violets. Here & there whins were in bloom in the commons but they hadn't that strong intoxicating perfume such as they have on Montrose Links on a hot day.[13]

Now that Tom MacDonald had left 18 Pyrland Road to finish *The Albannach* in Scotland, and with Peggy occupied with her interests (including duties as secretary to an art group), MacDiarmid tried hard to get a job in London. He went to the Caledonian Club to meet William Will, honorary Secretary of the Vernacular Circle of the London Burns Club and a director of Allied Newspapers, in the hope of securing some reviewing work for the *Daily Telegraph* and he asked Compton Mackenzie if he could help. In neither case had he any luck. Inadvertently he caused Mackenzie great embarrassment by his decision to publicise the existence of Clann Albain.

He announced, in the *Daily Record* of 10 May 1930, that radical nationalists were involved in a Scottish Sinn Fein movement and two days later was quoted, in the same paper, on the subject of Clann Albain. On Friday, 16 May, MacDiarmid was specific:

> Clann Albain is no new thing. It has been built up steadily during the past two years, The majority of its members are members of the national party [though] the latter has no responsibility for it. One of the most disinguished of living Scotsmen is the Chief of Clann Albain. I am not at liberty to divulge his name, or those of the other office bearers. The organisation is an exclusive one – no one is admitted to membership who is not thoroughly guaranteed and tested. The members, apart from an inner circle, do not know the names of any of the office bearers. The whole organisation is on a militaristic basis, and in this resembles the Fascist movement.[14]

As a result of this revelation Mackenzie was investigated by the Special Branch. Fortunately for Mackenzie his denial of conspiracy was accepted by the senior police officer who interviewed him.

MacDiarmid made his provocative statements, about a Scottish Sinn Fein and Clann Albain, in Glasgow in connection with the second annual delegate conference of the NPS on Saturday, 10 May. After his visit to Glasgow he did not return to Peggy, Christine, Walter and 18 Pyrland Road. He had found a job in Liverpool and arrived there on 12 May; Peggy thought it would be better if she remained in London, with Christine continuing at her convent school. MacDiarmid was employed as Publicity Officer for the Liverpool Organisation, founded in 1923 by a group of businessmen intent on promoting the city as a leading industrial centre. Established as a limited company in 1928 the Liverpool Organisation was supported by subscriptions from more than three hundred Merseyside firms and with grants from the various corporations involved: Liverpool, Birkenhead, Wallasey and Bootle. As Publicity Officer, MacDiarmid was required to produce technical articles on shipping and other matters for such journals as the *Ironmonger*. His office was on the Pier Head, in the Royal Liver Building: one of those massive Edwardian architectural monuments to the prosperous past of a city that had built its trade on slaves, sugar and other commodities.

About a month after he had arrived in Liverpool, MacDiarmid heard that Peggy was poorly, 'highly neurasthenic',[15] and was staying with the Muirs in Crowborough, Sussex. Separated from his family, the poet spent a fair amount of time drinking in Liverpool pubs but fortunately he also saw men with whom he could discuss his creative work. He resumed his old friendship with Roderick Watson Kerr who had been working on the *Liverpool Post* since 1926. (The Porpoise Press, co-founded by Kerr, published a new impression of *Annals of the Five Senses* in 1930).

AE visited Liverpool and was somewhat startled when MacDiarmid arrived at his hotel in formal evening attire. Obliged to attend a Lord Mayor's banquet, in his official capacity, MacDiarmid had donned an outfit complete with miniature medals. Though he had obtained an invitation for AE, the Irishman said he would not be seen dead at such a gathering. MacDiarmid left the function around one in the morning then made his way to AE's hotel where the pair talked until breakfast time.

The biggest creative problem MacDiarmid faced in Liverpool was the completion of *To Circumjack Cencrastus* which he had been working on for almost four years. On 30 June he sent two-thirds of the poem to Blackwood's and was ready with the complete text in July. Blackwood's asked him for a subtitle and he obliged with 'The Curly Snake', thus honouring one of his favourite places in Langholm. Before the poem was published, MacDiarmid orchestrated a press campaign designed to make *Cencrastus* a major issue in Scotland. In the *Daily Record* of 21 September an anonymous article appeared, under the lurid heading 'A Poet Runs Amok', drawing attention to the poem's violence of expression, its attacks on prominent Scots (Ramsay MacDonald, Sir Harry Lauder, Lauchlan Maclean Watt and others), and its determination to be 'blankly blasphemous'.[16] Writing under the pseudonym of 'Pteleon', in the *Scots Observer* of 2 October, MacDiarmid warned readers of the scurrilous nature of a poem that dared to attack British Imperialism and the Royal Family. On the day of publication, 29 October, the *Daily Record* gave additional publicity to the poem by printing two reviews. One, by William Power, hailed *Cencrastus* as an extraordinary achievement. The other, condemning the poem as an affront to civilised society, was by the Very Revd Dr Lauchlan Maclean Watt, Minister of Glasgow Cathedral and a popular writer, author of *The Grey Mother* and *Songs of Empire*, hymn writer and former contributor to *Northern Numbers*.

Watt was twice cursed in *Cencrastus*. First he was lumped together with two Scottish comedians and J. J. Bell, author of the enormously successful sentimental novel *Wee Macgreegor* (1902). MacDiarmid contemplated the appeal of such men with bitter irony:

> I wish I was Harry Lauder,
> Will Fyffe or J. J. Bell,

- Or Lauchlan Maclean Watt
For the maitter o' that!
- Dae I Hell!   (254)

A few pages on, in the poem, Watt's bestselling volume of verse was
ridiculed:

And gin we canna thraw aff the warld
Let's hear o' nae 'Auld grey Mither' ava,
But o' Middle Torridonian Arkose
     Wi' local breccias,
Or the pillow lavas at Loch Awe....   (261)

It is one of the most egregious flaws of *Cencrastus* that MacDiarmid
protests too much against men such as Watt, enemies not worthy of
attention in a major creative enterprise purporting to deal with universal
issues rather than Scottish petty squabbles. However, Watt rose to the
bait in his predictably rancorous review of *Cencrastus*:

> This is not genius, but the impudence of a gamin. It is not poetry. Here,
> most frequently, we have neither rhyme nor reason. We have the utterance
> of much that should never find expression in decent society, of the healthily
> sane.... It sounds like Homer after he had swallowed his false teeth.[17]

Unfortunately for MacDiarmid, Watt was not the only man who found
the poem unsatisfactory. F. G. Scott, who saw the manuscript in
Montrose, felt much disquiet: 'I couldn't give my approval of the poem'.[18]
Reservations from such a man as Scott must have wounded MacDiarmid.

It has to be said that, as a whole, *To Circumjack Cencrastus* lacks the
assurance that distinguished *A Drunk Man Looks at the Thistle*. In *A Drunk
Man* MacDiarmid uttered the provocatively blasphemous prophesy that
an inebriated Scotsman was capable of becoming, through the will to
creative power, 'A greater Christ, a greater Burns' (86). This ideal is
explicitly repudiated in *Cencrastus*:

A'e thing's certain: Christ's Second Comin'
'll no' be to Scotland whaurever it is.   (258)

Though *Cencrastus* is weakened by a faltering of faith in the spiritual
potential of the Scot, the poem has magnificent passages that stand out
clearly from the less intense bits and pieces that surround them. In *A*

Drunk Man the constant contradiction was a source of poetic tension; in *Cencrastus* the alternation of aspiration and desperation deprives the poem of a visionary unity. The contradictions are not contrapuntal but inconsistent. MacDiarmid's creative struggle, in this poem, is dragged down by his distress over those aspects of Scotland he abominated: an often provincial mentality, the veneration of well-paid mediocrities, the indifference to artistic integrity, the isolation of the man of genius.

MacDiarmid told George Ogilvie he had excised about one-third of *A Drunk Man* and some of this discarded material was certainly used in *Cencrastus* which consequently reads as a sequence of separate parts. The poem opens and closes majestically and all the material in between amounts to a massive parenthesis that is intended to illustrate the argument though it frequently obscures it. Some sections of *Cencrastus* were originally detached from the sequence for identifiable purposes; for example, 'Frae Anither Window in Thrums' – which begins 'Here in the hauf licht waiting' till the clock/Chops' (230) – once figured as the title poem of a proposed collection.[19] Structurally *Cencrastus* is a miscellany.

MacDiarmid started out with a plan of absorbing interest: to express in Scots verse the nobility of the Gaelic Idea, an indigenous alternative to the Russian Idea he had explored in *A Drunk Man* through his address to Dostoevsky. The poet, obliged to raise the consciousness of his race, attempts to reveal the beauty of the Gaelic Idea to his countrymen who should thereby be impelled to recover the Gaelic culture ruined after the catastrophic defeat of the clans at Culloden. Expressed in prose, the Gaelic Idea is the necessary counterpart to the Russian Idea. It is a dynamic intellectual device:

> It does not matter a rap whether the whole conception of this Gaelic idea is as far-fetched as Dostoevsky's Russian Idea – in which he pictured Russia as the sick man possessed of devils but who would yet 'sit at the feet of Jesus'. The point is that Dostoevsky's was a great creative idea – a dynamic myth – and in no way devalued by the difference of the actual happenings in Russia from any Dostoevsky dreamed or desired. So we in Scotland (in association with the other Gaelic elements with whose aid we may reduce England to a subordinate role in the economy of these islands) need not care how future events belie our anticipations so long as we polarize Russia effectively – proclaim that relationship between freedom and genius, between freedom and thought, which Russia is denying – help to rebalance Europe in accordance with our distinctive genius – rediscover and manifest anew our dynamic spirit as a nation. This Gaelic Idea ... calls us to a redefinition and extension of our national principle of freedom on the plane

of world-affairs, and in an abandonment alike of our monstrous neglect and ignorance of Gaelic and of the barren conservatism and loss of the creative spirit on the part of those professedly Gaelic and concerned with its maintenance and development.[20]

From his discussions with Mackenzie about Clann Albain, from his study of Scottish history, from his sympathy with the revolutionary achievements of the Russians, from his increasingly bitter resentment of English Imperialism, MacDiarmid had come to the conclusion that the Gaelic Idea was the modern answer to the quasi-genocidal destruction of Gaelic culture in Scotland. Scotland was, he believed, a quintessentially Gaelic nation that had been battered into submission but could be resurrected. The incongruity of advocating the Gaelic Idea in Scots did not discourage MacDiarmid who, after all, embraced the Russian Idea in *A Drunk Man* though he told Dostoevsky 'I ken nae Russian and you ken nae Scots' (151). As versified in *Cencrastus* the argument suggests that the realisation of the Gaelic Idea is a more urgent business than the creation of a Scots literature:

> If we turn to Europe and see
> Hoo the emergence o' the Russian Idea's
> Broken the balance o' the North and Sooth
> And needs a coonter that can only be
> The Gaelic Idea
> To mak' a parallelogram o' forces,
> Complete the Defence o' the West,
> And end the English betrayal o' Europe.
> (Time eneuch then to seek the Omnific Word
> In Jamieson yet.
> Or the new Dictionary in the makin' noo,
> Or coin it oorsels!)   (222-3)

What actually happens in *Cencrastus* is that the Gaelic Idea unfolds in asides rather than as the essence of the composition. The poet becomes distracted by disputation and allows his central argument to become blurred as he focuses on other obsessions. Following the method he had sustained with such conspicuous success in *A Drunk Man* MacDiarmid reworks in verse several notions derived from books that reinforced his own insights. He cites Leontiev, the Russian aesthete who detested democracy and the inexorable rise of the bourgeoisie. He mentions Valéry whose poem *Le Serpent* depicts the snake as it coils round the

Tree of Life and the Tree of Knowledge.[21] Shestov's *All Things Are Possible* is again an influence. Speculating on the evolutionary possibilities of a stone, Shestov wrote:

> [I]t might be that a stone changed into a plant before our eyes, and the plant into an animal. That *there is nothing unthinkable* in such a supposition is proved by the theory of evolution. This theory only puts centuries in place of seconds.[22]

MacDiarmid writes:

> The day is comin' when ilka stane
> 'll hae as guid as a human brain
> And frae what they are noo men
> Develop in proportion then ...   (221)

(That thought will recur in MacDiarmid's great poem 'On a Raised Beach'.)

Another strong influence on the poem is Denis Saurat's *The Three Conventions* (1926), first serialised in the *New Age*, a series of dialogues involving several speakers: the Psychologist, the Poet, the Dreamer and the Metaphysician who gets the best lines. It classifies the three conventions as Material, Moral and Metaphysical and argues that the purpose of life is the creation of the Metaphysical convention by the will of man. According to Saurat's Metaphysician:

> It is impossible to admit that being has no aim; that being does not reach its aim: consciousness of itself; and consciousness once reached, the preservation of consciousness, which is immortality.... We are creating our immortality and our God, even as we formerly created consciousness and man (Immortality being only an extension of consciousness, and God of man).[23]

Sympathising with such speculations, abstruse to the point of absurdity so that language escapes from the phenomenal world, MacDiarmid runs the risk of submerging his own observations under an ocean of unfathomable abstraction.

Fundamentally, *Cencrastus* seeks a coalescence between the Gaelic Idea and MacDiarmid's belief that 'The function of art is the extension of human consciousness.'[24] He elucidated his aim in a letter, of February 1939, to Helen Cruickshank:

As to *Cencrastus*, all I can say is that Cencrastus, the Curly Snake, is a Gaelic (or Scottish) version of the idea common to Indian and other mythologies that underlying Creation there is a great snake – and that its movements form the pattern of history. In my poem that snake represents not only an attempt to glimpse the underlying pattern of human history but identifies it with the evolution of human thought – the principle of change and the main factor in the revolutionary development of human consciousness, 'man's incredible variation', moving so intricately and swiftly that it is difficult to watch, and impossible to anticipate its next moves. The poem as a whole therefore is a poem of Homage to Consciousness – a paean to Creative Thought. In so far as it is specifically a Scottish poem, and concerned in particular to glorify the Gaelic element in our heritage (which I believe underlies our Scottish life and history in much the same way that consciousness underlies and informs the whole world of man) the doctrine it is filled with [concerns] World Consciousness which I believe to be the great function and destiny of Man – a historic mission of humanity in relation to the Cosmos in which we Scots can play our part in so far as we have that sharp awareness of our own nature in which, as in a mirror, we can see natures other than our own. I believe that this pursuit of World Consciousness is the phase of mankind's development upon which we are now entering.[25]

The clarity of this exposition, written some nine years after the completion of the poem, indicates the grandeur of the plan. At the time he actually put the finishing touches to *Cencrastus* MacDiarmid was too unsettled to sustain the serpentine symbolism.

He had touched on such symbolism in previous poems: in 'Sea-Serpent', from *Penny Wheep*, he affirmed that 'the serpent is movin' still,/A movement that a' thing shares' (50); in *A Drunk Man* Leviathan, the serpent of the deep, is linked to the restless roots of the thistle so that its 'coils like a thistle's leafs/Sweep space wi' levin sheafs' (98). As a creature of coils, the serpent represents the cycles of life; as an entity that perpetually renews its skin it is a symbol of resurrection. Renewal and resurrection are central to MacDiarmid's desire to repossess the Gaelic heritage. For the superlative opening of the poem Cencrastus is addressed in a sequence of nineteen stanzas, most of them structured in twelve contemplative rhymeless lines with a conversational half-line flourish. In the first stanza Cencrastus is separated from all other phenomena but identified as the serpent who gave excellent advice to Eve in the Garden of Eden.'There is nae movement in the warld like yours' (181), MacDiarmid tells Cencrastus then adds, in the second stanza, that one force equals the strength of the serpent, namely the faith that can move mountains. The poet's faith is not conventionally Christian for he accuses Christ of a failure to understand the contradictory complexity of the serpent. Cencrastus is a shaping force even Buddha and Christ were unable to direct.

Leaving aside the mental lethargy of 'maist folk' (181) – 'the dreich mob' (183) – the process of consciousness allows men to dream they might be Gods though even the best of men persistently fail to translate their dreams into reality. Dostoevsky, one of the heroes of *A Drunk Man*, is praised, but Burns, supposedly the soul of Scotland, is condemned as 'That Langfellow in a' but leid' (185), a forerunner of the despicable 'Whistle Binkie bards' (185). For MacDiarmid, history presents the sorry spectacle of generations unable to pass beyond the infantile stage of thinking. Still, there are glimpses of a higher consciousness in the spirit of Saint Sophia and the sound of Gaelic music. The poet must pursue thought towards a peak of perfection:

> The consciousness that maitter has entrapped
> In minerals, plants and beasts is strugglin' yet
> In men's minds only, seekin' to win free.
> As poets' ideas, in the fecht wi' words,
> Forced back upon themsel's and made mair clear,
> Owrecome a' thwarts whiles, miracles at last.   (187)

Having announced his theme, MacDiarmid settles down to details. Not for him the conventional Burnsian wisdom of a universal brotherhood. Instead, inspired by the ideal of 'Gaeldom regained' (188), he desires a vision that looks at the highest level of consciousness. His evolutionary impulse leads him 'To think nae thocht that's e'er been thocht afore' (189). However, *Cencrastus* begins to break up into a series of asides that seldom impinge on the central theme of the composition. There is a witty lyric on Scottish hunters cursing the darkness that descended on the day of Christ's crucifixion, a catalogue of German poets, a series of separate poems complete with titles. 'The Mavis of Pabal' expresses the poet's solitude since 'There's nae sign o' a mate to be seen' (192); 'The Parrot Cry', a fine piece of satire on the consequences of the Parliamentary Union of 1707, has little relation to the encounter with Cencrastus; a section of short pieces, 'From the Scots Anthology', confirms the loose structure of the poem.

Two reflective stanzas link 'The Mavis of Pabal', 'The Parrot Cry' and 'From the Scots Anthology' to an English translation of Rilke, a *tour de force* that stands on its own. MacDiarmid was drawn to Rilke because the German poet went further than Nietzsche in affirming the artistic nature of the superman. Rilke believed in salvation through art, implying that creativity was the highest aspiration of humanity. In 1908 Rilke conveyed his doctrine in two requiems (both composed within six days) for artists ultimately unable to put art above life: the painter Paula Modersohn-Becker (1867-1907), and the poet Wolf van Kalckreuth (1887-1906) who committed suicide at the age of nineteen. It is the requiem for Paula Modersohn-Becker that MacDiarmid translates.

Paula Becker had married Otto Modersohn, her teacher in the artists' colony of Worpswede. Twice she went to Paris to devote herself to her own painting and twice Modersohn persuaded her to return to look after himself and his daughter by a previous marriage. In February 1906 she left her husband for a third time and set up as a painter in Paris. Again Modersohn followed her and lured her back to Worpswede by offering a large studio of her own. Pregnant, she returned and painted such works as the self-portrait of 1906 in which she stands bare-breasted wearing beads and clutching flowers. She had reached her greatest moment as an artist but 'when the day came to rise from childbed after a difficult birth, she suffered an embolism and died'.[26]

MacDiarmid adapted Rilke's requiem inventively, deleting about a quarter of the text and ending on a passage originally occurring earlier in the poem.[27] Rebuking the dead woman, the poet complains of the manner of her going:

> You cannot see as even here you could
> Life's upward irreversible way, and fall
> By the dead weight of grievance from the spheres
> To which you now belong to this poor past.
> – *That* wakes me often like a thief at night.   (198)

The requiem prolongs the physical presence of Paula Modersohn-Becker through an accumulation of images about fruit: the fruits the artist painted, her appearance 'Fruit-like at last before the mirror here' (199), the eating of fruit 'till nothing but the core/Was left, full of the green seeds of your death' (200). This tasting of fruit, unforbidden on earth, invokes the sensuous appetite of the artist Modersohn-Becker when she eschewed domestic obligations. As translated by MacDiarmid, the poem ends with a plea to the artist's ghost:

> Hear me, help me, for see we disappear,
> Not knowing when, into anything beyond our thought
> Even as a landsman's eyesight fails to hold
> The Deity on the shoulders of a ship,
> When its own lightness lifts it suddenly
> Up and away into the bright sea wind.... (202)

The Rilke translation is followed by a two-line link leading into a complaint that Scotland's four universities (at that time) 'Are Scots but in name' (203) and another link introduces one of MacDiarmid's finest lyrics, a poem weighty with world-weariness about Scotland's resistance to change. The last of three stanzas reads:

> *Nae wonder if I think I see*
> *A lichter shadow than the neist*
> *I'm fain to cry: 'The dawn, the dawn!*
> *I see it brakin' in the East.'*
> > *But ah*
> > *— It's juist mair snaw!* (205)

Beautiful as such passages are, MacDiarmid is unable to develop his central theme through utterances that go against the argumentative grain of *Cencrastus*. He returns to the Gaelic Idea by hailing the brilliance of 'The Gaelic sun' (207), a shining ideal that replaces the nostalgic notion of the Celtic Twilight so popular with sentimentalists.

As Scotland needs an inspirational example to reveal the profundity of the Gaelic Idea he commends, as a heroic individual, the great Gaelic poet Alasdair MacMhaighstir Alasdair (Alexander MacDonald, *c.* 1695-*c.* 1770) who is addressed directly just as as Dostoevsky was addressed in *A Drunk Man*. MacDiarmid celebrates the Gaelic poet's masterpiece 'Birlinn Chlann Raghnaill' (The Galley of Clan Ranald), a description of a sea voyage from South Uist to Carrickfergus in Ireland:

> *Jaupin' the stars, or thrawin' lang strings*
> > *O' duileasg owre the sun*
> *Till like a jeelyfish it swings*
> > *In deeps rewon,*
> *And in your brain as in God's ain*
> > *A' thing's ane again!* (210)

254

Hope, MacDiarmid implies, can only be encouraged through an aware-
ness of men of genius, like Alasdair MacMhaighstir Alasdair or the Irish
Gaelic bard Aodhagán Ó Rathaille, author of the *aisling* (vision-poem)
'Gile na Gile' (Brightness of Brightness):

> *Aodhagán Ó Rathaille sang this sang*
> *That I maun sing again;*
> *For I've met the Brightness o' Brightness*
> *Like him in a lanely glen,*
> *And seen the hair that's plaited*
> *Like the generations o' men.*   (224)

With his knowledge of such figures MacDiarmid has no time at all for
those who lack vision which is why he dismisses the likes of 'Neil Munro
and Annie Swan' (231), popular Scottish novelists. Consciousness is
clear to individuals who see beneath surfaces and beyond everyday
appearance. MacDiarmid takes his stand with the Gaelic visionaries.

However, MacDiarmid acknowledges a problem that prevents him
from realising his poetic destiny. Turning to his personal life, he has to
cope with a grim reality that obliges him to make domestic ends meet.
He describes in anecdotal detail a humiliating encounter with an employer
(Foreman of the *Montrose Review*) who had the power to dismiss him.
The poet curses his colleagues, curses 'a'thing that gars me pretend or
feel/That life as maist folk hae't is real' (236), curses his 'dooble life and
dooble tongue,/ – Guid Scots wi' English a' hamstrung – ' (236).
Circumscribed by his circumstances, he worries that his vision is 'juist
provisional and 'll hae/A tea-change into something rich and Scots'
(239) – an unusually weak pun for MacDiarmid. MacDiarmid's autobiographical references in *Cencrastus* become more and more strident as
the poet succumbs to the realisation that he is fighting a losing battle as
a man of genius brought down by a series of misfortunes.

MacDiarmid began *Cencrastus* with a surge of ambition, certain he
could make a poem that would command all his abilities. He began
writing it in Montrose, went to London, lost his balance on a bus, lost
his job with *Vox*, lost daily contact with his wife and children when he
was in Liverpool finishing the poem. What is admirable in *Cencrastus* is
MacDiarmid's poetic resolution: he wants to 'sing as never Scotsman
sang afore' (241), wants to reveal the 'unkent God' (241), wants to
articulate the genuine voice of Scotland. When he finds, in the final

stretch of the poem, that he cannot achieve this he eschews confessional self-pity but collapses into grotesque self-portraiture:

> *Noo in synoptic lines*
> *A Scot becomes a God*
> *− A God in Murray tartan*
> *To whom nae star's abroad.* (246)

This self-mockery makes him think of his old enemy Harry Lauder, who amassed a fortune by a comical caricature of the supposedly typical Scotsman. MacDiarmid loses sight of *Cencrastus* as he bitterly defines his own position as the visionary poet impoverished by a society indifferent to culture:

> Up to the een in debt I stand
> My haill life built on shiftin' sand
> And feel the filthy grit gang grindin'
> Into my brain's maist delicate windin'. (252)

By this stage of *Cencrastus* MacDiarmid is agonisingly aware of his failure to follow through his grand conception. By comparing himself with Scots he despises (Lauder, Neil Munro, Annie Swan, Lauchlan Maclean Watt) he has descended to a base level and seen his work suffer as a consequence:

> The brilliance o' form nae langer shines
> Upon the subject-maitter o' my poem
> I've let owre muckle in't no' needfu' to
> The licht that su'd ha'e been my a'e concern,
> Dulled and debauched my work ... (254)

His language, he suggests, has likewise deteriorated, sounding more like English with a Scots accent than Synthetic Scots: 'my leid is scarcely Scots' (255). Before it ends *Cencrastus* fragments further with a series of twenty numbered poems − including a memorable couplet, 'Scots steel tempered wi' Irish fire/Is the weapon that I desire' (263) − and a reprint of 'A Moment in Eternity' from his first book, *Annals of the Five Senses*. All is not lost, though, for he eventually returns triumphantly to his theme by saluting the spirit of renewal in Cencrastus:

Up frae the slime, that a' but a handfu' o' men
Are grey wi' still. There's nae trace o't in you.
Clear withoot sediment. Day withoot nicht.
A' men's institutions and maist men's thochts
Are tryin' for aye to bring to an end
The insatiable thocht, the beautiful violent will,
The restless spirit of Man, the theme o' my sang   (285)

Uplifted by this challenge he projects himself not as the Scottish saviour
(as he did in *A Drunk Man*) but as perhaps the last chance available to
Scotland:

The problem is to find in Scotland some
Bricht coil o' you that hasna yet uncurled,
And, hoosoever petty I may be, the fact
That I think Scotland isna dune yet proves
There's something in it that fulfilment's lacked
And my vague hope through a' creation moves.   (288)

Understandably, MacDiarmid was unhappy with his finished product.
He told Ogilvie, 'I did not do in it what I intended – I deliberately
deserted my big plan.'[28]

For all that, the reviews were generally favourable in the periodicals
MacDiarmid took seriously. Edwin Muir reviewed *Cencrastus* twice, in
the *New Statesman* and the *Criterion*. He felt the poem contained some
of MacDiarmid's most masterly work, 'superbly rhythmical verse, firmly
managed, stabbed with a fleeting wit, fertile in experiment, with winking
lights of thought deepset in it, and occasional explosions of a large
humour'[29]; and that the language, essentially a Scots-cadenced English,
would 'give no very great difficulty to an English reader'.[30] In the *Modern
Scot*, a progressive magazine founded in St Andrews by a rich American,
James H. Whyte, in 1930, Denis Saurat wrote that the loose form of
Cencrastus allowed MacDiarmid to sing 'with that ecstasy which is
beyond criticism in its energy that wings itself home into the very bosom
of light'.[31]

With *Cencrastus* behind him, MacDiarmid was working on a new
poem. Sure that the quintessential Scot was a Faustian character he
planned to base a Scottish poem on the framework of Goethe's *Faust*,
much as Joyce had based *Ulysses* on Homer's *Odyssey*.

For several years MacDiarmid had been friendly with Kaikhosru Shapurji Sorabji, the composer who was to write a fiercely critical column on music for Orage's *New English Weekly*, the successor to the *New Age*. Sorabji (originally Leon Dudley Sorbaji), the son of a Parsi father and a Spanish-Sicilian mother, had completed an epic work for piano – *Opus Clavicembalisticum*, in three parts and twelve subdivisions, lasting two hours in performance – and had dedicated the score to 'my two friends ... Hugh M'Diarmid and C. M.Grieve'.[32] MacDiarmid was fascinated by Sorabji's esoteric and erudite manner and thrilled to be associated with a musical work of such complexity. He planned to go to Glasgow for the first two days of December since on 1 December Sorabji was performing *Opus Clavicembalisticum* and the following day the poet was to address Glasgow University Scottish Nationalist Association as its Vice President. He thought of taking Peggy but in the event arrived alone staying, prior to his visit to Glasgow, with Helen Cruickshank at her home in Edinburgh. In conversation with Cruickshank, MacDiarmid said he would have to 'resolve a domestic situation which would probably lead to the break-up of his marriage'.[33] News about the intensity of Peggy's relationship with McElroy had reached him in Liverpool and he must have pondered on the possibility that if his wife was forced to choose between a prosperous businessman and an impoverished poet then the poet was likely to be the loser.

Worried by this situation he still managed to press his claims as a writer. On 9 December he wrote to T. S. Eliot, offering an essay for the *Criterion*. Eliot accepted 'English Ascendancy in British Literature' (published in the *Criterion* the following July and collected in *At the Sign of the Thistle* in 1934). It is one of MacDiarmid's most lucid pieces of critical prose and explores issues already aired in *Cencrastus*: the visionary vitality of Gaelic, the greatness of the Irish Gaelic poet Aodhagán Ó Rathaille, the stature of the Scots Gaelic poet Alasdair MacMhaighstir Alasdair. MacDiarmid objected to the assumption that English was the supreme linguistic achievement of Britain and the indifference of the English to experimental writers as important as Charles Doughty (1845-1926), neglected because of his use of archaic words and his attempts to revive the tradition of Chaucer and Spenser. He cited the success of revivalist movements such as the Landsmaal in Norway and called for a reassessment of Scottish Gaelic culture. In Scotland, MacDiarmid argued, the arrogance of English imperialism had, when applied to education, relegated Gaelic and dialect writers to a limbo and he proposed three conditions to ensure the advance of the Scottish Renaissance Movement:

a rising tide of Scottish national consciousness; a reconcentration, in schools and universities, on native Scottish literature; and the bridging of the gulf between Gaelic and Scots. 'Scotsmen', he said, 'must remain creatively inferior unless their own line lies in a different direction than a mere subsidiary to English letters.'[34]

MacDiarmid met Eliot for lunch, at the Royal Societies Club in London, at the end of 1930. The two poets discussed the argument of 'English Ascendancy in British Literature' and MacDiarmid took the opportunity to ask Eliot if he could put in a good word for him with Bruce Richmond, editor of the *Times Literary Supplement*, in the hope (vain, as it transpired) that he might get some reviewing work for the paper. MacDiarmid was in a dilemma. He wanted regular work in London but could find nothing suitable. When he saw Peggy in London he realised she wanted to break completely from him. Certainly there was no chance of her coming to Liverpool. As MacDiarmid told his mother, on the subject of Peggy's attitude: 'I wanted her – she did not want me. That was why she would not come to Liverpool.'[35]

Returning to Liverpool on his own, MacDiarmid began to shape the Scottish *Faust* as an autobiographical poem, examining his own geographical and emotional roots as a Scottish Borderer. Writing while 'Sittin' in Liverpool' (1149) after being rejected by Peggy in London, which dates the poem 'Kinsfolk' to around April 1931, he looked back on a life that had separated him from his own parents and now threatened to deprive him of the family he had loved in Montrose. He had left part of himself behind in the Muckle Toon of Langholm and in Liverpool he was alone again, contemplating the loss of his 'wife and weans in London' (1149). MacDiarmid was adamant that his domestic trauma was not of his doing:

> I bein' a man made ither human ties
> But they – my choice – are broken (in this case
> No' a' my choice) as utterly as those
> That bound me to my kin and native place.
> My wife and bairns, is't tinin' them that thraws
>   Me back on my first cause?   (1147)

He answered the question defiantly. Born a Borderer, he had to live as a man 'sprung/Frae battles, mair than ballads' (1150). He was not entirely equal to the domestic battle.

Events now overwhelmed MacDiarmid. In London, Peggy had had

an abortion and contracted septicaemia as a result. In July, as MacDiarmid put it, she was 'rushed into a nursing home, went through a touch-and-go operation, emerged a wraith'.[36] Given the fact that abortion was a criminal offence at the time, MacDiarmid's statement diplomatically avoids the central issue. Peggy probably went into the nursing home for dilatation and curettage: the surgical scraping of tissue from the womb. Thinking that McElroy was the father of the aborted child, MacDiarmid phoned the coal-merchant who agreed to pay for Peggy's treatment though he was not directly responsible. Peggy's pregnancy was the result of an affair with a Breton nationalist named la Rue.[37] In August Peggy went to Scotland, to convalesce at her parents' house in Methil. Around the same time MacDiarmid, drinking more heavily than he had ever done before, lost his job with the Liverpool Organisation as his work was affected by incessant binges.[38] He arrived in London at the beginning of September and found an empty house at 18 Pyrland Road. Not only was Peggy staying in Scotland until the end of September but her sister, Ina, was on holiday in Germany.

As a 'grass widower'[39] MacDiarmid was in a position to combine business with pleasure. The Scottish *Faust* was now taking shape as a poem combining autobiography and political philosophy. Two sections of it, 'Charisma and My Relatives' and 'To Lenin' – a title later expanded to 'First Hymn to Lenin' – had been accepted for Lascelles Abercrombie's anthology *New English Poems* (1931) where the latter was footnoted as coming from *Clann Albann*, a work in progress. So now the Scottish *Faust* had a title – taken from the name of the movement initiated by MacDiarmid and Mackenzie – and a theme that projected MacDiarmid as a heroic outsider separated, by his creative gift, from 'faither, mither, brither, kin' (301). Dedicated to McElroy and dwelling on the combative connotations of the Scottish Borders, 'Charisma and My Relatives' suggests that MacDiarmid will have to fight his own battles:

> And fence the wondrous fire that in me's lit
> Wi' sicna barriers roond as hide frae'ts licht
>   Near a'body's sicht.   (302)

'First Hymn to Lenin', dedicated to Prince D. S. Mirsky, addresses the leader of the Russian Revolution as a greater Christ, a superman able to soar above 'the majority' (298) and 'the crood' (299). Subscribing to the notion that the end justifies the means, so that the activities of the Soviet secret police (the Cheka), are accepted as necessary atrocities,

MacDiarmid tells Lenin that political murder is an acceptable part of the revolutionary process:

> What maitters 't wha we kill
> To lessen that foulest murder that deprives
> Maist men o' real lives?   (298)

The language of 'Charisma and My Relatives' and 'First Hymn to Lenin' is not the Synthetic Scots of the 1920s but a didactic English with a Scots accent.

The poet who dismissed capitalism as 'that foulest murder' was, paradoxically, anxious to become a businessman in 1931. At the beginning of September he was offered a directorship with the Unicorn Press, the firm that was to publish his *First Hymn to Lenin and Other Poems* as a limited edition in December. In return for investing £500 capital in the firm, he would become literary adviser entitled to his share of the profits. MacDiarmid thought the Unicorn Press a 'tip-top proposition'[40] and felt he could trust his fellow directors, L. N. Cooper and J. F. Moore. In order to raise the capital he turned to the few men he thought would oblige him with money. McElroy provided £250, Neil Gunn sent him £200 on request, but Andrew Grieve refused to lend money, telling his brother he would 'never invest ... in a company with which you were remotely concerned'.[41] MacDiarmid's personal lack of capital was eventually to prove his undoing in this commercial adventure but he was accepted as a director of the Unicorn Press which meant he had the use of an office at 321 High Holborn and could rent a flat at 64 Chancery Lane.

With high hopes of financial security, MacDiarmid was intent on celebrating his return to London as enjoyably as possible. Looking for sexual company, in the absence of Peggy, he brought a woman to spend nights with him, at Pyrland Road, on 9 and 11 September. To use the official terminology, 'On both of these occasions [he] committed adultery with the said woman'.[42]

Settled, or unsettled, in Pyrland Road, MacDiarmid wanted to renew contact with the London literati. Since his new stamping ground, in connection with the Unicorn Press, was High Holborn he was drawn to Hennekey's pub where, on Friday nights, writers regularly gathered to drink and talk at its distinctive long bar. Irish writers such as Austin Clarke and Liam O'Flaherty attended these gathering and the Scottish poet felt especially at home with them (despite his scuffle with O'Flaherty). On the first or second Friday in September MacDiarmid was holding forth at Hennekey's when a young woman paid her first visit to the pub. Twenty-five, red-haired and petite, Valda Trevlyn had been invited along by a boyfriend interested in literature. MacDiarmid was attracted by Valda. She was amused by the poet's attentions. Every time she took out a cigarette he provided a light. Reversing the gesture symbolically, Valda provided a new light in MacDiarmid's life. This ardent, forceful, politically conscious young woman was to become his companion for the rest of his life.

Valda Trevlyn was born on 1 July 1906 at 472 Moorlands, Bude, Cornwall. Her unmarried mother was Florence Ann Rowlands, a domestic cook. Her father, not named on her birth certificate, was 'a jack of all trades'.[43] He died when Valda was a baby so she was brought up by her mother and an aunt who paid for her to go to the local grammar school. Valda remembered her early days in Bude with a mixture of wonder and pride:

> We were working-class, very poor. My aunt, the one we all lived with, was a real aristocrat, through all our poverty. We always had starched napkins, starched cloths on the table. There were few things for a girl to do at that time. You could be a domestic servant, work in a shop, be a nurse, that was about it. I decided, after leaving school, to leave Bude so I saved up some money and packed a suitcase and left with a friend. I was going to London. So I went to the station and found I only had enough money for a single ticket to Bristol.[44]

She arrived in Bristol, sporting a scarlet tammie, and met a woman who advised her to apply for a job as a shop assistant in Baker & Baker. After eighteen months in Bristol, she went to London, at the end of 1930. She found a job in the millinery department of Bourne & Hollingsworth – a prestigious shop whose customers included Lady Ottoline Morrell – and began to explore the sights of London.

When Valda's boyfriend asked her to come to a soirée, she thought it had 'something to do with a chapel, something like that'.[45] She was surprised when the soirée took place in a pub rather than a church. MacDiarmid's presence was unavoidable: he talked loudly and at length though he did not talk to Valda as he was intent on captivating his audience at Hennekey's. She accepted lights from him, that first night, and found him 'very interesting though I wasn't immediately attracted to him'.[46] Not long after this encounter, MacDiarmid phoned Valda at her London hostel and asked her out. They went to Hennekey's together, visited other pubs, and Valda quickly realised that this seemingly poised poet was an extremely vulnerable man. She was amazed at his appetite for alcohol and he told her he was drinking as a result of the depression he experienced through the breakdown of his marriage. 'He said', Valda noted, 'he could never commit suicide but he was trying to drink himself to death.'[47] In the clarity of the mornings after, however, MacDiarmid was trying to piece his shattered life together. He was working hard on *Clann Albann*, he was involved with the Unicorn Press, and he realised Valda was a woman with whom he could regain his sense of direction. Like him, she was defiant and unconventional: she believed in Communism, Cornish home-rule, creative people.

Listening to MacDiarmid's tale of the collapse of his relationship with Peggy, Valda was sympathetic to his plight. From MacDiarmid's point of view his wife had betrayed him, for Peggy had refused to come to Liverpool with him, preferring life in London with McElroy. Divorce was inevitable but MacDiarmid was in no position, financially, to fight for custody of his children. Peggy and MacDiarmid privately agreed on a solution to the marital impasse. If he allowed her to divorce him, rather than citing her adultery and criminal abortion, she would let him have access to the children, a promise she was to break. MacDiarmid asked Valda if she would be the co-respondent and she agreed though she knew he had slept with another woman at Pyrland Road while Peggy was in Scotland. Valda surprised herself by her willingness to become involved:

> I didn't mind though all my friends, and his friends, were against it. I said I'd rather it was me than the other woman. Deciding to stand by him *was* a difficult decision. I didn't really believe in the business of 'Hugh MacDiarmid' or any of that: this business of being a Scottish poet was all baloney. What really decided me was when I was standing in the Tottenham Court Road. Christopher had gone down to the lavatory and had gone into the women's. I thought, 'Oh, my God, I can't leave him.' A silly way to decide anything. I was never 'in love' with him. I loved him. It's quite different. If I'd been 'in love' with him I wouldn't have lasted six months.[48]

To facilitate the divorce, MacDiarmid and Valda spent the night of 26 September at the Strand Palace Hotel, signing the register as Mr and Mrs McDermott. As Valda recalls, she and MacDiarmid 'sat up all night, we didn't do anything'.[49] Peggy returned to London the following day and two days later met MacDiarmid to discuss details of the divorce.

With the divorce now a foregone conclusion, MacDiarmid was free of any commitment to Peggy. In October he and Valda became lovers. MacDiarmid suggested to Valda that they should marry after his divorce came through, but she resisted the idea. She was, however, willing to have a child by him:

> I thought he'd had one divorce and that we were two very different people. Different backgrounds, different ideas. I didn't know much about Scotland apart from Robert the Bruce and Wallace, I was more interested in Ireland because when I was a child there was a revolution going on there. I became pregnant – not accidentally. For Christopher it was a way of consolidating the bond between us. I said Yes, but wouldn't marry him.[50]

Materially, MacDiarmid was in a confused situation. Peggy and the children had the house in Pyrland Road, while he had his flat in Chancery Lane. With a divorce pending, and a relationship with a woman he wanted to marry, the poet had a complicated life.

As a director of the Unicorn Press, MacDiarmid could claim some credibility as a publisher and he sought ways of expanding his business interests. He attempted to launch a new magazine, *New English Monthly*, under the editorship of Orage (who settled for the *New English Weekly* to which MacDiarmid, and his friend Sorabji, contributed). He became an adviser to John Heritage, the publishing firm that (in 1932) brought out *The Albannach* by Fionn Mac Colla (Tom MacDonald). He became a director of two ventures, London Editorial Service and Combined Newspapers, aimed at supplying articles on Douglasite economics to the press. Through his close association with Orage, Douglas and the Social Credit movement, he became the sole agent for dealing with the publication of American editions and foreign translations of Douglas's work. Over the imprint C. M. Grieve, he published Douglas's *Warning Democracy* (1931), a collection of speeches and articles. On 11 November he introduced Douglas to Eliot over lunch at the Holborn Restaurant.

First Hymn to Lenin was published, by the Unicorn Press, in December 1931. All the poems in this volume were intended to form part of *The Muckle Toon* which was to be the first volume of *Clann Albann* as MacDiarmid explained when 'Kinsfolk' – then called 'From Work in Progress' and unfortunately omitted from *First Hymn to Lenin* – was published in J. H. Whyte's *Modern Scot* that July. Though 'First Hymn to Lenin' does not obviously relate to Langholm it does define MacDiarmid's considered political credo so puts the autobiographical texts in a theoretical context. Apart from the title poem the contents of the volume (containing seventeen poems in all) reach back lyrically to memories of Langholm.

Thematically, MacDiarmid insists on the difference between himself, as an intellectual, and the people he grew up with. He tells his dead father:

> I'm nae mair your son.
> It is my mind, nae son o' yours, that looks,
> And the great darkness o' your death comes up
> And equals it across the way.   (299)

As for Langholm folk in general, he asks God to drench them in a 'Prayer for a Second Flood':

> O arselins wi' them! Whummle them again!
> Coup them heels-owre-gowdy in a storm sae gundy
> That mony a lang fog-theekit face I ken
> 'll be sooked richt doon under through a cundy
> In the High Street, afore you get weel-sterted
>   And are still hauf-herted!   (300)

To counterpoint the sheer abandon of this, MacDiarmid puts a scientific gloss on the biblical story of the Flood in 'Water of Life' which invokes water — 'the ocean-flair' (315) — as the element from which humanity emerged in 'the time/We ploutered in the slime' (314). From water, a ubiquitous sight in Langholm, he had learned to appreciate the unstoppable torrent of change that runs through each life:

> It teach't me mony lessons I've ne'er forgot —
> That it's no' easy to thraw cauld water on life;
> The changes a man can safely undergang
> And bide essentially unchanged; the strife
> To tak' new forms and in it no' forget
>   We've never managed yet.   (318)

Though discursive in intention, the Langholm poems are richly sensuous as a result of the liquid imagery.

What separates the poet from the Langholm folk is, the book implies, the phenomenon of genius that has touched him. In 'The Burning Passion' MacDiarmid considers that genius falls fortuitously on the most unlikely individuals. Genius, he declares, transcends social class and biological probabilities:

> Juist as frae ony couple genius springs,
> There is nae telling' save wi' folk owre auld
> Or impotent. The stupidest pair on earth
> Are still as likely to strike in the blin' fauld
> Maze o' manseed upon the vital spark
>> As folk o' merit, means, or mark.   (305)

What MacDiarmid wants is 'a technique for genius' (305), an evolutionary leap forward to a world in which all individuals are born with genius. This evolutionary miracle is (after the manner of Lenin's revolutionary miracle) to be achieved by 'the measure o' oor will' (305). 'The Hole in the Wall' contemplates individuality as an experiment conducted by nature in the interests of evolutionary improvement. MacDiarmid is still mesmerised by the mystery of his own artistic gift.

'The Seamless Garment' links Langholm with MacDiarmid's political outlook. The poem − 'about the factory mill in Langholm in which my grandfather and several of my uncles and my cousins were employed'[51] − is addressed to a weaver, Wullie, whose professional expertise seems, to the poet, sadly at odds with his ignorance of international politics:

> Are you equal to life as to the loom.
>> Turnin' oot shoddy or what?
> Claith better than man? D'ye live to the full,
>> Your poo'er's a' deliverly taught?
> Or scamp a'thing else? Border claith's famous.
> Shall things o' mair consequence shame us?   (312)

The things of more consequence are the politics of Lenin and the poetry of Rilke. So long as the working man attends unthinkingly to his daily routine he will be merely an appendage to the machines he operates. The poem is an appeal for an expansion of proletarian consciousness. Its patronising tone, however, is self-defeating. In lecturing the working man on his apathy, MacDiarmid treats him like a backward child. It is not a poem calculated to comfort a proletarian reader.

On the evidence of *First Hymn to Lenin and Other Poems* MacDiarmid was, despite his personal traumas of 1931, in fine creative form. Following the stanzaic pattern established in 'Kinsfolk' he had a basic metrical structure for *The Muckle Toon*. A stanza rhyming *abcbdd* (and built essentially of five iambic pentameters leading to a truncated last line) is used in five of the poems from *First Hymn*: the title poem, 'Prayer for a Second Flood', 'Charisma and My Relatives', 'The Burning Passion',

'Water of Life'. Clearly the Muckle Toon stanza would carry the auto-biographical burden of the sequence and the simpler forms (usually quatrains as in 'Museum Piece', 'The Liquid Light', 'Country Folk', 'The Hole in the Wall', 'Another Turn of the Screw') would operate in asides.

By MacDiarmid's prolific standards, 1931 was a quiet year in terms of his published output. His edition of *Living Scottish Poets* had been published in September and *First Hymn* was the only collection of original MacDiarmid poems issued that year. For Christmas 1931, however, MacDiarmid's friend Charlie Lahr — an American socialist with a second-hand bookshop in London — brought out a special signed edition of *O wha's been here afore me lass*, reprinting the lyric from *A Drunk Man*. F. G. Scott's cousin, William Johnstone, then teaching at the Hackney School of Art and the Royal School of Needlework, tells an amusing anecdote about MacDiarmid selling a copy of this, for £30, to Eliot. MacDiarmid went to Eliot's office at Faber & Faber, in Russell Square, but failed to emerge for some time. When eventually MacDiarmid reappeared he explained that Eliot had wanted to discuss poetry: 'The pubs are opening and he's wanting to talk about poetry! ... Dammit, William, we've been sitting talking — just imagine Eliot talking about poetry anyway! Still, I got the money.'[52]

MacDiarmid spent the Christmas of 1931 and the New Year of 1932 abroad. As a delegate to the PEN Congress in The Hague he travelled to The Netherlands via France and Belgium. The highlight of his trip was a tour of the Zuider Zee reclamation scheme in the company of the brilliant Czech writer Karel Čapek. As Čapek was forty-one and MacDiarmid thirty-nine, the two men were contemporaries with 'a great deal in common'.[53] They talked of themes developed in Čapek's novel *Krakatit* (1924, translated by L. Hyde as *An Atomic Phantasy* in 1925) and in his travel books: that man's desire to dominate the earth could, by interfering with nature, lead to the destruction of humanity. 'Karel Čapek', MacDiarmid wrote, 'loved the trees and those forests that stand in their solid ranks across the Northern earth, as if they were still guarding earth's infancy.'[54]

Returning to London after his visit to The Hague, MacDiarmid reconciled himself to the reality of the divorce. He was not in Edinburgh when, on 16 January 1932, the decree of divorce was pronounced by Lord Pitman in the Court of Session. As stated briefly, in a newspaper report:

Evidence was led in an undefended action of divorce by Mrs Margaret Skinner or Grieve, 18 Pyrland Road, London N5, against Christopher

Murray Grieve, journalist, 64 Chancery Lane, London WC ... The pursuer's case was an allegation of infidelity on the part of her husband in the house at Pyrland Road on two occasions last September during the absence of the pursuer in Scotland for convalescence following an illness. Lord Pitman held infidelity proved, and granted decree of divorce, with custody of the two children, and aliment at the rate of £100 per annum for each child and expenses.[55]

After the divorce McElroy took Peggy to Ireland for a holiday, deserted his wife Kate, then set up homes for Peggy in Victoria Street, London, and Hindhead, Surrey. MacDiarmid was hurt by the terms of the divorce, saddened that Peggy had gone back on her word. Instead of citing, as agreed, the night he had spent with Valda at the Strand Palace Hotel she had added this to the poet's indiscretions so it seemed he had committed adultery with the same woman at Pyrland Road, at the Royal Oak Hotel, Rottingdean, and at the Strand Palace Hotel. Though MacDiarmid did not immediately understand the implications of the divorce, Peggy was determined to deny him access to Christine and Walter. He did not see his children again for more than twenty years.

In London, MacDiarmid's response to the divorce was expressed in prose and verse. Writing to his mother, who was horrified at the public revelation of his adultery,[56] MacDiarmid said:

I quite understand your feelings about the divorce case ... The whole matter has been a desperate blow to me. It is useless my going into details as you do not know the circumstances. Suffice it to say that I exhausted every possible means before I did the only thing left and acted in such a way as to enable her to claim her freedom and divorce me. I am passionately fond of her and would have given anything in the world to have retained her.[57]

In a poem 'Unfathered through Divorce'[58] the poet grieved for the loss of his daughter:

Christine, the light of my life and the approving eyes
Of famous people, or my muse herself,
Are nothing to many a remembered look
Of your fond childhood, my beloved elf.

The darkness that has sundered you and me,
If my blame bitterly we pay for it,
Nor dare I blame your mother if I can,
Since that might make it darker even yet.

11

Breid-and-Butter Problems

Oh, it's nonsense, nonsense, nonsense,
Nonsense at this time o' day
That breid-and-butter problems
S'ud be in ony man's way.
                    'Second Hymn to Lenin'   (325)

O N 13 January 1932, that is three days before Lord Pitman granted
a divorce to Margaret Skinner in Edinburgh, an odd incident
occurred outside the Old Bailey in London. It was to have important
implications for MacDiarmid. What happened was that two men
approached a constable on duty outside the court and asked him if he
knew of a typesetter who would set some erotic poems. Unabashed, the
constable directed the men to a printing house near the Old Bailey. As
this printer already set the *Methodist Recorder* he rejected the request,
telling the men 'I'm afraid we couldn't undertake a job of that sort.'[1]
Both men were doubtless highly amused. They were Douglas Glass, later
a photographer; and Count Geoffrey Wladislas Vaile Potocki of Montalk.

Born in New Zealand, the son of an architect and grandson of a
Polish professor, Potocki of Montalk was an egregious eccentric who
had shoulder-length hair and sported a long red cloak and leather
sandals. Virginia Woolf referred to him as 'that whining & complaining

269

disreputable egomaniac, the Polish Count'.[2] Montalk was convinced he was the heir to the Polish throne and his rampantly reactionary periodical, the *Right Review*, was described as the official organ of the Royal House of Poland. As well as being virulently anti-Semitic, Montalk was a connoisseur of erotic literature and, that day in 1932, sought a printer to set, for private circulation, a pamphlet *Here Lies John Penis*. As subsequently pirated it contained five items: three original poems and translations of Rabelais's 'Chanson de la Braguette' and Verlaine's 'Idylle High Life'.

Montalk and Glass finally found a printer, Mr De Lozey, who said he could set the manuscript for twenty-five shillings. Convinced the price was exorbitant Montalk nevertheless agreed to leave the manuscript with De Lozey while he secured quotations from other printers. Once Montalk and Glass had left, De Lozey phoned the police. The two men were arrested and taken to Brixton prison. Glass was discharged at Clerkenwell police court but on 8 February Montalk was back at the Old Bailey before Sir Ernest Wild, the Recorder of London, who summed up: 'Are you going to allow a man, because he calls himself a poet, to deflower our English language by popularising these words?'[3] Montalk was sentenced to six months' imprisonment, a decision W. B. Yeats described as 'criminally brutal'.[4] An appeal fund attracted subscriptions from Aldous Huxley, H. G. Wells, J. B. Priestley, Walter de la Mare, T. S. Eliot and Hugh Walpole but the appeal on 7 March was rejected and Montalk had to serve his time in Wormwood Scrubs. While Montalk was in prison he rented, for ten shillings a week, his country cottage to MacDiarmid and Valda. In April 1932 the poet and his pregnant companion moved to Cootes, a large cottage in Thakeham, west Sussex.

Montalk must rank as one of MacDiarmid's most unlikely, and unlikable, friends, It is one thing for a poet committed to socialism to overlook the pro-Mussolini politics of Ezra Pound, a man of integrity and a poet of genius. It is quite another for a self-respecting socialist to tolerate a fanatical racist reactionary who, in later years, sympathised with Hitler and the white supremacists of South Africa. Admittedly, MacDiarmid eventually denounced Montalk as one of the 'negligible scribblers' (1134) of the extreme right. In 1932, however, he considered Montalk a friend he needed. MacDiarmid's business affairs with the Unicorn Press were in tatters and he was desperate to find somewhere he could live and work on his *Clann Albann* project.

Before he left London for Thakeham, MacDiarmid had attempted unsuccessfully to interest Blackwood's in a new collection of poems, explaining (in a letter of 27 January) that he had in hand a new volume entitled *Alone With the Alone*. The work comprised a prelude – 'The Hydra', consisting of thirty-two poems – and the title poem 'Alone With the Alone'. Several of the poems in the prelude are from the *Sonnets of the Highland Hills* but there are important new poems, especially 'By Wauchopeside' (published in the *Modern Scot* of April 1932) and 'Second Hymn to Lenin' (published in the *Criterion* of July 1932). Both poems were intended for *The Muckle Toon*, the first volume of *Clann Albann*. In the surviving papers relating to *Alone With the Alone* the title poem is missing but must have been the work retitled 'Depth and the Chthonian Image' in *Scots Unbound and Other Poems* (1932).[5] It is possible that MacDiarmid changed the title of the poem by recalling an article in *transition*, a journal he enjoyed. The double issue for June/November 1929 had contained 'The Synthesist Universe: Dreams and the Chthonian Mind', a title certain to appeal to MacDiarmid.

'Depth and the Chthonian Image' was, MacDiarmid noted, 'designed as a perfectly clear and comprehensive expression of my whole aesthetic, political and general position'.[6] Written presumably in the period immediately prior to his divorce, it shows MacDiarmid seeking spiritual illumination in disinterested cogitation. His philosophical debt in this poem is to Plotinus who envisaged the Divine Being as an eternal triad comprising the One (the supreme Absolute, the source) from which emanates Intelligence (*Nous*, uniting the one and the many) from which emanates the Soul (the creative force forming the material universe). Illuminated by the Soul, the individual reaches the One by contemplation, achieving the mystical flight of the alone to the Alone. Plotinus expresses this notion in ecstatic terms:

> We may believe that we have really seen, when a sudden light illumines the Soul; for this light comes from the One and is the One.... The Soul must remove from itself good and evil and everything else that it may receive the One alone, as the One is alone.... If then a man sees himself become one with the One, he has in himself a likeness of the One, and if he passes out of himself, as an image to its archetype, he has reached the end of his journey.... Such is the life of gods and of godlike and blessed men; a liberation from all earthly bonds, a life that takes no pleasure in earthly things, a flight of the alone to the Alone.[7]

This mystical quest is central to MacDiarmid's vision.

The poem is inscribed 'On looking at a ruined mill and thinking of the greatest' (346), the greatest being the One, the Absolute, the spiritual source to which MacDiarmid aspires. According to Plotinus, 'When we [look towards the One] we attain the end of our existence, and our repose, and we no longer sing out of tune, but form in very truth a divine chorus around the One.'[8] MacDiarmid's divine chorus unfolds in ten 24-line stanzas rhyming *abcbddeffebbcbadgghihijj*. The One (the image refers back to *A Drunk Man*, with its Great Wheel) turns in a vast universal wheel which contains all other movement on earth and in space:

> There is nae nearer image gi'en to life
> O' that conclusive power by which you rin
> Even on, drawin' a' the universe in,
> Than this loose simile o' the heavenly hosts
> Vainly prefigurin' the unseen jaups
> Roond your vast wheel – or mair waesome ghosts
> O' that reality man's pairt o' and yet caps
> Wi' Gods in his ain likeness drawn
> > – Puir travesties o' your plan.   (347-8)

MacDiarmid seeks to simulate the majestic movement and cosmic complexity of this vast wheel through the expansive sweep of his stanzas and the alliterative texture of his language.

Human thought, MacDiarmid reasons, can approach the One only through schema and symbol. However, the poet understands that the One is essentially pluralistic and that it is not a symbol but the actual principle that informs the universe:

> You're no' its meanin' but the world itsel'.
> You let nae man think he can see you better
> By concentratin' on your aneness either.
> He pits his mind into a double fetter
> Wha hauds this airt or that, no' baith thegither.
> You are at aince the road a' croods ha' gane
> > And alane wi' the alane.   (349)

That restates MacDiarmid's view of the simultaneity of the visionary experience.

The idea of movement – of a ruined mill, of a planet or a mind, of a vast universal wheel – reminds MacDiarmid of his own position as the force behind the Scottish Renaissance Movement which can be respected only if it survives him, a man of the people:

> *Ein Mann aus dem Volke* – weel I ken
> Nae man or movement's worth a damn unless
> The movement 'ud gang on withoot him if
> He de'ed the morn. Wherefore in you I bless
> My sense o' the greatest man can typify
> And universalise himsel' maist fully by.   (351)

The poet needs to transcend conventional life, to soar beyond the earthly to the eternal, to enlarge himself through a vision of 'the terrible crystal, the ineffable glow' (352). A phrase from Ezekiel (1:22), 'the terrible crystal' became a key to MacDiarmid's concept of creativity: watching the river Esk he saw 'the terrible, the terrible crystal' (390); in a poem entitled 'The Terrible Crystal' he saw 'a gem-like transparence / All the colour and fire of life' (1094); in a statement of his poetic approach he insisted 'it is only in the Scots language I can achieve or maintain ... "the terrible crystal" '.[9] It is, so 'Depth and the Chthonian Image' indicates, the terrible crystal of creativity that makes the poet immortal, an imperishable part of a cosmic consciousness. In the last lines of the poem MacDiarmid asserts his external self:

> Eternity like a ring,
> Virile, masculine, abandoned at nae turn
> To enervatin' luxury
> Aboot me here shall ever clearer burn,
> And in its licht perchance at last men'll see
> Wi' the best works o' art, as wi' you tae,
> Chance can ha'e nocht to dae!   (353)

It is instructive to compare 'Depth and the Chthonian Image' with two other poems composed about the same period and also intended for *The Muckle Toon*. As always, when he was working on a major sequence, MacDiarmid tested his linguistic resources experimentally. 'Depth and the Chthonian Image' is composed in a heavy, almost clotted, Scots with none of the conversational connotations of *A Drunk Man*. Clearly, the poet felt this aggrandised Scots (as he came to call it) was especially suitable for philosophical discussion. By contrast, 'By Wauchopeside' uses a delicately lyrical Scots to recreate moments remembered from his Langholm childhood. The poem compares the movement of the poet's mind to the perpetual motion in and around the river Wauchope. MacDiarmid's delight in the memory is evident in the first stanza:

> Thrawn water? Aye, owre thrawn to be aye thrawn!
> I ha'e my wagtails like the Wauchope tae,
> Birds fu' o' fechtin' spirit, and o' fun,
> That whiles jig in the air in lichtsome play
> Like glass-ba's on a fountain, syne stand still
> Save for a quiver, shoot up an inch or twa, fa' back
> Like a swarm o' winter-gnats, or are tost aside,
> > By their inclination's kittle loup,
> > To balance efter hauf a coup.   (1083)

The ability to dissolve one simile into another – 'like the Wauchope', 'Like glass-ba's', 'Like a swarm o' winter-gnats' – in a sustained statement owes something to the multi-layered approach of Charles Doughty whose *The Dawn in Britain* (1906) is full of passages like the following, in which the similes add natural beauty to the argument of the poem:

> Smiles out, in firmament,
> The hoary girdled, infinite, night of stars,
> Above them: like as when, in sweet spring-time,
> With wind-flowers white, some glade is storied seen;
> Whereas, from part to part, like silver stream,
> Shine hemlocks, stichworts, sign of former path.[10]

As MacDiarmid said, in a letter of 18 February 1932 to T.S. Eliot, he was fascinated by such verse, 'making an intensive study ... of all the poetry of Charles Doughty'.[11]

Characteristically, throughout 'By Wauchopeside' MacDiarmid isolates an upward movement which brings him back to his evolutionary idealism, his determination to participate in a willed advance in the human condition. By the end of the poem he has suggested that poetry must deal with more than dazzling natural scenes. It must, so MacDiarmid supposes, contribute to a new consciousness that will create change. Or, as he puts it in 'Second Hymn to Lenin':

> Poetry like politics maun cut
> The cackle and pursue real ends,
> Unerringly as Lenin, and to that
> Its nature better tends.   (324)

'Second Hymn to Lenin' is a pugnacious statement of MacDiarmid's conviction that poetry is the supreme creative achievement of mankind. In comparison to poetry, with its cerebral complexity, 'politics is bairns' play' (328), a pursuit forced on political supermen such as Lenin because of the infantile state of the human race. MacDiarmid's love of paradox underlies the assertive nature of this poem. He begins by conceding to Lenin the necessity of politics then immediately claims that he, the poet, is involved in a superior activity. Ostensibly, MacDiarmid grants, the socialist poet should be writing simple poems for working men and women, making his work accessible to the masses. However it is not for the poet to descend to a common level (the poem contends), but for the masses to rise up to the evolutionary idealism of the poem – and the revolutionary realism of the gifted politician. At the end of the second hymn MacDiarmid answers his own question about the potential of poetry – 'what else can poetry be?' (328) – with a ringing declaration:

> *The core o' a' activity,*
> *Changin't in accordance wi'*
> *Its inward necessity*
> *And mede o' integrity.*
>
> Unremittin', relentless,
> Organized to the last degree,
> Ah, Lenin, politics is bairns' play
> To what this maun be!   (328)

Considering the mystical longing of 'Depth and the Chthonian Image', the lyrical tone of 'By Wauchopeside' and the didactic thrust of 'Second Hymn to Lenin' *The Muckle Toon* was on course to be a volume of great stylistic diversity as well as vast proportions, judging from the poems intended for the first of five volumes.

Stylistically, MacDiarmid was qualifying his modernism with Romantic traditions fondly remembered from his youthful exposure to poetry. There is more than a touch of Shelley in 'Second Hymn to Lenin'. The great English Romantic had written 'The Mask of Anarchy' after the Peterloo massacre of August 1819 and had articulated the radical voice of England in ringing tones of moral righteousness:

> Science, Poetry, and Thought
> Are thy lamps; they make the lot

> Of the dwellers in a cot
> So serene, they curse it not.[12]

Following Shelley's indignant example, MacDiarmid also composes quatrains advancing fundamental principles:

> *Sport, love, and parentage,*
> *Trade, politics and law*
> *S'ud be nae mair to us than braith*
> *We hardly ken we draw.* (325)

MacDiarmid's frequent declarations of anglophobia have misled critics in search of poetic precedents. Shelley, however, was a definite influence on MacDiarmid: not only did Shelley combine a poetic vision with a political passion, but the opening phrase of the Shelley quatrain quoted might have been MacDiarmid's motto.

'Second Hymn to Lenin' was recognised as an exceptionally important political poem: Eliot's decision to include it in the *Criterion* encouraged MacDiarmid at a very difficult time. Writing to Eliot, on 18 February, on hearing that the poem would appear in the July issue of the journal, MacDiarmid even accepted the suggestion that one stanza – the quatrain beginning 'Gin I canna win through to the man in the street' (323) – should be deleted from the poem, though it was eventually retained. MacDiarmid asked Eliot to keep the type of 'Second Hymn to Lenin' standing, once set, so a pamphlet of the poem could be issued in due course.

Soon after arriving in Thakeham he wrote to Eliot again – on 5 April – explaining his straitened circumstances. Thinking of his business problems in London and his consequent financial embarrassment, he said:

> Things have gone badly with me financially & otherwise recently and I am very anxious to obtain additional literary or journalistic work of any kind or any sort of job whatever. Alas, either is excessively ill to find these days. I have meanwhile 'parked' down here in a cottage where I can live very cheaply and am working hard to finish several new books, including a novel and my big poem (of which the Lenin hymns are separable short items) – which is, I think, making good progress.[13]

The novel was never finished though the *Glasgow Herald* on 15 August did publish an imaginative prose fragment, 'The Scab', about the earth under threat from the spread of 'a malign piece of ground ... stealthily but incessantly encroaching on Nature'.[14] Though *Clann Albann* was never finally completed MacDiarmid was indeed making magnificent progress on *The Muckle Toon* volume.

At a geographical distance of some fifty miles from London, MacDiarmid found Thakeham conducive to creative work. On 12 May he reported on his artistic optimism in a letter to his mother. He had, he said, experienced 'a tremendous rush of poetry'.[15] The torrential image was apposite, for the poet was alive with thoughts of the liquid features of the Langholm landscape. He had just completed the poem 'Tarras' which the *Free Man*, a Social Credit weekly edited in Edinburgh by Robin Black, was to publish (on 25 June, prior to its appearance as a pamphlet, limited to twenty copies, with a frontispiece by William Johnstone). Tarras — where the fastest river in Dumfriesshire runs through a lonely moor — had become for MacDiarmid a poetic symbol of his political struggle:

> *This Bolshevik bog! Suits me doon to the grun'!*
> *For by fike and finnick the world's no' run.*
> *Let fools set store by a simperin' face,*
> *Ithers seek to keep the purale in place*
> *Or grue at vermin — but by heck*
> *The purpose o' life needs them — if us.*   (337)

The inexorable movement of water through peat and over boulders had an elemental power the poet, attracted by the Marxist theory of historical inevitability, found more absorbing than any personal relationships.

The greatest of the poems about the liquid features of Langholm is 'Water Music'. Written in Thakeham, dedicated to William and Flora Johnstone, this onomatopoeic masterpiece is a Scotsman's answer to Joyce's prose poem 'Anna Livia Plurabelle' (from *Finnegans Wake*) about the river Liffey. MacDiarmid gives an extraordinary verbal impression of the rhythms of the rivers that run through Langholm:

> Archin' here and arrachin there,
>   Allevolie or allemand,
> Whiles appliable, whiles areird,
>   The polysemous poem's planned.

> Lively, louch, atweesh, atween,
>   Auchimuty or aspate,
> Threidin' through the averins
>   Or bightsom in the aftergait.   (333)

Helen Cruickshank, who visited MacDiarmid in Thakeham, heard the poet recite 'Water Music' after she had located him playing shove-ha'penny with Sussex yeomen in his new local, the White Lion. Meeting the pregnant Valda, Cruickshank thought the poet's new companion 'gay and hospitable and full of a wonderful courage'.[16]

Apparently MacDiarmid not only drank in the White Lion but occasionally wrote there. During an evening's drinking MacDiarmid announced that he wanted to commit a poem to paper. Valda went to the toilet and returned with several sheets of paper. Slightly inebriated and with toilet paper thus to hand, MacDiarmid noted down one of his most memorable lyrics, 'Milk-Wort and Bog-Cotton'. The first of two stanzas is an expression of MacDiarmid's affinity with the earth and shows an exquisite sense of rhythm as the lines ebb and flow around the traditional measure of the iambic pentameter:

> Cwa' een like milk-wort and bog-cotton hair!
> I love you, earth, in this mood best o' a'
> When the shy spirit like a laich wind moves
> And frae the lift nae shadow can fa'
> Since there's nocht left to thraw a shadow there
> Owre een like milk-wort and milk-white cotton hair.   (331)

In the following stanza, returning to a theme that runs through *A Drunk Man*, the poet observes that 'deep surroondin' darkness ... Is aye the price o' licht' (331).

As in all his concentrated periods of poetic composition MacDiarmid enjoyed, while in Thakeham, alternating between lyrical utterances and downright declarations. Hence the expressive distance between, say, 'Water Music' and 'Tarras'. Another striking example of his range can be seen by contrasting 'Milk-Wort and Bog-Cotton' with 'An Apprentice Angel' which is aimed at the poet's old enemy, Lauchlan Maclean Watt, and ends with a caustic couplet: 'I fancy your Presbyterian Heaven / 'll be haunted tae wi' a hellish leaven' (333). Writing to Neil Gunn from Thakeham, on 24 June, MacDiarmid commented on the emotional extremes of his new poems while anticipating that he would soon finish *The Muckle Toon*:

I can hang on by my toenails a little longer – and with luck long enough to finish Vol. 1 of *Clann Albann* (which – at present rate of progress – won't take me more than another month). I note what you say re violence; but my own conceptions of literary politics – as of Scottish politics – are extremely comprehensive and quite unshakeable. The leopard isn't going to change its spots. I agree with you, however, that certain forms of violence are too easy – weak – not really violent enough! And you can trust me to avoid these all right this time. My violent passages will be designed to kill. Did you see the second of my two poems to 'L. M. W.; An Apprentice Angel' (Lauchlan Maclean Watt) in Orage's *New English Weekly*? That is the true stuff – bitter as Hell, but poetry! But the percentage of stuff that does not raise any personal or political issues and depends upon 'beauty' and 'music' in the more usual acceptations of these very misleading (and really meaningless) terms is very much higher. Instance – my 'Water Music' in the *Scots Observer* ... and my 'Tarras' which is appearing in this week's *Free Man* ... I think you'll agree that stuff like these is ample to offset a great deal more of my more questionable tricks than I propose to inflict upon the readers of *Clann Albann*.[17]

While MacDiarmid was adamant that he was on the right lines as far as his creative work was concerned, he was unable to square with Gunn the complications arising from the money the novelist had advanced to establish MacDiarmid's directorship of the Unicorn Press.

As it related to MacDiarmid, the financial drama of the Unicorn Press was rapidly becoming a black comedy of confusion. MacDiarmid had found a friend in the firm when the publisher Stanley Nott (who was to bring out *At the Sign of the Thistle*, a collection of MacDiarmid essays, in 1934) became a director. Alas, Nott defaulted in paying up his share capital and he and MacDiarmid were dismissed from the firm by J. F. Moore and L. N. Cooper who wrote to Gunn demanding that he pay a liability of £24 8s on a £100 share certificate issued to MacDiarmid. Meanwhile, MacDiarmid had turned to McElroy and Peggy for legal advice on securing his shares.

Unable to draw any further income from the Unicorn Press, Mac-Diarmid was forced to run up debts to pay for his rent and his everyday expenses. Since 21 May he had been contributing a weekly column, 'At the Sign of the Thistle', to Robin Black's *Free Man* and on 1 July the *Scottish Educational Journal* (which had published the notorious 'Contemporary Scottish Studies' articles) began a new series by MacDiarmid, using the pseudonym James Maclaren. MacDiarmid was paid ten shillings for the *Free Man* column and not much more for the *Scottish Educational*

Journal series. However, he had an outlet for his ideas. 'The Course of Scottish Poetry' began, in the *Scottish Educational Journal*, with a general denunciation of the penury of Scottish aesthetics and a reminder of Lenin's call for party-political literature. In this connection, 'Maclaren' noted 'the relationship of *Hymns to Lenin* today with Burns's welcome to the French Revolution'.[18] (The series ran until 21 July 1933.)

Domestic life was, inevitably, a strain on Valda who had to cope with poverty as well as pregnancy. Like MacDiarmid, she had no private means and she had set aside savings of £30 to pay for the pamphlet publication of *Second Hymn to Lenin*. (Limited to one hundred copies and reprinted from the type used for the appearance of the poem in the *Criterion*, *Second Hymn to Lenin* came out in September over the imprint of Valda Trevlyn, Thakeham, with a portrait frontispiece by William Johnstone and a cover drawing by Johnstone's wife Flora.) Valda was encouraged by MacDiarmid to believe that childbirth was an uncomplicated business:

> I was going to have a baby and that was that. Christopher had always impressed on me about the mill girls in [Langholm], how marvellous they were. They came home for lunch and had their babies and went back to work. I thought, if the bloody mill girls can do that so can I. How naïve I was. I knew all about the theory of having babies, but those mill girls gave me a real hang-up. Anyway, I finally saw a doctor a few weeks before I was due.[19]

Advised to have the baby in hospital she went to Steyning where, on 28 July, she gave birth to James Michael Grieve. MacDiarmid told Neil Gunn on 4 August:

> Valda had a son to me last Thursday morning. Both are going on well now. But the confinement proved an altogether abnormal one and she will have to remain in the nursing home for at least a fortnight longer. Only her youth and exceptional vitality and the healthy country life we have been living down here pulled her through. I was at my wits end to get even the minimum charges together but we thought we could just pull through by the skin of our teeth, until this happened and of course upsets all calculations. Heaven only knows what's to happen.[20]

Having visited Valda and baby Michael at Steyning on 9 August, MacDiarmid got in touch with Helen Cruickshank, hoping she could put some work his way. If, he assured her, he could get a job paying at least £2 a week then he would willingly 'sign an absolute teetotal pledge in return for any such job – and keep it'.[21] He had unsuccessfully approached Sir Robert Bruce and David Anderson (respectively editors of the *Glasgow Herald* and *Daily Record*) for work and now expected to be evicted from the Thakeham cottage and have his furniture seized. Meeting his debts was impossible and he had allowed an additional complication into his life. La Rue, the Breton nationalist who had fathered Peggy's aborted child, had sought refuge under MacDiarmid's roof while the police were pursuing him as an illegal immigrant. MacDiarmid was thus technically harbouring a criminal and, to add to the stress of the situation, there were unpleasant repercussions from the Unicorn Press.

'My affairs are going steadily from bad to worse,' MacDiarmid informed Neil Gunn on 16 August.[22] He was hopelessly in arrears with his cottage rent and had dropped any pretence of extricating himself with dignity from the Unicorn Press affair. He formally transferred his shares to Peggy, McElroy and Gunn, then went to Steyning, collected Valda and Michael, and headed for London where the family was met by Donald and Catherine Carswell. The prodigal returned to Scotland, with Valda and Michael, on the overnight bus from London to Edinburgh, a tiring journey that took seventeen hours. When they got to Edinburgh Robin and Margaret Black were waiting to receive them as guests in their Portobello home.

The poetic legacy of the period culminating at Thakeham was displayed, towards the end of the year, in the volume *Scots Unbound and Other Poems*. It contained 'Milk-Wort and Bog-Cotton', 'An Apprentice Angel', 'Water Music', 'Tarras', 'Depth and the Chthonian Image' and other pieces including the title poem, dedicated to Robin and Margaret Black, celebrating the Scots sense of colour. A prefatory note explained that all the poems in *Scots Unbound*, like those in *First Hymn to Lenin and Other Poems* and like 'Second Hymn to Lenin', were separable items from the first volume of *Clann Albann*. Ironically, however, the *Clann Albann* project virtually ended with MacDiarmid's return to his native land.

12

Accepting the
Stones

But it is wrong to indulge in these illustrations
Instead of just accepting the stones.
It is a paltry business to try to drag down
The arduus furor of the stones to the futile imaginings of men,
To all that fears to grow roots into the common earth,
As it soon must, lest it be chilled to the core,
As it will be – and none the worse for that.
    'On a Raised Beach'   (425)

BEFORE hurrying away from Thakeham at the end of August 1932, MacDiarmid had told Helen Cruickshank that he could make ends meet provided he could earn £2 a week. Always helpful, Cruickshank discussed the matter with Robin Black, editor-publisher of the weekly *Free Man* which was financed by Dr Stanley Robertson, an affluent dental surgeon in Musselburgh, near Edinburgh. Black and Robertson agreed to hire MacDiarmid as assistant editor of the *Free Man* at a wage of £2 per week. This arrangement meant MacDiarmid had the use of the *Free Man* office at 1 India Buildings, Victoria Street, Edinburgh; there he wrote most of the editorial copy as well as continuing his weekly causerie 'At the Sign of the Thistle'.

Like the *New Age*, in its later years, and like Orage's other journal, the *New English Weekly*, the *Free Man* was committed to the economic policies of C. H. Douglas. It was also dedicated to the cause of Scottish nationalism. The issue of 10 September 1932 is typical. On the front page there is a declaration of principle:

> This journal stands for the right of the individual to a full life and that liberty which is the only true basis of an enduring social fabric. This faith implies a definite distrust of the prevailing tendency to mass acquiescence, and is opposed to the increasing centralisation of all forms of control.... A virile nationalism only can create a vital internationalism. It is the particular mission of the *Free Man* to give a lead to, and provide an open forum for, all those in Scotland who are dissatisfied with her present condition and are determined to make her once more the land of freedom and progress with a living voice in world affairs.[1]

The editorial comments on an address by Sir Alfred Ewing to the British Association and on a speech by Dingle Foot, Labour MP for Dundee, then ends – predictably given the Douglasite ethos of the journal – with an attack on the bankers. MacDiarmid's column develops an anti-English argument from a passage in Catherine Carswell's *The Savage Pilgrimage: A Narrative of D. H. Lawrence* (1932). There is a Douglasite analysis of the evolution of money and the back page of the eight-page paper advertises books by Douglas and his disciples.

During his first few weeks as assistant editor of the *Free Man*, MacDiarmid, Valda and Michael stayed with Robin and Margaret Black at 8 Esplanade in Joppa, a suburb of Edinburgh. Six miles east of Musselburgh, in Longniddry village, Stanley Robertson found a dilapidated two-roomed red-pantiled cottage for rent at ten shillings a week. MacDiarmid moved into this, furnishing the but-and-ben with a table and chairs lent to him by his mother Elizabeth – now widowed for a second time since James Dawson had died, on 15 September 1932, from cerebral concussion and cardiac failure. Situated in an old fruit farm to the south of Longniddry, Fruit Farm Cottage (as it is still known) was not a pleasant place to live. To reach the cottage the poet and his family had to walk through a railway arch and past a disused lime-kiln that, in the words of Helen Cruickshank, 'looked like a sinister back-cloth from a Wagner opera'.[2] Valda quickly became hostile to her new home:

> We were near a quarry and all the tramps used to sleep there. I'd be making up Mike's bottle and a tramp would peer in the window and, of course, the

bottle would be smashed and Mike and I would get on the bed to hide. I wasn't used to that sort of thing at that time.[3]

When MacDiarmid returned on the late-night bus from Edinburgh, Valda literally had to light his way through the railway arch as there was no light near the cottage. She rolled up newspapers and lit them under the arch: 'he suffered from night blindness and so going under the arch he had a beacon'.[4] Helen Cruickshank sympathised with the plight of the family and invited them to spend the Christmas of 1932 with her in Corstorphine. She hired a pram for the weekend 'and the poet, "domestic as a plate", wheeled it up and down our hilly roads with Valda and I laughing on either side'.[5]

In Cruickshank's opinion there were too many distractions for Mac-Diarmid in Edinburgh. During his lunch-break he liked to drink in Rutherford's Bar, off South Bridge, and on his way to get the bus back to Longniddry there was the temptation of Rose Street – Edinburgh's 'amber mile' of bars. MacDiarmid's friends could see he was unhappy. He was borrowing money from his brother Andrew – then working in Edinburgh for the Inland Revenue and living at Liberton – and he was running up debts at the grocer's in Longniddry. Cruickshank heard that David Orr, resident doctor on the Shetland island of Whalsay, wanted to help and was willing to accommodate the poet and family, in the hope that the arrangement would allow MacDiarmid to write and Valda to work as a housekeeper. Cruickshank discussed the opportunity with Robin Black on a sunny bench behind St John's Church in Princes Street:

> I was gazing in the direction of De Quincey's tomb in the adjoining churchyard of St Cuthbert's when Robin said, 'And, of course, Whalsay is a dry island.' At which, I heard myself say firmly, 'I think he should go.'[6]

When the proposal was put to MacDiarmid he readily agreed. Stanley Robertson cleared the poet's outstanding debts in Longniddry and MacDiarmid moved his mother's furniture into a flat in Bruntsfield, Edinburgh. The Bruntsfield address – care of Mrs Craik, 8 Westhall Gardens, off Leamington Terrace – was one MacDiarmid intended to return to as he thought that, at most, he would be in Shetland for a matter of months rather than years. At 7 p.m. on 2 May 1933 he boarded the Lerwick steamer at Leith, without Valda and Michael who (two days later) went down to Cornwall for a month's holiday with her mother. MacDiarmid was met in Lerwick by David Orr – the first meeting between the two men – and they sailed on the mail steamer, the *Earl of*

Zetland, from Lerwick to Whalsay, a journey lasting an hour and a half. Landing at Symbister harbour, MacDiarmid and Orr went to the doctor's house, a temporary address as Orr was having a new house built for him.

Whalsay ('whale island'), lying on the east side of the Shetland Mainland, measures less than six miles from the south-west to the north-east and has a maximum breadth of just over two miles. At the time of MacDiarmid's arrival it had a population of around nine hundred and was dependent on haddock and herring fishing, industries in decline. As an illuminating expression, collected by MacDiarmid, has it, 'the Orcadian is a farmer with a boat, the Shetlander is a fisherman with a croft'.[7] The fishermen-crofters had to endure considerable hardship on Whalsay: they had no lighting, sewage, rubbish disposal or other public services and most of the roads were in an atrocious condition. By contrast, W. A. Bruce, the laird of Whalsay, lived in style at Symbister House. Politically, MacDiarmid saw Whalsay as a microcosm of an unjust society.

Visually, however, Whalsay was a revelation to MacDiarmid. An undulating island of hills and valleys textured by sedge and heather, Whalsay is rich in archaeological relics – the Standing Stones of Yoxie, the neolithic Bunzie House, the Iron Age fort at the Loch of Huxter, the heel-shaped cairn of Pettigarths Field. More spectacular than these are the dazzling views of the islands scattered like a broken string of beads around Whalsay. The Shetland poet Vagaland (T. A. Robertson) described the West Isles as 'Gem-stones set in a sun-gilt sea'.[8] Similarly, the islands clustered around Whalsay glow, in the setting sun, like emeralds and amethysts. And the steep cliffs of the islands are alive with birds, allowing a 'poet of passion' to see himself as 'A bird cliff under the midnight sun' (482).

Within two weeks of settling on Whalsay MacDiarmid had written a new poem of some length, 'Ode to All Rebels'. The first poem completed on the island was an attempt to shrug off the pain of his recent past by transforming personal experience into an artistic statement. His aim was to return to the multi-layered mode of *A Drunk Man Looks at the Thistle*: whereas in his masterpiece he had built a magnificent poetic structure on the basis of his aspirations, he hoped he could now do something similar on the theme of his divorce from Peggy and his separation from Christine and Walter. Alas, the verbal majesty of *A Drunk Man* eluded him in 'Ode to All Rebels', a poem that reads as the product of an emotional after-effect from a domestic trauma. *A Drunk Man* had dealt with the notion of creative chaos in a lucid sequence,

'Ode to All Rebels' reassembles autobiographical events chaotically — and crudely. Gollancz, the publishers, deleted the poem from *Stony Limits* on the grounds of obscenity. It is no more erotically explicit than Joyce's *Ulysses* but it is obsessively unwholesome in its references to sex.

Stylistically, 'Ode to All Rebels' is MacDiarmid's most awkward effort to write an expressionist poem in Scots: Gothic elements, supernatural touches and deliberate bits of blasphemy are brought together in an assault on the expectations of the reader. Linguistically, the ode uses a conversationally casual dialect Scots fortified by rhyme. Indeed, after Gollancz's objections to the obscenity of the poem, MacDiarmid had little trouble anglicising parts of it for publication in *Second Hymn to Lenin and Other Poems*.[9] The neurotic nature of the poem accounts for its lack of focus. MacDiarmid never establishes a single speaking voice for his melodramatic monologue; instead he presents different voices that issue eerily from the same source. There is the voice of the poet (who comments on culture), the voice of the fictional narrator (who expatiates on sex), the voice of the Rebel Angel (who discourses on the evolutionary ideal), the voice of the outcast (who identifies with Ishmael). 'Ode to All Rebels' is a disturbed, and disturbing poem: pathological in tone, its texture is riddled with images of disease and death.

The first line of 'Ode to All Rebels', spoken by a fictional narrator who is supposedly an individual other than the poet, announces a death. The speaker recalls the death of his first wife, Kate, and goes on to examine the impact of her loss: 'My haill warld gane', 'The tender ties twixt us twa ... wantonly snapt' (487). In a necrophiliac fantasy, the speaker admits he was sexually aroused when watching Kate's coffin enter the earth:

> Even as frae lowerin' the coffin I raze
> Conscious o' my nature in a wud amaze
> And strauchtened up my muckle animal frame
> That kent what it wanted and kent nae shame
> And stood in a burst o' sun
> Glowerin' at the bit broken grun'. (488)

From Kate he turns to his second wife Jean (the name used for the wife in *A Drunk Man*) with a feeling of *déjà vu*: 'I felt / I'd seen her afore tho' I hadna' (489). United with Jean he felt his previous marriage to Kate 'was juist something I'd dreamed' (490). For the visionary, all women are aspects of an eternal ideal. Kate and Jean are interchangeable, both modelled on Peggy.

The speaker shifts from the eternal to the earthly in a confessional passage about his extra-marital adventures. Thinking of the sexual appetites of the opposite sex he allows a woman to articulate an erotic insight:

> 'The Colonel's too gallant, too romantic, too old,'
>   She sadly admitted, 'it's true,
> To appreciate the Great Discovery of the Age
>   – That women like It too'   (491)

That reads like wishful thinking about Peggy's relationship with an older man, McElroy. The thought of this brings the speaker, now the representative of the poet, to the implications of her liaison: 'I ha'ena seen the bairns / Since Jean divorced me' (491), 'I wadna ken the bairns / Even if I saw them again' (492). The speaker's answer to this is to create conditions that allow him to live an imaginative life free from the 'unspeakable horror' (495) of physical relationships. Suddenly the speaker reaches back to the time when he and Kate were medical students together at a harrowing examination of a corpse. Kate looks at the speaker:

>   I returned her look
> Wi' ane strictly accordin' to the book,
> As I fingered the vagina lyin' afore me
>   – Carcinoma o' the uterus – while o'er me
> Swept the thocht: 'Darlin' the neist may be you'
>   – I saw deep eneuch then, and saw true,
>   And yet lo'ed her, I confess,
>   Gin nane the mair certes nane the less.   (496)

The speaker marries Kate, convinced that women are merely sexual comforters.

At this point the speaker reveals that he is a rebel angel whose 'haill warld's vanished like Kate and Jean' (498) – one wife lost through death, the other through divorce (death and divorce being synonymous in the context of the poem). In his angelic state he has been 'born / Deaf and blind' (497): his eyes and ears are attuned only to the eternal. He is alone, he is shunned by humanity, 'I am Ishmael, the only man, / Wha's the freend o' a' men' (507). Alone – without the company of women and men – he is able to appeal to God as he does at the conclusion of the poem.

'Ode to All Rebels' is psychologically revealing, confirming the mental agony his divorce imposed on the poet. Unfortunately it tends to collapse into confusion as the identity of the speaker changes arbitrarily and alarmingly. It is a rambling composition because MacDiarmid clutches unconvincingly at concepts he has previously used with inventive brilliance: the spiritual challenge of sexuality, the superiority of darkness to light, the isolation of the iconoclast, the mediocrity of the majority, the pursuit of the impossible. One of the poetic asides in 'Ode to All Rebels' suggests that MacDiarmid was acutely aware of the drably discursive manner of the poem:

> I used to write sic bonny sangs
> A'body wi' pleasure and profit could read,
> Even yet a bit discipline's a' that I need
> To mak' mysel' ane o' the greatest poets
> Puir Scotland's ever managed to breed.
> Why dae I turn my back on a' that
> And write this horrible rubbish instead?
> – Sustain me, spirit o' God, that I pay
> These seductive voices nae heed!   (494-5)

The intended irony of these last two lines does not conceal the genuine reservations of the poet.

Writing 'Ode to All Rebels' (it was finished by the middle of May) was a cathartic exercise, providing at least a temporary release from memories of Peggy. MacDiarmid had come to Whalsay (the words are his own) 'in exceedingly bad state, psychologically and physically'.[10] As David Orr understood, the poet had to regain his sense of composure both mentally and physically. For the sake of his health, he needed to take advantage of his new environment. Thus MacDiarmid lost little time exploring the islands near Whalsay. He went, on a haddock boat, to the Out Skerries, a group of isles five miles north-east of Whalsay. Also on board was Thomas Robertson, one of HM Survey Geologists, who was particularly interested in the glaciation of Whalsay and the Out Skerries. For the next three months (before the geologist returned to Edinburgh) Robertson was one of MacDiarmid's closest friends on Whalsay. The poet listened attentively to Robertson's observations on such phenomena as the raised beaches of West Linga, the biggest of the islands between Whalsay and the Mainland.

While the experience of being out and about in boats invigorated MacDiarmid, he was given to dark moods. He described himself as a man 'brooding in uninhabited islands'[11] and sometimes the brooding was excessively bitter. Bruse Holm, a tiny island between Mainland and West Linga, is the 'uninhabited isle' (1272) that is the setting for the 'Letter to R. M. B.' – that is, Robin McKelvie Black of the *Free Man*. MacDiarmid expresses his disgust with Scotland in this poem, resolutely turns his back on his native land. His verdict on Scotland is pitiless:

> There is nae ither country 'neath the sun
> That's betrayed the human spirit as Scotland's done,
> And still the betrayal proceeds to the complete
> Dehumanisin' o' the Scottish breed.
> Oh, R. M. B., I looked frae Arthur's Seat
> On a waur Hell than ony God decreed.   (1273)

This outburst coincided with the poet's expulsion from the National Party of Scotland on the grounds of his Communist sympathies. On 19 May MacDiarmid received a letter from John MacCormick explaining that the NPS had no room for extremists. Party policy was to present a moderate front to the Scottish people by getting rid of men like Mac-Diarmid and merging (which it duly did in April of the following year) with the right-wing Scottish Party. To the poet, the modern nationalists were akin to 'a troupe of gibbering lunatics'.[12]

Two days after reading MacCormick's letter, MacDiarmid was off in another direction. He was given a place aboard a sailing boat bound for the herring fishing around Yell Sound. The *Valkyrie*, on which MacDiarmid travelled, was a sail drifter, one of the old square-sail boats that would soon be put out of business by the steam drifters. Skippered by John Irvine of Saltness, Whalsay, the *Valkyrie* had a crew comprising Irvine's sons Johnnie and Laurie, Wilfred Gilbertson, Robbie Williamson, Jimmy Williamson, James Hutchison and the cook Johnnie Polson.[13] MacDiarmid was taken along, at his own request, as an observer. Irvine's son John remembered the poet as an industrious insomniac: 'He was the only man I ever knew who never slept – that was a week at sea – he just lay in a bunk, leant against a beam six inches above his head, and wrote.'[14] The poet who had lamented, in 'Ode to All Rebels', that he had lost his touch for 'bonny sangs' now recovered his lyrical impulse at sea in a sequence of 'Shetland Lyrics'.

These lyrics are expressions of wonder at the apparently uncomplicated lives of the fishermen, Tormented by the calamitous complexity of his own private life, the poet took comfort in the way the fishermen overcame the elemental challenge of the sea. The first of ten 'Shetland Lyrics' is a verbal sketch of the herring fishers. Written in a simplified Scots, it rejoices in the way the fishermen sing to the herring 'Come, shove in your heids and growl' (437) – perhaps a mishearing of the phrase 'shove in your heids and growe' – that is, grow. In a moment of epiphany, MacDiarmid sees God as a singing fisherman who watches the indiscriminate mass of men struggling in a sea of doubt before being hauled up to Heaven:

> 'Left, right – O come in and see me,'
> Reid and yellow and black and white
> Toddlin' up into Heaven thegither
> At peep o' day frae the endless night.   (438)

The second Shetland lyric is uncharacteristically humble. Watching the idiotic faces of the fish and reflecting on the limited intellectual existence of the fishermen, the poet feels they have an intimate relationship with God that is denied to the man of letters:

> Aye, and I kent their animal forms
> And primitive minds, like fish frae the sea,
> Cam' faur mair naturally oot o' the bland
> Omnipotence o' God than a fribble like me.   (438)

On the evidence of the Shetland Lyrics, MacDiarmid was impressed, at this time, by the direct functional routine of the fisherman. As he was in an empathetic mood, on board the *Valkyrie*, it seems likely that the poem 'Off the Coast of Fiedeland' (not collected until 1947) refers to this trip in May 1933 though it is dated 'Shetland (West Side) Herring Fishing, June 1936' (723). As its title makes clear, this poem is set in the deep waters around the most northern point of the Shetland Mainland. MacDiarmid's intention is to produce a simple narrative conveying the consciousness of a fisherman, hence the determinedly commonplace trappings of the poem. Dedicated to John Irvine of the *Valkyrie* it establishes the outlook of the speaker who begins, appropriately enough, with a location:

Twenty miles out to the main deep
Due west o' the Ramna Stacks
And sou-west o' the Flugga Light
I ha'e a' that my pleasure lacks.   (723)

Disappointingly, this dramatic monologue succumbs to sentimentality. Temperamentally unable to adapt himself to the priorities of the fisherman, MacDiarmid lapses into moments of bathos. The speaker longs for his 'wee Whalsay lassie' (724) and comes out with a statement so banal as to be totally unconvincing:

For a workin' lad and a workin' lass
Can lo'e each ither juist at least as weel
As Royalty or the wealthiest folk
Or onybody trained in a public skeel.   (727)

As in 'The Seamless Garment', his previous attempt to write a populist poetry, MacDiarmid becomes patronising in his approach. Nevertheless, he was writing incessantly and experimenting with points of view.

Returning to Whalsay on 27 May MacDiarmid enthused over his stint at sea in a letter to his brother Andrew: 'I am just back from the herring fishing — one of the most marvellous experiences I have ever had, and one that has given me a wonderful tan and bucked me up immensely'.[15] He was happy that Valda and Michael were due in Whalsay at the beginning of June but had encountered an unexpected setback. David Orr had married — the poem 'Bedtime' is an epithalamium for David and Margaret Orr — and this development upset the plan for MacDiarmid and Valda to live with the doctor in his new house at Symbister. For a few weeks MacDiarmid moved, with Valda and Michael, into Brough Schoolhouse (Brough is a hamlet in north-west Whalsay) and looked for more suitable accommodation. Luckily he found a cottage on a hillside at Sodom, east of Symbister harbour. The semi-detached building had a fairly large livingroom and a back kitchen downstairs and two bedrooms upstairs. As the child of a previous tenant had died of tuberculosis in the cottage the locals were unwilling to consider it as a fit place for human habitation, assuming that the illness would linger on in the house. MacDiarmid, however, was delighted with his new home which he rented, from John Anderson of East Hamister, for twenty-six shillings a year — in addition to rates of seven shillings,

To facilitate his move to the cottage in the middle of July, MacDiarmid had his furniture sent up from Edinburgh and asked Helen

Cruickshank to mail him some blankets. MacDiarmid describes the conditions in the cottage, his home for eight years, in his autobiography:

> I succeeded in getting a nice commodious four-roomed cottage standing on a hillside and looking out over a tangled pattern of complicated tideways, *voes* and islands with snaggled coasts to the north Shetland Mainland and the Atlantic ... Comfort never mattered very much to me [and] I am not a 'knacky' person; what furniture we had at the beginning was made for the most part by my wife out of orange boxes, tea boxes, and the like.[16]

There were additional burdens. MacDiarmid had the right to cut peat for his open hearth fire but his peat stack was a quarter of a mile from the cottage, quite a distance to carry a full basket. Water had to be drawn from a well quarter of a mile in the opposite direction. There were compensations. The view of Linga Sound was magnificent and the poet's family soon acquired interesting 'pets': a scoury (wild herring gull chick) and a wild cat.

As he explained in letters to his brother and mother, MacDiarmid had another complication in his life. He was suffering from an anal fissure and had been advised that an operation must be arranged next time the symptoms became severe. Meanwhile, he felt he could procrastinate with this problem by taking an opportunity to visit the Faroe Islands for one week. Every two years the Shetlanders and the Faroese exchanged delegations and MacDiarmid's trip coincided with the Faroese National Festival of St Olaf. He sailed on the Faroese steamer, the *Tjaldur* (meaning 'oyster-catcher'), and was astonished at the sight, on the horizon, of 'the monstrous shapes of Litla Dimun and Stora Dimun [followed by] sterile pyramids rising to needle-points, sheer walls of basalt, fantastic ridges with razor edges'.[17] Though only in the Faroes for a short period at the beginning of August, MacDiarmid came to the conclusion that he was in the presence of a political and cultural renaissance. Sardonically, he compared the vitality of the Faroes with the failure of Shetland to treasure its own traditions:

> The preservation of the Faroese language – the carrying of it in recent years to the highest creative level – cannot be gainsaid. The Shetlands have all but completely lost their old Norse language ... The Shetlands are half-ruined; the population is rapidly declining; scores of crofts are falling into desuetude; the fishing is in a bad way; unemployment and poverty are rampant ... [By contrast, the Faroes] have won a very great measure of autonomy, and the predominant party is determined upon complete

independence ... [I believe] the Faroes are a wonderful object lesson and model to every other country in the world today ...[18]

While in the Faroes, MacDiarmid talked to writers and politicians and even watched three football matches between the Shetlanders and the Faroese. He noted, with relish, that the Faroese won two of the three games.

Coming back to Whalsay, MacDiarmid looked again at the Shetland landscape in the light of the sights he had seen in the Faroes. 'The Shetlands', he wrote, 'have a similar lack of trees which at first gives an impression of barrenness and monotony until closer acquaintance shows that, despite this strange lack, there is no absence of variety of colour and form and the landscape, however different to that to which one has been accustomed, has its own completeness and complexity.'[19] MacDiarmid had spent much of his boyhood in the woods around Langholm and his work was rich in references to trees; the strange new tree of 'A Moment in Eternity', the gigantic tree in *A Drunk Man Looks at the Thistle*, the trees of 'Whuchulls' (Whitshiels, a wood near Langholm) intended for *Clann Albann*.

It was apparent that the treeless, windswept world of Shetland demanded a special viewpoint and special linguistic resources. *Clann Albann* belonged to a past MacDiarmid had put behind him. An article of 12 August, in the *Scots Observer*, revealed that *Clann Albann* was no longer a priority. 'I cannot', he said, 'set any date for the finish of the undertaking [as] the whole scheme may never be carried out.'[20] He had written his *Muckle Toon* poems in Scots and continued in Scots with 'Ode to All Rebels' and the 'Shetland Lyrics'. Now he wanted an erudite alternative, an English capable of articulating his understanding of a world stripped to its essentials; he felt his internal struggle for survival was externalised in the loneliest reaches of the Shetland landscape. As he had done when he resuscitated Scots, MacDiarmid went back to the basics of language. Charles Doughty, a key figure for MacDiarmid in the 1930s, had disturbed the smooth surface of modern literary English by developing a vigorous antiquarian manner – 'Doughty', said MacDiarmid approvingly, 'had to abandon modern English and use a large infusion of Anglo-Saxon words and native syntactical forms.'[21] MacDiarmid, for his part, wanted to do something equally radical by – paradoxically – adopting a contrary position, a different direction. Instead of reverting to an archaic English he would evolve a Synthetic English by fleshing out the bones of the spoken language with the muscles of a scientific vocabulary. Technical terms, by their unfamiliarity, would compel the reader to consider the fundamental nature of language as a supreme reality rather than an incidental ornament. Hence MacDiarmid's reference, in an essay on Doughty, to 'the urgent and unescapable necessity of the poetic use of the full range of modern scientific terminology'.[22]

Through his friendship with Thomas Robertson (who left Shetland in August) MacDiarmid had gained an appreciation of geology and he began 'On a Raised Beach' — arguably his greatest poem in English — with a passage combining geological and spiritual allusions. The result is as strange and startling as the Scots he had synthesised in his earlier work. To the modern consciousness, accustomed to everyday English, the opening stanza sounds like an utterance from another world, which is precisely the impact MacDiarmid intended:

> All is lithogenesis — or lochia,
> Carpolite fruit of the forbidden tree,
> Stones blacker than any in the Caaba,
> Cream-coloured caen-stone, chatoyant pieces,
> Celadon and corbeau, bistre and beige,
> Glaucous, hoar, enfouldered, cyathiform,
> Making mere faculae of the sun and moon
> I study you glout and gloss, but have
> No cadrans to adjust you with, and turn again
> From optik to haptik and like a blind man run
> My fingers over you, arris by arris, burr by burr,
> Slickensides, truité, rugas, foveoles,
> Bringing my aesthesis in vain to bear,
> An angle-titch to all your corrugations and coigns,
> Hatched foraminous cavo-rilievo of the world,
> Deictic, fiducial stones. Chiliad by chiliad
> What bricole piled you here, stupendous cairn?
> What artist poses the Earth écorché thus,
> Pillar of creation engouled in me?
> What eburnation augments you with men's bones,
> Every energumen an Endymion yet?
> All the other stones are in this haecceity it seems,
> But where is the Christophanic rock that moved?
> What Cabirian song from this catasta comes?   (422-3)

There are various references to religion in that piece of verbal virtuosity: the forbidden tree, the Caaba (Meccan shrine containing a sacred black stone), the Cabirian mysteries (the Cabiri being ancient mystic divinities whose cult spread from Lemnos, Samothrace, and Imbros). But the crucial question comes in the penultimate line, 'where is the Christophanic rock that moved?' What in this stony world, asks MacDiarmid, permits any resurrection of the spirit? His poetic inquiry proceeds from this position.

Though there is a strongly speculative element in 'On a Raised Beach', the poem has a subjective dimension as the deracinated man, separated from Scotland, identifies with stones on an uninhabited island. From his cottage at Sodom he gazed on the uninhabited island of West Linga which he had certainly visited with Robertson. It was a place that fuelled his literary fantasies. In a prose piece, 'Life in the Shetland Islands', MacDiarmid tells us of a visit to West Linga:

I arranged with the boatman who took me over from the inhabited island of Whalsay to the uninhabited island of [West] Linga to train his telescope on a given spot on the third day afterwards, in the early afternoon, and if I was seen standing there, to come over and fetch me. If not, to keep on doing so every afternoon thereafter until I was so seen — if I ever was. That boatman suspected that I might commit suicide, but he did not communicate his suspicions to anyone else; he did as he was told; he trained his telescope on the arranged spot in the early afternoon of the third day, but he was a bit of a Nelson. I was not there, as a matter of fact, but, even if I had been, he could not have seen me for a thick wall of fog (one of the many little matters I had not foreseen or provided for in the arrangements I made). Nevertheless, he came, and I returned to Whalsay with him.

I took no food with me to Linga [and] I slept in a cave in the rocks.[23]

This extraordinary story is paralleled by a fine poem, 'Diamond Body', written — according to the inscription — in a cave of the sea:

Crossing the island I see the tail of my coat
Wave back and forth and know
It is the waves of the sea on my beach.
And now I am in the cave. A moment ago
I saw the broad leather-brown belts of tangleweed,
And the minute forms that fix themselves
In soft carmine lace-stencils upon the shingle ...
It seems as though it were the shingle
And the waving forest of sea-growth
That moves — and not the water!   (1088)

The close observation and anecdotal evidence show that MacDiarmid certainly looked carefully at the landscape of West Linga and peered into the caves on the island. His claim to have spent three days alone there, sleeping in a cave, is fiction not fact. Whalsay people remember him well and there is no oral record of him ever being left alone on the island for as long as a day[24]. Still, he imaginatively possessed his raised beach on West Linga.

Stepping outside his cottage at Sodom, MacDiarmid could see all of one raised beach on West Linga and – partly obscured by the Calf of Linga – some of a longer raised beach near Croo Wick where boats frequently land. According to locals who knew MacDiarmid, the shingle shelf at Croo Wick is the raised beach of MacDiarmid's great poem. It has been enlarged by his imagination since it is not so much a stupendous cairn as (conforming to the dictionary definition) the old sea-margin above the later water-level. After his return to Whalsay from the Faroes MacDiarmid took opportunities to scrutinise the raised beach. Up from his cottage was a general store owned by Jimmy Arthur who became the poet's friendly shopkeeper when he moved from the doctor's house in Symbister (by way of Brough Schoolhouse) to Sodom. In August 1933 Jimmy Arthur and his brother Hugh made several trips to Croo Wick to get shingle for mixing in concrete. Some days they went back and forward repeatedly and would leave MacDiarmid alone until it was time for the final journey back to Whalsay. While on the island MacDiarmid would write in the notebook he always carried on Whalsay but if the poem benefited from immediate impressions it was later rewritten as a formal philosophical statement. MacDiarmid was proud that the poems he wrote on Whalsay were composed systematically; drafted, then carefully polished.

Indeed, MacDiarmid sent a draft of the poem to F. G. Scott before he produced the final version. Absent from the draft is the majestic opening section quoted above and the final stanza of the text published in *Stony Limits and Other Poems*.[25] In place of the published final stanza is an alternative ending in which the poet stands up on the raised beach and walks on its surface, feeling no need to compete with the stones beneath his feet. Scott suggested that MacDiarmid should attenuate the tone of this poem, making it cerebral as well as subjective. MacDiarmid responded to this advice, though the poem remains a quest for an individual faith. Philosophically it is a reassessment of the issues announced in *A Drunk Man Looks at the Thistle*.

In *A Drunk Man* the central figure had collapsed on a hillside before rising to resurrection. In 'On a Raised Beach' the central figure is again in a fallen state: he is on his back, conscious that 'Nothing has stirred / Since I lay down this morning an eternity ago . But one bird' (423). Blake saw eternity in a grain of sand, MacDiarmid sees it in the stones of the raised beach and hears it in the song of a solitary bird. He knows that the secret of the bird's song is its natural openness – 'The inward gates of a bird are always open' (423) – and claims the same freedom. It is a difficult freedom for a man soured by poverty and faced with an everyday struggle for existence – 'Bread from stones is my sole and desperate dearth' (423). Still, poetry allows him to soar like a bird, to transcend imaginatively his fallen physical situation.

The medieval Scottish philosopher Duns Scotus held there was no difference between being and essence. What distinguishes one thing from another is form, not matter: his principle of individuation, *haecceity* (*haecceitas*, 'thisness') – cited by MacDiarmid in his first stanza – denotes the formal property by which an object (or person) is uniquely individuated. The stones are distinct from human beings, but an essential part of the same universe. In order to come to terms with this, human beings must become reconciled to the 'thisness' of the stones. More precisely, each individual must insist on the inviolability of his being, his separate identity:

> It will be ever increasingly necessary to find
> In the interests of all mankind
> Men capable of rejecting all that all other men
>   Think, as a stone remains
> Essential to the world, inseparable from it,
>   And rejects all other life yet.   (429)

Inseparable, yet separate. This is why MacDiarmid calls the stones 'Detached intellectuals' (432). Their 'thisness' is their strength. MacDiarmid's intellectual detachment is his strength. He can scrutinise his own unbreakable essence, whatever his existence.

As a metaphysical pursuit dealing with existence, ontology differentiates between existent reality and appearance. MacDiarmid accepts the stony reality of existence and acknowledges the illusion of appearance. It is the essential truth he seeks, a universal concept of coherence:

> We must be humble. We are so easily baffled by appearances
> And do not realise that these stones are one with the stars.
> It makes no difference to them whether they are high or low,

> Mountain peak or ocean floor, palace, or pigsty.
> There are plenty of ruined buildings in the world but no ruined
>   stones.
> No visitor comes from the stars
> But is the same as they are.   (425)

The humility he accepts is a consequence of the otherness of the stones, their absolute indifference to geocentric and anthropocentric illusions. Material structures of humankind are impermanent — ruined buildings but no ruined stones — and what endures is eternal essence. For the mystical poet the idea is stronger than its physical expression.

A scholarly commentator on the poem has remarked 'MacDiarmid writes as an atheist and his poem is eloquent testimony that out of an atheist ontology a great poem may spring.'[26] It is an odd kind of atheist who writes about stones as MacDiarmid does: 'Nothing can replace them / Except a new creation of God' (426), 'These stones go through Man, straight to God, if there is one' (427), 'Only in them / If in anything, can His creation confront Him' (427), 'Who thinks God is easier to know than they are?' (427). MacDiarmid is not denying the existence of a universal creative force — it is, after all, an assumption that runs through all his poetry — but he is reluctant to acknowledge the primitive patriarchal God of received religion. 'On a Raised Beach' is a religious poem that refuses to narrow religion down to a simple schematic solution. Its faith is expansive, founded on the mystical essence of material objects and expressed through a language that finally sinks into silence.

Looking at the stones MacDiarmid invests them with creative qualities. Eschewing the conceptual encumbrances of traditional philosophy and theological dogma, he is overwhelmed by the properties of the stones. The inhuman world they affirm is overwhelmingly beautiful to the human observer. Touching this world the poet searches for a simile: 'It fills me with a sense of perfect form, / The end seen from the beginning, as in a song' (428). However, no song sung on earth (even the song of a bird or a poet) can capture the eternal essence of the stones. MacDiarmid thinks of the music of the spheres produced (according to the Pythagoreans) by the movement of the heavenly bodies. And, as at the end of a *A Drunk Man*, he exalts silence as the closest the artist can come to the ultimate creative aim, the wordless essence of the ineffable:

> But the kindred form I am conscious of here
> Is the beginning and end of the world,
> The unsearchable masterpiece, the music of the spheres,

Alpha and Omega, the Omnific Word.
These stones have the silence of supreme creative power,
The direct and undisturbed way of working
Which alone leads to greatness.   (428-9)

Scrutiny of the stones has led MacDiarmid to an awareness of his
own isolation as an artist. His physical isolation from mainland Scotland
merely confirms his poetic isolation from other people. Reasserting the
élitism of his past he declares 'Great work cannot be combined with
surrender to the crowd' (429). Just as the stones are 'Detached intellectuals' (432) he must be a disinterested artist. In this mood he rejects
'other men' (430) along with their man-made answers to the challenge
of the universe. Cities crumble, but 'Truth is not crushed' (430):

Truth has no trouble in knowing itself.
This is it. The hard fact. The inoppugnable reality,
Here is something for you to digest.
Eat this and we'll see what appetite you have left
For a world hereafter.
I pledge you in the first and last crusta,
The rocks rattling in the bead-proof seas.   (430)

Other men, with their unexamined notion of 'a world hereafter', live in
the 'real' world that has limited interest for the visionary. MacDiarmid,
in pursuit of the eternal essence, is on his own.

Tenaciously, MacDiarmid probes further into the implications of his
isolation. He wishes to become as separate as a stone, to affirm the
quality of his uniqueness:

It is not a question of escaping from life
But the reverse – a question of acquiring the power
To exercise the loneliness, the independence, of stones,
And that only comes from knowing that our function remains
However isolated we seem fundamental to life as theirs.   (431)

Isolation is not escapist, MacDiarmid implies, because the particular
actions of an individual have a universal application. Just as the stone
on a raised beach is involved in a general motion, so the poet on the
planet earth is involved in a human movement. He has his responsibilities
to others. Silence is the supreme expression of art, stones symbolising
the ultimate essence, isolation as the aim of the individual: these seem
matters peculiar to poetry. Turning from the abstract essence to the

physical presence of the stones, MacDiarmid is reminded of his responsibility to others:

> These bare stones bring me straight back to reality.
>   I grasp one of them and I have in my grip
> The beginning and the end of the world,
> My own self, and as before I never saw
> The empty hand of my brother man,
> The humanity no culture has reached, the mob.
> Intelligentsia, our impossible and imperative job!   (432)

Still, the socialist poet decides against compromise and embraces complexity. For him the supreme reality is spiritual; the mob will rise up only by raising their consciousness. MacDiarmid's truth, after all, is a truth accessible to the mob: the mass of humankind is a multitude of individuals. They must be fed on truth, not dogma – must have essence *and* existence.

In his penultimate stanza, MacDiarmid queries the Christian solution. According to the New Testament, the Christian church would be built on the human rock of Peter (Matthew 16:18); again according to Christian gospel, 'love / Once made a stone move' (433) from the mouth of Christ's tomb. The symbolism is linked linguistically: the empty mouths of the mob, the open mouth of the Christian tomb, the poetic mouth that speaks of silence. MacDiarmid can derive no institutional message from the stones though he shuts out emptiness by allowing the individual spirit to soar above death:

> But let us not be afraid to die.
> No heavier and colder and quieter then,
> No more motionless, do stones lie
>   In death than in life to all men.
> It is not more difficult in death than here
> – Though slow as the stones the powers develop
> To rise from the grave – to get a life worth having;
> And in death – unlike life – we lose nothing that is truly
>   ours.   (433)

MacDiarmid is surely recalling, in that passage, Shestov's suggestion that 'it might be that a stone changed into a plant ... and the plant into an animal'.[27] It is no more unlikely, for the poet in pursuit of the impossible, than that spiritual life evolves after physical death. When MacDiarmid says 'in death – unlike life – we lose nothing that is truly ours' he is asserting the supremacy of the spirit. It is a sordid struggle for survival that kills the spirit – of the masses, of the individual – not the acceptance of death as part of a universal principle of change. What is 'truly ours', for this poet, is spiritual essence, not material existence. If the thought is paradoxical, it is also unmistakably mystical.

Finally, MacDiarmid returns to the music of the spheres: 'The end seen from the beginning, as in a song' (428). In the beginning was the word (the Omnific Word), a precept MacDiarmid accepted as a poet. In the end that word speaks of the silence of supreme creative power:

> Song, your apprentice encrinite, seems to sweep
> The Heavens with a last entrochal movement;
> And, with the same word that began it, closes
> Earth's vast epanadiplosis.   (433)

'On a Raised Beach' is an extraordinarily defiant interpretation of poetic isolation. Unwilling to be defeated by his apartness MacDiarmid creates a solipsistic credo that might otherwise be alarming but is saved, in this instance, by linguistic vitality.

The internal war in MacDiarmid's mind between contemplative quietism and political activism had, in the past, been resolved in single poems, albeit as long as *A Drunk Man*. Now, 'Busy as any man in those centres of the brain / Where consciousness flourishes' (411), he tends to produce two apparently irreconcilable modes: contemplative compositions as delicate as 'On a Raised Beach', with its quietist affirmation of silence; stridently propagandist pieces celebrating Social Credit. During 1933 he was disposed to quietism though he knew that, in a human context, it was an antisocial creed. The internal war carried the risk of making MacDiarmid a casualty of unbearable tension. He can write (in a poem first published in the July 1933 issue of the *Modern Scot*):

> I was better with the sounds of the sea
>   Than with the voices of men
> And in desolate and desert places
>   I found myself again.   (454)

The self could sustain a poem but it had a restricted application to everyday life.

There is a significant shift of emphasis in the verse MacDiarmid produced in 1933, in his most personal poems. During the 1920s his concept of self had been dynamic: 'To be yersel's – and to mak' that worth bein'. / Nae harder job to mortals has been gi'en' (107). Effort had to be made, will had to be exercised, the self had to be created. In Shetland, MacDiarmid took his self as static and unshakeable: he was in danger of becoming settled, to a pathological degree, in his solipsism. For a gregarious man like MacDiarmid, isolation had an irritating edge.

That he was frustrated by the antisocial implications of his position is evident in several poems. 'Etika Preobrazhennavo Erosa' asserts, initially, that the greatest goal for humankind is to aspire to proletarian virtues. Having said that, MacDiarmid withdraws from his fellow creatures:

> It is next to impossible still
> For me to bear any other man close – for deep
> Differences surge up like a blast from Hell ...   (407)

There is no spiritual solution covering the gulf between his political ideal of human harmony and his dislike of human contact so he reverts to slogans:

> This wisdom after the event is not the life or art
>   That's whitening every bourgeois heart,
>   There's no time to be arch
>   On the revolutionary march.   (409)

The poem ends with a salute to Lenin who 'kept his beat in Russia' (411). Between the agony of introspection and the desire for political change was a gulf that threatened to swallow MacDiarmid's stability.

'I am enamoured of the desert at last' (431), MacDiarmid says in 'On a Raised Beach'. The phrase alludes to Doughty's idiosyncratic prose classic, *Travels in Arabia Deserta* (1888). 'Stony Limits', MacDiarmid's tribute to Doughty, hails the author as a hero, an absolutely untypical Englishman, 'A plug suspended in England's false dreams' (420). Unable to tolerate living men, MacDiarmid empathises with a dead man, cherishes 'The lonely at-one-ment with all worth while' (421). Ending on another paean to silence, MacDiarmid suggests there is more vitality in the dead Doughty than in the living beings on earth:

> I have seen Silence lift his head
> And Song, like his double, lift yours,
> And know, while nearly all that seems living is dead,
> You were always consubstantial with all that endures.

> Would it were on Earth! Not since Ezekiel has that faw sun ringed
> A worthier head; red as Adam you stood
> In the desert, the horizon with vultures black-winged,
> And sang and died in this still greater solitude
> Where I sit by your skull whose emptiness is worth
> The sum of almost all the full heads now on Earth
> – By your roomy skull where most men might well spend
> Longer than you did in Arabia, friend!   (422)

That final exclamation is desperate: Doughty, dead, is a friend; others, 'most men', are enemies. A companion elegy, for Rilke (who died in the same year, 1926, as Doughty), specifically rejects 'love of our enemies' as 'stupid' (419).

Since he believed that language determines consciousness rather than vice versa, MacDiarmid tested his sensation of solitude in Scots as well as English. 'Harry Semen' – excluded from *Stony Limits* on the grounds of obscenity and considered by at least one critic as MacDiarmid's greatest poem[28] – uses Scots sensuously to assess the miraculous birth of an outstanding individual (a persistent theme in MacDiarmid). A profoundly personal poem, 'Harry Semen' is a monologue by a man who looks at an island and considers the vices and virtues of the solitary life. He knows, at his most vulnerable moments, that he can never be entirely alone since he is forever part of his past, a product of his sexual genesis. His island is likened to the moon-white belly of a dogfish that is caught on a fisherman's line: MacDiarmid, the fisherman of words, can neither land this symbol nor let it go. Its bright movement in the brine reminds him of the shock of his conception, 'the spasm frae which I was born' (484). Tormented by this thought, he considers that mental stability depends on an ability to distance the self from the seed:

> the difference 'twixt
> The sae-ca'd sane and insane
> Is that the latter whiles ha'e glimpses o't
> And the former nane.   (484)

By definition, then, having glimpsed the seed, MacDiarmid sides with the insane – knowing that poets have proverbially passed for mad.

In the second stanza, MacDiarmid invokes the 'pelvic experience' (484) of conception. With the sexual spasm, the semen separates and each seed strives for a distinct life, 'Nane o' them wi' ocht in common in the least' (484). Similarly, MacDiarmid admits that each strand of his thought is separate; the poet of harmony has stretches when nothing coheres. He has proliferated into pluralism from a single seed. The third stanza questions the justice of the survival of this seed in preference to others and regrets that the life of the one means the death of the many. Thinking along these lines the poet takes self-indulgence to a masturbatory conclusion. A poem that emerges from the creative spasm is sickeningly self-centred:

> What worth am I to a' that micht ha'e been?
> To a' the wasted slime I'm capable o'
> Appeals this lurid emission, whirlin' lint-white and green.   (484)

A poem, 'Harry Semen' itself, may be the result of 'sick-white onanism' (484).

Yet the poem, the 'lurid emission', is also an expression of purity – an immaculate conception because created by the self. Punning on his pseudonymous Christian name, MacDiarmid thinks of poems as scattered seeds, as competing colours, 'hue upon still mair dazzlin' hue' (485). Finally, he allows his creation, his poem, to dissolve into the Christian concept of immaculate conception. One poet seeds many poems and beyond that perhaps a larger creative force seeds the universe with a blizzard of seeds:

> Sae Joseph may ha'e pondered; sae a snawstorm
> Comes whirlin' in grey sheets frae the shaddowy sky
> And only in a sma' circle are the separate flakes seen.
> White, whiter, they cross and recross as capricious they fly,
> Mak' patterns on the grund and weave into wreaths,
> Load the bare boughs, and find lodgements in corners frae
> The scourin' wind that sends a snawstorm up frae the earth
> To meet that frae the sky, till which is which nae man can say.
> They melt in the waters. They fill the valleys. They scale the peaks.
> There's a tinkle o' icicles. The topmaist summit shines oot.
> Sae Joseph may ha'e pondered on the coiled fire in his seed,
> The transformation in Mary, and seen Jesus tak' root.   (485)

Compellingly, the symbol of the snowstorm moves into short spasmic sentences as MacDiarmid realises his metaphysical speculation in physical terms. The final stanza, quoted above, is one of his grandest triumphs in Scots, the work of a master of a medium he has created for himself; the poem finally illustrates its own argument.

Returning to such a rich Scots in 1933 brought MacDiarmid back to the Bible he studied in his youth as he moves from his self to thoughts of Mary and Joseph and Jesus. This involuntary regression is one reason why MacDiarmid wished to abandon Scots for Synthetic English. He felt that the oral rhythms of Scots spoke of the past whereas Synthetic English, an idiom devoid of conversational contact, afforded him the cerebral freedom to explore his own consciousness. 'Harry Semen', a poem about genesis, is an end, not a beginning: never again would MacDiarmid use Scots with such intensity.

On 24 September 1933, MacDiarmid informed his brother that he had eventually accepted treatment for his anal fissure:

> I went through the operation finally – but a modified form of it; not the bigger one originally contemplated. It is hoped that this may prevent any recurrence of the trouble beyond the extent of occasional minor inconvenience susceptible of fairly easy treatment. It was of course a damned nuisance and involved a considerable amount of subsequent pain and discomfort, but, as only a local anaesthetic was required and the cutting was not extensive, I did not suffer as I feared from any great reactions nor did I have to keep to bed except for three days. I'm feeling all right now, but infernally busy.[29]

As he was so involved with his literary efforts, he asked Andrew to pass the news of his operation to their mother. Having written so much in Synthetic Scots, MacDiarmid told Andrew, he though it was imperative to press on with his experiments in Synthetic English. As evidence of his success with this new idiom he enclosed 'In the Caledonian Forest', a poem dedicated to Andrew and his wife Chryssie. 'You can take it from me,' MacDiarmid assured Andrew, 'it's a good poem no matter how unfamiliar the diction may be.'[30] The first of three stanzas reads:

> The geo-selenic gimbal that moving makes
> A gerbe now of this tree now of that
> Or glomerates the whole earth in a galanty-show
>   Against the full moon caught
> Suddenly threw a fuscous halation round a druxy dryad
>   Lying among the fumet in this dwale wood
> As brooding on Scotland's indecrassifiable race
>   I wandered again in a hemicranic mood.   (391)

Apart from three lines – one in each stanza: 'Against the full moon caught', 'This freaked and forlorn creature was indeed', 'The moonshine flickered in the silent wood' (391-2) – the poem has been so composed that there is an unfamiliar word in every line. Usually the unusual word is an adjective: 'fuscous' (dingy), 'druxy' (of timber, having decayed spots concealed by healthy wood), 'epirhizous' (growing on a weed), 'frampold' (cross-grained). Recalling the woodland that once covered Scotland, MacDiarmid enters the Caledonian Forest through the mind and racial memory. Watching the reflected light of the full moon transform the earth into a shadow pantomime ('galanty-show') he sees a forlorn wood nymph lying among the dung of deer. Rooted to her position, she looks at the poet who wonders how he might honour her then realises that she, in her predicament, is a symbol of the decay of Scotland. He withdraws into cogitation, feeling unable to rescue the symbol for modern Scotland. It is a romantic notion eccentrically expressed.

When he included 'In the Caledonian Forest' in *Scottish Scene*, Mac-Diarmid added two sections: the second of these, beginning 'They are not endless these variations of form' (392), was subsequently incorporated into *In Memoriam James Joyce* (758-9); the third was 'Ephphatha', separated as a single poem in *Stony Limits*. 'Ephphatha' shows the extent of MacDiarmid's dictionary-dredging as all the unusual words in this short poem alliterate by virtue of their proximity in the dictionary: 'piaffer' (trotting gait), 'palaeocrystic' (consisting of ancient ice), 'phengites' (transparent stones used by the ancients for windows), 'panopticon' (prison in which all prisoners can be watched from one point), 'pellagra' (deadly deficiency disease marked by shrivelled skin, wasted body and insanity), 'paxwax' (strong tendon in an animal's neck), 'phosphene' (light seen when the eyeball is pressed), 'photopsia' (appearance of flashes of light due to irritation of the retina), 'pasilaly' (spoken language for universal use), 'pamphract' (protective covering).

In the Gospel according to St Mark, Christ is asked to help a deaf man who has an impediment in his speech. Christ takes the man aside, puts his fingers into his ears and touches his tongue, 'And looking up to heaven, he sighed, and saith unto him, Eph-pha-tha, that is, Be opened' (7:32). Instantly the deaf man can hear and speak plainly. MacDiarmid's poem opens impressively with a glimpse of the Shetland landscape: 'Only a sheep's fodder bush and a screw pine / And a dark sea going by at a piaffer' (393). The poet is painfully aware that he is imprisoned on an island, part of a doomed species. The light is harsh and when a solitary voice cries 'Ephphatha' it has no impact, being 'no more than a rattle of broken bones / On the invisible pamphract of God' (393). The underlying theme of the poem – the isolation of the eloquent individual – is deliberately buried under the forced dictionary diction.

Since his youth, MacDiarmid had taken great delight in 'adventuring in dictionaries' (823). Just as Jamieson's *Dictionary* had informed his Scots poetry, so *Chambers's 20th Century Dictionary* was his main source for Synthetic English.[31] No doubt he was as avid an enthusiast for this one-volume work as his friend William Soutar who recorded (on 29 July 1931) 'An historical moment – completed my odyssey through Chambers's *Dictionary* – I began 8 years and 8 months ago.'[32] MacDiarmid had neither the time nor the temperament to study the dictionary systematically, in Soutar's manner, but he looked on it as an indispensable source of linguistic inspiration.

One of the pre-eminent poems of this period, 'Lament for the Great Music' (included in *Stony Limits* as a substitute for 'Ode to All Rebels') does not depend on unusual English words though it derives textural strength from the use of Gaelic phrases. The lament is a long meditative poem addressed to the MacCrimmons who, as hereditary pipers to MacLeod of MacLeod, ran a college of piping at Boreraig on Skye and practised their art for two centuries before the college was closed in the aftermath of Culloden. Searching for an expansive alternative to the lyric, MacDiarmid attempts to emulate in verse the open-ended, yet formally disciplined, improvisatory quality of the pibroch. As a result, the lament is more solidly structured than the other meditative poems.

'Great Music' translates the Gaelic *Ceòl-Mór*, the most advanced form of pipe music. In pibroch the progression involves variations on a theme, or *urlar*. MacDiarmid's theme is the glory that was Gaeldom and he offers three variations inspired by this theme. First, he approaches the theme ironically in a section running from the first lines to the speculation 'Who can guarantee that two and two / Are not five on Jupiter?' (470). Second, he responds ecstatically to the theme and delivers himself of a mystical manifesto before invoking shadows as Hebridean 'grey rocks / Are gaining ground and the seas are black with their shadows' (475). Finally, he relates the haunting music of the MacCrimmons to his own physical isolation which, paradoxically, turns out to be a precondition for acting responsibly in the poetic service of humankind.

Opening on four lines of adaptation sustaining a pastoral note[33] MacDiarmid relates the image of Christ abandoned on the cross to the cultural crucifixion of Gaelic music. Both examples are aspects of betrayal. Just as Christianity has betrayed its founder by atrophying into an organisational routine so Scotland has turned its back on the Gaelic glory and degenerated into a small nation with small ambitions. Deprived of its greatest indigenous art form Scotland staggers forward into greater and greater banality, forever taking the idea of 'vast progress' (464) seriously. Emphasising the irony of it all MacDiarmid offers evidence of Scotland's appalling decline with regard to the Great Music:

> And, besides, as *The Scotsman* says, it is likely enough
> The great music has had a real if imponderable influence
> On subsequent piping after all – like Christ on the Kirk!
>   – My God, can you not read history and see
> They have never had what you are fain to save?   (464)

and again

> We have no use for the great music.
> All we need is a few good-going tunes.   (468)

The comparison between Christ and the Great Music is sustained and MacDiarmid realises that the use of this specific symbolism might only be approximate in this case and show 'how far from the great music I am' (466). The poet therefore expands his referential repertoire; animated by 'Platonic intellectualism' (470) and 'the style of Plotinus' (477) he pours withering scorn on the atrocious state that Scotland finds itself in. He would be happier if there was only a Platonic Idea of Scotland – an image uncontaminated by the hideous reality. It would have been better, he supposes, had the catastrophe of Culloden been followed by total destruction instead of a cultural genocide that permitted the survival of a collective memory of the vanished glory:

> Sumeria is buried in the desert sands,
> Atlantis in the ocean waves – happier these
> Than Scotland, for all is gone, no travesty
> Of their ancient glories lives
> On the lips of degenerate sons as here.   (467)

This first, heavily ironical section, ends on a powerful anecdote. MacDiarmid takes the reader into his confidence by telling him he would have loved to have witnessed the silence observed by pipers as a protest against the imprisonment of a MacCrimmon. The story has its own symbolism for a poet who is forever advancing towards a metaphysical silence.

308

   The second variation on the *urlar,* and central section of the poem, opens on an image of a sunset as a symbol of the fading of Gaelic culture as represented by the Great Music. Watching the light fading, however, the poet senses an inner light, a spiritual glow that is to spread through the remainder of the poem:

>   With the passing of the splendour from the
>   heights
>   The middle distance and foreground were suddenly lit up
>   With a light (like that in which shingle lies under the
>   sea-tide's forefoot)
>   Bursting from some hidden spring of the afterglow. All else
>   Was darker save the quickened feeling – like the sense
>   of a man
>   Who returns from foreign scenes to the country of his
>   blood and birth.   (471)

MacDiarmid is alone in the afterglow; he is illuminated by a vision of the Great Music which only emphasises the tragedy of modern Scotland. If the sun finally sets then the darkness of modern Scotland will be seen as a disaster, an inferno of urbanisation: 'How can I think of you / In these cities you never saw' (472). MacDiarmid turns scornfully to Scots who live their lives in ignorance of the Great Music, indifferent apparently to the extirpation of their cultural heritage. As a poet MacDiarmid has to grow into something greater than contemporary Scotland: 'My native land should be to me / As a root to a tree' (472). Moreover, he claims that all Scots are to some extent responsible for the perpetuation of the tragedy: 'These denationalised Scots have killed the soul / Which is universally human' (472). However, a sunset is a symbol with its own logic and MacDiarmid believes that Scotland might be lit up again by a turning of the earth toward a new light. In expressing this faith in the rediscovery of the creative source MacDiarmid issues a mystical manifesto:

>   It is the realisation of the light upon which
>   Not only life but the very existence of the universe
>   depends;
>   Not only animal life but earth, water, air.
>   If it faded it would mean the end of 'everything'.
>   It does not fade. Our spirit is of a being indestructible.
>   Its activity continues from eternity to eternity.
>   It is like the sun which seems to set to our earthly eyes

> But in reality shines on unceasingly.
> It is the movement which the mind invents
> For its own expression not otherwise than the stars.   (473)

The sunset is an illusion imagined by men; similarly the spirit of the
Great Music lives on in eternity and is accessible to the creative individual. What MacDiarmid seeks is neither the appearance of reality nor the
subjective illusion of reality but a spiritual unity with an evolutionary
ideal which is a different order of reality because 'The supreme reality is
visible to the mind alone' (475). MacDiarmid's neoplatonic intellectual
vision reveals this spiritual reality:

> It is the supreme reality (not the Deity of personal theism)
> Standing free of all historical events in past or future,
> Knowable – but visible to the mind alone   (474)

In this state of mind it is possible to have 'a rapt and mysterious / Communion with the spiritual world' (474). Such a metaphysical
assumption sustained the improvisatory genius of the Great Music and
it is the ultimate end of MacDiarmid's long poetic search for the hidden
source of creativity.

   In the last section of the poem MacDiarmid speaks for himself; tells
the great MacCrimmon pipers that he is with them and therefore cut off
from his fellow men. He is a man seeking spiritual harmony more than
human companionship:

> I am as lonely and unfrequented as your music is.
> I have had to get rid of all my friends,
> All those to whom I had to accommodate myself.
> If one's capital consists in a calling
> And a mission in life one cannot afford to keep friends.
> I could not stand undivided and true amongst them.
> Only in the solitude of my thought can I be myself
> Or remember you clearly.   (475-6)

The poet does not feel that his isolation condemns him as an antisocial
escapist. On the contrary the determination to inhabit the metaphysical
sphere allows MacDiarmid to serve others as his sacrifice saves humanity
by communicating the spiritual insight and solace of great art. Mac-
Diarmid's poetry is a gift he presents to humanity:

So those who have had to dwell
In solitude, at the furthest remove from their fellows,
Serve the community too. Their loneliness
Is only because they belong to a wider community
Than that of their immediate environment,
Not to one country or race, but to humanity,
Not to this age but to all time,
As your pibrochs reached to Eternity   (476-7)

Just because he is so serious about his sacrifice MacDiarmid is 'horrified by the triviality of life, by its corruption and helplessness' (477). He condemns urbanisation as an insult to the free spirit of humankind, then soars above cities by putting them beneath him. Socialism – or Social Credit – can solve all the economic problems: 'The struggle for material existence is over. It has been won' (478). But that is only a beginning, a means of clearing the way for the revelation of the great spiritual end. To attain that end humankind needs a poetic saviour who will discover the source of creativity which 'resembles the ray of a fountain; it rises, sparkles' (478). In earlier lines, MacDiarmid had referred to birdsong – 'a dipper's song' (476) – and he recalls the ornithological image. He is not a wanderer but a poet who has evolved according to the particular environment of Scotland; 'I am only that Job in feathers, a heron, myself, / Gaunt and unsubstantial' (479).

Aware that too much abstract speculation can lead to infinite regression, 'ultimate Incoherence' (480) he links his art to actuality. As a poet, however, his human obligation is to suffer solitude as a prelude to a personal resurrection and a cultural rebirth:

I dare not leave this dark and distracted scene.
I believe in the necessary and unavoidable responsibility of man
And in the ineluctable certainty of the resurrection
And know that the mind of man creates no ideas
Though it is ideas alone that create.
Mind is the organ through which the Universe reaches
Such consciousness of itself as is possible now, and I must not brood
On the intermittence of genius, the way consciousness varies
Or declines, as in Scotland here, till it seems
Heaven itself may be only the best that is feasible
For most people, but a sad declension from music like yours.
Yes, I am prepared to see the Heavens open
And find the celestial music poor by comparison.
Yet my duty is here.   (480)

Once more, MacDiarmid is prepared to be reborn, about to focus his 'cosmic consciousness' on 'the creative instant, the moment of divine realisation, / When the self is lit up by its own inner light' (481). Illuminated by the spirit of Scotland contained in the Great Music, he ends by saluting the MacCrimmons and sharing 'the eternal light' (482) with them as the future rises to resurrection. In this poem, MacDiarmid points to the future by looking back into the historical past in order to discover a cultural cradle for the new Scotland. The supreme reality is visible to the mind alone; the supreme reality of Scotland is visible to the mind open to the Gaelic quintessence of the country.

As the long Shetland winter drove MacDiarmid increasingly indoors – by the end of September the poet was complaining 'the winter darkness is heavy upon us'[34] – he put the final touches to his *Stony Limits* volume for Gollancz. His new contemplative poems (principally 'On a Raised Beach', for 'Lament for the Great Music' was not originally included in the volume) and Synthetic English compositions (such as 'In the Caledonian Forest') would, he anticipated, stand as the most arresting items. He also inserted poems from the abandoned *Muckle Toon* project – 'The Monument' and 'The Point of Honour'. Other poems were defiantly didactic. 'First Objectives' declares, in the last quatrain, 'And above all the Church must go' (394); 'The Belly Grip' rails against the immorality of politicians such as 'Mosley and Lloyd ... a MacDonald, a Baldwin, a Thomas' (395-6); 'Song of the New Economics' cites Social Credit propagandists as examples of evolutionary fulfilment for the poet hears, 'in an audience of countless millions' (396), a speaker say:

> Douglas, Orage, and a few
> Others of that highbrow crew! –
> Are further already from most men
> Than average humans from monkeys got ...   (397)

In contrast to such heroes, Ramsay MacDonald is, under the guise of MacStatesman, one of the 'Educated chimps' (399) cynically sacrificing humankind on the altar of a bankrupt economic policy.

Some of the argumentative poems, written rapidly in a combative English, rely on antiquated bits and pieces of poetic diction: 'I trow' (397, 401) appears in 'Song of the New Economics' and 'Genethliacon for the New World Order'. The second of these poems, dedicated to Orage's daughter Ann, celebrates the coming of a world made whole by Social Credit. Just as the pain of childbirth gives way to a joyful recognition of a new being, so the world will pass from pain to peace when it creates the new economic order. Related to the Social Credit poems are works in praise of Communist stalwarts. John Maclean is addressed as the supreme Scottish martyr, murdered by the destructive forces of capitalism. Lenin is perceived as an immortal in a succinct four-line poem, 'The Skeleton of the Future', which moves from description to deification. Thinking of Lenin's tomb, MacDiarmid writes:

> Red granite and black diorite, with the blue
> Of the labradorite crystals gleaming like precious stones
> In the light reflected from the snow; and behind them
> The eternal lightning of Lenin's bones.   (387)

MacDiarmid decided to dedicate the book to Valda and Michael and to open it with a playful poem in praise of Valda, 'Ho, My Little Sparrow'.

A slight poem, 'In a Neglected Graveyard', was prompted by a specific occasion. It offers an obituary for Walter Elliot, Minister of Agriculture in MacDonald's national government and MacDiarmid's rival in the Aberdeen University Rectorial election of 1933. Writing to Neil Gunn on 25 November, MacDiarmid declared himself well pleased with his showing in the election. Elliot (307 votes) won and MacDiarmid came third with 158 votes, a respectable showing for a controversial candidate. The poet was ahead of Aldous Huxley (117 votes) but behind G. K. Chesterton (220 votes) – ironically, in view of his reference to the 'huge eclipse' (85) caused by Chesterton in *A Drunk Man*. At the end of November, MacDiarmid sailed to Edinburgh so he could speak at the University Union, on 2 December, on the subject of the Scottish Renaissance. Next day he sailed back to Whalsay, and the ferociously severe Shetland winter.

Existing mainly on fish and potatoes gifted to them by Whalsay people, MacDiarmid and his family spent much of the winter huddling in front of the peat fire in their cottage. That first winter they spent in Shetland was 'one long nightmare of cold and damp and darkness and discomfort'.[35] MacDiarmid regretted the hardship he had, unavoidably, inflicted on Valda and Michael but found no difficulty in persevering with his literary work. In addition to *Stony Limits* he had another book to complete. Lewis Grassic Gibbon, whose Scots novel *Sunset Song* apeared in 1932, had approached MacDiarmid with a proposal to collaborate on a book and the poet had eagerly embraced the opportunity. *Scottish Scene*, as the book was to be called, would comprise polemical prose as well as creative verse and fiction. With MacDiarmid in Shetland and Gibbon living (since 1931) – somewhat improbably – in Welwyn Garden City it would eschew conventional scene-setting and concentrate on the essential matter of Scotland.

Thirty-two in 1933, Gibbon had less than two years of life left to him. Though different from MacDiarmid in background and temperament he shared with the poet a passionate love-hate relationship with Scotland and a belief in Communism (MacDiarmid was moving towards membership of the Communist Party). Born James Leslie Mitchell in 1901, Gibbon (the pseudonym was derived from his mother's maiden name) was eight when his family settled in Bloomfield, a farm-croft on a hill above Arbuthnott village in the Mearns (another name for Kincardineshire). This landscape featured as an enduring reality in the imaginative world of Gibbon.

He was educated at Mackie Academy in Stonehaven then left after a year to work as a reporter on the Aberdeen *Journal* and the *Scottish Farmer* in Glasgow. His experience as a journalist in Glasgow was even more unfortunate than MacDiarmid's experience as a journalist in Edinburgh; he was sacked for tampering with his expense account and, in a fit of depression, seriously considered suicide. From 1919 to 1929 Gibbon was a clerk employed by the Royal Army Service Corps then by the Royal Air Force. Thanks to his military service he travelled to the Middle East and Central America, experiences he used in several books. Indeed, after publishing his first book *Hanno*, in 1928, he published seventeen books before his untimely death at thirty-four. He was a compulsive writer who divided his day into three portions, planning to complete 1500 words in each portion: *Sunset Song*, his masterpiece, was written in six weeks.

Gibbon believed fervently in Diffusionism, holding that the Golden Age of the primitive hunter had been destroyed by the curse of civilisation. It was a notion he used in many works, including his autobiographical novel, *The Thirteenth Disciple* (1931) and his trilogy *A Scots Quair* – *Sunset Song, Cloud Howe* (1933), *Grey Granite* (1934). His essay, 'The Antique Scene', in *Scottish Scene*, declared his Diffusionist principles:

> All human civilizations orginated in Ancient Egypt.... Before the planning of [civilized] architecture enslaved the minds of men, man was a free and happy and undiseased animal wandering the world in the Golden Age of the poets (and reality) from the Shetlands to Tierra del Fuego.[36]

314

By contrast, MacDiarmid saw the Golden Age in the future, in a world economically emancipated by Social Credit. MacDiarmid's discursive essays in *Scottish Scene* advocated Douglasite reforms, a more politically conscious Scottish culture, a radical revision of language, the teaching of Scots literature and Gaelic language in schools, the creation of a revolutionary alternative to the bourgeois stance of the Scottish National Party. Generally, he found Scotland depressingly provincial and unable to understand that the future depended on Social Credit as 'the alternative to Fascism and the complement and corrective of Communism'.[37]

The most memorable parts of *Scottish Scene* are the creative contributions by Gibbon and MacDiarmid. Gibbon, using the richly rhythmic Scots prose that made *Sunset Song* arguably the most magnificent Scottish novel since *The House with the Green Shutters*, provided five superlative short stories ('Greenden', 'Smeddum', 'Forsaken', 'Sim', 'Clay'). Mac-Diarmid, too, offered Scots prose, in his dramatic sketches 'The Purple Patch' and 'Some Day', composed probably about 1927 when he wrote several stories in Scots. 'Some Day', in which country folk consider 'Resurrection day at Sleepyhillock'[38] is related thematically to the poem 'Crowdieknowe'. Sleepyhillock is the name of a cemetery at Montrose and one of the speakers in the sketch imagines 'a' the graves crackin' open an' the fowk loupin' oot'.[39]

Of the poems MacDiarmid chose for *Scottish Scene*, only 'In the Caledonian Forest' indicated the new direction his work had taken in Shetland. The six Shetland lyrics were a return to the Scots style of the 1920s, 'Envoi: On Coming Home' was originally intended for *The Muckle Toon*, 'Scotland' was a lively metrical prelude to the volume. 'Tam o' the Wilds', MacDiarmid's longest poetic offering in *Scottish Scene*, dates from the first months in Shetland (it was completed by July 1933) and is a measured verbal portrait, in Scots, of 'a common workin' man' (368) with an insatiable appetite for knowledge. Painstakingly it lists Tam's amateur interests in entomology, ornithology, icthyology and helmintology then closes with a tribute to William Soutar, to whom the poem is dedicated:

> I had written this and I suddenly thocht
> O' ane withdrawn frae the common life o' men
> Shut awa' frae the warld in a sick-room for aye,
> Yet livin' in what a wonderfu' world even then
> – The pure world o' the spirit; less kent
> To nearly a'body than Tam's interests even,
> And I saw in his sangs the variety o' creation
> Promise in a new airt mair than a' he was leavin'.   (378)

On one level MacDiarmid's tribute to Soutar is a reciprocal gift for 'The Auld Tree' for in that poem (published in the *Modern Scot* of April 1932) Soutar presented a vision of a Scotland reborn through the efforts of its prophets William Wallace, Burns and MacDiarmid. Yet the empathy with Soutar, in 'Tam o' the Wilds', is revealing. A man shut away from the world and existing in the 'pure world o' the spirit': such, MacDiarmid felt, was his own position on Shetland. He was as isolated as a bedfast invalid. Significantly, he referred to himself as being 'marooned on this little island of Whalsay'.[40]

The year 1933 had been momentous for MacDiarmid, an enormously prolific period. By the end of the year he had completed *Stony Limits* and his part in *Scottish Scene*. Elated by his artistic energy he was also depressed by the rigours of the Shetland winter and keen to return to mainland Scotland, at least for a while. Given his fascination with his own reputation he must have taken some cheer, in January 1934, when Eric Linklater's comic novel *Magnus Merriman* appeared complete with a portrait of MacDiarmid as Hugh Skene. Wyndham Lewis had recently cited the poet in his *One-Way Song* (1933) as part of a list of contemporary writers including 'Auden (most recent bust) with playground whistle: / MacDiarmid beneath a rampant thistle.[41] Now Linklater gave a portrait of MacDiarmid as the colourful leader of a Scottish literary revolution:

> But as Skene's genius matured he discovered that the Scots of Dunbar and Henryson was insufficient to contain both his emotion and his meaning, and he began to draw occasional buckets from the fountains of other tongues. At this time it was not uncommon to find in his verse, besides ancient Scots, an occasional Gaelic, German, or Russian phrase.... [Skene's] suit was unremarkably grey, but he wore a purple collar and shirt and a yellow tie with red spots. Apart from his clothes his appearance was sufficiently striking to suggest genius. He had a smooth white face, dwarfed by a great bush of hair, and in brisk, delicate, rather terrier-like features his eyes shone bright and steady. His hands were beautifully shaped and somewhat dirty.[42]

MacDiarmid relished this fictional account of himself. 'That's me to a T,' he exclaimed in his autobiography, adding that the dirty hands were due to his habit of placing his hands in pockets full of loose black tobacco.[43]

Early in the New Year of 1934 MacDiarmid resolved to return to London, albeit temporarily, in order to secure more literary work. He had several plans for books and was keen to secure contracts for these.

He also wanted to combine business with pleasure in addition to a grand political gesture. Having confronted stones poetically in Shetland, he turned his mind to a symbolic stone in London. In common with other Scottish nationalists he found it offensive that Scotland's ancient Stone of Destiny was kept in London rather than Scone. According to tradition, the Stone was brought to Scotland by Fergus Mor mac Erc when he established his Dalriadan dynasty in *c.* 500. Kenneth MacAlpin moved the Stone to the Pictish centre of Scone for his coronation as king of Scotia in 843 and successive Scottish kings were crowned on it. In 1296 Edward I, the 'Hammer of the Scots', captured the Stone and took it to Westminster Abbey where it rested under the coronation chair. MacDiarmid intended, in 1934, to bring back the Stone to Scotland. Recovering the Stone would be more than a gesture. So far as the English authorities were concerned, the Stone represented the continuity of the monarchy, so that its removal would be a constitutional affront as well as a criminal offence. For MacDiarmid, and like-minded nationalists, the restoration of the Stone to its rightful place in Scotland would mean the winning of a battle in the war with England and English assumptions. MacDiarmid longed to take part in such a battle, to 'hammer' the English.

13

Agonies and Abominations

Think not that I forget a single pang
O' a' that folk ha'e tholed,
Agonies and abominations 'yont a' tellin'
Sights to daunt the maist bold.
      'Ode to All Rebels'   (503)

PSYCHOLOGICALLY unsettled in Shetland and writing poems obsessed with his own isolation MacDiarmid decided, in 1934, that he would gain at least a semblance of security by once more associating himself with a political party. Having been expelled from the National Party of Scotland for his Communist leanings, he applied for membership of the Communist Party of Great Britain (CPGB). The hymnographer of Lenin was accepted though he had no intention of slavishly following the party line. Politically, MacDiarmid was convinced that John Maclean's concept of a Scottish Workers' Republic could be the salvation of Scotland. Maclean himself, he felt, was the necessary martyr of this movement.

After his trial for sedition in 1918 – he was savagely sentenced to five years' imprisonment but released at the end of the year after vociferous public protests – Maclean became interested in the views of MacDiarmid's Gaelic revivalist friend the Hon. Ruaraidh Erskine of Mar.

Maclean's leaflet *All Hail, the Scottish Workers' Republic!* (1920) put Communism in a Celtic context by calling for a revolutionary renewal of the camaraderie of the clans:

> Scotland must again have independence, but not to be ruled by traitor kings or chiefs, lawyers and politicians. The communism of the clans must be re-established on a modern basis.... The country must have but one clan, as it were – a united people working in co-operation and co-operatively, using the wealth that is created.
>
> We can safely say, then: back to communism and forward to communism.... [Revolutionary workers in Scotland are] carrying forward the tradition and instincts of the Celtic race.
>
> All hail, the Scottish Workers' Republic![1]

Maclean worked for an independent Scottish Workers' Republican Party, refusing to join the CPGB when it was established in 1920. Orthodox British Communists, such as Willie Gallacher (later a close friend of MacDiarmid) responded by spreading rumours that Maclean was mentally unbalanced as a result of his prison experiences: at Peterhead Prison in 1918 Maclean was convinced that drugs had been added to his food. He was force-fed after undertaking a hunger strike. Imprisoned again in 1921 and actively involved, as a candidate for the Gorbals district of Glasgow, in the General Election of 1923, Maclean died of pneumonia on 30 November 1923 at the age of forty-four. In MacDiarmid's opinion Maclean was 'the greatest leader the working class of Scotland had yet had'.[2] It was in accord with this conviction that MacDiarmid wrote of the martyred leader in 'John Maclean (1879-1923)'. In the poem Maclean is promoted as a proletarian Christ, crucified by the forces of capitalism:

> As Pilate and the Roman soldiers to Christ
> Were Law and Order to the finest Scot of his day,
> One of the few true men in our sordid breed,
> A flash of sun in a country all prison-grey.
> Speak to others of Christian charity; I cry again
> For vengeance on the murderers of John Maclean.   (486)

At the beginning of March 1934 MacDiarmid, Valda and Michael sailed from Shetland then headed south. The poet stayed on alone in London while Valda took Michael to her mother's house in Bude. Just before his departure from Whalsay, MacDiarmid received the proofs of *Stony Limits and Other Poems* and was irritated to encounter objections to some of the poems he had included in the collection. Writing to Dorothy Horsman (production manager of Gollancz) on 18 March, from a temporary address (6 Acacia Place, SW8) in London, he conceded he was 'guilty of frank expressions of Communist and anti-religious opinion and out-spoken sentiments on sexual matters'.[3] He had not, he argued, gone beyond the legal limits observed by publishers.

Nevertheless, the poem on John Maclean was removed from the book and replaced by two earlier poerms: 'Cattle Show' and 'The Little White Rose', a lyric first published anonymously in the *Modern Scot* of July 1931 and, again anonymously, in *Living Scottish Poets* (1931):

> The rose of all the world is not for me.
> I want for my part
> Only the little white rose of Scotland
> That smells sharp and sweet – and breaks the heart.   (461)

'Harry Semen' and 'Ode to All Rebels', considered obscene, were replaced by 'The Progress of Poetry' and 'Lament for the Great Music'. 'Edinburgh Toun' and 'A Judge Commits Suicide', respectively a quatrain and a couplet critical of capitalist law and order, were excised in exchange for 'First Love', a romantic substitute.

While the poet was willing to compromise in order to expedite the publication of *Stony Limits* he was determined not to waver in his plan to remove the Stone of Scone from Westminster Abbey. He found a suitable base by going to stay with Donald and Catherine Carswell in Hampstead. MacDiarmid's relationship with Catherine Carswell had got off to an acrimonious start when he took objection to an article she wrote about Burns in the *Radio Times* (14 Feb. 1930). Soon they found they had enough in common to become close friends.

Catherine Roxburgh Macfarlane was born in Glasgow on 27 March 1879, the daughter of a merchant. She became a socialist after reading Robert Blatchford at the age of seventeen, studied English at Glasgow University, experienced a disastrous first marriage (to Herbert Jackson, who tried to kill her) and made a reputation as dramatic and literary critic of the *Glasgow Herald* from 1907 to 1915 when she married Donald Carswell (born 1882 in Glasgow), then a sub-editor on the same paper. She lost her job with the *Glasgow Herald* after writing a glowing review of D. H. Lawrence's banned novel *The Rainbow* (1915) and it was Lawrence who encouraged her to complete her autobiographical Glasgow novel, *Open the Door!* (1920), and to do justice to the passionate nature of Burns in her *The Life of Burns* (1930). In London, both Catherine and Donald wrote, she as assistant dramatic critic of the *Observer* and as author of *The Savage Pilgrimage* (1932), her biography of Lawrence, and *Robert Burns* (1933); he as author of *Brother Scots* (1927), a study of Scottish presbyterianism, and *Sir Walter* (1930). In 1935 the Carswells were working on an anthology, *The Scots Week-End*, which contains five items by MacDiarmid.

The Carswells' home at 17 Keats Grove faced 7 Downshire Hill where Edwin and Willa Muir rented a house. Willa remembered how MacDiarmid turned up at Downshire Hill full of enthusiasm for his part in the projected removal of the Stone of Scone; he had, apparently, been given money by a rich friend (possibly Muirhead) to take the Stone to Scotland by car:

> The removal of the Stone of Scone was a pet scheme of Christopher's and he had been advertising it up north for some time. His enterprise was supposed to be a Top Secret, but he had already told the Carswells about it, confidentially, and he told us about it, confidentially. During the next few days we discovered that he was telling various other London Scots about it, confidentially.... I think he did not bother about the mere technical problem of prising the Stone loose; he was gloriously racing north with it in A Fast Car – he kept repeating these magic words, A Fast Car – and he was going to drop it in some Border stream where it would look like any other boulder until the time came to escort it through Scotland after the hue and cry had been baffled. The brilliance of this idea illuminated Christopher. His yellow hair fizzed up; he was radiant with sheer daftness.[4]

According to Willa, MacDiarmid made several visits to Westminster Abbey but spent more time in his favourite pub, the Plough, in Bloomsbury, where he generously stood drinks all round. When his two fellow-conspirators, both rugby forwards, arrived by train from Edinburgh the poet told them there was an insurmountable problem. He had spent the money and could not now secure A Fast Car.[5]

On Friday, 6 April, MacDiarmid had a meeting in London with McElroy and Peggy who had been secretary of McElroy's business for several months and was newly installed as a director, drawing a substantial salary and virtually running the company. Realising he was 'as fond of Peggy as ever'[6] MacDiarmid then travelled down to Cornwall to see Valda. He was staying at Valda's mother's house at 28 King Street, Bude, when he heard some distressing, but not totally unexpected, news from his brother Andrew. At 10 p.m. on Wednesday, 11 April, the poet's mother Elizabeth died of stomach cancer at Laurie's Close, Waterbeck, near Langholm. Andrew had gone down to Waterbeck and duly signed the death certificate. Unable to come up to Scotland for his mother's funeral (she was buried beside her first husband, in Langholm Cemetery) MacDiarmid wrote pugnaciously to Andrew on 12 April:

> I, of course, reproach myself for at least not even writing to her oftener — tho' I had improved in this respect of late. Yet my sense of failure in this respect would have been very greatly mitigated if I had known that she had received my last letter in time. I can imagine some of the reflections that are passing through your mind. Chryssie said to me last time I was in Edinburgh that she thought I was only concerned with one thing — my own self-glorification. She was wrong — because what I do, irrational as it is from ordinary standards, isn't even concerned with that but often diametrically opposed to the advancement even of my own reputation. I do serve certain ideas — quite disinterestedly, and to my own loss; and at the moment and for some time back I have been involved in very difficult matters; it has taken me all my time to keep going at all. If occasionally this has led me (and I am in no way apologising for it) into ways of living of which you could for one reason or another have disapproved, and which admittedly were disapprovable on both general and particular grounds, that does not mean that I was unconscious in any way, or failing to meet, my major problems, as is proven by the fact that I have no fewer than seven books coming out this year and others contracted for in advance.[7]

The fact that MacDiarmid was about to see several of his books published (five, not seven: *Five Bits of Miller, Scottish Scene, Stony Limits, At the Sign of the Thistle, Selected Poems*) was not at all calculated to comfort Andrew who felt, with each year and crisis that passed, that his wife was correct in her assessment of his brother.

As far as Andrew was concerned, worse was to follow for Mac-Diarmid urgently wanted whatever money was due to him on his mother's death. By 16 April MacDiarmid was back in London where he visited his friend Charlie Lahr in his bookshop at 68 Red Lion Street and saw John Gawsworth who wanted to use MacDiarmid stories, free of charge, in a proposed anthology. MacDiarmid gladly gave his permission to Gawsworth then decided to return to Shetland — alone, as Valda and Michael were still in Bude. He got as far as F. G. Scott's house in Glasgow. Writing on 7 May, from 44 Munro Road, he demanded that Andrew settle his mother's estate as he was desperately short of money.

Before returning to London MacDiarmid spent a few days in Edinburgh and received from Andrew £10 on account of his interest in the estate. Having a drink in Rutherford's Bar off South Bridge, he was introduced to Sorley MacLean by George Davie. A few months younger than MacLean, Davie studied classics and philosophy at Edinburgh University and became an ardent admirer of MacDiarmid's philosophically provocative poetry. His friend MacLean, subsequently celebrated as one of Scotland's greatest Gaelic poets, was born on the island of Raasay on 26 October 1911, attended school on Skye, and came to Edinburgh in 1929 to study English at the university. At the time of his first meeting with MacDiarmid, MacLean was at Moray House Teachers Training College. He was astonished by the quality of MacDiarmid's work, certain that his lyrical gift amounted to genius. For his part, MacDiarmid was delighted to encounter an admirer who was not only obviously intelligent but was also a native Gaelic speaker and an authority on Gaelic poetry. It was a friendship that was to have important repercussions for both men. Having met MacLean and obtained money from Andrew, MacDiarmid took the train to London, arriving on Sunday, 20 May.

On the Sunday evening he booked into the Royal Hotel, Woburn Place, Russell Square. Next morning he tried to contact publishers he thought might advance him money but was out of luck as most of them were out of town for the Whitsun holiday. He wrote to Andrew for a further £5 which was promptly wired to him next day. He then went on a binge and brought a woman back to the hotel. Meanwhile, back in Cornwall, Valda was worried. Her mother, who claimed second sight, told her that Christopher was planning to leave her. She quickly left for London, Michael remaining with her mother, and tracked the poet to his hotel:

> I went to the hotel and asked if Christopher Grieve was there. I asked if he was staying with a Mrs Grieve and was told yes. I said 'I'm the second Mrs Grieve and that makes her the third Mrs Grieve.' I went upstairs and they were in separate rooms.[8]

Confronted by an angry Valda, whose temper was a formidable weapon, MacDiarmid made his peace.

His situation improved in June as he had money due on the publication, that month, of *Scottish Scene* and *Stony Limits*. He was also elated by the appearance, in the June issue of the *Modern Scot*, of his polemical poem 'Welcome to the PEN Delegates'. For some time he had lamented that Scottish PEN had degenerated into a coterie of untalented amateurs and professional hacks. As the PEN Congress for 1934 was being held in Edinburgh, he took the opportunity to dissociate himself from the spectacle by arranging for his poem to coincide with the gathering. Composed in Drydenesque couplets, 'Welcome to the PEN Delegates' dwells on the incongruity of staging an international literary event in Scotland. MacDiarmid pours scorn on Scottish critics and condemns three of Scotland's leading literary lights – the novelist George Blake (a director of the Porpoise Press), Compton Mackenzie and Lewis Spence. The poet mentions 'novelists who, in huge remainders, now/Stampede the scene behind Blake's beefy brow', regrets (in a reference to Mackenzie on Barra, projecting himself as a second Bonnie Prince Charlie) how 'kilted Tearlach, standing cap in hand,/Cheers on the dirty work from Barra's strand', spits venom at 'the bald-faced Spence' (1302).

In June, too, MacDiarmid found a supportive place to stay in London for he moved, at the beginning of the month, into John Gawsworth's house at 33 Great James Street, while Valda returned to Michael and her mother in Bude. At that time Gawsworth – to whom 'The Little White Rose' is dedicated – was a young man of twenty-one who already had impressive literary credentials. Born Terence Ian Fytton Armstrong (on 29 June 1912) he had published *Poems 1930-1932* (1933), a critical study of Wyndham Lewis and the prose books *Above the River* (1931) and *Backwaters* (1932). He had now completed his anthology *New Tales of Horror* (1934), containing stories by MacDiarmid. Dating from 1927 are two Scots tales: 'A'body's Lassie', about the ghost of a girl; and 'Wound-Pie'[9] (originally entitled 'A Dish o' Whummle' when it appeared in the *Scots Observer*) about a mysterious old crone. 'The Stranger', one of two English stories, cleverly approaches the identity of an enigmatic incomer through the guesses of pub gossips. While staying with Gawsworth, MacDiarmid read the proofs of his verbal sketch *Five Bits of Miller* (1934) which he published himself in an edition of forty numbered copies. The five bits of the nauseatingly unpleasant Miller are the mucus from his nose, the phlegm from his throat, the wax from his ears, the parings from his nails, the squeezed muck from the blackheads on his chin. It is a bitter little study in disgust.

MacDiarmid had unsuccessfully approached the publishers Boriswood about a possible collection of all his extant stories. This contact had a curious outcome for Boriswood were on the point of publishing *Broken Record* (1934), a book of memoirs by Roy Campbell, the reactionary South African poet of Scottish descent. On being shown the proofs, MacDiarmid took objection to a reference to himself, presumably touching on his Communism and conviviality, as libellous and held up publication of the book until the offending page was removed by Boriswood. Other publishers offered more welcome news. Stanley Nott, who brought out a book of MacDiarmid essays in 1934, *At the Sign of the Thistle* (reflecting on Synthetic Scots and other topics and containing a hilarious account of 'The Last Burns Discovery', a water closet once used by the Bard), accepted *Forty New Songs* (retitled *Second Hymn to Lenin and Other Poems* in 1935). Macmillan agreed to bring out a *Selected Poems* (reprinting work from several volumes from *Sangschaw* to *Stony Limits*) and commissioned MacDiarmid to edit *The Golden Treasury of Scottish Poetry* for which he intended, with the help of Sorley MacLean, to translate a number of Gaelic texts.

Joined by Valda in July, and with Michael staying on at her mother's in Bude, the poet rented a flat at 12 Petherton Road, Highbury. Valda was alarmed at the deterioration in Christopher's condition as she explained in a frank letter of 6 August to Helen Cruickshank (incidentally thanking her friend for the gift of ten shillings):

> I should not bother you with my affairs [but] something has to be done – things are pretty serious apart from the financial side. Christopher's health is definitely breaking up, he had the Dr in on Saturday, he has to have preserves, ever since we've been here he has had blinding headaches a thing I've never known him have. Of course the preserves will probably put that right, when I went to fetch the medicine Dr Coidan told me that he must go very slow indeed, that apart from being on the verge of a nervous breakdown a few more heavy drinking bouts would finish things. You see Helen troubles never come singly. I'm afraid Hugh MacDiarmid and C. M. Grieve do not come first with me, it is Christopher that matters, Christopher that I love, I only wish they knew the beautiful side of his nature. They read poetry by Hugh MacDiarmid, they read articles full of 'rantings' by C. M. Grieve, some even see him reeling out of a pub, the others talk about it, and so they form opinions, when they are not in the position to do so.[10]

Valda herself was unwell, suffering from asthma, though she did not mention this to Helen Cruickshank. Her main concern was with Christopher whose nervous problems prevented him from sleeping. Drinking heavily may have knocked him out for a few hours at night but did nothing to diminish his sense of insecurity.

One of the elements in MacDiarmid's illness was the meeting with Peggy earlier in the year, bringing back memories of the best years of their married life. Under the terms of his divorce he was supposed to pay £100 a year for each of his children by Peggy but it was impossible for MacDiarmid to keep up with these payments and he was considerably in arrears. Though now a wealthy woman, Peggy wrote to Andrew about the situation. Andrew brought the matter to the attention of his brother who said he would write to Peggy in the hope of coming to a mutually acceptable arrangement. About to take a holiday in Orkney, Andrew sent MacDiarmid another £15 in connection with his mother's estate. The poet duly acknowledged that he had received the sum of £30 to date.

Despite his personal troubles MacDiarmid was writing as prolifically as ever. He had begun an autobiography, provisionally placed – for an advance of £50 – with Jarrolds, the publishers of *Scottish Scene*; and he was writing a new long poem, to be titled *The Red Lion*, projected as an urban counterpart of *A Drunk Man*, dealing with the slums of Glasgow and the whole range of contemporary working-class life. It seems likely that 'Third Hymn to Lenin' (quoted in *Lucky Poet* and first published in its entirety in the April 1955 issue of the *Voice of Scotland*) was conceived as part of this work: its topical reference to Michael Roberts's anthology *New Country* (1933) and its criticism of Ernest William Barnes's *Scientific Theory and Religion* (1933) tend to place the poem in 1934. In this third hymn, MacDiarmid calls on the spirit of the dead Lenin to light up Glasgow, deliberately drawing a religious parallel with Christ. He also dissociates himself from the English political poets – 'Auden, Spender, those bhoyos' (900) – who are dismissed as charlatans slumming, for artistic effect, with the working class. (Both Cecil Day Lewis in 1934 and John Lehmann in 1940 – in *A Hope for Poetry* and *New Writing in Europe* respectively – acknowledged that MacDiarmid's socialist poetry preceded the leftist verse of the school of Auden.)

Another segment from the Glasgow sequence, 'In the Slums of Glasgow' (collected as the penultimate poem in *Second Hymn to Lenin and Other Poems*) extends the quietist tone of the long poems written in Shetland the previous year. According to the Gospel of St John, when Christ had been crucified the soldiers took his garments including his coat which was 'without seam, woven from the top throughout' (John 19:23). Drawing on the Seamless Garment as a biblical symbol of spiritual purity MacDiarmid applies it to the slums so it contains the collective soul of the slum-dwellers. 'I have caught a glimpse of the seamless garment,' says MacDiarmid, 'And am blind to all else for evermore.' Uplifted by his awareness of the 'shining light' (562) of the slums, he declares that his vision amounts to a conversion. He puts personal mysticism above the received theology of his youth and the historical materialism of Marx:

> I have not gained a single definite belief that can be put
> In a scientific formula or hardened into a religious creed.
> A conversion is not, as mostly thought, a turning towards a belief,
> It is rather a turning round, a revolution indeed.
> It has no primary reference to any external object.
> It took place in me at last with lightning speed.
> I suddenly walk in light, my feet are barely touching the ground,
> I am free of a million words and forms I no longer need.　　　(563)

The poem seeks to resolve the tension between MacDiarmid's social conscience and his subjective longing for eternal silence. Observing the slums he considers how sexual ecstasy gives each slum-dweller an insight into eternity, 'The bliss of God glorifying every squalid lair' (564). This inadequate apology for material misery leads on to an affirmation of the poet's spiritual ecstasy: 'I am filled forever with a glorious aware-ness/Of the inner radiance, the mystery of the hidden light in these dens' (564).

Conscious of the solipsistic drift of such sentiments MacDiarmid, the declared Communist, also wrote a series of determinedly didactic poems, illustrating his argument that 'any utterance that is not pure/Propaganda is impure propaganda for sure' (558). Intended for *Second Hymn to Lenin and Other Poems*, these propagandist pieces employ shock tactics derived from the First World War poems of Sassoon and Owen. 'In the Children's Hospital' is a powerful riposte to the royal patronage of the poor and disabled as MacDiarmid imagines a princess patting the head of a legless boy and concludes with an angry couplet – 'But would the sound of your sticks on the floor/Thundered in her skull for evermore!' (547). Having dealt with royalty he makes religion his target in 'After Two Thousand Years', accusing the Christians of making 'the bloodiest and beastliest world ever seen/Under the sun' (559).

'Another Epitaph on an Army of Mercenaries' indignantly rejects the 'Epitaph on an Army of Mercenaries' A. E. Housman wrote in defence of the professional soldiers who fought at the First Battle of Ypres. Housman ends his poem by praising the professionals who saved the world by fighting for their money. MacDiarmid subjects Housman's argument to withering verbal fire:

> It is a God-damned lie to say that these
> Saved, or knew, anything worth any man's pride.
> They were professional murderers and they took
> Their blood money and impious risks and died.
> In spite of all their kind some elements of worth
> With difficulty persist here and there on earth. (551)

Here the monosyllabic rhymes and conversational rhythms give the poem an irrefutable authority. 'If I was not a Soldier' considers the likely fate of a professional murderer who chooses to fight for workers in the class war. He would, he anticipates, be tolerated 'Till I rose with the rest and was batoned or shot/By some cowardly brute – such as I am now!' (556).

The finest poems of this period attempt to fuse the poet's private and public concerns in a more artistically accessible manner than he managed with the vague mysticism of 'In the Slums of Glasgow'. With a delicacy of perception, MacDiarmid encourages readers to focus their attention on images. 'On the Ocean Floor' uses the image of the Foraminifera for the evolutionary sacrifice of the many in the development of individual genius. 'Lo! A Child is Born' uses the Marxist concept of a personified History to compare the creation of a new world to a difficult birth as the future emerges from the present (the similes are dynamic): 'Springing into history quivering like a fish,/Dropping into the world like a ripe fruit in due time' (548). Two poems draw on MacDiarmid's love of Valda. 'Birth of a Genius Among Men' describes sexual union as the earthly equivalent of the eternal act of creation. Though the poem ends with the evocation of abstract ideas these are first embodied in sensuous images: 'You were all female, ripe as a rose for the plucking,/I was all male and no longer resisted my need' (540). 'O Ease My Spirit' has the poet admitting his exhaustion with the burden of personal limitations and intellectual division. He asks for the ability to encompass all aspects of the world:

> And quicken me to the gloriously and terribly illuminating
> Integration of the physical and the spiritual till I feel how easily
> I could put my hand gently on the whole round world
> As on my sweetheart's head and draw it to me. (539)

Three years after meeting Valda in London, MacDiarmid married his sweetheart – on 12 September 1934 at Islington Register Office. (On 7 September he had received a further payment of £9 10s on his mother's

estate, making a total of £42 7s 10d.) On the marriage certificate Christopher Murray Grieve is described as a journalist of forty-two, Valda
Trevlyn Rowlands as a spinster of twenty-eight. The ceremony was
witnessed by Charlie Lahr and his friend Margaret Bressler. Five days
after the marriage MacDiarmid was looking for another commission, in
addition to *The Golden Treasury of Scottish Poetry* and his autobiography.
He wrote to the publishers George Routledge, offering a book, *Scottish
Eccentrics*, which, he explained, he had been researching for some time in
the Library of the British Museum.

Routledge's acceptance of the offer led to a contract for £40 on
publication and a meeting with A. J. B. Paterson, the firm's sales manager,
a man keen on Scottish literature and as fond of a drink as MacDiarmid.
Two positive decisions emerged from this meeting. First, Routledge had
asked Lewis Grassic Gibbon to edit a series ('Meanings in Scotland') of
ten books and MacDiarmid was contracted (again for £40 on publication)
to write *What Lenin Has Meant to Scotland*. MacDiarmid had met Gibbon
earlier in the year and now discussed the series with him in London and
at Gibbon's home in Welwyn Garden City where he lived with his wife
Ray, daughter of the original of Long Rob of the Mill in *Sunset Song*.
The poet urged the novelist to make the most of this opportunity by
stressing crucial Scottish issues. He noted approvingly that Gibbon was
to write on Burns, Compton Mackenzie on Catholicism and Scotland,
A. S. Neill on education and suggested that, as well as his own book,
the series should include Neil Gunn on whisky and Willa Muir on sex.
Gibbon regretted, he told MacDiarmid, that 'You and I, alas, are the
only Communists in the series'.[11] It was because of their ideological aims
in common (for Gibbon finally found Communism a more convincing
creed than Diffusionism) that *Grey Granite* (published Nov. 1934), the
last and most political part of the trilogy *A Scots Quair*, was dedicated
to MacDiarmid.

The second consequence of MacDiarmid's meeting with Paterson
presented the poet with the prospect of a little financial security. He was
offered a retainer of £52 per annum, payable quarterly in advance from
1 October, in return for introducing Scottish books and authors to
Routledge and editing and reporting on Scottish texts. This agreement
was confirmed in writing by 28 September by which time MacDiarmid,
Valda and Michael were back in Whalsay.

After seven months' absence the family found their cottage in
need of an overhaul. MacDiarmid's immediate reaction to the return to
Whalsay was directed at the weather which, he said, was 'simply hellish

(a cold hell!), torrential rain, hurricane winds and, at the moment for the sake of a little variety, snow'.[12] He looked forward, however, to a winter's work which he hoped would allow him to complete four books by March 1935 as he had promised his publishers: *The Golden Treasury of Scottish Poetry*, *Scottish Eccentrics*, *What Lenin Has Meant to Scotland* and, yet another commission, *The Wolfe of Badenoch* (about the fourteenth-century Scottish rebel Alexander Stewart, for the publishers Rich & Cowan). There were, inevitably, distractions. MacDiarmid saw in the New Year of 1935 quietly but had forgotten that the islanders adhered to the Old Calendar and so started their celebrations on 7 January. By 7 p.m. that Monday night, MacDiarmid's cottage was crammed with twenty-five men. As it was obligatory for every man to sample every other man's bottle, the busy poet reverted to his role of drunk man – when Helen Cruickshank had advised MacDiarmid to go to a dry island she did not anticipate that the absence of bars had little to do with the availability of alcohol. By 27 January MacDiarmid was seriously worried about the amount of work he had undertaken. He wrote to Gibbon:

> I have been in the horrible position of taking on too much – contracting to have far too much done by a given date. Apart from the various lets and hindrances connected with getting re-installed here and having various essential repairs carried out on the house, such a plight instead of spurring me to greater efforts semi-paralyses me and I keep on saying 'I'll never get it done' and not even trying to until the fateful date draws so near that I have to make a really heroic effort.... I have really been working hard, though my total of words per day falls far short of the requirements if my various MSS are to be delivered up to contracted dates.[13]

Working from literal line-by-line translations supplied by Sorley MacLean, MacDiarmid had already completed versions of some Gaelic poems for *The Golden Treasury of Scottish Poetry*. For example, the *Modern Scot* of January 1935 contained *The Birlinn of Clanranald* from the Scots Gaelic of Alexander MacDonald (James Whyte subsequently issued this as a booklet, limited to 100 signed and numbered copies, over the imprint of his Abbey Book Shop in St Andrews). MacDonald's poem, composed around 1750 and descriptive of a sea voyage from South Uist to Carrickfergus, is rendered into energetic verse with textural touches reminiscent of Gerard Manley Hopkins. Towards the close of the poem there is an explanation of how the ship's crew 'set up the right-royal, rocking, rowing,/Deft and timeous,/And made good harbour there at the top/Of Carrick-Fergus' (532).

On 7 February Lewis Grassic Gibbon died of peritonitis at the tragically early age of thirty-four; MacDiarmid added to his heavy literary workload by taking over his role as editorial adviser on 'Meanings for Scotland' (a slight change from 'Meanings in Scotland' as a title for the series). The series was now well under way; in addition to the contracts given to Gunn and A. S. Neill, Edwin Muir was writing on *Scott and Scotland*, Eric Linklater on *The Lion and the Unicorn*, William Power on *Literature and Oatmeal*. MacDiarmid suggested that Tom MacDonald should be commissioned to write a book on what Gaelic has meant to Scotland but Paterson felt this was too specialised a subject.

Having completed *Scottish Eccentrics* and *What Lenin Has Meant to Scotland* – both of which were written rapidly and packed with lengthy quotations – MacDiarmid went to Edinburgh at the beginning of May. He visited his brother at Liberton, borrowing two shillings for pipe tobacco, then went to stay for a few days with the dentist Stanley Robertson at Parsonage House in Musselburgh where his admirer supplied him with a new set of dentures free of charge. On 10 May he spoke at Manchester University, enlightening English students on the subject of the Scottish Renaissance Movement. When he got back to Whalsay he had to face problems with the books he had delivered to Routledge. The publishers objected to the arrangement of the material in *Scottish Eccentrics* and what they held to be excessively long sentences. Reluctantly MacDiarmid agreed to reshuffle his chapters (the book deals with colourful Scottish characters such as Sir Thomas Urquhart and William McGonagall) and to allow a Routledge copy-editor to shorten his sentences. The Lenin book was not so easily altered and it was a work MacDiarmid was anxious to see published before October when he would be standing as a candidate in the Edinburgh University Rectorial Election.

Routledge made one suggestion MacDiarmid accepted with alacrity, that the title of the book should be changed to *Red Scotland*. However, he was displeased by Paterson's first impression of the book. Having commissioned a text of 50,000 words, Paterson could not accept Mac-Diarmid's text of more than 100,000 words and asked him to consider cutting out most of the quotations. By the time MacDiarmid received this news, on 24 July, he was already ill and in no state to react favourably to the thought of revising *Red Scotland*. David Orr, who initially interpreted MacDiarmid's condition as pneumonia but realised his illness was psychosomatic, told the poet he must avoid any further work for at least a year. Yet MacDiarmid had to complete his book to the publisher's

331

satisfaction in order to earn advances due on publication. It was about this time that Routledge told him they intended to end his retainer, at the end of the year, and pay him instead the sum of £10 on each book they accepted on his advice.

Apart from overwork, MacDiarmid was severely depressed by a letter from Peggy. Kate McElroy intended to take Peggy to court for obtaining money by enticing McElroy away from her; Peggy wanted MacDiarmid to agree to come to London to speak in her favour in court. This possibility rang alarm bells in MacDiarmid's mind and, on an irrational impulse, he wrote to Sean O'Casey, McElroy's friend, asking if he should go back to Peggy. An astonished O'Casey, who had only once met MacDiarmid at that time, decided to ignore the letter, feeling that the poet's private life was none of his business.

The first week of August brought a visitor to Whalsay. Sorley MacLean came for a holiday, staying in MacDiarmid's cottage and taking a trip to West Linga with MacDiarmid and Michael. MacLean noticed that MacDiarmid had lost weight and was drawn and nervous but thought 'there was nothing wrong with him mentally'.[14] Orr, keeping a watchful eye on MacDiarmid, was frequently at the cottage and, as the doctor was as fervent a Douglasite and Scottish Nationalist as MacDiarmid, most of the conversations concerned politics. MacLean recalled one discussion with MacDiarmid:

> I remember arguing with him about his belief that Major Douglas's Social Credit could solve man's economic problems. His answer was to the effect that the bourgeoisie must be liquidated. I am not at all sure that 'liquidated' was the word he used but I took his answer to mean that the ethos of the bourgeoisie must be psychologically or morally destroyed.... His very poverty was itself a proof of the greatness of his uncompromising commitment.... It mattered very little to me that I thought him mistaken about Social Credit or that I thought him hard on Auden...[15]

Stimulated by his week in Whalsay, MacLean left — unaware that MacDiarmid was about to be plunged into a grave crisis, in Valda's words 'a matter of life and death'.[16] After MacLean's departure, Orr moved MacDiarmid into his own house so that he could monitor his diet and take constant care of him.

On Tuesday, 13 August, David Orr told MacDiarmid he could do nothing more for him. He had to seek psychiatric help. Valda turned to the one man she felt could, and would, exert a positive influence on her husband. She wired F. G. Scott in St Andrews and, on the Wednesday, went with MacDiarmid on the steamer to Aberdeen. Michael was left behind to be looked after by the old lady in the cottage next door, the locals were told that the poet had nicotine poisoning from his incessant pipe-smoking, and Valda was sure they thought they had seen the last of her and her husband.

St Andrews in 1935 could claim to be the cultural centre of the Scottish Renaissance, largely due to the activities of the wealthy American owner-editor of the *Modern Scot*. James H. Whyte had established the Abbey Book Shop and his own home at 3 South Street and in 1931 had bought the former coastguard building at 5-11 North Street which he had converted into an art-gallery with a house on either side. Since 1931 Scott had taken his annual summer holiday in St Andrews, staying at 5 North Street; at number 11, on the other side of the gallery, lived John Tonge, a journalist (who used the pseudonym A. T. Cunningham for his aesthetic writings), a homosexual, and Whyte's closest friend. A few hundred yards from North Street, at Castlelea, lived Edwin and Willa Muir. After a road-accident on Hampstead Heath, in which their son Gavin was knocked down by an oil-tanker, Edwin and Willa settled in St Andrews in 1935, at the time of MacDiarmid's breakdown.

Thus MacDiarmid arrived in a Scottish town that, fortuitously, accommodated a number of his friends and admirers: Scott, principally; but also Whyte and Tonge to whom MacDiarmid later dedicated *In Memoriam James Joyce* in recognition of their understanding of modernism. Muir, contemplating *Scott and Scotland*, was unhappy in St Andrews and had become disenchanted with MacDiarmid's Communism as he himself was moving towards a wholly Christian commitment (it was in St Andrews in 1939 that he finally accepted Christianity as the meaning of his life). Willa, who had been educated at St Andrews University, was in her element, making herself the centre of attention. Valda had an unpleasant memory of a day on the beach in St Andrews on account of Willa's insensitivity to MacDiarmid's illness. Some years later she recalled 'Willa sprawling on the beach in one of those modern bathing costumes – four sizes too small – just oozing with grossness & holding forth unnecessarily on her favourite topic – phallic symbolism'.[17] Willa was then writing, for the 'Meanings for Scotland' series, her book on sex and Scotland, *Mrs Grundy in Scotland*.

Scott, however, grasped the gravity of the situation and arranged for MacDiarmid to be admitted to Gilgal, a detached block of the Murray Royal Hospital in Perth, on 17 August. Opened in 1930, Gilgal Nursing Home welcomed voluntary patients seeking psychiatric help and was

established to put into practice the enlightened ideas of Dr Walter
Duncanson Chambers, Physician Superintendent at the Murray Royal
Hospital. Gilgal had one wing for men and another for women, each
with a small ward, rooms, and single rooms, amounting to some twenty
beds. Each ward had a large open-air veranda where patients could be
out of doors in bed by day. Interestingly, given MacDiarmid's religious
upbringing, the name Gilgal had biblical connotations. Gilgal ('circle of
stones') is identified, in Joshua, as the first camp of Israel after crossing
the Jordan: 'And those twelve stones, which they took out of Jordan,
did Joshua pitch in Gil-gal' (Joshua 4:20).

As the Murray Royal Hospital observes a strict rule of confidentiality,
it is difficult to define the exact nature of MacDiarmid's illness. Looking
back on 1935, David Orr cited 'a certain disorientation, which we later
surmised was due to a summation of numerous subconscious "insults"
arising from domestic difficulties a few years previous'.[18] Valda thought
the illness was the result of work weariness and the sudden intervention
of Peggy in the poet's life. In a letter to Andrew Graham Grieve on 28
August 1935, Valda wrote:

> I saw C. yesterday [Tuesday, 27 Aug.] – he was looking awfully rotten –
> poor fellow – having had a rather bad set-back over the week-end. The Dr
> says he is suffering from complete nervous exhaustion – the blood-tests
> have proved negative. He is very emaciated weighing just over 8 st....
> Only Mr Scott and I know his address – Dr Chamber[s] is the head of the
> Perth Mental Hospital & you know what people are like (& Christopher
> has so many enemies) the next thing we'd be hearing is the rumour that he
> was in the mental hospital.
>
> I feel I ought to mention this – please forgive me – but before long I
> expect you will hear a lot about Peggy – Mrs McElroy is suing her for
> seducing Mr McElroy & for the recovery of £25,000 he has made over to
> her – Christopher knows it is in the air – but nothing definite – we are
> trying to keep any further news of this from him – as any worry &
> excitement – may mean months of illness...[19]

That weekend setback mentioned by Valda was caused by Mac-
Diarmid's irrational and impulsive behaviour. On Friday, 23 August, he
got dressed and was told he could walk around the hospital grounds for
a while. Once he was outside, MacDiarmid decided to visit Soutar at his
home at 27 Wilson Street, in the Perth suburb of Craigie. He travelled
by taxi and stayed away for around three hours. When he returned to
Gilgal his temperature had risen and he was on the point of collapse.

Next day he went out on to the veranda and lay in the sun, causing his temperature to rise alarmingly. When Valda (who had spent the weekend with Helen Cruickshank in Edinburgh) arrived on the Tuesday (27 Aug.), MacDiarmid was still badly shaken. Dr Chambers told her the poet would have to have an operation for haemorrhoids as soon as he was stronger and he had agreed to this. On 28 August, Valda caught the 2 p.m. boat from Aberdeen to Shetland to await further developments. She had an unpleasant journey, suffering frequently from sea-sickness. Glad to be back with Michael, she busied herself by sorting out Mac-Diarmid's papers, filling a tea-chest with newspaper cuttings kept by the poet.

John Tonge drove F. G. Scott to Gilgal on 8 September to see MacDiarmid. Afterwards they visited Soutar who noted, in a letter to Helen Cruickshank, that Scott had seen a slight improvement, though not much to build on: 'F.G. said he was still very shaky on his legs [but] is submitting quietly to the treatment.'[20] Following Scott's visit, Andrew Grieve came to see his brother, bringing cigarettes and news of his holiday in Mull. On 22 September, MacDiarmid wrote to Andrew, asking for £10 which he urgently needed for his fare back to Shetland though he was not yet in a fit state to leave Gilgal.

The next letter to Andrew, undated but undoubtedly 24 September, showed dangerous signs of agitation. The cause of this was the prospect of a visit from Peggy, making MacDiarmid desperate for the money he had asked from Andrew:

> My good progress is continuing. A matter of which I have spoken to you before is advancing rapidly – viz. my reunion with my first family. Peggy (who left the man she has been living with since our divorce) is coming to see me here this weekend – with, I think, Christine. That means (I know because of the terms of our recent correspondence) she is now prepared to remarry me as soon as matters can be arranged. In view of this I urgently need money at once. I must for example make myself presentable with a new shirt and pair of flannel bags (my present shirt – the only one I have with me – having been laundered into a most ragged condition), while as matters stand I haven't a halfpenny to give them a cup of tea.[21]

The meeting with Peggy (who came alone) clarified MacDiarmid's position. Seeing her he realised that any reunion was impossible and that it would be self-destructive for him to become involved in her court case.

Unexpectedly, Andrew had not sent the money MacDiarmid

requested, a decision that prompted the poet to write angrily to his brother on 1 October. Protesting that he valued Andrew as a friend and not merely an easy financial touch, MacDiarmid said he would have been dead had he not experienced the 'miracle of specialist treatment'[22] at Gilgal. This admission led to a heartfelt tribute to F. G. Scott, designed to shame Andrew into contrition:

> Scott took the whole financial burden [of the medical expenses] on himself; Orr offered to go halves but Scott wouldn't let him (Orr has helped Valda all the while and would have telegraphed the cash I asked you to *lend* me by return if I'd had or cd have got enough to wire him the request). Nor would Scott tolerate any question of repayment; said he would regard it as an insult to the spirit in which he had undertaken to do it. Scott has visited me every Saturday here; brought two or three ounces of black tobacco every time latterly; and a fine, big-bowled new pipe. I've this moment received from him registered letter containing the amount I asked you for. Scott's in your position. A salaried man, with like you a lately acquired house to keep going, a wife, and 4 children at good schools. He could not have done it at all but for the fact that he had happened to receive payment for some extra inspectorial duties he'd done apart from his ordinary work. It has cost him at least (apart from railway fares, keeping Valda and I in St Andrews, paying the 'chief's – Dr Chambers' – £15/15 – fee for motoring through and inspecting me there when it was decided I needed hospital treatment, and apart from papers, tobacco, pipe etc. he's given me) – £31.10/– to my knowledge and likely more. So there you are.[23]

Confident that he had made a miraculous recovery and hopeful of securing a job as the editor of a new Oban newspaper, MacDiarmid was ready to return to Whalsay to pick up the pieces of his life. Discharged from Gilgal on 3 October, he travelled to Edinburgh and, that evening, caught the steamer from Leith to Shetland.

14

Mature Art

The Mature Art – alone with the Alone.
No voice not fully enfranchised,
No voice dispensable or undistinguishable
Like a man who needs uses words from many dialects
To say what he has to say as exactly and directly as possible.
In Memoriam James Joyce (786-7)

MACDIARMID's return to Whalsay in October 1935 was accompanied by physical and literary irritations. In his weakened condition he suffered a rough journey to Shetland: 'the worst sea-jostling I've ever had – a terrible experience for a fellow straight from a hospital bed'.[1] Rather than resting, as he had been advised to do, he decided to come to terms with the issue of *Red Scotland*. While he was in Gilgal 'The Voice of Scotland' series – a change from the planned series-title of 'Meanings for Scotland' – had started (in September) with Eric Linklater's *The Lion and the Unicorn* and Neil Gunn's *Whisky and Scotland*. Facing the title-page of Linklater's book was a list of volumes in the series, indicating that *Red Scotland* was shortly to be published. On Sunday, 13 October, MacDiarmid wrote to A. J. B. Paterson of Routledge, explaining that he intended to excise the irrelevancies from his text. Thankfully, all was well with *Scottish Eccentrics* (on course for its appearance in March), a book the poet dedicated to Paterson with gratitude and affection.

An extract from *Red Scotland* was published on 26 October on the front page of *New Scotland*, the weekly successor to the *Free Man* (which had ceased publication in 1934). Its tone was uncompromising and challenging:

> The Communist Party is right in regarding the official National Party of Scotland as a Fascist organisation.... All these people [associated with the new Scottish National Party] are Anglo-Scots, with no real knowledge of Scottish language or literature – insulated from it by English, and by the fact that they are cut off from the Scottish proletariat, all their concrete connections being with the denationalised Anglicised bourgeoisie.... Continued association with England, either in the present relationship or any other, or even continued allegiance to the dangerously and anti-democratically conspiring clique of cosmopolitan careerists in Windsor Castle, cannot but commit us to Fascism, the antithesis of the Scottish genius and the negation of its natural destiny and world-function. We can only rightly direct our affairs at the present time and in the future by rigid adherence to the policy that inspired us in the past – unbreakable alliance with France and continual war with England.[2]

Back in 1923 MacDiarmid had written in favour of Scottish Fascism. Now, with Hitler installed as Führer of Nazi Germany, the grisly nature of Fascism was apparent. A narrow Scottish nationalism, indifferent to culture and strong on bourgeois values, was anathema to MacDiarmid.

With eighty-eight votes (compared to 825 for the winner, Viscount Allenby, 792 for Douglas Chalmers Watson, 292 for Lord Clydesdale) MacDiarmid came bottom of the poll in the Edinburgh University Rectorial Election that October. At about the same time he heard that Rich & Cowan had rejected his study of *The Wolfe of Badenoch* so he submitted the book, without success, to Routledge. (It was never published though bits of it are incorporated in *Lucky Poet* where the ferocious Wolfe is presented as a fourteenth-century freedom fighter.[3]) On the positive side, various periodicals continued to print his poems. 'Art and the Workers', evidently a selection of the Glasgow sequence *The Red Lion*, appeared in the *Scottish Bookman* of December; the same month the *London Mercury* published 'Veuchen' and the prophetic 'Glasgow, 1960' which imagines the city buzzing over the discussion of a Turkish poem rather than a football match.

The year 1936 was to be a grim one, full of anger and indignation.

It began badly when MacDiarmid heard that Routledge had decided not to publish *Red Scotland*. The Routledge reader's report on the revised text of 50,000 words pointed out that more than half the book comprised quotations, that it included libellous passages about the royal family, and that it lacked commercial qualities. MacDiarmid was furious, writing to Paterson on 26 January:

> This – *Red Scotland* – is a book which is being eagerly awaited all over Scotland and elsewhere and the imminence of its publication has already had repercussions in Communist Headquarters. Friends of mine whose judgement I trust, who have seen portions of the typescript, are – in contradistinction to your reader – of the opinion that it strikes the nail on the head and is sure to create a furore and to have important consequences. You can appreciate from this the grave difficulties in which this eleventh-hour rejection places me, apart from its unheard-of character in relation to a book by any author of established reputation. This is bound to react very detrimentally on my influence, and the fact that you have advertised the book may very well increase my difficulties in now placing it elsewhere.[4]

MacDiarmid was correct in his assumption. *Red Scotland* was never published as a book though portions of it were used in his periodical, the *Voice of Scotland*, and in *Lucky Poet*. As Valda put it, the failure to place the book with Routledge was 'a crushing blow to Christopher'.[5]

At the beginning of April the national newspapers were full of reports of the enticement case brought by Kate McElroy against Peggy. In the King's Bench Division, in London on 2 April, it was alleged that Mrs McElroy, the fifty-nine-year-old mother of nine children (five of whom were still living), had suffered grievously as a result of Peggy's actions. According to Lord Reading, KC, Peggy pestered McElroy after their first meeting, succeeded in enticing him away from his wife, became a director and secretary of his company, dominated his business affairs, and obtained at least £10,000 from him. On 8 April Kate McElroy was awarded £3500 damages against Peggy. In fact, Peggy subsequently (26 Oct.) succeeded in reversing this judgement after an appeal, but the publicity given to the case in April brought great distress to MacDiarmid.

In his mood of dejection he was not much impressed by a collective tribute to his genius, presented to him that spring. A public testimonial – signed by Walter de la Mare and Sean O'Casey as well as several Scottish writers including Sir James Barrie, R. B. Cunninghame Graham, Compton Mackenzie and Eric Linklater – commented on 'the magic of a genius which is at the same time intimately Scottish and widely European'.[6]

MacDiarmid observed wryly, 'It is not wise to look a gift horse in the mouth, but I cannot forbear a shrewd glance at the teeth of this testimonial.'[7] He thought the testimonial would do him more harm than good, given the hostility to him from some quarters in Scotland, and that it was preposterous that it should come at a time when he was struggling to make ends meet.

After giving a broadcast for the BBC in Aberdeen, MacDiarmid went to Edinburgh in May. He booked into the George Hotel, then moved to 6 Claremont Street to stay with Tom and Mary MacDonald who had married in Montrose at the beginning of the year. MacDonald had converted to Catholicism in 1935, a decision that interested MacDiarmid. Mary recalled how the poet talked about romance and religion:

> I was in the early stages of pregnancy and often lay down in the afternoon because of sickness. Chris would come and sit on the bed beside me when he would speak to me of his marriage to Peggy, his first wife, and the damage he feared the break-up and loss of his children had done to his lyrical faculty. He seemed very depressed when he dwelt on this, and did so often when I was alone with him. Maybe it was the fact that he was living with very happy newly-weds that reopened the old wound. He discussed religion, too, and almost as if encouraging me said that were he to adopt any religion it would be Roman Catholicism.[8]

Mary was amazed at the number of students who came to her house to do homage to MacDiarmid; Tom was irritated by this, disapproving of the Communist influence MacDiarmid exerted on young Scots.

The following month, MacDiarmid experienced one of the most hurtful episodes of his career. J. H. Whyte's *Modern Scot* – the last issue of which, in January 1936, contained a lukewarm review of *Second Hymn to Lenin and Other Poems* – had amalgamated with the *Scottish Standard* to form *Outlook*, a new monthly edited by David MacEwen (a close friend of Neil Gunn) with Whyte as literary editor. The third issue of *Outlook*, appearing in June, contained a substantial extract from Edwin Muir's forthcoming book, *Scott and Scotland*, one of the volumes in 'The Voice of Scotland' series which MacDiarmid had helped to promote. Ostensibly about Scott as a writer, Muir's book amounted to an attack on Scots as a literary language. He asserted that 'Scotsmen feel in one language and think in another',[9] argued that only English could further the literary aspirations of modern Scotland, suggested that Scots was limited to the language of simple poetry, dismissed as anachronistic the attempt to resuscitate Scots and stated that MacDiarmid had 'left Scottish verse very much where it was before'.[10] Predictably, MacDiarmid was outraged by this assault on his own position as it clearly attempted to undermine the authority of his masterly work in Scots. In his opinion, Muir was the Judas who had betrayed the poetic saviour of Scotland.

Muir proclaimed that Scotland had lost a literature as well as a language as a result of historical change: the adoption by the Reformers of the English Bible (translated in 1560 by English refugees in Geneva); the transfer of the Scottish court to London after the Union of the Crowns in 1603; the hostility of the educated élite to indigenous Scottish culture after the parliamentary union of 1707. Great Scots makars (Dunbar and Henryson) had written adult poetry because they combined feeling and thought in a mature homogeneous language. However, a succession of shocks to the cultural system of Scotland meant that the poetry produced after the parliamentary union showed a painful split between emotion and intellect, between dialect and discourse. Even a man of genius such as Burns, argued Muir, turned to English when he needed to apply thought to his theme in passages of 'Tam o' Shanter'. And as for the popularity of Burns with the anglophiles of his time, Muir suggested that a sensuous Scots represented a psychological regression to childhood, the sound of something lost. Compared to a homogeneous language, dialect was an inadequate and infantile utterance.

With this thesis MacDiarmid could have had some sympathy. He, after all, had lamented the puerile matter and feeble-minded manner of post-Burnsian verse. He had likewise rejected simple dialect verse in favour of a modernist Synthetic Scots. Yet Muir had chosen to make an argumentative issue of MacDiarmid's own work. He conceded that MacDiarmid's attempt to revitalise Scots poetry by exposing it to European influences was an honourable effort; and he regretted that Scottish critics preferred the lyrics to *A Drunk Man*. Still, MacDiarmid's poetry did nothing to alter Muir's opinion that Scots was a lost cause. The implication was that MacDiarmid was only a gifted literary oddity; a man whose literary experiments were interesting but did nothing to advance Scots as a linguistic option worthy of the attention of mature minds.

Muir set out to produce a polemical work in a series designed to challenge the complacency of Scotland, a country (according to Muir) where criticism was more like a disease of literature than a corrective. In terms of his editorial brief, he succeeded for his work was powerfully provocative. Yet in treating *A Drunk Man* as a linguistic experiment rather than a poetic achievement he missed the point of MacDiarmid's

341

masterpiece and so undermined his own argument. If one man could combine intellect and emotion so triumphantly in a great poem then that was more than enough to demonstrate that Scots could still serve the Scottish poet. Muir's conclusion that 'Scotland can only create a national literature by writing in English'[11] is itself immature; *A Drunk Man* revealed that a Scot could contribute to international literature by writing in Scots. Muir's presumption that English was superior to Scots as a literary medium was itself a parochial attitude arising out of a limited understanding of the poetic potential of speech. Even with the evidence of *A Drunk Man* before him he was unable to admit that a work of genius transcends conventional expectations. In thinking of his own future as a poet writing in English, Muir ignored what others had done with dialect: the precedent of Dante, the presence of MacDiarmid.

Henceforth MacDiarmid treated Muir with the utmost hostility. He lost no opportunity of condemning his former friend, even claiming (in a letter to Soutar) that 'Whyte and Muir were responsible for preventing the publication of *Red Scotland*'.[12] By way of reply to Muir's extract, MacDiarmid sent a letter to *Outlook*. Offended by its belligerent tone and personal abuse of Muir, Whyte rejected it. MacDiarmid then circulated an open letter to Whyte, prepared as a press handout with the headline 'Proletarian-Separatist Literary Line in Scotland'. Dated Whalsay, 1 July 1936, MacDiarmid's letter amounted to a declaration of literary war on Whyte, Muir and the 'fascist-nationalist' line of *Outlook*:

> I must obviously completely dissociate myself from this line and do so now with the direct warning that you are betraying the Scottish Movement — that the people who took no previous interest in that Movement with whom you are now getting into touch are not worth getting into touch with, but are a worthless set of people — a historically doomed class of petit-bourgeois due for speedy liquidation.[13]

Though he had initiated the literary feud through his contention that the Scots language was intellectually exhausted and incapable of revival, Muir refused to be drawn into verbal combat with MacDiarmid. Willa thought that 'Edwin's indifference to all this invective was genuine [for the attack] on himself seemed a small issue to what was happening in the world at large'.[14] Perhaps. It is equally arguable that he was haunted by the experience. Muir based many of his poems on his dreams and one of his best-known works, 'The Combat' (first published in 1947 and collected two years later in *The Labyrinth*), describes a nightmare possibly prompted by the way he had fractured a friendship dating back to 1924. In the poem two unevenly matched antagonists fight a perpetual battle. The aggressor is a crested animal, arrayed in royal hues, who uses his claws to tear the heart out of his enemy – a submissively soft and gentle creature. Poetic logic would allow Muir to see MacDiarmid as a pitiless enemy and himself as a perpetual victim.

Despite his poor showing in the 1935 Edinburgh University Rectorial Election, MacDiarmid agreed to stand again in 1936, mainly to secure a platform for his political aims. During the autumn he formed, with the support of Scottish students, the Red Scotland Group who issued 'The Red Scotland Thesis'. At this time MacDiarmid was working on a biography of John Maclean in collaboration with Maclean's daughter Nan Milton.[15] 'The Red Scotland Thesis' advocated Scottish Workers' Republicanism as conceived by Maclean:

> We claim that we have, along this Red Scotland line, the end of Scottish Nationalism and the beginning of Workers' Republicanism. *Our line represents a complete break with recent Scottish cultural developments, and the realisation that further such developments must of necessity be revolutionary.* The Communist and Social Democratic neglect of and side-tracking of the Scottish Cause up to now has been responsible for the long confused and inefficient Scottish Nationalist grouping, and the extent to which the whole thing has now played into Fascist hands ... *No Scottish Socialist can read this exposition of the John Maclean line with any feeling other than shame at not having been engaged in pushing it all along.*[16]

MacDiarmid's stand on Scottish Workers' Republicanism was tested in two votes. At the Edinburgh University Rectorial Election, in October, he came second bottom of the poll though the 266 votes cast for him represented a marked improvement on his position the previous year. The following month, on 30 November, the Communist Party wrote to tell him he had been expelled by a unanimous vote of the Scottish District Committee. MacDiarmid was in no mood to accept that information passively.

Having been expelled for 'nationalist deviationism'[17] MacDiarmid appealed to the Communist International. Moscow remitted his expulsion back to the CPGB and the issue was examined at the Party Congress where the vote was by delegation – Welsh, Scottish, N.E. England, and so on. As F. G. Scott told MacDiarmid, several Scots – including the Muirs – hoped that the poet would be humiliated by the Party.[18] Only the Scottish delegation voted in favour of MacDiarmid's expulsion, all the others voted against it. Not only was he reinstated but the Scottish Secretariat of the CPGB eventually admitted it had been mistaken in ignoring the national issue; it changed its policy to include a measure of autonomy for Scotland though it continued to resist MacDiarmid's arguments in favour of Scottish Workers' Republicanism.

On 16 April 1937, MacDiarmid was at the BBC in Aberdeen broadcasting on the literary differences between 'The Shetlands and the Faroes'. His main point was that whereas the Faroese had established a modern literary movement by using their native language, the Shetlanders had allowed the Norn language to atrophy through indifference to its expressive potential. On Whalsay, some of the fishermen joined Valda to listen to the broadcast on the only radio set on the island, in Jimmy Arthur's shop. They were not amused by what they took to be MacDiarmid's onslaught on their collective ignorance. 'Wait till he comes back!' they said to Valda. 'I slunk out', she said, 'in fear and trembling.'[19]

The day after giving the broadcast, MacDiarmid visited Soutar in Perth. By this time the poet's sartorial appearance proclaimed his Scottish commitment for he wore a kilt of the red Murray of Tullibardine tartan[20] and other accoutrements. Soutar described MacDiarmid's arrival on the Saturday afternoon with a mixture of amusement and fascination:

> About 3.30, C.M.G. came striding in, resplendent in full Highland rig-out. He had been celebrating his descent upon the South – but hadn't reached the blethering stage, so we had a hearty time, with much loud laughter. He had a number of MSS with him and read part of his *Red Scotland*, which sounded quite convincing. As he read, he supported himself at an angle over my table, and the angle increased with the reading until he was literally dropping cigarette-ash and dialectical materialism all about me. I thought it might relieve the congestion if he removed his plaid – but discovered that it was part of the regalia.[21]

As he had done the previous year, MacDiarmid went to Edinburgh, signing in at the George Hotel then moving in with Tom and Mary MacDonald at 6 West Claremont Street. On 15 May Helen Cruickshank celebrated her fifty-first birthday at the George Hotel with MacDiarmid and the MacDonalds and it was decided that, for the poet's last night in Edinburgh, a party should be held at West Claremont Street so he could meet his many admirers. Having arranged for the jollifications to begin at 7.30 p.m. Tom MacDonald was annoyed when MacDiarmid failed to materialise at the appointed time. After about two hours had elapsed the bell rang and MacDonald went on to the landing to open the downstairs door. MacDiarmid staggered up the two flights of stairs, clutching a bottle of whisky in his arms. He wore his red kilt, a red shirt[22] and was clearly the worse for wear.

Leaving the assembled guests in the spacious sitting room, Mary took the poet to the dining room where she confiscated his bottle and tried to sober him up with black coffee. When he made his entrance to the sitting room he was still unsteady, tripping on a rug and missing the chair that had been kept vacant for him. 'Unperturbed,' said Mary, 'he picked himself up, sat in the chair, and delivered a most brilliant discourse, well peppered with oaths.'[23] At 2 a.m. Helen Cruickshank left to catch the night bus to Corstorphine but not before she had been embraced by MacDiarmid who told her he would have married her if they had met twenty years before. When the party finally broke up, at 7 a.m., MacDiarmid was still going strong though agitated by the absence of the bottle of whisky he had brought. Mary now returned it to him and, after a few drinks, he slept. In the evening he caught the steamer at Leith, having borrowed his fare from Tom and Mary.

No longer receiving his retainer of £52 per year from Routledge, MacDiarmid was forced to take on further commissions though his priority was to be the completion of an epic vision of a world language, a sequence (cast in a multilingual idiom though essentially in English) he intended to call *Cornish Heroic Song for Valda Trevlyn*. He was still working on *The Golden Treasury of Scottish Poetry*, still writing his autobiography, and now took on two more books: *The Islands of Scotland* for Batsford and *Scottish Doctors* for Harrap. With all this work he still found time to entertain visitors. W. R. Aitken – later his bibliographer and co-editor of *The Complete Poems of Hugh MacDiarmid* – came to Whalsay in July, one of several visitors that summer (another was G. E. Davie). In September, MacDiarmid researched *The Islands of Scotland* by visiting Eigg, Skye, South Uist, Barra, Mull and Iona. He was accompanied on this trip by W. D. McColl (a Gaelic revivalist who, like MacDiarmid, had been expelled from the National Party of Scotland in 1933) and he stayed with Sorley MacLean (then teaching at Portree Secondary School) on Skye and with Compton Mackenzie on Barra. It was a welcome working holiday for the poet; the weather was good and he enjoyed the company of close friends.

On his return to Shetland, MacDiarmid settled into a routine as he worked on his four commissions and spent as much time as he could on his projected epic *Cornish Heroic Song for Valda Trevlyn*. Michael was now attending the local school on Whalsay – 'It was quite a long walk, around $1\frac{1}{2}$ miles, even taking the shortcut across the rigs and moorland'[24] – and Valda (with some financial help from Helen Cruickshank) was doing her best to make domestic ends meet. It was a task that had its dramatic moments as she had to climb cliffs to get gulls' eggs for pickling for the winter. Michael has recalled how galvanised buckets 'stood around filled with seagulls' eggs, obscene in their white-coating of preservative'.[25]

The Grieves varied their diet thanks to the mackerel and cods' roe the islanders, who cared for neither, gave them and they bought herring from the boats for fivepence a dozen. To warm them during the winter they had to prepare their stack of peat and there were frequent calls for credit at Jimmy Arthur's shop. Opportunities for relaxation were limited. Sometimes David Orr brought round a bottle of whisky, sometimes MacDiarmid and Valda went to Symbister House for a game of bridge with the laird and his wife (who was the sister of Herbert Grierson of Edinburgh University). And MacDiarmid enjoyed light reading, poring over American Western magazines, chuckling at the antics of Jeeves and Bertie Wooster in the P. G. Wodehouse novels, thrilling to the convoluted plots of detective stories by Margery Allingham, Peter Cheyney and others. At such times MacDiarmid was content with a thriller in his hand and a pipeful of black twist tobacco in his mouth. While he read by the light of the Aladdin lamp, Valda knitted an 'intricate dazzle of Fair Isle patterns'.[26]

However, there was an intolerable strain on the poet as he worked at his epic composition. Michael watched the manuscript

> scrunched so hard into a ball of desperate irritation and neglect that it destroyed the carefully built peat fire like a cannon-shot, sending red sparks clouding aloft to grow black on the book spines. Its very tightness, however, saved it from extinction, the outer pages tea-coloured to a crisp as my mother – an eye to the hurricane of creativity – burned her fingers, ignoring the angry torment that urged its abandonment to the nethermost reaches of his own personal hell.
>
> Beneath the card table, sorting tangles of wool, I watched and wondered at the raging quiet of violence, and quaked at the great bang that almost lifted the front door from its hinges. But on an island such as Whalsay there are no places to go; the neighbours few and far; the pubs non-existent.[27]

When the fury and the frustration faded, MacDiarmid returned to his epic task.

The years 1937-9 represent the last great creative effort of Mac-Diarmid's poetic career. In that period he produced more than 20,000 lines of poetry – which he envisaged as about one-third the complete *Cornish Heroic Song for Valda Trevlyn*. In this composition he changed his direction for reasons relating to his breakdown of 1935 which he described as 'no ordinary illness but a touch-and-go one – a horrible imminence of death'.[28] Elsewhere he referred to his illness as 'the crisis which so completely altered the nature of my work'.[29] Though his epic poem contains lyrical asides he was now suspicious of the emotional demands of the concentrated lyric. Henceforth his work was to be intricately intellectual, calculated and controlled. That, anyway, was the theory.

David Orr noted that MacDiarmid 'never allowed himself to dream the same dream more than twice [as he] considered repeated dreams as a waste of nervous and psychic energy'.[30] Since MacDiarmid's divorce, though, he had dreamed repeatedly of Peggy, to his psychological cost, and he decided, after his breakdown, that he would remove her presence from his mind:

> So one night [he explained to a friend, Henry Grant Taylor], by a tremendous effort of will, he 'exorcised' the haunting, and once and for all cleared the image of Peggy from his mind. His recovery began almost from that moment, and his life slowly returned to normal.[31]

The *Cornish Heroic Song for Valda Trevlyn* was, stylistically at least, intended as an alternative to the Scots lyrics he had written while married to Peggy. 'Cornish Heroic Song for Valda Trevlyn', the fragment from the sequence of the same name, was once described by MacDiarmid as the opening section but, in June 1938, it was described as the 'First Appendix (Cornwall)'.[32] MacDiarmid rejected any supposition that Valda was English, praising her as 'a Cornish girl, symbolizing the further development of my pro-Celtic ideas'.[33] She therefore takes her place as the Spirit of Cornwall, '*Spyrys Kernow*, be with me now' (1103); as an embodiment of 'The Celtic genius – Cornwall, Scotland, Ireland, Wales' (708). In *In Memoriam James Joyce*, MacDiarmid himself represents Scotland, Joyce Ireland, Dylan Thomas (in a section revised after the death of the Welsh poet in 1953) Wales. One of the political issues underpinning the poem is the author's 'concern to get rid of the English Ascendancy and work for the establishment of Workers' Republics in Scotland, Ireland, Wales and Cornwall, and, indeed, make a sort of Celtic Union of Socialist Soviet Republics'.[34]

A related notion is that of the East-West Synthesis, an attempt to link the idea of a Scottish Workers' Republic with the actuality of the Soviet Union. This accounts for the jarring presence, in the poem, of 'Stalin, the Georgian' (745). From his reading of L. A. Waddell's *The British Edda* (1930) and L. Albert's *Six Thousand Years of Gaelic Grandeur Unearthed* (1936) MacDiarmid had come to the conclusion that 'the original impetus to civilisation was an Ur-Gaelic initiative, *nota bene* in the very region, Georgia, the original home of the Scots, which has given Stalin to the world'.[35] This theory of the Georgian genesis of the Scots has an obvious eccentricity and shows MacDiarmid casting around for connections that will make his poem cohere though it must be remembered that he took great delight in irrational assumptions and, a follower of Shestov, did not regard conventional logic as the concern of the poet. In 'The Fingers of Baal Contract in the Communist Salute' – a poem intended as part of the *Cornish Heroic Song for Valda Trevlyn* as witness the phrase 'This is a Cornish song' (677) – he mentions 'Stalin the Georgian' before adding 'We are Georgians all./We Gaels' (679). In 'Dìreadh III' he affirms that the Scottish Gael initiated the idea of civilisation currently being renewed at its native source 'since Georgia,/ Stalin's native country, was also the first home of the Scots' (1191). And in 'Lamh Dearg Aboo', dedicated to Stalin, he claims to speak for 'we Scots who had our first home/In Caucasian Georgia like your-self' (1323) when he welcomes the rapid evolution of the East-West Synthesis.

The Celtic Genius, the Caledonian Antisyzygy, the Gaelic Idea, the East-West Synthesis; these idiosyncratic obsessions are integrated into the poem along with a mass of material derived from the books he had read and the periodicals he had piled up in his Whalsay cottage. Though the poem expresses eccentric opinions, MacDiarmid insisted that he was conveying incontrovertible facts. 'I seek a poetry of facts' (630) he said. His aim was 'A poetry full of erudition, expertise, and ecstasy' (1019), 'A learned poetry wholly free/From the brutal love of ignorance' (1030). MacDiarmid still conceived of poetry as an art with its genesis in the inspirational logos. Words still existed as a vast treasure to be plundered by the poet with the abandon of a Border reiver about his business. Since 'lack of money does not mean poverty of spirit' (820) the poet could accumulate words in a privacy he willingly shared with the public, or that select part of the reading public sympathetic to ostentatiously intellectual long poems. He wanted to exchange his Scots poetry of suggestion for a poetry of statement. His interest was no longer with unusual nouns, as it had been in the poems in Synthetic Scots and

Synthetic English. He was now fascinated by exotic names and esoteric titles, as he acknowledged in a humorous parenthesis:

> Amos Tutuola, the Yoruba writer,
> Who has begun the structure of new African literature;
> Paul Bohannan on the Tiv of Central Nigeria;
> The metaphysical system, so complex and yet so tidy,
> Of the Dogon of French West Africa;
> Nahuatl, Mazatec, and Tarāhumara;
> Shirokogoroff's *Psychomental Complex of the Tungus*;
> (If that line is not great poetry in itself
> Then I don't know what poetry is.)   (793)

Sections of the poem read like the raw material for an ambitious bibliography, dealing mainly with linguistics.

Because of the fragmentary nature of its publication it is important to establish how MacDiarmid saw the shape of *Cornish Heroic Song for Valda Trevlyn*. By February 1938 he had arranged some 5000 lines of the poem as *Mature Art* and by December 1939 *Mature Art* had grown to 20,000 lines. *Mature Art*, he told Soutar, was 'a separable section of the *Cornish Heroic Song*'.[36] 'Dìreadh', which first appeared in the *Voice of Scotland* in December 1938, was described as 'one of the shorter separable lyrics interspersed in an immensely long as-yet-unpublished poem, *Cornish Heroic Song for Valda Trevlyn*'.[37] *The Kind of Poetry I Want* was 'a sequence which runs, appearing and reappearing at intervals, through the entire immense bulk of [the] *Cornish Heroic Song*'.[38] The three *Poems of the East-West Synthesis* (1946) were taken from the *Cornish Heroic Song* as MacDiarmid made clear in a note to one of them, 'Tristan and Iseult', when he printed it in the *Voice of Scotland* in 1946.[39] The title section of *In Memoriam James Joyce* was offered to T. S. Eliot as a small portion of *Mature Art*, itself a segment of the *Cornish Heroic Song*.[40] When sections of *Impavidi Progrediamur* were broadcast on the BBC Third Programme in December 1956 they were attributed to 'the second instalment of the vast poem whose opening section, *In Memoriam James Joyce*, was published last year'.[41] And the *Collected Poems* of 1962 contained eleven poems from *Impavidi Progrediamur*, footnoted as 'One of the four volumes of the huge poem of which *In Memoriam James Joyce* (1955) was the first'.[42]

At the end of his life MacDiarmid said there was no proper sequence in which poems from *Impavidi Progrediamur* (or *Haud Forrit* as he had intended to retitle it) could be presented and that the complete *Cornish Heroic Song for Valda Trevlyn* had been abandoned, parts of it subsumed in other works.[43] It is unfortunate that he was not able to complete the poem as originally conceived for it was his intention to compose a work of around 60,000 lines which, he reckoned, would make the *Cornish Heroic Song* the longest single poem in world literature. Even *Mature Art*, the 20,000-line portion completed by December 1939, never appeared as an ordered sequence with its multi-referential text, its use of more than twenty languages, its eighty separate lyrics.[44] As *In Memoriam James Joyce* is more than 5000 lines and *The Kind of Poetry I Want* more than 1000 lines, it can be safely assumed that almost everything MacDiarmid published after *Second Hymn to Lenin and Others Poems* – with obvious exceptions such as *The Battle Continues* (1957), remnants from the pre-Whalsay days, occasional poems and commissions such as 'The Borders' (for BBC television) – came from the *Cornish Heroic Song*.

The length of the project was important to MacDiarmid for he wanted to write an epic equal to the challenge of 'the epical age of Communism' (740). He had been greatly impressed by Lenin's eulogy of erudition in his last public speech, delivered in November 1922 at the Fourth Congress of the Communist International:

> It would be a very serious mistake to suppose that one can become a Communist without making one's own the treasures of human knowledge.... Communism becomes an empty phrase, a mere façade, and the Communist a mere bluffer, if he has not worked over in his consciousness the whole inheritance of human knowledge – made his own and worked over anew all that was of value in the more than two thousand years of development of human thought.[45]

It was with this intellectual ideal in mind that he declared 'the poetry of the age/Should be brought into conformity with its scientific spirit' (766), that he cited Rilke's dictum 'the poet must know everything' (1016), that (in a passage dated 1938 by its opening line) he contended:

> – I am forty-six; of tenacious, long-lived country folk.
> Fools regret my poetic change – from my 'enchanting early lyrics' –
> But I have found in Marxism all that I need –
> (I on my mother's side of long-lived Scottish peasant stock
> And on my father's of hardy keen-brained Border mill-workers).
> It only remains to perfect myself in this new mode.
> This is the poetry I want – all

I can regard now as poetry at all,
As poetry of to-day, not of the past,
A Communist poetry that bases itself
On the Resolution of the C.C. of the R.C.P.
In Spring 1925: 'The Party must vigorously oppose
Thoughtless and contemptuous treatment
Of the old cultural heritage
As well as of the literary specialists ...
It must likewise combat the tendency
Towards a purely hothouse proletarian literature.'   (615)

As the poem unfolds, however, MacDiarmid is shown as no dogmatic Communist. At the time of writing the *Cornish Heroic Song* he was also, for example, a follower of Shankara's Vedanta philosophy – 'And a greater interest in Indian thoughts and ideas/Exists nowhere in the world than in my mind' (856). As Shankara held that the eternal Being is the only authentic reality, the everyday world being an illusion (*maya*), it will be understood that MacDiarmid's historical materialism coexisted easily with his mysticism. His epic was to be all-embracing. As he said in an essay on Charles Doughty (one of the heroes of the epic) 'It is epic – and no lesser form – that equates with the classless society.'[46]

MacDiarmid's friend Barker Fairley – author of *Charles Doughty* (1927) and editor of *Selected Passages from 'The Dawn in Britain' of C. M. Doughty* (1935) – had moved from the Chair of German at Manchester University to the Chair of German at Queen's University College, Toronto. MacDiarmid told Soutar that 'Barker Fairley – the Doughty man – is introducing me to Canada'.[47] The *Canadian Forum* of July 1937 contained a new MacDiarmid poem, 'The Glass of Pure Water', footnoted as one of 'the shorter separable incidental poems from an extremely long as-yet-unpublished poem, *Cornish Heroic Song for Valda Trevlyn*.'[48] Its opening lines

Hold a glass of pure water to the eye of the sun!
It is difficult to tell the one from the other
Save by the tiny hardly visible trembling of the water.   (1041)

alludes to a passage in 'Lament for the Great Music' where the poet addresses the MacCrimmons:

I know your music best when as it were an island pool
Away here I hold a glass of water between me and the sun

> And can only tell the one from the other by the lint-white quiver,
> The trembling life of the water   (473)

There follows, in 'The Glass of Pure Water', a gesture towards 'these particular slum people/I am chiefly concerned with' (1041) which recalls 'In the Slums of Glasgow' in particular and the planned Glasgow slum sequence in general. MacDiarmid pulls in strands of his previous work – a stanza (1010) of *The Kind of Poetry I Want* quotes the concluding quatrain of 'Second Hymn to Lenin' – to establish his artistic maturity. 'The Glass of Pure Water' connects the timeless Celtic world to the contemporary iniquity of capitalism. One of the main arguments of the *Cornish Heroic Song* is expressed in a passage urging humankind to eliminate the evils of capitalism so the individual can come face to face with the eternal. MacDiarmid thinks of gestures expressing more than words, of the spiritual primacy of the Celtic people:

> Our duty is to free that water, to make these gestures,
> To help humanity to shed all else,
> All that stands between any life and the sun,
> The quintessence of any life and the sun;
> To still all sound save that talking to God;
> To end all movements save movements like these.
> India had that great opportunity centuries ago
> And India lost it – and became a vast morass,
> Where no water wins free; a monstrous jungle
> Of useless movement; a babel
> Of stupid voices, drowning the still small voice.
> It is our turn now; the call is to the Celt.   (1043)

MacDiarmid's desire is to create, through his poem, a bridge between political activism and philosophical quietism.

Like 'The Glass of Pure Water', the three 'Dìreadh' poems (*dìreadh* is Gaelic for the act of ascending) are lyrical interludes from the *Cornish Heroic Song*. Together they clarify the vision produced by a Celtic consciousness. 'Dìreadh I' begins with a parade of Gaelic words whose meanings are either given in parentheses or footnotes. The poet – 'looking, *cromadh*, at all Scotland below us' (1164) – is in danger of producing a primer of Gaelic expressions but manages to surmount this philological obstacle by considering the nature of his own work. He offers a passage on the purpose of his poetry (though the irony of the first line of the following extract should be noted):

> Without the least self-consciousness
> I achieve the ideal of so many poets,
> The union of poetry and science,
> My theme being nature *in solido,*
> That mysterious presence of surrounding things
> Which imposes itself on any separate element
> That we set up as an individual for its own sake.   (1167)

Nature, so far as the 'Dìreadh' poems are concerned, means Scottish nature in a psychological as well as a topographical sense. MacDiarmid indicates that his own nature is a product of the Scottish earth-mother:

> I am the primitive man, Antaeus-like,
> Deriving my strength from the warm, brown, kindly earth,
> My mother.   (1167)

Such a man will not succumb passively to the sensuous charm of traditional nature poetry. He intends to impose himself on any environment that appeals to him, to free his Scotocentric outlook from parochial limitations:

> To raise his theme to a higher level
> And transform it into a philosophic ideal
> In successive poems, realistic, idealistic, historical,
> And, finally, triumphantly, all three combined,
> Like the clear, sharp, changing looks of the Shetland Islands
> That gain by not being a separate fact.   (1168-9)

This higher level of consciousness is attainable by metaphysical effort, as the poet demonstrates by placing himself on spiritual summits. Regarding 'all Scotland/In my vision now' (1170) he discerns in the diversity of the Scottish landscape the source of the Caledonian Antisyzygy which enables the sensitive Scot to be 'a world in himself ... full of darkness like a mountain' (1170). The nationalism of such a man is not small-minded as MacDiarmid shows by asking and answering a question that takes him back to the lush landscape of his youth:

> Scotland small? Our multiform, our infinite Scotland *small?*
> Only as a patch of hillside may be a cliché corner
> To a fool who cries 'Nothing but heather!' where in September another
> Sitting there and resting and gazing around

353

Sees not only the heather but blaeberries
With bright green leaves and leaves already turned scarlet
Hiding ripe blue berries; and amongst the sage-green leaves
Of the bog-myrtle the golden flowers of the tormentil shining;
And on the small bare places, where the little Blackface sheep
Found grazing, milkworts blue as summer skies;
And down in neglected peat-hags, not worked
Within living memory, sphagnum moss in pastel shades
Of yellow, green, and pink; sundew and butterwort
Waiting with wide-open sticky leaves for their tiny winged prey;
And nodding harebells vying in their colour
With the blue butterflies that poise themselves delicately upon them;
And stunted rowans with harsh dry-leaves of glorious colour.
'Nothing but heather!' – How marvellously descriptive! And
    incomplete!   (1170-1)

There is no loss of the lyrical faculty in that passage, often detached from its context by enthusiastic anthologists.

Scotland, then, is both microcosm and world-in-itself; both universal and particular. In the same way, the poet is both part of a collective and apart from it;

Remember, I speak
Never of the representative individual man as man,
But always of the artist as the great exception
To the whole human order of things   (1172)

Pursuing his individuality in 'Dìreadh II' MacDiarmid surveys Scotland from the viewpoint of Berwickshire. Indeed the essentially rural character of MacDiarmid's background is seen in an ecstatic passage near the beginning of the poem when he recounts an experience that came to him at the top of a glen when, in the presence of stags, he saw 'golden eagles, safe/In their empyrean liberty' and knew that 'squadrons of bomber planes' would never take their place:

I cried: Here is the real Scotland,
The Scotland of the leaping salmon,
The soaring eagle, the unstalked stag,
And the leaping mountain hare.
Here, above the tree-line, where the track
Is the bed of an amethystine burn
In a bare world of shining quartz and purple heather,

354

> Is the Scotland that is one of the sights of the earth
> And once seen can never be forgotten.   (1175)

That evocation of the land of the mountain and the flood is as romantic as anything in Sir Walter Scott.

In comparison to the 'Scotland of the leaping salmon', cities, including Edinburgh and Glasgow, are 'rubbish' (1175) which is why this poet cannot empathise with the industrial proletariat. He is always the figure in the landscape (or the library), present as person in various anecdotes or as a natural metaphor:

> Chafing always upon a rocky bed
> The river gathers round it
> All that fine tangle of foliage
> You see only upon impetuous streams.   (1180)

MacDiarmid has said that these four lines are 'applicable to and give a picture of my own life'.[49] His search for the source of creativity runs back to the river of Langholm.

'Dìreadh III' begins with a glorious description of the poet standing on the summit of Sgurr Alasdair looking at the Cuillin peaks of Skye:

> Here near the summit of Sgurr Alasdair
> The air is very still and warm,
> The Outer Isles look as though
> They were cut out of black paper
> And stuck on a brilliant silver background ...
> The western sea and sky undivided by horizon,
> So dazzling is the sun
> And its glass image in the sea.
> The Cuillin peaks seem miniature
> And nearer than is natural
> And they move like liquid ripples
> In the molten breath
> Of the corries which divide them.
> I light my pipe and the match burns steadily
> Without the shielding of my hands,
> The flame hardly visible in the intensity of light
> Which drenches the mountain top.   (1186-7)

Here MacDiarmid uses traditional techniques such as alliteration (summit/still, stuck/silver, nearer/natural) and euphony with masterly effect and the rhythm seems to conform to conversational requirements so the line-endings provide natural pauses. Significantly, in *The Islands of Scotland*, he reproduced this passage almost verbatim in prose.[50] As other parts of the *Cornish Heroic Song* make clear, he no longer saw an intrinsic virtue in the linear conventions of verse. In the lyrical interludes, the rhythm is persuasive; in the discursive passages it often seems arbitrary.

On the summit of Sgurr Alasdair, MacDiarmid is in his natural element, 'a simple place of clean rock and crystal water' (1186), alone with nature which is seen as a spiritual manifestation (as with Wordsworth, one of the poets MacDiarmid most admired in his youth); a mystical configuration; as a work of natural art both actual and ideal. A man 'possessed by this purity' (1187) MacDiarmid is visited by 'the Gaelic genius' (1187) that sustains him and his poetic work. He is pushed back into memories that matter to him: he thinks of the first rock-pigeon he ever saw, of his early lyrics in Scots, and goes forward from the past into a new level of perception so that he can 'covet the mystery of our Gaelic speech' (1191). MacDiarmid signals his ascension to a spiritual and poetic summit. He is a man transfigured by his Celtic consciousness, is 'with Alba – with Deirdre' (1193). As the third 'Dìreadh' poem moves towards a climax the poet avails himself of a liquid euphony and finally reaches the summit where he sees the legendary deer whose reappearance signifies the resurrection of Scotland:

> Let what can be shaken, be shaken,
> And the unshakeable remain.
> The Inaccessible Pinnacle is not inaccessible.
> So does Alba surpass the warriors
> As a graceful ash surpasses a thorn.
> Or the deer who moves sprinkled with the dewfall
> Is far above all other beasts
> – Its horns glittering to Heaven itself.   (1193)

Dedicated to Helen Cruickshank, and planned as long before as 1932,[51] the 'Dìreadh' sequence is the most memorable section of the *Cornish Heroic Song*. Elsewhere in his epic, MacDiarmid describes the kind of poetry he wants; in 'Dìreadh' he demonstrates its quality.

Turning from lyrical interludes to the main body of the *Cornish Heroic Song* requires an adjustment. The landscape is replaced by the library; for the most part the poet speaks of books instead of singing of 'the cool and gracious greenery' (1187). MacDiarmid's idiosyncratic approach is evident from the first lines of that part of the *Cornish Heroic Song* entitled *In Memorian James Joyce*:

> I remember how you laughed like Hell
> When I read you from Pape's 'Politics of the Aryan Road':
> 'English is destined to become the Universal Language! . . .'   (738)

This is a speculative scenario. MacDiarmid had never met Joyce and, if he had, it is doubtful if the Irish master would have tolerated a reading from a man MacDiarmid described as 'A. G. Pape, whose ancestors on either side embraced almost all the great diplomats of France and of Great Britain and with whom, for a time, I had a good deal to do in Edinburgh'.[52] Joyce is present not as a person, but as a supreme example of the creative genius of the Celtic race. He is addressed as a spiritual familiar, just as Dostoevsky was in *A Drunk Man*, Alexander MacDonald in *To Circumjack Cencrastus*, and Lenin in the hymns.

As a Celtic lord of language, Joyce is invited to the rarefied heights inhabited by those who worship words, who believe 'There lie hidden in language elements that effectively combined/Can utterly change the nature of man' (781). Using the Gaelic word *aonach*, meaning both a solitary place and a place of union, MacDiarmid beckons Joyce to join him:

> Welcome then, Joyce, to our *aonach* here,
> Here where alone we can live . . .
> Where nothing matters save Implex and Noösphere   (746)

That last line combines a zoological term (implex defines an inturning of the integument for attachment of muscles in Arthropoda) with a metaphysical expression (used by Teilhard de Chardin for the sphere of the mind, the collective racial memory). In MacDiarmid's poem, where language is more sacred than any institutional religion, Joyce is to be deified.

Summons to Joyce also provide the poem with a frame. After the invitation to the *aonach*, Joyce is mentioned mainly in passing – for example, 'unlike you, Joyce, I am more concerned/With the East than the West' (801) – until the close of *In Memoriam James Joyce* when

MacDiarmid abruptly brings his poem to an end by completing the frame:

> And so I come to the end of this poem
> And bid you, Joyce – what is the word
> They have in Peru for *adios*? – *Chau*, that's it!
>   Well, Chau for now.   (888)

Framing is not the only well-worn structural device that MacDiarmid employs. When he discusses his own poem, he draws attention to its lack of sequential solidity. It is 'This rag-bag, this Loch Ness Monster' (755); he is 'confronted with a gigantic maze/Of faulty knowledge, indirections, and distortions of all kinds' (852). Though the multilingual texture of the poem connects it with Eliot's *The Waste Land* and Pound's *Cantos* – he mentions 'the Pound-Eliot *olla podrida* of tongues' (761) – the linear technique is not modernistic. Eliot used juxtaposition in *The Waste Land*, Pound adopted an ideogrammatic method. MacDiarmid, a past master of counterpoint and dialectical contrast, relies on the medieval device of the catalogue in the discursive bulk of the *Cornish Heroic Song*.

Lyrical interludes apart, the poem is a monument to MacDiarmid's reading, and not only his omnivorous reading of intellectually demanding books for there is a place for Al Capp (817), the creator of the *Li'l Abner* comic strip; enough room for Thurber's animals 'the Goad, the female Shriek,/The Garble with an Utter in its claws' (804-5); and (in *The Kind of Poetry I Want*) a simile drawn from MacDiarmid's fondness for American Western magazines:

> as when the butts of a man's twin Colt guns
> Seem fairly to leap into his palms
> As the weapons flash out
> In smooth, eye-defying movements.   (609)

Again and again, MacDiarmid provides lists of words, books and names as he proclaims his omniscience – 'we know them all/And every detail of their works' (759). A virtuoso namedropper by nature, he takes great delight in these lists in deference to his provocative contention that 'consummate learning is far more rare/Than genius' (753). In *In Memoriam James Joyce* there are lists of treatises:

Carr on 'The Visual Illusion of Depth',
Titchener's 'Experimental Psychology of the Thought Processes',
Henry Cowell on 'The Process of Musical Creation' ...   (807)

and lists of authors:

Mistral, Carl Spitteler, these are my friends
And Rubén Darío, Vasile Alecsandri, Uys Krige,
Otokar Březina, Jens Peter Jacobsen, Paavo Cajander,
Svatopluk Cech, Arne Garborg, Jaroslav Vrchlicky,
Rasmus Effersoe, and Ceiriog ...   (817)

and (most effectively) lists of the crimes of political gangsters:

The concentration camps, the cat o' nine tails,
The law more lawless than any criminal,
The beatings-up by the police,
The countless thuggeries of Jacks-in-office,
The vile society women, infernal parasites,
The endless sadism, Gorilla-rule,
The live men hanging in the plaza
With butcher's hooks through their jaws ...   (841)

Two other structural procedures should be mentioned. In *The Kind of Poetry I Want*, MacDiarmid's love of similes is elevated into a structural principle as he elucidates his literary aesthetic: 'poems like the bread-knife/Which cuts three slices at once' (1005), 'A language like the magnetic needle' (1015), 'A poetry like Pushkin's in the morning sky of Russia' (1017), 'A poetry abstruse as hedge-laying' (1025), 'A poetry ... like a wrestling bout on a village green' (1027). The fourth structural principle goes back to 'Lament for the Great Music' with its attempt to simulate the open-minded improvisatory manner of the pibroch by producing verbal variations on a central theme. In 'Bagpipe Music' (identified as an extract from *Impavidi Progrediamur* when it appeared in the *Saltire Review* of Spring 1957) he invokes 'tunes without measure or end' (665) and in *The Kind of Poetry I Want*, referring to pipe music, he acclaims

Songs like the transition from the *ùrlar* to the *crunluath*,
Those variations which suggest hidden reserves
Of strength, of ingenuity, to follow,
Of undreamed-of gracenotes hidden in the fingers,

359

Then into the *crunluath breabach*,
Before the merciless variety, the ranting arrogance of which
Even the wonders of the *crunluath* pale to insignificance,
And finally into the fourth and greatest movement of the *pìob mhòr*,
The most fantastic music in all the range of the pipes,
The *crunluath a-mach* — where miracles of improvisation
Form themselves of their own volution under the fingers   (1007)

Without doubt, MacDiarmid wanted his great song to display merciless variety and ranting arrogance.

In Memoriam James Joyce is grandly subtitled 'From A Vision of World Language' and a world language, or linguistic internationalism, is a subject that runs through the poem. MacDiarmid specifically rejects as imperialistic the global pretensions of the English language and dismisses the limited scope of Basic English as designed by C. K. Ogden and developed by I. A. Richards:

— All dreams of 'imperialism' must be exorcised,
Including linguistic imperialism, which sums up all the rest.
The best policy would be to apply
The method of Basic, not to English,
But to the vast international vocabulary which already
      exists.   (790)

This vast international vocabulary is accessible to the author of the *Cornish Heroic Song* though he is fluent only in English and Scots, admitting, in a rare moment of modesty, 'alas I can speak no Greek/And am now too old to learn' (797). Nevertheless he uses phrases from many languages including Greek, German, French, Dutch, Norn, Gaelic, Welsh, Sanskrit and Hebrew — not always accurately as apparently two Hebrew words (793) are upside down. Clearly the world language MacDiarmid wants, like the kind of poetry he wants, is an artistic amalgam along the lines of *Finnegans Wake* so he can hold 'all language in my vision now' (819). It is a language for an impossibly ideal world inhabited exclusively by poets and scholars; a language that will 'heal the breach/Between genius and scholarship, literature and learning' (752) and so repair the 'broken unity of the human spirit' (753).

Theoretically, world language is the aim of the poet. In practice, though, MacDiarmid is confined largely to English coloured with exotic quotations. Gaelic is invoked as an ideal rather than applied and Scots

is used sparingly and with little impact in a quatrain which would lose
nothing if presented entirely in English:

> To fules the spirit seems to be active
> When the senses alane are really spry
> Even as the mune appears to move
> When it's nocht but the clouds ga'en by.   (798)

In an attempt to vary the verbal texture of the poem, MacDiarmid
punctuates the text with colloquial expressions – 'the salt of the earth'
(741), 'knocked about in the world' (743), 'we've gone stone winnick'
(752), 'Ah Joyce, enough said, enough said!/Mum's the word now!
Mum's the word!' (884) – which bring light relief to the work.

The reader should not forget, in considering the notion of a world
language, that MacDiarmid's sense of humour is, as always, part of the
creative process. This is not seen only in the colloquialisms, or in jokes –
such as the one about 'the "fu' po"/As the old Scotswoman called the
faux pas' (748) – but in the extended paradox that enables a writer to
reject the English language in a poem written in English. It should also
be remembered that two of MacDiarmid's indigenous predecessors
played verbal games with the concept of an expanded language. Sir
Thomas Urquhart, the celebrated translator of Rabelais, wrote (while
in prison after fighting on the royalist side at Worcester in 1651)
Ekskubalauron – 'the Discovery of a most Exquisite Jewel' – which drew
up fanciful rules for a universal language. Another Scottish writer, Robert
Fergusson, anticipated MacDiarmid's 'adventuring in dictionaries' in his
humorous address 'To Dr Samuel Johnson: Food for a new Edition of
his Dictionary' which uses epithets such as Scoticanian, Loch-Lomondian,
perpendicularian, lignarian, usquebalian and plumb-puddenian. Mac-
Diarmid was aware of the comical aspects of Scottish pedantry, especially
in a poem which has words with an Irish comic genius: the first line of
In Memoriam James Joyce, after all, has Joyce laughing like Hell.

If the main subject of the *Cornish Heroic Song* is language, as illuminated by the Celtic genius, the visionary theme of the work is the
potential of poetry to restore the 'unity of the human spirit' (753).
Disturbed for decades by the incessant cerebration that involved him in
the endless options of pluralism, MacDiarmid seeks a mystical union by
embracing 'the complex vision of everything in one' (823), by focusing
on 'a single creative ray' (823). Addressing Joyce, he says:

> Ah, Joyce, this is our task,
> Making what a moving, thrilling, mystical, tropical,
> Maniacal, magical creation of all these oppositions,
> Of good to evil, greed to self-sacrifice,
> Selfishness to selflessness, of this all-pervading atmosphere,
> Of the seen merging with the unseen,
> Of the beautiful sacrificed to the ugly,
> Of the ugly transformed to the beautiful,
> Of this intricate yet always lucid and clear-sighted
> Agglomeration of passions, manias, occult influences,
> Historical and classical references
> – Sombre, insane, brilliant and sane,
> Timeless, a symbol of the reality
> That lies beyond and through the apparent,
> Written with the sweeping assurance, the inspired beauty,
> The intimated truth of genius,
> With natures like ours in which a magnetic fluidity
> That is neither 'good' nor 'bad' is forever
> Taking new shapes under the pressure of circumstances,
> Taking new shapes, and then again,
> As Kwang makes Confucius complain of Laotze,
> 'Shooting up like a dragon.'   (821)

Language is the ladder on which the poet ascends to the 'intimated truth of genius'. Creativity is the credo of MacDiarmid's epic.

Mystical assumptions about the nature of creative genius had informed MacDiarmid's verse since the beginning. He felt, as the years passed, that it had become too easy, too effortless, for him directly to declare his metaphysic without qualification. He wanted to surmount the simplicity of the short lyric, wanted to confirm the depth of his conviction through the breadth of his references. So he establishes his intellectual credentials by his erudite awareness of linguistics (742), physics (782), experimental music (796), mathematics (803), astronomy (844), Indian thought (855), psychology (880), Western philosophy (884) and so on. Yet the most revealing and memorable lines of *In Memoriam James Joyce* are not the lists that testify to MacDiarmid's reading but the affirmative utterances that shoot, meteor-like, from the obscurity of the surrounding references.

> Poetry is human existence come to life,
> The glorious energy that once employed
> Turns all else in creation null and void   (757)

Once one's attuned to the elemental
One's banished by the superficial for ever.   (798)

        my certain knowledge,
Derived from the complex vision of everything in me,
That the whole astronomical universe, however illimitable,
Is only one part and parcel of the mystery of Life;
Of this I am as certain as I am certain that I am I.
The astronomical universe is *not* all there is.   (822)

It is death that most of all reveals love ...
Because the function of death is, more than all else,
To mark off that which is timeless
From that which is merely living.   (834)

There is neither good nor evil,
Better nor worse,
But only the harmony
Of that which is,
The pure phenomenon
Abiding in the eternal radiance.   (835)

For beyond the four dimensions of space-time
There is the fifth dimension, individuality   (836)

The universal *is* the particular.   (845)

It does not after all seem certain
That the peace I have found is entirely
Free from mystical elements.   (881)

– The supreme reality is visible to the mind *alone*.   (888)

MacDiarmid had insisted, in 'Lament for the Great Music', that 'The supreme reality is visible to the mind alone' (475); at the end of *In Memoriam James Joyce* he adds that important emphasis, 'The supreme reality is visible to the mind *alone*'. Punning on 'alone' as signifying both exclusivity and solitude, he acknowledges the spiritual essence of his art. Physical reality is an illusion – unthinking existence 'The very definition of vulgarity' (884) – whereas metaphysical reality is a certainty for the inspired artist. Such an artist exhibits the passion of the Celtic race since 'this fanatic devotion to art/Is alien to the English poetic temperament' (757). MacDiarmid's lyrical affirmations are to be seen as the product of an intellectual struggle, a universal quest that is light years away from the 'magnificent insularity ... of the Anglo-Saxon mind' (789). One section of *In Memoriam James Joyce* is pointedly entitled 'England is Our Enemy', England standing in the poem for imperialism.

For MacDiarmid, the answer to imperialism is individuality, conceived as a heroic quality. The epithet heroic in his overall title refers to the effort involved in surpassing everyday existence and achieving a spiritual essence that is 'The final reality to which human life can attain' (884). This essence is dependent on a free choice that is, paradoxically, obligatory on every responsible individual; 'Freedom is only really possible/In proportion as all are free' (884). To MacDiarmid the spiritual essence is an authentic experience not an example of mindless escapism which is why he considers himself to be uncontaminated by escapist options:

> The 'distraction' of Pascal,
> The 'aesthetic stage' of Kierkegaard,
> The 'inauthentic life' of Heidegger,
> The 'alienation' of Marx,
> The self-deception (*mauvaise foi*) of Sartre.   (884)

That list includes intellectual heroes of MacDiarmid and the inclusion of such figures supports the heroic mood of the poem.

Joyce, obviously, is first among MacDiarmid's favourites but the poem goes on to praise 'Doughty and Hopkins ... Doughty, by far the greatest of them all' (740), 'my great master, Shestov' (745), 'That heroic genius, Antonio Gramsci' (745), 'Yeats and others who are dead' (757), Pound – 'in the English-speaking world there is at least Ezra Pound' (857) – and scores of others. Parts of the epic intended for *Impavidi Progrediamur* project MacDiarmid himself as the supreme Scottish hero. He is 'The Man for Whom Gaeldom is waiting' (1372), the prophet who is finally honoured in a reborn Scotland. His work is eventually to be valued, his heroic song understood:

> In him were incarnate at that moment
> The liberties and the rights of man asserted in the face of power,
> The independence of the spirit which demands
> That conscience be satisfied
> Even against one who ranks himself higher than its claims.
> Scotland felt at that moment
> That no man ever personified her,

> Ever would represent her,
> As he did,
> And she grew in glory
> And was transfigured with pride.
> It was not a Scottish moment;
> It was a universal moment.   (1376-7)

'King Over Himself', another section from the sequence, has the prophet 'summing up in himself/The whole range of Gaelic wisdom' (1386). Ultimately, the hero of the work is the poet who created it; MacDiarmid as a saviour omniscient enough to address the universe.

All the contradictions the poet has lived with are to come together in a personal unity made by his own imagination. He no longer feels fragmented by inconsistency for, in this mystical poem, everything is contained in the expansive evolution of his art:

> Let the only consistency
> In the course of my poetry
> Be like that of the hawthorn tree
> Which in early Spring breaks
> Fresh emerald, then by nature's law
> Darkens and deepens and takes
> Tints of purple-maroon, rose-madder and straw.   (756)

With such verbal gestures towards the exhilarating eloquence of his earliest poems (the elaborate tree-imagery of this passage harks back to the strange tree of 'A Moment in Eternity') MacDiarmid offers the *Cornish Heroic Song* as a summation of his creative life. On it, he believed in the throes of composition, would rest his claim to poetic immortality – 'All else must be sacrificed to this great cause./I fear no hardships. I have counted the cost' (756). In the sense that Wordsworth saw the child as father of the man, the mature artist who fears no hardships is descended from the youth who was taught, in Langholm, to fear no evil.

Naturally, MacDiarmid's epic, as a summation, accommodates some old obsessions. They include Nietzschean amorality, since 'There is neither good nor evil' (835); creative evolution, as 'It is unlikely that man will develop into anything higher/Unless he desires to and is prepared to pay the cost' (842); cosmic consciousness; metaphysical afterlife; the articulation of the ineffable; the spirituality of silence, 'the dumbness finally desired by Tyutchev and Pasternak' (742). Though the work contains a more elaborate apparatus of allusion than any previous

MacDiarmid poem, the most recently acquired references tend to confirm insights he already held.

During the composition of his epic MacDiarmid was constantly on the lookout for intellectual allies and he found these in books and periodicals. Through the Carnegie Library he borrowed bound volumes of the *Revue Philosophique* of Paris so he could make use, for example, of essays on Kierkegaard, Heidegger and Martin Buber. Given the solipsism of his work, his interest in this trio is understandable. He felt an affinity for Kierkegaard's doctrine of subjective truth and emphasis on the primary importance of the existing individual. He understood why Heidegger held that existence can be apprehended only through the analysis and description of being (*Dasein*, 'being there') and confronted death as the limit of possibility. He was predisposed to Buber's philosophy of dialogue as formulated in *Ich und Du* (1923) which contrasts the reciprocal I/Thou relationship between subject and subject with the I/It attitude of subject to object; and maintains that God, as the eternal Thou, is the sole subject that wholly absorbs the individual. In *The Kind of Poetry I Want* Kierkegaard and Buber (oddly, since Buber lived until 1965) are linked with Dostoevsky as 'the greatest spirits/Of the nineteenth century' (618). A passage on Heidegger shows MacDiarmid simply reproducing the French commentary from the *Revue Philosophique*:

> Comme la Zeitlichkeit de Heidegger,
> La temporalité est une durée finie.
> La perfection mélodique tient essentiellement
> Au caractère fine de cette durée,
> Aux limites que celle-ci impose à l'art musical
> Et dont il faut
> Qu'il triomphe en les transcendant.   (622)

MacDiarmid was no respecter of the notion of other authors' private property in literature; whatever appeared in print was in the public domain, a body of literature that could be cannibalised by the omnivorous poet. The notion of copyright was a legal distraction that had little interest for him. (He was careless with his own copyright and one inebriated night in Newcastle, in his later years, signed over the rights of a Scots lyric to a group of students who, sensibly, declined the gift.)

The regurgitant aspect of MacDiarmid's epic became more apparent in later years when he was wont to add to the poem passages he came across in the course of his reading. Before the publication of *In Memoriam James Joyce* in 1955, for example, he added a long section on Karl Kraus, beginning 'And, above all, Karl Kraus' (767). This, in fact, was lifted from an anonymous article on Kraus which appeared on the front page of the *Times Literary Supplement* of 8 May 1953. MacDiarmid was reprimanded (in the *TLS* of 6 May 1965) for apparently appropriating this passage which, it transpired, had been written by Erich Heller. In the fourth edition of his *The Disinherited Mind* (1975) Heller pointed out that MacDiarmid's Kraus passage 'consists of 157 lines of which 149 are taken from my essay – with their essential identity preserved – even though they suffered a little breakage in the process of being lifted up into the poetic mode'.[53] Another passage from *In Memoriam James Joyce*, beginning 'Come, follow me into the realm of music' (871), comprises a quotation from the composer Ferruccio Busoni.[54] In footnotes Mac-Diarmid briefly acknowledges the *TLS* and Busoni; however, unless the reader had the original sources to hand, there would be no way of knowing the extent of MacDiarmid's borrowing.

Concerned with the 'painful and ecstatic awareness/Of language as the central mystery/Of the intellectual life' (763) the whole *Cornish Heroic Song* was to be the result of one man's omnivorous reading. MacDiarmid thought nothing of 'integrating' into his text material from books or newspapers. Thus 'When the Birds Come Back to Rhiannon' (part of *Impavidi Progrediamur*) is lifted from Angus Robertson's *Children of the Fore-World* (1933); a seven-line passage beginning 'Till above every line we might imagine' (1019), from *The Kind of Poetry I Want*, is an unattri-buted quotation from F. R. Leavis's *Revaluation* (1936); the verse-para-graph about the human foetus, beginning 'Even so long before the foetus' (887) in *In Memoriam James Joyce*, is from Sir Charles Sherrington's *Man on his Nature* (1940); a six-line passage, beginning 'When a Chinese calligrapher' (765), again from *In Memoriam James Joyce*, is verbatim from a review by Hugh Gordon Porteus. These are only a few examples.

No longer able to rely entirely on the inspirational urge that sustained him through the lyrics and *A Drunk Man* (a poem with many quotations and allusions) MacDiarmid came to value quantity at least as much as quality. He was forever advocating the intrinsic merits of the long poem, sure that length was poetic proof of artistic integrity. When he was possessed by his creative gift he continued to write passages of intel-lectual power and linguistic purity. When he was unable to rise to the artistic occasion he relied on material plundered from his reading. At the time of his discovery of the potential of Scots, he wrote easily and rapidly and later decided that such inspirational work was too easy. He claimed that 'consummate learning is far more rare/Than genius' (753) and thought that booklore was synonymous with scholarship. If this meant borrowing the words of others without acknowledgement, then so be it; MacDiarmid had never set much store on conventional morality. As a schoolboy he had lifted books from a favourite teacher; as a self-styled scholarly poet he lifted bits of books from his favourite writers. If he was guilty of theft in both instances, then MacDiarmid was unrepentant.

A modernist who admired the compositional methods of Eliot and Pound, MacDiarmid defended himself by quoting Eliot's axiom, 'Minor poets borrow, major poets steal'.[55] He saw no virtue in being untouched by other talents, no vice in reprocessing literary material. One section of *The Kind of Poetry I Want* indicates the positive and negative aspects of his anthological approach:

> A poetry not for those who do not love a gaping pig
> Or those made mad if they behold a cat
> And least, those who, when the bagpipe sings i' the nose,
> Cannot contain their urine.

> The poetry of one the Russians call 'a broad nature'
> And the Japanese call 'flower heart'
> And we, in Scottish Gaeldom, *'ionraic'*.
> The poetry of one who practises his art
> Not like a man who works that he may live
> But as one who is bent on doing nothing but work,
> Confident that he who lives does not work,
> That one must die to life in order to be
> Utterly a creator   (1021)

There are two types of indebtedness here. The first four lines are obviously allusive for MacDiarmid could have justifiably taken it for granted that the reader would recognise their source in *The Merchant of Venice*.[56] The following stanza incorporates, without acknowledgement, some fine phrases from Thomas Mann's story 'Tonio Kröger', published in an English translation of 1928:

> He worked, not like a man who works that he may live; but as one who is bent on doing nothing but work [knowing] that he who lives does not work; that one must die to life in order to be utterly a creator.[57]

Yet the charge of plagiarism was meaningless to MacDiarmid. The closest he came to excusing his practice was to indicate that he often noted down passages in notebooks then subsequently forgot the source and assumed the words were his own.[58]

For all its aberrations – no more than Pound's *Cantos* with their loose structure, their mass of quotations, their alternating lyrical and discursive sections – the open-ended epic is a work of dazzling intellectual energy and considerable emotional power. It is certainly one of the finest long poems of the twentieth century: more coherent than William Carlos Williams's *Paterson* (1946-58), more intelligent than Charles Olson's *Maximus* (1953-70), more accessible than Louis Zukofsky's *'A'* (1959-78), more pugnacious than Derek Walcott's *Another Life* (1973). It can stand comparison with the *Cantos* (1917-70) and though it lacks the grand design of Pablo Neruda's *Canto General* (1950) it has passionate qualities in common with the masterpiece of the Chilean poet. It is perhaps better appreciated alongside a Romantic than a modernist composition. Like Wordsworth's *The Prelude* it shows the growth of a poet's mind. It is a mind that moves among books with an infectious enthusiasm:

> This is the testament of a man who has had
> The supreme good luck ever since he was a lad
> To find in himself and foster a vast will
> To devote himself to Arts and Letters, and still
> (Constantly in 'devout prayer to that eternal Spirit
> Who can enrich with all utterance and knowledge')
> Is happily in middle age insatiable yet,
> An omnivorous reader and passionate lover
> Of every creative effort the whole world over   (1030)

It is also a mind that, albeit subjectively and solipsistically, advances an ideal for its readers:

> The spiritual evolution from vile humanity
> To authentic manhood and onward
> To participation in self-universal ...
> I do not agree that contempt of the simple-minded
> Is a limitation that is destructive
> Of any poise of the spirit.   (877)

Though that adamantly élitist notion may offend some, it is the essence of MacDiarmid. The *Cornish Heroic Song for Valda Trevlyn* reveals, in startling detail, the kind of poet he is.

Unable to find remunerative work as a journalist and exhausted by his efforts on the epic, MacDiarmid nevertheless spent the Christmas of 1937 pleasantly enough thanks to the generosity of Helen Cruickshank (who sent money as well as cake and shortbread) and an invitation to celebrate the festive season with the Bruces at Symbister House. By 11 January 1938 Valda was depressed over her husband's uphill struggle. In his epic MacDiarmid had written 'lack of money does not spell poverty of spirit' (820) but the financial strain was telling on the Grieves. They were living on credit from Jimmy Arthur's shop and there was little prospect of ready cash as MacDiarmid had still to deliver *The Golden Treasury, The Islands of Scotland, Scottish Doctors*, the autobiography (now placed provisionally with Gollancz) to the publishers who commissioned them. Valda wrote a candid letter to Helen Cruickshank on 11 January:

> I'm not in a cheerful mood & cannot pretend to be for I cannot help remembering how full of hope – of fighting spirit – of humanity – Christopher was when he came back from Gilgal – then how one thing after another happened – first the beastly court case – the Muirs' dastardly behaviour & the failure to get a publisher for Red Scotland – that was a crushing blow to Christopher – one damn thing after another – just when he was trying so hard – & really Helen although he looks quite fit – he's very far from strong physically (the least thing knocks him over – a night up & he's useless for a couple of days) & just a bundle of nerves – He's plenty of pot-boilers on hand – but is quite unfit to tackle them – we have a young boy coming up in about 10 days time – to take the typing & some of the other things of[f] Christopher's hands – I don't know how it will turn out I'm sure – but how thankful I'd be if it could only give him a break – a chance to clear his decks & then get on with poetry – after all it is the only thing that matters – these books he is doing & working so hard over – any other writer in Scotland could do them just as well – perhaps much better – & certainly much more easily – it's a damnable (sorry I keep on swearing) such a shame – that none of the Scottish papers won't give him an article – or book reviews – one a week would keep us going – & give him a chance to get on with the only thing that matters – to the long view. It's not Christopher's fault that he's not – this Helen I realise is our *last chance* – if we cannot pull through when Taylor comes up – it's the end – & I'll end the whole thing & us as well – rather than let Scotland break him & crow over it.[59]

That heartfelt letter clarifies the conditions in which MacDiarmid wrote the first part of his epic.

The 'young boy' was Henry Grant Taylor, twenty-four when he arrived in Whalsay in January 1938. He was born on 10 February 1914 on the estate of Culgruff (Crossmichael, Kirkcudbrightshire) where his father was head gardener. After attending Dumfries Academy, Taylor went on a bursary to read French and German at Edinburgh University where he first heard of MacDiarmid as a candidate in the Rectorial Elections of 1935 and 1936. He did not vote for the poet, having little taste for nationalist politics at the time. His main interest at university, outside his course, was athletics.

In his graduation year, 1936, Taylor became friendly with Robert Garioch Sutherland, later to make a name for himself as a Scots poet but at that time teaching at an Edinburgh school. Leaving university, Taylor returned to stay with his mother in the Kirkcudbrightshire village of Southwick. Apart from relief work as a rural postman he was unable to find a job so was responsive when he received a letter from Sutherland stating that MacDiarmid was in desperate need of secretarial assistance in Whalsay. Impulsively, and with the approval of his mother, Taylor decided to help the poet. When he arrived at Symbister harbour he was met by the poet who impressed him instantly and received him warmly. Taylor was given one of the two upstairs bedrooms in the poet's cottage, MacDiarmid, Valda and Michael using the other.

In return for typing for MacDiarmid, Taylor received no payment though he was happy to be treated virtually as a member of the family, eating when they ate and adjusting to their considerable intake of tea. Taylor worked rapidly on MacDiarmid's poetic manuscript, managing about forty words a minute on an old Smith-Corona machine. By 4 February MacDiarmid wrote to T. S. Eliot offering Faber the typescript of 'an important long poem – between 4000 and 5000 lines – entitled *Mature Art*'.[60] MacDiarmid took the opportunity to elaborate on the scope of what he regarded as the first portion of his *Cornish Heroic Song*:

I define it as a 'hapax legomenon of a poem – an exercise in schlabone, bordatini, and prolonged scordatura' and it is, I am very safe in saying, a very advanced example of 'learned poetry', much of it written in a multi-linguistic diction embracing not only many European but also Asiatic languages, and prolific in allusions and 'synthetic poetry', demanding for their complete comprehension an extremely detailed knowledge of numerous fields of world-literature. At the same time the logic of the whole is

371

clear, and most of the poem should be understood by almost anyone who reads while he runs – if he runs fast enough.[61]

Eliot replied, on 8 February, saying he was interested in the poem even if he found the title *Mature Art* forbidding.

Shortly after typing MacDiarmid's letter to Eliot, Taylor heard that his mother was seriously ill. She died of cancer in Dumfries and on 22 February he went south for the funeral. He was thankful to come back to a mass of work in Whalsay, *Mature Art* having grown in the interval. On 3 April Valda told Helen Cruickshank that 'Christopher is still wrestling with his huge poem – Mature Art – in between other stuff & wishes he had ten years to devote himself to it'.[62] There were other matters to discuss with Cruickshank. First, Valda was happier since she had acted, with David Orr and Taylor, in an amateur production of Chekhov's *The Bear* (on 25 March). On a more serious level, Valda was optimistic about the attempts of Cruickshank, Donald Carswell and the Blackwood brothers to persuade the Royal Literary Fund to make an award to MacDiarmid. In support of Cruickshank's plan, Valda provided details of her weekly bill, just under £5 for necessities (coal, oil, food) and sundries (stationery and black twist tobacco). MacDiarmid also wrote to Cruickshank explaining that, because of the delay in completing his four commissioned books, he had no income and was £75 in debt to local shops.

By 4 May MacDiarmid had sent to Eliot a 10,000-line typescript of *Mature Art* and Valda noticed how much the effort had taken out of him: 'I swear it's added twenty years to all of us – hysterics – sudden flaps – ravings – rescuing MSS from the flames and such like'.[63] Good news, however, came after the mid-May meeting of the RLF. MacDiarmid was awarded £125; a cheque for £75 was sent to him immediately and the remainder paid at the rate of £5 per month. Elated by the good news, MacDiarmid forged ahead. Part of *Scottish Doctors* had already been typed by an agency and Taylor quickly completed the typescript for Harrap. It seems the firm asked MacDiarmid to revise the book which, for various reasons, never appeared.[64]

Now that he could rely on a fast and enthusiastic typist, and had a temporary release from debt, MacDiarmid planned – with the backing of David Orr – to launch a new magazine which he first thought of calling the *Scottish Republic* before he settled on the *Voice of Scotland* (the title of the series *Red Scotland* should have enhanced). W. R. Aitken, then working as a librarian in Dunfermline, agreed to be business manager, and the quarterly was designed to provide a platform for 'Scottish Republicanism and the Leninist line in regard to Scotland of the late John Maclean, and the detailed analysis of Scottish issues in the light of dialectical materialism'.[65] Meanwhile, MacDiarmid was waiting for word from Eliot on *Mature Art*.

Eliot gave his verdict on 8 June. He thought the poem 'a very remarkable piece of work ... that ought to be published'.[66] Yet he was unable to persuade his colleagues at Faber to take the financial risk of publishing the book. Were MacDiarmid to approach another publisher, said Eliot, then he would gladly give the poem his personal support. At least the renewal of contact with Eliot had two positive results. Eliot accepted 'Cornish Heroic Song for Valda Trevlyn' for the *Criterion* and asked MacDiarmid to review Keith Henderson's *Burns — By Himself* for the journal. (Both items appeared in the final issue of the *Criterion*, January 1939, along with a letter from MacDiarmid on the restrictions of the urban mind.) MacDiarmid asked Eliot to forward *Mature Art* to Macmillan (who had published his *Selected Poems* in November 1934 and commissioned *The Golden Treasury of Scottish Poetry*) but they too turned it down.

The first issue of the *Voice of Scotland*, dated June-August 1938, printed 'The Red Scotland Thesis' and included poems by MacDiarmid ('The Glen of Silence', from the *Cornish Heroic Song*), J. F. Hendry, Soutar, Sorley MacLean and — reviving MacDiarmid's oldest pseudonym — A. K. Laidlaw, credited with writing 'Three Wars', a short poem condemning 'The War Makers, the War Profiteers' (1312). The following issue, for September-November, ran on much the same lines with poems by MacDiarmid ('A Golden Wine in the Gaidhealtachd'), Soutar and Hendry and book reviews by A. K. Laidlaw. The most controversial item in this issue was not verbal but visual: a caricature by 'B.N.' of the Muirs, showing Willa as a monstrous figure in a bathing-suit stroking the ear of a tiny lamb in the likeness of Edwin. Clearly based on Valda's memory of Willa holding forth on the beach at St Andrews in 1935, it also owed something to the verbal sketch of the Muirs in Wyndham Lewis's satirical masterpiece, *The Apes of God* (1930). In Lewis's book, Edwin is Keith of Ravelstone, a 'very earnest, rather melancholy freckled little being [who] fell in with that massive, elderly Scottish lady next to him — that is his wife. She opened her jaws and swallowed him comfortably.'[67]

'B.N.', the caricaturist, was Barbara Niven who had come, with her husband Ern Brooks, to spend the summer of 1938 with MacDiarmid. Then forty-two she was the daughter of Manchester's Medical Officer of Health and had studied mathematics at Cambridge and painting and sculpture at Manchester School of Art. Brooks, fifteen years younger than Niven, had also studied art in Manchester. The couple were committed Communists (Niven became the main fund-raising force for the *Daily Worker*, the Party newspaper) and were active in the Artists International Association, rallying support for the Spanish Republicans. In 1938, indeed, Niven arranged for Picasso's *Guernica* to go on exhibition in London and Manchester. She was a bright and vibrant woman and a skilful artist, influenced by the pictorial approach of Wyndham Lewis. She drew MacDiarmid in the Vorticist style.

It was Valda who came up with the idea of the caricature and asked Barbara to draw it. When she heard that Helen Cruickshank was appalled at the cruelty of the caricature, Valda was unrepentant. 'It's really extraordinarily funny to me', she wrote to Cruickshank, 'that Christopher cannot make a perfectly legitimate attack on anyone without its being branded as libellous and so forth.'[68] Valda had heard reliable reports of Willa's malicious gossip: how she was in the habit of denouncing MacDiarmid as a charlatan and how she told a company of people (including W. R. Aitken) that MacDiarmid had failed to complete *Red Scotland*, hence its non-appearance in the 'Voice of Scotland' series. MacDiarmid, too, wrote to Cruickshank, justifying the caricature:

> I'm not surprised to receive your clip on the lug re the Muir cartoon. I'd heard it had affected quite a number of people in the same way; I even had an official wigging about it from the Communist Party! ... [I feel] the real grievance against the cartoon is precisely the devastating and unanswerable truth of the essential point it makes – Willa's overpowering presence which has always been a nuisance to friends of Edwin's.[69]

As he made clear to Cruickshank, MacDiarmid was more than willing to make enemies. Certainly there was considerable resentment in the Communist Party over the Scottish Workers' Republicanism he was pursuing in the *Voice of Scotland* and the Muir caricature gave the Scottish District Committee an opportunity to categorise him as a wildly unscientific socialist.

Glad to be, once again, involved with a journal, MacDiarmid was pleased by the impact of the *Voice of Scotland*. Gradually his health was improving and, as he told his brother Andrew on 23 October, he was 'about twice as heavy (i.e. fat) now as I've ever been before and have a full, curly but rather greyish beard to boot! (not to my boots!)'.[70] His quarterly brought him into contact with other writers and lessened the feeling of isolation he experienced on Whalsay. For the third issue of the *Voice of Scotland* (Dec. 1938-Feb. 1939) he assembled a 'Celtic Front Number', printing work from Scotland ('Dìreadh I', for Helen Cruickshank, by himself and poems by others including J. F. Hendry and Ruthven Todd), Ireland (Donagh MacDonagh), Cornwall (Dorian Cooke) and Wales (Dylan Thomas with 'The tombstone told when she died'). He also inserted a provocative note on the Celtic contingent in the Spanish Civil War, claiming

> the Celtic members – Scottish, Irish, and Welsh – of the International Brigade found it impossible to work hand in hand with their English comrades and had to break away from them and join up in a body with the Americans instead.... It is obvious at all events that a similar breaking-away from the English must take place in other connections.[71]

This was too much for his opponents within the Communist Party and they began to move for another expulsion.

Poetically, MacDiarmid moved into action over the Spanish Civil War as a result of his hatred of Roy Campbell whose *Flowering Rifle*, a 5000-line poem in iambic couplets, was published on 6 February 1939 by Longman (after Faber rejected it). Campbell, the grandson of a Glaswegian who emigrated to South Africa, projected himself as the scourge of the Spanish Republicans though this was a piece of wishful thinking as he never fought for Franco; he visited Spain in 1936 and returned as a war correspondent. MacDiarmid rushed to reply to *Flowering Rifle* in a long poem, *The Battle Continues*, which excoriated his enemy:

> Campbell, they call him – 'crooked mouth', that is –
> But even Clan Campbell's records show no previous case
> Of such extreme distortion, of a mouth like this
> Slewed round to a man's bottom from his face
> And speaking with a voice not only banal.
>   But absolutely anal.
> Franco has made no more horrible shambles
> Than this poem of Campbell's,
> The foulest outrage his breed has to show
> Since the massacre of Glencoe!   (905)

Containing poignant as well as prosaic passages, and sustaining a relentlessly didactic tone, *The Battle Continues* is a minor MacDiarmid work but an effective rejoinder to Campbell. It would have been seen as such if it had been published at the time. However, the complete poem was not issued until 1957 which added to the irony of the opening phrase, 'Anti-Fascism is a bit out of date' (905).

Apart from his poetic contributions to the *Voice of Scotland* and his *Speaking for Scotland* (in a broadsheet series edited by Paul Potts) MacDiarmid was most visible during 1939 as a writer of prose. (Another aspect of 1939 was his unsuccessful attempt in applying for the post of Director of Glasgow Art Galleries and Museums, a job that went to T. J. Honeyman, who had been with the poet on the staff of the 42nd General Hospital in Salonika.) Published in June and dedicated to David Orr, *The Islands of Scotland* was no conventional travel book; the author's lack of interest in topography was shown by the paucity of references to Whalsay, the island he knew best. Like his recent poetry, *The Islands of Scotland* was the result of reading rather than direct observation and had the by now obligatory references to John Davidson and Charles Doughty, the Caledonian Antisyzygy and the Gaelic Idea, the artistic vigour of the Faroes compared to the cultural provincialism of Shetland. 'I have no patience', MacDiarmid wrote in his Author's Note, 'with the *olla podrida* of old wives' tales, day-trippers' ecstasies, trite moralisings, mawkish sentimentality, supernatural fancies, factual spinach, and outrageous banality which fills most books on this subject'.[72] Still, the poems MacDiarmid contributed to the book are of considerable interest as fragments from the *Cornish Heroic Song*. 'The Stone Called Saxagonus' denounces the fantasy of the Celtic Twilight; 'In the Shetland Islands' – the first stanza of which reappears in *In Memoriam James Joyce* (780) – praises 'The pleasure of my own company' (574); and 'Island Funeral', a descriptive poem, appeals to the 'Gaelic spirit' (582). The book is now remembered for the first publication of 'Perfect' printed in the text without attribution, but in fact lifted (apart from the first line) from a prose passage in Glyn Jones's *The Blue Bed and Other Stories* (1937). 'Perfect', years later, became the centrepiece of a literary *cause célèbre*.

Having typed *Mature Art* (which was still maturing), part of *Scottish Doctors* and *The Islands of Scotland*, Taylor was now busy typing *The Golden Treasury of Scottish Poetry* (though MacDiarmid prepared some of the texts from cutouts) and translating whatever the poet wanted from the *Revue Philosophique*. The two men now had an office of sorts. For a rent of £2 12s a year, MacDiarmid obtained, from Bruce the laird, a two-room cottage at Hillhead, opposite Symbister House. There he retired with Taylor to work for long periods under pressure. Taylor was now seeing the girl he was later to marry – Mary Hughson, Michael Grieve's schoolteacher – and was glad the way things were going in Whalsay. When Ern Brooks and Barbara Niven revisited Whalsay in the summer of 1939 she decorated the poet's office with murals of Cencrastus the Curly Snake and a Cavorting Cow, developed from a doodle by Michael. MacDiarmid put up photographs of writers such as Pound, Eliot, Joyce and the Turkish poet Nazim Khikmet and displayed, as a motto, a quotation from Marcus Aurelius: 'How all things upon Earth are pesle mesle; and how miraculously things contrary one to another, concurre to the beautie and perfection of the Universe.'[73]

This tranquil period ended on 3 September 1939 when Britain and France declared war on Germany. Taylor, a member of the Peace Pledge Union, registered immediately as a conscientious objector. The word spread and there were even rumours that MacDiarmid was a spy; since Germany and Russia had signed a non-aggression pact the Communist poet was investigated by one Captain Hay. Ironically, MacDiarmid was no longer a member of the Communist Party. He had been expelled, at last, for his personal attacks on others, for championing Scottish Workers' Republicanism and for his statement on the Scottish hostility to the English members of the International Brigade. In the *Voice of Scotland* for June-August, MacDiarmid made a personal issue of his expulsion. He noted 'the fact that the Scottish District Committee of the C.P. expelled Hugh MacDiarmid for daring to criticise and caricature Edwin Muir'.[74] With a world war on, MacDiarmid had to cease publication of the *Voice of Scotland* after that issue.

During September, MacDiarmid became a champion of a local cause, speaking on behalf of fifteen Whalsay cottars who had been served with increased valuations on their houses, a decision that would affect their rates. Both MacDiarmid and Taylor spoke against the new assessments at a meeting in Symbister Hall where the poet pointed out that the new valuation of £4 on £1 houses represented an increase of 300 per cent. Thomas Johnston, the County Assessor, was furious and declared that MacDiarmid was a misguided individual. Defiantly the poet attempted to enlist the legal services of Sir Alexander MacEwen (one of the stalwarts of the Scottish National Party and unsympathetic to MacDiarmid's political extremism); unfortunately, MacEwen was not able to come at short notice and the appeals were dismissed. MacDiarmid denounced the County Assessor in a letter to the *Shetland Times* (16 Sept.), calling Johnston one of 'the yes-men of the County Council' and insisting on his own right to speak for the cottars 'since the Shetland workers are for the most part entirely unorganized and have scarcely begun to awaken to class-consciousness and Dialectical Materialism'.[75]

Earlier in the year Taylor had been to Paris to see Jack Kahane of the Obelisk Press who had agreed to publish *Mature Art*, now expanded from the text Eliot had seen. Kahane had died in the autumn but his son wanted to go ahead with the book. On 18 December, MacDiarmid sent out prospectuses for *Mature Art*:

> It is an enormous poem of over 20,000 lines, dealing with the interrelated themes of the evolution of world literature and world consciousness, the problems of linguistics, the place and potentialities of the Gaelic genius, from its origin in Georgia to its modern expressions in Scotland, Ireland, Wales, Cornwall, Galicia and the Pays Basque, the synthesis of East and West, and the future of civilisation.
>
> It is a very learned poem involving a stupendous range of reference, especially to Gaelic, Russian, Italian and Indian literatures, German literature and philosophy, and modern physics and the physiology of the brain, and while mainly in English, utilises elements of over a score of languages, Oriental and Occidental.[76]

After quoting Eliot's opinion of the work, MacDiarmid asked subscribers to reserve copies of the book at two guineas a time.

The Golden Treasury of Scottish Poetry came out in December, dedicated (like *A Drunk Man Looks at the Thistle*) to F. G. Scott. It is an ambitious anthology, presenting not only Scottish classics (ballads, Barbour, the Scots makars, Fergusson, Burns and so on) but translations (by the editor with the help of G. E. Davie) from the Latin of George Buchanan and Arthur Johnstone; and translations (by the editor with the help of Sorley MacLean) from the Gaelic of Iain Lom, Alexander MacDonald, Duncan Ban MacIntyre, William Ross, William Livingston and MacDiarmid's friend Donald Sinclair (who had died in 1932). Contemporary poets included Soutar, Cruickshank, Albert Mackie and MacDiarmid himself (with five poems) and there was an apology for the omission of young poets such as Norman MacCaig (later one of MacDiarmid's closest friends). Edwin Muir was not only conspicuous by his exclusion but was the subject of yet another attack in an introduction which asserted the superiority of Scots over English and the supremacy of Gaelic. F. G. Scott thought MacDiarmid had made a serious mistake by 'carrying into the introd. a personal feud'.[77] Still, the anthology was well received in the *Times Literary Supplement* and elsewhere.[78]

By the end of December MacDiarmid felt he had completed his

autobiography to his own satisfaction. Much of the manuscript had been typed not by Taylor in Whalsay but by Tom MacDonald in Edinburgh. Estimates of the length of the original work, as sent by MacDiarmid to his London agent Gilbert White vary; at different times MacDiarmid mentioned that it amounted to 200,000 words, 500,000 words and 'over half a million words' whereas Valda thought it nearer one million words and that the effort of writing it longhand had made its author shrink physically.[79] Even allowing for exaggeration, the autobiography was too bulky for publication during a war that imposed paper shortage and censorship on publishers. Gollancz could not handle such a big book and Methuen agreed to issue it only in instalments, a volume at a time: *Lucky Poet, A Poet and His Friends, Lament for the Children* and (excepting those parts dealing exclusively with the subject) *Scottish Politics, 1707-1940*. MacDiarmid hoped that *Lucky Poet* would come out the following year.

In January 1940 MacDiarmid heard that Donald Carswell had been killed in a car accident when leaving in the darkness for his job in the Home Office. On 5 February he wrote to Andrew Grieve after hearing of the death of his wife Chryssie, following a short illness. It was a devastating blow to Andrew who was then living in Woking, Surrey, having been promoted by the Inland Revenue. He was transferred to Glasgow where he stayed in furnished rooms with his son Angus and daughter Morag until he settled in Cambuslang, near Glasgow. The house was soon to provide the setting for a scene that would finally break relations between MacDiarmid and his brother.

On 14 June the Germans entered Paris, and in consequence the Obelisk Press were unable to publish *Mature Art*. MacDiarmid then submitted the work to Methuen and the Hogarth Press but both firms turned it down. Life was beginning to grow grimmer for MacDiarmid and Valda (whose mother had recently died in Cornwall). As for Taylor, he was summoned that summer to a tribunal in Aberdeen where his case, as a conscientious objector, was turned down. An Appeals Tribunal in Edinburgh confirmed the Aberdeen decision and Taylor drifted out of MacDiarmid's life to face imprisonment in Dumfries and military service overseas.[80]

Unsure how the war would affect him, MacDiarmid asked Andrew if he could get him a temporary clerkship with the Civil Service in Glasgow as the war had created so many vacancies. Andrew was unable to help and, inexorably, the poet was claimed by the War Reserve. Too old, at forty-nine, for active service MacDiarmid was nevertheless considered to be fit enough to work as a labourer on the roads. Hearing of this plan, Helen Cruickshank used her influence in the Civil Service to secure MacDiarmid a job that would, it was hoped, be less physically demanding. After a period of training in Glasgow, he was to work in a munitions factory. On 9 January 1942 MacDiarmid complained to Soutar of being 'caught in a curious eddy of the industrial conscription'.[81] With Valda and Michael waving him off, MacDiarmid left Whalsay for the last time (still somewhat in debt to Jimmy Arthur) on 13 January. He arrived in Aberdeen the next day then travelled south to report for duty in Glasgow.

15

Returning to Glasgow

> Returning to Glasgow after long exile
> Nothing seemed to me to have changed its style.
> Buses and trams all labelled 'To Ibrox'
> Swung past packed tight as they'd hold with folks.
>   'Glasgow, 1960'   (1040)

DRAWN unwillingly into the Second World War as a result of the industrial conscription scheme of Herbert Morrison, the Home Secretary, MacDiarmid felt, for all his reservations about Shetland, that Glasgow was a poor exchange for Whalsay. He had always abhorred big cities – on the biblical grounds that 'Cain, the murderer, was also the first city-builder'[1] – and wartime Glasgow had its deadly aspects. At first, MacDiarmid thought of staying with F. G. Scott in Jordanhill but accepted his brother's invitation to stay at his home: Benachie, 70 Grenville Drive, Cambuslang, a town some five miles south-east of Glasgow. Andrew was now a widower, doing staffing investigation work for the Inland Revenue in Glasgow, which meant he was away from home for several days at a time. His son Angus was with the Merchant Navy, though occasionally home on leave. Morag, Andrew's daughter, then nineteen, was a lively intelligent woman, interested in literature and psychology. She enjoyed the work of Eliot, read Freud with fascination.

Though she was aware that, as Hugh MacDiarmid, her Uncle Chris was a controversial and famous figure in Scottish life, she felt no awe in his presence. She had been aware of the strained relationship between her father and uncle for some time. In March 1936 Andrew and his family had come home to their house in Liberton to a note, written on toilet paper, from the poet: he had found the bathroom window open, had admitted himself to the house, and had been and gone. Morag had heard her father complain bitterly that Uncle Chris had not come to see his mother when she was dying, a situation redolent of the memory of the old woman constantly asking for her favourite son.

In 1942 Morag found herself in the role of her father's brother's keeper. She made his meals, washed his clothes and when – after his initial period of training in precision engineering at Thorniebank Training College – he worked night shifts at the Mond Nickel factory, she made sure there was food available for him. In his few periods of spare time, MacDiarmid enjoyed the company of Morag. She recalled:

> We got on extremely well. I can remember being amazed when he used to help me wash up, and peg out the laundry. My father never did such things, nor any of the other husbands and fathers I had encountered! We went to the pictures together – saw *Citizen Kane*, I recall – and he took me to Glasgow University to hear T. S. Eliot give a talk. ... He addressed meetings in Glasgow, and various people would telephone with messages for him and sometimes make the journey out to Cambuslang to see him.[2]

Andrew was not happy about the use of his home as a political and cultural fixture; and not amused by his brother's references to him being bourgeois.

The poet left Cambuslang following a fearful row with his brother. After attending a political rally, MacDiarmid came back to Cambuslang, obviously drunk. He suggested to Angus, then home on leave, that he should consider seditious actions against the military authorities. Andrew exploded in anger, telling his brother he would not tolerate such talk. Insults were traded, Andrew denouncing Christopher as a megalomaniac. 'I', MacDiarmid replied, 'shall be famous long after you're dead and forgotten.'[3] He was ordered out of the house. Staggering into the street, he managed to get a taxi to take him to F. G. Scott's home in Jordanhill. After this scene which occurred about the middle of July, MacDiarmid never saw his brother again.[4]

382

Arranging to come on a day when Andrew was away, the poet returned to Cambuslang, one week after his fraternal eviction, to collect his books and papers. However, as letters continued to arrive at Cambuslang, sometimes confusingly addressed to 'Mr Grieve' who could be either brother, Andrew wrote to Christopher asking him to inform the postal authorities of his new address. An acerbic exchange followed and then on 5 August MacDiarmid made a powerful epistolary attack on his brother. In response to Andrew's accusation that he was paranoid, MacDiarmid pointed out that there was no evidence for this in his medical history. Andrew commented in a note written (presumably in the heat of the moment on receiving it) at the top of MacDiarmid's letter:

> He *has* chronic monomania both in relation to persecution (one of the forms)
> & in relation to a sense of high importance (politically) in another. I didn't
> *say* it was due to his medical history but he himself told me in the Gilgal
> Home in Perth before [Dr Chambers] that his illness there was due to
> *Syphilis*. What about *that* History?[5]

Obviously, Andrew was beside himself with rage as his marginal annotations to this letter show.

To Andrew's astonishment MacDiarmid denied he had often borrowed sums of money, denied he had ever been drunk at Cambuslang, denied he had been ordered out of the house during a scene witnessed by Angus and Morag:

> So far am I, as I have always been, from wishing to make a convenience of
> you, my dear brother, that you will find it not only difficult, but impossible,
> to reconcile any such suggestion with the alacrity and finality with which
> I now cease to have any relations whatever with you. And in that connection
> I must point out (since I am keeping a copy of this letter too) that despite
> all my (according to you) heinous offences it was I who took umbrage and
> forthwith left your house – not (as you will probably say, and no doubt
> probably already believe yourself) you who in self-righteous wrath ordered
> me out of it. And I got here all right – a remarkable achievement for a
> drunk![6]

This little fraternal fracas did nothing for MacDiarmid's peace of mind.

By the time he moved into Scott's home, MacDiarmid had started work at Mechan's Engineering Company in Scotstoun, on Clydeside. Initially, he was required to do physically exhausting filing work in the gunshield department and his inability to discharge these duties made him the despair of his foreman who told Mechan's supervisor, 'this man's no bloody good to me, can I get him changed'.[7] Charles Nicoll, foreman of the Copper Shell-Band Section, agreed to take the poet in his charge. Now the work was a little easier. MacDiarmid turned the bands off copper cups and carried them into the machine shop. It was lighter work than filing and he was fortunate in finding a friend in his foreman. Charles Nicoll, a Glaswegian then aged thirty-six, was a skilled engineer, an amateur poet, an accomplished photographer and a member of the Scottish National Party.

MacDiarmid himself had settled some of his differences with the SNP. In May Douglas Young, who was to go to prison for refusing to take his medical examination for the Armed Forces, had been elected Chairman of the SNP by a small minority. Several members, including John MacCormick, resigned as they regarded Young as a nationalist in the MacDiarmid mould (Young's volumes of Scots verse certainly established him as a poetic disciple of MacDiarmid). After meeting Young, MacDiarmid began to associate with men such as Dr Robert McIntyre, Secretary of the SNP (and later the first Scottish Nationalist MP, after the Motherwell by-election of 1945); and Robert Blair Wilkie, a member of the SNP National Council, and subsequently editor of the *Scots Independent*, the Party newspaper. Wilkie was astonished that a man of MacDiarmid's intellectual calibre should be working on Clydeside:

> The insanity of the London Government's anti-cultural bias was manifested in the flesh by his appearance and his predicament. Here was a highly educated and cultured individual uprooted, utterly weary and insanely harassed, consigned to a labouring job to which he was ill-suited.... It was obviously an act of reprisal against a notorious and emphatic dissident. ... He was so utterly weary and dejected, and yet, in this plight, there was an underlying steely acceptance of Life which spoke of a most courageous and resourceful man.[8]

On 22 August, MacDiarmid went with McIntyre to Elderslie, Renfrewshire, for the Wallace Day Rally then returned to his routine at Mechan's.

According to Nicoll, MacDiarmid did not mix with the workers outside the Copper Shell-Band Section. There was no canteen so the men brought food in with them and boiled their tea on a fire in the yard. Nicoll, who took several photographs of the poet, was amused by his friend's appearance:

> Chris used to wear a great big Kilmarnock bonnet. Now Chris was very
> fond of his head of hair but when he was going up and down the yard like
> this he looked like a very small man under a great big bonnet.[9]

MacDiarmid visited Nicoll at his home at the foot of Shakespeare Street,
Maryhill, and planned to form a cultural association in Glasgow. The
plans came to nothing as MacDiarmid's activities were curtailed, for a
while, when he sustained serious injuries at Mechan's at the end of
August. Nicoll remembered that a heavy copper plate fell onto Mac-
Diarmid's foot and 'could have cut the foot off altogether'.[10] MacDiarmid
described the accident in a letter to Douglas Young; 'I had a very serious
accident at work – pulled a pile of copper plate down on myself and
disabled both legs and one of my arms. I was extremely lucky not to be
killed.'[11] He recuperated at 2 Park Terrace, the Glasgow home of Robin
Black, who had relaunched the *Free Man*.

Characteristically, MacDiarmid was ready to return to work after a
few weeks. He hobbled about Mechan's with the help of walking sticks
and with a limp in his left leg. Anticipating the arrival from Shetland of
Valda and Michael, MacDiarmid found rented accommodation with a
Mrs Donnelly at 35 Havelock Street, Partick, and in December his
wife and son arrived, bringing with them forty tea-chests packed with
manuscripts and books. Then aged ten, Michael was sent to Kilquhanity,
a progressive co-education boarding school run by John and Morag
Aitkenhead. Valda got a job in the book department of Lyons' store, on
the corner of Sauchiehall Street and Elmbank Street. As for MacDiarmid,
he was working from 8 a.m. to 5.30 daily and doing compulsory overtime
three Sundays out of four. Despite the nature of the job he felt 'in
excellent form and none the worse of my adventure into practical
proletarianism'.[12]

Lucky Poet, published by Methuen in September 1943, briefly mentioned
MacDiarmid's work 'doing hard manual labour in big Clydeside engineering shops'[13] but, as it had been completed some time before, concentrated on his creative life. Just as *The Islands of Scotland* was no
conventional travel book, so *Lucky Poet* is no ordinary autobiography.
Grandiosely subtitled 'A Self-Study in Literature and Political Ideas' it
offers little confessional material and less intimacy though it is 'the story
of an absolutist whose absolutes came to grief in his private life'.[14] Of
course, MacDiarmid's original typescript had been reduced to *Lucky Poet*
which was supposed to be the first of several volumes, leading on to *A*

Poet and His Friends (on Yeats, Orage, Douglas, Cunninghame Graham, Compton Mackenzie, John Buchan and others), *Lament for the Children* (about his divorce, two marriages and children by Peggy and Valda) and *Scottish Politics, 1707-1940*. As it stands, *Lucky Poet* is a prolonged and lively advertisement for the poet himself. A belligerent book that pulls no punches, *Lucky Poet* is MacDiarmid's finest prose work.

A large part of the book consists of polemic. 'My function in Scotland during the past twenty to thirty years', says MacDiarmid, 'has been that of the cat-fish that vitalizes the other torpid denizens of the aquarium.'[15] Or, moving from metaphor to simile, his duty is 'to keep up perpetually a sort of Berserker rage, or *riastral*, in the way of the old heroes'.[16] MacDiarmid has no timidity, advancing his ideas with the indignation of a man who has, he says, been sentenced to virtual death by the capitalist system. He is a man made for Communism, an admirer of Lenin, John Maclean and Stalin, though:

> I would like, say, Stalin a great deal better if ... he spent his long nights in drunken orgies with his boon companions, his 'Desperadoes', and his women – night after night – and yet carrying on his immense work, relentless as steel ... I totally lack – and detest – the Puritanism that goes with most so-called Communism or Socialism.[17]

Apart from his literary and political heroes MacDiarmid has 'no love of humanity', identifying not with other people but only with 'the higher brain-centres, the human mind'.[18] Regarding the moneyed classes as subhuman, he has 'no use for anything between genius and the working man'.[19] He answers proletarian diffidence with élitist arrogance, reconciling his intellectualism and his Communism with a belief that every individual should, like himself, aspire to genius and thus create a new social order of excellence. This levelling-up is a practical possibility for a poet possessed by an evolutionary ideal:

> I believe ... that scientific development and a better social order can tap genius in every human being and create a society in which men like the greatest philosophers, poets, and scientists in human history will no longer be, as they have always been hitherto, very rare exceptions, but the rule – most men will be of a stature like that of Plato or Homer or Shakespeare.[20]

From his own genius (and that fact is taken for granted throughout his book) MacDiarmid has derived no comfort, no security, no tranquillity.

Instead he has been subjected to 'eye-popping hatred from all sorts of vibrantly commonplace people'.[21]

Thus MacDiarmid presents himself as a poet in a beleaguered position, a man living a desperate struggle with no wish for simple human relationships since these would reduce him to intellectual infantilism. He is a loner, an outcast, a man regarded as a public enemy because he is too spiritual for a degenerate Scotland: a 'sort of Ishmael'.[22] Although in love with his eternal idea of Scotland, he detests the reality of contemporary Scotland. So he proclaims his faith in 'the shining vision of Alba'[23] and describes the beauty of the country, especially the landscape around Langholm. Yet he hates cities and the brutally ignorant Scots who stay in them. MacDiarmid, the quintessential Scot, becomes a new hammer of the Scots: 'Modern Scotland is a disease in which almost everything has turned into mud'[24]; and, again, 'Scotland is simply a big Inebriates' Home, the deadly tipple responsible being the English Idea.'[25]

Constantly the book turns viciously on MacDiarmid's enemies, real and imagined. Edwin Muir, regardless of his qualities as a poet and critic, is top of the hate-list, 'a leader of the white-mouse faction of the Anglo-Scottish *literati* and a paladin in mental fight with the presence of a Larry the Lamb'.[26] Old enemies such as Harry Lauder, Lauchlan Maclean Watt and Sir Alexander MacEwen are dealt with in passing. A coruscating passage of invective condemns

> the whole gang of high mucky-mucks, famous fatheads, old wives of both sexes, stuffed shirts, hollow men with headpieces stuffed with straw, bird-wits, lookers-under-beds, trained seals, creeping Jesuses, Scots who Ha'evers, village idiots, policemen, leaders of white-mouse factions and noted connoisseurs of bread and butter, glorified gangsters, and what 'Billy' Phelps called Medlar Novelists (the medlar being a fruit that becomes rotten before it is ripe), Commercial Calvinists, makers of 'noises like a turnip', and all the touts and toadies and lickspittles of the English Ascendancy, and their infernal women-folk, and all their skunkoil skulduggery.[27]

Less admirably T. S. Cairncross, MacDiarmid's Langholm mentor, is dismissed as a hypocritical careerist, a charge that not only hurt Cairncross but horrified MacDiarmid's cousin Bob and his wife Alice, Cairncross's sister-in-law. Langholm never forgave MacDiarmid for his treatment of the town and townspeople in *Lucky Poet*. For he told (to them) embarrassing tales out of school; how one teacher got another pregnant, how two twelve-year-old pupils gave a demonstration of sexual intercourse on top of a desk.

Yet Langholm is identified as the inspiration of MacDiarmid's art. Acknowledging that the epithet 'lucky' covers both good and bad luck, he says 'My first bit of luck was ... to be born in the wonderful little Border burgh of Langholm'.[28] Langholm, with its public library, is the reason for his omnivorous reading. Langholm, with its three rivers, is the source of his appreciation of light and colour. Langholm, with its lush surrounding landscape, is another Eden. Langholm, with its eccentric characters, is a constant presence. In Langholm, too, he absorbed the oral rhythms of Scots. Claiming that he could have written his autobiography in Scots as easily as in English MacDiarmid declares that English is not his native language and that 'it is only in the Scots language I can achieve ... "the terrible crystal".'[29]

Language itself is a recurrent topic in the book. MacDiarmid's use of Scots is justified and he rejoices that Scots and Gaelic are the roots of the national culture. Scots is to be extended, Gaelic to be recovered, English is to be left to the English – apart from Synthetic English which is a poetic law unto itself. Language, the book explains, is fundamental to MacDiarmid since he is a kinsman of the linguists Alexander Murray and Lindley Murray. Therefore, 'so far from being mere affectation, one of my main prepossessions as a writer – my concern with linguistics – is hereditary'.[30]

A creative confrontation with language is the essence of poetry, according to MacDiarmid. In the beginning is the word, technique being a secondary matter since the creation of poems 'is very like diamond-polishing'.[31] A poet is a man inspired, in this case by the Scottish Muse, Audh (meaning 'the deep-minded'). MacDiarmid's poetic destiny is to honour Audh:

> To serve Scotland – to develop an Audhology comparable in spiritual reach and intellectual elaboration to the Sophiology that has been developed elsewhere; and, first and foremost all the time, to write (alternately, and happily now and again – and perhaps, with increasing frequency, simultaneously) a poetry of strange architecture ...[32]

He embraces Audh in his poems and his examination of the Caledonian Antisyzygy, the Gaelic Idea, the East-West Synthesis and the Celtic Union of Soviet Republics.

A bewildering variety of beliefs inform the book. Not only does MacDiarmid describe himself as a Communist and a Nationalist but he contends that 'Communism is a stage on the way to Anarchism'[33] and that his nationalism requires him 'to be a Republican, with an utter hatred of all Royalty, and in particular our present Royal Family'.[34] Though he endorses Hume's sceptical attitude to religion he has known all the great mystical experiences and regards himself as 'an Advaitin, holding Sankara's Vedanta philosophy'.[35] He follows Kant and Bergson in perceiving the external world subjectively but also accepts the universal objectivism of Einstein. He is a student of the Scholasticism of Duns Scotus but also of the non-Aristotelian biology of C. M. Child. Like Shestov he is an irrationalist, like Alfred Korzybski a scientific determinist, like Major Douglas an advocate of Social Credit, like Lenin a believer in revolution. If these ideas clash, they thereby contribute to 'the seeming paradoxes of my work'.[36] Everything is reconciled in the imagination of the poet. MacDiarmid's anthological approach allows him to move easily from opinion and anecdote to long quotations from his own verse, principally passages from the *Cornish Heroic Song*.

At the beginning of the book he reflects bitterly on the life he led in Shetland where he heard 'nothing but the inane phrases of women'[37] and, in a postscript to his Author's Note, commends the company of the 'barbarous and illiterate lower classes of workers'[38] he has known through his Clydeside experiences. When he speaks in his own voice, he produces superlative examples of invective; when he quotes (at large and at length) it is usually to the point. Appropriately, the book ends with a quotation. MacDiarmid says he would choose for a motto on his tombstone the words of Mr Justice Mugge: 'A disgrace to the community.'[39]

Lucky Poet was designed to unsettle its readers. It delighted those who already admired MacDiarmid, confirmed the worst suspicions of those who resented his arrogance and élitism, and won him many new followers. Edgell Rickword, the left-wing poet, objected to a passage describing him as a former member of the Black-and-Tans and the book was temporarily withheld from sale until MacDiarmid made a diplomatic substitution.[40] The best review of the book was by Sylvia Townsend Warner, author of the supernatural novel *Lolly Willowes* (1926) and (since 1935) a member of the Communist Party that had expelled MacDiarmid. Writing in *Our Time* she saw *Lucky Poet* as a magnificent if confused self-portrait of the artist as a man divided:

> *Lucky Poet* is a more complicated affair [than Berlioz's *Mémoires* and Stendhal's *Henri Brulard*], a flaw runs through the crystal, for this is a self-study of a compound personality, a long conversation during which Hugh MacDiarmid and C. M. Grieve explain themselves to each other, both

bringing a profusion of learning, experience, and versatility to the common task, and going at it hammer and tongs. The result makes difficult reading, rather as though the pages of two encyclopaedias were being turned by a sixty-mile gale; but the confusion is a relevant confusion, since both authors are Scottish nationalists; and how, without a little confusion, could there be an adequate treatment of the nationalism of a nation possessing two languages, two cultures, and a considerable tradition of being two nations?[41]

MacDiarmid had made his marks on the minds he most valued.

In the middle of October 1943 the author of *Lucky Poet* went to Perth for the funeral of Soutar, who died on 15 October. Soon after this he had to look for a new address in Glasgow after an argument between Valda and Mrs Donnelly, the landlady at 35 Havelock Street. Valda owned a bitch and Mrs Donnelly was annoyed when it was on heat. 'It's quite natural,' Valda told her, 'or did you and Mr Donnelly have a child by miraculous conception?'[42] For that the Grieves were asked to leave and, while looking for another place to stay, lived for a bit at the Argyle Street office of Robin Black. They moved into 27 Arundel Drive, Battlefield, Glasgow, at the end of 1943 and from that address MacDiarmid corresponded with Nancy Cunard who requested a poem for her anthology *Poems for France*. MacDiarmid obliged with 'The Fall of France' which appeared in the anthology in 1944, as a portion of a long, unpublished poem; in fact, *Cornish Heroic Song*.

By March 1944 the poet was weary of physical work, telling Nancy Cunard:

I have literally no time to myself at all these days – working seven days a week from 7 a.m. to 6.30 p.m., and two nights to 9.30 and when I say working I mean it – real hard physical toil. So I have no time for anything at all save work, eat, and sleep. I'm not complaining – only explaining, why I can't keep track of things properly, reply in reasonable time to letters, etc. And of course one of these things I simply can't do is to keep abreast of reading. So I miss all sorts of things; and missed alas! Miss Warner's review of *Lucky Poet* in *Our Time*. Many thanks for telling me about it.[43]

It was the mind-numbing strain of his working conditions that led MacDiarmid to request a transfer to the Merchant Service. According to Robert Blair Wilkie, Dr Robert McIntyre used his influence to secure MacDiarmid a job as Postal Officer to the Allied fleets in Greenock, 'whence each morning he set out in a boat with the mail for the Free French, Canadian, Norwegian, Polish, British and American ships in the Allies' busiest port in Britain'.[44] The poet told a different story:

I became first a deck-hand – and then first engineer – on a Norwegian vessel, MFV *Gurli*, chartered by the British Admiralty and engaged in servicing vessels of the British and American Navies in the waters of the Clyde Estuary. The other members of the crew were all Norwegians. They were excellent ship-mates, and I soon became an expert at making lobscouse, jam soup, and other specialities, doing the local purchasing, and helping with any necessary secretarial work. With Anders Olsen as skipper and later Arvid Carllson, I had a splendid time – all the more so since we were based on Greenock and the Albert Harbour there held the biggest small boat pool in Great Britain, with French, Belgian, Dutch, Scandinavian and other vessels. Greenock was as a consequence highly internationalised then and each of its public houses a veritable Babel. My wife was in Glasgow, but as I received 'seamen's rations' (which were several times as much as ordinary civilian rations) and she got these, since I ate on board ship, we managed well enough.[45]

He was certainly in a more fortunate position in Greenock than that of the few Scottish poets he admired, especially two Gaelic poets. George Campbell Hay, whose essay on 'Gaelic and Literary Form' had appeared in the last issue of the *Voice of Scotland*, had been imprisoned in Edinburgh then sent to North Africa as a soldier, an experience that permanently affected his mental health. Sorley MacLean had been seriously injured, in both feet, at the Battle of El Alamein and had been hospitalised in England before returning to Scotland to resume teaching at Boroughmuir School in Edinburgh. MacLean's book *Dàin do Eimhir agus Dàin Eile* had appeared in November 1943 and in 1944 he arranged a meeting with MacDiarmid:

MacDiarmid's lyrics [had] made me despair of any poetry that either I or anyone else could produce [so in 1944] Christopher and I argued through most of the night and early hours in the morning about his lyrics, and I remember asking him who he thought he was or what did he think had been given to him when he hoped to write greater poetry than those lyrics. I think I wore him down.[46]

More likely, MacDiarmid was generally worn down by his war work.

By May 1944 MacDiarmid had completed his edition of Soutar's *Collected Poems*. His introduction placed Soutar as a courageous man and interesting minor poet who wrote his best work in Scots but was too infrequently inspired and too pedestrian in his use of rhythm. Unfortunately, MacDiarmid omitted all Soutar's extended poems (including 'The Auld Tree', dedicated to MacDiarmid) and some of his finest short poems with the result that when the edition was eventually published in 1948 it caused a literary scandal in Scotland.

No collections of recent poetry by MacDiarmid appeared in 1944 but he had become friendly with William Maclellan, a printer (of Hope Street, Glasgow) turned publisher. Maclellan brought out *Selected Poems of Hugh MacDiarmid*, in 1944, a thoughtful selection edited by R. Crombie Saunders from volumes from *Sangschaw* to *The Islands of Scotland*. Maclellan also published *Poetry Scotland*, a periodical anthology edited by Maurice Lindsay (a soldier when he supervised the first number in 1943) and this printed poems by MacDiarmid as well as by a new generation of Scottish poets, many of them admirers of MacDiarmid: Sydney Goodsir Smith, Douglas Young, Alexander Scott and Lindsay himself.

Young, one of the most vocal of MacDiarmid's followers, grouped the new generation of Scots poets together under the linguistic banner of Lallans, a term he preferred to MacDiarmid's Synthetic Scots. Burns had used the word Lallans (meaning Lowlands) in his epistle 'To William Simpson' so it had a good poetic pedigree.[47] MacDiarmid actively encouraged his followers and, in 1944, participated in a public reading with Young, Lindsay and George Bruce at Glasgow's Stevenson Hall. Lindsay later gave his impression of the evening:

> When it came to MacDiarmid's turn to perform he moved to the platform, opened his book, but remained silent. There was an embarrassed ripple among the audience. Douglas Young rose, looked over MacDiarmid's shoulder, removed the book from his hand, turned it the other way round and sat down again. As if nothing odd had happened MacDiarmid then began reading: like a needle being placed on the edge of a 78 rpm gramophone record. For all his praises of 'the golden wine of the ghaidealtachd', MacDiarmid had a poor head for drink. A couple of double whiskies was enough to blur the clarity of his speech. Someone had been detailed to make sure there was no 'strong drink taken' before MacDiarmid's turn to read came, but the poet had given his watchdog the slip.[48]

As with Sorley MacLean's anecdote, it is important to remember what the war had taken out of MacDiarmid in physical wear and tear.

Victory in Europe Day was celebrated on 8 May 1945 but the poet had little cause for celebration as he was now redundant and had to register as unemployed in Glasgow when he returned to Arundel Drive. For a controversial figure in his fifties there was little opportunity for remunerative work so MacDiarmid once again plunged himself into politics. At Douglas Young's invitation he had (in 1943) become a member of the SNP National Council and agreed to stand as a candidate for the Party at the General Election of 26 July. In the Labour landslide all eight SNP candidates lost (McIntyre being turned out of Parliament after six months' membership). In Kelvingrove, MacDiarmid lost his deposit, the result being: J. L. Williams (Lab) 12,273; Col. Walter Elliot (Con) 12,185; C. M. Grieve (SNP) 1314; Capt. C. J. Morgan (Lib) 919.

The Second World War ended officially with the surrender of Japan on 14 August 1945, three days after MacDiarmid's fifty-third birthday. The unemployed poet was still anxious to place some parts of his *Cornish Heroic Song* with a publisher; on 2 September, in the hope that the paper shortage had improved, he resubmitted *In Memoriam James Joyce* (that is, the title section of the sequence as published in 1955 with some revisions) to T. S. Eliot. Eliot replied on 4 February 1946:

> I have had your Joyce poem for a long time. I found my Board indisposed to take it on but I am afraid I have been hanging on to it and brooding over it by myself from time to time to try to think whether anything could be done. It is a magnificent tribute to language and even the least sympathetic critic could not deny that it is an astonishing piece of work. I don't believe that more than very few people would read it because I don't think that more than very few people have the right infatuation with language. But I still don't see what can be done and I at last reluctantly return it.[49]

MacDiarmid had to hold back his typescript for some time though he continued to release parts of the *Cornish Heroic Song* when he could, as in the two books he published in 1946. *Speaking for Scotland: Selected Poems*, the first American edition of his verse, was published in Baltimore with an introduction by Compton Mackenzie. It virtually comprises the *Selected Poems* of 1934 but adds the uncollected 'Two Memories', a fragment of the *Cornish Heroic Song*. *Poems of the East-West Synthesis* consists of three poems ('The Fingers of Baal Contract in the Communist Salute', 'Ceol Mor', 'Tristan and Iseult') from the same epic.

Though MacDiarmid had done relief work for the Post Office at Christmas and Valda moved from Lyons' book department to work for £2 a week as bookshop assistant in John Smith's in St Vincent Street, he was impecunious and unhappy at Arundel Drive. During 1946 he was delighted when offered an opportunity to move. The invitation came from Walter and Sadie Pritchard who offered the Grieves the basement below their splendid three-storey house at 32 Victoria Crescent

Road, Dowanhill. It was a pleasant part of Glasgow and there was an excellent bar, the Curlers, round the corner in Byres Road. MacDiarmid quickly became a local at the Curlers though Sadie wanted to make him the centrepiece of a cultural salon at her home.

Walter and Sadie Pritchard both taught art, he at Glasgow School of Art, she at Edinburgh College of Art: Walter painted a mural for the Curlers (it is still there) showing MacDiarmid and his friends in Jacobean costume. Sadie was the sister of Robert McLellan, one of Scotland's finest dramatists. For a time MacDiarmid thought McLellan's skilful use of Scots might form the basis of a Scottish National Drama. The Curtain Theatre (which put on a production of MacDiarmid's *Nisbet*, featuring Duncan Macrae in the title role) had achieved considerable success with McLellan's historical plays including *Jeddart Justice* (1933) and *Jamie the Saxt* (1937).

When, in November 1946, the correspondence columns of the *Glasgow Herald* were dominated by letters for and against the experimental use of Scots, MacDiarmid proclaimed that Scots verse, prose and drama had been advanced inventively by himself, the late Lewis Grassic Gibbon and McLellan. The controversy began after a broadcast lecture in which James Fergusson used the term 'plastic Scots' to ridicule the Scottish Renaissance Movement which by then comprised a school of poets attempting to emulate MacDiarmid. Fergusson complained that the users of 'plastic Scots' wrote bad poetry in a bastard language. MacDiarmid (who was supported in the correspondence by Maurice Lindsay, Edwin Morgan, Douglas Young and R. Crombie Saunders) made the point that Scottish poets wrote best in Scots:

> There is no question of my trying to enforce ... Lallans on our Southern neighbours. What I object to is their enforcing their English on us.... The entire Scottish contribution to English poetry could be excised without noticeable detriment to the latter. In these circumstances it has simply been my contention that it would be better for Scottish poets to cease using a medium in which time has shown they have an irremediable inferiority and see if they cannot do better in the very different Scottish tradition, first of all in the 'halfway house' of Scots, and ultimately in a resumption of Gaelic.[50]

Apart from such epistolary outbursts, MacDiarmid's life in Glasgow had settled into a routine which consisted of drinking at the Curlers, talking to the friends who flocked to see him, occasionally speaking in public and sometimes going out for an entertaining evening. On 30 March 1947 he gave the Dunedin Society's third Sunday lecture at

Glasgow's Saltire Club in Wellington Street. The following night he went to see a revival of *Jamie the Saxt* with Duncan Macrae in the title role, repeating his triumph of the first production. Back in Victoria Crescent Road he enjoyed his contact with the Pritchards. He dedicated 'The Terrible Crystal' (a fragment from the *Cornish Heroic Song*) to Sadie and her presence prompted a new poem, a quatrain:

> You remind me, young, lovely, a wife and a mother,
>   And capital artist to boot,
> Of orange groves seen with their simultaneous burden
>   Of leaves and flowers and fruit.   (1340)

Valda, however, rather resented Sadie's familiar attitude towards the poet. 'She made up to Christopher', Valda complained. 'One evening she leaned forward – she had boobs like gooseberries – and said "am I embarrassing you, Christopher" and I said, "in the pub they'd call you a pricktease".'[51]

Valda felt miserable when, at the beginning of May, MacDiarmid accepted a job in Carlisle: 'I was afraid to run a bath in case I'd be criticised for using hot water'.[52] The poet had accepted an invitation to join the staff of the *Carlisle Journal*, then edited by his friend Fred Sleath. As the paper came out twice weekly two reporters, Rodney Hallworth and Dick Allen, were able to have some verbal fun with the poet on the Monday and Thursday press nights. They would look up words in a one-volume *Oxford Dictionary* and test MacDiarmid's vocabulary. 'We never beat him,' Dick Allen remembered; 'he was always able to give us almost verbatim the Latin derivatives or French connections of each and every word.'[53] During his time in Carlisle, MacDiarmid worked at the office in 60 English Street (a name that must have afforded him some amusement) and lived at the privately owned and teetotal Viaduct Hotel. He claimed he needed only three hours' sleep and his fellow reporters took that as gospel.

Though he stayed at a temperance hotel, MacDiarmid continued to enjoy drinking, frequenting rough-and-ready workingmen's pubs. Dick Allen was struck by the poet's sensitivity to the sun:

> He had strange ideas like wearing a fur coat in the middle of summer to keep the sun out. I recall the Cumberland Show on one of the hottest days of the year. C.M. covered it, writing in pencil on newsprint copy paper. There was so much sweat came out of his curly head that the whole thing

had to be re-written back at the office because the printers wouldn't accept it.[54]

During his stint with the *Carlisle Journal* MacDiarmid covered, in addition to the Cumberland Show, a ceremony in Carlisle Cathedral and a boxing tournament.

Marginally better off financially for his brief return to journalism, MacDiarmid was back in Glasgow before the end of 1947. Maclellan published his *A Kist of Whistles* in September, a volume consisting mainly of poems from the *Cornish Heroic Song*. He published a poem ('Happy on Heimay', from the *Cornish Heroic Song*) in the *New Shetlander* (Nov.-Dec.) and on 27 November gave a broadcast talk on the Cumbrian poet Susanna Blamire for the BBC Scottish Home Service. On the last day of the year he had to go to Glasgow Infirmary to receive treatment for plantar warts and an X-ray which revealed a blood-clot and calcium deposit on the muscle of his leg. Still, it was a good homecoming for the family. Valda was relieved to see him return from a boozy period in Carlisle in one piece and Michael was home on his school holiday.

On Saturday, 28 August 1948, MacDiarmid was honoured in Edinburgh at a special luncheon given by his friends and admirers at the Scotia Hotel. He was presented with a drawing of himself (see frontispiece) by the late David Foggie, a gift from the guests who included the sculptor Benno Schotz, F. G. Scott, Albert Mackie, Neil Gunn, Eric Linklater, James Bridie and Joseph Chiari. During the luncheon Chiari made a speech acclaiming MacDiarmid as one of the few men of vision alive and Albert Mackie, as chairman, read out a tribute from T. S. Eliot who was unable to be present:

> There are two reasons why I should have wished to be present on this occasion. The first is my respect for the great contribution of the Poet to Poetry – in general – in my time; the second is my respect for his contribution to Scottish Poetry – in particular.... It will eventually be admitted that he has done more also for English poetry, by committing some of his finest verse to Scots, than if he had elected to write exclusively in the Southern dialect.[55]

With one of the ironies characteristic of MacDiarmid's career the man so honoured was shortly at loggerheads with some of his countrymen.

His edition of Soutar's *Collected Poems* was published in October and Soutar's friends James A. Finlayson and William Montgomerie wrote to the *Scotsman* deploring the omissions in the edition. James Bridie, one of the guests at the Scotia Hotel luncheon, stated in the *Scotsman* (22 Nov.) that 'there is a clear case for the setting up of a committee of inquiry by either the Saltire Society or Scottish PEN while Soutar's friends are still alive and the truth is still available'.[56] Though aware of the implication that he had deliberately suppressed Soutar's best work in order to promote his own excellence, MacDiarmid treated the whole matter philosophically, making no public comment but writing privately to Douglas Young on 25 November:

> I am not a member of either [the Saltire Society or Scottish PEN]; nor have they any official standing. Bridie might as well have suggested that I should be hauled at once before a Court Martial in Edinburgh Castle. Scottish Command has certainly as much right to intervene in the matter as either the Saltire or PEN ... and I would on the whole expect fairer treatment from Scottish Command.... My position is therefore that the editing by me of S's poems was a private arrangement with his parents and that I am answerable to no one else. I have a letter from Mr Soutar himself expressing his complete satisfaction that I 'had made a fine job of it'. That being so, I regard the matter as closed.[57]

This is one of the rare instances of MacDiarmid avoiding a public row.

Young was an academic as well as a poet, teaching classics at University College, Dundee, so was well placed to gather signatures for a diplomatically worded appeal to the Prime Minister, Clement Attlee, on MacDiarmid's behalf. Young intended to secure a Civil List Pension for the poet who, just back from a trip to Oxford and Manchester on 28 February 1949, confirmed to his friend that if offered a pension he would accept it gratefully. By 24 March he was able to tell Young that Attlee had been in touch and that the news was good. While waiting for an official offer he went about his usual radical business, contributing regularly to the *National Weekly*, a recently established nationalist journal published by the Caledonian Press (who had brought out *Poems of the East-West Synthesis*).

It was becoming impossible for the Grieves to continue living beneath the Pritchards at Victoria Crescent Road. There was Valda's hostility to Sadie and the Pritchards' resentment at some of the noisy visitors – including the poet James Burns Singer, then a student of zoology – who came to call on MacDiarmid. On top of this, MacDiarmid had decided that Ewan MacColl and not Robert McLellan represented the best hope for a significant Scottish contribution to the theatre. Born Jimmy Miller in Auchterarder, Perthshire, in 1915, MacColl married the

actress Joan Littlewood in 1935 and in 1945 they formed Theatre
Workshop, a company committed to socialist drama broadly on Brechtian
lines. MacDiarmid accepted an invitation to become a director of Theatre
Workshop and was greatly impressed by the production, at the Edinburgh International Festival of 1949, of MacColl's play *The Other
Animals*. The event coincided with his departure from the Pritchards'
basement.

At a meeting of the Saltire Society, MacDiarmid's work had been
praised by the Earl of Selkirk whose brother, the Duke of Hamilton –
'Scotland's premier duke' no less, as MacDiarmid gleefully noted[58] –
offered to help out the poet by letting him stay in the laundry cottage
attached to his Lanarkshire mansion of Dungavel. Six miles south-west
of Strathaven, and – ironically – near Lauder Ha' where Sir Harry Lauder
lived until his death in 1950. Dungavel House had become the ducal
home of the Hamiltons after the demolition of Hamilton Palace, their
ancestral home, in 1922. During the Second World War, the mansion
was used as a hospital and convalescent home for personnel of the
Women's Auxiliary Air Force. In June 1949 the Duke of Hamilton put
the property up for sale.

MacDiarmid and Valda moved into the laundry cottage, 'a fine
commodious house in the middle of a pine wood',[59] in the autumn of
1949. Soon after settling in they were visited by Arnold Wesker, then
an aspiring writer of seventeen. Wesker had written to MacDiarmid who
replied with some kind words about the poems he had sent. On holiday
with a girlfriend, Wesker decided to visit the poet at Dungavel:

> He and his patient wife [Valda] fed us and gave us a bed for the night
> though we said we had our tent. In return my friend gave him a haircut.
> But then came an excruciating honour. He announced that he'd read his
> new poem. Or the new section of a long poem.... One of the long, political
> prose poems. I know only that I was not understanding it, that it went on,
> that even had I been able to understand it I'd not have heard it because I
> spent most of the time working out what I was going to say. Talk about
> casting pearls before swine. Though in fairness to myself I was as nervous
> as hell. It was not that I thought *him* dotty, but that I felt ashamed not to
> be able to follow the great man's work. I also felt very flattered. It was,
> nevertheless, a memorable event for me, a boy from a council flat in Hackney
> being welcomed into the home of a real writer. It was perhaps the first step
> on a ladder of encouragements that I'd received – my family and English
> teacher aside. And I shall always be grateful.[60]

As Wesker's observations confirm, MacDiarmid felt completely at home at Dungavel.

At the end of 1949 MacDiarmid again went his own way as a nationalist. John MacCormick launched, that October, the Scottish Covenant which attracted more than two million signatures; however MacDiarmid felt that the Scottish Covenant Committee was betraying the trust of so many people by failing to contest the forthcoming General Election. Meanwhile, Robert Blair Wilkie, a candidate at the Camlachie by-election, was expelled by the SNP as an extremist and formed the Scottish Resistance Committee (later the Scottish National Congress) of which MacDiarmid became a member. This Committee decided to put up MacDiarmid as an Independent Scottish Nationalist candidate and his election leaflet stressed 'I belong to no political party, but believe that in Scotland the Scottish cause should come first and foremost all the time'.[61] The General Election of 23 February 1950 resulted in a reduced Labour majority and another lost deposit for MacDiarmid. At Kelvingrove the result was: Rt Hon Walter Elliot (Con) 15,197; J.L. Williams (Lab) 13,973; S.J. Ranger (Lib) 831; C.M. Grieve (Ind. Scot. Nat.) 639.

On 10 March 1950 MacDiarmid wrote to Attlee after a formal offer of a Civil List Pension of £150 per annum: 'I beg to thank you for your letter ... telling me that His Majesty the King has been graciously pleased on your recommendation to grant me a Civil List Pension.'[62] News of his acceptance of this award was announced in the press under the headline 'Scots Republican Accepts King's Pension'. MacDiarmid commented:

> I was very glad to accept Mr Attlee's offer of the pension even though I am a Republican and it is a Royal grant. I refused to sign the Scottish Covenant because for one thing it meant giving allegiance to the throne, and secondly, I am a separatist and the Covenant calls for 'Ulster-model' Home Rule, while I prefer complete independence for Scotland. At any rate I shall be glad of the £150 a year because poetry is in the doldrums today and a man like me, primarily a poet, finds it difficult to make a living.[63]

One of the first men to send congratulations to MacDiarmid was Robert McLellan, evidently unaware of MacDiarmid's dramatic dispute with his sister.

As MacDiarmid told McLellan, and F.G. Scott, he hoped to write some important new work at Dungavel. What he did write was a long essay on *Aesthetics in Scotland* which was developed from the script for a lecture he intended to deliver in the spring at the invitation of Glasgow Corporation. In an expansive mood, encouraged by the idyllic environment at Dungavel, MacDiarmid surveyed the state of art in Scotland and made a general case for more culture. Opposed to the notion that the artist should simplify his art in order to make it easily accessible to the public, he argues that it is the responsibility of the masses to lift themselves up into the Olympian heights inhabited by the great artists. What he is doing is combining his intellectual élitism with a belief in the untapped resources of the Scottish people for he categorises the ordinary man and woman in the street as culturally underprivileged and looks forward to the day when the spiritual light of the Scottish Renaissance will dawn on Scotland so that all Scots will be in a position to comprehend their own culture. For this reason he attacks the financial élitism of the Edinburgh International Festival:

> The Scottish dichotomy between experience and consciousness – the dissociation in our midst between energy and sensibility, between conduct and theories of conduct, between life conceived as an opportunity and life conceived as a discipline – cannot be healed in the Edinburgh Festival way. Our national culture suffers from all the ills of split personality. The Edinburgh Festival's high prices excluding most of our people, together with its importation of foreign arts and artists and the virtual exclusion of our own, simply accentuate this schizophrenia.[64]

Unpublished until 1984, *Aesthetics in Scotland* is one of MacDiarmid's most calm and considered prose works.

In June 1950 Dungavel House, with its sixty-two acres of land (fifty-two of them woodland), was bought by the Scottish Division of the National Coal Board in order to establish the first permanent residential training school for young miners.[65] MacDiarmid was asked to vacate the laundry house by the end of August, though the notice of eviction was later extended to the end of the year. This development contributed to a hectic end to 1950 for MacDiarmid had other matters on his mind. His son had registered as a conscientious objector and on 13 September the poet wrote to Douglas Young seeking his assistance in Michael's forthcoming case. (Valda's anger at official indifference to Michael's predicament was vented when she attended a meeting at Strathaven, addressed by Emmanuel Shinwell, MP, and pelted the War Minister with eggs.) On 26 October MacDiarmid left for Moscow on a trip organised by the Scottish-USSR Friendship Society. He met Samuel Marshak, the Russian translator of Burns, and other Soviet writers and returned to

London on 11 November just in time to go to Sheffield, the following day, for the World Peace Congress. He still had to find somewhere to live but through William Maclellan, who had a home at Thankerton, near Biggar, he met a Lanarkshire farmer, Tweedie, who agreed to let rent-free to the Grieves a farm cottage at Candymill, by Biggar. MacDiarmid was heading back to the Borders.

16

A Single and Separate Person

A single and separate person
Indubitably alive during a particular stretch of time,
He contrived to weave a singularly brilliant
Unbroken thread of evidence that this *was* so.
　　　'The Kulturkampf'　　(702)

BROWNSBANK Cottage, Candymill, the house that was to be home for MacDiarmid for the rest of his life, stands on a hill-farm a few miles from Biggar – which is about forty miles north-east of Langholm. When the Grieves moved into their but-and-ben it provided a somewhat primitive haven. There was an outside toilet, no electricity, and water had to be carried from a tap in the garden. The previous tenant, a ploughman, had kept hens in the front garden but Valda intended to cultivate the ground for flowers and plants. She also decided to line an outhouse with orange boxes so her husband would have somewhere to keep his books and papers. MacDiarmid noted that Brownsbank offered easy access to Edinburgh by bus (a journey of an hour and a half) though Glasgow was more difficult to get to, the route going through Lanark, Carluke, Wishaw and Motherwell.

　　Best of all, MacDiarmid acknowledged, Brownsbank 'had the supreme advantage of being rent-free, and my wife speedily made it not only habitable but comfortable'.[1] She lit the house with oil-lamps and using a single-burner oil stove, a primus and the open fire in the sitting room managed to cook three-course meals. Fortunately both Valda and MacDiarmid liked curries and continental food which could be prepared slowly in this way. Over the years the couple acquired home comforts: Edinburgh University students and members of the Young Communist League regularly came out to help improve the cottage which gradually acquired a kitchenette, bathroom, hot and cold water, flush lavatory and electric light.

As the Grieves installed themselves in Brownsbank at the beginning of January 1951 they had to cope with heavy snow and a frozen water supply, residential hazards. The snow did not, however, insulate them from the outside world and they had to face the certainty of Michael going to prison. In December the Edinburgh Appellate Tribunal had rejected his application to be registered as a conscientious objector and the family had to wait for the grim outcome of that decision.

MacDiarmid visited Germany and Poland in 1951 – meeting Pablo Neruda and Nazim Khikmet at the Writers' Club in East Berlin – and finally heard, on 16 June the following year, that Michael had been sentenced to six months' imprisonment by Glasgow Sheriff Court. Then working as the full-time cook at Kilquhanity, Michael was found guilty of failing to submit himself for a National Service medical examination when ordered to do so by the court. Michael, who was not legally represented, objected to the competency and relevance of the proceedings and said the case against him was contrary to the law of Scotland and should be dismissed as an infringement of his civil rights. Michael served his sentence in Barlinnie and Saughton.

That MacDiarmid was never far away from controversy was illustrated by his angry front-page article in the *National Weekly* of 28 June 1952. It was the culmination of a quarrel with Maurice Lindsay whose volume of Scots verse, *Hurlygush*, he had introduced in 1948. Lindsay was now established as music critic of the Glasgow *Bulletin* and editor-presenter of *Scottish Life and Letters* on the BBC Scottish Home Service. On 6 June the Dunedin Society, of which MacDiarmid was President, arranged a recital of music by Francis George Scott and Erik Chisholm at the Institute of Contemporary Arts in London. Joan Alexander, accompanied by Allie Cullen, sang eighteen songs by Scott; Agnes Walker played six pieces by Chisholm. According to Lindsay's review of the recital in the *Bulletin* of 7 June:

before Miss Alexander could sing a note we had to listen to a discourse (lasting 50 minutes) by Mr C. M. Grieve (Hugh MacDiarmid), and further diatribes amounting to another 20 minutes. The purpose of these remarks was to introduce the evening's music, but Mr Grieve's speech did not suggest that this was a very suitable assignment for him.[2]

Recalling this occasion years later, Lindsay claimed that Eric Blom, the distinguished critic, departed after twenty minutes of MacDiarmid's 'arguably irrelevant ranting' and argued that by driving Blom and other members of the audience away, 'MacDiarmid had once again done his old friend and collaborator a major disservice'.[3]

Furious at Lindsay's notice in the *Bulletin*, MacDiarmid wrote a reply to the paper and when this appeared in a drastically reduced form contributed his feature to the *National Weekly*. It is another example of MacDiarmid's desire to wound his opponents in literary warfare:

> I remember well when Mr Lindsay first climbed on to the band-wagon of the Scottish Renaissance Movement. He came to see me about it. I had no difficulty whatever in appreciating that under his natty khaki shirt what may be described as his bosom was warming with the glowing ecstasy of a dog sighting a new and hitherto undreamed-of lamp-post. With scant knowledge, he proceeded to spread himself all over the place with tremendous go-getting zeal and no nice feelings whatever about horning in where he wasn't wanted.... Several days before the [Scott recital] he phoned to a friend of mine in Glasgow, suggested that I was the wrong sort of person to chair such a function, and implied that he should do so instead. This suggestion not being accepted, he determined that he must be present – and present he was.[4]

MacDiarmid had no intention of mellowing into a Grand Old Man. Though the flow of poetry was not forthcoming he was actively involved in Scottish culture.

In 1952 MacDiarmid helped launch the Edinburgh People's Festival as a radical alternative to the official Edinburgh International Festival. He wanted to write a play on the Macbeth theme with Ewan MacColl and hoped to persuade Sean O'Casey to participate in the Edinburgh People's Festival. Neither wish was fulfilled though he did renew contact with O'Casey, sending him a copy of his centenary study of *Cunninghame Graham* (1952). O'Casey had long since severed relations with McElroy – 'the most egotistic & selfish mortal that ever crossed my path'[5] – and corresponded with MacDiarmid on friendly terms. There was, however, an ironic aftermath to the McElroy affair. On 4 May 1953, Sean and

Eileen O'Casey were in Edinburgh for the first night of the King's Theatre presentation of *Purple Dust*. MacDiarmid and Valda were there, too, and MacDiarmid was unaware that Poges and Souhaun in the play were modelled on McElroy and Peggy.

After the performance MacDiarmid and O'Casey were guests of honour at a party in Norman MacCaig's Edinburgh flat. According to MacDiarmid's memory of the night, O'Casey was quiet until he took a glass of brandy then broke into song.[6] For his part, O'Casey recalled that he 'embraced Scotland's greatest poet, Hugh McDiarmuid'.[7] Eileen O'Casey gives a third version of what was evidently a wild party for members of the cast and some forty people including singers and bagpipe players:

> Though Sean never drank much, whisky that night was so plentiful that he did not realize how much he was drinking ... He loved Edinburgh so much that he felt, if it had been less cold and far off, that it was a place in which he could have lived. Actually it was because he had found in Hugh MacDiarmid a man with whom ... he could be entirely at ease: a poet and a writer with the same political opinions.[8]

O'Casey later dedicated his autobiographical *Sunset and Evening Star* to 'My dear Friend Hugh MacDiarmid, Alba's Poet and one of Alba's first men' and paid tribute to his Scots volumes, 'books of new thought, daring, and lyrical with fine songs'.[9]

Poetically, it was MacDiarmid's desire in the early 1950s to write 'a whole host of new Scots lyrics' for, as he told F. G. Scott, 'I am quite unwilling to write an occasional lyric. I must be able to write to my own satisfaction the complete sequences I have in mind – or nothing.'[10] Nevertheless the Scots poems he produced were occasional in the technical sense, written for or around particular occasions. Apart from 'A Poem for Christmas 1952' – a slight piece supposing that a modern Christ would be classified 'as a Commie' (1368) – he wrote some poems prompted by the coronation, on 2 June 1952, of Elizabeth II. 'A Coronation Dream' commented on the ephemeral nature of the occasion:

> The pomp and glory lasts a wheen 'oors,
> Syne if ony trace can be seen it's
> In lumps o' sodden papers on the pavements
> And cherry stanes and husks o' peanuts.   (1380)

Objecting to the principle of monarchy and to the erroneous title of the new queen as the second Elizabeth of Scotland, a group calling themselves the Scottish Republican Army made noisy gestures of protest. Mac-Diarmid addressed a poem, 'Faugh-a-Ballagh', to the SRA and prophesied that their actions – 'bombin' a wheen windas,/Daubin' oot the damned English numbers' (1369) – would lead to an upswelling of republican opinion in Scotland.

He wrote a poem ridiculing the cultural pretensions of the Edinburgh International Festival, amused that 'only a guid-gaen military tat-too/Appeals to the taste o' ilka yahoo' (1370); and he composed a satirical sixain, 'Nuts in May', about two television programmes:

> I saw twa items on
> The TV programme yesterday.
> 'General Assembly of the Church of Scotland'
> Said ane – the ither 'Nuts in May'.
> I lookit at the picters syne
> But which was which I couldna say.   (1371)

The most ambitious of these new Scots poems, 'Miracle in the Horribals', used the device of topicality by specifying the date 5 October 1953 in the second line. On that date, according to MacDiarmid's fanciful scenario, the Gorbals ('the Horribals'), Glasgow's notorious slum-quarter, renounced crime – to the consternation of the authorities and the professional do-gooders. The point of the poem is to suggest that the apparatus of capitalism depends on crime:

> Bitterest o' a' were the Salvation Airmy,
> Licensed victuallers, health visitors, nuns, and charity agents,
> And it became clear as glaur that a'thing in life
> Hings thegither, and a' Society's pageants
> Need a' the auld elements if they're to gang on
> As they've dune in the past. Whaur there's nae crime
> Lawyers, court officers, polis'll ha'e a thin time
> And wi' them a' the thoosands that to them hang on!   (1378)

The difference between these poems and MacDiarmid's great work in Scots is obvious in the loose rhythms, the purely functional rhymes (agents/pageants) and the substitution of value judgement for vision.

It seemed as if his visionary gift had gone. As William Maclellan had expressed his willingness to publish at least a large portion of *Mature Art*, MacDiarmid had to assemble a coherent text from those parts of his typescript he could recover since some of his papers were still in storage. Fortunately, part of the typescript was kept in crates at Maclellan's garage at Thankerton but even with this the poet 'had to write fresh stuff to fill [in] gaps'.[11] The fresh stuff was mainly reprocessed material written by others. For example he found the long Karl Kraus section in the *Times Literary Supplement* of 8 May 1953 as explained in chapter 14. When Dylan Thomas died on 9 November 1953 he adapted a passage inspired by T. H. White's *The Sword in the Stone* (one of his favourite books in Shetland) to read as an elegy for the Welsh poet:

> I rejoiced when from Wales once again
> Came the ffff-putt of a triple-feathred arrow
> Which looked as if it had never moved.   (828)

Elsewhere in the poem, MacDiarmid made small adjustments in accordance with his changed circumstances. A reference to 'the Shetland Islands where I live' appeared in the past tense as 'the Shetland Islands where I lived' (763). A long parenthesis was added about MacDiarmid's 'angling friend Norman MacCaig' (851). MacCaig, a tall, handsome, highly articulate man – who had been imprisoned as a conscientious objector in the Second World War – was one of the few younger Scottish poets erudite enough to impress MacDiarmid. Born in Edinburgh in 1910 and a classics graduate of Edinburgh University, MacCaig worked as a schoolteacher in Edinburgh. His background, however, had Gaelic connections for his mother was a Gaelic speaker from Scalpay, Harris. MacDiarmid appreciated MacCaig's intellectual clarity, his acerbic wit, his capacity for keeping a clear head while drinking malt whisky, and the fact that he was one of the few Scottish poets of his generation who eschewed the MacDiarmid manner. After dabbling with the Apocalyptic mode in his early collections, MacCaig wrote beautifully crafted neo-Metaphysical poems influenced by Wallace Stevens in their concern for the problems of perception. MacDiarmid was glad to have MacCaig's help in preparing a text of *In Memoriam James Joyce* for publication. By the end of 1953 the two poets had made enough progress to satisfy Maclellan that he could successfully publish the book by attracting subscribers.

About the same time MacDiarmid had a sad falling-out with F. G. Scott, one of his closest friends for years: the man who encouraged him through the composition of *A Drunk Man* – which was reprinted in 1953 with a perceptive introduction by David Daiches – and who had paid for his medical treatment in Gilgal. MacDiarmid tells the sorry tale with little ceremony: 'Scott became increasingly reactionary in the last decade of his life. One day I took Jankel Adler, the painter, to see him, and Scott immediately expressed himself of the most violent anti-semitic opinions. I signalled to Adler and we rose and left.'[12] It is an odd anecdote that issues from some psychological need on MacDiarmid's part to reject those to whom he felt indebted. He had rejected Cairncross in *Lucky Poet* and now he rejected Scott. The jibe about anti-Semitism is not entirely convincing. MacDiarmid had once accepted a cottage from Potocki de Montalk, a virulent anti-Semite; he often sang the praises of Major Douglas, another anti-Semite; and one of the most important figures in his poetic pantheon was Ezra Pound whose anti-Semitic views were well known to his admirers. All that can be said in defence of MacDiarmid is that he had some reason to resent Scott's habit of lecturing his former pupil. Even the sweet-tempered Soutar had noticed Scott's 'mentor-relationship with Grieve' and the composer's tendency 'to patronize Grieve'.[13] At any rate, an important friendship was at an end. 'The rift between us', said MacDiarmid, 'was complete.'[14] When, more than a year after the incident, MacDiarmid sent Scott a copy of *Francis George Scott*, his essay on the occasion of the composer's seventy-fifth birthday, there was no response. Similarly, when (in 1957) Glasgow University conferred an honorary degree on Scott, MacDiarmid's congratulations were not acknowledged.

In 1954 Maclellan began to send out circulars advertising the publication of *In Memoriam James Joyce*, incidentally quoting the high opinion T. S. Eliot had expressed about the poem in letters to MacDiarmid. Eliot took exception to this use of his words without permission and MacDiarmid apologised, informing Eliot that 'the text as it is now being printed ... is not substantially altered from the typescript you read – only tightened up in places'.[15] Eliot gladly accepted the apology and said he stood by his previous assessment of the poem.

For the summer of 1955 MacDiarmid went to Prague as one of the guests of Spartakiade, the quinquennial national physical culture festival. He relaunched the *Voice of Scotland* that year and had four new publications: *Selected Poems*, edited by Oliver Brown; his booklet on F. G. Scott, his edition of the *Selected Poems of William Dunbar* and, after years of waiting, *In Memoriam James Joyce*. The Joyce poem was reviewed in the *New Statesman* (10 Sept.) by G. S. Fraser, a Poundian scholar and Scottish poet, who acknowledged the genius of MacDiarmid's early verse but found the new title the work of an 'agonised existentialist sage (in Marxist fancy dress) talking at endless length to himself rather than others in hodden-grey blank verse'.[16] MacDiarmid replied, affably enough, observing 'I *am* a Communist and not a wearer of "Marxist fancy dress".'[17]

Despite his public declaration of Communist commitment MacDiarmid was not, of course, a member of the Communist Party of Great Britain, having been expelled for the second time in 1939. At the beginning of 1956 the CPGB had 33,095 members including some prominent intellectuals such as the novelist Doris Lessing and the historian Christopher Hill. Some had grave doubts about the Stalinist years and these were confirmed from an unexpected source. In February Nikita Khrushchev, First Secretary, addressed a secret session of the Twentieth Congress of the Communist Party of the Soviet Union and denounced Stalin as a tyrant who had used terror to sustain his regime and destroy loyal Communists.

Meeting in London in April 1956 the Twenty-Fourth Congress of the CPGB passed a resolution regretting that the Soviets had not yet published the text of Khrushchev's speech. John Gollan, an Edinburgh man, became the new General Secretary of the CPGB and the executive committee accepted that the Party had been guilty of dogmatism and sectarianism. On 4 June the US Department of State published the text of Khrushchev's speech and the political committee of the CPGB issued a statement admitting that it would be necessary to make a Marxist reassessment of the degeneration of Soviet democracy under Stalin.

International events seemed to conspire to add to the confusion of the CPGB. On 30 October, a week after Imre Nagy had been appointed minister-president of Hungary, Soviet troops invaded north-east Hungary. The following day Anglo-French troops bombed Egyptian airfields, provoking anger from some quarters in Britain over the nature of the Suez War. Nagy's Hungarian government renounced, on 2 November, the Warsaw treaty and appealed to the United Nations against Soviet invasion. Two days later Soviet forces attacked Budapest forcing Nagy to take refuge in the Yugoslav embassy and Janos Kadar to form a government sympathetic to the USSR. It has been frequently observed that the involvement of Britain and France in the Suez crisis encouraged the Soviets to intervene in Hungary and suppress the forces hostile to them.

The impact of the Soviet invasion of Hungary divided the CPGB. Around a third of the staff of the *Daily Worker* resigned. MacDiarmid, however, was convinced that the Soviet action had ended a reactionary counter-revolution in Hungary and wrote to John Gollan on 15 November: 'In view of the resignations from the Party reported in the press, I feel that the time has come for me to express my complete agreement with the line taken by your Executive and to renew my membership of the party.'[18] Gollan referred the matter to Gordon McLennan, Scottish District Secretary of the CPGB.

Although his private letter to Gollan supported the official party line of apologising for the Soviet invasion, MacDiarmid also put his name to a collective letter which was sent to the *Daily Worker* on 18 November. Rejected by the Party newspaper, it was printed in the *New Statesman* of 1 December. Signed by fifteen self-confessed Marxists, including Doris Lessing and Christopher Hill as well as by MacDiarmid, the letter attacked the CPGB for slavishly following a Stalinist line:

> We feel that the uncritical support given by the Executive Committee of the Communist Party to the Soviet action in Hungary is the undesirable culmination of years of distortion of fact, and failure by British Communists to think out political problems for themselves. We had hoped that the revelations made at the 20th Congress of the Communist Party of the Soviet Union would have made our leadership and press realise that Marxist ideas will only be acceptable in the British Labour movement if they arise from the truth about the world we live in.[19]

Though there were clear contradictions in MacDiarmid's private letter to Gollan and his participation in the collective letter, the Party were willing to overlook their differences with the poet. At a time when so many intellectuals were leaving, the Party welcomed a man whose cultural credentials were sound. During 1956 a third edition of *A Drunk Man* and an edition of *Stony Limits and Scots Unbound* had appeared; on 19 December D. G. Bridson broadcast a production of selected passages from *Impavidi Progrediamur* on the BBC Third Programme. For a Party trawling for support, MacDiarmid had become a catch.

Some 7000 members, including Hill and Lessing, left the CPGB as a result of the Khrushchev revelations and the Party line on the Soviet invasion of Hungary. MacDiarmid chose the moment to contribute an article, 'Why I Rejoined', to the *Daily Worker* of 28 March 1957:

> While many members have left the Communist Party, allegedly on account of the 'de-Stalinising revelations', or Hungary, I have felt, on the contrary, that this was precisely the time to rally the Party again and throw all my energies into the fight.... Mistakes and distortions there have been, of

course. But even if the figures of the enemies of Communism were accurate, the killings, starvings, frame-ups, unjust judgements and all the rest of it are a mere bagatelle to the utterly mercenary and unjustified wars, the ruthless exploitation, the preventable deaths due to slums, and other damnable consequences of the profit motive, which must be laid to the account of the so-called 'free nations of the West'.... In the light of [the counter-revolutionary danger in Hungary], the Russian intervention was not only justified, but imperative, if unfortunately necessary.... I have had the privilege of travelling in the past few years in the Soviet Union, in Poland, and in Czechoslovakia, and I am writing this on the eve of going to China. Everything I have seen in these countries and all my intercourse with their public men, their writers and other artists, and their ordinary folk, has abundantly strengthened and confirmed my Communist faith.[20]

This statement gravely disappointed many of the poet's most fervent admirers though, as a man who regarded the business of being provocative as part of his life's work, he was indifferent to their disapproval. And though the accumulation of evidence over the years showed Mac-Diarmid's assessment of Soviet injustice as a 'mere bagatelle' to be wildly inaccurate, he never deviated from his opinion that the Party had adopted the right course. There is a strong parallel with Pound's adherence to the ideas that led to his incarceration in Washington.

MacDiarmid mentioned in his *Daily Worker* article that he was about to go to China. He flew to Beijing by way of Belgium, Czechoslovakia and the Soviet Union and, on 29 April, attended a reception given by the Ministry of Culture. MacDiarmid was part of a group from the British-Chinese Friendship Society, one of forty-six such delegations which had come to celebrate May Day in Communist China. On 2 May, the British party were taken to the Great Wall of China, an experience MacDiarmid remembered best because of an unusual contest with

Lord Chorley, the lawyer and President of the British Alpine Club, whom I raced up and down the Great Wall of China, and beat – an achievement he attributed to my Border blood and experience in running and jumping among banks of heather bushes and peat bogs...[21]

At Chungking, Sichuan province, he had a chance to talk to Graham Greene who came to his hotel with a gift:

It was a small stoneware jar of *Moh Tih*, or, as it is called, 'white Wuchang wine'. He said he daren't take it with him [to Canton] as it was liable to explode and wreck the plane, and he enjoined me to be extremely careful too. 'Well,' I said, 'I can't imagine it can do any harm to a confirmed whisky drinker.' So I uncorked it there and then, and drank it. It tasted like a mixture of petrol and vodka, but I suffered no ill-effects beyond the initial 'grue' at its taste.[22]

Greene was less effusive about the memory of this meeting. 'At my only encounter,' he said, 'I thought him a little hostile, but he became friendly when I started talking about different brands of Scotch Whisky.'[23] The Chinese visit produced another of MacDiarmid's occasional poems, 'The Chinese Genius Wakes Up':

> For it's not the colour of your skin
> Any longer that's going to matter,
> It's the colour of your politics –
> And the Chinese are right with the latter.   (1411)

The poem contains thirty-two similarly rough-and-ready quatrains.

On his return from China, MacDiarmid stopped for a few days in London where he was met by Valda. He gave a poetry reading at the Geneva Club before heading north for Scotland for a surprise. Edinburgh University approached him to see if he would accept an honorary LL.D. He accepted, so he said, 'for the Party's sake, if not for my own'.[24] At sixty-five MacDiarmid remained a fiercely controversial figure. The two books he published in 1957 (*Three Hymns to Lenin* and *The Battle Continues*) proclaimed his political colours; he was notorious for his decision to rejoin the Communist Party; he was just back from China. Moreover, he still asserted his Scottish Workers' Republicanism at every opportunity and he listed his hobby in *Who's Who* as anglophobia. Yet along with such pillars of the establishment as Dr Michael Ramsay, then Archbishop of York, he was capped and given his honorary degree by Sir Edward Appleton, Principal of Edinburgh University, in a ceremony in the McEwan Hall, on 5 July 1957. A citation hailed MacDiarmid as a great Scot worthy to be ranged alongside George Buchanan, David Hume and Thomas Carlyle.

Honoured by Edinburgh University at the same time as MacDiarmid was Sir Sydney Smith who had come to Edinburgh from New Zealand in 1927 when appointed to the Chair of Forensic Medicine. In his book about his career as a flamboyant forensic expert, *Mostly Murder*, he describes how he sent his son, Sydney Goodsir Smith (born in Wellington in 1915), to study medicine at Edinburgh University but soon discovered 'he had no bent in that direction, and transferred him to Oxford, where he read history and literature.... He writes, strangely enough for a New Zealander, in broad Scots, inclined somewhat to obscurity and occasional bawdiness'.[25] Sydney Goodsir Smith had become one of MacDiarmid's most talented followers and one of his closest friends. He was boisterous and boozy, garrulous and gregarious, and gleefully projected a persona as the boozy bard of Auld Reekie. His finest achievement is the long sequence of twenty-four elegies, *Under the Eildon Tree*, which was composed in Edinburgh in 1946-7, published in 1948 and revised in 1954. In this work Smith draws on the courtly love convention which makes the poet a passive and unworthy worshipper at the shrine of a beautiful and unattainable lady. Smith is the courtly lover with a hangover, a subject on which he could rightly claim to be an expert.

Smith was almost a permanent fixture in the literary bars of Rose Street: Milne's and the Abbotsford. Milne's, downstairs at the corner of Hanover Street, was a workingmen's pub which attracted thirsty Communists; they had their own alcove, dubbed the Little Kremlin, and they welcomed MacDiarmid to their ranks. In the backroom of Milne's the poets gathered to discuss the contents of *Lines Review* (launched in 1952 in honour of MacDiarmid's sixtieth birthday) with its printer and publisher, Callum Macdonald. MacDiarmid, MacCaig and Smith were recognised as the unholy poetic trinity of Milne's and were described as such in a modern Scottish novel:

> The bar was crowded except where three men stood in a small open space created by the attention of the other customers. One had a sombre pouchy face and upstanding hair which seemed too like thistledown to be natural, one looked like a tall sarcastic lizard, one like a small sly shy bear. 'Our three best since Burns,' a bystander informed me, 'barring Sorley of course.'[26]

The Abbotsford was a more elegant establishment than Milne's, numbering lawyers and businessmen among its clientele. There too Mac-Diarmid, MacCaig and Smith held forth: MacDiarmid alternating between affability and intensity, MacCaig delivering swift sarcastic verbal thrusts, Smith with a monocle in his eye and a glass in his hand and sometimes an inhaler at his throat to ward off attacks of asthma. All three poets were incessant smokers as well as heavy drinkers so their presence was surrounded by a tobacco cloud of unknowing.

Inevitably, the three men were labelled the Rose Street Poets. To celebrate the bicentenary of the birth of Burns, some of the Milne's Bar regulars formed a 200 Burns Club and at their first meeting – on 20

January 1959 at the Peacock Hotel, Newhaven, Edinburgh – installed MacDiarmid, MacCaig and Smith as club bards. The following month MacDiarmid went to Czechoslovakia, Hungary and Bulgaria for the Burns celebrations in these countries; MacCaig drily commented that the poet's membership of the Communist Party was not dissimilar to free membership of an international travel agency.[27]

MacDiarmid was involved in two books marking the Burns bicentenary. His own *Burns Today and Tomorrow* (1959) was a résumé of his persistent attacks on Burns, seeing him as a great songwriter and inferior poet, and his detestation of the Burns Cult (though he rarely turned down an opportunity to address a Burns Club). According to MacDiarmid, it was the mindless adulation and imitation of Burns that had lowered Scottish literature to a pitiful level of self-congratulatory sentimentalism:

> Burns led directly to this sorry pass through his anti-intellectualism and his xenophobia. It is nonsense to say that he embodies all the great elements of the Scottish tradition when in these two main respects he in fact completely betrayed it.... It is a betrayal of Dunbar and Gavin Douglas and the other great *makars* to whom Burns owed so much, and it has been largely responsible for landing the Scottish Muse in the horrible mess it has occupied since.[28]

In his book MacDiarmid found room to praise MacCaig as 'one of the best living Scottish poets'.[29]

MacCaig's contribution to the bicentenary celebrations was to edit an anthology, *Honour'd Shade*, which so heavily featured the Rose Street Poets than an anonymous reviewer in the *Scotsman* suggested the book 'might perhaps almost have been called, like one of the poems it contains, "The Muse in Rose Street"'.[30] This led to another of the newspaper correspondences MacDiarmid relished. On 20 November 1959 he wrote to the *Scotsman*:

> The Rose Street group of contributors are certainly head and shoulders above all the contemporary Scottish versifiers and several of them, in the opinion of leading critics in England and other countries, are of very high rank indeed.[31]

After another letter, in which MacDiarmid compared the Rose Street Poets to small but significant literary groups in Greece, France, Russia, Austria and Spain, Helen Cruickshank sent the *Scotsman* an epistle making fun of the fact that *Honour'd Shade* had been published by Chambers, best known for their dictionaries:

> Noo, wha dis Hughoc think he can impress
> Wi's fremit learnin'? Fegs, wha is't unless
> It's Chambers' Brithers, whase braw Dictionar'
> Supplied the borrowed words he writes wi' vir.[32]

In his reply MacDiarmid was quick to dismiss his old friend's contribution to the correspondence as 'an inane giggle which lets loose more than a whiff of sour grapes'.[33]

Travel, cultural controversy, political engagements and public speaking were now MacDiarmid's main activities. Sometimes they clashed as when on 27 February 1960, the car in which MacDiarmid and Valda were travelling knocked over a telegraph pole and overturned. They were taken to Law Hospital, Lanarkshire, to recover. Valda suffered internal injuries to her right side and a recurrence of back trouble. The poet sustained facial injuries, the most troublesome of which was 'the fact that my dentures were smashed in my mouth and the splinters of the vulcanite plates gashed my gums and pierced the roof of my mouth, with the consequence that I cannot get new dentures until my mouth heals'.[34] He was thus obliged to cancel various engagements. However, he was well enough to give a talk on Lewis Grassic Gibbon to the Communist Party in Edinburgh on 9 September and he stood as a candidate in the Aberdeen University Rectorial Election towards the end of the year. In 1958 MacDiarmid had been bottom of the poll at St Andrews (with 262 votes, well behind Lord Boothby with 723 votes); in 1960 he came close to winning at Aberdeen, receiving 248 votes, only twenty-nine less than the winner, the painter and naturalist Peter Scott. To ease MacDiarmid's financial problems, that year the actor Alex McCrindle wrote to Scottish writers (such as Compton Mackenzie) asking them to contribute £50 to a fund that would enable improvements to be made to Brownsbank Cottage.

By the end of 1960 MacDiarmid had become a member of the Committee of 100, an organisation founded by Bertrand Russell as a more active extension of the Campaign for Nuclear Disarmament, which, the philosopher felt, had lapsed into timid respectability. Pledged to a campaign of civil disobedience, the Committee of 100 attracted a number of intellectuals, including Doris Lessing and Arnold Wesker as well as MacDiarmid. On 18 February 1961 MacDiarmid was one of several celebrities who spoke in Trafalgar Square, London, before a crowd of about 20,000 people. After the speeches Russell, MacDiarmid, and other Committee members marched down Whitehall towards the Ministry of Defence. There Russell attached a declaration of principle to the Ministry's front door in Storey's Gate, St James's Park, and the group took part in a sit-down that lasted for about two hours until darkness had fallen. MacDiarmid sat proudly beside Lord and Lady Russell.

MacDiarmid was involved in another accident in 1961 when, on 29 March, a car struck him in Edinburgh and he recovered consciousness in the Out-Patients' Department of Edinburgh Royal Infirmary with stitches in the back of his head. Apart from that unexpected blow, it was a fulfilling year for him. Kulgin Duval published a sumptuous edition of *The Kind of Poetry I Want*, consisting of 300 numbered and signed copies printed by Dr Giovanni Mardersteig on the hand-press of the Officina Bodoni in Verona. Duval was a bibliophile and book-dealer with a flat-cum-office at 112 Rose Street, conveniently close to Milne's and the Abbotsford where he frequently met MacDiarmid. Born in Girvan, of Huguenot ancestry, in 1930 Duval was working as a wine-waiter at the Ritz, in London, when he first started to collect rare first editions for sale to Americans staying at the hotel. His friend and partner, Colin Hamilton, found a lost MacDiarmid manuscript, 'Bracken Hills in Autumn' (from *The Muckle Toon* project), in an antiquarian bookshop in Mayfair and subsequently published it as a pamphlet. Duval and Hamilton helped to ease the financial strain of MacDiarmid's life as they were able to sell his manuscripts and fair copies.

It was 1962, the year that Peggy died in Kent, that MacDiarmid experienced 'the real breakthrough'.[35] To celebrate his seventieth birthday on Saturday, 11 August, his *Collected Poems* was published in the United States by Macmillan of New York, with a small British edition by Oliver & Boyd of Edinburgh made possible by the intelligent opportunism of the firm; the 200 Burns Club reprinted *A Drunk Man Looks at the Thistle*; and Sydney Goodsir Smith and Duval edited a *Festschrift* containing critical essays on his work. The BBC broadcast programmes featuring MacDiarmid's poetry and personality and the Communist Party organised birthday parties in Edinburgh and Glasgow. A fund was established to present the poet with his portrait by Peter Westwater and the press generally acclaimed the Grand Old Man, the *Observer* (12 Aug.) running a long laudatory profile on the 'Poet of the Gaelic World'. Though the *Collected Poems* of 1962 contained many mistakes and made the egregious error of subdividing *A Drunk Man* into a series of separately titled sections, the volume led to a general consensus of opinion that MacDiarmid was one of the greatest living poets.

Since its inception in 1947 the Edinburgh International Festival had been attacked by MacDiarmid as an expensive irrelevance. However, he accepted an invitation to participate in the International Writers' Conference held, during the Festival, shortly after his seventieth birthday. Organised by the publisher John Calder, the conference was held in the McEwan Hall and designed to discuss five topics on successive days. On Monday, 20 August, the conference started with a debate on the status of the novel; various writers, including Henry Miller and Edinburgh's own Muriel Spark, paraded their prejudices but the discussion failed to reach any particular conclusion. Tuesday's session was a different matter, an explosive encounter between MacDiarmid and Alexander Trocchi, the Glasgow-born novelist who had achieved recognition in the USA with *Young Adam* (1954) and *Cain's Book* (1960).

In the course of the session on 'Scottish Writing Today', Trocchi called MacDiarmid 'an old so-and-so' and told the poet 'You have a few rather old-fashioned quaintnesses'.[36] MacDiarmid dismissed the novel, in general, as an inferior art-form and ridiculed Trocchi, whose work he had not read, as an exponent of an entirely spurious internationalism. Trocchi, a self-confessed heroin-addict, walked out in protest. As MacDiarmid recalled later, most of the speakers were drunk since 'some wag had put on the speakers' table what we all took to be a carafe of water but which actually held pure malt whisky with which ... we refreshed ourselves copiously'.[37]

Wednesday's session, in which 'Commitment' was considered, brought even more criticism MacDiarmid's way. Norman Mailer began the discussion, calling commitment a lifebelt in the oceanic collision of values in the contemporary world. MacDiarmid was not interested in being similarly vague. He stood up and declared he was a Communist. There were hisses and boos from the audience as MacDiarmid continued, trembling (perhaps as an after-effect of the day before) and speaking loudly above the protests. As a Communist, he claimed to be the only entirely committed writer present. Mary McCarthy objected to this, observing that MacDiarmid was 'claiming to be the most committed writer as if boasting he were the best writer'.[38] MacDiarmid greatly enjoyed the occasion.

Early in 1963 MacDiarmid featured as the joint-author of a new Swedish translation. In collaboration with Elspeth Harley Schubert he produced a version of Harry Martinson's science-fiction poem *Aniara*. This gave him an opportunity to exercise his enthusiasm for scientific imagery:

> Thus it was when the solar system closed
> its gateway of purest crystal and cut off
> the space-ship Aniara from all
> the associations and promises of the sun.[39]

As a translation it was a respectable performance though the *Times Literary Supplement* was disappointed, suggesting that the book was 'unlikely to add many to the large numbers of Mr MacDiarmid's admirers who consider him to be among the finest of modern translators'.[40] MacDiarmid also brought out, through Duval, a sequence of eight *Poems to Paintings by William Johnstone* though these were not new but fragments from *Mature Art*. The hero of the sequence was not the painter but the poet – 'A visionary, a lover of facts' (1072).

On 14 March 1963, MacDiarmid was in London at the Dorchester Hotel to receive the William Foyle Poetry Prize of £250 for his *Collected Poems*. A fortnight after this he was again resisting Grand Old Manhood. Hearing rumours that Langholm Town Council were considering proposals to give him the Freedom of the Burgh he wrote to the Langholm Town Clerk, Edward Armstrong, on 28 March: 'Please inform your Council that if at any future time they should offer me the Freedom I will refuse it, and will also refuse any other public recognition offered to me by Langholm.'[41] MacDiarmid felt it was pointless of the Council to discuss the matter further as they were hostile to him on account of *Lucky Poet* linking Langholm with 'two scandalous stories'.[42] He thought he had sufficient honours anyway: the Civil List Pension, the LL.D, the Andrew Fletcher of Saltoun Medal (from Edinburgh University Nationalist Club, for services to Scotland), the Foyle Poetry Prize. 'I am', he said, 'a little tired now of public honours and in no way anxious for more.'[43] As MacDiarmid rightly realised, he represented Langholm in a way no Council official ever could.

If the poet ever privately entertained hopes of a peaceful old age, his opponents in Scotland made sure that was impossible. At the close of 1963 Forbes Macgregor, an Edinburgh schoolteacher and writer of humorous verse in the vernacular, published *The Gowks of Mowdieknowes: A Study of Literary Lunacy*. This satire on the Scottish Renaissance Movement centred on its leader, identified as Kirsty MacGrumphy (an allusion to the MacDiarmid pseudonym and the fact that the poet was known as Kirsty as a boy in Langholm). As presented in Macgregor's book MacGrumphy is a megalomaniacal opportunist:

> With that naive cunning ... which is so often the greater part of the Scotch village idiot's stock-in-trade, young MacGrumphy early realised with what facility he could obtain that adulation his soul thirsted for.... [So] by perusing one or two obsolete volumes of Geography, or Cosmography, History and Astronomy, which the scientific world had finished referring to for the best part of four generations, the stripling MacGrumphy, like that other stripling of destiny before him, readily had to hand the equivalent of the five smooth stones from the brook, wherewith to conquer the Goliath of popular incredulance.[44]

Appalled at this insult to his integrity, MacDiarmid wrote to Macgregor, on 12 February 1964:

> If, as I am told, you are a school teacher I will call a meeting of the parents of the pupils of any school in which you may be still teaching ... and at the same time I will issue a pamphlet dealing faithfully with your booklet.[45]

The following month he was again imbroiled in argument as the correspondence columns of the *Scotsman* printed letters for and against the merits of Scottish folksong. An advocate of intellectualism in art, MacDiarmid rejected folksong as an insult to the intelligence, as little more than 'rubbish'.[46]

In May, MacDiarmid went to Canada for a reunion with his daughter Christine with whom he had first re-established relations in 1953 when she was a nurse in Dundee, married to Dr Alistair McIntosh. Peggy had asked her children not to see their father when she was alive but Christine, as the older child with fond memories of her father, had felt this an unfair obligation and had welcomed his approach in Dundee. Her brother, on the other hand, only three at the time of the divorce, had honoured his mother's request and had not seen MacDiarmid until 1963 by which time Walter was a mining engineer in Rochdale (he subsequently settled in Cincinatti). Christine had emigrated from Scotland to Georgetown, Ontario, where she became matron of Lakeside School.

MacDiarmid was delighted to see his daughter, his son-in-law and his four Canadian grandchildren Elspeth, Donald, Alison and Roderick. (The dedication of *The Company I've Kept* mentions Christine's children and the poet's other grandchildren: Walter's children Judith, Angela and Jane; Michael's children Christopher and Lucien.) In Georgetown,

MacDiarmid was determined to relax and spent some time at the Muskoka Lakes where his son-in-law had a chalet and a motor-boat. However, while at Georgetown, he did agree to travel the twenty-five miles to Toronto to read some of his poems at the university. He also sat for his portrait by Aba Bayevsky and, at the request of the university, made a recording of *A Drunk Man*.

On his return to Scotland he heard that the BBC Scottish Home Service had, in his absence, broadcast a review of Kenneth Buthlay's *Hugh MacDiarmid* (1964) and that Alexander Scott, a sympathetic critic, had described MacDiarmid as the worst poet in Scotland. George Bruce, the producer of the programme, explained that the remark had been intended facetiously for MacCaig had praised MacDiarmid as the best poet in Scotland before Scott had added 'and the worst'.[47] MacDiarmid was satisfied and wrote a memorable letter to Bruce on 1 July:

> The necessity of being honest with oneself – i.e. exhibiting one's weaknesses as well as one's strengths – is not generally understood. Alex Scott is quite right – but it is part of the image I have always tried to project that it should be so. It would not have suited my book at all to be faultless. My job, as I see it, has never been to lay a tit's egg, but to erupt like a volcano, emitting not only flame, but a lot of rubbish.[48]

Many of MacDiarmid's most provocative statements should be considered in that context.

On 4 September 1964 MacDiarmid made front-page news in most of the newspapers and was the subject of the lead story in the *Daily Worker*. 'Communist to Fight Home', declared the banner headline; 'MacDiarmid raising TV rights issue' was the subheading to the story. MacDiarmid was going to challenge the Prime Minister, Sir Alec Douglas-Home, with a purpose. He wanted to use the constituency of Kinross & West Perthshire as the scene for a battle to secure the Communist Party a share in party political broadcasts. To qualify for the right to participate in such broadcasts it was necessary to field at least fifty candidates which the Communist Party could not afford to do. MacDiarmid felt this was unfair to minority interests and told a London press conference that he would demand the right to appear on television and radio every time Sir Alec, his opponent, did. Speaking at the Communist Party Headquarters in Covent Garden, MacDiarmid stated that if he was not granted similar facilities to Sir Alec he would attempt to get his election annulled on the grounds of a breach of election law. MacDiarmid then turned to the personality of his opponent in a vintage piece of invective:

> He is in fact a zombie, personifying the obsolescent traditions of an aristocratic and big landlord order, of which Thomas Carlyle said that no country had been oppressed by a worse gang of hyenas than Scotland. He is not really a Scotsman, of course, but only a sixteenth part of one, and all his education and social affiliations are anti-Scottish. Sir Walter warned long ago that a Scotsman unscotched would become only a damned mischievous Englishman, and that is precisely what has happened in this case.[49]

With the energetic assistance of Alex Clark as his Election Agent, MacDiarmid had no difficulty in getting signatories for his nomination papers and made his appeal to the 32,000 voters of Kinross & West Perthshire mainly through the press which took a great interest in his campaign since he was a colourful candidate and a complete contrast to the Prime Minister. MacDiarmid was recognised as a major poet yet lived in relative poverty in a little hill-farm cottage. Sir Alec was a landed aristocrat owning, through his estate company, some 60,000 acres, mainly in the Borders. MacDiarmid savaged Sir Alec in his election pamphlet:

> He is a yes-man of the Pentagon as was exemplified by his statement that the British people would willingly be reduced to atomic ash in defence of his [Sir Alec's] notions of freedom. He supported Chamberlain's policy of appeasement to Hitler.... The powers that be [Sir Alec and the Tory Party and the establishment in general] are obviously afraid that if the Communists were once allowed to state their case [on radio and television] the gaff would be blown on the pretensions of the major parties.[50]

At the General Election of 15 October, Sir Alec Douglas-Home polled 16,659 votes and MacDiarmid, predictably bottom of the poll, managed only 127 votes. (Labour narrowly ousted the Conservatives nationally.) For the Communist Party the result was not important, the broadcasting issue was. MacDiarmid duly presented his petition to have Sir Alec's election annulled, accusing the former Prime Minister of corrupt and illegal practices under the Representation of the People Act (1949). A hearing in the Scottish Election Court was set for 21 December.

Tired by his exertions as a Communist candidate MacDiarmid intended to spend some time relaxing at Biggar before the election hearing. He was at home on 28 October when he was visited, unexpectedly, by Colin Wilson, author of *The Outsider* (1956) and various books on existentialism and mysticism. Wilson was on holiday in Scotland with his wife Joy, looked up MacDiarmid's address in *Who's Who*, and decided to call on him as the poet was not on the phone. An Angry Young Man of the 1950s arrived armed with a bottle of whisky for the Angry Old Man of Scotland:

> Valda answered the door, and was absolutely charming – she invited us in immediately. Chris was ... sitting in his armchair – but I remember that strange lined forehead, and the vast mop of grey/white hair. I was also surprised at the extremely small nose, which gave the face a schoolboyish appearance. I can't remember whether Chris had read any of my books, but he had certainly heard about me, and when we opened the bottle of whisky, we got into one of those long amazing conversations that move over an immense area of intellectual interest – only the Scots seem capable of this kind of thing. At some point in the evening ... Chris's son Michael came in, and so did the poet Norman [MacCaig]. What *did* surprise me is that when the subject of Communism came up, Norman and Michael both said they thought it was a lot of nonsense, and Chris took this with the utmost good humour.[51]

In November, MacDiarmid went to a launching party in the Edinburgh Bookshop, George Street, for Duncan Glen's *Hugh MacDiarmid and the Scottish Renaissance* (Glen had by then also embarked on his series of small editions of MacDiarmid's verse) and on 3 December he took part in a televised debate from the Oxford Union. MacDiarmid spoke for the motion 'Extremism in the defence of Liberty is no vice; moderation in the pursuit of Justice is no virtue' (a quotation from Barry Goldwater, US Presidential candidate in 1964). He was supported by Malcolm X, the black American revolutionary, and opposed by Lord Stoneham and Humphry Berkeley, MP.

Before Court of Session judges, Lord Migdale and Lord Kilbrandon, MacDiarmid appeared at the Scottish Election Court hearing in Parliament House, Edinburgh, on 21 December. Sir Alec Douglas-Home attended the court for the morning session but did not return to the hearing in the afternoon, being given permission to leave to attend to other business. Cross-examined by Sir Alec's counsel, MacDiarmid was asked if he considered everybody should have a chance of broadcasting even if they had only one candidate. He replied in the affirmative. MacDiarmid's complaint was that whereas Sir Alec had benefited from five Conservative Party political broadcasts he had not been allowed to participate even in a literary discussion on the radio because of his status as a parliamentary candidate. Had he been accorded equal broadcasting facilities to Sir Alec, he suggested, he would have polled more than 127 votes. On 23 December, both judges rejected MacDiarmid's attempt to have Sir Alec's election declared void and certified that the former Prime Minister had been duly elected. Expenses against MacDiarmid were awarded but these were later recovered. MacDiarmid was well pleased with the outcome:

> I lost the case but I, and the Communist Party, were greatly comforted by the general expressions in the Press and elsewhere that we ought to have won, and that the political broadcasts and telecasts arrangements would have to be altered in the way we wished. We were satisfied too with the enormous publicity throughout the world the matter received, and with our thus having been able to so effectively expose a piece of characteristic anti-Democratic trickery.[52]

For MacDiarmid this political defeat was a moral victory.

A week after the Scottish Election Court hearing decision against MacDiarmid, yet another controversy surfaced. On 31 December the *Times Literary Supplement* published an anonymous review of the critical books by Buthlay and Glen. After commenting on the poet's use of Scots the reviewer endorsed Buthlay's judgement of the poem 'Perfect' as an Imagist masterpiece. 'Perfect', according to Buthlay, was 'the poem that Ezra Pound and the Imagists talked about but did not write ... It is also, in its second verse, an object lesson in the meaningful use of vowel-music, consonance, and alliteration.'[53] Here is 'Perfect' as included, without any reference to authorship, in *The Islands of Scotland*:

> I found a pigeon's skull on the machair,
> All the bones pure white and dry, and chalky,
> But perfect,
> Without a crack or a flaw anywhere.
>
> At the back, rising out of the beak,
> Were twin domes like bubbles of thin bone,
> Almost transparent, where the brain had been
> That fixed the tilt of the wings.   (573)

It was certainly an impressive piece of writing though more concise than any of the English poems MacDiarmid produced in Shetland.

The explanation was simple. On 21 January 1965 the Welsh writer,

Glyn Jones, published a letter in the *TLS* explaining that he, and not MacDiarmid, had written the words, except for the opening line:

> These words ... were written by me – except the first line – as prose in a volume of short stories entitled *The Blue Bed* and published by Cape in 1937. This is not a question of similarity or echoes; the words are identical – apart, I repeat, from the first line – and describe in my story the skull of a seagull found on the shore.... I ought to add that I have no personal quarrel with Hugh MacDiarmid at all and that I have long been an admirer of his poetry.[54]

MacDiarmid responded cautiously. He had not read *The Blue Bed* but may have seen the 'Perfect' passage quoted in a review of the book: 'I either automatically memorized it and subsequently thought it my own, or wrote it into one of my notebooks with the same result. Any plagiarism was certainly unconscious.'[55] In conclusion, MacDiarmid assured Jones that the poem would never again appear over his name, though this promise was later forgotten.[56]

Rather than leave the matter at that, as an amusing if embarrassing literary incident settled by the two men it most affected, Edwin Morgan and Buthlay wrote letters to the *TLS* implying that the poetic act of creation was mainly a matter of lineation. That opened the floodgates to *TLS* readers who cited further examples of prose that had been 'rearranged' by MacDiarmid: critical rather than fictional prose at that (as explained in chapter 14). MacDiarmid's riposte to these revelations was to quote T. S. Eliot, 'Minor poets borrow, major poets steal.'[57] He then retired to the Olympian heights as if above the battle. However in a private letter of 10 April, he wrote:

> The 'Perfect' matter was most unfortunate.... We don't invent the infor-mation – we get it somewhere – and retail it without acknowledging sources. It's the use we put things to that counts. If part of a loaf is torn out, beaten up into dough, and baked anew as a biscuit, that is not plagiarism of the loaf.... Quotations show a proper social spirit.[58]

That neatly ignored the main point at issue, namely that MacDiarmid presented 'Perfect' without indicating that it was a quotation. Some time later, when he met Glyn Jones in Wales, he told the Welsh writer that he should have been delighted by the affair since it brought so much publicity his way.[59] The poet certainly felt that way.

A second volume of autobiography, *The Company I've Kept*, was published in 1966. Not surprisingly, given the age of the author, it fell far short of the polemical passion of *Lucky Poet*, comprising mainly previously printed articles on men he admired (John Maclean and Major Douglas), tributes to Sorabji, O'Casey and Pound, and some anecdotes about his recent activities as a Communist candidate at the General Election and as the boon companion of MacCaig and Smith: 'Norman, Sydney, and I may not resemble the Three Musketeers in the least, but we make an excellent trio.'[60] The book contained a poem written in 1961, at the request of the Communist Party, for the eightieth birthday of Willie Gallacher (who represented West Fife as a Communist MP for fifteen years from 1935, and who died in 1965). Part of it read:

> Willie Gallacher shines out, single of purpose,
> Lovely in his integrity, exemplifying
> All that is best in public service – distinct,
> Clear-headed and hearted,
> A great humanist, true comrade and friend.   (1079)

It was an occasional poem with little of MacDiarmid's sense of occasion.

Another recent MacDiarmid poem was released that year when, on 17 March, BBC Scotland televised (as a verbal counterpoint to still photographs by Alan Daiches, son of David Daiches) a work they had commissioned. 'The Borders', a longish poem consisting mainly of quatrains in a conversational Scots, is MacDiarmid's most sentimental offering, a heartfelt declaration of his love for Langholm:

> And a' the rivers, the Esk, the Ewes,
> The Wauchope, the Nith, I dooked in and fished,
> Guddled and girned – the hert o' a loon
> Nae better playgr'und could ever ha'e wished.
>
> And the wuds o' the Langfall and Kernigal
> Whaur we picked the hines and got oor conkers
> And dung the squirrels oot o' the trees
> In the happy days when we were younkers.   (1429)

It was a long way in quality from 'Whuchulls' – exploring the same territory, complete with 'Here I dung doon the squirrels wi' my sling' (1902) – which Duncan Glen published as a pamphlet that year. 'Whuchulls', from *The Muckle Toon* project, was ancient history to the ageing poet.

Tying up the loose ends of his life in *The Company I've Kept*,

MacDiarmid mentioned that he had been invited to read his poems to the Poetry Center of New York though Valda was worried in case he'd 'do a Dylan Thomas'[61] on her and die in America through an excess of alcoholic hospitality. However, after some visa problems concerning his Communist credentials, he decided to go following a trip of 28 April 1967 to Sweden where he gave a lecture on 'Poetry and Science' at the University of Lund. It was a lively talk, affirming scientific insights and Santayana's spiritual perception of the material world; he had, after all, asked in *In Memoriam James Joyce* 'Have I found/No salvation but only Santayana again?' (881). He flew to New York on 20 April to celebrate John Weston's revised edition of his *Collected Poems* and five days later repeated his lecture on poetry and science in Amherst.

At 8.30 p.m. on 4 May MacDiarmid was at New York's celebrated Poetry Center where the finest poets had read and where Dylan Thomas's *Under Milk Wood* was first performed. MacDiarmid was introduced to the audience by Norman MacCaig then read a selection of his poems including 'On a Raised Beach' and, after an intermission, lyrics from *Sangschaw* and *Penny Wheep* and sections of *A Drunk Man*. On 6 May he flew to Canada, where he saw Barker Fairley, and returned to Scotland at the end of the month.

In June MacDiarmid became first president of the 1320 Club, a radical nationalist organisation whose title honoured the Declaration of Arbroath which insisted that Scotland would never submit to the English so long as one hundred patriots lived. (He contributed to the club's magazine, *Catalyst*, but gradually realised that the organisation had been penetrated by a police agent.) Less contentiously he read at the Poetry International Festival in London on 12 July and took part in several events centred on his seventy-fifth birthday on 11 August. The National Library of Scotland mounted a birthday exhibition of books and manuscripts; the BBC broadcast a television tribute and four radio programmes; the Communist Party held a public celebration in the Royal Lyceum Theatre, Edinburgh; and MacGibbon & Kee published *A Lap of Honour*, containing some previously uncollected poems as well as a prefatory note in which MacDiarmid defended his poems in 'aggrandised Scots',[62] that is the sections of *The Muckle Toon* which appeared in the volume. After the birthday celebrations he travelled to Budapest with Valda for a week's holiday.

Though he was still living an active life with his intellectual energy not noticeably diminished, MacDiarmid was beginning to suffer from internal pains. On 5 January 1968 he went to Chalmers Hospital in

Edinburgh for tests. However, he recovered fairly rapidly after a spell in hospital and was in Glasgow on 6 April to address a 1320 Club symposium[63]; in Langholm on 26 July for the Common Riding festival; in Cheltenham on 1 September for a poetry reading; and in Dublin on 16 November for another poetry reading.

Duval and Hamilton brought out an elegant edition of *A Drunk Man* (with woodcuts by Frans Masereel) in 1969 and on 18 June the poet flew from Prestwick to Toronto, noting in his diary 'a beautiful proof that someday somehow the human race is going to make it'.[64] Staying with his daughter he was afflicted by what he took to be a virus infection which 'upset most of my internal organs and culminated in a bout of pneumonia'.[65] He was treated by his son-in-law, Dr Alistair McIntosh, and given a course of antibiotic drugs. However, when he returned to Scotland he still felt ill and returned to Chalmers Hospital for treatment on 14 July. Again he made strenuous efforts to get back on his feet; after being discharged, on 22 July, he travelled to Langholm for another Common Riding festival.

Penguin Books published his *Selected Poems*, edited by David Craig and John Manson, in 1970 but the highlight of that year was his first meeting with Ezra Pound. On 10 November 1970 – two years before Pound's death in Venice on 31 October 1972 – MacDiarmid visited Pound in the Venice house he shared with Olga Rudge. An unrepentant Pound had come back to Italy in 1958 after thirteen years in the prison ward of St Elizabeth's Hospital, the federal asylum for the insane in Washington. He had continued for some time to adhere to the Fascist ideals that had led to his arrest by the American authorities but by 1967 he admitted, in an interview with Allen Ginsberg, that 'the worst mistake. I made was that stupid suburban prejudice of anti-Semitism [which] spoiled everything'.[66] Most of the time Pound was mute, maintaining a mysterious silence rather than raking over the traumatic past.

MacDiarmid, however, found Pound willing to talk about their mutual friends Eliot, Orage and Major Douglas. Pound and Rudge took their visitors – MacDiarmid was accompanied by Valda, Duval and Hamilton – to lunch in a restaurant near their home then crossed the Grand Canal in a vaporetto. MacDiarmid and Pound had coffee together in St Mark's Square. MacDiarmid treasured this meeting even above the memorable night he spent with Yeats in Dublin in 1928. 'Of all the men I have known,' MacDiarmid declared after this one meeting, 'I loved Ezra Pound.'[67] He had long been exhilarated by Pound's poetry and critical prose, had corresponded with him in 1933 and was overjoyed to meet a man who had created the climate for modernism, composed music as well as verse, produced brilliant translations, revitalised Yeats in a way no operation ever could, and had established himself as one of the immortals of modern literature:

> My impression of him [in 1970] was of surprising sturdiness and inde-
> pendence and a wonderful directness and self-sufficiency. He must have
> been frail but he did not feel frail; as he linked arms with me the impression
> was one of his strength and self-sufficiency. He was in high spirits too and
> extremely genial.[68]

MacDiarmid met another distinguished American poet on 2 June 1971, when Robert Lowell came as a guest to a Scottish Arts Council reception in Edinburgh. The cause of celebration, on this occasion, was the release by Claddagh Records of Dublin of a double LP of the poet reading *A Drunk Man Looks at the Thistle*. MacDiarmid was in splendid form, mischievously teasing the assembled company about the quality of his greatest poem. 'I know exactly what to make of this poem,' he said in a short speech: 'it's absolute rubbish.'[69] Among the guests was Helen Cruickshank, and Valda, with her splendid henna-red hair, talked at length with her old friend. To those present, MacDiarmid looked remarkably healthy for a man of his age.

Yet his physical condition was deteriorating. On 11 August he was at Brownsbank, preparing to go out for a seventy-ninth birthday party with Valda and his most welcome visitors from Canada: Christine, her husband and children. Suddenly, MacDiarmid felt an intense inner pain and his son-in-law, a consultant physician, had him rushed into the Western General Hospital, Edinburgh, for a genito-urological operation. Discharged at the end of the month to recuperate at Brownsbank, he felt extremely weak. He had hoped to go to the USA for a second visit but was eventually persuaded to abandon the idea.

Still, he was able to look forward to enjoying his eightieth birthday in some style. On 10 February 1972 he was in London for the opening night of his adaptation of Brecht's *The Threepenny Opera* at the Prince of Wales Theatre. Lotte Lenya, widow of the composer Kurt Weill, turned up to give her support, a gesture much appreciated by MacDiarmid. On 27 May the poet went to a MacDiarmid symposium at Edinburgh University to hear his work praised by David Daiches and other enthusi-asts. In honour of his birthday there were exhibitions in Edinburgh

University Library and the Old Glasgow Museum. The BBC transmitted a colour film, *Rebel Poet*, and broadcast a reading of *A Drunk Man*. Valda wrote a poem for the birthday, published in the *Scotsman* (12 Aug.). It began:

> Over the years you've dreamed your dreams
> And as always
> You go back to your past
> In Langholm − your tap-root.[70]

Valda went with MacDiarmid to the Netherlands in the middle of June 1973 for the Rotterdam Poetry Festival and at the end of the month he again read at the Poetry International Festival in London. He was in Langholm in July for the Common Riding, as he explained to the poet David Wright:

> I felt quite O.K. on the Common Riding morning ... It was a splendid morning and I was looking forward to a very happy day. I went down to the Market Place − looked into the Eskdale Bar to see if you'd arrived, and then stood outside awaiting the second Crying of the Fair. And then suddenly collapsed. A doctor was sent for and sounded me, took my blood pressure, etc. − and found nothing whatever the matter with me. He simply thought I'd be[en] standing in the sunshine too long and that my collapse was due to some inadequacy of the blood supply to the brain − but he could discover no cause for that.
>
> A few years ago I used to take these collapses fairly frequently, but had not had any for a long time.[71]

These collapses were due to erratic syncope, occasioned by the arterial wear-and-tear of old age.

By 1975, however, the consultant surgeon at Chalmers knew that MacDiarmid had an inoperable cancer of the large bowel though the precise nature of the illness was not disclosed to the poet. Instead he was persuaded that he had a rectal ulcer and accepted treatment first by cauterisation under anaesthesia then by radiotherapy. Knowing he was gravely ill, both Christine and Walter saw their father in 1975.

Even at this late stage in his life MacDiarmid was not immune from aggravation. Maurice Lindsay's anthology of *Modern Scottish Poetry* was published towards the end of 1976 and printed 'The Little White Rose' as a motto for the whole collection. Lindsay, however, attributed the poem not to MacDiarmid but to Compton Mackenzie. The mistake confounded a confusion that had circulated as gossip. In November 1929

Mackenzie had said, in a radio broadcast, 'You know our wild Scots rose? It is white, and small, and prickly, and possesses a sharp sweet scent which makes the heart ache.'[72] Parts of this speech were published in the *Scots Independent* (Dec. 1929); when MacDiarmid published 'The Little White Rose' in 1931 (in the *Modern Scot* for July of that year and in *Living Scottish Poets*) he did so anonymously and with acknowledgements to Mackenzie. It then appeared in *Stony Limits*. Unquestionably, the lyric was his own work, a creative transmutation and not a direct borrowing like 'Perfect'. MacDiarmid was distressed by the error and though Lindsay and the publishers Carcanet apologised and promised to correct the blunder, MacDiarmid felt he had been, once again, shabbily treated in his own country.[73]

On 26 January 1977 MacDiarmid went to Chalmers for another operation. Seemingly indestructible he survived and was able to attend a concert, held in the Edinburgh Music Hall, on 13 August, to mark his eighty-fifth birthday. By 1978 MacDiarmid was a frail shadow of his former robust self. He hoped, however, he would live long enough to see the *Complete Poems* which his son Michael and his bibliographer W. R. Aitken were editing in two volumes. On 18 June he wrote to Bill Aitken:

> I've been a week out of hospital now and as I think I told you had two major operations there – one of which confirmed the fact that the basic cause of my troubles is a cancer of the rectum. It is temporarily quiescent. Cancers do that – go into latencies. The doctors had told Valda and Mike I'd probably 6 months to live, but I'm a tough old guy and may live far longer. I'm not anxious to and feel I've done my best work and am unlikely to be able now to add to that, so there's no point living on.
>
> I still expect to go to Dublin for the July 6th affair. But I am very weak and apt to have a lot of pain.[74]

Just over two months before he died the poet travelled to Dublin to receive, on 6 July, the honorary degree of Litt.D. from Trinity College. Terminally ill, he knew this would be his last public appearance. Though in constant severe pain and doubtful of having the physical strength to stand for the ceremony, he acted with characteristic courage. Here is MacDiarmid's account of the occasion in a letter of 12 July to Sorley MacLean:

> The Dublin ceremony went off splendidly. I was shaking in my shoes and afraid I might collapse at any moment. But the authorities were most

understanding and had posted a stalwart 6-foot graduate at my elbow, alert to see I didn't stumble and giving me a helping hand whenever I had occasion to move.... I kept a very low profile but tho' tired out enjoyed the occasion, as did Valda. Needless to say the kindness, courtesy and helpfulness of the Irish left nothing to be desired. I've had to rest since I got home and have had a fearful lot of pain, but I do not think my going to Dublin, tho' a great risk, did me any real harm.[75]

On his return to Scotland he was shown the proofs of his *Complete Poems* and realised, as he had anticipated, that the publication would be posthumous. At 3 a.m. on 9 September 1978 Christopher Murray Grieve died in Chalmers Hospital, Edinburgh.

Hugh MacDiarmid, the poet, lives on.

Epilogue

Christopher Murray Grieve was eighty-six when he died in Chalmers Hospital, Edinburgh, on 9 September 1978. He had outlived not only his mentors but most of his colleagues and contemporaries. George Ogilvie died in 1934; Pittendrigh Macgillivray in 1938; William Soutar in 1943; Catherine Carswell in 1946; Denis Saurat and F. G. Scott in 1958; Edwin Muir in 1959; T. S. Cairncross in 1961; Peggy (who remarried and became Mrs Harry J. Tilar) in 1962; Sean O'Casey and R. E. Muirhead in 1964; T. S. Eliot in 1965; Willa Muir in 1970; Barbara Niven, Andrew Grieve, Ezra Pound and Sir Compton Mackenzie in 1972; Neil Gunn in 1973; Helen Cruickshank, Sydney Goodsir Smith and Tom MacDonald in 1975. Though he advanced the ideal of being 'self-universal' (877) MacDiarmid was aware of his identity as a witness to a particular period. He had no desire to live on into another era as an invalid.

As news of his death was announced to the public, the name Grieve was mentioned only by way of explaining that this was the actual identity of Scotland's greatest modern poet who was internationally known by the pseudonym he adopted in 1922: Hugh MacDiarmid. I remember sitting at home and listening to the lunchtime news. MacDiarmid was dead and, as if in defiance of that fact, the poet's voice was reproduced through a recording. That he remained a living presence was evident. Shortly after the announcement there was a knock on my door. The actor Henry Stamper, my near neighbour, had also heard. 'Chris', said Henry, 'was a great man. Now we'll see how he is remembered.'

On Wednesday, 13 September, my wife and I were driven down to Langholm, for the funeral, by our close friend Trevor Royle, then Literature Director of the Scottish Arts Council. It was a dreich day and umbrellas were out to protect heads against the drizzle. There were distinguished heads at the gathering of several hundred admirers. Most of them were bowed down, grieving for MacDiarmid.

As the mist settled on the hillside of Langholm Cemetery tears were shed unashamedly by the graveside. Alex Clark, MacDiarmid's election agent in his campaign against Sir Alec Douglas-Home, spoke about MacDiarmid's political commitment: 'Having been greatly influenced by the Russian Revolution, and by Marxism, he wanted to see Socialism here in Scotland and believed that given full recognition of Nationhood, Scotland would lead Britain to Socialist change.' Norman MacCaig, poet and one of the closest friends during MacDiarmid's final years, delivered a more subjective statement. 'He would', said MacCaig, 'walk into my mind as if it were a town and he a torchlight procession of one, lighting up the streets of my mind and some of the nasty little things that were burrowing into the corners.' MacCaig described MacDiarmid as 'a gregarious, genuinely friendly, and most courteous man, who savaged hypocrisy and fought for the enlargement of life.'

A piper, Seamus MacNeill of the Glasgow College of Piping, played the pibroch 'Lament for the Children'. Valda Grieve, the poet's widow, placed white roses on the coffin. Christopher Murray Grieve was thus laid to rest in his native Langholm. The restless spirit of Hugh Mac-Diarmid could not be similarly confined.

After the funeral the mourners gathered for a drink in Langholm. Valda expressed her opinion that it was appropriate that her husband should be buried in the Muckle Toon so 'those who rejected him will now have to live with him'. Many of us got drunk and, this being Scotland, there were discussions that turned into fierce arguments. Norman MacCaig had anticipated, in his poem 'After His Death', that MacDiarmid's death would be observed by two minutes' pandemonium. Doubtless MacDiarmid would have liked it that way.

At the end of *Lucky Poet* MacDiarmid had chosen the phrase 'A disgrace to the community' as the motto for his tombstone. In fact the ochre-coloured headstone reproduced a celebrated quatrain from *A Drunk Man Looks at the Thistle*:

> I'll ha'e nae hauf-way hoose, but aye be whaur
> Extremes meet – it's the only way I ken
> To dodge the curst conceit o' being' richt
> That damns the vast majority o' men. (87)

It was an apposite statement. MacDiarmid had spent his creative life in pursuit of extremes. He had been a poet of pluralism and paradox who avoided neat solutions and enjoyed the artistic tension of seemingly irreconcilable opposites. Judged solely in the context of consistency, he had been frequently erratic. Judged solely in the interests of orthodox ethics he had been occasionally eccentric. His vision did not focus on one object or issue. It was as large as his creative life. After all, he believed in a spiritual dimension; and held that 'Poetry is human existence come to life' (757). A close inspection of his work reveals him as a mystic with a metaphysical view of the external world. 'The supreme reality', he said, 'is visible to the mind alone' (475). And his mind was triumphantly the imaginative mind of a poet.

Assessing any poet is a problem; literary fashions come and go, big names fade into the shadows cast by each generation. MacDiarmid, however, has all the hallmarks of the major poet. He had a wonderfully vital vision which he could express with astonishing eloquence, he had a restless personality which eschewed complacency and avoided stylistic repetition, he had a lifelong love affair with language. As a Scottish poet, animated by 'a mystical sense / Of the high destiny of a nation' (476), he stands supreme. For linguistic ingenuity only Dunbar and Burns come near him and it must be remembered that MacDiarmid had to renew a tradition that his great predecessors took for granted. Finding Scots reduced to a parochial idiom suitable for isolated outbursts of sentimentality, he shook that language to its linguistic roots and created, in *A Drunk Man Looks at the Thistle*, not only the most revolutionary work in Scots literature, but one of the most powerfully imaginative achievements in twentieth-century poetry.

Because he enjoyed (and sometimes endured) such a long life Mac-Diarmid inevitably produced poems below his own exalted standards. Pathological poems, such as 'Ex-Parte Statement on the Project of Cancer', contain more frustration than philosophy and do not show the poet at his best. The occasional poems he wrote towards the close of his creative career sometimes descend into doggerel. No matter. MacDiarmid is to be judged on his finest poems: the early lyrics, *A Drunk Man*, the vigorous verse intended for *The Muckle Toon*, 'self-universal' poems such as 'On a Raised Beach' and 'Lament for the Great Music', the subjective sections of the *Cornish Heroic Song* project. With such works to his credit he becomes an international figure, a national poet accessible to all.

Metrically, MacDiarmid was a traditionalist. He favoured the couplet and the quatrain (as *A Drunk Man* demonstrates) and when he used free verse, in the *Cornish Heroic Song*, he did not depart radically from convention: line-endings occur after emphatic phrases, enjambement is the exception rather than the rule. Stylistically, he proclaimed himself a modernist and his reverence for Joyce is seen most readily in his sensuous manipulation of unusual words, as witness 'Water Music':

> Brade-up or sclafferin', rouchled, sleek,
> Abstraklous or austerne,
> In belths below the brae-hags
> And bebbles in the fern.　(334)

However he understood modernism to be a method of renewing, not replacing, tradition. Several of his most masterly compositions make use of medieval techniques. *A Drunk Man* brilliantly adapts the dream-vision as well as alluding to ballads; the *Cornish Heroic Song* project is structured as a series of catalogues. His innovative use of language was linked to a profound regard for the enduring forms of literature.

For MacDiarmid, as for Joyce, words were sacred objects in themselves, phenomena that enabled the poet to receive the realistic world through a series of epiphanies. MacDiarmid's tendency to regard dictionaries as treasurehouses of sacred linguistic objects accounts for his love of alliteration: the word, he felt, came first and he experienced mystical delight as well as aesthetic pleasure from 'adventuring in dictionaries' (823). Yet he was able to impose his artistic will on words and, in his finest works, to pressure them with poetic tension. He is one of the few poets to make genuinely creative use of the dialectic.

Pound was one of MacDiarmid's literary heroes yet MacDiarmid was more of a Symbolist than an Imagist. Too expansive to isolate images as aperçus, he set great store by symbols that would stretch the intellectual resources of the reader: the strange tree of 'A Moment in Eternity', the thistle of *A Drunk Man*, the curly snake of *Cencrastus*, the torrent of *The Muckle Toon*, the pebbles of 'On a Raised Beach'. Such symbols enabled him to give poetic substance to the metaphysical abstractions that absorbed him.

Characteristically his imagery is a combination of the old and the new. Brought up as the churchgoing child of committed Christians, he became an authority on the Bible and made frequent use of biblical iconography. God and Christ are familiar figures in MacDiarmid's poetry and his concept of poetry endorsed St John's assertion 'In the beginning was the Word'. At the same time he avoided theological dogma and often expressed his vision through scientific images. From the early Scots lyrics to the long poems in idiosyncratic English there is a cosmic consciousness, an awareness that the earth is a tiny body floating in a vast space. An inspirational poet, he nevertheless made it his business to know about advances in scientific knowledge. He was fond of quoting Rilke's belief that the poet must know everything.

MacDiarmid achieved artistic equality with the poets who most impressed him. He could be as provocatively paradoxical as Blake, as delicately discursive as Wordsworth, as verbally exhilarating as Hopkins, as fanciful as Doughty, as speculative as Rilke, as assertive as Pound. He takes his place as easily with the old masters as with the moderns. Indeed he is one of the immortals of twentieth-century poetry, the peer of Pound, Eliot and Neruda.

As for MacDiarmid's legacy, it has to be confined to his own achievement. Since MacDiarmid wanted a nation of individuals, not generations of imitators, he remains a stimulating example rather than a figure to be followed unthinkingly. He said enough about the Burns Cult in particular to demonstrate his hostility to convivial cults in general. MacDiarmid wanted to be remembered as a national poet of international importance and those who take him seriously will take him at his word.

He continues to be discussed as a controversial character. There are the inevitable anecdotes about MacDiarmid the drinker and polemicist. Some of these, of course, are apocryphal. I remember when it was known I was writing this book that I received a letter from a citizen of Edinburgh who claimed to know MacDiarmid. The poet, this correspondent insisted, was daily to be seen in Milne's Bar almost always in a state of intoxication soon after opening hours. I recalled my own days of drinking regularly in Milne's and how MacDiarmid's visits were confined mainly to Saturday lunchtime sessions when he was invariably accompanied by Norman MacCaig who either saw him safely on the Biggar bus afterwards or put him up at his own house. At no time was MacDiarmid a solitary drinker soaking his sorrows in the Rose Street bars. Then I remembered: there was a Milne's regular, who faintly resembled MacDiarmid as he too had a shock of white hair, wore glasses (as the poet did in later years) and was fond of asserting his Communist principles. A retired miner, he fitted the description of the daily drinker. A case of mistaken identity then, but such mistakes are the stuff of poetic legends.

When he was going through his hardest times, MacDiarmid had a few close friends. When he was a household name in Scotland, a frequent contributor to radio and television and the subject of several films, everybody wanted to know him and buy him a drink and come away with a story to tell. He was eminently approachable and spoke warmly to admirers, often playing to the gallery. 'Great poets, such as myself,' he would begin a sentence, a twinkle in his eye. But the great poet had few pretensions as a person. The first time I drank with him in Milne's I addressed him as 'Dr Grieve' in deference to the honorary degree he had received from Edinburgh University in 1957. 'Don't call me Dr Grieve,' he chuckled. 'What should I call you?' I asked. 'Chris.' In these years, Chris was an easy man to know; the mystery was, and remains, MacDiarmid.

Throughout his life MacDiarmid exuded immense energy. As he grew older he lost little of his essential vitality and was usually the life and soul of any gathering he attended. His sense of occasion prevented him from becoming grim and humourless; his sense of destiny prevented him from becoming trivial. A colourful character, especially when he wore the kilt, he and Valda were Scottish celebrities with their own style. It was not wise to take him for granted. The poet's disarmingly courteous manner could occasionally be tested beyond endurance and he would reveal the combative core of his personality. Valda, always supportive of MacDiarmid, never tolerated fools gladly and several times showed the fierce temper of her Cornish temperament.

In his native Langholm, MacDiarmid was regarded with suspicion even after his death. A proposal to erect a bronze monument, ten feet high and fifteen feet across, on Whita Hill, a mile east of Langholm, was rejected as aesthetically unacceptable by Dumfries and Galloway Regional Council planning committee. A controversy ensued, during which MacDiarmid's reputation was heatedly discussed in various quarters. Eventually, in 1985, Jake Harvey's bronze monument (cast in the form of an open book containing some key symbols) was placed on a new site near Whita Yett, Langholm. The whole episode, with its acerbic tone and exchange of insults, is fairly typical of the way MacDiarmid is treated as an issue in Scotland. Nevertheless, the poetry is the priority.

Before he died MacDiarmid saw the proofs of his *Complete Poems* and pronounced himself content with his achievement. Though he suffered physical distress in his last days he had attained a measure of serenity through the knowledge that he had fulfilled his own potential. He had changed Scotland, given the nation an ideal made in his own image. He had been internationally acknowledged as a major poet. He had lived his life uncompromisingly, always preserving his artistic integrity. His monument is his poetry. His belief in 'the ineluctable certainty of the resurrection' (480) is no facile dogma, but, ultimately, a religious revererence towards his own art. The poet lives as long as his lines and images are imprinted on the minds of his readers.

Notes on Sources

In preparing this book, MacDiarmid archives in the following locations have been consulted: BBC Written Archives Centre, Reading; Beinecke Rare Book and Manuscript Library, Yale University; Ellen Clarke Bertrand Library, Bucknell University; Edinburgh University Library; Harry Ransom Humanities Research Center, University of Texas at Austin; Lilly Library, Indiana University; McMaster University Library, Hamilton, Ontario; National Library of Scotland; Poetry/Rare Books Collection, State University of New York at Buffalo; Sterling Library, University of London; University of Delaware Library; University of Reading Library; University of Victoria Library. Many of the MacDiarmid letters in these archives have been published in *The Letters of Hugh MacDiarmid*; unpublished letters are so indicated in the Notes.

1 THE MUCKLE TOON

1 *Scotsman*, 9 March 1972. This report opened by explaining 'Traditional Scottish tartan has become moonstruck, a new tartan being designed in the colours of the lunar landscape — black, brown, silver and grey.'
2 Hugh MacDiarmid, *Lucky Poet* (1943; rept. London: Jonathan Cape, 1972), p. 402.
3 Alan Bold (ed.), *The Thistle Rises: a MacDiarmid Miscellany* (London: Hamish Hamilton, 1984), p. 276.
4 Ibid., p. 149.
5 Ibid., p. 153.
6 *Lucky Poet*, p. 220.
7 Ibid., p. 232.
8 Ibid., p. 225.
9 Hugh MacDiarmid, *The Company I've Kept* (London: Hutchinson, 1966), p. 256.
10 *Lucky Poet*, p. 37.
11 Alan Bold (ed.), *Sir Walter Scott: The Long-Forgotten Melody* (London: Vision Press, 1983), p. 7.
12 *Lucky Poet*, p. 200. In the same book, MacDiarmid refers to 'impossible old Tories like Sir Walter Scott and Lord Tweedsmuir' (p. 28).
13 Dorothy Wordsworth, *Recollections of a Tour Made in Scotland A.D. 1803*, ed. J. C. Sharp (London: David Douglas, 1894), p. 272.
14 *Lucky Poet*, p. 4.
15 Ibid.
16 Ibid., p. 2.
17 Ibid., p. 349.
18 Ibid., p. 2.
19 Ibid., p. 4.
20 Ibid., p. 3.
21 Gordon Wright, *MacDiarmid: An Illustrated Biography* (Edinburgh: Gordon Wright, 1977), p. 21.
22 *Lucky Poet*, p. 218.
23 Ibid.
24 Ibid., pp. 218-19.
25 *The Thistle Rises*, p. 153
26 *Lucky Poet*, p. 18n.
27 Ibid., p. 226.

28 Ibid., p. 191. 'Burns ... was taboo in my father's house and quite unknown to me as a boy' MacDiarmid writes.
29 Ibid., p. 8.
30 Ibid., p. 224.
31 Ibid., p. 77.
32 Ibid., p. 234.
33 Ibid., p. 225.
34 Ibid., p. 5.
35 For the paragraph about Millom I am indebted to Mrs Isabella Andrews, whose sisters were the Little friends of Grieve's; and to the poet Norman Nicholson (born in Millom in 1914) who writes (in a letter of 29 April 1986) 'apart from the language which he draws from Classical Scots, much of MacDiarmid's vernacular is not too far removed from that of the old Cumberland dialect vocabulary, especially that spoken in the northern part of the country'.
36 *Lucky Poet*, p. 231.
37 *The Thistle Rises*, p. 387.
38 John and Robert Hyslop, *Langholm As It Was* (Langholm: Robert Scott, 1912), p. 557.
39 *Lucky Poet*, p. 16.
40 Ibid., p. 34.
41 *The Thistle Rises*, p. 259
42 Ibid., p. 349.
43 There is no Walligate in Langholm. However MacDiarmid explained that he 'used it since there are all sorts of street-names ending "gate" in Scottish burghs'. See John Weston's edition of *A Drunk Man Looks at the Thistle* (Amherst: University of Massachusetts Press, 1971, p. 25n.).
44 *The Thistle Rises*, p. 282.
45 *Lucky Poet*, p. 77.
46 Ibid., p. 8.
47 *The Thistle Rises*, p. 357.
48 Ibid., p. 379.
49 Ibid., p. 385.
50 Ibid., pp. 385-7.
51 *Lucky Poet*, p. 40. MacDiarmid writes: 'I was no child prodigy ... my brother did much better at school than I did — I had an insuperable objection to medal and bursary competitions and the like, an objection which has since made me continuously contemptuous of the directions in which one competes with one's fellows ...'
52 Hurt by the hostile remarks Hugh MacDiarmid made about him in *Lucky Poet*, Cairncross destroyed the letters he had received from his erstwhile admirer.
53 The postcard was preserved by Morag Enticknap, daughter of Andrew Graham Grieve. It is undated and the postmark has been obliterated.
54 For information about T. S. Cairncross I am indebted to his son-in-law, the Revd Inglis Finnie.
55 The doctrinal history of the Church of Scotland is a complex one. In 1799 tension in the kirk caused a division between the progressive New Lichts and the reactionary Auld Lichts. The New Lichts believed there should be no state church but a kirk sustained by the congregation on a voluntary basis; the Auld Lichts claimed to represent a national established church. In 1820 the New Lichts joined the United Secession Church which, in 1847, amalgamated with the Relief Church to form the United Presbyterian Church to uphold the voluntary principle. At the theological Disruption of 1843, 474 ministers (out of some 1200) signed the Deed of Demission and formed the Free Church of Scotland which relied on its own membership for financial as well as spiritual support. In 1900 the Free Church and the United Presbyterian Church amalgamated as the United Free Church. As a member of Langholm South United Free Church, therefore, Christopher Grieve was bathed, theologically, in a New Licht.
56 *Lucky Poet*, p. 223.
57 *The Thistle Rises*, p. 259.
58 T. S. Cairncross, *The Steps of the Pulpit* (London: Hodder & Stoughton, 1910), pp. 164-6.
59 Hugh MacDiarmid, *At the Sign of the Thistle* (London: Stanley Nott, 1934), p. 67.
60 In *The Thistle Rises*, p. 251, Mac-

Diarmid says 'I am a materialist and an atheist'.

61 *Lucky Poet*, p. 224.
62 T. S. Cairncross, *Blawearie* (London: Hodder & Stoughton, 1911), p. 125.
63 T. S. Cairncross, *The Steps of the Pulpit*, p. 32. The phrase occurs in an essay entitled 'Blawearie', Cairncross's fictional name for Langholm. 'Blawearie' begins with phrases reminiscent of the poem 'Langholm': 'It lies on a Southern slope, basking in the glow of the Solway, and from the hills above it can be seen the polished floor of the firth stretching away in beaten gold into space, beyond Criffel to the sea.' (p. 30).
64 *Lucky Poet*, p. 49.
65 Ibid., p. 8.
66 Alan Bold (ed.), *The Letters of Hugh MacDiarmid* (London: Hamish Hamilton, 1984), p. 631.
67 *Lucky Poet*, p. 8.
68 *The Letters of Hugh MacDiarmid*, p. 629.
69 Cf. 'my early recollections carry me back to the time I was four'. *Lucky Poet*, p. 40.
70 Ibid., p. 222.
71 Ibid., p. 231.
72 *The Thistle Rises*, p. 357.
73 *Lucky Poet*, p. 5.
74 Ibid., p. 228.

75 Ibid., p. 227. MacDiarmid took revenge on his anonymous enemy in his autobiography: she left school, supposedly seriously ill but the pupils 'gloated over the news that the cause of her illness was that she had been "carrying on" up one of the hills with one of the men teachers, and had got "a straw in her womb"'.
76 Ibid. p. 228.
77 Ibid.
78 Ibid., p. 229.
79 *The Thistle Rises*, p. 246.
80 Ibid., p. 275.
81 Maurice Lindsay, *Francis George Scott and the Scottish Renaissance* (Edinburgh: Paul Harris, 1980), p. 13.
82 Ibid., p. 24.
83 Ibid.
84 Ibid., p. 25.
85 *The Thistle Rises*, p. 276.
86 *Lucky Poet*, p. 229.
87 Maurice Lindsay, *Francis George Scott*, p. 24.
88 *Lucky Poet*, p. 227.
89 Ibid., p. 338.
90 Ibid., p. 229.
91 *The Thistle Rises*, p. 283.
92 *Eskdale and Liddesdale Advertiser*, 25 Nov. 1908, p. 4. The poem is uncollected.

2 A Man Sae Shunned

1 T. S. Cairncross has a facetious passage about the Langholm train in *The Steps of the Pulpit*: 'The Blawearie [that is, Langholm] express, it is true, once came in before time, but the stationmaster got such a fright the experiment was never repeated. This memorable institution does a steady nine miles an hour, rests and drinks included, and there are sometimes people who travel by it.' (p. 30).
2 *Lucky Poet*, p. 105.
3 MacDiarmid often implied – for example in *Scottish Biographies 1938* (London: E. J. Thurston) – that he had been educated at Edinburgh University.

sity. J. K. Annand, in a letter to A.B. (15 Feb. 1982), mentions MacDiarmid's 'claim to have been educated at Edinburgh University, which is quite untrue, as C.M.G. once admitted to me when I challenged him about it'.
4 Hugh MacDiarmid and Lewis Grassic Gibbon, *Scottish Scene* (London: Jarrolds, 1934), p. 81.
5 All his life MacDiarmid claimed to be taller than he actually was. He says in *Lucky Poet* (p. 2) that he was 'considerably taller' than his grandfather Andrew Graham. His passports record different heights but reach 5 ft $10\frac{1}{2}$ in. My own impression is that he was

about 5 ft 7 in. Commenting on the contradictory evidence of the poet's passports, Colin Hamilton says (in a letter to A.B. of 2 Sept. 1986) 'You're in the growth industry. [One] passport gives the height of 5 ft $10\frac{1}{2}$ in. which seems impossible! I think that you should abandon passports as reliable evidence.'

6 *Lucky Poet*, p. 64.
7 Ibid.
8 George Ogilvie, *Broughton Magazine*, Christmas 1920; quoted in Gordon Wright, *MacDiarmid: An Illustrated Biography*, pp. 25-6.
9 John Sinclair, 'An Old Master', *Broughton Magazine*, Christmas 1960, p. 15.
10 Ibid. Sinclair taught at Broughton after Ogilvie. He became Principal Teacher of English and, latterly, deputy Headmaster. A.B. was taught English by Sinclair in the 1950s.
11 J. K. Annand (ed.), *Early Lyrics by Hugh MacDiarmid* (Preston: Akros Publications, 1968), pp. 21-2.
12 Gordon Wright, *MacDiarmid: An Illustrated Biography*, p. 25.
13 Ibid., p. 26.
14 A. R. Orage, *Friedrich Nietzsche: The Dionysian Spirit of the Age* (Edinburgh: T. N. Foulis, 1906), p. 13.
15 Ibid., p. 24.
16 *The Thistle Rises*, p. 137.
17 A. R. Orage, *Consciousness: Animal, Human, and Superman* (London: Theosophical Society, 1907), pp. 85-6.
18 Norman and Jeanne Mackenzie, *The Time Traveller: The Life of H. G. Wells* (London: Weidenfeld & Nicolson, 1973), p. 225.
19 *The Thistle Rises*, p. 196.
20 A. R. Orage, *Friedrich Nietzsche: The Dionysian Spirit of the Age*, p. 65.
21 Maurice Lindsay (ed.), *John Davidson: A Selection of his Poems* (London: Hutchinson, 1961), p. 47. As well as MacDiarmid's essay 'John Davidson: Influences and Influence' (pp. 47-54) this useful selection has a preface by T. S. Eliot, who acknowledges the influence on him of Davidson's 'Thirty Bob a Week', calling it 'a great poem for ever'.
22 Ibid., p. 23.
23 J. K. Annand, *Early Lyrics by Hugh MacDiarmid*, p. 19.
24 John Bogue Nisbet, 'Sea Weed and Sand', *Broughton Magazine*, Summer 1909, p. 150.
25 *The Letters of Hugh MacDiarmid*, p. 10.
26 Jethro Bithell (ed.), *Contemporary German Poetry*, (London: Walter Scott, 1909), p. 26.
27 Ibid., p. xxvi.
28 *Broughton Magazine*, Christmas 1909, p. 29.
29 *Broughton Magazine*, Easter 1910, pp. 31-2.
30 Jerred Metz, 'Flammarion and the Comet's Poisonous Tail', *Astronomy*, Oct. 1985, p. 26.
31 *Broughton Magazine*, Summer 1910, p. 29.
32 Gordon Wright, *MacDiarmid: An Illustrated Biography*, p. 24.
33 C. M. Grieve, *Annals of the Five Senses* (1923; rept. Edinburgh: Polygon Books, 1983), p. 159.
34 Ibid., p. 60.
35 *New Age*, 12 May 1910, p. 26.
36 Friedrich Nietzsche, *Beyond Good and Evil* (Edinburgh: Good European Society, 1907), pp. 5-34. Translated by Helen Zimmern. The emphases are in the original; the quotation draws on sections 1, 4, 8, 23.
37 I am indebted to Linda Christie, Librarian of Broughton High School, for showing me the relevant entries in the Broughton school log.
38 Albert Mackie, in conversation with A.B. Mackie (1904-85) was one of MacDiarmid's greatest admirers. After leaving Broughton he went to Edinburgh University then had a stint as a schoolteacher. He became one of Scotland's best-known journalists, editing the *Edinburgh Evening Dispatch* from 1946 to 1954. As 'Macnib' he published humorous verse on topical subjects; his serious Scots writing in *Poems in Two Tongues* (1928) was well received as a real contribution to the Scottish Literary Renaissance initiated by MacDiarmid. Mackie's poem 'To

Hugh M'Diarmid' describes how 'a deid M'Diarmid turns/Tae form a Twae-in-Yin wi Burns'. MacDiarmid included Mackie's poem 'Molecatcher' in *The Golden Treasury of Scottish Poetry* (1940).

39 *Lucky Poet*, pp. 228-9.
40 J. K. Annand, in conversation with A.B. Like MacDiarmid and Albert Mackie before him, Annand attended Broughton and edited the *Broughton Magazine* (in 1925-6). He, too, was taught by Ogilvie; he, too, published Scots verse, for example *Sing it Aince for Pleisure* (1965).

41 *The Thistle Rises*, p. 286.
42 Ibid., pp. 286-7.
43 *Lucky Poet*, p. 36.
44 *The Letters of Hugh MacDiarmid*, p. 66.
45 Ibid., pp. 66-7.
46 Ibid., p. 832.
47 *New Age*, 9 Feb. 1911, p. 349.
48 *New Age*, 23 Feb. 1911, p. 397.
49 *The Company I've Kept*, p. 271.
50 C. M. Grieve, 'The Young Astrology', *New Age*, 20 July 1911, p. 274.
51 *Annals of the Five Senses*, p. 160.
52 Ibid., p. 32.
53 Ibid., p. 159.
54 *Lucky Poet*, p. 40.

3 An Ardent Spirit

1 Kenneth O. Morgan, *Rebirth of a Nation: Wales 1880-1980* (1981; rept. Oxford: Oxford University Press, 1982), pp 54-5.
2 *The Letters of Hugh MacDiarmid*, p. 4.
3 Ibid., p. 5.
4 Michael Foot, *Aneurin Bevan* (1962; rept. Frogmore: Granada, 1975), p. 25.
5 *The Letters of Hugh MacDiarmid*, p. 5.
6 Colin Holmes, 'The Tredegar Riots of 1911: Anti-Jewish Disturbances in South Wales', *Welsh History Review*, Oct. 1982, p. 216.
7 *The Letters of Hugh MacDiarmid*, p. 5.
8 Ibid., p. 4.
9 Ibid., p. 6.
10 *Scottish Scene*, p. 252.
11 *The Letters of Hugh MacDiarmid*, p. 5.
12 Ibid., p. 11.
13 Ibid.
14 George Bernard Shaw, *The Complete Plays* (London: Paul Hamlyn, 1965), p. 341.
15 *The Letters of Hugh MacDiarmid*, p. 11.
16 *Glasgow Herald*, 21 Feb. 1912. Uncollected. A cutting of the poem is preserved in the Andrew Graham Grieve collection in Edinburgh University Library (Gen. 2236), hereafter AGG.
17 *People's Journal*, 15 March 1912. AGG.
18 *The Letters of Hugh MacDiarmid*, p. 390.
19 Gordon Wright, *MacDiarmid: An Illustrated Biography*, p. 62.

20 *The Letters of Hugh MacDiarmid*, p. 11.
21 William Cookson (ed.), *Ezra Pound: Selected Prose 1909-1965* (London: Faber & Faber, 1973), p. 35.
22 *The Letters of Hugh MacDiarmid*, p. 11.
23 AGG. Uncollected.
24 *The Letters of Hugh MacDiarmid*, p. 12.
25 Neil Munro, *The Clyde: River and Firth* (London, Adam & Charles Black, 1907), pp. 96-7. Munro's text is accompanied by illustrations by Mary Y. Hunter and J. Young Hunter.
26 *The Company I've Kept*, p. 125.
27 *The Letters of Hugh MacDiarmid*, p. 12.
28 William Knox (ed.), *Scottish Labour Leaders 1918-1939* (Edinburgh: Mainstream, 1984), p. 206. The Maxton quotation is taken from a speech he made in Glasgow in 1925 and represents views he had held for years. Knox adds: 'Over the years Maxton held to his belief in Scottish self-determination and independence, but in the 1930s he had grown less enthusiastic, saying that "a struggle these days for mere political liberty is out of date, whether it takes place in India, Ireland or Scotland".' (p. 207).
29 *The Letters of Hugh MacDiarmid*, p. 12.
30 *The Thistle Rises*, p. 262.
31 *The Letters of Hugh MacDiarmid*, p. 12.
32 Ibid.
33 Ibid.

34 Ibid., pp. 12-13.
35 Alan Bold (ed.), *The Martial Muse* (Exeter: Wheaton, 1976), p. 34.
36 John Maclean, *In the Rapids of Revolution* (London: Allison & Busby, 1978), pp. 76-7. Edited by Maclean's daughter Nan Milton, the book contains essays, articles and letters written from 1902 to 1923.
37 Alan Bold (ed.), *The Martial Muse*, p. 35.
38 Timothy Rogers, *Rupert Brooke* (London: Routledge & Kegan Paul, 1971), p. 36.
39 Alan Bold (ed.), *The Martial Muse*, p. 37.
40 Hugh MacDiarmid, in conversation with A.B. Compare the following quatrain in 'Towards a New Scotland', from *Stony Limits*: 'Was it for little Belgium's sake/Sae mony thoosand Scotsmen dee'd? / And never ane for Scotland fegs / Wi' twenty thoosand times mair need!' (451).

41 *The Letters of Hugh MacDiarmid*, p. 13.
42 As late as 1937 Grieve contributed to an anthology entitled *Neo-Georgian Poetry, 1936-7* edited by his friend 'John Gawsworth' (T.I.F. Armstrong).
43 *The Letters of Hugh MacDiarmid*, p. 13.
44 P. Berresford Ellis, *James Connolly: Selected Writings* (Harmondsworth: Penguin Books, 1973), p. 32.
45 Yeats's poem was completed on 25 September 1916 and collected in *Michael Robartes and the Dancer* (1921). It is annotated helpfully in Richard J. Finneran (ed.), *W. B. Yeats: The Poems* (London: Macmillan, 1983), p. 645.
46 *The Thistle Rises*, p. 289.
47 *The Letters of Hugh MacDiarmid*, p. 13.
48 *The Company I've Kept*, p. 104.
49 *The Letters of Hugh MacDiarmid*, p. 367.
50 Following the publication of 'The Cabbage' (attributed to 'P') in the *Glasgow Herald* of 12 Feb. 1912, 'A Disappointing Man' appeared, in the same paper, on 7 Dec. 1912.

4 THISTLEONICA

1 *Annals of the Five Senses*, p. 69.
2 Ibid., p. 71.
3 John Terraine, *The First World War* (1965; rept. London: Secker & Warburg, 1983), p. 86.
4 Sheila Duffy, interview with Hugh MacDiarmid, Nov. 1975. I am most grateful to Sheila Duffy for providing me with a copy of this interview, hereafter cited as Duffy.
5 Monica Krippner, *The Quality of Mercy* (London: David & Charles, 1980), p. 184.
6 'Salonikan Grave' is part of Kipling's sequence 'Epitaphs of the War 1914-18'. See T.S. Eliot (ed.), *A Choice of Kipling's Verse* (London: Faber & Faber, 1941), p. 167. In his introduction (p. 16) Eliot advises the reader to 'look attentively' at the sequence as proof of Kipling's skill as an epigrammist.
7 AGG. Uncollected.
8 *The Letters of Hugh MacDiarmid*, p. 7.
9 Ibid, pp. 7-8. The poem by T. Sturge

Moore is 'Sent from Egypt with a Fair Robe of Tissue to a Sicilian Vine-Dresser. 276 BC'. In the opening lines of 'Cornish Heroic Song for Valda Trevlyn', MacDiarmid refers to 'the Coan wine my friend Sturge Moore has sung / In one of the first longish poems my boyhood knew' (704).
10 Ibid., p. 8.
11 Ibid., p. 10.
12 Ibid., pp. 13-14.
13 Ibid., p. 16.
14 Ibid.
15 Ibid., p. 17.
16 Duffy.
17 *The Letters of Hugh MacDiarmid*, pp. 32-3.
18 Ibid., p. 22.
19 Ibid., p. 23.
20 Ibid., p. 22.
21 Maurice Hewlett, *The Song of the Plow* (London: Heinemann, 1916), p. vi.
22 *The Letters of Hugh MacDiarmid*, p. 19.
23 Ibid., p. 24.

24 Ivan Turgenev, *Rudin* (Harmonds-worth: Penguin Books, 1975), p. 63. Translated by Richard Freeborn who draws attention, in his introduction, to the influence of Thomas Carlyle on Turgenev.

25 Alan Shelston (ed.), *Thomas Carlyle: Selected Writings* (Harmondsworth: Penguin Books, 1971), p. 236. The Carlyle quotation comes from 'The Hero as Man of Letters', the fifth of the lectures delivered in May 1840.

26 *Annals of the Five Senses*, p. 22.

27 Ibid., p. 23.

28 Ibid., p. 27.

29 Ibid., p. 28.

30 Ibid., pp. 31-2.

31 Ibid., p. 27.

32 Ibid., p. 28.

33 Ibid., p. 31.

34 *Lucky Poet*, p. xi.

35 *Annals of the Five Senses*, p. 69.

36 Ibid.

37 D. H. Lawrence, *The Complete Poems* (1964; rept. Harmondsworth; Penguin Books, 1977), pp. 123-5. Edited with an Introduction and Notes by Vivian de Sola Pinto and F. Warren Roberts.

38 *The Letters of Hugh MacDiarmid*, p. 19.

39 Ibid., p. 20.

40 AGG.

41 T. S. Eliot (ed.), *Literary Essays of Ezra Pound* (London: Faber & Faber, 1954), p. 5. The quotation comes from an essay which includes 'A Few Don'ts', first printed in *Poetry*, March 1913.

42 *The Letters of Hugh MacDiarmid*, p. 23.

43 Ibid., p. 25.

44 Ibid., p. 11.

45 Ibid., p. 25.

46 *The Thistle Rises*, p. 290.

47 *Lucky Poet*, p. 105.

48 *The Letters of Hugh MacDiarmid*, p. 25.

49 *Lucky Poet*, p. 105.

50 *The Letters of Hugh MacDiarmid*, p. 29.

51 Ibid., p. 26.

52 Ibid., p. 27.

53 Ibid., p. 30.

54 *Annals of the Five Senses*, p. 66.

55 *The Letters of Hugh MacDiarmid*, p. 29.

56 *The Company I've Kept*, p. 184.

57 Duffy.

58 *Annals of the Five Senses*, p. 81.

59 *The Letters of Hugh MacDiarmid*, p. 33.

60 Ibid.

61 *Lucky Poet*, p. 106.

62 *The Letters of Hugh MacDiarmid*, pp. 34-5.

63 Ibid., p. 29.

64 Compare Grieve's 'And I, the stranger, who had been afraid' with A. E. Housman's 'I, a stranger and afraid / In a world I never made.' Housman's lines occur in the twelfth poem of *Last Poems* (1922): see A. E. Housman, *Collected Poems* (Harmondsworth: Penguin Books, 1956), p. 117.

65 *The Thistle Rises*, p. 300.

66 *The Letters of Hugh MacDiarmid*, p. 368.

67 Ibid., p. 37.

68 Ibid., p. 38.

69 *Lucky Poet*, p. 404.

5 ODDMAN OUT

1 Lang's poem was first published in 1887 and appears in standard Scottish anthologies as well as his *Poetical Works* (4 vols., 1923); he also wrote a history, *St Andrews* (1893).

2 *The Letters of Hugh MacDiarmid*, p. 41.

3 Ibid., p. 45.

4 Ibid., p. 40.

5 Ibid., p. 41.

6 Ibid., pp. 41-2.

7 Ibid., p. 44.

8 Duncan Cameron, in conversation

with A.B. Duncan Cameron became Head Stalker at Kildermorie.

9 C. M. Grieve (ed.), *Northern Numbers* (Edinburgh; T. N. Foulis, 1920), p. 9.

10 *Lucky Poet*, p. 179.

11 Henley (1849-1903) came to Edinburgh after English doctors had recommended the amputation of his right leg because of tubercular infection; as he had already, at the age of sixteen, had his left leg amputated beneath the knee he was anxious to try an alter-

native. Lister saved Henley's leg though the treatment was agonising. John Connell, in *W. E. Henley* (London: Constable, 1949), suggests that Henley's suffering led to his poetic innovations: 'His poetic response to a prolonged physical and spiritual challenge and bombardment was deeply similar to that of the poets of the 1914-18 War ... Hospital life, as Henley knew it in the Seventies, was a new kind of human experience – as new as the factories, the mills, the slums and the mass-war which were other products of the Industrial Revolution.' (pp. 58-9).

12 *Northern Numbers*, p. 128.
13 Ibid., p. 109.
14 Ibid., p. 9.
15 *The Letters of Hugh MacDiarmid*, p. 51n, p. 53n.
16 Ibid., p. 45
17 AGG.
18 *The Letters of Hugh MacDiarmid*, pp. 49-50.
19 Ibid., p. 51n.
20 Ibid., p. 40.
21 W. H. Gardner (ed.), *Poems and Prose of Gerard Manley Hopkins* (Harmondsworth: Penguin Books, 1953), p. 27. In view of Grieve's political affiliation in later years it is interesting to note that Hopkins wrote, in a letter of 2 Aug. 1871, 'I must tell you I am always thinking of the Communist future ... Horrible to say, in a manner I am a Communist.' (pp. 172-3).

22 Ibid., p. 61.
23 J. C. Donaldson (ed.), *Munro's Tables* (Edinburgh: Scottish Mountaineering Trust, 1981), p. 132.
24 *The Letters of Hugh MacDiarmid*, p. 48.
25 Ibid.
26 Ibid., p. 43.
27 Ibid., p. 47.
28 Ibid.
29 C. M. Grieve, 'T. S. Cairncross', *National Outlook*, Dec. 1920, p. 121.
30 Ibid., p. 120.
31 *The Letters of Hugh MacDiarmid*, p. 52.
32 Ibid., p. 56.
33 Thomas Hutchinson (ed.), *The Poetical Works of William Wordsworth* (Oxford: Oxford University Press, 1913), pp. 587-90.
34 Kenneth Allott (ed.), *Matthew Arnold: A Selection* (Harmondsworth: Penguin Books, 1954), pp. 181-4.
35 Hugh MacDiarmid and Duncan Glen, *A Conversation* (Preston: Akros Publications, 1970), p. 58. The conversation was recorded on 25 Oct. 1968.
36 A.K.L., 'Edinburgh Poets: Is the Doric Necessary?', *Edinburgh Evening News*, 1 Sept. 1921, p. 3. A.K.L. (or Alister K. Laidlaw) was a pseudonym frequently used by Grieve.
37 Ibid.

6 MONTROSE OR NAZARETH

1 For information about Grieve's conditions at the *Montrose Review* I am indebted to Judith Sutherland, Managing Director of the paper.
2 William Cowper, *Poetical Works* (Edinburgh: Nimmo, Hay & Mitchell, 1891), p. 51.
3 *The Thistle Rises*, p. 288.
4 *Lucky Poet*, p. 56.
5 *The Thistle Rises*, p. 288.
6 William J. Tyrie, in conversation with Judith Sutherland. Tyrie began his working life as an apprentice printer on the *Montrose Review* and became a director of the paper.
7 Ibid.
8 *The Letters of Hugh MacDiarmid*, p. 59,
9 'A.K.L.', 'The Yellow Bride', *Edinburgh Evening News*, 12 Jan. 1922, p. 4.
10 Arnold Silcock (ed.), *Verse and Worse* (London: Faber & Faber, 1958), p. 75.
11 'The Complete Poetical Works of T. E. Hulme' in Ezra Pound, *Personae: Collected Shorter Poems* (London: Faber & Faber, 1952), p. 260.

12 T. S. Eliot (ed.), *Literary Essays of Ezra Pound*, p. 4.

13 Ezra Pound, *Personae*, p. 93.

14 Hugh MacDiarmid, *David Hume: Scotland's Greatest Son* (Edinburgh: Paperback Bookshop, 1962).

15 Ironically, the actor was an Irishman, Thomas Sheridan (1721-88), father of Richard Brinsley Sheridan.

16 David Robertson (ed.), *Whistle-Binkie* (Glasgow: David Robertson, 1890), p. 93. 'Dr Jamieson, in defining "Whistle-binkie," thus illustrates the term in its application: "One who attends a penny wedding, but without paying any thing, and therefore has no right to take any share of the entertainment; a mere spectator, who is, as it were, left to sit on a bench by himself, and who, if he pleases, may whistle for his own amusement."'

17 Ibid., p. 470. William Carnie was not one of the original Whistlebinkies but a latecomer to the fold.

18 G. Gregory Smith, *Scottish Literature* (London: Macmillan, 1919), pp. 138-45.

19 *The Letters of Hugh MacDiarmid*, p. 107.

20 Hugh MacDiarmid, *Contemporary Scottish Studies* (1926; rept. Edinburgh: Scottish Educational Journal, 1976), p. 89.

21 *The Letters of Hugh MacDiarmid*, p. 69n.

22 Ibid., p. 69.

23 'A.K.L.', 'Edinburgh Poets: Is the Doric Necessary?' *Edinburgh Evening News*, 1 Sept. 1921, p. 3.

24 William Will (ed.), *The Scottish Tongue* (London: Cassell, 1924), pp. x-xi.

25 In the Postscript to his epistle 'To William Simpson of Ochiltree', Burns wrote 'In days when mankind were but callans; / At grammar, logic an' sic talents, / They took nae pains their speech to balance, / Or rules to gie; / But spak their thoughts in plain, braid Lallans, / Like you or me.' James Barke (ed.), *Poems and Songs of Robert Burns* (London: Collins, 1960), p. 150. Stevenson, in 'The Maker to Posterity', used the Burns Stanza to justify his vernacular verse: ' "*What tongue does your auld bookie speak?*" / He'll speir; an' I, his mou to steik: / "No bein' fit to write in Greek, / I wrote in Lallan, / Dear to my heart as the peat reek, / Auld as Tantallon."' Robert Louis Stevenson, *Underwoods* (London: Chatto & Windus, 1887), p. 78.

26 William Will (ed.), *The Scottish Tongue*, p. x.

27 Ibid., p. 45.

28 Ibid., p. 88.

29 Ibid., p. 123.

30 *The Letters of Hugh MacDiarmid*, p. 750.

31 Ibid., p. 750.

32 Ibid., p. 751.

33 Ibid., p. 753.

34 Lewis Spence, 'The Fiery Cross', *Edinburgh Evening News*, 2 Jan. 1922, p. 4.

35 Lewis Spence, 'A Scottish Free State', *Edinburgh Evening News*, 2 Jan. 1922, p. 4. The Declaration of Arbroath, the classic statement of Scottish independence, comprises a letter, composed by Bernard de Linton, sent by the Scottish clergy to Pope John XXII in April 1320 as an act of allegiance to Robert the Bruce. Its most famous section reads 'For so long as one hundred men remain alive, we shall never under any conditions submit to the domination of the English. It is not for glory or riches or honours that we fight, but only liberty, which no good man will consent to lose but with his life.' Translated fom the Latin by Lord Cooper of Culross and cited in A. Bold (ed.), *Scottish Quotations* (Edinburgh: Mercat Press, 1985), p. 173.

36 *Edinburgh Evening News*, 9 Jan. 1922, p. 4.

37 Ibid., 13 Jan. 1922, p. 4.

38 Ibid., 16 Jan. 1922, p. 4.

39 *The Letters of Hugh MacDiarmid*, p. 754.

40 Lewis Spence, 'Literary Scotland: 1910-35', *Scots Magazine*, May 1935, p. 93.

447

41 *Edinburgh Evening News*, 22 Feb. 1922, p. 4.
42 Ibid., 24 Feb. 1922, p. 4. 'An Auld Scots Sonnet' was reprinted in Spence's *The Phoenix and Other Poems* (Edinburgh: Porpoise Press, 1923), p. 8. And again (as 'Sonnet in Auld Scots') in Spence's *Plumes of Time* (London: Allen & Unwin, 1926), p. 51.
43 *Contemporary Scottish Studies*, p. 62. The quotation is from an article by Grieve in the *Scottish Educational Journal* of 27 Nov. 1925 and generously places Spence as 'the first Scot for five hundred years to write "pure poetry" in the vernacular. The achievement was unquestionably related to his nationalism ...'
44 Lewis Spence, 'Poets at Loggerheads', *Scotland's Magazine*, Aug. 1954, p. 34. In the same article Spence says 'I cannot believe that [MacDiarmid's] efforts were founded on any tolerably scientific or rational basis'.
45 Richard Ellman, *James Joyce* (1959; revd. Oxford: Oxford University Press, 1983), p. 421.
46 Hugh MacDiarmid, in conversation with A.B. Discussing his early enthusiasm for Joyce (in Milne's Bar, Edinburgh) Grieve deeply regretted that he had never met the Irish master 'though of course I knew Yeats'. In the third issue of the *Scottish Chapbook*, Oct. 1922, p. 69, Grieve refers in a footnote to 'James Joyce's *Ulysses*, published in France by Sylvia Beach'.
47 *The Letters of Hugh MacDiarmid*, p. 71.
48 Ibid.
49 Ibid.
50 Ibid., p. 72.
51 Ibid., p. 757.
52 'Modern Scottish Verse', *Glasgow Herald*, 16 May 1922, p. 3.
53 Helen B. Cruickshank, 'Mainly Domestic', K.D. Duval and Sydney Goodsir Smith (eds.), *Hugh MacDiarmid: A Festschrift* (Edinburgh: K.D. Duval, 1962), p. 188.
54 *Contemporary Scottish Studies*, p. 97.
55 Francis Russell Hart and J. B. Pick, *Neil M. Gunn: A Highland Life* (London: John Murray, 1981), p. 76.
56 Alexander Scott, *Still Life* (Edinburgh: Chambers, 1958), p. 26.
57 *The Letters of Hugh MacDiarmid*, p. 137.
58 Ibid.
59 Trevor Johns, 'MacDiarmid the Montrosian', *Montrose Review*, 24 April 1986, p. 14.
60 *Scottish Chapbook*, Aug. 1922, p. iii.
61 Ibid., pp. 2-3. The quotation comes from Leo Shestov, *All Things Are Possible* (London; Martin Secker, 1920), p. 111. Authorised translation by S. S. Koteliansky. Although Koteliansky's name appears on the title page as translator, the text was extensively revised by D. H. Lawrence, who also wrote a foreword to the book. See Harry T. Moore, *The Priest of Love* (1974; rept. Harmondsworth; Penguin Books, 1976), pp. 441-2.
62 *The Letters of Hugh MacDiarmid*, p. 10.
63 *The Thistle Rises*, p. 323.
64 John and Robert Hyslop, *Langholm As It Was*, pp. 395-7.
65 *Lucky Poet*, pp. 6-8.
66 Hugh MacDiarmid and Duncan Glen, *A Conversation*, p. 60.
67 Leo Shestov, *All Things Are Possible*, p. 38.
68 Walt Whitman, 'Song of Myself', Section 51. In *Leaves of Grass* (1855; rept. London: J. M. Dent, 1947), p. 78. The phrase occurs in parenthesis in three lines often quoted by Mac-Diarmid in conversation: 'Do I contradict myself? / Very well then I contradict myself, / (I am large, I contain multitudes.)'
69 *The Letters of Hugh MacDiarmid*, p. 75.
70 Ibid., p. 77.
71 'At Birmingham', *Scottish Chapbook*, Sept. 1922, p. 41.
72 Ibid., pp. 42-3.
73 *The Letters of Hugh MacDiarmid*, p. 76.
74 C.M. Grieve, 'Scottish Books and Bookmen', *Dunfermline Press*, 30 Sept. 1922, p. 7.
75 Ibid.

76 Ibid.
77 Sir James Wilson, *Lowland Scotch as spoken in the Lower Strathearn District of Perthshire* (London: Oxford University Press, 1915), p. 169.
78 Ibid., p. 190.
79 J. Logie Robertson (ed.), *Burns: Poetical Works* (London: Oxford University Press, 1904), p. 536.
80 Hugh MacDiarmid and Duncan Glen, *A Conversation*, p. 17.
81 'Causerie', *Scottish Chapbook*, Oct. 1922, pp. 62-3.
82 Hugh M'Diarmid, 'Following Rebecca West in Edinburgh', *Scottish Chapbook*, Oct. 1922, pp. 69-73.
83 *The Letters of Hugh MacDiarmid*, p. 198.
84 Ibid., p. 759.
85 Ibid., p. 761.
86 C. M. Grieve, 'A Scotsman Looks at His World', *Dunfermline Press*, 25 Nov. 1922, p. 6.
87 *The Thistle Rises*, p. 247.
88 Ibid., p. 224.
89 Ibid.
90 Ibid., p. 247.
91 Ibid., p. 225.
92 Ibid., p. 288.
93 Trevor Johns, 'MacDiarmid the Montrosian', *Montrose Review*, 17 April 1986, p. 14.
94 *The Letters of Hugh MacDiarmid*, p. 81.
95 *The Thistle Rises*, pp. 128-9.
96 C. M. Grieve, 'Plea for a Scottish Fascism', *Scottish Nation*, 5 June 1923, p. 6.
97 Ibid.
98 Ibid., p. 7.
99 C. M. Grieve, 'Programme for a Scottish Fascism', *Scottish Nation*, 19 June 1923, p. 10.
100 *Lucky Poet*, p. 137.
101 Hugh MacDiarmid and Duncan Glen, *A Conversation*, p. 23.
102 Ezra Pound, *The Cantos* (London: Faber & Faber, 1954), p. 451. Pound is referring to the fate of Mussolini: in April 1945 he and his mistress were captured at Lake Como by partisans and shot; their bodies were then hung up before the mob in Milan.
103 George Orwell, *Collected Essays* (London, Mercury Books, 1961), p. 265. Orwell's essay, 'Notes on Nationalism', dates from 1945.
104 C. M. Grieve, 'Programme for a Scottish Fascism', p. 10.
105 George Orwell, *Collected Essays*, p. 278.
106 *The Letters of Hugh MacDiarmid*, p. 875.
107 Quoted in the *Scottish Chapbook*, May 1923, p. 297.
108 *New Age*, 15 Nov. 1923. Quoted in P. H. Butter, *Edwin Muir: Man and Poet* (Edinburgh: Oliver & Boyd, 1966), p. 38.
109 *Annals of the Five Senses*, p. 15.
110 G. Gregory Smith, *Scottish Literature*, p. 33.
111 *Annals of the Five Senses*, p. 155n.
112 Dostoevsky, *Letters from the Underworld* (London: J. M. Dent, 1913), p. 88. Translated by C. J. Hogarth.
113 *Annals of the Five Senses*, p. 52.
114 Ibid., p. 102.
115 Denis Saurat, 'A Moment in Eternity', *Scottish Nation*, 3 July 1923, p. 5. Introducing Saurat's article, Grieve writes: 'The following article is an interpretation, in the light of the Actuel philosophy, by Professor Denis Saurat ... The Actuel philosophy has been expounded by Professor Saurat in his *Principia Metaphysica*, and his *Dialogues Métaphysiques*, and informs his stupendous poem *L'Actuel* [which] was described in the *Scottish Nation* a fortnight ago, by Miss Isobel Guthrie [that is, Grieve] as "the science of comparative religion set to music – in the key of prophecy".'
116 AGG.
117 Maurice Lindsay, *Francis George Scott and the Scottish Renaissance*, p. 45.
118 Ibid., p. 25.
119 *The Company I've Kept*, pp. 89-90.
120 Ibid., p. 98.
121 MacDiarmid's assertion, in *The Company I've Kept*, that Scott was anti-semitic because he was 'partly of Jewish blood' (p. 98) astonished the

composer's widow Burges and son George who wrote to the poet asking 'how you came by this information'; no reply was forthcoming. See Maurice Lindsay, *Francis George Scott and the Scottish Renaissance*, p. 212.

122 *Annals of the Five Senses*, p. 32.

123 Francis Steegmuller (ed.), *The Letters of Gustave Flaubert 1830-1857* (London: Faber & Faber, 1982), p. 79.

124 *Lucky Poet*, p. 34.

125 *The Letters of Hugh MacDiarmid*, p. 47. The quotation comes from a letter of 15 Nov. 1920 to Ogilvie: 'My ear is faulty, I know — I am as you know tone-deaf in music and that does affect my work ...' Maurice Lindsay, in *Francis George Scott and the Scottish Renaissance* (p. 55), relates an anecdote in which MacDiarmid, Scott and George Bruce were waiting for a bus in Perth, after the funeral of William Soutar: 'As they stood waiting, Scott suddenly said to Bruce: "D'you know who the greatest music-critic in the world is?" "No," said the surprised Bruce. "Chris here," said Scott, "he's tone deaf!" The poet, who never outgrew his pupil-teacher relationship with Scott, said nothing.'

126 *Lucky Poet*, p. xxiii.

127 'A Scottish Literary Renaissance', *Glasgow Herald*, 31 Dec. 1923, p. 6.

128 AGG.

129 Paul Selver, *Orage and the 'New Age' Circle* (London: Allen & Unwin, 1959), p. 76.

130 Ezra Pound, *Selected Prose 1909-1965*, p. 180.

131 Ibid., p. 182.

132 *The Company I've Kept*, p. 105.

133 Paul Selver, *Orage and the 'New Age' Circle*, p. 28.

134 *The Company I've Kept*, p. 271.

135 C. M. Grieve, 'Mannigfaltig: the Scottish Muse', *New Age*, 11 Sept. 1924, p. 234.

136 Ibid.

137 Ibid.

138 Helen B. Cruickshank, 'Mainly Domestic', p. 189.

139 P. H. Butter, *Edwin Muir* (Edinburgh: Oliver & Boyd, 1962), p. 30.

140 Edwin Muir, *An Autobiography* (London: The Hogarth Press, 1954), p. 154.

141 *Scottish Chapbook*, Nov.-Dec. 1923, p. 63.

142 Willa Muir, *Belonging* (London: The Hogarth Press, 1968), p. 116.

143 Ibid. Willa Muir refers to Peggy as being 'pregnant with their second child'. As Christine Grieve was born in 1924 and Walter in 1928 (when the Muirs were again in Montrose) it seems that Willa's account of MacDiarmid in Montrose conflates several occasions, in 1924, 1925 and 1928.

144 Ibid.

145 Ibid., p. 115.

146 AGG.

147 Trevor Johns, 'MacDiarmid the Montrosian', *Montrose Review*, 17 April 1986, p. 14.

148 George Kitchin, 'The "Scottish Renaissance" Group, *Scotsman*, 8 Nov. 1924, p. 8.

149 *The Letters of Hugh MacDiarmid*, pp. 84-5.

150 Ibid., p. 308.

151 Ibid., p. 309.

152 *Contemporary Scottish Studies*, pp. 1-2.

153 John Buchan, Preface to Hugh M'Diarmid, *Sangschaw* (Edinburgh: William Blackwood, 1925), p. x.

7 WEE BIT SANGS

1 Scott's prize produced one of the lighter moments in the history of the modern Scottish Renaissance. Hugh Roberton, founder and conductor of the Glasgow Orpheus Choir, organised part-song competitions in 1919 and 1924. Scott won the first competition with his 'Aye she kaimed her

yellow hair' but in 1924, having fallen out with Roberton, entered 'O Jesu Parvule' under the name of his friend William Burt. It won first prize to the embarrassment of Burt, the fury of Roberton, and the delight of Scott and Grieve. No further competitions were arranged by Roberton.

2 Maurice Lindsay, *Francis George Scott and the Scottish Renaissance*, p. 48.

3 A.K., 'From a Scottish Study', Aberdeen *Press and Journal*, 12 Sept. 1925, p. 5.

4 W.J., 'Verdicts', *Glasgow Evening Times*, 24 Sept. 1925, p. 2.

5 'Poetry and Plays', *Scotsman*, 28 Sept. 1925, p. 2.

6 Theta, 'The Scots Renaissance and Mr C.M. Grieve', *Scottish Educational Journal*, 30 Oct. 1925, p. 1171. Theta was the pseudonym of Thomas Henderson, editor of the *Scottish Educational Journal*.

7 'Sangschaw', *Glasgow Herald*, 3 Dec. 1925, p. 4.

8 Lewis Spence, 'The Scottish Literary Renaissance', *Nineteenth Century and After*, July 1926, p. 127.

9 Grieve's article, 'Towards a Scottish Renaissance', appeared in the *Irish Statesman*, 16 Jan. 1926.

10 'A Scottish Renaissance', *Times Literary Supplement*, 7 Jan. 1926, p. 8.

11 Edwin Muir, 'The Scottish Renaissance', *Saturday Review of Literature*, 31 Oct. 1925, p. 259.

12 *The Letters of Hugh MacDiarmid*, p. 87.

13 When MacDiarmid quoted French, in conversation or at poetry readings, he made no attempt to give a French sound to the words.

14 *The Thistle Rises*, p. 248.

15 Hugh MacDiarmid and Duncan Glen, *A Conversation*, p. 53.

16 J. Y. Simpson, *Man and the Attainment of Immortality* (London: Hodder & Stoughton, 1922), pp. 306-7.

17 Geoffrey Keynes, *Poetry and Prose of William Blake* (London: Nonesuch Library, 1961), p. 118.

18 *The Letters of Hugh MacDiarmid*, p. 309.

19 Ibid., p. 86.

20 Ibid., p. 87.

21 Helen B. Cruickshank, 'Mainly Domestic', p. 189.

22 *Contemporary Scottish Studies*, p. 118.

23 Ibid., p. 6.

24 Ibid.

25 Ibid., p. 100.

26 Ibid., p. 19.

27 Ibid., p. 118.

28 *The Thistle Rises*, p. 131.

29 *Scottish Chapbook*, Nov.-Dec. 1923, p. 64.

30 *The Letters of Hugh MacDiarmid*, p. 310.

31 *Contemporary Scottish Studies*, p. 61.

32 James Kinsley (ed.), *The Poems of William Dunbar* (Oxford: Clarendon Press, 1979), p. 79.

33 A. R. Orage, *Friedrich Nietzsche: The Dionysian Spirit of the Age*, p. 65.

34 'Penny Wheep', *Times Literary Supplement*, 24 March 1927, p. 214.

35 Ibid.

36 See George Bruce's essay 'Between Any Life and the Sun' in K. D. Duval and Sydney Goodsir Smith (eds.), *Hugh MacDiarmid: A Festschrift*, pp. 57-72.

37 *New Age*, 5 June 1924, p. 66.

38 Nancy Gish, 'An Interview with Hugh MacDiarmid', *Contemporary Literature*, 20, no 2 (1979), p. 144.

8 Sic a Nicht

1 *The Company I've Kept*, p. 96.

2 Hugh MacDiarmid, *A Drunk Man Looks at the Thistle* (Edinburgh: Wm. Blackwood & Sons; 1926; 2nd edn., Glasgow: Caledonian Press, 1953; 3rd edn, Edinburgh: Castle Wynd Printers, 1956), p. vii.

3 Duffy.

4 Maurice Lindsay, *Francis George Scott and the Scottish Renaissance*, p. 55. Scott's Autobiographical Letter, in the Maurice Lindsay Archive in the National Library of Scotland, clearly specifies the Glen Clovis Hotel but

Lindsay, and the composer's son George Scott, both agree with A.B. that F. G. Scott meant the Clova Hotel, in Glen Clova.

5 In *Lucky Poet*, p. 231, MacDiarmid described himself as 'a great walker ... and to go sixteen miles back in a day and climb a fairish hill between the going and the returning was quite within my compass'. The entry on C.M. Grieve in *Scottish Biographies 1938* (London: E. J. Thurston, 1938), pp. 311-12, states: 'Played Rugby and Hockey for many teams; long-distance runner.' MacDiarmid, in *Lucky Poet*, p. 1, says he played rugby for Broughton and the British Army; in the Duffy interview, however, he confines his rugby experience to playing for the Marseilles Base Team at St Raphael in March 1919.

6 Maurice Lindsay, *Francis George Scott and the Scottish Renaissance*, p. 62.

7 'Braid Scots in Verse', *Glasgow Herald*, 13 Feb. 1926, p. 4.

8 Ibid.

9 Albert Mackie, 'Encounters with the stormy petrel', *Edinburgh Evening News*, 12 Sept. 1981. Item 82 in Box XPR 6013 R55 in Scottish Library, Edinburgh Central Library. Mackie describes his first meeting with Mac-Diarmid in 1925; the poem he saw in this form was 'I Heard Christ Sing', included in *Sangschaw*.

10 Gordon Wright, *MacDiarmid: An Illustrated Biography*, p. 56. The poem written on toilet paper was 'Milk-Wort and Bog-Cotton', from *Scots Unbound and Other Poems*.

11 *The Letters of Hugh MacDiarmid*, p. 322.

12 'Editorial', *Voice of Scotland*, 9, no 1 (1959), p. 5.

13 *The Letters of Hugh MacDiarmid*, p. 206.

14 Ibid., p. 362.

15 *The Thistle Rises*, p. 282.

16 *The Company I've Kept*, p. 158.

17 *The Letters of Hugh MacDiarmid*, p. 364.

18 Ibid., p. 365.

19 Maurice Lindsay, *Francis George Scott and the Scottish Renaissance*, pp. 54-5.

The quotation is fom the Auto-biographical Letter of 20 May 1945.

20 William Johnstone, *Points in Time* (London: Barrie & Jenkins, 1980), p. 73.

21 Bernard Landis, Letter of 28 July 1986 to A.B.

22 *The Letters of Hugh MacDiarmid*, p. 89.

23 Ibid., p. 320.

24 Ibid., p. 319. In *The Letters of Hugh MacDiarmid* this letter reproduces the date the poet attached to it, 10/6/26. However, what MacDiarmid meant was 6/10/26 (he often misdated letters) so this letter should come after that on pp. 328-9 of *Letters*.

25 Ibid., p. 331.

26 *Annals of the Five Senses*, p. 17.

27 J. Logie Robertson (ed.), *Burns: Poetical Works*, p. 1.

28 *The Thistle Rises*, p. 278.

29 Hugh MacDiarmid, *At the Sign of the Thistle* (London: Stanley Nott, 1934), p. 184.

30 Harvey Oxenhorn, *Elemental Things: The Poetry of Hugh MacDiarmid* (Edinburgh: Edinburgh University Press, 1984), p. 2. 'The opening phrase [of *A Drunk Man*] recalls Burns's well-known drinking song ("We are na' fou, we're nae that fou' / But just a drappie in our e'e ...").'

31 *The Thistle Rises*, p. 257.

32 Jackson Mathews (ed.), *The Collected Works of Paul Valéry, Volume 1* (London: Routledge & Kegan Paul, 1971), p. 451.

33 Ibid., p. 96. David Paul's translation of Valéry's lines reads: 'I even saw myself changed to that misty tree / Whose majesty diaphanously lost / Surrenders to the love of infinite space. / Immense being invades me, the burning incense / Of my divine heart breathes a shape without end ... / All the forms of light quiver in my essence! ...' (p. 97).

34 Avril Pyman, *The Life of Aleksandr Blok: The Distant Thunder 1880-1908* (Oxford: Oxford University Press, 1979), p. 241n.

35 Babette Deutsch and Avrahm Yarmolinsky (eds.), *Modern Russian Poetry*

(London: The Bodley Head, 1923), p. 129.

36 *The Letters of Hugh MacDiarmid*, p. 363.

37 In *Lucky Poet* (p. 345) MacDiarmid mentions 'Tyutchev's famous masterpiece, *Silentium'*; introducing Lydia Pasternak Slater's translation of *Poems by Boris Pasternak* (Fairwarp, Sussex: Peter Russell, 1954) he again cites 'Tyutchev's famous masterpice Silentium' (p. 7). In *To Circumjack Cencrastus* he declares 'Tyutchev was richt' (219) on the subject of darkness; in *In Memoriam James Joyce* he draws attention to 'the dumbness finally desired by Tyutchev and Pasternak' (742).

38 Babette Deutsch and Avrahm Yarmolinsky (eds.), *Modern Russian Poetry*, p. 29.

39 *Lucky Poet*, p. 105.

40 Babette Deutsch and Avrahm Yarmolinsky (eds.), *Modern Russian Poetry*, p. 29.

41 *The Works of Oscar Wilde* (London: Spring Books, 1963,), p. 914. The sentence occurs in the essay 'The Truth of Masks'.

42 Hugh MacDiarmid, *A Drunk Man Looks at the Thistle*, p. vii.

43 G. Gregory Smith, *Scottish Literature*, p. 4.

44 Ibid., pp. 34-5.

45 George Davie, *The Crisis of the Democratic Intellect* (Edinburgh: Polygon Books, 1986), p. 112.

46 D. S. Mirsky, *Modern Russian Literature* (London: Oxford University Press, 1925), p. 51.

47 Leo Shestov, *All Things Are Possible* (London: Martin Secker, 1920), p. 24.

48 Ibid., p. 144.

49 Ibid., p. 135.

50 *The Thistle Rises*, p. 137.

51 A. R. Orage, *Friedrich Nietzsche: The Dionysian Spirit of the Age*, p. 65.

52 A. R. Orage, *Nietzsche in Outline and Aphorism*, p. 12.

53 *The Thistle Rises*, p. 131.

54 Ibid., p. 136.

55 Janko Lavrin, *Dostoevsky and His Creation* (London: Collins, 1920), p. 177.

56 Ibid., p. 182.

57 *The Thistle Rises*, p. 137.

58 D. S. Mirsky, *Modern Russian Literature* (London: Oxford University Press, 1925), p. 48. Reviewing Mirsky's book in the *New Age* (25 June 1925, p. 92) MacDiarmid regretted the limited coverage of contemporary Russian poetry, a fault corrected by Mirsky's *Contemporary Russian Literature: 1881-1925* (London: Routledge, 1926) of which MacDiarmid accordingly approved (*New Age*, 4 Nov. 1926, p. 9).

59 *Selected Essays of Hugh MacDiarmid*, p. 40.

60 *Scottish Chapbook*, Nov.-Dec. 1923, p. 70. After printing the text of 'Braid Scots' MacDiarmid announced 'other sections of this poem . . . as follows: IV., The Voice of Scotland; V., Invocation to the Old Makars; VI., Scotland as Mystical Bride; VII., Braid Scots and the Sense of Smell; VIII., Braid Scots, Colour, and Sound; IX., Address to the World-Poets of To-day; X., Edinburgh; XI., Glasgow; XII., Sunrise Over Scotland and an Epilogue'. Commenting on this plan Ann Edwards Boutelle, in *Thistle and Rose* (Loanhead: Macdonald Publishers, 1980, p. 79) calls 'Braid Scots' the 'missing link between the Lallans lyrics [and] *A Drunk Man Looks at the Thistle*'.

61 G. Wright, *MacDiarmid: An Illustrated Biography*, p. 21. The poet's mother described the infant Christopher Grieve as 'an eaten an' spewed lookin' wee thing'.

62 Quoted in Harold Beaver (ed.), *Herman Melville: Moby-Dick* (Harmondsworth: Penguin Books, 1975), pp. 23-4.

63 *Annals of the Five Senses*, p. 27.

64 John C. Weston, in his annotated edition of *A Drunk Man Looks at the Thistle* (Amherst: University of Massachusetts Press, 1971, p. 99), wonders if the Drunk Man is thinking of 'Ezekiel's vision of the four man-creatures forming "a wheel in the middle of a wheel"'.

65 W. B. Yeats, *A Vision* (London: T. Werner Laurie, 1925), p. 152.

66 Ibid., p. 155.

67 Ludwig Wittgenstein, *Tractatus Logico-Philosophicus* (London: Routledge & Kegan Paul, 1961), p. xxii. This edition reprints Wittgenstein's German text alongside a new translation by D. F. Pears and B. F. McGuinness. It also contains Russell's introduction to the first English translation.

68 Ibid., p. 151.

69 *Annals of the Five Senses*, p. 70.

70 *The Letters of Hugh MacDiarmid*, p. 332.

71 Ibid., p. 331.

72 Ibid., p. 332.

73 *Glasgow Evening News*, 25 Nov. 1926.

74 Aberdeen *Press and Journal*, 27 Nov. 1926, p. 5.

75 *The Letters of Hugh MacDiarmid*, pp. 90-1.

76 'Gog' (Oliver St John Gogarty), 'Literature and Life: A Drunk Man Looks at the Thistle', *Irish Statesman*, 8 Jan. 1927, p. 432.

77 *The Letters of Hugh MacDiarmid*, p. 377.

78 Edwin Muir, 'Verse', *Nation and Athenaeum*, 22 Jan. 1927, p. 568.

9 THE 'REVIEW' REPORTER STILL

1 Michael Grieve and Alexander Scott (eds.), *The Hugh MacDiarmid Anthology* (London: Routledge & Kegan Paul, 1972), p. xiii. The quotation comes from the introductory essay, 'Hugh MacDiarmid: The Man', by MacDiarmid's son, Michael Grieve.

2 *The Letters of Hugh MacDiarmid*, pp. 91-2.

3 Ibid., p. 209.

4 MacDiarmid planned to call his collection of Scots stories *The Muckle Toon*, a title he also applied to the first volume of his projected poetic sequence *Clann Albann*, The Scots short stories of MacDiarmid appeared in 1927 as follows: 'Old Miss Beattie' (*Gallovidian Annual*), 'The Common Riding' (*Glasgow Herald*, 12 March), 'Murtholm Hill' (*Scots Magazine*), 'The Waterside' (*Glasgow Herald*, 16 April), 'A'body's Lassie' (*Scots Observer*, 14 May), 'The Moon Through Glass' (*Glasgow Herald*, 16 July), 'Maria' (*Glasgow Herald*, 27 Aug.), 'The Visitor' (*Scots Observer*, 1 Oct.), 'Andy' (*Glasgow Herald*, 22 Oct.). They are reprinted in *The Thistle Rises*, pp. 341-89.

5 Trevor Johns, 'MacDiarmid the Montrosian', *Montrose Review*, 24 Apr. 1986, p. 14.

6 Though Spanish was not a language MacDiarmid knew well, he succeeded in translating the novel as *The Handmaid of the Lord*. It was published by Secker in 1930 as an anonymous translation and first listed among MacDiarmid's works in *Second Hymn to Lenin* (1935).

7 *The Letters of Hugh MacDiarmid*, p. 219.

8 *Glasgow Evening News*, 26 Jan. 1928.

9 *Glasgow Evening Times*, 26 Jan. 1928.

10 *Lucky Poet*, p. 91.

11 Compton Mackenzie, *My Life and Times: Octave Six 1923-1930* (London: Chatto & Windus, 1967), pp. 138-9.

12 Maurice Lindsay, *Francis George Scott and the Scottish Renaissance*, p. 60. Scott also described Mackenzie as a 'facile play-actor' whose intrusion into the Scottish Renaissance was 'a disastrous blow'.

13 Compton Mackenzie, *My Life and Times*, p. 133.

14 *Contemporary Scottish Studies*, p. 11.

15 John MacCormick, *The Flag in the Wind* (London: Victor Gollancz, 1955), p. 34.

16 *Selected Essays*, p. 127.

17 Compton Mackenzie, *My Life and Times*, p. 134.

18 Ibid., p. 132.

19 Gordon Wright, *MacDiarmid: An Illustrated Biography*, p. 48.

20 *The Thistle Rises*, p. 291. Yeats admired MacDiarmid's verse and included four MacDiarmid poems in his *Oxford Book of Modern Verse* (1936) — 'O Wha's Been Here Afore Me Lass' (from *A*

Drunk Man), 'Parley of Beasts', 'Cattle Show', 'The Skeleton of the Future'.

21 MacCormick, in *The Flag in the Wind* (p. 30), says 'Baldwin crept in by a meagre majority of sixty votes over Cunninghame Graham.' However, the figures, as given by Compton Mackenzie in *My Life and Times* (p. 160), are as follows: Baldwin 1014, Cunninghame Graham 978, Samuel 396, Mitchell 226. Mackenzie notes that Cunninghame Graham had a majority of 211 among male students while the women supported Baldwin. For this reason Baldwin was known, at Glasgow, as the first Lady Rector.

22 John MacCormick, *The Flag in the Wind*, p. 35.

23 Compton Mackenzie, *My Life and Times*, p. 161.

24 *The Letters of Hugh MacDiarmid*, p. 297-8.

25 Ibid., p. 396.

26 *Lucky Poet*, p. 106.

27 *The Letters of Hugh MacDiarmid*, p. 397.

28 Compton Mackenzie, *My Life and Times*, p. 189.

29 *The Letters of Hugh MacDiarmid*, p. 394.

30 Letter of 15 Dec. 1954 to George Malcolm Thomson. In 1927 MacDiarmid had been exhilarated by the appearance of Thomson's book *Caledonia* as it provided him with a splendid opportunity for propaganda; he disagreed with Thomson's doubts about the ability of the Scots to determine their own destiny but recommended *Caledonia* in several reviews published in 1927: in *Forward* on 5 Nov., the *New Age* on 10 Nov., *Outlook* on 12 Nov. In a letter, of 1 June 1983 to A.B., Thomson said: 'He was an odd bird, wasn't he? A small but real genius and a great force.'

10 GRIEF IN HIS PRIVATE LIFE

1 Compton Mackenzie, *My Life and Times*, p. 196.

2 *The Company I've Kept*, p. 115.

3 *Vox*, 7 Dec. 1929, p. 156. As well as using the initials A.K.L., as he did when discussing Bridges, MacDiarmid made other contributions to *Vox* anonymously or as 'Stentor'.

4 *The Letters of Hugh MacDiarmid*, p. 379.

5 *Lucky Poet*, p. 38. Several pub gossips spread the story that the fall from the bus had ruined MacDiarmid's sense of rhythm but such a supposition has no medical foundation.

6 *Vox*, 28 Dec. 1929, p. 282.

7 Sean O'Casey, *Collected Plays: Volume Three* (London: Macmillan, 1951), p. 6.

8 Ibid.

9 Eileen O'Casey, *Eileen* (London: Macmillan, 1976), p. 147. Eileen O'Casey disguises Peggy Grieve as 'Kathleen' in her account, but, in a letter to A.B. of 6 Aug 1984, confirmed that Kathleen and Peggy were one.

10 *Daily Mail*, 4 April 1936, p. 9.

11 Peggy Grieve, Undated letter in Helen Cruickshank Archive, Edinburgh University Library.

12 Peggy Grieve, Letter dated 'Easter Monday' [1930] in Helen Cruickshank Archive, Edinburgh University Library.

13 Ibid.

14 Fionn Mac Colla, *Too Long In This Condition* (Thurso: Caithness Books, 1975), p. 93. In this posthumously published autobiography, Mac Colla says (pp. 93-4) 'as far as I know Clann Albain was totally imaginary ... As for C. M. Grieve's part in the matter, one can only say that conspiracy was not his métier. Neither by temperament nor habit of life was he suited to it.'

15 *The Letters of Hugh MacDiarmid*, p. 229.

16 Ibid., p. 355n.

17 *Lucky Poet*, p. 39.

18 Maurice Lindsay, *Francis George Scott and the Scottish Renaissance*, p. 56.

19 *The Letters of Hugh MacDiarmid*, p. 383. In a letter of 16 Jan. 1930 to Gogarty MacDiarmid quotes some lines that appear in *Cencrastus* and attributes

them to his projected collection *Another Window in Thrums*. He then explains that *Another Window in Thrums* derives from an early draft of *Cencrastus* which 'will bear no resemblance whatever to this early draft'.

20 *Selected Essays*, pp. 67-8.

21 While he was writing *Cencrastus* Mac-Diarmid wrote to Neil Gunn, on 27 Aug. 1928, asking for a copy of Valéry's *Le Serpent* which was translated by Mark Wardle and published, with an introduction by T. S. Eliot, as a *Criterion* pamphlet in 1924.

22 Leo Shestov, *All Things Are Possible*, p. 128.

23 Denis Saurat, *The Three Conventions* (London: Unicorn Press, 1932), pp. 126-8.

24 *Selected Essays*, p. 44.

25 *The Letters of Hugh MacDiarmid*, p. 128.

26 Germaine Greer, *The Obstacle Race* (London: Secker & Warburg, 1979), p. 50. In this book Greer discusses Modersohn-Becker in a feminist context and suggests (p. 50), 'She was isolated and undervalued in Worpswede, and would have been much happier living like a gypsy in Paris.'

27 Kenneth Buthlay, *Hugh MacDiarmid* (Edinburgh: Oliver & Boyd, 1964), p. 76.

28 *The Letters of Hugh MacDiarmid*, p. 103.

29 Edwin Muir, 'A Star in the North Sky', *New Statesman*, 6 Dec. 1930, p. xxiv. Christmas Book Supplement.

30 *Criterion*, April 1931, p. 519.

31 *Modern Scot*, Jan. 1931, p. 62.

32 Gordon Wright, *MacDiarmid: An Illustrated Biography*, p. 52.

33 Helen B. Cruickshank, *Octobiography*, (Montrose: Standard Press, 1976), p. 80.

34 Hugh MacDiarmid, *The Uncanny Scot*, ed. Kenneth Buthlay (London: Mac-Gibbon & Kee, 1968), p. 123.

35 Undated letter. AGG.

36 *The Letters of Hugh MacDiarmid*, p. 233.

37 Interview with Valda Grieve, 11 Feb. 1984. Hereafter Valda.

38 In a letter of 10 Aug. 1932 to Helen Cruickshank, MacDiarmid said: 'Now the fact is that (with the sole exception of Liverpool) any drinking or other proclivities have never interfered with the diligent discharge of my duties.' *The Letters of Hugh MacDiarmid*, p. 114. In *Lucky Poet* he makes two significant references to Liverpool: he calls his period in Liverpool 'unfortunate [for] painful reasons, and owing perhaps to a considerable extent to my own blame' (p. 41); and he refers to 'a wild year as Publicity Officer of the Liverpool Organisation' (p. 105).

39 *The Letters of Hugh MacDiarmid*, p. 233.

40 Ibid., p. 234.

41 Andrew Grieve, Letter of 10 Oct. 1932 to MacDiarmid. AGG.

42 'Summons of Divorce in case of Mrs Margaret Skinner or Grieve against Christopher Murray Grieve'. Scottish Record Office, CS 253/4498/1933, p. 5.

43 Valda.

44 Ibid.

45 Ibid.

46 Ibid.

47 Ibid.

48 Ibid.

49 Ibid.

50 Ibid.

51 *Lucky Poet*, p. 20.

52 William Johnstone, *Points in Time*, pp. 162-3. As told in Johnstone's book, the story has MacDiarmid trying to sell Eliot the lyric for publication which is unlikely as it had already appeared in *A Drunk Man*. However, the anecdote was clarified by A.B. in conversation with Johnstone.

53 *Lucky Poet*, p. 107.

54 Ibid., p. 108.

55 *Scotsman*, 18 Jan. 1932, p. 14.

56 On 23 Nov. 1931, Elizabeth Dawson had written to her son Andrew, MacDiarmid's brother, '[News of the divorce] fell like a bomb shell on us for we thought it would be Peggie that would be to blame but alas who ever can he have been carrying on with, it is too awful.' AGG.

57 Undated letter, but certainly Jan. 1932, from MacDiarmid to his mother. AGG.
58 Unpublished. Hugh MacDiarmid Papers, University of Delaware Library.

11 Breid-and-Butter Problems

1 Alec Craig, *The Banned Books of England* (London: Allen & Unwin, 1962), p. 85.
2 Anne Olivier Bell and Andrew Mc-Neillie (eds.), *The Diary of Virginia Woolf: Volume IV, 1931-5* (1982; rept. Harmondsworth: Penguin Books, 1983), p. 320.
3 A. Craig, *The Banned Books of England* p. 89.
4 Ibid.
5 A manuscript and typescript of *Alone With the Alone* is part of the Hugh MacDiarmid Papers, University of Delaware Library. MacDiarmid's use of the phrase 'alane wi' the alane' (349) in 'Depth and the Chthonian Image' is strong evidence that this is the poem originally entitled 'Alone With the Alone'.
6 *The Letters of Hugh MacDiarmid*, p. 116.
7 William Ralph Inge, *The Philosophy of Plotinus: Volume Two* (London: Longmans, Green, 1929), pp. 134, 135, 143.
8 Ibid., p. 139.
9 *Lucky Poet*, p. 35.
10 Barker Fairley (ed.), *Selected Passages from 'The Dawn in Britain' of Charles Doughty* (London: Duckworth, 1935), p. 13.
11 *The Letters of Hugh MacDiarmid*, p. 444.
12 Edmund Blunden (ed.), *Selected Poems: Percy Bysshe Shelley* (London: Collins, 1954), p. 367.
13 Ibid., p. 445.
14 *The Thistle Rises*, pp. 390-1.
15 AGG.
16 Helen Cruickshank, 'Mainly Domestic', p. 192.
17 *The Letters of Hugh MacDiarmid*, pp. 243-4.
18 James MacLaren, 'The Course of Scottish Poetry', *Scottish Educational Journal*, 1 July 1932, p. 829.
19 Raymond Ross, 'Valda', *Scotsman* (weekend supp; 1 Sept. 1984), p. 6.
20 *The Letters of Hugh MacDiarmid*, p. 248.
21 Ibid., p. 115.
22 Ibid., p. 248.

12 Accepting the Stones

1 C. M. Grieve, 'At the Sign of the Thistle', *Free Man*, 10 Sept. 1932, p. 4.
2 Helen Cruickshank, 'Mainly Domestic', p. 192.
3 Valda.
4 Ibid.
5 Helen Cruickshank, 'Mainly Domestic', p. 192.
6 Ibid., p. 193.
7 Hugh MacDiarmid, *The Islands of Scotland* (London: Batsford, 1939), p. 57.
8 M. Robertson (ed.), *The Collected Poems of Vagaland* (Lerwick: Shetland Times, 1975), p. 181.
9 'Kate's eyes were sea-green' became 'A Pair of Sea-Green Eyes' (552); 'Here at the heicht o' passion' (495) became 'As Lovers Do' (540); 'Are the livin' sae muckle use' (501) became 'At the Cenotaph' (538); 'O weel may timid and graspin' folk' (502) became 'Thanksgiving' (546); 'Think not that I forget a single pang' (503) became 'Think Not That I Forget' (548). There is also an anglicised extract from the Ode beginning 'As the heavy earth is the same below' (543) which corresponds to the lines starting from 'But as the lourd earth is the same alow' (505). The differences between the Scots and English versions are so minimal as to

suggest that the Scots texture of the Ode is simply a matter of orthography.

10 *Lucky Poet*, p. 45.

11 *The Letters of Hugh MacDiarmid*, p. 250.

12 Ibid.

13 Ruth McQuillan and Agnes Shearer, *In Line with the Ramna Stacks* (Edinburgh: Challister Press, 1980), p. 2.

14 John Irvine, in conversation with A.B.

15 AGG.

16 *Lucky Poet*, pp. 45-6.

17 *At the Sign of the Thistle*, p. 129.

18 Ibid., pp. 128-9.

19 Hugh MacDiarmid, 'Faeroerne', *Scottish Educational Journal*, 12 Jan. 1934, p. 55.

20 W.R. Aitken, 'Hugh MacDiarmid's "Unpublished" Books', in F. McAdams (ed.), *Of One Accord* (Glasgow; Scottish Library Association, 1977), p. 65.

21 *Selected Essays*, p. 75.

22 Ibid., p. 80.

23 *The Uncanny Scot*, pp. 80-3.

24 Jimmy Arthur, whose uncle owned the general store at Sodom in MacDiarmid's time, discussed this with A.B.

25 In Nov. 1985 Valda Grieve, the poet's widow, published a limited edition of *On a Raised Beach* containing both the *Stony Limits* text of the poem and the draft version sent to F.G. Scott and preserved in Edinburgh University Library.

26 D.M. MacKinnon, *The Problem of Metaphysics* (Cambridge: Cambridge University Press, 1974), pp. 167-8.

27 Leo Shestov, *All Things Are Possible*, p. 128.

28 Harvey Oxenhorn, *Elemental Things* (Edinburgh: Edinburgh University Press, 1984), p. 171.

29 AGG. Dr Hannah Royle told A.B. on 5 February 1987, that there is 'no link whatsoever' between the anal fissure of 1933 and the rectal carcinoma that eventually killed the poet.

30 Ibid.

31 Ruth McQuillan, 'MacDiarmid's Other Dictionary', *Lines Review*, Sept. 1978, p. 10.

32 William Soutar, *Diaries of a Dying Man*, ed. Alexander Scott (Edinburgh: W. & R. Chambers, 1954), p. 26.

33 In an essay on 'The Seamless Garment and the Muse', *Agenda*, Autumn-Winter 1967-8, the Irish poet John Montague points out that MacDiarmid's opening lines

> Fold of value in the world west from Greece
> Over whom it has been our duty to keep guard
> Have we slept on our watch; have death and dishonour
> Reached you through our neglect and left you in lasting sleep?

are derived from Eoin MacNeill's translation of Grainne's lullaby over Diarmid in the *Duanaire Finn*:

> O fold of valour of the world west from Greece,
> over whom I stay watching,
> my heart will well-nigh burst
> if I see thee not at any time.

34 Letter of 25 Sept. 1933. AGG.

35 *Lucky Poet*, p. 45.

36 Hugh MacDiarmid and Lewis Grassic Gibbon, *Scottish Scene* (London: Jarrolds, 1934), p. 20.

37 Ibid., p. 340.

38 Ibid., p. 130.

39 Ibid.

40 *Lucky Poet*, p. 45.

41 Wyndham Lewis, *One-Way Song* (London: Faber & Faber, 1933), p. 74.

42 Eric Linklater, *Magnus Merriman* (London: Jonathan Cape, 1934), pp. 73-4.

43 *Lucky Poet*, p. 230.

13 Agonies and Abominations

1 John Maclean, *In the Rapids of Revolution*, ed. Nan Milton (London: Allison & Busby, 1978), p. 218.

2 *The Company I've Kept*, p. 125.

3 *The Letters of Hugh MacDiarmid*, p. 847.

4 Willa Muir, *Belonging*, pp. 164-5.

5 As Willa Muir noted (*Belonging*, p. 165) the idea of returning the Stone to Scotland 'had been let loose into the air of Scotland, with all the panache of Christopher's personality, and the queer thing was that it stayed alive there until the fifties'. In 1950 a group of young Scots removed the Stone from Westminster Abbey and deposited it at Arbroath Abbey but it was taken back to London. MacDiarmid wrote a sonnet 'On the Asportation of the Scone Stone': 'Since David with a pebble in his sling / Goliath slew, now with this heavier stone / A little nation marks the opening / Of a like unequal battle for its own / And splits the atom of Earth's greatest throne' (1362). Ian Robertson Hamilton, who organised the removal of the Stone on Christmas morning 1950, describes the significance of his action in *No Stone Unturned* (London: Gollancz, 1952, pp. 26-7): 'The origin of this Stone shines dimly through the mists of history, but it has always been associated with the right of government. ... Thus it is not surprising the value that Scotsmen place on this piece of Stone. It was taken from them as the symbol of their liberty, and while it remained in England the superstition, if one can call the faith of a people superstition, was maintained that Scotland could never be prosperous until the Stone was returned.' In *The North Wind of Love* (1945) Compton Mackenzie imagines a botched attempt to remove the Stone on St Andrew's Day 1932.

6 Letter of 12 April 1934 to Andrew Graham Grieve. AGG.

7 Ibid.

8 Valda.

9 '"A Dish of Whummle" appeared as "Wound-Pie" [*sic*] ... It was altered by the editor to accord with his misunderstanding of the Scots *wund* (= wind).' Kenneth Buthlay, *Hugh MacDiarmid* (Edinburgh: Oliver & Boyd, 1964), p. 81n.

10 Letter in Helen Cruickshank Archive, Edinburgh University Library.

11 Ian S. Munro, *Leslie Mitchell: Lewis Grassic Gibbon* (Edinburgh: Oliver & Boyd, 1966), p. 173. Munro's book has a Foreword by MacDiarmid.

12 *The Letters of Hugh MacDiarmid*, p. 534.

13 Ibid., p. 558.

14 Sorley MacLean, in conversation with A.B., 17 March 1984.

15 Sorley MacLean, 'MacDiarmid 1933-1944', in P. H. Scott and A. C. Davis (eds.), *The Age of MacDiarmid* (Edinburgh: Mainstream, 1980), p. 18.

16 Letter of 20 August 1935 to the publishers Routledge. Routledge Archive, Reading University Library.

17 Undated letter, but probably Sept. 1938, to Helen Cruickshank. Helen Cruickshank Archive, Edinburgh University Library.

18 David Orr, 'MacDiarmid – the Man', *Jabberwock* (5, 1958), p. 15.

19 AGG.

20 Maurice Lindsay, *Francis George Scott and the Scottish Renaissance*, p. 58.

21 AGG. The letter has only the date 'Tuesday' but the reference to 'a few days ago', in connection with the request of 22 Sept. for money, establishes this as a letter of 24 Sept. 1935.

22 AGG. Dating of 1 Oct. is conjectural.

23 Ibid.

14 Mature Art

1 *The Letters of Hugh MacDiarmid*, p. 548.
2 Hugh MacDiarmid, 'Scotland, France and Working Class Interests', *New Scotland*, 26 Oct. 1935.
3 In the *Voice of Scotland* (Mar.-May 1939) there is a section on 'The Wolfe of Badenoch' (pp. 7-11). A note (on p. 7) mentions that the contribution is from 'an unpublished book on the Wolfe by Mrs N. K. Wells ... and Hugh MacDiarmid'. Nannie Wells was known as 'the nanny of the Scottish National Party'. The *Voice of Scotland* article on the Wolfe was duly incorporated in *Lucky Poet*.
4 *The Letters of Hugh MacDiarmid*, pp. 554-5. The reader's report on *Red Scotland* is contained in the Routledge Archive in Reading University Library.
5 Letter dated 'Tuesday 11th' (11 Jan. 1938) in Helen Cruickshank Archive, Edinburgh University Library.
6 *Lucky Poet*, p. 42.
7 Ibid.
8 Mary MacDonald, 'I Raise My Glass', unpublished typescript.
9 Edwin Muir, *Scott and Scotland* (London: Routledge, 1936), p. 21.
10 Ibid., p. 22.
11 Ibid., p. 178.
12 *The Letters of Hugh MacDiarmid*, p. 157.
13 Ibid., p. 853.
14 Willa Muir, *Belonging*, p. 195.
15 MacDiarmid never completed his work on the Maclean biography. He eventually turned all his material over to John Broom whose *John Maclean* was published in 1973. Nan Milton's *John Maclean* also appeared in 1973.
16 'The Red Scotland Thesis', *Voice of Scotland* (June-Aug. 1938), pp. 10-11.
17 Hugh MacDiarmid, Foreword, P. Berresford Ellis and Seumas Mac a' Ghobhainn, *The Scottish Insurrection of 1820* (London: Gollancz, 1970), p. 13.
18 Maurice Lindsay, *Francis George Scott and the Scottish Renaissance*, p. 196. Scott also wrote to MacDiarmid: 'I don't see why you should bother at all about the C.P. Surely to goodness you can't imagine at your time of life that *any* party in its official capacity can be worth a docken or would be likely to fit you into its ranks.' (Ibid., p. 197).
19 Raymond Ross, 'Valda', *Scotsman* (weekend supp; 1 Sept. 1984), p. 6.
20 In *Lucky Poet* (p. 2) MacDiarmid explains his choice of tartan: 'I took [my middle initial, "M"], and my Christian name of Christopher, from my paternal grandmother, Christina Murray, and it is through her that I claim the right to wear the red Murray of Tullibardine tartan'.
21 William Soutar, *Diaries of a Dying Man*, p. 111.
22 The red shirt had political connotations: 'I fight in red for the same reasons / That Garibaldi chose the red shirt / Because a few men in a field wearing red / Look like many men ... But, best reason of all, / A man in a red shirt can neither hide nor retreat' (603-4).
23 Mary MacDonald, 'I Raise My Glass'.
24 Michael Grieve, letter to A.B., 19 Jan. 1987.
25 Michael Grieve and Alexander Scott (eds.), *The Hugh MacDiarmid Anthology* (London: Routledge & Kegan Paul, 1972), p. xi.
26 Ibid., p. xii.
27 Ibid., pp. xii-xiii.
28 *The Letters of Hugh MacDiarmid*, p. 548.
29 Hugh MacDiarmid, *In Memoriam James Joyce* (Glasgow: William Maclellan, 1955), p. 12.
30 David Orr, 'MacDiarmid – the Man', *Jabberwock* (5, 1958), p. 15.
31 Henry Grant Taylor, letter to A.B., 9 Mar. 1984.
32 When MacDiarmid published *Cornish Heroic Song for Valda Trevlyn* (Glasgow: Caledonian Press, 1943) he indicated that this was the opening section of an extremely long unpublished poem; in a letter of 18 June 1938, to T. S. Eliot, he offered the 'First

Appendix (Cornwall)' for publication in the *Criterion* where it appeared in January 1939 as 'Cornish Heroic Song for Valda Trevlyn' – the same text as the Caledonian Press booklet.

33 *Lucky Poet*, p. 7.

34 Ibid., p. 26.

35 Ibid., pp. 369-70.

36 *The Letters of Hugh MacDiarmid*, p. 169.

37 W. R. Aitken, 'Hugh MacDiarmid's "Unpublished" Books', in F. McAdams (ed.), *Of One Accord* (Glasgow: Scottish Library Association, 1977), p. 67.

38 *Lucky Poet*, p. 165.

39 W. R. Aitken, 'Hugh MacDiarmid's "Unpublished" Books', p. 67.

40 *The Letters of Hugh MacDiarmid*, p. 453.

41 W. R. Aitken, 'Hugh MacDiarmid's "Unpublished" Books', pp. 69-70.

42 Hugh MacDiarmid, *Collected Poems* (Edinburgh: Oliver & Boyd, 1962), p. 418n.

43 Michael Grieve and W. R. Aitken (eds.), *The Complete Poems of Hugh MacDiarmid* (Harmondsworth: Penguin Books, 1985), p. vi.

44 Henry Grant Taylor, letter to A.B., 9 Mar. 1984.

45 *Lucky Poet*, p. 153.

46 *Selected Essays*, p. 76.

47 *The Letters of Hugh MacDiarmid*, p. 155.

48 *Canadian Forum* (July 1937), p. 129.

49 *Lucky Poet*, p. 261.

50 Hugh MacDiarmid, *The Islands of Scotland* (London: Batsford, 1939), p. 120.

51 In the postscript of a letter of 10 Aug. 1932, MacDiarmid tells Helen Cruickshank, 'I did a couple of hill poems for the suite I mean to dedicate to you – but I'm not satisfied with them yet and am recasting them'. *The Letters of Hugh MacDiarmid*, p. 116. The reference to 'the Shetland Islands' (1169) and to sights he had seen in his trip to Skye and other Scottish islands in September 1937 shows that whatever MacDiarmid had drafted by August 1932 was entirely recast and rewritten in 1937-9.

52 *Lucky Poet*, p. 48.

53 Erich Heller, *The Disinherited Mind* (London: Bowes & Bowes, 1975), p. x.

54 Ronald Stevenson, 'MacDiarmid, Joyce and Busoni', in *MacDiarmid: A Festschrift*, p. 146: MacDiarmid's text is 'a huge quotation from an essay which Busoni wrote in America in 1910, entitled "The Realm of Music" '. For the prose translation see Ferruccio Busoni, *The Essence of Music*, tr. Rosamond Ley (London: Rockcliff, 1957), pp. 188-9.

55 *The Letters of Hugh MacDiarmid*, p. 832.

56 Shakespeare, *The Merchant of Venice* (IV.i.47-50): 'Some men there are love not a gaping pig; / Some that are mad if they behold a cat; / And others, when the bagpipe sings i' the' nose, / Cannot contain their urine'.

57 Thomas Mann, *Death in Venice. Tristan. Tonio Kröger*, tr. H. T. Lowe-Porter (1928; rept. Harmondsworth: Penguin Books, 1955), pp. 148-9.

58 *The Letters of Hugh MacDiarmid*, p. 829. Referring to his use of Glyn Jones's prose in his poem 'Perfect', MacDiarmid says 'I either automatically memorized it and subsequently thought it my own, or wrote it into one of my notebooks with the same result.'

59 Letter dated 'Tuesday 11th' but certainly Jan. 1938 because of the reference to the imminent arrival of Henry Grant Taylor. Helen Cruickshank Archive, Edinburgh University Library.

60 *The Letters of Hugh MacDiarmid*, p. 446.

61 Ibid.

62 Helen Cruickshank Archive, Edinburgh University Library.

63 Letter dated 'Friday morning' but probably early May 1938. Helen Cruickshank Archive, Edinburgh University Library.

64 Anticipating early delivery of the book, Harrap advertised *A Pageant of Scottish Doctors* during 1937 and it was listed in the 1938 edition of Whitaker's *Reference Catalogue of Current Literature*. In a letter of September 1940 Mac-

Diarmid mentioned (*The Letters of Hugh MacDiarmid*, p. 132) that he had a history of Scottish doctors 'on the stocks' which means he was revising the typescript that, Taylor confirms, was sent to Harrap in 1938. Eventually the book may have been destroyed in the Blitz. A letter of 6 March 1984 to A.B. from Richard Butterworth, a director of Harrap, explains that the firm has 'no records of the manuscript entitled *Scottish Doctors* by Hugh MacDiarmid, which apparently was delivered to this firm in 1938 ... Unfortunately, all our pre-war records were destroyed when our former offices in High Holborn were blitzed in 1941.' So *Scottish Doctors* joins *Red Scotland* and *The Wolfe of Badenoch* in the list of MacDiarmid's missing books.

65 *The Letters of Hugh MacDiarmid*, p. 265.
66 Ibid., p. 447n.
67 Wyndham Lewis, *The Apes of God* (1930; rept. Harmondsworth: Penguin Books, 1965), p. 315.
68 Letter dated 'Thursday or Friday morning', Helen Cruickshank Archive, Edinburgh University Library.
69 *The Letters of Hugh MacDiarmid*, pp. 125-6.
70 AGG.
71 *Voice of Scotland*, Dec. 1938-Feb. 1939. The statement on 'Spain and the Celtic Volunteers' appears on the inside front cover, opposite p. 1.
72 Hugh MacDiarmid, *The Islands of Scotland* (London: Batsford, 1939), p. vii.
73 *Lucky Poet*, p. 423.
74 *Voice of Scotland* (June-Aug. 1939), p. 6.
75 *Lucky Poet*, pp. 87-9.
76 Prospectus for *Mature Art*, in the William Soutar Archive, National Library of Scotland.
77 Maurice Lindsay, *Francis George Scott and the Scottish Renaissance*, p. 206.
78 *Times Literary Supplement* (15 Feb. 1941) noted MacDiarmid's combative introduction; praised the scope of the anthology and the quality of the Latin and Gaelic translations; and concluded (p. 84) that 'this new Golden Treasury is a very heartening, as well as a very pleasing, volume'.
79 See *The Letters of Hugh MacDiarmid* (pp. 131, 173) and *Lucky Poet* (p. xvii) for estimates. Valda's anecdote about the poet shrinking is repeated in Taylor's letter of 9 Mar. 1984: 'MacDiarmid has worked at high pressure for most of the day. Now, very tired, he has fallen asleep in his old armchair at one side of the fireplace. I look hard at him, and am amazed. He has shrunk. It is an illusion, of course.... Could a tremendous expenditure of mental energy result in a bodily shrinkage?'
80 After his appeal had been turned down in Aberdeen and Edinburgh, Taylor got a job with the Forestry Commission near Southwick. From there he returned his call-up papers and served two weeks in jail in Dumfries before being drafted into the Royal Corps of Signals. He served for five years, including eighteen months in Persia and Iraq. When demobilised he returned to Shetland to marry Mary Hughson, back in her home island of Fetlar. In 1947 he fell victim to Multiple Sclerosis and in 1966 left Fetlar with his wife. She died, aged fifty-six, in Galashiels where Taylor settled.
81 *The Letters of Hugh MacDiarmid*, p. 189.

15 RETURNING TO GLASGOW

1 *Lucky Poet*, p. 105.
2 Morag Enticknap, Andrew Grieve's daughter, in a letter to A.B., 14 July 1984.
3 Ibid.
4 At the end of the Second World War, Andrew was again promoted by the Inland Revenue and transferred to Head Office London, then de-centralised to Llandudno. He remarried in 1956 and moved with his new wife, Irene Mary Abbott (also a tax officer),

to Maida Vale, London. After a partial gastrectomy, he took early retirement and settled near Bournemouth, then Winchester where, after a long and painful illness, he died of kidney failure in 1972, aged seventy-eight.

5 AGG.
6 AGG.
7 Charles Nicoll, in conversation with A.B., 3 Feb. 1984.
8 Robert Blair Wilkie, letter to A.B., 15 July 1984.
9 Charles Nicoll, in conversation.
10 Ibid.
11 *The Letters of Hugh MacDiarmid*, p. 600.
12 Ibid., p. 191.
13 *Lucky Poet*, p. xxxiii.
14 Ibid., p. 44.
15 Ibid., p. xxv.
16 Ibid., p. 79.
17 Ibid., p. 239.
18 Ibid., p. 78.
19 Ibid., p. 402.
20 Ibid., p. 237.
21 Ibid., p. 78.
22 Ibid., p. 234.
23 Ibid., p. 404.
24 Ibid., p. 236.
25 Ibid., p. 248.
26 Ibid., p. 21.
27 Ibid., p. 149.
28 Ibid., p. 218.
29 Ibid., p. 35.
30 Ibid., p. 3.
31 Ibid., p. 56.
32 Ibid., p. 423.
33 Ibid., p. 67.
34 Ibid., p. 93.
35 Ibid., p. 408.
36 Ibid., p. 307.
37 Ibid., p. xxvii.
38 Ibid., p. xxxiii.
39 Ibid., p. 426.
40 Originally the reference in *Lucky Poet* (p. 172) read 'Edgell Rickword is about the only person with some idea of Nationalism, but even he was in the Black-and-Tans....' After Rickword had complained to the publisher, pp. 171-2 were removed and a replacement page was tipped in which deleted the reference to Rickword and sub-

stituted the following sentence; 'Hardly one of the London *literati* has any idea of Nationalism or does not aid and abet Imperialism in one way or another.'
41 Sylvia Townsend Warner, 'Cock of the North', *Our Time*, Feb. 1944, p. 12.
42 Valda.
43 *The Letters of Hugh MacDiarmid*, p. 616.
44 Robert Blair Wilkie, letter to A.B., 15 July 1984.
45 *The Company I've Kept*, pp. 187-8.
46 Sorley MacLean, 'MacDiarmid 1933-1944', p. 19.
47 See note 25 to Ch. 6, p. 447.
48 Maurice Lindsay, *Thank You for Having Me* (London: Robert Hale, 1983), p. 75.
49 *The Letters of Hugh MacDiarmid*, p. 455n.
50 Ibid., p. 788.
51 Valda.
52 Ibid.
53 Dick Allen, letter to A.B., 21 Aug. 1984. Allen's anecdote is complemented by one from the poet's son, Michael Grieve: '[As a boy in Shetland] I eagerly thumbed through the hand-heavy dictionary in an attempt to catch this smoke-hazed figure out – not just at spelling, that would have been too difficult ... It was the meanings of the words, their shimmering sugestiveness, the exciting exactness, the image-conjuring. It was a game not to be won; the dictionary and he had established a rare accord of mutual esteem.' Michael Grieve and Alexander Scott (eds.), *The Hugh MacDiarmid Anthology*, p. xii.
54 Dick Allen, Ibid.
55 *The Letters of Hugh MacDiarmid*, p. 456n.
56 Ibid., p. 602n.
57 Ibid., pp. 602-3.
58 Ibid., p. 861.
59 Ibid., p. 270.
60 Arnold Wesker, letter to A.B., 10 May 1984.
61 Gordon Wright, *MacDiarmid: An Illustrated Biography*, p. 87.
62 *The Letters of Hugh MacDiarmid*, p. 860.

63 Gordon Wright, *MacDiarmid: An Illustrated Biography*, p. 83; from *Scottish Daily Express* report.

64 Hugh MacDiarmid, *Aesthetics in Scotland*, ed. Alan Bold (Edinburgh: Mainstream, 1984), p. 90.

65 Dungavel House was used as a training school for miners from 1951 to 1969 when it was bought by the Prison Service. In 1974 it reopened as HM Prison Dungavel.

16 A Single and Separate Person

1 *The Company I've Kept*, p. 188.

2 *Bulletin*, 7 June 1952, p. 8.

3 Maurice Lindsay, *Francis George Scott and the Scottish Renaissance*, p. 140.

4 Hugh MacDiarmid, 'A Soldier's Farewell to Maurice Lindsay', *National Weekly*, front and back page.

5 *The Letters of Hugh MacDiarmid*, p. 634.

6 *The Company I've Kept*, p. 161.

7 David Krause (ed.), *The Letters of Sean O'Casey* (New York; Macmillan, 1980, vol. 2), p. 967.

8 Eileen O'Casey, *Sean* (1971, rept. London: Pan Books, 1973), p. 203.

9 Sean O'Casey, *Sunset and Evening Star* (1954, rept. London: Pan Books, 1973), p. 86.

10 *The Letters of Hugh MacDiarmid*, p. 491.

11 Ibid., p. 656.

12 *The Company I've Kept*, p. 98.

13 William Soutar, *Diaries of a Dying Man*, p. 60.

14 *The Company I've Kept*, p. 98.

15 *The Letters of Hugh MacDiarmid*, p. 456.

16 *New Statesman*, 10 Sept. 1955, p. 306.

17 *New Statesman*, 17 Sept. 1955, p. 328.

18 The letter is kept in the Communist Party Library, Picture Library and Archive. George Matthews, who kindly provided A.B. with a photocopy, explains that Gordon McLennan, Scottish District Secretary of the CPGB in 1956, went to see MacDiarmid at Biggar. In a letter of 9 Oct. 1986 to A.B., Alex Clark, Scottish Organiser of the CPGB in 1956, says; 'I do know that [MacDiarmid] wrote to John Gollan, and I had the responsibility for giving him his new card ... he continued to pay his subscriptions from that date through me, even when I had left that post.'

19 *New Statesman*, 1 Dec. 1956, p. 701.

20 Hugh MacDiarmid, 'Why I Rejoined', *Daily Worker*, 28 March 1957, p. 2.

21 *The Company I've Kept*, p. 198.

22 Ibid., pp. 198-9.

23 Graham Greene, letter of 9 May 1986 to A.B.

24 *The Company I've Kept*, p. 196.

25 Sir Sydney Smith, *Mostly Murder*, (1959; rept. London: Companion Book Club, 1961), p. 319.

26 Alasdair Gray, *1982 Janine* (London: Jonathan Cape, 1984), p. 282. In an epilogue to his novel, Gray (p. 343) says, 'The matter of Scotland refracted through alcoholic reverie is from MacDiarmid's *A Drunk Man Looks at the Thistle*.'

27 Norman MacCaig, in conversation with A.B.

28 Hugh MacDiarmid, *Burns: Today and Tomorrow* (Edinburgh: Castle Wynd Printers, 1959), p. 23.

29 Ibid., p. 19.

30 *The Letters of Hugh MacDiarmid*, p. 798.

31 Ibid., p. 799.

32 Ibid., p. 806n.

33 Ibid., p. 807.

34 Ibid., p. 659.

35 *The Company I've Kept*, p. 189.

36 *Scotsman*, 22 Aug. 1962, p. 10. MacDiarmid was an avowed enemy of what he regarded as the antisocial experimentalism of some younger Scottish writers. In 1962, for example, he published the pamphlet *The Ugly Birds Without Wings* in which he denounced the 'concrete poetry' of Ian Hamilton Finlay. In conversation he was wont to associate 'the likes of' (a favourite phrase) Trocchi and Finlay with a spurious internationalism.

37 *The Company I've Kept*, p. 33.

38 *Scotsman*, 23 Aug. 1962, p. 6.

39 Harry Martinson, *Aniara*, adapted from the Swedish by Hugh Mac-Diarmid and Elspeth Harley Schubert (London: Hutchinson, 1963), p. 4.

40 *The Letters of Hugh MacDiarmid*, p. 588n. The *TLS* review appeared on 15 Feb. 1963.

41 Ibid., pp. 865-6.

42 Ibid., p. 815.

43 Ibid., p. 816.

44 Forbes Macgregor, *The Gowks of Mowdieknowes* (Edinburgh: Pinetrees Press, 1963), p. 14.

45 *The Letters of Hugh MacDiarmid*, p. 867.

46 Ibid., p. 823.

47 Ibid., p. 531n.

48 Ibid., p. 531.

49 *Daily Worker*, 4 Sept. 1964, p. 1.

50 'Vote for Dr C. M. Grieve (Hugh Mac-Diarmid) Communist Candidate', (Crieff: Alex Clark, 1964).

51 Colin Wilson, letter of 30 April 1986 to A.B.

52 *The Company I've Kept*, p. 214.

53 Kenneth Buthlay, *Hugh MacDiarmid*, p. 89.

54 *The Letters of Hugh MacDiarmid*, pp. 828-9.

55 Ibid., p. 829.

56 'Perfect' was excised from John Weston's revised edition of the *Collected Poems* (1967) and replaced, ironically, with a poem plagiarised from Hart Crane's *The Bridge*. However 'Perfect' appeared, without Glyn Jones's concurrence, in *Complete Poems* (1978). In a telephone conversation with A.B., Jones said he was irritated by this but had no objection to the poem appearing in a MacDiarmid collection so long as he was credited with providing the words. 'Perfect' returned to the MacDiarmid canon in the *Complete Poems* of 1985, with an explanatory note.

57 *The Letters of Hugh MacDiarmid*, p. 832.

58 Ibid., p. 662.

59 Glyn Jones, in conversation with A.B.

60 *The Company I've Kept*, p. 236.

61 Ibid., p. 200.

62 Hugh MacDiarmid, *A Lap of Honour* (London: MacGibbon & Kee, 1967), p. 11.

63 This address was published as *A Political Speech* (Edinburgh: Reprographia, 1972); and reprinted in *The Thistle Rises* (pp. 233-43).

64 Entry in MacDiarmid's SNP Diary for 1969. The poet's diaries were shown to A.B. by Colin Hamilton.

65 *The Letters of Hugh MacDiarmid*, p. 684.

66 John Tytell, *Ezra Pound: The Solitary Volcano* (London: Bloomsbury, 1987), p. 337.

67 *Paideuma*, Fall 1974, pp. 151-2.

68 Ibid., p. 152.

69 A.B. was a guest at this reception.

70 Gordon Wright, *MacDiarmid: An Illustrated Biography*, p. 151.

71 *The Letters of Hugh MacDiarmid*, p. 713.

72 Gordon Wright, *MacDiarmid: An Illustrated Biography*, p. 50.

73 In a letter of October 1987 to A.B., Maurice Lindsay writes: 'Being a bad proof reader, I showed Alexander Scott the proofs of [*Modern Scottish Poetry*], on the eve of a trip abroad.... So far as I can remember his words were: "You can't credit 'The Little White Rose' to MacDiarmid. He's renounced the authorship." At that time I had been resident in England for three years and had not regularly seen Scottish papers. I said: "Are you quite sure? He certainly has renounced the authorship of 'Perfect'." "Yes, I'm sure he's renounced both," said Alex; "Then who is the author?" said I. Alex had no suggestions. Remembering the direct lift of 'Perfect' from the prose of a Welshman, and the fact that 'The Little White Rose' originally appeared with acknowledgements to Mackenzie, I concluded that this must be a parallel case.'

74 *The Letters of Hugh MacDiarmid*, p. 592.

75 Ibid., p. 614.

Selected Bibliography

This selected bibliography by W. R. Aitken lists in chronological order books by Hugh MacDiarmid, omitting the limited printings of a single poem or two or a short essay in pamphlets and small editions not always to be found in even the largest libraries; books he has edited or translated; periodicals he has edited; and collections and selections of his writings, whether made by MacDiarmid himself or by others. This primary bibliography is followed by a chronological list of some twenty books discussing MacDiarmid and his work, from the time of the *Festschrift*, published on his seventieth birthday in 1962, to 1987.

BOOKS

Annals of the Five Senses. Montrose: C. M. Grieve 1923; Edinburgh: Porpoise Press 1930; introd. Alan Bold, Edinburgh: Polygon 1983.

Sangschaw. Edinburgh: Blackwood 1925.

Penny Wheep. Edinburgh: Blackwood 1926.

A Drunk Man Looks at the Thistle. Edinburgh: Blackwood 1926; introd. David Daiches, Glasgow: Caledonian Press 1953; Edinburgh: Castle Wynd Printers 1956; Edinburgh: 200 Burns Club 1962; illus. Frans Masereel, Falkland: Duval & Hamilton 1969; ed. John C. Weston, Amherst: University of Massachusetts Press 1971; ed. Kenneth Buthlay, Edinburgh: Scottish Academic Press 1987.

Contemporary Scottish Studies. London: Leonard Parsons 1926; with further studies and the 'furious and fascinating' correspondence they evoked, but omitting the introductory chapter, conclusion, and bibliography of the 1926 edition, Edinburgh: *Scottish Educational Journal* 1976.

Albyn, or Scotland and the Future. London: Kegan Paul 1927.

The Lucky Bag. Edinburgh: Porpoise Press 1927.

To Circumjack Cencrastus, or The Curly Snake. Edinburgh: Blackwood 1930.

First Hymn to Lenin, and other poems. London: Unicorn Press 1931.

Scots Unbound, and other poems. Stirling: Eneas Mackay 1932.

Scottish Scene, or The Intelligent Man's Guide to Albyn. With Lewis Grassic Gibbon. London: Jarrolds 1934; London: Hutchinson, for National Book Association nd; Bath: Cedric Chivers 1974.

Stony Limits, and other poems. London: Gollancz 1934.

At the Sign of the Thistle: a collection of essays. London: Stanley Nott 1934.

Second Hymn to Lenin, and other poems. London: Stanley Nott 1935.

Scottish Eccentrics. London: Routledge 1936; New York: Johnson Reprint Corporation 1972.

The Islands of Scotland: Hebrides, Orkneys, and Shetlands. London: Batsford 1939; New York: Scribners 1939.

Lucky Poet: A Self-Study in Literature and Political Ideas. London: Methuen 1943; London: Cape 1972.

A Kist of Whistles: new poems. Glasgow: Maclellan 1947.

Cunninghame Graham: a centenary study. Glasgow: Caledonian Press 1952.

Francis George Scott: an essay on the occasion of his seventy-fifth birthday. Edinburgh: Macdonald 1955.

In Memoriam James Joyce: From A Vision of World Language. Glasgow: Maclellan 1955; rpt with corrections 1956.

Stony Limits and Scots Unbound, and other poems. Edinburgh: Castle Wynd Printers 1956.

Three Hymns to Lenin. Edinburgh: Castle Wynd Printers 1957.

The Battle Continues. Edinburgh: Castle Wynd Printers 1957.

Burns Today and Tomorrow. Edinburgh: Castle Wynd Printers 1959.

The Kind of Poetry I Want. Edinburgh: Duval 1961.

The Company I've Kept. London: Hutchinson 1966; Berkeley, Calif: University of California Press 1967.

Celtic Nationalism. With Owen Dudley Edwards, Gwynfor Evans and Ioan Rhys. London: Routledge & Kegan Paul 1968.

Dìreadh I, II, and III. Frenich, Foss: Duval & Hamilton 1974.

Scotch Whisky. As tasted by Bill Simpson and others. London: Macmillan 1974. MacDiarmid writes on 'Great Malt Whiskies'.

John Knox. With Campbell Maclean and Anthony Ross. Edinburgh: Ramsay Head Press 1976.

Aesthetics in Scotland. Ed. Alan Bold. Edinburgh: Mainstream 1984.

BOOKS EDITED OR TRANSLATED

Northern Numbers, being representative selections from certain living Scottish poets. Edinburgh: T. N. Foulis 1920; 2nd ser, Edinburgh: T. N. Foulis 1921; 3rd ser, Montrose: C. M. Grieve 1922.

Robert Burns 1759-1796. London: Benn 1926. (Augustan Books of Poetry)

The Handmaid of the Lord. By Ramon Maria Tenreiro. London: Secker 1930. Anon trn by MacDiarmid.

Living Scottish Poets. London: Benn 1931. (Augustan Books of Poetry)

The Golden Treasury of Scottish Poetry. London: Macmillan 1940.

William Soutar: Collected Poems. London: Andrew Dakers 1948.

Robert Burns: Poems. London: Grey Walls Press 1949.

Selections from the Poems of William Dunbar. Edinburgh: Oliver & Boyd for the Saltire Society 1952.

Selected Poems of William Dunbar. Glasgow: Maclellan 1955.

Robert Burns: Love Songs. London: Vista Books 1962.

Aniara: A Review of Man in Time and Space. By Harry Martinson. Adapted from the Swedish by MacDiarmid and Elspeth Harley Schubert. London: Hutchinson 1963; New York: Knopf 1963; Stockholm: Bonnier 1963.

Henryson. Harmondsworth: Penguin Books 1973. (Poet to Poet)

The Threepenny Opera. By Bertolt Brecht. London: Eyre Methuen 1973.

PERIODICALS EDITED

The Scottish Chapbook. Montrose 1922-3. Monthly.

The Scottish Nation. Montrose 1923. Weekly.

The Northern Review. Edinburgh 1924. Monthly.

The Voice of Scotland. Dunfermline 1938-9; Glasgow 1944-9; Edinburgh 1955-8. Quarterly, irregular.

Poetry Scotland. No 4. Guest editor. Edinburgh: Serif Books 1949.

Scottish Art and Letters. Fifth miscellany. PEN Congress Number. Literary editor. Glasgow: Maclellan 1950.

COLLECTIONS AND SELECTIONS

Selected Poems. London: Macmillan 1934.

Selected Poems. Ed. R. Crombie Saunders. Glasgow: Maclellan 1944.

Speaking for Scotland: selected poems. Baltimore: Contemporary Poetry 1946.

Selected Poems. Ed. Oliver Brown. Glasgow: Maclellan 1945; as *Poems,* Glasgow: Scottish Secretariat 1955.

Collected Poems. New York: Macmillan Co 1962; Edinburgh: Oliver & Boyd 1962; rev. edn. with enlarged glossary by John C. Weston, New York: Macmillan Co 1967; London: Collier-Macmillan 1967.

>The *Collected Poems* is in fact 'only a big selection' of MacDiarmid's poetry. It was supplemented by three later collections:
>
>*A Lap of Honour.* London: MacGibbon & Kee 1967; Chicago: Swallow Press 1969.
>
>*A Clyack-Sheaf.* London: MacGibbon & Kee 1969.
>
>*More Collected Poems.* London: MacGibbon & Kee 1970; Chicago: Swallow Press 1970.

These collections are now superseded by the *Complete Poems* (1978; 1985).

The Uncanny Scot: a selection of prose. Ed. Kenneth Buthlay. London: MacGibbon & Kee 1968.

Selected Essays. Ed. Duncan Glen. London: Cape 1969; Berkeley, Calif: University of California Press 1970.

Selected Poems. Ed. David Craig and John Manson. Harmondsworth: Penguin Books 1970.

The Hugh MacDiarmid Anthology: Poems in Scots and English. Ed. Michael Grieve and Alexander Scott. London: Routledge & Kegan Paul 1972.

The Socialist Poems of Hugh MacDiarmid. Ed. T.S. Law and Thurso Berwick. London: Routledge & Kegan Paul 1978.

Complete Poems, 1920-1976. Ed. Michael Grieve and W.R. Aitken. 2 vols London: Martin Brian & O'Keeffe 1978; with corrections and an appendix, Harmondsworth: Penguin Books 1985.

The Thistle Rises: an anthology of poetry and prose. Ed. Alan Bold. London: Hamish Hamilton 1984.

The Letters of Hugh MacDiarmid. Ed. Alan Bold. London: Hamish Hamilton 1984.

BOOKS ABOUT MacDIARMID

Duval, Kulgin D. and Sydney Goodsir Smith, eds. *Hugh MacDiarmid: a Festschrift.* Edinburgh: Duval 1962.

Buthlay, Kenneth. *Hugh MacDiarmid (C. M. Grieve).* Edinburgh: Oliver & Boyd 1964 (Writers and Critics); rev. and enl., Edinburgh: Scottish Academic Press 1982 (Scottish Writers).

Glen, Duncan. *Hugh MacDiarmid (Christopher Murray Grieve) and the Scottish Renaissance.* Edinburgh: Chambers 1964.

Glen, Duncan, ed. *Hugh MacDiarmid: a critical survey.* Edinburgh: Scottish Academic Press 1972.

Morgan, Edwin. *Hugh MacDiarmid.* Harlow: Longman, for the British Council 1976 (Writers and their Work).

Watson, Roderick. *Hugh MacDiarmid.* Milton Keynes: Open University Press 1976.

Wright, Gordon. *MacDiarmid: an illustrated biography.* Edinburgh: Gordon Wright 1977.

Johnstone, William. *Points in Time: an autobiography.* London: Barrie & Jenkins 1980.

Lindsay, Maurice. *Francis George Scott and the Scottish Renaissance.* Edinburgh: Paul Harris 1980.

Scott, Paul H. and Albert C. Davis, eds. *The Age of MacDiarmid: essays on Hugh MacDiarmid and his influence on contemporary Scotland.* Edinburgh: Mainstream 1980.

Boutelle, Ann Edwards. *Thistle and Rose: a study of Hugh MacDiarmid's poetry.* Loanhead: Macdonald 1981.

Bold, Alan. *MacDiarmid: The Terrible Crystal.* London: Routledge & Kegan Paul 1983.

Kerrigan, Catherine. *'Whaur Extremes Meet': the poetry of Hugh MacDiarmid, 1920-1934.* Edinburgh: Mercat Press 1983.

Gish, Nancy K. *Hugh MacDiarmid: the man and his work.* London: Macmillan 1984.

Oxenhorn, Harvey. *Elemental Things: the poetry of Hugh MacDiarmid.* Edinburgh: Edinburgh University Press 1984.

Watson, Roderick. *MacDiarmid*. Milton Keynes: Open University Press 1985.

Davie, George Elder. *The Crisis of the Democratic Intellect: the problem of generalism and specialisation in twentieth-century Scotland*. Edinburgh: Polygon 1986.

McCarey, Peter. *Hugh MacDiarmid and the Russians*. Edinburgh: Scottish Academic Press 1987.

Glossary

The glossary is based on that printed in *The Complete Poems of Hugh MacDiarmid* which collates glossaries from the poet's published volumes. MacDiarmid's main linguistic source for Scots was J. Jamieson's *An Etymological Dictionary of the Scottish Tongue* (1808). Scholars of Scots are referred to *The Scottish National Dictionary* (ten volumes, 1929-76), by W. Grant and D. Murison. Useful one-volume dictionaries are A. Warrack's *Chambers's Scots Dictionary* (1911) and M. Robinson's *The Concise Scots Dictionary* (1985).

abstraklous: *outrageous*
aftergait: *outcome*
aiblins: *perhaps*
allemand: *orderly*
allevolie: *volatile*
ane: *one*
antrin: *occasional, rare*
appliable: *complaint*
archin': *flowing smoothly*
areird: *troublesome*
arnuts: *earth-nuts*
arrachin': *tumultuous*
aspate: *in full flood*
aucht-fit: *eight-foot*
auld: *old*
austerne: *austere*
averins: *heather-stems*

bairnie: *baby*
baith: *both*
bebbles: *tiny beads*
beek: *show*
belth: *sudden swirl, whirlpool*
bide: *stay, await*
bightsom: *ample*
blaw: *blow*
blinterin': *gleaming*
brade-up: *with address*
brae-hags: *wooded cliffs*

breenge: *burst*
bricht: *bright*
broukit: *neglected*
bubblyjock: *turkey*
bumclocks: *flying beetles*
byspale: *precocious child*

ca': *call*
cairney: *hillock*
cay: *jackdaw*
chitterin': *shivering*
claith: *cloth*
coof: *fool*
cornskreich: *corncrake*
cray: *pigsty*
cundy: *drain*
cwa': *come away*

datchie: *sly, secret*
deed: *died*
deltit: *pampered*
dern: *hide*
dirl: *throb*
dooks: *ducks*
draiks (i' the): *in a slovenly condition*
druntin': *whining*
drush: *smush, refuse*

eemis: *insecure*

een: *eyes*
elbuck: *elbow*

faddom: *fathom*
fash: *trouble, worry*
fecht: *fight*
feck: *great deal, majority*
fegs: *faith*
fell: *clever (adj.), very (adv.)*
ferlie: *wonder, marvel, surprise*
fochin': *turning over*
fog-theekit: *moss-hatched*
forenicht: *early evening*
fu': *full*

gang: *go*
gar: *make*
gin: *if*
golochs: *earwigs*
grat: *wept*
grue: *revulsion*
grun': *ground*
guissay: *pig*

hairst: *harvest*
heels-owre-gowdy: *head-over-heels*
heich: *high, height*
heich-skeitch: *crazy, irresponsible*
heid: *head*
hines: *raspberries*
how-dumb-deid: *the very dead of night*
howe: *bottom, hollow*

ilka: *every*

jaup: *splash*

ken: *know*
kittle: *tickle, (adj.) ticklish, difficult*
kyths: *appears, becomes known, emerges*

laich, laigh: *low*
lave: *rest, remainder*
laverock: *lark*
liddenin': *going backwards and forwards*
lift: *sky*
lochan: *little loch*
lo'e: *love*
loon: *lad*
louch: *come-hither, downcast*
loup: *jump*
lourd: *heavy, overcharged, cloudy*
lowe: *flame*

maun: *must*
mither: *mother*
mony: *many*
muckle: *big*
Muckle Toon: *Langholm, Dumfries-shire*
mune: *moon*

neist: *next*
nicht: *night*
nocht: *nothing*

on-ding: *downpour*
or: *before*
owre: *over*

peerie-weerie: *diminished to a mere thread of sound*
poo'er: *power*
puir: *poor*

rax: *stretch*
reek: *smoke (There was nae reek i' the laverock's hoose = it was a dark and stormy night)*
reid e'en: *traditionally the one night in the year when harts and hinds mate, in November*
reistit: *dried*
rouch: *rough, plentiful*

saul: *soul*
scaut-heid: *scrofulous, disfigured*
sclafferin': *slovenly*
seek: *sick*
ser': *serve*
sic: *such*
siccar (to mak'): *to make certain*
skime: *gleam*
skinkle: *gleam*
skrymorrie: *frightful and terrific*
stane: *stone*
straucht: *straight*
swack: *ample, supple*
syne: *afterwards, since, then, thereafter*

thrang: *busy*
thrawn: *contrary, stubborn*
tine: *lose*
tint: *lost*
tousie: *rumpled, untidy*

ugsome: *horrible, repulsive*

unkennable: *unknowable*

vennel: *lane, narrow street*
verra: *very*
virr: *stamina, force, vigour*

wa': *wall*
wae, waesome: *woeful*
watergaw: *indistinct rainbow*
waun'ert: *confused*
waur: *worse*
wecht: *weight*
weel: *well*
wrocht: *worked*
wunds: *winds*

yirdit: *buried*
yowdendrift: *counter-swirl of snow from the earth, gale driving down, opposite of earth-drift*
yow-trummle: *ewe-tremble (cold spell at end of July after sheep-shearing)*

Index